Staging the Nation

Plays from the American Theater
1787–1909

Staging the Nation

Plays from the American Theater
1787–1909

—⟫⟪—

DON B. WILMETH
Brown University

Bedford Books BOSTON

For Bedford Books

President and Publisher: Charles H. Christensen
General Manager and Associate Publisher: Joan E. Feinberg
Managing Editor: Elizabeth M. Schaaf
Developmental Editor: Jane Betz
Editorial Assistant: Maura Shea
Production Editor: Bridget Leahy
Copyeditor: Mary Tonkinson
Text Design: Claire Seng-Niemoeller
Cover Design: Isaac Stone
Cover Art: Detail from *Interior of Park Theatre*, New York, ca. 1821. Woodcut frontispiece from *Rejected Address.* © Collection of the New-York Historical Society.
Composition: Stratford Publishing Services, Inc.
Printing and Binding: Haddon Craftsmen, Inc.

For information, write: Bedford Books, 75 Arlington Street, Boston, MA 02116 (617–426–7440)

ISBN: 0–312–17091–2

Acknowledgments

James A. Herne, *Shore Acres.* From *Shore Acres*, by James A. Herne. Copyright © 1928 by Katherine C. Herne. Copyright © 1929 by Katherine C. Herne. Copyright © 1956 (renewal) by John T. Herne. Copyright © 1957 (renewal) by John T. Herne. Reprinted by permission of Samuel French, Inc.
Figure 1. Act V, scene II of *The Contrast.* Engraving by William Dunlap of the original production. By permission of the Wilmeth Collection.
Figure 2. Actor Edwin Forrest as Metamora. Illustration based on a Mathew Brady photograph. By permission of the Wilmeth Collection.
Figure 3. Parody of Forrest as Metamora. From J. K. Philander Doesticks (i.e., Mortimer Neal Thomson), *Doesticks What He Says* (New York, 1855). By permission of the Laurence Senelick Collection.
Figure 4. Image of Enid Markey and Will Geer in *Fashion.* Reprinted by permission of the Harvard Theatre Collection and The Houghton Library.
Figure 5. Image of the Griswold Opera House poster advertising *Uncle Tom's Cabin.* Reprinted by permission of the Harvard Theatre Collection and The Houghton Library.

Preface

Students of the American theater have been hardpressed in recent years to
locate in print major playtexts from the formative years of our dramatic past.
With one notable exception (a large collection of plays spanning the Colonial to the contemporary periods), volumes of plays from the pre-twentieth-
century American theater have been unavailable. *Staging the Nation: Plays
from the American Theater, 1787–1909* modestly attempts to redress this situation, reprinting key plays written prior to the emergence of what many
would consider mature modern American drama (the plays of Eugene
O'Neill and Susan Glaspell, for example).

Explanation of specific choices appears in the introduction that follows.
It is worth stating here, however, that the selections in this volume were
chosen in large measure as examples of successful ventures in the theater of
their time. Collectively, they serve as a circumscribed window into both the
developing country and its culture, while individually each play in this volume furnishes some insight into an ever-expanding and ever-more-complex
society. Plays about the nation did not emerge first in our own century. For
example, European affectation on these shores was pantomimed and paro-
died in American drama almost a hundred years before Dickens caricatured
the country's "small-dealing" capitalist. Staging the spectacle of American
society in absurd imitation of its English and European equivalents, Royall

Tyler and, later, Anna Cora Mowatt and others created a stock theme of American theater and nurtured the beginnings of an art form.

In like manner, bullying businessmen, desperate slaves, emancipated women, and savages (both murderous and noble) emerge from the fabric of the newly independent nation, proclaiming the merits of homespun virtue over foreign folly or directing the native gaze toward social consciousness in comedies of manners and morals, in melodrama and burlesque, and in the earliest attempts at American Realism.

Although the study of American theater and drama has long been viable, rewarding, and exciting, scholars have all too often marginalized or dismissed the study of American drama (and to a lesser extent the theater that produced its plays), a casualty, as Susan Harris Smith so elegantly argues in *American Drama: The Bastard Art* (Cambridge University Press, 1997), "of the wars of legitimation fought in the academy" (3), excluded as neither a "highbrow" literary genre or a "lowbrow" form of popular entertainment. Nevertheless, even though these particular plays may not be judged as literary samples of a high order, they are nonetheless of enormous value as cultural artifacts, telling us, as I suggest above, much about our past and offering glimpses into the theater of the time, for regardless of past judgments — sometimes puritanical, frequently flawed, and often elitist — American drama, including the best of the pre-twentieth-century canon, undeniably belongs in the panoply of American writing alongside fiction and poetry. Much of this drama, if not all, was, of course, written to be performed, and thus without this added dimension (and the presence of an audience — sometimes receptive, sometimes hostile, but rarely indifferent), the impact may be lessened. Fortunately, however, in recent years a large number of critically acclaimed works have appeared that address various issues raised in the annals of American theater, many focused on the years covered by these plays, the audiences that attended the theater, the dramas themselves, and certainly the context in which our theater belonged. These include Lawrence W. Levine's *Highbrow/Lowbrow: The Emergence of Cultural Hierarchy in America* (1988), Bruce McConachie's *Melodramatic Formations: American Theatre and Society 1820–1870* (1992), and Rosemarie Bank's *Theatre Culture in America, 1925–1860* (1997), to mention only three (see *Suggestions for Further Reading* for additional titles). Other indicators of the intensified interest in American theater and drama include the commitment of Cambridge University Press to publish a three-volume history of American theater, with equal attention paid to text and performance, and the same press's support of the series "Studies in American Theatre and Drama." I hope, then, that *Staging the Nation* will serve not only as a discrete collection of value on its own terms but as a complement to the growing scholarly literature on American theater and drama, supplying the much-needed texts that should be read alongside complementary historical, theoretical, and analytical studies.

To enhance the usefulness of this collection, I have included a number of editorial aids. An introduction provides basic information about the selected texts, and brief biographies of each author precede each play. In addition, I have included play summaries, not as shortcuts, keys to interpretation, or substitutions for the actual texts (for, like all forms of narrative literature, the story is only one small part of the whole) — they neither accomplish these tasks nor were they designed to be detailed plot synopses — but as a way to enter the playtexts or, more appropriately, as an aid to be used as a reminder of certain major plot devices after having read the texts. I have also included the prologues used in the original productions of *The Contrast,* Stone's *Metamora,* and *Fashion,* as well as historical and theatrical/cultural chronologies, and suggestions for further reading.

NOTE ON THE TEXTS

The text of *The Contrast* follows the 1787 first edition. The version of Stone's *Metamora* included here, a reconstruction by the late Richard Moody and first published by him in 1966 (*Dramas from the American Theatre, 1762–1909*), was drawn from partial versions originally at the Edwin Forrest home in Philadelphia and the University of Utah Library plus a copy (lacking Act V) found by Moody among the Lord Chamberlain's plays in the British Library. Brougham's burlesque *Metamora* replicates an edition published in Boston, circa 1857. *Fashion* follows the 1845 first edition. *Uncle Tom's Cabin,* based on Harriet Beecher Stowe's novel, is from an undated edition published in New York by Dick and Fitzgerald. Boucicault's *The Poor of New York* is reproduced from his original 1857 print edition (see introduction for other versions), adapted from Brisebarre and Nus's *Les Pauvres de Paris.* The text of *Shore Acres* is based on the version in Herne's *Shore Acres and Other Plays* (1928), its first publication. The text for *Secret Service* is essentially the one published in 1898 by Samuel French, with emendations found in the revised version published by Arthur Hobson Quinn in 1917. Fitch's *The City* follows the text found in *Plays by Clyde Fitch* (Little, Brown, 1915). Most obsolete stage directions have been regularized or eliminated where not textually necessary.

ACKNOWLEDGMENTS

For assistance in the preparation of this volume, I gratefully acknowledge the assistance of Rosemary Cullen, Curator of the Harris Collection of

American Poetry and Drama, and Ann Patrick, staff member in Special Collections, both at Brown University Library. I am pleased to acknowledge Christopher Bigsby, American drama expert par excellence, who encouraged the creation of this collection in the first place; Brown University, which provided a sabbatical leave that allowed me to undertake this project; my editor, Jane Betz; and Chuck Christensen and Joan Feinberg at Bedford Books, who rescued this volume when Everyman Paperbacks was unable to complete its task. Also at Bedford, my production editor, Bridget Leahy, and editorial assistant, Maura Shea. Hilary Laurie, publisher of Everyman, was supportive from the beginning and magnanimous in effecting the transition to Bedford. The late Richard Moody deserves to be recognized for his pioneering work in American theater scholarship, his reconstruction of Stone's *Metamora,* and for his encouragement of this effort. Colleagues from around the country endorsed this collection when it was first proposed, and their support served as an important catalyst toward its completion, for which I am most grateful. Particular thanks are due to Jonathan Curley for his research efforts on my behalf and especially for his suggestions, which have been incorporated into play summaries and the introduction. As always, my wife Judy has used her critical eye to good advantage. Her support and assistance are continuously valued.

Don B. Wilmeth
Brown University

Contents

><

Illustrations

—————————————— ✥ ——————————————

Staging the Nation

Plays from the American Theater
1787–1909

—————————— ✄ ——————————

Introduction for Students

>⟨⟨

The plays in this collection represent American drama from the earliest native comedy to be staged professionally, in 1787, to the emergence of American realism with some semblance of a social consciousness at the turn of the century. There are two comedies of manners, a social comedy, a burlesque, four melodramas (the dominant serious form of the period), and an early example of American realism subtitled a domestic comedy but with serious overtones. The selection of these nine examples from the hundreds possible was made in part because of their historical importance but also to highlight some of the more prominent stage successes seen on the American stage over more than a century of its history.

Other more literary or aesthetically satisfying selections could have been made, but few of these can claim a true stage history. Indeed, as many critics have suggested, few early American dramas are true masterpieces, and some are almost subliterary despite their apparent stage success. Yet no apologies are needed if these plays are examined on their own terms. And with some historical perspective, it is even possible to tolerate the excrescences of sentimentality, hackneyed clichés, stereotypical characters, and the general lack of intellectual underpinning found in many early American plays. Indeed, this particular collection actually illustrates that there was in the United States a developing native drama with distinct strengths and weaknesses well before Eugene O'Neill emerged in 1916 as a produced playwright.

While O'Neill has frequently been credited as the first American playwright to deal successfully with American themes, each of the selections in this volume emphasizes American topics, subjects, characters, or a combination of these. Though generally driven by plot, these early plays nevertheless offer prime examples of native playwrights searching for ways to stage the nation.

Tyler's *The Contrast* (1787), though a somewhat derivative effort (it resembles somewhat R. B. Sheridan's comedies of wit, in particular *The School for Scandal*), conceals its eccentricities and sophistication behind a simple veneer. It is a play that explores the fabric of contemporary eighteenth-century American culture, stark and separate from British influence. Yet with its emphasis on sentiment and cynicism, decorum and excessive behavior, style and substance, life and art, *The Contrast* is a comedy that more significantly reflects the bifurcation of a postcolonial nation in search of an identity. Historically, it is remembered for the introduction of the first stage Yankee, Jonathan, a type character that appears in dozens of American plays into the early twentieth century, including Herne's *Shore Acres* (also reprinted here). Following its premiere at New York's John Street Theatre (visited by Jonathan in *The Contrast*) on April 16, 1787, the play had several additional performances in the colonies and in recent years has found some success in a musical version.

Stone's *Metamora* (1829), based loosely on King Philip's War (1675–76) in New England and the most successful of the so-called Indian plays (and my research has identified over six hundred plays that fit this category from 1606 to the present), reverses the stereotype of the "bad" Indian and the popular prejudice against Native Americans of the nineteenth century. Instead, Stone undertakes a sharply honed moral investigation of human treachery and virtue, with the rather idealized and two-dimensional (though with some character weaknesses) Indian chief, Metamora, as the doomed but uncorrupted hero of his people. Furthermore, Stone attacks British convention and character, finding a moral purity and Native American tradition of honor immiscible with the white man's reproachable demeanor. As the first winner in a contest sponsored by actor Edwin Forrest (1806–1872) for a drama on an aboriginal theme written by an American, the play became, after its premiere on December 15, 1829, at New York's Park Theatre, a mainstay of Forrest's repertoire for some forty years.

The Indian play reached its apogee in the 1830s, but as the Indian problem grew more severe in the 1860s, its popularity began to recede, the Indian character becoming a more villainous and dangerous antagonist or, as seen in John Brougham's *Metamora* (1847), a burlesqued figure. With its ironic, comic objective, Brougham's ribald send-up of the Stone melodrama explodes the original play's seriousness and moral didacticism. Produced originally at Boston's Adelphi Theatre on November 29 with Brougham in the title role, the burlesque was repeated frequently over the following decade.

Fashion; or, Life in New York (1845) is historically important as one of the first successful American plays written by a woman, Anna Cora Mowatt. More so than *The Contrast,* despite similar themes, Mowatt's play is a melding of morality tale and comedy of manners, one of the most successful of its day, albeit typical of the naïveté in much American drama in its depiction of American goodness. Mowatt's self-conscious comedy, acknowledging the yoke of European custom on burgeoning American culture, elucidates the social conflicts between nativity and foreign influence, genuine sentiment and sentimental artifice. When it opened at the Park Theatre in New York on March 24, 1845, it provoked early critical comments from Edgar Allan Poe in the *Broadway Journal* on March 29 and April 5. Though Poe found faults, especially a lack of verisimilitude, an excess of artificial characters, and "no literary quality," he nonetheless concluded that "there is much merit . . . and in many respects (and those of a *telling* character) it is superior to any American play. The entire getting-up was admirable. . . . Compared with the generality of modern dramas, it is a good play — compared with most American dramas it is a *very* good one."[1]

Uncle Tom's Cabin (1852), in its various versions, is arguably the most successful play of the nineteenth century. Certainly George Aiken's scaled-down melodramatic version of the Harriet Beecher Stowe novel, though with complete narrative intact, had a pace and immediate impact lacking in Stowe's astonishingly popular novel.[2] Thomas Gossett notes how strongly the play has affected American and international thinking on the character of African Americans, the nature of life in the old South, and the struggle between good and evil.[3] Though the play is not essentially antislavery, it nevertheless served as propaganda for abolition. And it was seen by countless individuals from 1852 through the 1920s. By the 1890s at least four hundred troupes were performing various versions of the play throughout the United States. As late as 1927 a dozen companies were still barnstorming the country. In the early 1990s, as racial tensions in the United States escalated,

---

[1] Barnard Hewitt, *Theatre U.S.A. 1668 to 1957* (New York: McGraw-Hill Book Co., 1959), p. 138.
[2] Aiken's version was written for the Howard family (starring the four-year-old Cordelia Howard as Little Eva) and was first seen in Troy, New York, in September 1852.
[3] Thomas Gossett, *Uncle Tom's Cabin and American Culture* (Dallas: Southern Methodist University Press, 1985).

Uncle Tom's Cabin reemerged as a vehicle for investigating collective racial images and attitudes.

Dion Boucicault's *The Poor of New York* (1857), the general plot of which derives from the French play *Les Pauvre de Paris* by Edouard Brisebarre and Eugène Nus, is nonetheless, in Boucicault's first version,[4] a creative hybrid effort that is far removed from its original Paris setting.[5] It is centered around specific incidents resulting from two financial crises in America (in 1837 and 1857). Boucicault shows us the poverty of a segment of American society, focusing the action on the poor of New York living in tenements (with a climactic onstage slum-apartment fire)[6] as contrasted with the richness of some of its citizens. Furthermore, to localize his melodrama, Boucicault captures the look and dynamics of the New York streets, providing rich local details and allusions and settings recognizable to the audience of the day.

During the quarter of a century following Boucicault's melodrama, a few American dramatists became conscious of dramaturgical changes in Europe and sought to create a new, more realistic or aesthetically satisfying drama. Such efforts rarely met with popular success, for the American theater prior to the second decade of this century was almost exclusively a commercial

---

[4] Boucicault was later able to adapt his original play to many locales, changing the title to *The Poor of Liverpool, The Poor of Leeds, The Poor of Manchester, The Streets of London, The Poor of the London Streets, The Streets of Dublin, The Streets of Philadelphia,* and *The Money Panic of '57.*

[5] For a comparison of the French original and Boucicault's version, see Daniel Gerould, ed., *American Melodrama* (New York: Performing Arts Journal Publications, 1983), pp. 10–14. It first played at Wallack's Theatre in New York, on December 8, 1857.

[6] Boucicault is often credited with the introduction of what was known as a "sensation" scene, a climactic, spectacular moment onstage requiring inventive stage design and machinery. Such scenes actually date back to the Middle Ages. Nevertheless, Boucicault's "sensation" scenes were extraordinary, and the one in Act V of *The Poor of New York* was no exception. In the middle of a snowstorm, a decaying Union Square tenement goes up in flames and ultimately collapses onstage. In a rare theatrical revelation, practical man-of-the-theater Boucicault explained in "Illusions of the Stage" (*Scientific American*, supplement X [1881]: 4265–66) how the effects could be achieved:

> The house is painted on three separate pieces, the top one of which is swung from the flies; this constitutes the roof. Upon the second is painted half the wall, and it is joined to the bottom piece in an irregular zig-zag line. The simple dropping in succession of these pieces to the stage produces the falling of the roof and wall. The fire itself is represented by chemical red fire and powered lycopodium used separately, the former to give a red glow and the latter to represent flames. The shutters, which are to fall, are fastened to the scene with a preparation called "quick-match." This is made of powder (possibly gunpowder,) alcohol, and a lamp wick. The window frame and sashes are made of sheet iron. They are covered in oakum soaked in alcohol or naphtha. These sashes and frames are not fastened to the scene at all, but are placed a short distance behind it upon platforms. The quickest possible touch of flame ignites the oakum, and, in a moment, the fire runs round the sash, and nothing is apparently left but the blackened and charred wood. Steam is used to represent the smoke that issues from crannies in the walls of the burning building; and an occasional crash, fol-

venture, dominated for almost twenty years, beginning in 1896, by a group of six entrepreneurs, booking agents, and producers, known collectively as the Theatrical Syndicate. Their power prevented most dramaturgical experimentation and innovation. However, several adventurous playwrights, including George Henry Boker, William Vaughn Moody, and James A. Herne, attempted to follow their individual instincts and felt they were creating literary dramas.[7]

Of the three dramatists, Herne came the closest to becoming an American realist. A seasoned actor and theater manager, and thus a playwright who clearly understood the stage, Herne was introduced by the critic-theorist Hamlin Garland to realism and to the influential writer and apostle of realism, William Dean Howells, who encouraged Herne in the writing of his most controversial and subsequently influential play, *Margaret Fleming* (1890), an effort that led to Herne being dubbed "the American Ibsen."[8] But this play met with little popular success, and its critical acceptance was

---

lowed by the ignition of a little powder to produce a sudden puff of smoke, gives the spectator an idea of a falling rafter. Behind the entire scene is placed a very large endless towel upon which is painted a mass of flames. This is kept in constant upward motion; and, when viewed through an open window of the house, gives a good idea of the raging furnace within. Add to these things a real fire engine on the stage, a host of yelling supernumeraries in discarded firemen's uniforms, and the spectator is easily filled with a sense of tremendous danger. Nevertheless the only flames upon the stage are those arising from the burning lycopodium in a "flash torch," and they are only allowed to blaze up for a second or two at a time.

Boucicault borrowed ideas for "sensation" scenes from many sources, including other playwright's plays. In *After Dark* (1878), for example, Boucicault stole the gimmick of tying a character to a railroad track with a last-minute rescue used first by American playwright Augustin Daly in *Under the Gaslight* (1867). Daly, interestingly, was, along with Boucicault, the most successful purveyor of "sensation" scenes in such plays as *Gaslight, A Flash of Lightning* (1868), *The Red Scarf* (1868), and *Horizon* (1871). Examples of Daly's plays and details on his career can be found in Don B. Wilmeth and Rosemary Cullen, eds., *Plays by Augustin Daly* (Cambridge and New York: Cambridge University Press, 1984).

[7] Boker's best-known play was *Francesca da Rimini* (1855, but not successfully staged until 1883), considered the best romantic tragedy written by an American; Moody, recognized as the best lyric poet of his generation, wrote verse dramas but turned to prose for his most highly regarded plays, *The Great Divide* (1906) and *The Faith Healer* (1909).

[8] Herne's own principles for dramaturgy were clearly articulated in "Art for Truth's Sake in the Drama," published in the avant-garde magazine *Arena* 17 (February 1897): 361–70. It has been reprinted in *Theatre in the United States: A Documentary History, 1750–1915*, comp. Martha Mahard, Don B. Wilmeth, and David Rinear, ed. Barry Witham (New York and Cambridge: Cambridge University Press, 1996). In part, Herne wrote:

Art for truth's sake . . . emphasizes humanity. It is not sufficient that the subject be attractive or beautiful, or that it does not offend. It must first of all express some *large* truth. That is to say, it must always be representative. Truth is not always beautiful, but in art for truth's sake it is indispensable.

Art for art's sake may be likened to the exquisite decoration of some noble building; while art for truth's sake might be the building itself.

largely limited to the circle of literati that numbered Garland and Howells. Certainly *Margaret Fleming* was a landmark, and, in spite of its lack of theatrical success, as Brenda Murphy notes, "it raised the issues of realism as they applied to drama" in a way the more literary dramatic efforts of Howells never could. "It alerted playwrights, critics, and public alike to the change that was on the horizon."[9]

Herne's only commercial success was *Shore Acres*, begun in 1888 (as *The Hawthornes*, then *Shore Acres Subdivision* and *Uncle Nat*) before *Margaret Fleming* but completed afterwards in 1892.[10] Ultimately, Herne's reputation would rest on these two plays, embracing what Herne termed "Continental realism." As Herne explained in "Art for Truth's Sake," the play "grew, and I grew with it; and while I did not realize all its spirituality until its stage presentation set that spirituality free, still it must have had possession of me while writing, or I could not so have written."[11] Certainly, as was often the case with his plays, Herne provided himself with a wonderfully sympathetic role, the Yankee farmer Uncle Nat, a part that apparently captured Herne's own special personal qualities of gentleness, generosity, and humaneness, illustrating vividly why Herne was called the "apostle of simplicity." Part redemptive myth and part tragic realism, Herne's domestic comedy is set in rural coastal Maine and deals with the potential destruction of a family's harmony due to greed. The play expounds a simple puritan morality of truth unsurpassed, wrongdoing punished, and hypocrisy converted into a soul-strong symmetry of goodness and justice. The play had a long run at the theater of the Boston Museum in 1893 and ran in New York for almost seven months in 1893–94 before it began a four-year trek on the road. Herne performed Uncle Nat almost constantly until his final appearance in Boston on

---

Art for truth's sake is serious. Its highest purpose has ever been to perpetuate the life of its time. The higher the form of expression the greater the art. . . . But in expressing a truth through art, it should be borne in mind that selection is an important principle. If a disagreeable truth is not also an essential, it should not be used in art. . . . Truth is an essential of all art. I do not well see how there can be art without some truth. . . . In all art, ancient and modern, that which is in touch with contemporaneous life adheres closest to truth, because it is produced through some peculiar social condition. . . .

Art is a personal expression of life. The finer the form and color and the larger the truth, the higher the art. . . . I stand for art for truth's sake because it perpetuates the everyday life of its time, because it develops the latent beauty of the so-called commonplaces of life, because it dignifies labor and reveals the divinity of the common man.

[9] Brenda Murphy, *American Realism and American Drama, 1880–1940* (New York and Cambridge: Cambridge University Press, 1987), p. 85.

[10] *Shore Acres* opened in its final form on February 20, 1893, at the Boston Museum, having been staged at McVicker's Theatre in Chicago as *Shore Acres Subdivision*, and with substantial differences, in May 1892.

[11] Herne, p. 368.

December 3, 1898, earning a fortune and enjoying one of the few truly happy intervals in his life.

Not as controversial or daring in its brand of realism as *Margaret Fleming*, *Shore Acres* nonetheless drew enthusiastic responses from reviewers, including Herne's strongest detractors, who found the play truthful and epoch-marking (one critic even compared it to Hugo's *Hernani*). Such praise was overstatement, yet Herne's play does display many realistic details in setting (and action indicated in stage direction, climaxing in a final, gentle pantomime performed by Herne as Uncle Nat) and in its characters, though the latter tend toward exaggeration in Herne's attempt to create vivid and often comical local-color roles. Indeed, even Uncle Nat is an echo of Royall Tyler's Jonathan, but Herne's creation has a truthfulness and dimension missing in that early Yankee. Yet in the same household is Nat's niece, Helen Berry, an emancipated woman who reads daring books by advanced thinkers and finally evades her father's domination by running away with the free-thinking local doctor. Still, as compared to *Margaret Fleming*, it is clear that Herne made necessary compromises with his own ideals in order to produce a successful play.

If the detailed pantomime by Uncle Nat provides a sense of surface reality in *Shore Acres*, the far more extensive stage business specified in William Gillette's suspenseful melodrama *Secret Service* (1895), which premiered in its final form on October 5, 1896, at New York's Garrick Theatre, carries realism of action to a dramaturgical summit. Though set during the American Civil War and like other plays that chose this bitter conflict as a springboard for action with a melodramatic or romantic intent, Gillette's play in fact has little to do with the War between the States and nothing to do with the underlying cause or the true devastation of that protracted struggle.[12] For Gillette the Civil War serves merely as background for commentary on the dislocation of communication between North and South and the mental espionage that results in perpetual games of metaphors, lies, and euphemisms; the major theme of the play is actually far more universal. In the central character of Captain Thorne (the role played by Gillette almost eighteen hundred times), the play dramatizes how the scrupulous recognition of intentions and moral character can nonetheless lead to a crooked road of deceit and dissimulation, as well as redemptive reckonings with the true self.

Gillette wrote plays with roles tailored for his own understated acting style. Of his twenty full-length plays, nine featured roles acted successfully

---

[12] All major Civil War plays were written well after the fact. After 1875 none seem to have been partisan in nature. Other prime examples are: Boucicault's *Belle Lamar* (1874), Gillette's *Held by the Enemy* (1886), Bronson Howard's *Shenandoah* (1888), David Belasco's *The Heart of Maryland* (1895), Fitch's *Barbara Frietchie* (1899), and Herne's *The Reverend Griffith Davenport* (1899), the latter only one that deals directly with the effects of the issues on character.

by him. Like Thorne (or Sherlock Holmes, the character he first adapted for stage presentation in 1899), Gillette's vehicles are invariably calm, clear-headed persons who work quietly, quickly, and effectively in very trying circumstances. Gillette, articulate in regard to his ideas of good acting, first explicated his theories in a lecture given in 1913 at the fifth joint session of the American Academy of Arts and Letters and the National Institute of Arts and Letters in Chicago. Published two years later as "The Illusion of the First Time in Acting," Gillette's lecture/essay laid great stress on the use of the actor's personality in the creation of the role and provided a clear explanation for a technique that had long been explicit in his stage portrayals.[13] For a Gillette play to work successfully, all its details had to serve some purpose, and fast-moving action, suspense, and the tension between the demands of love and duty became his dramaturgical trademarks. An extremely intelligent man, Gillette ironically failed to apply his erudition to his plays or to challenge his audiences intellectually; rather, he wrote plays, both melodramas and comedies, designed for popular consumption. Nevertheless, he moved American drama one step closer to twentieth-century realism.

The final play in this collection, Clyde Fitch's *The City* (1909), subtitled "A Modern Play of American Life," is undeniably of the twentieth century. Indeed, it is a muckraking drama with cosmopolitan New York exposed as a breeding ground for sin, malice, and even murder. The City is a latter-day Sodom and Gomorrah contrasted with the pastoral sanctity of country life — sinister, incorrigible, and negligent toward the humanity that created it. It is enlightening to compare Fitch's City with the eighteenth-century New

---

[13] In part, Gillette explained his theory as follows:

... unfortunately for the actor he knows or is supposed to know his part. He is fully aware — especially after several performances — of what he is going to say. The Character he is representing, however, does *not* know what he is going to say, but, if he is a human being, various thoughts occur to him one by one, and he puts such of these thoughts as he decides to, into such speech as he happens to be able to command at the time. Now it is a very difficult thing — and even now rather an uncommon thing — for an actor who knows exactly what he is going to say to behave exactly as tho he didn't; to let his thought (apparently) occur to him as he goes along, even tho they are there in his mind already; and (apparently) to search for and find the words by which to express those thoughts, even tho these words are at his tongue's very end. That's the terrible thing — at his tongue's very end! Living and breathing creatures do not carry their words in that part of their systems: they have to find them and send them there — with more or less rapidity according to their facility in that respect — as occasion arises.

The Illusion of the First Time in Acting (New York: Dramatic Museum of Columbia University, 1915), pp. 40–41. For other Gillette plays and details on his career, see Rosemary Cullen and Don B. Wilmeth, eds. *Plays by William Hooker Gillette* (Cambridge and New York: Cambridge University Press, 1983).

York of Tyler (and the implied idea of the village versus the city) and even the mid-nineteenth-century New York setting used by Boucicault.

Fitch, a contemporary of British playwrights Arthur Wing Pinero and Henry Arthur Jones and in many ways comparable to them, was a deft and careful craftsman yet a playwright who never quite reached his potential. Though often serious, his plays lacked intellectual content. Nevertheless, he wrote entertaining dramas with intriguing plots and interesting characters whose human foibles and frailties are carefully explored, often in sprightly, witty dialogue — and he was enormously successful.[14] In 1901 four of his plays were running in New York; during the 1900–01 season ten were seen simultaneously in New York and on the road. He was the first American playwright to attain a truly international reputation.

The City, arguably Fitch's most mature play (it opened posthumously on December 21, 1909, at New York's Lyric Theatre), demonstrates Fitch's fondness for vivid real-life details (so pronounced that the expression "Fitchian details" entered the language) and other unique dramaturgical elements; yet, as Richard Moody notes, "his last play dug more deeply under the surface, grasped more firmly at the basic drives that propel men into action, and allowed them to express their passions in more highly charged language."[15] It is, in fact, hard to believe, given the language of much of today's drama (in the United States, for instance, the plays of Sam Shepard and David Mamet) that *The City* caused an uproar when Tully Marshall, the drug-crazed family parasite, uttered the line, "You're a God damn liar!" — the first time the phrase "God damn" had been uttered onstage. The reaction was no doubt similar to that in 1914 when Shaw allowed the word "bloody" to be spoken in *Pygmalion*.

---

[14]Like Herne, Bronson Howard, and other contemporary playwrights, Fitch recorded his thoughts on playwriting in an essay, "The Play and the Public," reprinted in Volume 4 of the Memorial Edition of *Clyde Fitch's Plays* (Boston: Little, Brown, 1915). He wrote in part:

> I feel myself very strongly the particular value . . . in a modern play of reflecting absolutely and truthfully the life and environment about us; every class, every kind, every emotion, every motive, every occupation, every business, every idleness! Never was life so varied, so complex; what a choice then! . . . Be truthful, and then nothing can be too big, nothing should be too small, so long as it is here, and *there*! . . . If you inculcate an idea in your play, so much the better for your play and for you — and for your audience. In fact, there is small hope for your play *as* a play if you haven't some small idea in it somewhere and somehow, even if it is hidden — it is sometimes better for you if it is hidden, but it must of course be integral.

[15]Richard Moody, *Dramas from the American Theatre, 1762–1909* (Cleveland: The World Publishing Co., 1966), p. 820.

FIGURE 1 *Act V, scene II of* The Contrast; *engraving by William Dunlap of the original production, with actor Thomas Wignell as Jonathan pictured at center.*

ROYALL TYLER

The Contrast

—————————————————— ➤❖ ——————————————————

Royall Tyler (1757–1826) was born in Boston, studied law at Harvard, and served in the army. Before being admitted to the bar, Tyler showed some early literary talent. After seeing a production of Sheridan's *The School for Scandal* in New York and being encouraged by actor-manager Thomas Wignell, Tyler wrote *The Contrast,* the first comedy by an American to be produced professionally (New York's John Street Theatre, April 16, 1787). *The Contrast* was followed a month later by *May Day in Town; or, New York in an Uproar,* a satirical farce with music satirizing the practice of spring cleaning and moving. A third play, *The Georgia Spec; or, Land in the Moon,* the title suggesting a theme dealing with land speculation in Yazoo County, Georgia, was staged in Boston and New York a decade later. Both of these texts are lost. Two other lost plays, *The Farm House* (produced in Boston, May 1796, and apparently adapted from a play with the same title by J. P. Kemble) and an adaptation of Molière's *The Doctor in Spite of Himself* (circa 1795) have been attributed to Tyler. Likely unperformed were *The Island of Barrataria* and three sacred dramas in verse, *The Judgement of Solomon, The Origin of the Feast of Purim; or, The Destinies of Haman and Mordecai,* and *Joseph and His Brethren.* These were published by Princeton University Press in 1941 as part of the America's Lost Plays series. In addition, Tyler wrote pamphlets, broadsides, law books, and poetry (his collected verse was not published until 1967). From 1807 through 1813, Tyler served as Chief Justice of the Vermont Supreme Court and taught jurisprudence at the University of Vermont from 1811 to 1814.

The Contrast

1787

Dramatis Personae

COLONEL MANLY
DIMPLE
VAN ROUGH
JESSAMY
JONATHAN

CHARLOTTE
MARIA
LETITIA
JENNY
SERVANTS

Act I, Scene I

An apartment at Charlotte's. Charlotte and Letitia discovered.

LETITIA: And so, Charlotte, you really think the pocket-hoop unbecoming.

CHARLOTTE: No, I don't say so: It may be very becoming to saunter round the house of a rainy day; to visit my grand-mamma, or go to Quakers' meeting: but to swim in a minuet, with the eyes of fifty well-dressed beaux upon me, to trip it in the Mall, or walk on the battery, give me the luxurious, jaunty, flowing, bell-hoop. It would have delighted you to have seen me the last evening, my charming girl! I was dangling o'er the battery with Billy Dimple; a knot of young fellows were upon the platform; as I passed them I faultered with one of the most bewitching false steps you ever saw, and then recovered myself with such a pretty confusion, flirting my hoop to discover a jet black shoe and brilliant buckle. Gad! how my little heart thrilled to hear the confused raptures of — "*Demme, Jack, what a delicate foot!*" "*Ha! General, what a well-turn'd —*"

LETITIA: Fie! fie! Charlotte (*Stopping her mouth*), I protest you are quite a libertine.

CHARLOTTE: Why, my dear little prude, are we not all such libertines? Do you think, when I sat tortured two hours under the hands of my friseur, and an hour more at my toilet, that I had any thoughts of my aunt Susan, or my cousin Betsey? though they are both allowed to be critical judges of dress.

LETITIA: Why, who should we dress to please, but those who are judges of its merit?

CHARLOTTE: Why a creature who does not know *Buffon* from *Souflee* — Man! — my Letitia — Man! for whom we dress, walk, dance, talk, lisp, languish, and smile. Does not the grave Spectator assure us, that even our much bepraised diffidence, modesty, and blushes, are all directed to make ourselves good wives and mothers as fast as we can. Why, I'll undertake with one flirt of this hoop to bring more beaux to my feet in one week, than the grave Maria, and her sentimental circle, can do, by sighing sen- ㅤ30 timent till their hairs are grey.

LETITIA: ㅤWell, I won't argue with you; you always out talk me; let us change the subject. I hear that Mr. Dimple and Maria are soon to be married.

CHARLOTTE: ㅤYou hear true. I was consulted in the choice of the wedding ㅤ35 clothes. She is to be married in a delicate white sattin, and has a monstrous pretty brocaded lutestring for the second day. It would have done you good to have seen with what an affected indifference the dear sentimentalist turned over a thousand pretty things, just as if her heart did not palpitate with her approaching happiness, and at last made her choice, ㅤ40 and arranged her dress with such apathy, as if she did not know that plain white sattin, and a simple blond lace, would shew her clear skin, and dark hair, to the greatest advantage.

LETITIA: ㅤBut they say her indifference to dress, and even to the gentleman himself, is not entirely affected.

ㅤ45

CHARLOTTE: ㅤHow?

LETITIA: ㅤIt is whispered, that if Maria gives her hand to Mr. Dimple, it will be without her heart.

CHARLOTTE: ㅤThough the giving the heart is one of the last of all laughable considerations in the marriage of a girl of spirit, yet I should like to ㅤ50 hear what antiquated notions the dear little piece of old fashioned prudery has got in her head.

LETITIA: ㅤWhy you know that old Mr. John-Richard-Robert-Jacob-Isaac-Abraham-Cornelius Van Dumpling, Billy Dimple's father (for he has thought fit to soften his name, as well as manners, during his English ㅤ55 tour), was the most intimate friend of Maria's father. The old folks, about a year before Mr. Van Dumpling's death, proposed this match: the young folks were accordingly introduced, and told they must love one another. Billy was then a good natured, decent, dressing young fellow, with a little dash of the coxcomb, such as our young fellows of fortune usually have. At ㅤ60 this time, I really believe she thought she loved him; and had they then been married, I doubt not, they might have jogged on, to the end of the chapter, a good kind of a sing-song lack-a-daysaical life, as other honest married folks do.

CHARLOTTE: ㅤWhy did they not then marry?

ㅤ65

LETITIA: ㅤUpon the death of his father, Billy went to England to see the world, and rub off a little of the patroon rust. During his absence, Maria like a good girl, to keep herself constant to her *nown true-love*, avoided company, and betook herself, for her amusement, to her books, and her

dear Billy's letters. But, alas! how many ways has the mischievous demon 70
of inconstancy of stealing into a woman's heart! Her love was destroyed
by the very means she took to support it.

CHARLOTTE: How? — Oh! I have it — some likely young beau found the
way to her study.

LETITIA: Be patient, Charlotte — your head so runs upon beaux. — 75
Why she read *Sir Charles Grandison, Clarissa Harlowe,* Shenstone, and
the *Sentimental Journey;* and between whiles, as I said, Billy's letters. But
as her taste improved, her love declined. The contrast was so striking be-
twixt the good sense of her books, and the flimsiness of her love-letters,
that she discovered she had unthinkingly engaged her hand without her 80
heart; and then the whole transaction managed by the old folks, now appeared so unsentimental, and looked so like bargaining for a bale of
goods, that she found she ought to have rejected, according to every rule
of romance, even the man of her choice, if imposed upon her in that
manner — Clary Harlowe would have scorned such a match. 85

CHARLOTTE: Well, how was it on Mr. Dimple's return? Did he meet a
more favourable reception than his letters?

LETITIA: Much the same. She spoke of him with respect abroad, and with
contempt in her closet. She watched his conduct and conversation, and
found that he had by travelling acquired the wickedness of Lovelace 90
without his wit, and the politeness of Sir Charles Grandison without his
generosity. The ruddy youth who washed his face at the cistern every
morning, and swore and looked eternal love and constancy, was now
metamorphosed into a flippant, pallid, polite beau, who devotes the
morning to his toilet, reads a few pages of Chesterfield's letters, and then 95
minces out, to put the infamous principles in practice upon every woman
he meets.

CHARLOTTE: But, if she is so apt at conjuring up these sentimental bug-
bears, why does she not discard him at once?

LETITIA: Why, she thinks her word too sacred to be trifled with. Besides, 100
her father, who has a great respect for the memory of his deceased friend,
is ever telling her how he shall renew his years in their union, and repeating the dying injunctions of old Van Dumpling.

CHARLOTTE: A mighty pretty story! And so you would make me believe,
that the sensible Maria would give up Dumpling manor, and the all- 105
accomplished Dimple as a husband, for the absurd, ridiculous reason, forsooth, because she despises and abhors him. Just as if a lady could not be
privileged to spend a man's fortune, ride in his carriage, be called after his
name, and call him her *nown dear lovee* when she wants money, without

loving and respecting the great he-creature. Oh! my dear girl, you are a monstrous prude. 110

LETITIA: I don't say what I would do; I only intimate how I suppose she wishes to act.

CHARLOTTE: No, no, no! A fig for sentiment. If she breaks, or wishes to break, with Mr. Dimple, depend upon it, she has some other man in her 115 eye. A woman rarely discards one lover, until she is sure of another. — Letitia little thinks what a clue I have to Dimple's conduct. The generous man submits to render himself disgusting to Maria, in order that she may leave him at liberty to address me. (*Aside, and rings a bell.*) I must change the subject. 120

(*Enter servant.*)

Frank, order the horses to. — Talking of marriage — did you hear that Sally Bloomsbury is going to be married next week to Mr. Indigo, the rich Carolinian?

LETITIA: Sally Bloomsbury married! — Why, she is not yet in her teens.

CHARLOTTE: I do not know how that is, but, you may depend upon it, 't is 125 a done affair. I have it from the best authority. There is my aunt Wyerley's Hannah (you know Hannah — though a black, she is a wench that was never caught in a lie in her life); now Hannah has a brother who courts Sarah, Mrs. Catgut the milliner's girl, and she told Hannah's brother, and Hannah, who, as I said before, is a girl of undoubted veracity, told it di- 130 rectly to me, that Mrs. Catgut was making a new cap for Miss Blooms-bury, which, as it was very dressy, it is very probable is designed for a wedding cap: now, as she is to be married, who can it be to, but to Mr. In-digo? Why, there is no other gentleman that visits at her papa's.

LETITIA: Say not a word more, Charlotte. Your intelligence is so direct 135 and well grounded, it is almost a pity that it is not a piece of scandal.

CHARLOTTE: Oh! I am the pink of prudence. Though I cannot charge myself with ever having discredited a tea-party by my silence, yet I take care never to report any thing of my acquaintance, especially if it is to their credit — *discredit*, I mean — until I have searched to the bottom of it. It 140 is true, there is infinite pleasure in this charitable pursuit. Oh! how delicious to go and condole with the friends of some backsliding sister, or to retire with some old dowager or maiden aunt of the family, who love scandal so well, that they cannot forbear gratifying their appetite at the expence of the reputation of their nearest relations! And then to return 145 full fraught with a rich collection of circumstances, to retail to the next circle of our acquaintance under the strongest injunctions of secrecy —

ha, ha, ha! — interlarding the melancholy tale with so many doleful shakes of the head, and more doleful, "Ah! who would have thought it! so amiable, so prudent a young lady, as we all thought her, what a monstrous pity! well, I have nothing to charge myself with; I acted the part of a friend, I warned her of the principles of that rake, I told her what would be the consequence; I told her so, I told her so." — Ha, ha, ha! 150

LETITIA: Ha, ha, ha! Well, but Charlotte, you don't tell me what you think of Miss Bloomsbury's match. 155

CHARLOTTE: Think! why I think it is probable she cried for a plaything, and they have given her a husband. Well, well, well, the puling chit shall not be deprived of her plaything: 't is only exchanging London dolls for American babies — Apropos, of babies, have you heard what Mrs. Affable's high-flying notions of delicacy have come to? 160

LETITIA: Who, she that was Miss Lovely?

CHARLOTTE: The same; she married Bob Affable of Schenectady. Don't you remember?

SERVANT (*enters*):   Madam, the carriage is ready.

LETITIA: Shall we go to the stores first, or visiting? 16

CHARLOTTE: I should think it rather too early to visit; especially Mrs. Prim: you know she is so particular.

LETITIA: Well, but what of Mrs. Affable?

CHARLOTTE: Oh, I'll tell you as we go; come, come, let us hasten. I hear Mrs. Catgut has some of the prettiest caps arrived you ever saw. I shall 17 die if I have not the first sight of them.   (*Exeunt.*)

SCENE II

A room in Van Rough's house. Maria sitting disconsolate at a table, with books, etc.

Song[1]

The sun sets in night, and the stars shun the day;
But glory remains when their lights fade away!
Begin, ye tormentors! your threats are in vain,
For the son of Alknomook shall never complain.

Remember the arrows he shot from his bow;
No — the son of Alknomook will never complain.

---

[1] This popular song of the period was published in New York by G. Gilfert (undated) under the title of *Alknomook* and carried the subtitle "The Death Song of the Cherokee Indians." It was published in London by Longman and Broderip in 1786.

Remember your chiefs by his hatchet laid low:
Why so slow? — do you wait till I shrink from the pain?

Remember the wood where in ambush we lay;
And the scalps which we bore from your nation away: 10
Now the flame rises fast, you exult in my pain;
But the son of Alknomook can never complain.

I go to the land where my father is gone;
His ghost shall rejoice in the fame of his son:
Death comes like a friend, he relieves me from pain;   15
And thy son, Oh Alknomook! has scorn'd to complain.

There is something in this song which ever calls forth my affections.
The manly virtue of courage, that fortitude which steels the heart against
the keenest misfortunes, which interweaves the laurel of glory amidst the
instruments of torture and death, displays something so noble, so exalted,   20
that in despite of the prejudices of education, I cannot but admire it, even
in a savage. The prepossession which our sex is supposed to entertain for
the character of a soldier is, I know, a standing piece of raillery among
the wits. A cockade, a lapell'd coat, and a feather, they will tell you, are ir-
resistible by a female heart. Let it be so. — Who is it that considers the   25
helpless situation of our sex, that does not see we each moment stand in
need of a protector, and that a brave one too. Formed of the more delicate materials of nature, endowed only with the softer passions, inca-
pable, from our ignorance of the world, to guard against the wiles of
mankind, our security for happiness often depends upon their generosity   30
and courage: — Alas! how little of the former do we find. How inconsis-
tent! that man should be leagued to destroy that honour, upon which
solely rests his respect and esteem. Ten thousand temptations allure us,
ten thousand passions betray us; yet the smallest deviation from the path
of rectitude is followed by the contempt and insult of man, and the more   35
remorseless pity of woman: years of penitence and tears cannot wash
away the stain, nor a life of virtue obliterate its remembrance. Reputation
is the life of woman; yet courage to protect it is masculine and disgusting;
and the only safe asylum a woman of delicacy can find is in the arms of a
man of honour. How naturally, then, should we love the brave, and the   40
generous; how gratefully should we bless the arm raised for our protection, when nerv'd by virtue, and directed by honour! Heaven grant that
the man with whom I may be connected — may be connected! —
Whither has my imagination transported me — whither does it now lead
me? — Am I not indissolubly engaged by every obligation of honour,   45

which my own consent, and my father's approbation can give, to a man who can never share my affections, and whom a few days hence it will be criminal for me to disapprove — to disapprove! would to heaven that were all — to despise. For, can the most frivolous manners, actuated by the most depraved heart, meet, or merit, anything but contempt from every woman of delicacy and sentiment?

VAN ROUGH (*without*): Mary!

MARIA: Ha, my father's voice — Sir! —

VAN ROUGH (*enters*): What, Mary, always singing doleful ditties, and moping over these plaguy books.

MARIA: I hope, Sir, that it is not criminal to improve my mind with books; or to divert my melancholy with singing at my leisure hours.

VAN ROUGH: Why, I don't know that, child; I don't know that. They us'd to say when I was a young man, that if a woman knew how to make a pudding, and to keep herself out of fire and water, she knew enough for a wife. Now, what good have these books done you? have they not made you melancholy? as you call it. Pray, what right has a girl of your age to be in the dumps? haven't you every thing your heart can wish; an't you going to be married to a young man of great fortune; an't you going to have the quit-rent of twenty miles square?

MARIA: One hundredth part of the land, and a lease for life of the heart of a man I could love, would satisfy me.

VAN ROUGH: Pho, pho, pho! child; nonsense, downright nonsense, child. This comes of your reading your storybooks; your Charles Grandisons, your Sentimental Journals, and your Robinson Crusoes, and such other trumpery. No, no, no! child, it is money makes the mare go; keep your eye upon the main chance, Mary.

MARIA: Marriage, Sir, is, indeed, a very serious affair.

VAN ROUGH: You are right, child; you are right. I am sure I found it so to my cost.

MARIA: I mean, Sir, that as marriage is a portion for life, and so intimately involves our happiness, we cannot be too considerate in the choice of our companion.

VAN ROUGH: Right, child; very right. A young woman should be very sober when she is making her choice, but when she has once made it, as you have done, I don't see why she should not be as merry as a grig; I am sure she has reason enough to be so — Solomon says, that "there is a time to laugh, and a time to weep"; now a time for a young woman to laugh is when she has made sure of a good rich husband. Now a time to cry, according to you, Mary, is when she is making choice of him: but, I should think that a young woman's time to cry was when she despaired of *get-*

ting one. — Why, there was your mother now; to be sure when I popp'd the question to her, she did look a little silly; but when she had once looked down on her apron strings, as all modest young women us'd to do, and drawled out ye-s, she was as brisk and as merry as a bee. 90

MARIA: My honoured mother, Sir, had no motive to melancholy; she married the man of her choice.

VAN ROUGH: The man of her choice! And pray, Mary, an't you going to marry the man of your choice — what trumpery notion is this? — It is these vile books. (*Throwing them away*) I'd have you to know, Mary, if you 95 won't make young Van Dumpling the man of *your* choice, you shall marry him as the man of *my* choice.

MARIA: You terrify me, Sir. Indeed, Sir, I am all submission. My will is yours.

VAN ROUGH: Why, that is the way your mother us'd to talk. "My will is 100 yours, my dear Mr. Van Rough, my will is yours": but she took special care to have her own way though for all that.

MARIA: Do not reflect upon my mother's memory, Sir —

VAN ROUGH: Why not, Mary, why not? She kept me from speaking my mind all her *life*, and do you think she shall henpeck me now she is *dead* 105 too? Come, come; don't go to sniveling: be a good girl, and mind the main chance. I'll see you well settled in the world.

MARIA: I do not doubt your love, Sir; and it is my duty to obey you. — I will endeavor to make my duty and inclination go hand in hand.

VAN ROUGH: Well, well, Mary; do you be a good girl, mind the main 110 chance, and never mind inclination. — Why, do you know that I have been down in the cellar this very morning to examine a pipe of Madeira which I purchased the week you were born, and mean to tap on your wedding day. — That pipe cost me fifty pounds sterling. It was well worth sixty pounds; but I overreached Ben Bulkhead, the supercargo: I'll 115 tell you the whole story. You must know that —

SERVANT (*enters*): Sir, Mr. Transfer, the broker, is below. (*Exit.*)

VAN ROUGH: Well, Mary, I must go. — Remember, and be a good girl, and mind the main chance. (*Exit.*)

MARIA (*alone*): How deplorable is my situation! How distressing for a 120 daughter to find her heart militating with her filial duty! I know my father loves me tenderly, why then do I reluctantly obey him? Heaven knows! with what reluctance I should oppose the will of a parent, or set an example of filial disobedience; at a parent's command I could wed awkwardness and deformity. Were the heart of my husband good, I 125 would so magnify his good qualities with the eye of conjugal affection that the defects of his person and manners should be lost in the emanation of his virtues. At a father's command, I could embrace poverty. Were the poor man my husband, I would learn resignation to my lot; I would enliven our frugal meal with good humour, and chase away misfortune 13(something) from our cottage with a smile. At a father's command, I could almost submit to what every female heart knows to be the most mortifying, to marry a weak man, and blush at my husband's folly in every company I visited. — But to marry a depraved wretch, whose only virtue is a polished exterior; who is actuated by the unmanly ambition of conquering 13 the defenceless; whose heart, insensible to the emotions of patriotism, dilates at the plaudits of every unthinking girl: whose laurels are the sighs and tears of the miserable victims of his specious behaviour. — Can he, who has no regard for the peace and happiness of other families, ever have a due regard for the peace and happiness of his own! Would to 14(something) heaven that my father were not so hasty in his temper! Surely, if I were to state my reasons for declining this match, he would not compel me to marry a man — whom, though my lips may solemnly promise to honour, I find my heart must ever despise.   (*Exit.*)

ACT II, SCENE I

Enter Charlotte and Letitia.

CHARLOTTE (*at entering*):   Betty, take those things out of the carriage and carry them to my chamber; see that you don't tumble them. — My dear, I protest, I think it was the homeliest of the whole. I declare I was almost tempted to return and change it.

LETITIA: Why would you take it?

CHARLOTTE: Didn't Mrs. Catgut say it was the most fashionable?

LETITIA: But, my dear, it will never sit becomingly on you.

CHARLOTTE: I know that; but did not you hear Mrs. Catgut say it was fashionable?

LETITIA: Did you see that sweet airy cap with the white sprig?

CHARLOTTE: Yes, and I longed to take it; but, my dear, what could I do? — Did not Mrs. Catgut say it was the most fashionable; and if I had not taken it, was not that awkward gawky, Sally Slender, ready to purchase it immediately?

LETITIA: Did you observe how she tumbled over the things at the next shop, and then went off without purchasing any thing, nor even thanking the poor man for his trouble? — But of all the awkward creatures, did you see Miss Blouze, endeavouring to thrust her unmerciful arm into those small kid gloves?

CHARLOTTE: Ha, ha, ha, ha!   20

LETITIA: Then did you take notice, with what an affected warmth
of friendship she and Miss Wasp met? when all their acquaintances
know how much pleasure they take in abusing each other in every
company?

CHARLOTTE: Lud! Letitia, is that so extraordinary? Why, my dear, I hope   25
you are not going to turn sentimentalist. — Scandal, you know, is but
amusing ourselves with the faults, foibles, follies and reputations of our
friends — indeed, I don't know why we should have friends if we are not
at liberty to make use of them. But no person is so ignorant of the world
as to suppose, because I amuse myself with a lady's faults, that I am   30
obliged to quarrel with her person, every time we meet; believe me, my
dear, we should have very few acquaintances at that rate.

(*Servant enters and delivers a letter to Charlotte, and goes out.*)

CHARLOTTE: You'll excuse me, my dear. (*Opens and reads to herself.*)

LETITIA: Oh, quite excusable.

CHARLOTTE: As I hope to be married, my brother Henry is in the city.   35

LETITIA: What, your brother, Colonel Manly?

CHARLOTTE: Yes, my dear; the only brother I have in the world.

LETITIA: Was he never in this city?

CHARLOTTE: Never nearer than Harlem Heights, where he lay with his
regiment.   40

LETITIA: What sort of a being is this brother of yours? If he is as chatty, as
pretty, as sprightly as you, half the belles in the city will be pulling caps
for him.

CHARLOTTE: My brother is the very counterpart and reverse of me: I am
gay, he is grave; I am airy, he is solid; I am ever selecting the most pleas- 45
ing objects for my laughter, he has a tear for every pitiful one. And thus,
whilst he is plucking the briars and thorns from the path of the unfortunate, I am strewing my own path with roses.

LETITIA: My sweet friend, not quite so poetical, and little more particular.

CHARLOTTE: Hands off, Letitia. I feel the rage of simile upon me; I can't   50
talk to you in any other way. My brother has a heart replete with the no-
blest sentiments, but then, it is like — it is like — Oh! you provoking
girl, you have deranged all my ideas — it is like — Oh! I have it — his
heart is like an old maiden lady's bandbox; it contains many costly things,
arranged with the most scrupulous nicety, yet the misfortune is that they   55
are too delicate, costly, and antiquated, for common use.

LETITIA: By what I can pick out of your flowery description, your brother
is no beau.

CHARLOTTE: No, indeed; he makes no pretension to the character. He'd ride, or rather fly, an hundred miles to relieve a distressed object, or to do 60 a gallant act in the service of his country: but, should you drop your fan or bouquet in his presence, it is ten to one that some beau at the farther end of the room would have the honour of presenting it to you, before he had observed that it fell. I'll tell you one of his antiquated, anti-gallant notions. — He said once in my presence, in a room full of company — 65 would you believe it — in a large circle of ladies, that the best evidence a gentleman could give a young lady of his respect and affection was to endeavour in a friendly manner to rectify her foibles. I protest I was crimson to the eyes, upon reflecting that I was known as his sister.

LETITIA: Insupportable creature! tell a lady of her faults! If he is so grave, 70 I fear I have no chance of captivating him.

CHARLOTTE: His conversation is like a rich old fashioned brocade, it will stand alone; every sentence is a sentiment. Now you may judge what a time I had with him, in my twelve months' visit to my father. He read me such lectures, out of pure brotherly affection, against the extremes of 75 fashion, dress, flirting, and coquetry, and all the other dear things which he knows I doat upon, that, I protest, his conversation made me as melancholy as if I had been at church; and heaven knows, though I never prayed to go there but on one occasion, yet I would have exchanged his conversation for a psalm and a sermon. Church is rather melancholy, to 80 be sure; but then I can ogle the beaux, and be regaled with "here endeth the first lesson"; but his brotherly *here,* you would think, had no end. You captivate him! Why, my dear, he would as soon fall in love with a box of Italian flowers. There is Maria now, if she were not engaged, she might do something. — Oh! how I should like to see that pair of penserosos 85 together, looking as grave as two sailors' wives of a stormy night, with a flow of sentiment meandering through their conversation like purling streams in modern poetry.

LETITIA: Oh! my dear fanciful —

CHARLOTTE: Hush! I hear some person coming through the entry. 90

SERVANT (*enters*): Madam, there's a gentleman below who calls himself Colonel Manly; do you chuse to be at home?

CHARLOTTE: Shew him in. (*Exit servant.*) Now for a sober face.

MANLY (*enters*): My dear Charlotte, I am happy that I once more enfold you within the arms of fraternal affection. I know you are going to ask 95 (amiable impatience!) how our parents do — the venerable pair transmit you their blessing by me — they totter on the verge of a well-spent life, and wish only to see their children settled in the world, to depart in peace.

CHARLOTTE: I am very happy to hear that they are well. (*Coolly*) Brother, will you give me leave to introduce you to our uncle's ward, one of my most intimate friends.

MANLY (*saluting Letitia*): I ought to regard your friends as my own.

CHARLOTTE: Come, Letitia, do give us a little dash of your vivacity; my brother is so sentimental, and so grave, that I protest he'll give us the vapours.

MANLY: Though sentiment and gravity, I know, are banished the polite world, yet, I hoped, they might find some countenance in the meeting of such near connections as brother and sister.

CHARLOTTE: Positively, brother, if you go one step further in this strain, you will set me crying, and that, you know, would spoil my eyes; and then I should never get the husband which our good papa and mamma have so kindly wished me — never be established in the world.

MANLY: Forgive me, my sister — I am no enemy to mirth; I love your sprightliness; and I hope it will one day enliven the hours of some worthy man; but when I mention the respectable authors of my existence — the cherishers and protectors of my helpless infancy, whose hearts glow with such fondness and attachment, that they would willingly lay down their lives for my welfare, you will excuse me if I am so unfashionable as to speak of them with some degree of respect and reverence.

CHARLOTTE: Well, well, brother; if you won't be gay, we'll not differ; I will be as grave as you wish. (*She affects gravity.*) And so, brother, you have come to the city to exchange some of your commutation notes for a little pleasure.

MANLY: Indeed, you are mistaken; my errand is not of amusement, but business and as I neither drink nor game, my expences will be so trivial, I shall have no occasion to sell my notes.

CHARLOTTE: Then you won't have occasion to do a very good thing. Why, there was the Vermont General — he came down some time since, sold all his musty notes at one stroke, and then laid the cash out in trinkets for his dear Fanny. I want a dozen pretty things myself; have you got the notes with you?

MANLY: I shall be ever willing to contribute as far as it is in my power, to adorn, or in any way to please my sister; yet, I hope, I shall never be obliged for this to sell my notes. I may be romantic, but I preserve them as a sacred deposit. Their full amount is justly due to me, but as embarrassments, the natural consequences of a long war, disable my country from supporting its credit, I shall wait with patience until it is rich enough to discharge them. If that is not in my day, they shall be transmitted as an honourable certificate to posterity, that I have humbly imitated our illustrious Washington, in having exposed my health and life in the service of my country, without reaping any other reward than the glory of conquering in so arduous a contest.

CHARLOTTE: Well said heroics. Why, my dear Henry, you have such a lofty way of saying things, that I protest I almost tremble at the thought 145 of introducing you to the polite circles in the city. The belles would think you were a player run mad, with your head filled with old scraps of tragedy; and, as to the beaux, they might admire, because they would not understand you. — But, however, I must, I believe, venture to introduce you to two or three ladies of my acquaintance. 150

LETITIA: And that will make him acquainted with thirty or forty beaux.

CHARLOTTE: Oh! brother, you don't know what a fund of happiness you have in store.

MANLY: I fear, sister, I have not refinement sufficient to enjoy it.

CHARLOTTE: Oh! you cannot fail being pleased. 155

LETITIA: Our ladies are so delicate and dressy.

CHARLOTTE: And our beaux so dressy and delicate.

LETITIA: Our ladies chat and flirt so agreeably.

CHARLOTTE: And our beaux simper and bow so gracefully.

LETITIA: With their hair so trim and neat. 160

CHARLOTTE: And their faces so soft and sleek.

LETITIA: Their buckles so tonish and bright.

CHARLOTTE: And their hands so slender and white.

LETITIA: I vow, Charlotte, we are quite poetical.

CHARLOTTE: And then, brother, the faces of the beaux are of such a lily 165 white hue! None of that horrid robustness of constitution, that vulgar corn-fed glow of health, which can only serve to alarm an unmarried lady with apprehensions, and prove a melancholy memento to a married one, that she can never hope for the happiness of being a widow. I will say this to the credit of our city beaux, that such is the delicacy of their complex- 170 ion, dress, and address, that, even had I no reliance upon the honour of the dear Adonises, I would trust myself in any possible situation with them, without the least apprehensions of rudeness.

MANLY: Sister Charlotte!

CHARLOTTE: Now, now, now brother (*Interrupting him*), now don't go to 175 spoil my mirth with a dash of your gravity; I am so glad to see you, I am in tip-top spirits. Oh! that you could be with us at a little snug party. There is Billy Simper, Jack Chassé, and Colonel Van Titter, Miss Promonade, and the two Miss Tambours, sometimes make a party, with some other ladies, in a side-box at the play. Everything is conducted with 180 such decorum — first we bow round to the company in general, then to

each one in particular, then we have so many inquiries after each other's
health, and we are so happy to meet each other, and it is so many ages
since we last had that pleasure, and, if a married lady is in company, we
have such a sweet dissertation upon her son Bobby's chin-cough, then   185
the curtain rises, then our sensibility is all awake, and then by the mere
force of apprehension, we torture some harmless expression into a double
meaning, which the poor author never dreamt of, and then we have recourse to our fans, and then we blush, and then the gentlemen jog one
another, peep under the fan, and make the prettiest remarks; and then we   190
giggle and they simper, and they giggle and we simper, and then the curtain drops, and then for nuts and oranges, and then we bow, and it's pray
Ma'am take it, and pray Sir keep it, and oh! not for the world, Sir: and
then the curtain rises again, and then we blush, and giggle, and simper,
and bow, all over again. Oh! the sentimental charms of a side-box con-   195
versation! (*All laugh.*)

MANLY: Well, sister, I join heartily with you in the laugh; for, in my
opinion, it is as justifiable to laugh at folly, as it is reprehensible to ridicule misfortune.

CHARLOTTE: Well, but brother, positively, I can't introduce you in these   200
clothes: why, your coat looks as if it were calculated for the vulgar purpose of keeping yourself comfortable.

MANLY: This coat was my regimental coat in the late war. The public tu-
mults of our state have induced me to buckle on the sword in support of
that government which I once fought to establish. I can only say, sister,   205
that there was a time when this coat was respectable, and some people
even thought that those men who had endured so many winter campaigns
in the service of their country, without bread, clothing, or pay, at least de-
served that the poverty of their appearance should not be ridiculed.

CHARLOTTE: We agree in opinion entirely, brother, though it would not   210
have done for me to have said it: it is the coat makes the man respectable.
In the time of the war, when we were almost frightened to death, why,
your coat was respectable, that is, fashionable; now another kind of coat
is fashionable, that is, respectable. And pray direct the tailor to make
yours the height of the fashion.   215

MANLY: Though it is of little consequence to me of what shape my coat is,
yet, as to the height of the fashion, there you will please to excuse me, sister. You know my sentiments on that subject. I have often lamented the
advantage which the French have over us in that particular. In Paris, the
fashions have their dawnings, their routine and declensions, and depend   220
as much upon the caprice of the day as in other countries; but there every
lady assumes a right to deviate from the general *ton*, as far as will be of

advantage to her own appearance. In America, the cry is, what is the fashion? and we follow it, indiscriminately, because it is so.

CHARLOTTE: Therefore it is, that when large hoops are in fashion, we often see many a plump girl lost in the immensity of a hoop petticoat, whose want of height and *em–bon–point* would never have been remarked in any other dress. When the high headdress is the mode, how then do we see a lofty cushion, with a profusion of gauze, feathers, and ribband, supported by a face no bigger than an apple; whilst a broad full-faced lady, who really would have appeared tolerably handsome in a large headdress, looks with her smart chapeau as masculine as a soldier.

MANLY: But remember, my dear sister, and I wish all my fair countrywomen would recollect, that the only excuse a young lady can have for going extravagantly into a fashion, is, because it makes her look extravagantly handsome. — Ladies, I must wish you a good morning.

CHARLOTTE: But, brother, you are going to make home with us.

MANLY: Indeed, I cannot. I have seen my uncle, and explained that matter.

CHARLOTTE: Come and dine with us, then. We have a family dinner about half past four o'clock.

MANLY: I am engaged to dine with the Spanish ambassador. I was introduced to him by an old brother officer; and instead of freezing me with a cold card of compliment to dine with him ten days hence, he, with the true old Castilian frankness, in a friendly manner, asked me to dine with him today — an honour I could not refuse. Sister, adieu — Madam, your most obedient —   (*Exit.*)

CHARLOTTE: I will wait upon you to the door, brother; I have something particular to say to you.   (*Exit.*)

LETITIA (*alone*):   What a pair! — She the pink of flirtation, he the essence of everything that is *outré* and gloomy. — I think I have completely deceived Charlotte by my manner of speaking of Mr. Dimple; she's too much the friend of Maria to be confided in. He is certainly rendering himself disagreeable to Maria, in order to break with her and proffer his hand to me. This is what the delicate fellow hinted in our last conversation.   (*Exit.*)

SCENE II

The Mall.

JESSAMY (*enters*):   Positively this Mall is a very pretty place. I hope the city won't ruin it by repairs. To be sure, it won't do to speak of in the same day with Ranelagh or Vauxhall; however, it's a fine place for a young fellow to display his person to advantage. Indeed, nothing is lost here; the girls have taste, and I am very happy to find they have adopted the elegant London fashion of looking back, after a genteel fellow like me has passed them. Ah! who comes here? This, by his awkwardness, must be the Yankee colonel's servant. I'll accost him.

(*Enter Jonathan.*)

Votre très — humble serviteur, Monsieur. I understand Colonel Manly, the Yankee officer, has the honour of your services.

JONATHAN: Sir! —

JESSAMY: I say, Sir, I understand that Colonel Manly has the honour of having you for a servant.

JONATHAN: Servant! Sir, do you take me for a neger — I am Colonel Manly's waiter.

JESSAMY: A true Yankee distinction, egad, without a difference. Why, Sir, do you not perform all the offices of a servant? Do you not even blacken his boots?

JONATHAN: Yes; I do grease them a bit sometimes; but I am a true blue son of liberty, for all that. Father said I should come as Colonel Manly's waiter to see the world, and all that; but no man shall master me: my father has as good a farm as the colonel.

JESSAMY: Well, Sir, we will not quarrel about terms upon the eve of an acquaintance, from which I promise myself so much satisfaction — therefore *sans cérémonie* —

JONATHAN: What? —

JESSAMY: I say, I am extremely happy to see Colonel Manly's waiter.

JONATHAN: Well, and I vow, too, I am pretty considerably glad to see you — but what the dogs need of all this outlandish lingo? Who may you be, Sir, if I may be so bold?

JESSAMY: I have the honour to be Mr. Dimple's servant, or, if you please, waiter. We lodge under the same roof, and should be glad of the honour of your acquaintance.

JONATHAN: You a waiter! By the living jingo, you look so topping, I took you for one of the agents to Congress.

JESSAMY: The brute has discernment notwithstanding his appearance. — Give me leave to say I wonder then at your familiarity.

JONATHAN: Why, as to the matter of that, Mr. — pray, what's your name?

JESSAMY: Jessamy, at your service.

JONATHAN: Why, I swear we don't make any great matter of distinction in our state, between quality and other folks.

JESSAMY: This is, indeed, a levelling principle. I hope, Mr. Jonathan, you have not taken part with the insurgents.

JONATHAN: Why, since General Shays has sneaked off, and given us the
bag to hold, I don't care to give my opinion; but you'll promise not to tell   45
— put your ear this way — you won't tell? — I vow, I did think the stur-
geons were right.

JESSAMY: I thought, Mr. Jonathan, you Massachusetts men always argued
with a gun in your hand. — Why didn't you join them?

JONATHAN: Why, the colonel is one of those folks called the Shin — shin   50
— dang it all, I can't speak them lignum vitæ words — you know who I
mean — there is a company of them — they wear a China goose at their
buttonhole — a kind of gilt thing. — Now the colonel told father and
brother — you must know there are, let me see — there is Elnathan,
Silas, and Barnabas, Tabitha — no, no, she's a she — tarnation, now I   55
have it — there's Elnathan, Silas, Barnabas, Jonathan, that's I — seven
of us, six went into the wars, and I stayed at home to take care of mother.
Colonel said that it was a burning shame for the true blue Bunker-hill
sons of liberty, who had fought Governor Hutchinson, Lord North, and
the Devil, to have any hand in kicking up a cursed dust against a govern-   60
ment, which we had every mother's son of us a hand in making.

JESSAMY: Bravo! — Well, have you been abroad in the city since your arrival? What have you seen that is curious and entertaining?

JONATHAN: Oh! I have seen a power of fine sights. I went to see two
marble-stone men and a leaden horse, that stands out in doors in all   65
weathers; and when I came where they was, one had got no head, and t'
other weren't there. They said as how the leaden man was a damn'd tory,
and that he took wit in his anger and rode off in the time of the troubles.

JESSAMY: But this was not the end of your excursion.

JONATHAN: Oh, no; I went to a place they call Holy Ground. Now I   70
counted this was a place where folks go to meeting; so I put my hymn-
book in my pocket, and walked softly and grave as a minister; and when
I came there, the dogs a bit of a meetinghouse could I see. At last I spied
a young gentlewoman standing by one of the seats, which they have here
at the doors — I took her to be the deacon's daughter, and she looked so   75
kind, and so obliging, that I thought I would go and ask her the way to
lecture, and would you think it — she called me dear, and sweeting, and
honey, just as if we were married; by the living jingo, I had a month's
mind to buss her.

JESSAMY: Well, but how did it end?   80

JONATHAN: Why, as I was standing talking with her, a parcel of sailor men
and boys got round me, the snarl headed curs fell a-kicking and cursing
of me at such a tarnal rate, that, I vow, I was glad to take to my heels and
split home, right off, tail on end like a stream of chalk.

JESSAMY: Why, my dear friend, you are not acquainted with the city; that   85
girl you saw was a — (*Whispers.*)

JONATHAN: Mercy on my soul! was that young woman a harlot! — Well,
if this is New York Holy Ground, what must the Holy-day Ground be!

JESSAMY: Well, you should not judge of the city too rashly. We have a
number of elegant fine girls here, that make a man's leisure hours pass   90
very agreeably. I would esteem it an honour to announce you to some of
them. — Gad! that announce is a select word; I wonder where I picked
it up.

JONATHAN: I don't want to know them.

JESSAMY: Come, come, my dear friend, I see that I must assume the honour   95
of being the director of your amusements. Nature has given us passions,
and youth and opportunity stimulate to gratify them. It is no shame, my
dear Blueskin, for a man to amuse himself with a little gallantry.

JONATHAN: Girl huntry! I don't altogether understand. I never played at
that game. I know how to play hunt the squirrel, but I can't play anything   100
with the girls; I am as good as married.

JESSAMY: Vulgar, horrid brute! Married, and above a hundred miles from
his wife, and think that an objection to his making love to every woman
he meets! He never can have read, no, he never can have been in a room
with a volume of the divine Chesterfield. — So you are married?   105

JONATHAN: No, I don't say so; I said I was as good as married, a kind of
promise.

JESSAMY: As good as married! —

JONATHAN: Why, yes; there's Tabitha Wymen, the deacon's daughter, at
home, she and I have been courting a great while, and folks say as how   110
we are to be married; and so I broke a piece of money with her when we
parted, and she promised not to spark it with Solomon Dyer while I am
gone. You wouldn't have me false to my true love, would you?

JESSAMY: May be you have another reason for constancy; possibly the
young lady has a fortune? Ha! Mr. Jonathan, the solid charms; the chains   115
of love are never so binding as when the links are made of gold.

JONATHAN: Why, as to fortune, I must needs say her father is pretty dumb
rich; he went representative for our town last year. He will give her —
let me see — four times seven is — seven times four — nought and
carry one — he will give her twenty acres of land — somewhat rocky   120
though — a Bible, and a cow.

JESSAMY: Twenty acres of rock, a Bible, and a cow! Why, my dear Mr.
Jonathan, we have servant maids, or, as you would more elegantly express
it, wait'resses, in this city, who collect more in one year from their mis-
tresses' cast clothes.   125

JONATHAN: You don't say so! —

JESSAMY: Yes, and I'll introduce you to one of them. There is a little lump of flesh and delicacy that lives at next door, wait'ress to Miss Maria; we often see her on the stoop.

JONATHAN: But are you sure she would be courted by me?   130

JESSAMY: Never doubt it; remember a faint heart never — blisters on my tongue — I was going to be guilty of a vile proverb; flat against the authority of Chesterfield. — I say there can be no doubt that the brilliancy of your merit will secure you a favourable reception.

JONATHAN: Well, but what must I say to her?   135

JESSAMY: Say to her! why, my dear friend, though I admire your profound knowledge on every other subject, yet, you will pardon my saying, that your want of opportunity has made the female heart escape the poignancy of your penetration. Say to her! — Why, when a man goes a-courting, and hopes for success, he must begin with doing, and not saying.   140

JONATHAN: Well, what must I do?

JESSAMY: Why, when you are introduced you must make five or six elegant bows.

JONATHAN: Six elegant bows! I understand that; six, you say? Well —

JESSAMY: Then you must press and kiss her hand; then press and kiss and   145 so on to her lips and cheeks; then talk as much as you can about hearts, darts, flames, nectar and ambrosia — the more incoherent the better.

JONATHAN: Well, but suppose she should be angry with I?

JESSAMY: Why, if she should pretend — please to observe, Mr. Jonathan — if she should pretend to be offended, you must — But I'll tell you how   150 my master acted in such a case: He was seated by a young lady of eighteen upon a sofa, plucking with a wanton hand the blooming sweets of youth and beauty. When the lady thought it necessary to check his ardour, she called up a frown upon her lovely face so irresistibly alluring that it would have warmed the frozen bosom of age: "Remember," said   155 she, putting her delicate arm upon his, "remember your character and my honour." My master instantly dropped upon his knees, with eyes swimming with love, cheeks glowing with desire, and in the gentlest modulation of voice, he said — "My dear Caroline, in a few months our hands will be indissolubly united at the altar; our hearts I feel are already so —   160 the favours you now grant as evidence of your affection, are favours indeed; yet when the ceremony is once past, what will now be received with rapture will then be attributed to duty."

JONATHAN: Well, and what was the consequence?

JESSAMY: The consequence! — Ah! forgive me, my dear friend, but you   165 New England gentlemen have such a laudable curiosity of seeing the bottom of every thing — why, to be honest, I confess I saw the blooming cherub of a consequence smiling in its angelic mother's arms, about ten months afterwards.

JONATHAN: Well, if I follow all your plans, make them six bows, and all that; shall I have such little cherubim consequences? 170

JESSAMY: Undoubtedly. — What are you musing upon?

JONATHAN: You say you'll certainly make me acquainted? — Why, I was thinking then how I should contrive to pass this broken piece of silver — won't it buy a sugar-dram? 175

JESSAMY: What is that, the love-token from the deacon's daughter? — You come on bravely. But I must hasten to my master. Adieu, my dear friend.

JONATHAN: Stay, Mr. Jessamy — must I buss her when I am introduced to her? 180

JESSAMY: I told you, you must kiss her.

JONATHAN: Well, but must I buss her?

JESSAMY: Why, kiss and buss, and buss and kiss, is all one.

JONATHAN: Oh! my dear friend, though you have a profound knowledge of all, a pugnancy of tribulation, you don't know everything. (*Exit.*) 185

JESSAMY (*alone*):   Well, certainly I improve; my master could not have insinuated himself with more address into the heart of a man he despised. — Now will this blundering dog sicken Jenny with his nauseous pawings, until she flies into my arms for very ease. How sweet will the contrast be, between the blundering Jonathan, and the courtly and ac- 190 complished Jessamy!

ACT III, SCENE I

Dimple's room.

DIMPLE (*discovered at a toilet, reading*):   "Women have in general but one object, which is their beauty." Very true, my lord; positively very true. "Nature has hardly formed a woman ugly enough to be insensible to flattery upon her person." Extremely just, my lord; every day's delightful experience confirms this. "If her face is so shocking that she must, in some degree, be conscious of it, her figure and air, she thinks, make ample amends for it." The sallow Miss Wan is a proof of this. — Upon my telling the distasteful wretch, the other day, that her countenance spoke the pensive language of sentiment, and that Lady Wortley Montague declared, that if the ladies were arrayed in the garb of innocence, the face 10 would be the last part which would be admired, as Monsieur Milton expresses it, she grin'd horribly a ghastly smile. "If her figure is deformed, she thinks her face counterbalances it."

(*Enter Jessamy with letters.*)

DIMPLE: Where got you these, Jessamy?
JESSAMY: Sir, the English packet is arrived.   15

(*Dimple opens and reads a letter enclosing notes.*)

"Sir,
"I have drawn bills on you in favour of Messrs. Van Cash and Co. as per margin. I have taken up your note to Col. Piquet, and discharged your debts to my Lord Lurcher and Sir Harry Rook. I herewith enclose you copies of the bills, which I have no doubt will be immediately honoured.   20
On failure, I shall empower some lawyer in your country to recover the amounts.
   "I am, Sir,
      "Your most humble servant,
         "JOHN HAZARD."   25

Now, did not my lord expressly say that it was unbecoming a well-bred man to be in a passion, I confess I should be ruffled. (*Reads.*) "There is no accident so unfortunate, which a wise man may not turn to his advantage; nor any accident so fortunate, which a fool will not turn to his disadvantage." True, my lord: but how advantage can be derived from this, I   30
can't see. Chesterfield himself, who made, however, the worst practice of the most excellent precepts, was never in so embarrassing a situation. I love the person of Charlotte, and it is necessary I should command the fortune of Letitia. As to Maria! — I doubt not by my *sang-froid* behavior I shall compel her to decline the match; but the blame must not fall upon   35
me. A prudent man, as my lord says, should take all the credit of a good action to himself, and throw the discredit of a bad one upon others. I must break with Maria, marry Letitia, and as for Charlotte — why, Charlotte must be a companion to my wife. — Here, Jessamy! (*Enter Jessamy.*)
DIMPLE (*folds and seals two letters*):   Here, Jessamy, take this letter to my love.   40
(*Gives him one.*)
JESSAMY: To which of your honour's loves? — Oh! (*Reading*) to Miss Letitia, your honour's rich love.
DIMPLE: And this (*Delivering another*) to Miss Charlotte Manly. See that you deliver them privately.
JESSAMY (*going*):   Yes, your honour.   45

DIMPLE: Jessamy, who are these strange lodgers that came to the house last night?

JESSAMY: Why, the master is a Yankee colonel; I have not seen much of him; but the man is the most unpolished animal your honour ever disgraced your eyes by looking upon. I have had one of the most *outré* conversations with him! — He really has a most prodigious effect upon my risibility.

DIMPLE: I ought, according to every rule of Chesterfield, to wait on him and insinuate myself into his good graces. — Jessamy, wait on the colonel with my compliments, and if he is disengaged, I will do myself the honour of paying him my respects. — Some ignorant unpolished boor —

JESSAMY (*goes off and returns*): Sir, the colonel is gone out, and Jonathan, his servant, says that he is gone to stretch his legs upon the Mall — Stretch his legs! what an indelicacy of diction!

DIMPLE: Very well. Reach me my hat and sword. I'll accost him there, in my way to Letitia's, as by accident; pretend to be struck with his person and address, and endeavour to steal into his confidence. Jessamy, I have no business for you at present. (*Exit.*)

JESSAMY (*taking up the book*): My master and I obtain our knowledge from the same source — though, gad! I think myself much the prettier fellow of the two. (*Surveying himself in the glass*) That was a brilliant thought, to insinuate that I folded my master's letters for him; the folding is so neat, that it does honour to the operator. I once intended to have insinuated that I wrote his letters too; but that was before I saw them; it won't do now; no honour there, positively. — "Nothing looks more vulgar (*Reading affectedly*), ordinary, and illiberal, than ugly, uneven, and ragged nails; the ends of which should be kept even and clean, not tipped with black, and cut in small segments of circles" — Segments of circles! surely my lord did not consider that he wrote for the beaux. Segments of circles! what a crabbed term! Now I dare answer, that my master, with all his learning, does not know that this means, according to the present mode, to let the nails grow long, and then cut them off even at top. (*Laughing without*) Ha! that's Jenny's titter. I protest I despair of ever teaching that girl to laugh; she has something so execrably natural in her laugh, that I declare it absolutely discomposes my nerves. How came she into our house! — (*Calling*) Jenny!

(*Enter Jenny.*)

JESSAMY: Prythee, Jenny, don't spoil your fine face with laughing.

JENNY: Why, mustn't I laugh, Mr. Jessamy?

JESSAMY: You may smile; but, as my lord says, nothing can authorise a   85
laugh.

JENNY: Well, but I can't help laughing — Have you seen him, Mr. Jessamy? Ha, ha, ha!

JESSAMY: Seen whom? —

JENNY: Why, Jonathan, the New England colonel's servant. Do you know   90
he was at the play last night, and the stupid creature don't know where he
has been. He would not go to a play for the world; he thinks it was a
show, as he calls it.

JESSAMY: As ignorant and unpolished as he is, do you know, Miss Jenny,
that I propose to introduce him to the honour of your acquaintance.   95

JENNY: Introduce him to me! for what?

JESSAMY: Why, my lovely girl, that you may take him under your protection, as Madam Rambouillet did young Stanhope; that you may, by your
plastic hand, mould this uncouth cub into a gentleman. He is to make
love to you.   100

JENNY: Make love to me! —

JESSAMY: Yes, Mistress Jenny, make love to you; and, I doubt not, when he
shall become domesticated in your kitchen, that this boor, under your
auspices, will soon become *un amiable petit Jonathan.*

JENNY: I must say, Mr. Jessamy, if he copies after me, he will be vastly   105
monstrously polite.

JESSAMY: Stay here one moment, and I will call him. — Jonathan! —
(*Calling*) Mr. Jonathan! —

JONATHAN (*within*):   Holla! there. — (*Entering*) You promise to stand by
me — six bows you say. (*Bows.*)   110

JESSAMY: Mrs. Jenny, I have the honour of presenting Mr. Jonathan,
Colonel Manly's waiter, to you. I am extremely happy that I have it in my
power to make two worthy people acquainted with each other's merit.

JENNY: So, Mr. Jonathan, I hear you were at the play last night.

JONATHAN: At the play! why, did you think I went to the devil's drawing   115
room!

JENNY: The devil's drawing room!

JONATHAN: Yes; why an't cards and dice the devil's device; and the playhouse, the shop where the devil hangs out the vanities of the world, upon
the tenterhooks of temptation. I believe you have not heard how they   120
were acting the old boy one night, and the wicked one came among them
sure enough; and went right off in a storm, and carried one quarter of the
playhouse with him. Oh! no, no, no! you won't catch me at a playhouse, I
warrant you.

JENNY: Well, Mr. Jonathan, though I don't scruple your veracity, I have   125
some reasons for believing you were there; pray, where were you about six
o'clock?

JONATHAN: Why, I went to see one Mr. Morrison, the *hocus pocus* man;
they said as how he could eat a case knife.

JENNY: Well, and how did you find the place?   130

JONATHAN: As I was going about here and there, to and again, to find it, I
saw a great crowd of folks going into a long entry, that had lanterns over
the door; so I asked a man, whether that was not the place where they
played *hocus pocus*? He was a very civil kind man, though he did speak like
the Hessians; he lifted up his eyes and said — "they play *hocus pocus* tricks   135
enough there, Got knows, mine friend."

JENNY: Well —

JONATHAN: So I went right in, and they showed me away clean up to the
garret, just like a meetinghouse gallery. And so I saw a power of topping
folks, all sitting round in little cabbins, just like father's corncribs — and   140
then there was such a squeaking with the fiddles, and such a tarnal blaze
with the lights, my head was near turned. At last the people that sat near
me set up such a hissing — hiss — like so many mad cats; and then they
went thump, thump, thump, just like our Peleg threshing wheat, and
stampt away, just like the nation; and called out for one Mr. Langolee —   145
I suppose he helps act the tricks.

JENNY: Well, and what did you do all this time?

JONATHAN: Gor, I — I liked the fun, and so I thumpt away, and hiss'd as
lustily as the best of 'em. One sailor-looking man that sat by me, seeing
me stamp, and knowing I was a cute fellow, because I could make a roar-   150
ing noise, clapt me on the shoulder and said, you are a damned hearty
cock, smite my timbers! I told him so I was, but I thought he need not
swear so, and make use of such naughty words.

JESSAMY: The savage! — Well, and did you see the man with his tricks?

JONATHAN: Why, I vow, as I was looking out for him, they lifted up a great   155
green cloth, and let us look right into the next neighbour's house. Have
you a good many houses in New York made so in that 'ere way?

JENNY: Not many, but did you see the family?

JONATHAN: Yes, swamp it; I see'd the family.

JENNY: Well, and how did you like them?   160

JONATHAN: Why, I vow they were pretty much like other families — there
was a poor, good-natured, curse of a husband, and a sad rantipole of a
wife.

JENNY: But did you see no other folks?

JONATHAN: Yes. There was one youngster, they called him Mr. Joseph; he   165
talked as sober and as pious as a minister; but like some ministers that I
know, he was a sly tike in his heart for all that: He was going to ask a
young woman to spark it with him, and — the Lord have mercy on my
soul! — she was another man's wife.

JESSAMY: The Wabash!   170

JENNY: And did you see any more folks?

JONATHAN: Why they came on as thick as mustard. For my part, I thought
the house was haunted. There was a soldier fellow, who talked about his
row de dow dow, and courted a young woman; but of all the cute folk I
saw, I liked one little fellow —   175

JENNY: Aye! who was he?

JONATHAN: Why, he had red hair, and a little round plump face like mine,
only not altogether so handsome. His name was Darby — that was his
baptizing name, his other name I forgot. Oh! it was, Wig — Wag —
Wag-all, Darby Wag-all — pray, do you know him? — I should like to   180
take a sling with him, or a drap of cyder with a pepper pod in it, to make
it warm and comfortable.

JENNY: I can't say I have that pleasure.

JONATHAN: I wish you did, he is a cute fellow. But there was one thing I
didn't like in that Mr. Darby; and that was, he was afraid of some of them   185
'ere shooting irons, such as your troopers wear on training days. Now, I'm
a true born Yankee American son of liberty, and I never was afraid of a
gun yet in all my life.

JENNY: Well, Mr. Jonathan, you were certainly at the playhouse.

JONATHAN: I at the playhouse! — Why didn't I see the play then?   190

JENNY: Why, the people you saw were players.

JONATHAN: Mercy on my soul! did I see the wicked players? — Mayhap
that 'ere Darby that I liked so, was the old serpent himself, and had
his cloven foot in his pocket. Why, I vow, now I come to think on 't, the
candles seemed to burn blue, and I am sure where I sat it smelt tarnally   195
of brimstone.

JESSAMY: Well, Mr. Jonathan, from your account, which I confess is very
accurate, you must have been at the playhouse.

JONATHAN: Why, I vow I began to smell a rat. When I came away, I went
to the man for my money again: "You want your money," says he. "Yes,"   200
says I. "For what," says he. "Why," says I, "no man shall jocky me out of
my money; I paid my money to see sights, and the dogs a bit of a sight
have I seen, unless you call listening to people's private business a sight."
"Why," says he, "it is the School for Scandalization." — "The School for

Scandalization! — Oh, ho! no wonder you New York folks are so cute at   205
it, when you go to school to learn it": and so I jogged off.

JESSAMY: My dear Jenny, my master's business drags me from you; would
to heaven I knew no other servitude than to your charms.

JONATHAN: Well, but don't go; you won't leave me so. —

JESSAMY: Excuse me. (*Aside to him*) Remember the cash.   (*Exit.*)   210

JENNY: Mr. Jonathan, won't you please to sit down. Mr. Jessamy tells me
you wanted to have some conversation with me.

(*Having brought forward two chairs, they sit.*)

JONATHAN: Ma'am! —

JENNY: Sir! —

JONATHAN: Ma'am! —   215

JENNY: Pray, how do you like the city, Sir?

JONATHAN: Ma'am! —

JENNY: I say, Sir, how do you like New York?

JONATHAN: Ma'am! —

JENNY: The stupid creature! but I must pass some little time with him, if   220
it is only to endeavour to learn whether it was his master that made such
an abrupt entrance into our house, and my young mistress's heart, this
morning. (*Aside*) As you don't seem to like to talk, Mr. Jonathan — do
you sing?

JONATHAN: Gor, I — I am glad she asked that, for I forgot what Mr. Jes-   225
samy bid me say, and I dare as well be hanged as act what he bid me do,
I'm so ashamed. (*Aside*) Yes, Ma'am, I can sing — I can sing "Mear," "Old
Hundred," and "Bangor."

JENNY: Oh! I don't mean psalm tunes. Have you no little song to please
the ladies; such as "Roslin Castle" or "The Maid of the Mill"?   230

JONATHAN: Why, all my tunes go to meeting tunes, save one, and I count
you won't altogether like that 'ere.

JENNY: What is it called?

JONATHAN: I am sure you have heard folks talk about it, it is called "Yankee Doodle."[2]   235

JENNY: Oh! it is the tune I am fond of; and, if I know anything of my mistress, she would be glad to dance to it. Pray, sing?

---

[2]The date, authorship, and composer of this popular song are the source of much debate. It was
well known in the colonies in the 1760s and during the balance of the eighteenth century references are commonplace. Although the song may have been written as early as 1745, its
printed history begins in April 1767. The words were published in the *Bath Chronicle* in 1776.

JONATHAN (*he sings*):

> Father and I went up to camp,
> Along with Captain Goodwin;
> And there we saw the men and boys, 240
> As thick as hasty pudding.
> > Yankee Doodle do, etc.

> And there we saw a swamping gun,
> Big as log of maple,
> On a little deuced cart, 245
> A load for father's cattle.
> > Yankee Doodle do, etc.

> And every time they fired it off
> It took a horn of powder,
> It made a noise — like father's gun, 250
> Only a nation louder.
> > Yankee Doodle do, etc.

> There was a man in our town,
> His name was —

No, no, that won't do. Now, if I was with Tabitha Wymen and Jemima 255
Cawley, down at father Chase's, I shouldn't mind singing this all out before them — you would be affronted if I was to sing that, though that's a
lucky thought; if you should be affronted, I have something dang'd cute,
which Jessamy told me to say to you.

JENNY: Is that all! I assure you I like it of all things. 260

JONATHAN: No, no; I can sing more, some other time, when you and I are
better acquainted, I'll sing the whole of it — no, no — that's a fib — I
can't sing but a hundred and ninety verses: our Tabitha at home can sing
it all. — (*Sings.*)

> Marblehead's a rocky place, 265
> And Cape-Cod is sandy;
> Charleston is burnt down,
> Boston is the dandy.
> > Yankee Doodle do, etc.

I vow, my own town song has put me into such topping spirits, that I be- 270
lieve I'll begin to do a little, as Jessamy says we must when we go a-court-

ing — (*Runs and kisses her.*) Burning rivers! cooling flames! red hot roses! pignuts! hasty pudding and ambrosia!

JENNY: What means this freedom! (*Striking him*) you insulting wretch.

JONATHAN: Are you affronted?   275

JENNY: Affronted! with what looks shall I express my anger?

JONATHAN: Looks! why, as to the matter of looks, you look as cross as a witch.

JENNY: Have you no feeling for the delicacy of my sex?

JONATHAN: Feeling! Gor, I — I feel the delicacy of your sex pretty smartly   280
(*Rubbing his cheek*), though, I vow, I thought when you city ladies courted and married, and all that, you put feeling out of the question. But I want to know whether you are really affronted, or only pretend to be so? 'Cause, if you are certainly right down affronted, I am at the end of my tether; — Jessamy didn't tell me what to say to you.   285

JENNY: Pretend to be affronted!

JONATHAN: Aye, aye, if you only pretend, you shall hear how I'll go to work to make cherubim consequences. (*He runs up to her.*)

JENNY: Begone, you brute!

JONATHAN: That looks like mad; but I won't lose my speech. My dearest   290
Jenny — your name is Jenny, I think? My dearest Jenny, though I have the highest esteem for the sweet favours you have just now granted me — Gor, that's a fib though, but Jessamy says it is not wicked to tell lies to the women. (*Aside*) I say, though I have the highest esteem for the favours you have just now granted me, yet, you will consider, that as soon as the   295
dissolvable knot is tied, they will no longer be favours, but only matters of duty, and matters of course.

JENNY: Marry you! you audacious monster! get out of my sight, or rather let me fly from you.   (*Exit hastily.*)

JONATHAN: Gor! she's gone off in a swinging passion, before I had time to   300
think of consequences. If this is the way with your city ladies, give me the twenty acres of rock, the Bible, the cow, and Tabitha, and a little peaceable bundling.

Scene II

The Mall. Manly enters.

MANLY: It must be so, Montague! and it is not all the tribe of Mandevilles shall convince me, that a nation, to become great, must first become dissipated. Luxury is surely the bane of a nation: Luxury! which enervates both soul and body, by opening a thousand new sources of enjoyment,

opens, also, a thousand new sources of contention and want: Luxury! 5
which renders a people weak at home, and accessible to bribery, corruption, and force from abroad. When the Grecian states knew no other
tools than the axe and the saw, the Grecians were a great, a free, and a
happy people. The kings of Greece devoted their lives to the service of
their country, and her senators knew no other superiority over their fel- 10
low citizens than a glorious preeminence in danger and virtue. They exhibited to the world a noble spectacle, — a number of independent
states united by a similarity of language, sentiment, manners, common
interest, and common consent, in one grand mutual league of protection. — And, thus united, long might they have continued the cherish- 15
ers of arts and sciences, the protectors of the oppressed, the scourge of
tyrants, and the safe asylum of liberty: But when foreign gold, and still
more pernicious, foreign luxury, had crept among them, they sapped the
vitals of their virtue. The virtues of their ancestors were only found in
their writings. Envy and suspicion, the vices of little minds, possessed 20
them. The various states engendered jealousies of each other; and, more
unfortunately, growing jealous of their great federal council, the Amphictyons, they forgot that their common safety had existed, and would
exist, in giving them an honourable extensive prerogative. The common
good was lost in the pursuit of private interest; and that people, who, by 25
uniting, might have stood against the world in arms, by dividing, crumbled into ruin; — their name is now only known in the page of the historian, and what they once were, is all we have left to admire. Oh! that
America! Oh! that my country, would in this her day, learn the things
which belong to her peace! 30

DIMPLE (*enters*): You are Colonel Manly, I presume?

MANLY: At your service, Sir.

DIMPLE: My name is Dimple, Sir. I have the honour to be a lodger in the
same house with you, and hearing you were in the Mall, came hither to
take the liberty of joining you. 35

MANLY: You are very obliging, Sir.

DIMPLE: As I understand you are a stranger here, Sir, I have taken the liberty to introduce myself to your acquaintance, as possibly I may have it in
my power to point out some things in this city worthy your notice.

MANLY: An attention to strangers is worthy a liberal mind, and must ever 40
be gratefully received. But to a soldier, who has no fixed abode, such attentions are particularly pleasing.

DIMPLE: Sir, there is no character so respectable as that of a soldier. And,
indeed, when we reflect how much we owe to those brave men who have
suffered so much in the service of their country, and secured to us those 45

inestimable blessings that we now enjoy, our liberty and independence, they demand every attention which gratitude can pay. For my own part, I never meet an officer, but I embrace him as my friend, nor a private in distress, but I insensibly extend my charity to him. (*Aside*) I have hit the Bumpkin off very tolerably. 50

MANLY: Give me your hand, Sir! I do not proffer this hand to everybody; but you steal into my heart. I hope I am as insensible to flattery as most men; but I declare (it may be my weak side), that I never hear the name of soldier mentioned with respect, but I experience a thrill of pleasure, which I never feel on any other occasion. 55

DIMPLE: Will you give me leave, my dear colonel, to confer an obligation on myself, by shewing you some civilities during your stay here, and giving a similar opportunity to some of my friends?

MANLY: Sir, I thank you; but I believe my stay in this city will be very short. 60

DIMPLE: I can introduce you to some men of excellent sense, in whose company you will esteem yourself happy; and, by way of amusement, to some fine girls, who will listen to your soft things with pleasure.

MANLY: Sir, I should be proud of the honour of being acquainted with those gentlemen — but, as for the ladies, I don't understand you. 65

DIMPLE: Why, Sir, I need not tell you, that when a young gentleman is alone with a young lady, he must say some soft things to her fair cheek — indeed, the lady will expect it. To be sure, there is not much pleasure, when a man of the world and a finished coquette meet, who perfectly know each other; but how delicious is it to excite the emotions of joy, 70 hope, expectation, and delight, in the bosom of a lovely girl, who believes every tittle of what you say to be serious.

MANLY: Serious, Sir! In my opinion, the man, who, under pretensions of marriage, can plant thorns in the bosom of an innocent, unsuspecting girl, is more detestable than a common robber, in the same proportion, as 75 private violence is more despicable than open force, and money of less value than happiness.

DIMPLE (*aside*):   How he awes me by the superiority of his sentiments. As you say, Sir, a gentleman should be cautious how he mentions marriage.

MANLY: Cautious, Sir! No person more approves of an intercourse be- 80 tween the sexes than I do. Female conversation softens our manners, whilst our discourse, from the superiority of our literary advantages, improves their minds. But, in our young country, where there is no such thing as gallantry, when a gentleman speaks of love to a lady, whether he mentions marriage, or not, she ought to conclude, either that he meant 85 to insult her, or, that his intentions are the most serious and honourable.

How mean, how cruel, is it, by a thousand tender assiduities, to win the affections of an amiable girl, and though you leave her virtue unspotted, to betray her into the appearance of so many tender partialities, that every man of delicacy would suppress his inclination towards her, by supposing her heart engaged! Can any man, for the trivial gratification of his leisure hours, affect the happiness of a whole life! His not having spoken of marriage may add to his perfidy, but can be no excuse for his conduct. 90

DIMPLE: Sir, I admire your sentiments — they are mine. The light observations that fell from me, were only a principle of the tongue; they came not from the heart — my practice has ever disapproved these principles. 95

MANLY: I believe you, Sir. I should with reluctance suppose that those pernicious sentiments could find admittance into the heart of a gentleman.

DIMPLE: I am now, Sir, going to visit a family, where, if you please, I will have the honour of introducing you. Mr. Manly's ward, Miss Letitia, is a young lady of immense fortune; and his niece, Miss Charlotte Manly, is a young lady of great sprightliness and beauty. 100

MANLY: That gentleman, Sir, is my uncle, and Miss Manly my sister.

DIMPLE (aside):   The devil she is! Miss Manly your sister, Sir? I rejoice to hear it, and feel a double pleasure in being known to you. (Aside) Plague on him! I wish he was at Boston again with all my soul. 105

MANLY: Come, Sir, will you go?

DIMPLE: I will follow you in a moment, Sir. (Exit Manly.) Plague on it! this is unlucky. A fighting brother is a cursed appendage to a fine girl. Egad! I just stopped in time; had he not discovered himself, in two minutes more I should have told him how well I was with his sister. — Indeed, I cannot see the satisfaction of an intrigue, if one can't have the pleasure of communicating it to our friends. (Exit.) 110

ACT IV, SCENE I

Charlotte's apartment. Charlotte leads in Maria.

CHARLOTTE: This is so kind, my sweet friend, to come to see me at this moment. I declare, if I were going to be married in a few days, as you are, I should scarce have found time to visit my friends.

MARIA: Do you think then that there is an impropriety in it? — How should you dispose of your time?

CHARLOTTE: Why, I should be shut up in my chamber; and my head would so run upon — upon — upon the solemn ceremony that I was to pass through — I declare it would take me above two hours merely to learn that little monosyllable — *Yes*. Ah! my dear, your sentimental imagination does not conceive what that little tiny word implies.

MARIA: Spare me your raillery, my sweet friend; I should love your agreeable vivacity at any other time.

CHARLOTTE: Why this is the very time to amuse you. You grieve me to see you look so unhappy.

MARIA: Have I not reason to look so?

CHARLOTTE: What new grief distresses you?

MARIA: Oh! how sweet it is, when the heart is borne down with misfortune, to recline and repose on the bosom of friendship! Heaven knows, that, although it is improper for a young lady to praise a gentleman, yet I have ever concealed Mr. Dimple's foibles, and spoke of him as of one whose reputation I expected would be linked with mine: but his late conduct towards me has turned my coolness into contempt. He behaves as if he meant to insult and disgust me; whilst my father, in the last conversation on the subject of our marriage, spoke of it as a matter which laid near his heart, and in which he would not bear contradiction.

CHARLOTTE (*aside*): This works well: oh! the generous Dimple. I'll endeavour to excite her to discharge him. But, my dear friend, your happiness depends on yourself: Why don't you discard him? Though the match has been of long standing, I would not be forced to make myself miserable: No parent in the world should oblige me to marry the man I did not like.

MARIA: Oh! my dear, you never lived with your parents, and do not know what influence a father's frowns have upon a daughter's heart. Besides, what have I to allege against Mr. Dimple, to justify myself to the world? He carries himself so smoothly, that every one would impute the blame to me, and call me capricious.

CHARLOTTE: And call her capricious! Did ever such an objection start into the heart of woman? For my part, I wish I had fifty lovers to discard, for no other reason, than because I did not fancy them. My dear Maria, you will forgive me; I know your candour and confidence in me; but I have at times, I confess, been led to suppose, that some other gentleman was the cause of your aversion to Mr. Dimple.

MARIA: No, my sweet friend, you may be assured, that though I have seen many gentlemen I could prefer to Mr. Dimple, yet I never saw one that I thought I could give my hand to, until this morning.

CHARLOTTE: This morning!

MARIA: Yes! — one of the strangest accidents in the world. The odious Dimple, after disgusting me with his conversation, had just left me when a gentleman, who, it seems, boards in the same house with him, saw him coming out of our door, and the houses looking very much alike, he came into our house instead of his lodgings; nor did he discover his mistake until he got into the parlour, where I was: he then bowed so gracefully; made such a genteel apology, and looked so manly and noble! —

CHARLOTTE (*aside*): I see some folks, though it is so great an impropriety, can praise a gentleman, when he happens to be the man of their fancy.

MARIA: I don't know how it was — I hope he did not think me indelicate — but I asked him, I believe, to sit down, or pointed to a chair. He sat down, and instead of having recourse to observations upon the weather, or hackneyed criticisms upon the theatre, he entered readily into a conversation worthy a man of sense to speak, and a lady of delicacy and sentiment to hear. He was not strictly handsome, but he spoke the language of sentiment, and his eyes looked tenderness and honour.

CHARLOTTE: Oh! (*Eagerly*) you sentimental grave girls, when your hearts are once touched, beat us rattles a bar's length. And so, you are quite in love with this he-angel?

MARIA: In love with him! How can you rattle so, Charlotte? am I not going to be miserable? (*Sighing*) In love with a gentleman I never saw but one hour in my life, and don't know his name! — No: I only wished that the man I shall marry may look, and talk, and act, just like him. Besides, my dear, he is a married man.

CHARLOTTE: Why, that was good natured. — He told you so, I suppose, in mere charity, to prevent your falling in love with him?

MARIA (*peevishly*): He didn't tell me so; he looked as if he was married.

CHARLOTTE: How, my dear, did he look sheepish?

MARIA: I am sure he has a susceptible heart, and the ladies of his acquaintance must be very stupid not to —

CHARLOTTE: Hush! I hear some person coming.

LETITIA (*enters*): My dear Maria, I am happy to see you. Lud! what a pity it is that you have purchased your wedding clothes.

MARIA: I think so. (*Sighing.*)

LETITIA: Why, my dear, there is the sweetest parcel of silks come over you ever saw. Nancy Brilliant has a full suit come; she sent over her measure, and it fits her to a hair; it is immensely dressy, and made for a court-hoop. I thought they said the large hoops were going out of fashion.

CHARLOTTE: Did you see the hat? — Is it a fact, that the deep laces round the border is still the fashion?

DIMPLE (*within*): Upon my honour, Sir!

MARIA: Ha! Dimple's voice! My dear, I must take leave of you. There are some things necessary to be done at our house. — Can't I go through the other room? 90

(*Enter Dimple and Manly.*)

DIMPLE: Ladies, your most obedient.

CHARLOTTE: Miss Van Rough, shall I present my brother Henry to you? Colonel Manly, Maria — Miss Van Rough, brother.

MARIA: Her brother! (*Turns and sees Manly.*) Oh! my heart! The very gentle- 95 man I have been praising.

MANLY: The same amiable girl I saw this morning!

CHARLOTTE: Why, you look as if you were acquainted.

MANLY: I unintentionally intruded into this lady's presence this morning, for which she was so good as to promise me her forgiveness. 100

CHARLOTTE (*aside*): Oh! ho! is that the case! Have these two penserosos been together? Were they Henry's eyes that looked so tenderly? — And so you promised to pardon him? and could you be so good natured? — have you really forgiven him? I beg you would do it for my sake. (*Whispering loud to Maria*) But, my dear, as you are in such haste, it would be 105 cruel to detain you: I can show you the way through the other room.

MARIA: Spare me, my sprightly friend.

MANLY: The lady does not, I hope, intend to deprive us of the pleasure of her company so soon.

CHARLOTTE: She has only a mantua-maker who waits for her at home. 110 But, as I am to give my opinion of the dress, I think she cannot go yet. We were talking of the fashions when you came in; but I suppose the subject must be changed to something of more importance now. — Mr. Dimple, will you favour us with an account of the public entertainments?

DIMPLE: Why, really, Miss Manly, you could not have asked me a question 115 more *malapropos*. For my part, I must confess, that to a man who has travelled, there is nothing that is worthy the name of amusement to be found in this city.

CHARLOTTE: Except visiting the ladies.

DIMPLE: Pardon me, Madam; that is the avocation of a man of taste. But, 120 for amusement, I positively know of nothing that can be called so, unless you dignify with that title the hopping once a fortnight to the sound of two or three squeaking fiddles, and the clattering of the old tavern windows, or sitting to see the miserable mummers, whom you call actors, murder comedy, and make a farce of tragedy. 125

MANLY: Do you never attend the theatre, Sir?

DIMPLE: I was tortured there once.

CHARLOTTE: Pray, Mr. Dimple, was it a tragedy or a comedy?

DIMPLE: Faith, Madam, I cannot tell; for I sat with my back to the stage all the time, admiring a much better actress than any there — a lady who 130 played the fine woman to perfection — though, by the laugh of the horrid creatures around me, I suppose it was comedy. Yet, on second thoughts, it might be some hero in a tragedy, dying so comically as to set the whole house in an uproar. — Colonel, I presume you have been in Europe?

MANLY: Indeed, Sir, I was never ten leagues from the continent. 135

DIMPLE: Believe me, Colonel, you have an immense pleasure to come; and when you shall have seen the brilliant exhibitions of Europe, you will learn to despise the amusements of this country as much as I do.

MANLY: Therefore I do not wish to see them; for I can never esteem that knowledge valuable, which tends to give me a distaste for my native 140 country.

DIMPLE: Well, Colonel, though you have not travelled, you have read.

MANLY: I have, a little: and by it have discovered that there is a laudable partiality, which ignorant, untravelled men entertain for everything that belongs to their native country. I call it laudable; — it injures no one; 145 adds to their own happiness; and, when extended, becomes the noble principle of patriotism. Travelled gentlemen rise superior, in their own opinion, to this: but, if the contempt which they contract for their country is the most valuable acquisition of their travels, I am far from thinking that their time and money are well spent. 150

MARIA: What noble sentiments!

CHARLOTTE: Let my brother set out from where he will in the fields of conversation, he is sure to end his tour in the temple of gravity.

MANLY: Forgive me, my sister. I love my country; it has its foibles undoubtedly — some foreigners will with pleasure remark them — but 155 such remarks fall very ungracefully from the lips of her citizens.

DIMPLE: You are perfectly in the right. Colonel — America has her faults.

MANLY: Yes, Sir; and we, her children, should blush for them in private, and endeavour, as individuals, to reform them. But, if our country has its errors in common with other countries, I am proud to say America, I 160 mean the United States, has displayed virtues and achievements which modern nations may admire, but of which they have seldom set us the example.

CHARLOTTE: But, brother, we must introduce you to some of our gay folks, and let you see the city, such as it is. Mr. Dimple is known to almost every 165 family in town — he will doubtless take a pleasure in introducing you.

DIMPLE: I shall esteem every service I can render your brother an honour.

MANLY: I fear the business I am upon will take up all my time, and my family will be anxious to hear from me.

MARIA (*aside*):   His family! But what is it to me that he is married! Pray, how did you leave your lady, Sir?   170

CHARLOTTE (*observing her anxiety*):   My brother is not married; it is only an odd way he has of expressing himself. — Pray, brother, is this business, which you make your continual excuse, a secret?

MANLY: No, sister: I came hither to solicit the honourable Congress that a number of my brave old soldiers may be put upon the pension list, who were, at first, not judged to be so materially wounded as to need the public assistance. — My sister says true: (*to Maria*) I call my late soldiers my family. — Those who were not in the field in the late glorious contest, and those who were, have their respective merits; but, I confess, my old brother-soldiers are dearer to me than the former description. Friendships made in adversity are lasting; our countrymen may forget us; but that is no reason why we should forget one another. But I must leave you; my time of engagement approaches.   175   180

CHARLOTTE: Well, but brother, if you will go, will you please to conduct my fair friend home? You live in the same street — I was to have gone with her myself — (*Aside*) A lucky thought.   185

MARIA: I am obliged to your sister, Sir, and was just intending to go. (*Going.*)

MANLY: I shall attend her with pleasure. (*Exits with Maria, followed by Dimple and Charlotte.*)

MARIA: Now, pray don't betray me to your brother.   190

CHARLOTTE (*just as she sees him make a motion to take his leave*):   One word with you, brother, if you please. (*She follows them out.*)

(*Manent Dimple and Letitia.*)

DIMPLE: You received the billet I sent you, I presume?

LETITIA: Hush! — Yes.

DIMPLE: When shall I pay my respects to you?   195

LETITIA: At eight I shall be unengaged.

(*Re-enter Charlotte.*)

DIMPLE (*to Charlotte*):   Did my lovely angel receive my billet?

CHARLOTTE: Yes.

DIMPLE: What hour shall I expect with impatience?

CHARLOTTE: At eight I shall be at home, unengaged.   200

DIMPLE: Unfortunate! I have a horrid engagement of business at that hour. — Can't you finish your visit earlier, and let six be the happy hour?

CHARLOTTE: You know your influence over me.

(They go out severally.)

SCENE II

Van Rough's house.

VAN ROUGH (*alone*): It cannot possibly be true! The son of my old friend can't have acted so unadvisedly. Seventeen thousand pounds! in bills! — Mr. Transfer must have been mistaken. He always appeared so prudent, and talked so well upon money matters, and even assured me that he intended to change his dress for a suit of clothes which would not cost so much, and look more substantial, as soon as he married. No, no, no! it can't be; it cannot be. — But, however, I must look out sharp. I did not care what his principles or his actions were, so long as he minded the main chance. Seventeen thousand pounds! — If he had lost it in trade, why the best men may have ill-luck; but to game it away, as Transfer says — why, at this rate, his whole estate may go in one night, and, what is ten times worse, mine into the bargain. No, no; Mary is right. Leave women to look out in these matters; for all they look as if they didn't know a journal from a ledger, when their interest is concerned, they know what's what; they mind the main chance as well as the best of us. — I wonder Mary did not tell me she knew of his spending his money so foolishly. Seventeen thousand pounds! Why, if my daughter was standing up to be married, I would forbid the banns, if I found it was to a man who did not mind the main chance. — Hush! I hear somebody coming. 'T is Mary's voice: a man with her too! I shouldn't be surprised if this should be the other string to her bow. — Aye, aye, let them alone; women understand the main chance. — Though, i' faith, I'll listen a little. (*Retires into a closet.*)

(Enter Manly leading in Maria.)

MANLY: I hope you will excuse my speaking upon so important a subject, so abruptly; but the moment I entered your room, you struck me as the lady whom I had long loved in imagination, and never hoped to see.

MARIA: Indeed, Sir, I have been led to hear more upon this subject than I ought.

MANLY: Do you then disapprove my suit, Madam, or the abruptness of my introducing it? If the latter, my peculiar situation, being obliged to leave the city in a few days, will, I hope, be my excuse; if the former, I will retire: for I am sure I would not give a moment's inquietude to her, whom I could devote my life to please. I am not so indelicate as to seek your immediate approbation; permit me only to be near you, and by a thousand tender assiduities to endeavour to excite a grateful return. 35

MARIA: I have a father, whom I would die to make happy — he will disapprove —

MANLY: Do you think me so ungenerous as to seek a place in your esteem without his consent? You must — you ever ought to consider that man as unworthy of you, who seeks an interest in your heart, contrary to a father's 40 approbation. A young lady should reflect that the loss of a lover may be supplied, but nothing can compensate for the loss of a parent's affection. Yet, why do you suppose your father would disapprove? In our country, the affections are not sacrificed to riches, or family aggrandizement: — should you approve, my family is decent, and my rank honourable. 45

MARIA: You distress me, Sir.

MANLY: Then I will sincerely beg your excuse for obtruding so disagreeable a subject and retire. (*He starts to leave.*)

MARIA: Stay, Sir! your generosity and good opinion of me deserve a return; but why must I declare what, for these few hours, I have scarce suf- 50 fered myself to think? — I am —

MANLY: What? —

MARIA: Engaged, Sir — and, in a few days, to he married to the gentleman you saw at your sister's.

MANLY: Engaged to be married! And have I been basely invading the 55 rights of another? Why have you permitted this? — Is this the return for the partiality I declared for you?

MARIA: You distress me, Sir. What would you have me say? You are too generous to wish the truth: ought I to say that I dared not suffer myself to think of my engagement, and that I am going to give my hand with- 60 out my heart? — Would you have me confess a partiality for you? If so, your triumph is complete; and can be only more so, when days of misery, with the man I cannot love, will make me think of him whom I could prefer.

MANLY (*after a pause*):   We are both unhappy; but it is your duty to obey your 65 parent — mine to obey my honour. Let us, therefore, both follow the path of rectitude; and of this we may be assured, that if we are not happy, we shall, at least, deserve to be so. Adieu! I dare not trust myself longer with you.

(*They go out severally.*)

Act v, Scene i

Dimple's lodgings, Jessamy meeting Jonathan.

JESSAMY: Well, Mr. Jonathan, what success with the fair?

JONATHAN: Why, such a tarnal cross tike you never saw! — You would have counted she had lived upon crab apples and vinegar for a fortnight. But what the rattle makes you look so tarnation glum?

JESSAMY: I was thinking, Mr. Jonathan, what could be the reason of her carrying herself so coolly to you.

JONATHAN: Coolly, do you call it? Why, I vow, she was fire-hot angry: may be it was because I buss'd her.

JESSAMY: No, no, Mr. Jonathan; there must be some other cause: I never yet knew a lady angry at being kissed.

JONATHAN: Well, if it is not the young woman's bashfulness, I vow I can't conceive why she shouldn't like me.

JESSAMY: May be it is because you have not the Graces, Mr. Jonathan.

JONATHAN: Grace! Why, does the young woman expect I must be converted before I court her?

JESSAMY: I mean graces of person; for instance, my lord tells us that we must cut off our nails even at top, in small segments of circles — though you won't understand that — In the next place, you must regulate your laugh.

JONATHAN: Maple-log seize it! don't I laugh natural?

JESSAMY: That's the very fault, Mr. Jonathan. Besides, you absolutely misplace it. I was told by a friend of mine that you laughed outright at the play the other night, when you ought only to have tittered.

JONATHAN: Gor! I — what does one go to see fun for if they can't laugh?

JESSAMY: You may laugh — but you must laugh by rule.

JONATHAN: Swamp it — laugh by rule! Well, I should like that tarnally.

JESSAMY: Why you know, Mr. Jonathan, that to dance, a lady to play with her fan, or a gentleman with his cane, and all other natural motions, are regulated by art. My master has composed an immensely pretty gamut, by which any lady, or gentleman, with a few years' close application, may learn to laugh as gracefully as if they were born and bred to it.

JONATHAN: Mercy on my soul! A gamut for laughing — just like fa, la, sol?

JESSAMY: Yes. It comprises every possible display of jocularity, from an *affettuoso* smile to a *piano* titter, or full chorus *fortissimo* ha, ha, ha! My master employs his leisure hours in marking out the plays, like a cathedral chanting-book, that the ignorant may know where to laugh; and that pit, box, and gallery may keep time together, and not have a snigger in one part of the house, a broad grin in the other, and a damned grum look in the third. How delightful to see the audience all smile together, then look on their books, then twist their mouths into an agreeable simper, then altogether shake the house with a general ha ha, ha! loud as a full chorus of Handel's, at an Abbey commemoration.

JONATHAN: Ha, ha, ha! that's dang'd cute, I swear.

JESSAMY: The gentlemen, you see, will laugh the tenor; the ladies will play the countertenor; the beaux will squeak the treble; and our jolly friends in the gallery a thorough bass, ho, ho, ho!

JONATHAN: Well, can't you let me see that gamut?

JESSAMY: Oh! yes, Mr. Jonathan; here it is. (*Takes out a book.*) Oh! no, this is only a titter with its variations. Ah, here it is. (*Takes out another.*) Now you must know, Mr. Jonathan, this is a piece written by Ben Jonson, which I have set to my master's gamut. The places where you must smile, look grave, or laugh outright, are marked below the line. Now look over me: "There was a certain man" — now you must smile.

JONATHAN: Well, read it again; I warrant I'll mind my eye.

JESSAMY: "There was a certain man, who had a sad scolding wife" — now you must laugh.

JONATHAN: Tarnation! That's no laughing matter, though.

JESSAMY: "And she lay sick a-dying" — now you must titter.

JONATHAN: What, snigger when the good woman's a-dying! Gor, I —

JESSAMY: Yes; the notes say you must — "And she asked her husband leave to make a will" — now you must begin to look grave — "and her husband said" —

JONATHAN: Ay, what did her husband say? — Something dang'd cute, I reckon.

JESSAMY: "And her husband said, you have had your will all your lifetime, and would you have it after you are dead too?"

JONATHAN: Ho, ho, ho! There the old man was even with her; he was up to the notch — ha, ha, ha!

JESSAMY: But, Mr. Jonathan, you must not laugh so. Why, you ought to have tittered *piano,* and you have laughed *fortissimo.* Look here; you see these marks, A. B. C. and so on; these are the references to the other part of the book. Let us turn to it, and you will see the directions how to manage the muscles. This (*Turns over.*) was note D you blundered at. — "You must purse the mouth into a smile, then titter, discovering the lower part of the three front upper teeth."

JONATHAN: How! read it again.

JESSAMY: "There was a certain man" — very well! — "who had a sad scolding wife" — why don't you laugh?

JONATHAN: Now, that scolding wife sticks in my gizzard so pluckily, that I   80
can't laugh for the blood and nowns of me. Let me look grave here, and
I'll laugh your belly full where the old creature's a-dying. —

JESSAMY: "And she asked her husband" — (*Bell rings.*) My master's bell!
he's returned, I fear — Here, Mr. Jonathan, take this gamut; and, I make
no doubt but with a few years' close application you may be able to smile   85
gracefully.

(*They go out severally.*)

SCENE II

Charlotte's apartment.

MANLY (*enters*):   What, no one at home? How unfortunate to meet the only
lady my heart was ever moved by, to find her engaged to another, and
confessing her partiality for me! Yet engaged to a man, who, by her inti-
mation, and his libertine conversation with me, I fear, does not merit her.
Aye! there's the sting; for, were I assured that Maria was happy, my heart   5
is not so selfish but that it would dilate in knowing it, even though it
were with another. — But to know she is unhappy! — I must drive these
thoughts from me. Charlotte has some books; and this is what I believe
she calls her little library. (*Enters a closet.*)

(*Enter Dimple leading Letitia.*)

LETITIA: And will you pretend to say, now, Mr. Dimple, that you propose   10
to break with Maria? Are not the banns published? Are not the clothes
purchased? Are not the friends invited? In short, is it not a done affair?

DIMPLE: Believe me, my dear Letitia, I would not marry her.

LETITIA: Why have you not broke with her before this, as you all along
deluded me by saying you would?   15

DIMPLE: Because I was in hopes she would ere this have broke with me.

LETITIA: You could not expect it.

DIMPLE: Nay, but be calm a moment; 't was from my regard to you that I
did not discard her.

LETITIA: Regard to me!   20

DIMPLE: Yes; I have done everything in my power to break with her, but
the foolish girl is so fond of me that nothing can accomplish it. Besides,
how can I offer her my hand, when my heart is indissolubly engaged to
you? —

LETITIA: There may be reason in this; but why so attentive to Miss Manly?   25

DIMPLE: Attentive to Miss Manly! For heaven's sake, if you have no better opinion of my constancy, pay not so ill a compliment to my taste.

LETITIA: Did I not see you whisper her today?

DIMPLE: Possibly I might — but something of so very trifling a nature, that I have already forgot what it was.   30

LETITIA: I believe, she has not forgot it.

DIMPLE: My dear creature, how can you for a moment suppose I should have any serious thoughts of that trifling, gay, flighty coquette, that disagreeable —

(*Enter Charlotte.*)

DIMPLE: My dear Miss Manly, I rejoice to see you; there is a charm in your   35
conversation that always marks your entrance into company as fortunate.

LETITIA: Where have you been, my dear?

CHARLOTTE: Why, I have been about to twenty shops, turning over pretty things, and so have left twenty visits unpaid. I wish you would step into the carriage and whisk round, make my apology, and leave my cards   40
where our friends are not at home; that you know will serve as a visit. Come, do go.

LETITIA (*aside*):   So anxious to get me out! but I'll watch you. — Oh! yes, I'll go; I want a little exercise. — Positively (*Dimple offering to accompany her*), Mr. Dimple, you shall not go, why, half my visits are cake and caudle   45
visits; it won't do, you know, for you to go. — (*Exit, but returns to the door in the back scene and listens.*)

DIMPLE: This attachment of your brother to Maria is fortunate.

CHARLOTTE: How did you come to the knowledge of it?

DIMPLE: I read it in their eyes.

CHARLOTTE: And I had it from her mouth. It would have amused you to   50
have seen her! She that thought it so great an impropriety to praise a gentleman that she could not bring out one word in your favour, found a redundancy to praise him.

DIMPLE: I have done everything in my power to assist his passion there: your delicacy, my dearest girl, would be shocked at half the instances of   55
neglect and misbehaviour.

CHARLOTTE: I don't know how I should bear neglect; but Mr. Dimple must misbehave himself, indeed, to forfeit my good opinion.

DIMPLE: Your good opinion, my angel, is the pride and pleasure of my heart; and if the most respectful tenderness for you and an utter indiffer-   60
ence for all your sex, besides, can make me worthy of your esteem, I shall richly merit it.

CHARLOTTE: All my sex besides, Mr. Dimple — you forgot your tête-à-tête with Letitia.

DIMPLE: How can you, my lovely angel, cast a thought on that insipid, 65 wry-mouthed, ugly creature!

CHARLOTTE: But her fortune may have charms?

DIMPLE: Not to a heart like mine. The man who has been blessed with the good opinion of my Charlotte must despise the allurements of fortune.

CHARLOTTE: I am satisfied. 70

DIMPLE: Let us think no more on the odious subject, but devote the present hour to happiness.

CHARLOTTE: Can I be happy, when I see the man I prefer going to be married to another?

DIMPLE: Have I not already satisfied my charming angel that I can never 75 think of marrying the puling Maria. But, even if it were so, could that be any bar to our happiness; for, as the poet sings —

> Love, free as air, at sight of human ties,
> Spreads his light wings, and in a moment flies.

Come then, my charming angel! why delay our bliss! The present mo- 80 ment is ours; the next is in the hand of fate.

(*Kissing her.*)

CHARLOTTE: Begone, Sir! By your delusions you had almost lulled my honour asleep.

DIMPLE: Let me lull the demon to sleep again with kisses. (*He struggles with her; she screams.*)

MANLY (*enters*): Turn, villain! and defend yourself. — (*Draws. Van Rough en-* 85 *ters and beats down their swords.*)

VAN ROUGH (*holding Dimple*): Is the devil in you? are you going to murder one another?

DIMPLE: Hold him, hold him — I can command my passion.

JONATHAN (*enters*): What the rattle ails you? Is the old one in you? Let the colonel alone, can't you? I feel chock full of fight — do you want to kill 90 the colonel? —

MANLY: Be still, Jonathan; the gentleman does not want to hurt me.

JONATHAN: Gor! I — I wish he did; I'd shew him Yankee boys' play, pretty quick — Don't you see you have frightened the young woman into the *hystrikes*? 95

VAN ROUGH: Pray, some of you explain this; what has been the occasion of all this racket?

MANLY: That gentleman can explain it to you; it will be a very diverting story for an intended father-in-law to hear.

VAN ROUGH: How was this matter, Mr. Van Dumpling?   100

DIMPLE: Sir — upon my honour — all I know is, that I was talking to this young lady, and this gentleman broke in on us, in a very extraordinary manner.

VAN ROUGH: Why, all this is nothing to the purpose. (*To Charlotte*) Can you explain it, Miss?   105

LETITIA (*entering through the back scene*):   I can explain it to that gentleman's confusion. (*To Van Rough*) Though long betrothed to your daughter, yet allured by my fortune, it seems (with shame do I speak it), he has privately paid his addresses to me. I was drawn in to listen to him by his assuring me that the match was made by his father without his consent, and that   110 he proposed to break with Maria, whether he married me or not. But whatever were his intentions respecting your daughter, Sir, even to me he was false; for he has repeated the same story, with some cruel reflections upon my person, to Miss Manly.

JONATHAN: What a tarnal curse!   115

LETITIA: Nor is this all, Miss Manly. When he was with me this very morning, he made the same ungenerous reflections upon the weakness of your mind as he has so recently done upon the defects of my person.

JONATHAN: What a tarnal curse and damn too!

DIMPLE (*aside*):   Ha! since I have lost Letitia, I believe I had as good make it   120 up with Maria — Mr. Van Rough, at present I cannot enter into particulars; but, I believe I can explain everything to your satisfaction in private.

VAN ROUGH: There is another matter, Mr. Van Dumpling, which I would have you explain — pray, Sir, have Messrs. Van Cash and Co. presented you those bills for acceptance?   125

DIMPLE (*aside*):   The deuce! Has he heard of those bills! Nay, then, all's up with Maria, too; but an affair of this sort can never prejudice me among the ladies; they will rather long to know what the dear creature possesses to make him so agreeable. (*To Manly*) Sir, you'll hear from me.

MANLY: And you from me, Sir. —   130

DIMPLE: Sir, you wear a sword. —

MANLY: Yes, Sir — This sword was presented to me by that brave Gallic hero, the Marquis de La Fayette. I have drawn it in the service of my country, and in private life, on the only occasion where a man is justified in drawing his sword, in defence of a lady's honour. I have fought too   135 many battles in the service of my country to dread the imputation of cowardice. — Death from a man of honour would be a glory you do not

merit; you shall live to bear the insult of man, and the contempt of that
sex whose general smiles afforded you all your happiness.

DIMPLE: You won't meet me, Sir? — Then I'll post you for a coward.   140

MANLY: I'll venture that, Sir. — The reputation of my life does not depend upon the breath of a Mr. Dimple. I would have you to know, however, Sir, that I have a cane to chastise the insolence of a scoundrel, and a
sword and the good laws of my country, to protect me from the attempts
of an assassin. —   145

DIMPLE: Mighty well! Very fine, indeed! — ladies and gentlemen, I take
my leave, and you will please to observe, in the case of my deportment,
the contrast between a gentleman, who has read Chesterfield and received the polish of Europe, and an unpolished, untraveled American.

(*Exit.*)

MARIA (*enters*):   Is he indeed gone? —   150

LETITIA: I hope never to return.

VAN ROUGH: I am glad I heard of those bills; though it's plaguy unlucky: I
hoped to see Mary married before I died.

MANLY: Will you permit a gentleman, Sir, to offer himself as a suitor to
your daughter? Though a stranger to you, he is not altogether so to her,   155
or unknown in this city. You may find a son-in-law of more fortune, but
you can never meet with one who is richer in love for her, or respect for
you.

VAN ROUGH: Why, Mary, you have not let this gentleman make love to you
without my leave?   160

MANLY: I did not say, Sir —

MARIA: Say, Sir! — I — the gentleman, to be sure, met me accidentally.

VAN ROUGH: Ha, ha, ha! Mark me, Mary; young folks think old folks to be
fools; but old folks know young folks to be fools. — Why, I knew all
about this affair: — This was only a cunning way I had to bring it about   165
— Hark ye! I was in the closet when you and he were at our house. (*Turns
to the company.*) I heard that little baggage say she loved her old father, and
would die to make him happy! Oh! how I loved the little baggage! —
And you talked very prudently, young man. I have inquired into your
character, and find you to be a man of punctuality and mind the main   170
chance. And so, as you love Mary, and Mary loves you, you shall have my
consent immediately to be married. I'll settle my fortune on you, and go
and live with you the remainder of my life.

MANLY: Sir, I hope —

VAN ROUGH: Come, come, no fine speeches; mind the main chance, young   175
man, and you and I shall always agree.

LETITIA: I sincerely wish you joy (*Advancing to Maria*); and hope your pardon for my conduct.

MARIA: I thank you for your congratulations, and hope we shall at once forget the wretch who has given us so much disquiet, and the trouble that he has occasioned. 180

CHARLOTTE: And I, my dear Maria — how shall I look up to you for forgiveness? I, who, in the practice of the meanest arts, have violated the most sacred rights of friendship? I can never forgive myself, or hope charity from the world, but I confess I have much to hope from such a brother; and I am happy that I may soon say, such a sister. — 185

MARIA: My dear, you distress me; you have all my love.

MANLY: And mine.

CHARLOTTE: If repentance can entitle me to forgiveness, I have already much merit; for I despise the littleness of my past conduct. I now find, 190 that the heart of any worthy man cannot be gained by invidious attacks upon the rights and characters of others — by countenancing the addresses of a thousand — or that the finest assemblage of features, the greatest taste in dress, the genteelest address, or the most brilliant wit, cannot eventually secure a coquette from contempt and ridicule. 195

MANLY: And I have learned that probity, virtue, honour, though they should not have received the polish of Europe, will secure to an honest American the good graces of his fair countrywoman, and, I hope, the applause of *the public*.

FIGURE 2 *Actor Edwin Forrest (1806–1872) in his tribal costume as Metamora. Illustration based on a Mathew Brady photograph.*

JOHN AUGUSTUS STONE

Metamora; or, The Last of the Wampanoags

>‹

John Augustus Stone (1800–1834) began his career as an actor at age twenty, performing, as he did throughout his short life, character roles — eccentric comics or old men. Never a star, he was nonetheless popular in New York from 1822 to 1831 and thereafter in Philadelphia, although during this latter period of his life he was frequently ill. Married in 1821 to the actress Mrs. Legge, Stone had two sons, both of whom became actors. In 1829 Stone became the first winner in actor Edwin Forrest's playwriting contest for "the best tragedy, in five acts, of which the hero, or principal character, shall be an aboriginal of this country." The play, *Metamora; or, The Last of the Wampanoags,* became Forrest's property after its first performance on December 15, 1829, at New York's Park Theatre, and his "war-horse" vehicle throughout much of his career. Stone wrote nine other plays, including *Restoration; or, the Diamond Cross* (1824), *Tancred, King of Sicily* (1827 and the only play of his published during his lifetime), *The Demoniac* (1831), a revision of J. K. Paulding's *The Lion of the West* (1831), *The Ancient Briton* (1833), and *The Knight of the Golden Fleece; or, The Yankee of Spain* (1834). Despondent over his ill health and his inability to repeat the success of *Metamora,* Stone committed suicide in 1834 by jumping into Philadelphia's Schuylkill River.

✈ Metamora; or, The Last of the Wampanoags

1829

DRAMATIS PERSONAE

METAMORA, *chief of the Wampanoags*
KANESHINE, *an Indian prophet*
ANNAWANDAH, *the traitor*
OTAH, *an Indian boy*   } *Indians*
INDIAN BOY, *child of Metamora*
NAHMEOKEE, *wife of Metamora*
INDIANS, WARRIORS, ETC.

LORD FITZARNOLD
SIR ARTHUR VAUGHAN
MORDAUNT
ERRINGTON, *chief of the council*
WALTER, *an orphan*
CAPTAIN CHURCH   } *English*
WOLFE
GOODENOUGH
TRAMP
OCEANA, *Mordaunt's daughter*
SOLDIERS, SAILORS, PEASANTS, ETC.

ACT I, SCENE I

Sunset. A wild, picturesque scene; high, craggy rocks in distance; dark pine trees, etc. Rocks cross stage, with platform cross behind. Steps, etc., at back. A rude tomb, flowers growing around it. Half dark. Mordaunt discovered leaning on tomb. Slow music.

MORDAUNT: The sun has sunk behind yon craggy rocks; and day's last beams are fading from the clouds that fleet in hurrying masses through the sky, like tattered banners of a flying host! England, my home! When will thy parent arms again enfold me? Oh! When for me will dawn a day of hope? Will not sincere repentance from my scathed brow efface the brand of regicide?

TRAMP (*Outside*):   What ho! Good Master Mordaunt! (*Cannon*)

MORDAUNT: Ha! What mean those sounds? Now, your news? (*Enter Tramp*)

TRAMP: A gallant bark, urged by the favoring breeze, makes for the crowded shore.

MORDAUNT: From England! Ha!

TRAMP: St. George's banner floats from her high mast, and her long signal pennon gleams with green and gold.

MORDAUNT: 'Tis he — he comes and with him hope arrives. Go, hasten,
fellow; seek my daughter; say the Lord Fitzarnold comes to greet her.   15
(*Tramp crosses to the right behind.*) Marshal my followers in their best array
— away to the beach and let loud music welcome him ashore. (*Exit
Tramp.*) What mingled feelings crowd about my heart, blended so
strange and wild? Sunned by his sovereign's smile, Fitzarnold comes to
woo and wed my daughter. Born on the heaving deep, the child of   20
storms, and reared in savage wilds, her worth and beauty well may grace
the courtly halls of England. And yet, to force her gentle will, whose
every thought has been to soothe my sorrows and relieve my cares! Yet
must she wed Fitzarnold. His alliance can with oblivion shroud the past,
clear from my scutcheon every rebel stain, and give my franchised spirit   25
liberty.

(*Exit. Slow music, four bars. Enter Oceana, looking around as if in search.*)

OCEANA: Sure, 'twas my father's voice, and loud in converse. Father! Dear
father! Not here? And yet I thought — (*Flute heard, distant*) Ha! whence
that strain? So soft yet strange. Methinks some pious minstrel seeks the
moonlight hour to breathe devotion forth in melody. (*Music changes.*)   30
Hark! It changes place and measure, too. Now deeper in the woods it
warbles, now it seems aloft floating in plaintive tones through the air.
This place — the hour — the day — heavens! 'tis my mother's birthday,
and her grave undecked with flowers! O my mother, my dear mother!
Perhaps her angel spirit hovers here o'er her lone daughter's steps, a   35
guardian still. (*Kneels to tomb*) Ah, what flower is this? "Forgetmenot!"
(*Music ceases.*) My mother, look from thy seraph home upon thy child,
and when for those thou lovest on earth thou breathest a prayer, oh, then
forget me not. (*Places flower in bosom. Enter Walter.*)

WALTER: Oceana!   40

OCEANA: Walter, was thine the strain but now I heard?

WALTER: 'Twas but an humble tribute to thy beauty, but could not match
the sweetness of thy voice, whose every tone, attuned to dulcet sounds,
can melt the soul to nature's harmony.

OCEANA: Walter, this from thee.   45

WALTER: Nay, blame me not; although dependent on Sir Arthur Vaughan,
nameless and poor, yet do I not despair, for in my heart a sacred treasure
lies I would not barter for my patron's gold.

OCEANA: What means't thou, Walter?

WALTER: Thine own sweet image, which naught on earth can banish or   50
efface — a whispered hope I dare not speak aloud — a light thine own
bright eyes have kindled up.

OCEANA: Nay, Walter, you ask not of the danger I escaped!

WALTER: Danger! What danger? When?

OCEANA: 'Twas yestere'en, when I was lingering on the eastern beach, all   55
heedless of the coming night, a panther growling from the thicket rushed
and marked me for his prey. Powerless I stood — my blood stood still —
I shrieked as I strove to fly, when at the instant, from a ready hand, swift
as the lightning's flash, an arrow came and felled the monster as he
crouched to spring.   60

WALTER: Didst mark who sent it?

OCEANA: Full well I did. High on a craggy rock an Indian stood, with
sinewy arm and eye that pierced the glen. His bowstring drawn to wing
a second death, a robe of fur was o'er his shoulder thrown, and o'er his
long, dark hair an eagle's plume waved in the breeze, a feathery diadem.   65
Firmly he stood upon the jutting height, as if a sculptor's hand had
carved him there. With awe I gazed as on the cliff he turned the grand-
est model of a mighty man.

WALTER: 'Twas Haups' great chieftain, Metamora called; our people love
him not, nor is it strange; he stands between them and extended sway,   70
ready alike with words of power to urge, or gleaming weapon force his
princely dues.

METAMORA (*Outside*):   Hah! Ha!

OCEANA (*Going up*):   Behold his dread encounter with a wolf. His vanquished foe with mighty arm he hurls down the steep height where mor-   75
tal never trod.

METAMORA: Hah! Hah! (*Enters on rock, passes across and off.*)

WALTER (*At Metamora's exit*):   'Tis Metamora, the noble sachem of a valiant
race — the white man's dread, the Wampanoag's hope. (*Enter Metamora.*)

METAMORA: Ha, ha, ha! Turned on me — brave beast; he died like a red   80
man.

OCEANA: Chief, you are hurt; this scarf will staunch the wound. (*Offers it*)

METAMORA: No! (*Rejects it*)

WALTER: 'Tis Oceana — she whose life you saved.

METAMORA: Metamora will take the white maiden's gift. (*Oceana ties his arm*   85
with scarf.)

OCEANA: But yestere'en thou savedst my life, great chief; how can I pay
thee for the generous deed?

METAMORA: Hearken, daughter of the pale face; Metamora forgives not a
wrong and forgets not a kindness. In the days of his age, Massasoit, my
father, was in the white man's dwelling; while there, the spirit of the grave   90
touched him and he laid down to die. A soft hand was stretched out to
save him; it was the hand of thy mother. She that healed him sleeps in
yonder tomb; but why should Metamora let his arrows sleep in the quiver
when her daughter's life was in danger and her limbs shook with fear?
Metamora loves the mild-eyed and the kind, for such is Nahmeokee.   95

WALTER: Such words, and more than all, such deeds, should win you,
chief, the love of all our people. Would you were more among us. Why
never seek our homes? Sir Arthur Vaughan's doors will open to the Indian chief.

OCEANA: My sire will thank thee for his daughter's life.   100

METAMORA: The red man's heart is on the hills where his father's shafts
have flown in the chase. Ha! I have been upon the high mountain top
where the grey mists were beneath my feet, and the Great Spirit passed
by me in his wrath. He spake in anger and the old rocks crumbled beneath the flash of his spear. Then I was proud and smiled, for I had slain   105
the great bird whose wing never tires, and whose eye never shrinks; and
his feathers would adorn the long black hair of Nahmeokee, daughter of
Miantonemo, the great hunter. The war and the chase are the red man's
brother and sister. The storm cloud in its fury frights him not. Wrapt in
the spoils he has won, he lays him down and no one comes near to steal.   110
The Great Spirit hears his evening prayer, and he sleeps amidst the roar
of a mighty cataract.

WALTER: Were all thy nation mild and good like thee, how soon the fire of
discord might be quenched.

METAMORA: Metamora has been the friend of the white man; yet if the   115
flint be smitten too hard it will show that in its heart is fire. The
Wampanoag will not wrong his white brother who comes from the land
that is first touched by the rising sun; but he owns no master, save that
One who holds the sun in his right hand, who rides on a dark storm, and
who cannot die. (*Crosses to the left*)   120

WALTER: That lofty bearing — that majestic mien — the regal impress
sits upon his brow, and earth seems conscious of her proudest son. (*Conch
shell heard sounding from the right*)

METAMORA: Ha! My young men return from their evening toil, and their
hands are filled with the sweet fish of the lake. Come to my wigwam; ye
shall eat of fish that the Great Spirit of the waters sends, and your hearts   125
shall be made glad. (*Going to the right, but returns and takes from his head an*

eagle plume) Maiden, take this; it means speed and safety; when the startling whoop is heard and the war hatchet gleams in the red blaze, let it be
found in thy braided hair. Despise not the red man's gift; it will bring
more good to you than the yellow earth the white man worships as his 130
god. Take it — no Wampanoag's hand will e'er be raised against the head
or hand that bears the eagle plume. (*Crosses to Walter*) Young man, be thou
like the oak in its spreading power and let thy tough branches shelter the
tender flower that springs up under them. Look to the maiden of the
eagle plume, and — come to my wigwam. (*Exit.*) 135

OCEANA: Teach him, Walter; make him like to us.

WALTER: 'Twould cost him half his native virtues. Is justice goodly? Metamora's just. Is bravery virtue? Metamora's brave. If love of country, child
and wife and home, be to deserve them all — he merits them.

OCEANA: Yet he is a heathen. 140

WALTER: True, Oceana, but his worship though untaught and rude flows
from his heart, and Heaven alone must judge of it. (*Enter Tramp.*)

TRAMP: Your father, lady, requires your presence.

OCEANA: Say I come. (*A distant drum*)

WALTER: What is that? 145

TRAMP: The drum that summons Lord Fitzarnold's escort. He comes a
suitor for my lady's hand. (*Exit Tramp.*)

WALTER: Deny it, Oceana — say 'tis false!

OCEANA: It is —

WALTER: Untrue? 150

OCEANA: Oh, most unwelcome.

WALTER: Heavens! You tremble — and your cheek is pale — my Lord
Fitzarnold, that most courtly gentleman, and must my hopes —

OCEANA: Walter, dost thou mean —

WALTER: Obey thy sire. I cannot say farewell. But, oh, when highborn rev- 155
elers carouse, and proud Fitzarnold lords it at the board, give one brief
thought to me! That blessed thought shall soothe the fond complainings
of my heart and hush them to repose. (*Exit Walter and Oceana.*)

SCENE II

Lights up. A room in Sir Arthur's house. Enter Sir Arthur and Walter.

WALTER: Yet hear me, sir.

SIR ARTHUR: Forbear; thou art too hot.

WALTER: 'Tis not the meanness of our state that galls us, but men's opin-
ions. Poverty and toil and consciousness of lowly destiny sit lightly where

no scorn is heaped upon them. But yesterday I was indeed content, for 5
none despised, none had learned to scoff the son of charity, the wretched
ship boy who could trace existence no further than the wreck from which
you plucked him; but now 'tis changed, all suddenly begin to find me
base.

SIR ARTHUR: Marry, go to! You wrong yourself and me. Have I not fos- 10
tered you — like a father tutored you? In early life bereft of wife and
child, wearied of discord and fierce civil strife, I left the haunts of wild
and factious men, to woo contentment in this wilderness. My heart was
vacant and received thee in. Do not by any rash, unworthy act forsake
that heart. Who is it finds thee base? 15

WALTER: All, since Fitzarnold is expected here.

SIR ARTHUR: Fitzarnold! What a plague! There is naught talked of or
thought of but Lord Fitzarnold! And yet this noble viscount, but for his
coat and title were a man to look with scorn upon — a profligate and
spendthrift as fame already has too truly shown him. 20

WALTER: And 'tis for such a man that Master Mordaunt sets me aside —
for such a man his daughter must cast me off.

SIR ARTHUR: Tut! Master Mordaunt is too wise a man to give his daughter to this Lord Fitzarnold. Patience awhile, and watch the progress of
this meteor. Patience, and trust to fortune.   (*Exit.*) 25

WALTER: This lordly suitor comes to wake me from my cherished dreams,
and crush the hopes which lately looked so fair. And shall I yield the glorious prize I deemed was wholly mine? Yield, and without a struggle?
No, by heaven! Look to thyself, Fitzarnold. Let Oceana be but true, I
heed not all thy power, thy wealth, thy titles, backed though they be by 30
Mordaunt's selfish views.   (*Exit.*)

SCENE III

*The harbor. Ships anchored in the distance. Military music. Mordaunt, Errington,
Goodenough, Church, Soldiers, Citizens (male and female) discovered. A boat comes on
from the left with Fitzarnold, Wolfe, and Sailors, who land. Shout.*

MORDAUNT: Long live the king! Welcome Fitzarnold! Rest to the sea-
worn! Joy to each and all!

FITZARNOLD: I thank thee, Mordaunt! But I did not think to see such
faces in the wilderness! Thy woody shores are bright with sparkling eyes,
like Argonaut's adventurous sailors. But where's the golden boon we look 5
for, sir? Fair Oceana — Mordaunt, where is she? (*Walter enters from the left
and stands against the wing.*)

MORDAUNT: So please you, my lord, at home, eager to pay your lordship's kindness back, and prove she can discern thy courtesy.

WALTER (*Aside*): Indeed! Dost say so, worldling?

MORDAUNT: Pray thee, regard these gentlemen, my lord — our council's father, Errington — and this our army's leader; elders of the State.   10

(*Introducing them severally; Fitzarnold salutes them, and at last approaching Walter, extends his hand; Walter bows coldly but does not take it. Music eight bars.*)

FITZARNOLD: How now, young sir? Mordaunt, who is this?

MORDAUNT: My noble lord, I pray thee, heed him not! A wayward youth, somewhat o'er worn with study. (*Crosses to Walter*) Rash boy! Be wise and tempt me not; I can destroy —   15

WALTER: Thy daughter's peace and wed her there. (*Mordaunt gives Walter a look of hate and turns from him.*)

MORDAUNT: Forth to the hall — a strain of music there. (*Crosses to the right*)

FITZARNOLD: Young sir, I shall desire some further converse with you.

WALTER: At injury's prompting, deeds, not words, were best. My lord, you shall find me. (*Touches his sword*)   20

FITZARNOLD: Now for thy fair daughter, Mordaunt, come.

(*Music. Exeunt all but Walter and Wolfe. Peasants and Soldiers exeunt.*)

WOLFE: Thou goest not with them?

WALTER: No, nor before, nor follow after. But why dost thou ask?

WOLFE: Because I know thee.

WALTER: Then thou knowest one who will not take a lordling by the   25
hand, because his fingers shine with hoops of gold — nor shun the beggar's grasp if it be honest. Thou knowest me?

WOLFE: Yes!

WALTER: To know oneself was thought task enough in olden time. What dost thou know?   30

WOLFE: That thou wert wrecked and saved.

WALTER: Aye, more's the pity! (*Aside*) Had I been drowned I had not lived to love and have no hope.

WOLFE: Thou art a good man's son.

WALTER: A pity then, again. Were I a rascal's offspring, I might thrive.   35
What more?

WOLFE: Thou shalt possess thy mistress.

WALTER: Didst mark that lord?

WOLFE: He is my master.

WALTER: Then I am dumb. Be faithful to him, and now farewell. (*Crosses to   40
the left*)

WOLFE: Yet in good time I will say that you will bestow a blessing for.
WALTER: Indeed! What mean you?

(*Enter Tramp with packet.*)

TRAMP: News from the Indians. (*Shows packet*) 'Tis for the council by a
horseman left, who bade me see it with all haste delivered. The Indian
tribes conspire from east to west and faithful Sasamond has found his   45
grave! This packet must be borne to Mordaunt.
WALTER: Trust it with me.
TRAMP: That I will readily, so thou wilt bear it safely.
WALTER: Aye, and quickly, too. (*Takes packet, crosses to the right*) Let me remember Metamora's words — "Look to the maiden of the eagle plume."   50

(*Exit hastily, followed by Wolfe, and Tramp. Quick curtain.*)

ACT II, SCENE I

*Music. Interior of a wigwam; a skin rolled. Stage covered with skins, etc. Child on skin
near entrance. Nahmeokee near it. Metamora at the left, preparing for the chase.*

NAHMEOKEE: Thou wilt soon be back from the chase.
METAMORA: Yes, before the otter has tasted his midday food on the bank
of the stream, his skin shall make a garment for Nahmeokee when the
snow whitens the hunting grounds and the cold wind whistles through
the trees. Nahmeokee, take our little one from his rest; he sleeps too   5
much.
NAHMEOKEE: Oh, no! But thou, Metamora, sleepst too little. In the still
hour of midnight when Wekolis has sung his song, and the great light
has gone down behind the hills, when Nahmeokee's arms like the growing vine were round thee — as if some danger lay waiting in the thick   10
wood — thou didst bid me bring thy tomahawk and the spear that Massasoit had borne when the war cry of the Wampanoags was loudest in the
place of blood! Why is thy rest like the green lake when the sudden blast
passes across its bosom?
METAMORA: Nahmeokee, the power of dreams has been on me, and the   15
shadows of things that are to be have passed before me. My heart is big
with a great thought. When I sleep I think the knife is red in my hand,
and the scalp of the white man is streaming.
NAHMEOKEE: Metamora, is not the white man our brother? And does
not the Great Spirit look on him as he does on us? Do not go towards   20
his home today because thy wrath is kindled and it spreads like the
flames which the white man makes in the dark bosom of the forest. Let

Nahmeokee clasp her arms around thee; rest thy head upon her bosom, for it is hot and thy eye is red with the thoughts that burn! Our old men counsel peace, and the aim of the white man will spare.   25

METAMORA: Yes, when our fires are no longer red, on the high places of our fathers; when the bones of our kindred make fruitful the fields of the stranger, which he has planted amidst the ashes of our wigwams; when we are hunted back like the wounded elk far toward the going down of the sun, our hatchets broken, our bows unstrung and war-whoop hushed;   30 then will the stranger spare, for we will be too small for his eye to see.

(*Trumpet. Enter Otah.*)

OTAH: O son of Massasoit, the power of the white man approaches, and he looks not like one who seeks the Wampanoag's friendship! Look where the bright weapons flash through the clouds of his track.

METAMORA: Ha! Let the paleface come with the calumet or with the   35 knife, Metamora does not fear their power. Where is Annawandah, skilled in talk? Let him approach me.

(*Exit Otah.*)

NAHMEOKEE: Our child would not rest in the mid-hour of night for the hidden snake had bitten him as he lay stretched in the rays of the sun. I rose from my seat to get the dried leaves the Good Spirit has filled with   40 power to heal; the moon was bright and a shadow passed me. It was Annawandah passed our wigwam; his step was like the course of the serpent and he paused and listened. My eye followed him to the seaside, and his light canoe shot like an arrow across the slumbering waters.

METAMORA: Humph! Was he alone?   45

NAHMEOKEE: Alone.

METAMORA: And he went with fear?

NAHMEOKEE: Like one who goes to steal.

(*Trumpet. Enter Otah.*)

OTAH: Look! The white warrior comes.

(*Enter Church, Sir Arthur Vaughan, and Goodenough, with musqueteers.*)

CHURCH: Although we come unbidden, chieftain, yet is our purpose   50 friendly.

METAMORA: Why do you bring your fire weapons if you come to hold a talk of peace?

CHURCH: It is our custom.

METAMORA: Well, speak; my ears are open to hear.   55

SIR ARTHUR: Philip, our mission is —

METAMORA: Philip! I am the Wampanoag chief, Metamora.

SIR ARTHUR: We are directed by our council's head, for the times are filled with doubt, and to make *sure* our bond of peace and love to urge your presence at the council. 60

NAHMEOKEE (*Aside*): Do not go.

METAMORA: Daughter of Miantinemo, peace! (*To them*) I will go.

CHURCH: Our troops shall form thy escort there.

METAMORA: I know the path.

SIR ARTHUR: We must not go without thee, chief. 65

METAMORA: I have breasted the cold winds of forty winters and to those that spoke kindly to me in the words of love I have been pliant — aye, very yielding like the willow that droops over the stream, but till with a single arm you can move the mighty rock that mocks the lightning and the storm seek not to stir Metamora when his heart says no. I will come! 70 (*Crosses to the right*)

CHURCH: We shall expect thee, chief.

METAMORA: Metamora cannot lie.

CHURCH: Stand to your arms.

(*Trumpet. Exit Church, Goodenough, Otah and Soldiers.*)

SIR ARTHUR: Be thou not rash, but with thy tongue of manly truth dispel all charge that wrongs thy noble nature. Throw not the brand that kin- 75 dles bloody war lest thou thyself should be the victim. (*Sir Arthur going to the left*)

METAMORA: My father's deeds shall be my counsellors, and the Great Spirit will hear the words of my mouth. (*Exit Sir Arthur.*) Now, Nahme- okee, I will talk to thee. Dost thou not love this little one, Nahmeokee?

NAHMEOKEE: Oh, yes! 80

METAMORA: When first his little eyes unclosed, thou saidst they were like mine; and my people rejoiced with a mighty joy, that the grandson of Mas- sasoit, the white man's friend, should rule in the high places of his kindred; and hoped that his days would be long and full of glory. Nahmeokee, by the blood of his warlike race, he shall not be the white man's slave. 85

NAHMEOKEE: Thy talk is strange, and fear creeps over me. Thy heart is beating at thy side, as if thy bosom could not hold it.

METAMORA: Because 'tis full of thee — and thee, my little one. Humph! Bring me the knife thy brother wore in battle — my hatchet — the spear that was thy father's when Uncas slew him for the white man's favor. 90 Humph! These things thou gavest me with thyself; thinkest thou this arm can wield them in the fight?

NAHMEOKEE: Ah! Thy bravery will lose thee to me.

METAMORA: Let not thy heart be troubled. If I require assistance from my people, I will lift up a flame on the lofty hill that shall gleam afar through   95
the thick darkness.

NAHMEOKEE: I shall remember thy words.

METAMORA: Take in thy babe; I am going. (*Crosses to the left*)

NAHMEOKEE: Metamora, dost thou go alone?

METAMORA: No; Manito is with me.   100

(*Exit. Nahmeokee exit.*)

Scene ii

A room in the house of Mordaunt. Enter Oceana.

OCEANA: Free from Fitzarnold's gaze, I feel myself again. Why came he here? His looks appalled me yet my father smiled — ah! he comes.

(*Enter Mordaunt.*)

MORDAUNT: How now, my daughter; how is this? Why have you left his lordship thus?

OCEANA: I thought 'twas time.   5

MORDAUNT: It is not time to play the prude, when noble men confess thy charms and come fair suitors to thee. Fitzarnold loves thee and his alliance is so dear to me, I'll have no scruples of a timid girl to weigh against it. For long years I've nursed this fondness and I now command obedience.   10

OCEANA: That union must remain unblessed wherein the helpless hand is giving no heart to bear it company. O my father, how at the altar can I take that vow my heart now whispers never can be kept.

MORDAUNT: Hear me, rash girl, now that none o'erhear our converse. Learn thy father's destiny — the name I bear is not my own!   15

OCEANA: My father!

MORDAUNT: Thou didst not know my former life and deeds. Hardy adventure and the shock of arms, civil contention and a monarch's death make up the past, and poison all who come! 'Tis thou alone can clothe my future days with peace and shed one cheering ray o'er a dark scene of   20
terror.

OCEANA: Art thou distraught?

MORDAUNT: Do not deny me, girl, and make me so! I am an outcast and a man forbid. Fitzarnold knows me and he asks my child — has power, and gaining thee preserves thy sire. Speak, Oceana! Thy resolve: what is it?   25

OCEANA: Thou canst not mean it, father! No, it cannot be!

MORDAUNT: Girl, it is as certain as our earthly doom. Decide, then, now between my honor and my instant death! For by thy mother's memory and by my soul, if my despair do find thee pitiless, my own right hand shall end a wretched life and leave thee nothing for a bridal dower but my curses and a blighted name. (*Crosses to the right*) 30

OCEANA: My throat is parched! I pray a moment's peace, a moment's pause.

(*Business. Mordaunt paces the stage in great agitation, at last falls on his knee to Oceana. Walter enters, starts at seeing them and remains at back.*)

MORDAUNT: Look at thy father, lowly begging life of thee. I will not swear, I will not rave, my child, but I'll implore thee! If thou hast ever loved me and dost so still, show that affection now! Let not thy father's name for- 35 ever stand a mark for men to heap their curses on — relent, my child.

OCEANA: I can endure no more — rise, my father.

MORDAUNT: Dost thou promise?

OCEANA: All, all!

MORDAUNT: Swear, by truth! by honor! By the dead — 40

OCEANA: To wed Fitzarnold —

WALTER (*Comes up*): Hold! Hold, rash girl, forebear! Thou art ensnared and wouldst pronounce thy doom.

MORDAUNT: Lightning consume thee, meddling fool! What bringst thou here? 45

WALTER: No pleasant duty, sir; a message which the council sends thee here. (*Gives packet to Mordaunt*) I am no spy, nor do I care to know secrets too dread for thine own heart to hold.

MORDAUNT: Beggar, begone!

(*Strikes him with packet and crosses to the left. Walter draws sword. Oceana interposes.*)

OCEANA: It is my father, Walter, mine. 50

WALTER: A blow.

OCEANA: Oh, thou wilt forgive him!

WALTER: Never! I will forth, and ere he shall enforce thee where thou hast no joy, will rend the mask he cheats us with. (*Crosses to the left*)

OCEANA: And if thou dost, by heaven I'll ne'er be thine. 55

WALTER (*Sheathes sword*): Old man, an angel's bosom shelters thine. Instruct Fitzarnold in our quarrel's cause. No daughter bars my way to him.

(*Exit. Enter Fitzarnold.*)

FITZARNOLD: How now, you tremble; what has chanced?

MORDAUNT: A moody beggar who abused my love and I chastised him for it — that's all.   60

OCEANA: My father —

MORDAUNT: Go to thy chamber.

OCEANA: Would it were my grave.   (*Exit.*)

MORDAUNT: My noble lord, that moody stripling whom you saw last night — whether set on by Vaughan, his patron, or by the vainness of his   65
own conceits, resolves to break my daughter's marriage.

FITZARNOLD: And wilt thou suffer this? What is the villain's state?

MORDAUNT: Dependence on Sir Arthur Vaughan; his wealth, a goodly person, and the law of schools. (*Bell tolls.*) Hark! I am summoned to the council. Wilt thou along?   70

(*Fitzarnold crosses to the left.*)

FITZARNOLD: I trust he finds no favor with your daughter.

MORDAUNT: She shall be thine, my lord; thine with free will and full contentment. Now for the council.

(*Exeunt.*)

SCENE III

Flourish. The council chamber. Errington, Sir Arthur and Church on raised platform. Mordaunt and Fitzarnold seated at table at the left; Elders, etc. Goodenough and Soldiers at the right. Villagers, etc. Walter and Tramp.

ERRINGTON: 'Tis news that asks from us most speedy action. Heaven has in sounds most audible and strange, in sights, too, that amazed the lookers-on, forewarned our people of their peril. 'Tis time to lift the arm so long supine, and with one blow cut off this heathen race, who spite of reason and the word revealed, continue hardened in their devious ways, and   5
make the chosen tremble. Colleagues, your voices — speak — are you for peace or war?

SIR ARTHUR: What is your proof your Indian neighbors mean not as fairly towards our settlements as did King Philip's father, Massasoit?

ERRINGTON: Sir, we have full proof that Philip is our foe. Sasamond, the   10
faithful servant of our cause, has been dispatched by Philip's men, set on to murder him. One of his tribe confessed the horrid truth — and will, when time shall call, give horrid proof on't. I say this chieftain is a man of blood, and Heaven will bless the valiant arm that slays him.

(*Metamora enters suddenly and remains at the center. When Metamora enters, all start and grasp their swords. The soldiers prepare to fire. All are silent and confused.*)

METAMORA: You sent for me and I am come. Humph! If you have noth-   15
ing to say I will go back — if you fear to question, Metamora does not
fear to answer.

ERRINGTON: Philip, 'tis thought you love us not, and all unmindful of our
league of peace, plot with the Narragansetts, and contrive fatal disorder
to our colony.   20

METAMORA: Do your fears counsel you? What is it makes your old men
grave? And your young men grasp their fire weapons as if they awaited
the onset of the foe? Brothers, what has Metamora done that doubt is in
all your faces and your spirits seem troubled? The good man's heart is a
stranger to fear, and his tongue is ready to speak the words of truth.   25

ERRINGTON: We are informed that thou gavest shelter to a banished man,
whose deeds unchristian met our just reproof — one by our holy synod
doomed — whom it is said you housed, and thereby hast incurred our
church's censure — and given just cause to doubt thy honesty.

METAMORA: Why was that man sent away from the home of his joy? Be-   30
cause the Great Spirit did not speak to him as he had spoken to you? Did
you not come across the great waters and leave the smoke of your father's
hearth because the iron hand was held out against you, and your hearts
were sorrowful in the high places of prayer. Why do you that have just
plucked the red knife from your own wounded sides, strive to stab your   35
brother?

ERRINGTON: Indian, this is no reply for us. Didst thou not know the sentence of the court on him whom thou didst shelter?

METAMORA: If my rarest enemy had crept unarmed into my wigwam and
his heart was sore, I would not have driven him from my fire nor forbid-   40
den him to lie down upon my mat. Why then should the Wampanoag
shut out the man of peace when he came with tears in his eyes and his
limbs torn by the sharp thorns of the thicket? Your great book, you say,
tells you to give good gifts to the stranger and deal kindly with him
whose heart is sad; the Wampanoag needs no such counselor, for the   45
Great Spirit has with his own fingers written it upon his heart.

MORDAUNT: Why dost thou put arms into thy people's hands, thereby en-
gendering mischief towards us?

METAMORA: If my people do wrong, I am quick to punish. Do you not set
a snare for them that they may fall, and make them mad with the fire wa-   50
ter the Great Spirit gave you in his wrath? The red man sickens in the
house of the palefaces, and the leaping stream of the mountains is made
impure by the foul brooks that mingle with it.

SIR ARTHUR: Chieftain, since these things are so, sell us thy lands and seek
another biding place.   55

METAMORA: And if I did, would you not stretch out your hand to seize that also? No! White man, no! Never will Metamora forsake the home of his fathers, and let the plough of the strangers disturb the bones of his kindred.

CHURCH: These are bold words, chief. 60

METAMORA: They are true ones.

ERRINGTON: They give no token of thy love of peace. We would deal fairly with thee — nay, be generous.

METAMORA: Then would you pay back that which fifty snows ago you received from the hands of my father, Massasoit. Ye had been tossed about 65 like small things upon the face of the great waters, and there was no earth for your feet to rest on; your backs were turned upon the land of your fathers. The red man took you as a little child and opened the door of his wigwam. The keen blast of the north howled in the leafless wood, but the Indian covered you with his broad right hand and put it back. Your little 70 ones smiled when they heard the loud voice of the storm, for our fires were warm and the Indian was the white man's friend.

ERRINGTON: Such words are needless now.

METAMORA: I will speak no more; I am going.

MORDAUNT: Hold! A moment, Philip; we have yet to tell of the death of 75 Sasamond, who fell in secret and by treachery.

METAMORA: So should the treacherous man fall, by the keen knife in the darkness and not ascend from the strife of battle to the bright haven where the dead warrior dwells in glory.

ERRINGTON: Didst thou contrive his murder? 80

METAMORA: I will not answer.

ERRINGTON: We have those can prove thou didst.

METAMORA: I have spoken.

ERRINGTON: Bring in the witness. (*Exit Goodenough.*) We, too, long have stayed the arm of power from execution. Come, we parley with a serpent 85 and his wiles are deep.

METAMORA: Injurious white man! Do not tread too hard upon the serpent's folds. His fangs are not taken out, nor has its venom lost the power to kill.

ERRINGTON: Approach! 90

(*Goodenough returns with Annawandah.*)

METAMORA: Annawandah!

ERRINGTON: Behold, deceitful man, thy deeds are known.

METAMORA: Let me see his eye. Art thou he whom I snatched from the

war club of the Mohigan, when thou hadst sung thy death song, and the
lips of the foe were thirsty for thy blood? Has Metamora cherished thee   95
in his wigwam and hast thou put a knife into the white man's hand to slay
him! The foul spirit hath entered thee, and the pure blood of the
Wampanoag has left thy veins. Thy heart is a lie, and thine eye cannot
rest upon the face of truth, when like the great light it shines on thee in
unclouded glory. Elders, can he speak to you the words of truth, when he   100
is false to his brother, his country and his god?

ERRINGTON: He was thy trusty agent, Philip, and conscience-smote revealed thy wickedness.

METAMORA: You believe his words?

ERRINGTON: We do, and will reward his honesty.   105

METAMORA: Wampanoag! No, I will not call thee so. Red man, say unto
these people they have bought thy tongue, and thou hast uttered a lie!

ERRINGTON: He does not answer.

METAMORA: I am Metamora, thy father and thy king.

ERRINGTON: Philip o'erawes him — send the witness home.   110

METAMORA: I will do that! Slave of the white man, go follow Sasamond.

(*Stabs Annawandah, who staggers off. All stand up, general movement.*)

ERRINGTON: Seize and bind him.

(*Soldiers make a forward movement.*)

METAMORA: Come! My knife has drunk the blood of the false one, yet it
is not satisfied! White man, beware! The mighty spirits of the Wampanoag race are hovering o'er your heads; they stretch out their shadowy   115
arms to me and ask for vengeance; they shall have it. The wrath of the
wronged Indian shall fall upon you like a cataract that dashes the up-
rooted oak down the mighty chasms. The war whoop shall start you from
your dreams at night, and the red hatchet gleam in the blaze of your
burning dwellings! From the east to the west, in the north and in the   120
south shall cry of vengeance burst, till the lands you have stolen groan
under your feet no more!

ERRINGTON: Secure him!

METAMORA: Thus do I smite your nation and defy your power.

ERRINGTON: Fire on him.   125

(*Business. Metamora hurls hatchet into stage, and rushes out. Soldiers fire after him.
Mordaunt, who has moved forward, receives a shot and falls in chair. Tableau. Drums,
trumpets, and general confusion. Quick curtain.*)

Act iii, Scene i

A chamber in Mordaunt's house. Enter Fitzarnold.

FITZARNOLD: Mordaunt wounded, and perhaps to death, struck by a shot that was leveled at the chief; and the fierce storm of war at distance heard, which soon may burst tremendous o'er our heads! This is no place for me. She must be mine tonight! Aye, this night, for fear his death may snatch his gold and daughter from me. Within there, Wolfe. (*Enter Wolfe.*)   5
Go get a surgeon for this Mordaunt's wounds, a scribe and priest for me — wilt be silent?

WOLFE: I will observe! Does my lord wed tomorrow?

FITZARNOLD: No, this night; and with tomorrow's sun I spread my sail for England.   10

WOLFE: Ha!

FITZARNOLD: How now! What meanest thou? Wouldst thou to rival me?

WOLFE: My lord!

FITZARNOLD: Well, well; go see thy duty done.   (*Exit.*)

WOLFE: My lord, be sure on't. Now for young Walter. I will fulfill my duty   15
but not to thee, my Lord Fitzarnold! Thou wilt not thank me for the priest I'll bring.   (*Exit.*)

Scene ii

An Indian village, deep wood, wigwam. Lights half down. Conch shell heard. Nahmeokee enters from wigwam.

NAHMEOKEE: Sure 'twas the shell of Metamora, and spoke the strain it was wont when the old men were called to council, or when the scout returns from his long travel.

METAMORA (*Outside*):   Nahmeokee!

NAHMEOKEE: It is — it is Metamora.   5

(*Enter Metamora.*)

METAMORA: Is our little one well, Nahmeokee?

NAHMEOKEE: He is. How didst thou leave the white man with whom thou hast been to hold a talk?

METAMORA: Like the great stream of the mountain when the spirit of the storm passes furiously over its bosom. Where are my people?   10

NAHMEOKEE: Here in the deep woods where Kaneshine, the aged priest, tells them the mighty deeds of their people, and interprets to them the will of the Great Spirit.

METAMORA: Otah! (*Otah enters.*) Summon my warriors; bid them with speed to council. (*Exit Otah.*) I have escaped the swift flight of the white man's bullets but like the bounding elk when the hunters who follow close upon his heels. (*Reenter Otah with Kaneshine and all the Indians. Indian march, eight bars. Indians form at the left.*) Warriors, I took a prisoner from the uplifted weapon of the Mohigan, when the victor's limbs were bloody and the scalps at his belt had no number. He lived in my wigwam; I made him my brother. When the spirit of sleep was upon me, he crept like a guilty thing away, and put into the white man's hand a brand of fire to consume me, and drive my people far away where there are no hunting grounds and where the Wampanoag has no protecting Spirit.

KANESHINE: Annawandah?

METAMORA: Annawandah!

KANESHINE: Where is he, chief of thy people, and where is the dog whose head the Great Spirit will smite with fire?

METAMORA: Where the ravenous bird of night may eat the flesh of his body. Here is the blood of the traitor's heart! (*Shows knife*) My people, shall I tell you the thoughts that fill me?

KANESHINE: Speak, Metamora, speak!

METAMORA: When the strangers came from afar off, they were like a little tree; but now they are grown up and their spreading branches threaten to keep the light from you. They ate of your corn and drank of your cup, and now they lift up their arms against you. Oh my people, the race of the red man has fallen away like the trees of the forest before the axes of the pale-faces. The fair places of his father's triumphs hear no more the sound of his footsteps. He moves in the region his proud fathers bequeathed him, not like a lord of the soil, but like a wretch who comes for plunder and for prey.

(*Distant thunder and lightning*)

KANESHINE: The chief has spoken truly and the stranger is worthy to die! But the fire of our warriors is burnt out and their hatchets have no edge. O son of Massasoit, thy words are to me like the warm blood of the foe, and I will drink till I am full! Speak again!

METAMORA: "Chief of the people," said a voice from the deep as I lay by the seaside in the eyes of the moon — "Chief of the people, wake from thy dream of peace, and make sharp the point of thy spear, for the destroyer's arm is made bare to smite. O son of my old age, arise like the tiger in great wrath and snatch thy people from the devourer's jaws!" My father spoke no more; a mist passed before me, and from the mist the Spirit bent his eyes imploringly on me. I started to my feet and shouted the shrill battle cry of the Wampanoags. The high hills sent back the echo, and rock, hill and ocean, earth and air opened their giant throats and cried with me, "Red man, arouse! Freedom! Revenge or death!" (*Thunder and lightning. All quail but Metamora.*) Hark, warriors! The Great 55 Spirit hears me and pours forth his mighty voice with mine. Let your voice in battle be like his, and the flash from your fire weapons as quick to kill. Nahmeokee, take this knife, carry it to the Narragansett, to thy brother; tell him the hatchet is dug from the grave where the grass is grown old above it; thy tongue will move him more than the voice of all 60 our tribe in the loud talk of war.

NAHMEOKEE: Nahmeokee will not fail in her path; and her eyes will be quick to see where the stranger has set his snare.

METAMORA: Warriors! Your old and infirm must you send into the country of the Narragansett, that your hearts may not be made soft in the 65 hour of battle.

NAHMEOKEE: Go you tonight, Metamora?

METAMORA: Tonight! I will not lay down in my wigwam till the foe has drawn himself together and comes in his height to destroy. Nahmeokee, I still will be the red man's father and his king, or the sacred rock 70 whereon my father spoke so long the words of wisdom shall be made red with the blood of his race.

(*Hurried music. Metamora and Indians exeunt. Nahmeokee goes in wigwam.*)

SCENE III

A chamber in Mordaunt's house. Clock strikes twelve as scene opens. Thunder distant. Enter Oceana in plain attire.

OCEANA: I know not how it is but every thunder peal seems to bear words portentous. The moaning blast has meaning in its sound and tells of distant horror — it is the hour when I bade Walter come! Can he have braved the tempest? Hark, I hear a step! (*Knock*) How my heart beats. (*Enter Fitzarnold.*) It is — it is Fitzarnold!

FITZARNOLD: Fitzarnold, lady! Why this wonder? Is it fear? Can she whom thunder frights not shrink from me?

OCEANA: My lord, the hour is late; I feign would know who sent thee hither.

FITZARNOLD: Thy honored father. 10

OCEANA: Thy purpose?

FITZARNOLD: Read it there. (*Gives letter*)

OCEANA: Ha! Tonight! Be thine tonight?

FITZARNOLD: Aye, tonight. I have thy father's secret.

OCEANA: I know thou hast, and in that mean advantage wouldst mar his daughter's happiness forever — away! I blush that thus I parley words with thee — get thee gone. (*Crosses to the left*)

FITZARNOLD: Yes, when thou goest with me; not till then, lady. I will not waste the time that grows more precious every moment to me. (*Thunder*) What though the lightning flash and thunder roll — what though the tempest pours its fury down, Fitzarnold's soul does swell above the din! Nay more, dares brave the storm within thy breast, and shrinks not from the lightning of thine eye.

OCEANA: Would it could kill thee!

FITZARNOLD: It can do more — can conquer like the fiery serpent. It pierces, and as it pierces charms — Oceana!

OCEANA: Stand back! I will alarm my sire.

FITZARNOLD: And if thou dost, he will not aid thee. My treasures are embarked, aye, all but thee; thy father gives consent, the priest waits and ere morning, father, daughter, son, shall all be riding on the wave for England.

OCEANA: No, never!

FITZARNOLD: Convince thyself — (*Stamps his foot. Walter enters disguised as a priest.*) Now, scornful lady, thy bridal hour has come; thy tauntings do but fan the flame that rages here.

OCEANA: Is there no refuge?

FITZARNOLD: None, but in these arms.

OCEANA: No hope — no rescue!

FITZARNOLD: None! None!

OCEANA: Walter, on thee I call — Walter, where art thou?

WALTER (*Throws off disguise*): Walter is here.

FITZARNOLD: Villain! Thy life or mine!

(*Fitzarnold draws, Oceana throws herself between them.*)

OCEANA: Forebear! No blood! (*To Walter*) Thou must come stainless to these arms.

WALTER: Sayest thou? Wilt thou take me to them?

OCEANA: I will — I do.

(*They embrace.*)

FITZARNOLD: Thy father's blood be on thee; he is Fitzarnold's victim.

(*Exit. Bell rings. Enter Tramp.*)

TRAMP: The savages approach! The Wampanoag chieftain and his crew, at distance, peal their startling yell of war! Haste, sir, to meet them.

WALTER: Retire thee for a while, my Oceana — thou, sir, on the instant follow me — your sword! your sword!   50

(*Exit with Oceana; Tramp follows.*)

SCENE IV

A view of Mordaunt's house on the beach. Sea in distance, ship on fire. Garden and staircase leading down to the water. Lights down at opening of scene. Distant yells heard. Enter Fitzarnold hastily.

FITZARNOLD: Almighty powers! Hemmed in on every side! No hope. (*War-whoop*) Hark to their savage yells! No means are left for flight, for on the waves my precious vessel burns — by the fell savage mastered! No retreat!

(*War whoops. Exit Fitzarnold hastily. Metamora and all the Indians enter up staircase entrances. Music hurried, forte till all are on.*)

METAMORA (*Pointing to Fitzarnold*):   Follow him! (*To others*) Go into the   5
white man's dwelling and drag him to me that my eye can look upon his torture and his scalp may tell Metamora's triumph to his tribe — go.

(*Otah and Kaneshine are about to enter the house when Oceana appears.*)

OCEANA: Forebear, ye shall not enter.
METAMORA: Warriors, have I not spoken.

(*Throws her around to the left; Indians go in.*)

OCEANA: Great Chieftain! Dost thou not know me?   10
METAMORA: I am a Wampanoag in the home of mine enemy; I ride on my wrongs, and vengeance cries out for blood.
OCEANA: Wilt thou not hear me?
METAMORA: Talk to the rattling storm or melt the high rocks with tears; thou canst not move me. My foe! my foe! my foe!   15
OCEANA: Have mercy, Heaven!

(*The Indians return dragging in Mordaunt.*)

METAMORA: Hah!
MORDAUNT: Mercy! Mercy!
OCEANA: My father! Spare my father! (*Rushes to Mordaunt*)
METAMORA: He must die! Drag him away to the fire of the sacrifice that   20
my ear may drink the music of his dying groans.
OCEANA: Fiends and murderers!
METAMORA: The white man has made us such. Prepare.

(*Business*)

OCEANA: Then smite his heart through mine; our mangled breasts shall meet in death — one grave shall hold us. Metamora, dost thou remember this? (*Shows eagle plume*)   25

METAMORA: Yes.

OCEANA: It was thy father's. Chieftain, thou gavest it to me.

METAMORA: Say on.

OCEANA: Thou saidst it would prove a guardian to me when the conflict   30
raged. Were thy words true when with thy father's tongue thou saidst, whatever being wore the gift, no Indian of thy tribe should do that being harm.

METAMORA: The Wampanoag cannot lie.

OCEANA: Then do I place it here. (*Places it on Mordaunt's bosom*)   35

METAMORA: Hah!

OCEANA: The Wampanoag cannot lie, and I can die for him who gave existence to me.

MORDAUNT: My child! my child!

(*Red fire in house*)

METAMORA: Take them apart! (*Indians separate them.*) Old man, I cannot let   40
the tomahawk descend upon thy head, or bear thee to the place of sacrifice; but here is that shall appease the red man's wrath. (*Seizes Oceana; flames seen in house*) The fire is kindled in thy dwelling, and I will plunge her in the hot fury of the flames.

MORDAUNT: No, no, thou wilt not harm her.   45

OCEANA: Father, farewell! Thy nation, savage, will repent this act of thine.

METAMORA: If thou art just, it will not. Old man, take thy child. (*Throws her to him*) Metamora cannot forth with the maiden of the eagle plume; and he disdains a victim who has no color in his face nor fire in his eye.

(*Bugle sounds.*)

MORDAUNT: Gracious heavens!   50

METAMORA: Hark! The power of the white man comes! Launch your canoes! We have drunk blood enough. Spirit of my father, be at rest! Thou art obeyed, thy people are avenged.

(*Exit hastily followed by the Indians. Drums and trumpet till curtain. Enter Walter, Goodenough, Church, Soldiers, Peasants, male and female, all from behind house. Soldiers are about to fire, when Walter throws himself before them and exclaims.*)

WALTER: Forebear! Forebear!

(*Walter and Oceana embrace. Tableau. Curtain.*)

Act iv, Scene i

Enter Errington, Lord Fitzarnold, Walter, and Church. A room in Sir Arthur's house.

SIR ARTHUR: Welcome my brother.

ERRINGTON: The strife is over: but the wail of those who mourn some captive friend still wounds the ear and fills our hearts with sadness.

FITZARNOLD: The follower of mine, surprised or else too venturous in the fight, was dragged away in bondage.   5

SIR ARTHUR: Old Wolfe.

FITZARNOLD: The same — a moody but a faithful man doomed no doubt to torture or to death.

WALTER (*Aside*):   Faithful indeed. But not to him thou think'st.

ERRINGTON: He will avenge the captives' fall.   10

WALTER: But must they fall — is there no way to save them?

ERRINGTON: None, young sir, unless thy wisdom find it.

WALTER: They might be ransomed.

SIR ARTHUR: True they might. And from my wealth I'll pay whatever price the Indians' power will yield them for.   15

ERRINGTON: But who so rash to bear such offer unto Philip in his present mood?

FITZARNOLD (*Aside*):   Could I but tempt this stripling to his death.

ERRINGTON: Say is there one so reckless and so brave will dare the peril to preserve his fellows?   20

FITZARNOLD: Grave sirs, I know of none more truly fit than young Walter to achieve the deed. How proud the name required by such an act. How vast the joy his daring heart must feel. Whose arm against such terror shall prevail. And rescue numbers from a lingering death.

WALTER:

If my Lord so dearly holds the prize,   25
Why not himself adventure to attain it?
But I will go — for I have reasons for it
Would move me, felt I not my Lord's great pity for the captives' woe.

SIR ARTHUR:

Bravely said, thou deserve'st our thanks,
And if thou canst persuade the hostile chief   30
To draw his arm'd bands away and save the blood, that else must flow so terribly.

ERRINGTON:

Take swiftest horse young man and Heaven protect thee.

WALTER:

No tongue so blest as that which heralds peace —

No heart so mailed as that which beats, warm for his fellow man.
Fare you well.   (*Exit Walter.*)   35

ERRINGTON:

Now to our labours — those new levies made —
We may exterminate, with one full blow
This savage race, hated of man — unblessed of Heaven —
Surely a land so fair was ne'er designed to feed the heartless infidel.

(*Cry: "Indians! Indians!"*)

ERRINGTON: Hah! More massacre! Mercy, Heaven!   40

(*Enter Oceana.*)

OCEANA: Oh, Sirs, shew pity to a captive wretch whom heartless men
abuse with taunts and blows. If ye are men oh let the helpless find in you
kind pity — mercy and protection.

ERRINGTON:

Maiden,
Whom dost thou speak of?   45

OCEANA:

An Indian woman
And her infant child, by these made prisoners. Look there, they have
ta'en her child from her.

(*Enter Nahmeokee with Officer, two Guards, as prisoner. Goodenough with the child.*)

ERRINGTON:

How now, who hast thou there?

GOODENOUGH:

An Indian woman, we captured in the glen.
A spy, 'tis thought sent by the cursed foe.   50

ERRINGTON:

Came she alone?

GOODENOUGH:

No, a young and nimble man
Was with her, but he 'scap'd pursuit.
I am sure he is wounded, for I saw him fall.

ERRINGTON: Woman what art thou?   55

NAHMEOKEE: Give poor woman her child?

ERRINGTON: Dost thou hear my question?

NAHMEOKEE: Give poor Indian woman her child?

OCEANA: Do so.

GOODENOUGH: Why 'twas I that caught the creature — and —   60

OCEANA: Man, didst thou hear me? (*Takes child from him*)

GOODENOUGH: Hard times indeed to lose so good a prize. [The brat is saleable.][1] 'Tis mine.

OCEANA: Measureless brute.

GOODENOUGH: For what? 'Tis only an Indian boy.   65

(*Oceana gives Nahmeokee her child, who touch'd with her kindness, takes her scarf to wipe Oceana's eyes. The latter recognises it to be the one bound round Metamora's arm in first scene.*)

OCEANA: Nahmeokee!

NAHMEOKEE: Hush!

ERRINGTON: Who art thou, woman?

NAHMEOKEE: I am the servant of the Great Spirit.

ERRINGTON: Who is thy husband?   70

NAHMEOKEE: One thou dost not love.

ERRINGTON: His name?

NAHMEOKEE: I will not tell thee.

ERRINGTON: We can enforce an answer.

NAHMEOKEE: Poor Indian woman cannot keep her limbs from pain; but   75
she can keep silence.

ERRINGTON: Woman, what is thy nation and thy race?

NAHMEOKEE: White man, the Sun is my father and the Earth my mother —
I will speak no more.

ERRINGTON:
Captain, take charge of this same stubborn wretch   80
Who neither will her name nor purpose tell.
If she do prove as alleg'd a spy,
Nothing shall save her from a public death;
We must o'erawe our treacherous foe.
[And this obdurate and blasphemous witch   85
May in her death, keep death from many more.]
Summon our Elders — my Lord Fitzarnold,
Your counsel now may aid us.

FITZARNOLD: 'Tis thine, — and my poor service.

ERRINGTON: Take her away. (*Cross to right*) Justice is sometimes slow, Yet is   90
she sure.

NAHMEOKEE: Thy nation, white man, yet may find it so.

(*Exeunt Errington, Goodenough, Church, Nahmeokee and Soldiers.*)

[1] Lines in brackets were crossed out in the original version.

OCEANA: Fitzarnold of the Council — could I move His sympathy? (*Approaching him tremblingly*) My lord.
FITZARNOLD: Well lady? 95
OCEANA: I have offended thee.
FITZARNOLD: I have forgotten it.
OCEANA: I have a boon to ask.
FITZARNOLD: Sayst thou — of me?
OCEANA: It will not cost thee much. 100
FITZARNOLD: No price too great to purchase thy sweet smiles of thee.
OCEANA:
Then be this female's advocate, my lord.
Thou canst be eloquent and the heart of good,
But much misguided men may by thy speech
Be moved to pity and to pardon her. 105
FITZARNOLD: How so — a wandering wretch unknown?
OCEANA: Metamora has helpless prisoners.
FITZARNOLD:
'Tis true — and thou dost deeply feel for them.
Young Walter now seeks their enfranchisement.
OCEANA:
I know it sir. (*Aside*) Be still my throbbing heart. 110
My lord, what vengeance will her husband take.
Think you will aught appease dread Philip's wrath —
When he is told — chieftain, thy wife's a slave?
FITZARNOLD:
His wife — the Queen! Indeed! Dost say so?
OCEANA:
Give not the secret unto mortal ear — 115
It might destroy all hopes of unity.
Preserve this captive from impending doom
And countless prayers shall pay thee for it.
FITZARNOLD:
Thy kind approval is reward enough.
OCEANA: Shall she be saved? 120
FITZARNOLD: She shall be free — a word of mine can do it.
OCEANA: Thanks! Thanks! My Lord deceive me not.
FITZARNOLD: Fear not, fair Lady. I have pledged my word.

(*Exit Oceana.*)

FITZARNOLD: Thou thinks't me kind — ha! ha! I will be so. Philip has
Captives — and young Walter's there. 125

The Council dare not take this woman's life for that would doom their captive countrymen. Imprisoned she is free from danger for the law protects her. But turn her loose to the wild fury of the senseless crowd *she dies* ere justice or the Elders' arms can reach her. Ah! This way conducts me straight to the goal. I am resolved to reach and seal at once my hated rival's doom. 130

[Oh! I will plead as Angels do in Heaven
For mortals when they err and mourn for it.]
Her freedom is her death — the zealot crowd
Will rush upon her like the loosen'd winds 135
And prove as merciless — while the lion husband,
Madden'd with his loss, sheds blood to surfeiting.
Oh yes, dear pleader for the captive one,
Thy boon is granted. She shall be free! (*Exit.*)

SCENE II

One-half dark. An Indian Retreat. Wolfe bound to the Stake at the right. Metamora at a distance leaning on his rifle. Kaneshine and Warriors. Lights one-half down.

KANESHINE: Warriors, our enemies have been met, and the blood of the Stranger has sunk deep into the sand — yet the spirit of those who have fallen by the power of the foe are not yet appeas'd — prepare the captives for their hour of death. Come round the tree of sacrifice and lift up the flame, till it devour in its fiery rage, the abhor'd usurpers (*Gun*) of the red 5 man's soil! Come, my lips are dry for the captives' blood.

(*As they are about to fire the pile, a shot is heard. Enter Walter.*)

METAMORA: Hold! Let the young man say why he comes into our country unbidden. Why does he tempt the ire of our warriors, when their weapons are red with the blood of the battle?

WALTER:
That I come friendly let this emblem speak. 10
To check the dire advance of bloody war,
To urge the Wampanoag to disarm his band
And once again renew with us the bond
That made the white and red man brothers.

METAMORA: No, young man, the blood my warriors have tasted, has made 15 their hearts glad and their hands are thrust out for more. Let the white man fear. The arrow he has shot into the mountain has turned back and pierced his own side. What are the Elders' words?

WALTER:

    Let Philip take our wampum and our coin
    Restore his captives and remove his dead   20
    And rest from causeless and destructive war,
    Until such terms of lasting peace are made
    As shall forever quell our angry feuds
    And sink the hatchet to be raised no more.

METAMORA: *Humph!* And meanwhile he sharpens his long weapons in se- 25
cret, and each day grows more numerous. When the great stream of the
mountains first springs from the earth it is very weak, and I can stand up
against its waters, but when the great rain descends, it is swift and
swollen, death dwells in its white bosom and it will not spare.

WALTER:

    By Him who moves the stars and lights the Sun,   30
    If thou dost shed the trembling captives' blood,
    A thousand warlike men will rush to arms
    And terribly avenge their countrymen.

METAMORA: Well, let them come! Our arms are as strong as the white
man's. And the use of the fire-weapon he has taught us. My ears are shut 35
against thee.

WALTER (*To Wolfe*): Oh, my friend! I will achieve thy rescue if gold or prayers
can move them.

WOLFE:

    I was prepared to die, and only mourned
    For I am childless and a lonely man.   40
    I had not told the secret of thy birth.
    And shewn thy father to thee.

WALTER: My Father! Sayst thou?

WOLFE: Walter, listen to me.

OTAH (*Speaks without*): Metamora!   45

METAMORA: Ha! (*Enter Otah*)

OTAH: Nahmeokee!

METAMORA: Dead!

OTAH: Our feet grew weary in the path, and we sate down to rest in the
dark wood — the fire-weapons blazed in the thicket, and my arm was 50
wounded, with the other I grasped the keen knife you gave Nahmeokee,
but I sank down powerless and the white men bore off the queen a
captive.

METAMORA: *Humph* — Nahmeokee is the white man's prisoner. Where is
thy horse?   55

WALTER: Beneath yonder tree.

METAMORA: Unbind the captive! Young man! You must abide with the Wampanoag till Nahmeokee returns to her home. Woe unto you if the hard hand has been laid upon her. Take the white man to my wigwam.   60

WALTER: I thank thee, Chieftain, this is kindness to me. Come, good Wolfe, tell me my father's name.

METAMORA: If one drop fall from Nahmeokee's eye, one hair from her head, the axe shall hew your quivering limbs asunder and the ashes of your bones be carried away on the rushing winds. Come, old man.   65

(*Exeunt*)

SCENE III

(*Enter Fitzarnold*)

FITZARNOLD: Nahmeokee now is free, and the fanatic herd all cry aloud, "Oh mad rulers! Mercy to her" — she comes — and witch, hag and Indian din her ears. They come this way — I must avoid their clamor. (*Enter Nahmeokee.*)

NAHMEOKEE: Let them not kill the poor Indian woman.

FITZARNOLD: Woman away.   5

NAHMEOKEE: They will murder my child.

FITZARNOLD: Hold off — I cannot help thee. (*Exit Fitzarnold.*)

NAHMEOKEE: They come upon me from every side of the path. My limbs can bear me no farther. Mercy! Hah! They have missed my track and seek in the wood, and in the caves for my blood. Who is he that rides a   10
swift horse there, through the narrow path way of the glen! The shade of the coming night is over him and he dimly appears a red man riding the swift cloud. (*Shouts*) Ha, they have traced me by the white garment, the brambles tore from me in my flight. They come. Cling to me my child. Cling to thy mother's bosom. (*Enter Goodenough and four Peasants.*)   15

GOODENOUGH: Foul Indian witch, thy race is run. Drag her to the lake. Take her child from her. (*Enter Metamora.*)

METAMORA: Stand back! or the swift death shall take wing. Which of you has lived too long? Let him lift up his arm against her.

OFFICER: How is this? King Philip ventures here? What comest thou for?   20

METAMORA: Boy! Thou art a child, there is no mark of the war upon thee. Send me thy Elder, or thy Chief. I'll make my talk to him.

GOODENOUGH: Here comes Master Errington. (*Enter Errington and Soldiers*)

ERRINGTON: Philip a Prisoner!

METAMORA: No! He has arms in his hand and courage in his heart, he   25
comes near you of his own will, and when he has done his work, he'll go
back to his wigwam.

ERRINGTON: Indian, you answer boldly.

METAMORA: What is there I should fear?

ERRINGTON: Savage! The wrath of him who hates the Heathen and the   30
man of blood.

METAMORA: Does he love mercy; and is he the white man's friend?

ERRINGTON: Yes.

METAMORA: How did Nahmeokee and her infant wrong you, that you
hunted her through the thorny pathway of the glen, and scented her   35
blood like the fierce red wolf in his hunger?

CHURCH: Why hold parley with him! Call our musqueteers and bear them
both to trial and to doom. Heaven smiles on us — Philip in our power.
His cursed followers would sue for peace.

METAMORA: Not till the blood of twenty English captives be poured out   40
as a sacrifice. Elders beware, the knife is sharpened — the stake is fixed —
and the captives' limbs tremble under the burning gaze of the prophet of
wrath. Woe come to them when my people shall hear their chief has been
slain by the pale faces or is bound in the dark place of doom.

NAHMEOKEE: Do not tempt them, Metamora, they are many like the   45
leaves of the forest and we are but as two lone trees standing in their
midst.

METAMORA: Which can easier escape the hunter's spear? The tiger that
turns on it in his wrath, or the lamb that sinks down and trembles? Thou
has seen me look unmoved at a torturing death — shall mine eye be   50
turned downward when the white man frowns?

ERRINGTON: Philip, the peace our young man offered thee. Didst thou regard his words?

METAMORA: Yes.

ERRINGTON: And wilt thou yield compliance?   55

METAMORA: I will. Nahmeokee shall bear the tidings to my people that
the prisoners may return to their homes, and the war-whoop shall not go
forth on the evening gale.

ERRINGTON:

Let her set forth. Friends, let me advise you,   60
Keep the Chieftain prisoner, let's muster men.
And in unlook'd for hour with one blow we will overwhelm
This accursed race. And furthermore — (*Converses apart*)

NAHMEOKEE (*To Metamora*):   I will remember thy words.

METAMORA: Grieve not that I linger in the dark place of the condemned, for the eye of the Great Spirit will be on me there.   65

ERRINGTON: We greet thee, Philip, and accept thy love. Nahmeokee may return.

METAMORA: 'Tis very good. The horse stands 'neath the brow of the hill — speak not — I read thy thought in thy eye. Go — go, Nahmeokee. I am ready to follow you.   70

ERRINGTON: Conduct him forth to prison. (*Soldiers attempt to take his gun.*)

METAMORA: No! This shall be to me as my child and I will talk to it, until I go back to my people.

GOODENOUGH: Right well conceived, could it but talk.

METAMORA: It can — when the land of my great forefathers is trampled   75
on by the foot of the foe — or when treachery lurks round the Wampanoag, while he bides in the white man's home.

ACT V, SCENE I

Same as Act I, Scene I. Lights down. Oceana discovered leaning against tomb. Slow music, four bars.

OCEANA: Tomb of the silent dead, thou seemest my only refuge! O Walter, where art thou? Alas! the kindly promptings of thy noble heart have led thee to captivity, perhaps to death! Welcome the hour when these dark portals shall unfold again, and reunite parent and child in the long sleep of death. (*Enter Fitzarnold.*) Ah! Fitzarnold here!   5

FITZARNOLD: I come with words of comfort to thee and fain would soothe thy sorrow.

OCEANA: I do not ask your sympathy, my lord.

FITZARNOLD: A sea of danger is around thee, lady, and I would be the skillful pilot to guide thy struggling bark to safety.   10

OCEANA: Nay, but let me rather perish in the waves than reach a haven to be shared with thee.

FITZARNOLD: Thou hast no choice; thy father willed thee mine, and with his latest breath bequeathed thee to me. Walter, my stripling rival in thy love, has left thee here defenseless and alone. I deem as nothing thy un-   15
natural hate, and only see thy fair and lovely form; and though thy flashing eyes were armed with lightning, thus would my arms enfold thee.

OCEANA (*Clings to tomb*):   Now, if thou darest, approach me — now whilst with my mother's spirit hovering o'er me — whilst thus with tearful eyes and breaking heart I call on Heaven to blast the bold audacious wretch,   20
who seeks a daughter's ruin o'er her parent's grave.

FITZARNOLD: Aye, despite of all.

METAMORA (*In tomb*): Hold! Touch her not!

OCEANA: Hark to that voice! Kind Heaven has heard my prayers.

(*The door of the tomb opens, and Metamora appears. Oceana faints and falls.*)

FITZARNOLD: Philip here! 25

METAMORA: He is. The Great Spirit has sent me;[2] the ghosts are waiting for thee in the dark place of doom! Now thou must go. Tremble, for the loud cry is terrible and the blaze of their eyes, like the red fire of war, gleams awfully in the night.

FITZARNOLD: I have not wronged thee. 30

METAMORA: Not? Didst thou not contrive the death of Nahmeokee, when the treacherous white man thirsted for her blood? Did she not with bended knees, her eyes streaming with woes of the heart, catch hold of thy shining broad garment thinking it covered man? Was not thy hand upraised against her, and thy heart, like thy hand, flint that wounds the 35 weary one who rests upon it?

FITZARNOLD: No! no!

METAMORA: I saw thee when my quick step was on the hills, and the joy of Metamora's eyes felt thy blows. I feel them now! "Revenge!" cried the shadow of my father as he looked on with me. I, too, cried revenge and 40 now I have it! The blood of my heart grows hotter as I look on him who smote the red cheek of Nahmeokee.

FITZARNOLD: As reparation I will give thee gold.

METAMORA: No! Give me back the happy days, the fair hunting ground, and the dominion my great forefathers bequeathed me. 45

FITZARNOLD: I have not robbed thee of them.

METAMORA: Thou art a white man, and thy veins hold the blood of a robber! Hark! The spirits of the air howl for thee! Prepare — (*Throws him around to the right*)

FITZARNOLD: Thou shalt not conquer ere thou killest me. This sword a royal hand bestowed! This arm can wield it still. 50

(*Draws; Metamora disarms and kills him.*)

METAMORA: Metamora's arm has saved thee from a common death; who dies by me dies nobly! (*Turns to Oceana*) For thee, Metamora's home shall screen thee from the spreading fury of his nation's wrath.

(*Hurry till change. Exit bearing Oceana.*)

---

[2] The original manuscript reads "He is the Great Spirit has sent me." Richard Moody suggests this alternative is more plausible.

SCENE II

A chamber. Enter Sir Arthur, meeting Errington and Church.

SIR ARTHUR: I have news will startle you.

ERRINGTON: Is't of the chief?

SIR ARTHUR: It is; he has escaped our power!

ERRINGTON: Escaped! Confusion! How?

SIR ARTHUR: But now we sought his prison and found it tenantless.   5

ERRINGTON: But how escaped he? There was no egress thence, unless some treacherous hand unlocked the door.

SIR ARTHUR: And so we thought, at first; but on minute search we found some stones displaced, which showed a narrow opening into a subterranean passage, dark and deep, through which we crept until, to our surprise, we reached the tomb of Mordaunt.   10

ERRINGTON: The tomb of Mordaunt?

SIR ARTHUR: The ruined pile which now serves as our prison was, years since, when first he sought these shores, the residence of Mordaunt, and this secret passage, doubtless, was formed by him for concealment or escape in time of danger.   15

ERRINGTON: Indeed!

SIR ARTHUR: Yes, and he had cause to be so guarded, for once, unseen by him, I heard that wretched man commune with Heaven, and sue for pardon for the heinous sin of Hammond of Harrington!   20

ERRINGTON: Hammond! The outlawed regicide?

SIR ARTHUR: Even so; it was himself he prayed for, the guilty man who gave to death the king, his lord, the royal martyr Charles. As Mordaunt, he here sought refuge from the wrath of the rightful heir now seated on the throne.   25

ERRINGTON: Think you the chieftain knew this secret way?

SIR ARTHUR: 'Tis likely that he did, or else by chance discovered it and thus has won his freedom and his life.

CHURCH: We must summon our men. Double the guard and have their range extended.   30

(Exeunt Church and Errington.)

WOLFE *(Without)*: Where is Sir Arthur Vaughan?

SIR ARTHUR: Who calls? *(Enter Wolfe.)* Now, who art thou?

WOLFE: A suppliant for pardon.

SIR ARTHUR: Pardon — for what?

WOLFE: A grievous sin, I now would fain confess.   35

SIR ARTHUR: Indeed! Go on! Declare it then; I will forgive thee!

WOLFE: Long years have passed since then, but you must still remember when at Naples with your wife and child.

SIR ARTHUR: Ha! Dost thou mean —

WOLFE: The flames consumed thy dwelling and thou together with thy wife and boy, escaped almost by miracle.

SIR ARTHUR: Ha!

WOLFE: I there looked on midst the assembled throng, a stranger mariner. Urged by the fiend, and aided by the wild confusion of the scene, I snatched your boy and through the noisy throng I bore him to my anchored bark, thinking his waiting parents soon would claim with gold their darling. Next day came on a tempest and the furious winds far from the city drove us and thy child.

SIR ARTHUR: Heavens! Can this be true?

WOLFE: He grew up the sharer of my sea-born perils. One awful night our vessel struck upon the rocks near these shores and the greedy ocean swelled over her shattered frame — thy son —

SIR ARTHUR: Go on — go on —

WOLFE: Was by mysterious power preserved and guided to his unconscious father. Walter is thy son.

SIR ARTHUR: Man! Why didst thou not tell me?

WOLFE: I feared thy just anger and the force of law. I became Fitzarnold's follower but to this hour has memory tortured me.

SIR ARTHUR: And Walter is a hostage to the savage foe; perchance they have murdered him!

WOLFE: No! Oceana's kindness to the Indian queen has purchased his freedom and my own.

SIR ARTHUR: Where is he?

WOLFE: Looking for her he loves, fair Oceana! Whom 'tis said, a party of the foe carried off.

SIR ARTHUR: Quick, let us arm and follow him. For thee, this act of justice pardons thee.

(*Exeunt.*)

Scene III

Indian village. Groups of Indians. Kaneshine and Otah discovered. Kaneshine has been addressing them. His looks are gloomy and bewildered.

METAMORA (*Outside, at change of scene*):   Where are my people?

KANESHINE: Ha! 'Tis our chief — I know the sound of his voice, and some quick danger follows him.

(*Metamora enters, bearing Oceana. Nahmeokee enters from wigwam.*)

METAMORA: Nahmeokee, take the white maiden in; I would speak to my
people; go in and follow not the track of the warrior's band.   5

NAHMEOKEE: Come in, my mat is soft, and the juice of the sweet berry
shall give joy to thy lips. Come in, thou art pale and yielding, like the lily,
when it is borne down by the running waters.

(*She leads Oceana into wigwam.*)

METAMORA: Warriors, I have escaped from the hands of the white man,
when the fire was kindled to devour me. Prepare for the approaching   10
hour if ye love the high places your fathers trod in majesty and strength.
Snatch your keen weapons and follow me! If ye love the silent spots
where the bones of your kindred repose, sing the dread song of war and
follow me! If you love the bright lakes which the Great Spirit gave you
when the sun first blazed with the fires of his torch, shout the war song   15
of the Wampanoag race, and on to the battle follow me! Look at the
bright glory that is wrapped like a mantle around the slain in battle! Call
on the happy spirits of the warriors dead, and cry, "Our lands! Our nation's freedom! Or the grave!"

KANESHINE: O chieftain, take my counsel and hold out to the palefaces   20
the pipe of peace. Ayantic and the great Mohigan join with our foes
against us, and the power of our brother, the Narragansett, is no more!
List, o chieftain, to the words that I tell of the time to come.

METAMORA: Ha! Dost thou prophesy?

KANESHINE: In the deep wood, when the moon shone bright, my spirit   25
was sad and I sought the ear of Manito in the sacred places; I heard the
sound as of one in pain, and I beheld gasping under a hemlock, the lightning had sometime torn, a panther wounded and dying in his thick red
gore. I thought of the tales of our forefathers who told us that such was
an omen of coming evil. I spoke loudly the name of Metamora, and the   30
monster's eyes closed instantly and he writhed no more. I turned and
mourned, for I said, Manito loves no more the Wampanoag and our foes
will prevail.

METAMORA: Didst thou tell my people this?

KANESHINE: Chieftain, yes; my spirit was troubled.   35

METAMORA: Shame of the tribe, thou art no Wampanoag, thy blood is
tainted — thou art half Mohigan, thy breath has sapped the courage of
my warriors' hearts. Begone, old man, thy life is in danger.

KANESHINE: I have spoken the words of truth, and the Great Manito has
heard them.   40

METAMORA: Liar and coward! Let him preserve thee now!

(*About to stab him when Nahmeokee enters from wigwam and interposes*)

NAHMEOKEE: He is a poor old man — he healed the deep wound of our little one. (*Gets to the left of Metamora*)

METAMORA: Any breast but Nahmeokee's had felt the keen edge of my knife! Go, corrupted one, thy presence makes the air unwholesome   45
round hope's high places. Begone!

KANESHINE: Metamora drives me from the wigwam before the lightning descends to set it on fire. Chieftain, beware the omen.   (*Exit.*)

NAHMEOKEE (*Aside*):   Will he not become the white man's friend and show him the secret path of our warriors? Manito guard the Wampanoag!   50

METAMORA: Men of Po-hon-e-ket, the palefaces come towards your dwellings and no warrior's hatchet is raised for vengeance. The war whoop is hushed in the camp and we hear no more the triumph of battle. Manito hates you, for you have fallen from the high path of your fathers and Metamora must alone avenge the Wampanoag's wrongs.   55

OMNES: Battle! Battle!

METAMORA: Ha! The flame springs up afresh in your bosoms; a woman's breath has brought back the lost treasure of your souls. (*Distant march, drums and trumpet heard*) Ha! they come! Go, warriors, and meet them, and remember the eye of a thousand ages looks upon you. (*Warriors exeunt   60
silently.*) Nahmeokee, should the palefaces o'ercome our strength, go thou with our infant to the sacred place of safety. My followers slain, there will the last of the Wampanoags pour out his heart's blood on the giant rock, his father's throne.

NAHMEOKEE: O Metamora!   65

METAMORA: Come not near me or thou wilt make my heart soft, when I would have it hard like the iron and gifted with many lives. Go in, Nahmeokee. (*Distant trumpets. Nahmeokee goes in wigwam. Metamora kneels.*) The knee that never bent to man I bend to thee, Manito. As the arm was broken that was put out again Nahmeokee, so break thou the strength of the   70
oppressor's nation, and hurl them down from the high hill of their pride and power, with the loud thunder of thy voice. Confound them — smite them with the lightning of thine eye — while thus I bare my red war arm — while thus I wait the onset of the foe — (*Loud alarm*) They come! Death! Death, or my nation's freedom!   75

(*Rushes off. Loud shouts. Drums and trumpets till change.*)

SCENE IV

Rocky pass. Trumpet sounds retreat. Enter Errington and Church.

ERRINGTON: They fly! They fly — the field is ours! This blow destroys them. Victory cheaply bought at twice our loss; the red man's power is broken now forever. (*Enter Walter.*) Is Oceana slain?

WALTER: No; the chieftain Metamora rescued her from the base passions of the Lord Fitzarnold whom Metamora slew to avenge the wrongs he of- 5 fered to his wife, and Oceana by the chief was borne in safety to his lodge.

ERRINGTON: In safety?

WALTER: Yes; from the hands of Nahmeokee I received her, just as some Indians, maddened by defeat, prepared to offer her a sacrifice.

ERRINGTON: Away then, Walter. (*Walter crosses to the right.*) Sir Arthur now 10 seeks thee out to claim thee as his own son.

WALTER: My father! I fly to seek him.   (*Exit.*)

ERRINGTON: The victory is ours; yet while Philip lives we are in peril! Come, let us find this Indian prophet whom Metamora banished from his tribe. He may be bribed to show us the chieftain's place of safety.   15

(*Exeunt. Change.*)

SCENE V

Metamora's stronghold. Rocks, bridge and waterfall. Nahmeokee discovered listening. The child lies under a tree at the right, covered with furs. Slow music, four bars.

NAHMEOKEE: He comes not, yet the sound of the battle has died away like the last breath of a storm! Can he be slain? O cruel white man, this day will stain your name forever.

(*Slow music, sixteen bars. Metamora enters on bridge.*)

METAMORA: Nahmeokee, I am weary of the strife of blood. Where is our little one? Let me take him to my burning heart and he may quell its 5 mighty torrent.

NAHMEOKEE (*With broken utterance*):   He is here!

(*Lifts the furs and shows the child dead*)

METAMORA: Ha! Dead! Dead! Cold!

NAHMEOKEE: Nahmeokee could not cover him with her body, for the white men were around her and over her. I plunged into the stream and 10 the unseen shafts of the fire weapons flew with a great noise over my head. One smote my babe and he sunk into the deep water; the foe shouted with a mighty shout, for he thought Nahmeokee and her babe had sunk to rise no more.

METAMORA: His little arms will never clasp thee more; his little lips will never press the pure bosom which nourished him so long! Well, is he not happy? Better to die by the stranger's hand than live his slave.

NAHMEOKEE: O Metamora! (*Falls on his neck*)

METAMORA: Nay, do not bow down thy head; let me kiss off the hot drops that are running down thy red cheeks. Thou wilt see him again in the peaceful land of spirits, and he will look smilingly as — as — as I do now, Nahmeokee.

NAHMEOKEE: Metamora, is our nation dead? Are we alone in the land of our fathers?

METAMORA: The palefaces are all around us, and they tread in blood. The blaze of our burning wigwams flashes awfully in the darkness of their path. We are destroyed — not vanquished; we are no more, yet we are forever — Nahmeokee.

NAHMEOKEE: What wouldst thou?

METAMORA: Dost thou not fear the power of the white man?

NAHMEOKEE: No.

METAMORA: He may come hither in his might and slay thee.

NAHMEOKEE: Thou art with me.

METAMORA: He may seize thee, and bear thee off to the far country, bind these arms that have so often clasped me in the dear embrace of love, scourge thy soft flesh in the hour of his wrath, and force thee to carry burdens like the beasts of the fields.

NAHMEOKEE: Thou wilt not let them.

METAMORA: We cannot fly, for the foe is all about us; we cannot fight, for this is the only weapon I have saved from the strife of blood.

NAHMEOKEE: It was my brother's — Coanchett's.

METAMORA: It has tasted the white man's blood, and reached the cold heart of the traitor; it has been our truest friend; it is our only treasure.

NAHMEOKEE: Thine eyes tell me the thought of thy heart, and I rejoice at it. (*Sinks on his bosom*)

METAMORA: Nahmeokee, I look up through the long path of thin air, and I think I see our infant borne onward to the land of the happy, where the fair hunting grounds know no storms or snows, and where the immortal brave feast in the eyes of the giver of good. Look upwards, Nahmeokee, the spirit of thy murdered father beckons thee.

NAHMEOKEE: I will go to him.

METAMORA: Embrace me, Nahmeokee — t'was the first you gave me in the days of our strength and joy — they are gone. (*Places his ear to the ground*) Hark! In the distant wood I faintly hear the cautious tread of men! They are upon us, Nahmeokee — the home of the happy is made ready for thee. (*Stabs her, she dies.*) She felt no white man's bondage — free as the air she lived — pure as the snow she died! In smiles she died! Let me taste it, ere her lips are cold as the ice. 55

(*Loud shouts. Roll of drums. Kaneshine leads Church and Soldiers on bridge.*)

CHURCH: He is found! Philip is our prisoner.

METAMORA: No! He lives — last of his race — but still your enemy — lives to defy you still. Though numbers overpower me and treachery surround me, though friends desert me, I defy you still. Come to me — come singly to me! And this true knife that has tasted the foul blood of your nation and now is red with the purest of mine, will feel a grasp as strong as when it flashed in the blaze of your burning dwellings, or was lifted terribly over the fallen in battle. 60 65

CHURCH: Fire upon him!

METAMORA: Do so, I am weary of the world for ye are dwellers in it; I would not turn upon my heel to save my life.

CHURCH: Your duty, soldiers. 70

(*They fire. Metamora falls. Enter Walter, Oceana, Wolfe, Sir Arthur, Errington, Goodenough, Tramp, and Peasants. Roll of drums and trumpet till all on.*)

METAMORA: My curses on you, white men! May the Great Spirit curse you when he speaks in his war voice from the clouds! Murderers! The last of the Wampanoags' curse be on you! May your graves and the graves of your children be in the path the red man shall trace! And may the wolf and the panther howl o'er your fleshless bones, fit banquet for the destroyers! Spirits of the grave, I come! But the curse of Metamora stays with the white man! I die! My wife! My Queen! My Nahmeokee! 75

(*Falls and dies; a tableau is formed. Drums and trumpet sound a retreat till curtain. Slow curtain.*)

JOHN BROUGHAM

Metamora; or, The Last of the Pollywogs

———————————— >< ————————————

Born in Dublin, John Brougham (1810–1880) performed in amateur theatricals at Trinity College, appeared with Madame Vestris in 1830 at London's Olympic Theatre and later at Covent Garden, and in 1840 leased the Lyceum Theatre. But his real success as playwright, manager, poet, humorist, and sometime actor came with his immigration to the United States in 1842. Much of his career in America was ostensibly as an actor-manager, including short-lived attempts at management at Brougham's Broadway Lyceum (1850–52) and the old Bowery (1856–57). But he was far more successful as an actor-playwright at Wallack's Theatre for seven years and, after spending the Civil War years in London, serving again in that capacity at the Winter Garden Theatre and at Daly's Fifth Avenue Theatre. Being a humorous writer brought him the most recognition, earning him in 1890 Laurence Hutton's appellation of the American Aristophanes. Brougham wrote over 160 scripts for the stage; of these, more than fifty (ten extant) took the form of burlesques, extravaganzas, and dramatic novelties. The most successful were *Po-ca-hon-tas; or, the Gentle Savage* (1855), *Columbus El Filibustero!!* (1857), and *Metamora; or, The Last of the Pollywogs* (first staged in 1847). Other efforts included the adaptations *Dombey and Son* (1848), *Jane Eyre* (1849), and *Vanity Fair* (1849); melodramas *Night and Morning* (1855), *The Gunmaker of Moscow* (1857), and *The Duke's Motto* (1863); the social satire *The Game of Love* (1856); and the burlesque *Much Ado About the Merchant of Venice* (1869). Brougham's last appearance on the stage was in Dion Boucicault's *Felix O'Reilly* (1879).

The Great "American Tragedian."

FIGURE 3 *Parody of Forrest as Metamora. From J. K. Philander Doesticks (i.e., Mortimer Neal Thomson)*, Doesticks What He Says *(New York, 1855)*.

Metamora; or, The Last of the Pollywogs

1847

A Burlesque, in Two Acts

Dramatis Personae

PAPPY VAUGHAN, *an influential early settler, early settled*
LORD FITZFADDLE, *a highly-to-be-envied individual, who has the honor to die by Metamora's knife*
MASTER WALTER, *not the hunchback, but over head and ears in love*
BADENOUGH, *a most unpleasant individual*
WORSER, *much the same, only more so*
OCEANA, *old Vaughan's daughter, a chip of the old block*

} *Anglo-Saxons*

METAMORA, *the ultimate Pollywog, an aboriginal hero, and a favorite child of the Forrest*
KANTSHINE, *a friend, who gives excellent advice, and is treated as all are who do it*
OLD TAR, *Indian Interpreter, from the Junk, half savage, half sailor*
WHISKEETODDI, *skilled in talk, so we are informed*
ANACONDA, *a recreant red man, rather serpentine*
TAPIOKEE, La Belle Sauvage, *the squalling Squaw of Metamora, killed with kindness*
PAPPOOSE, *being the last of the Last of the Pollywogs*

} *Pollywogs*

ACT I, SCENE I. —*A Wood.*

Enter Oceana and Walter.

OCEANA:
"Fathers have flinty hearts." O, what a bore!
WALTER:
So, my beloved, somebody said before;
But how to soften it fain would I know.
OCEANA:
I, too, indeed; I fear it is no go.
Three times today I've dared my daddy's frown —
Wandered forth unattended and alone
To meet my love. And while through yonder wood
I picked my steps, I didn't feel so good:
A hungry bear I saw my steps pursuing,

5

Which made me think there was some mischief brewing;   10
He licked his chops, and really seemed to say,
"My duck, I mean to dine on you today."
WALTER:
    How did you 'scape the awful danger, dear?
OCEANA:
    Well, do not interrupt me, and you'll hear:
    Just as my chance of life I'd given o'er,   15
    And thought the bear a most uncommon bore,
    The forest echoed with a mighty roar;
    And soon I saw before my pathway stand
    One of the na-*tyres* of this favored land,
    With rifle, belt, plume, moccasons, and all,   20
    Just as you see them at a fancy ball;
    His hair was glossy as the raven's wing;
    He looked and moved a sort of savage king;
    His speech was pointed, at the same time blunt —
    Something between a whisper and a grunt.   25
    "Ugh!" said he, "pale-face, why linger here?
    Afraid of that ungentlemanly bear?"
    "Just so," said I. With that he gave a yell,
    So sharp, so loud, the bear dropped down and fell;
    Pierced through the brain, he tumbled on his side,   30
    Instantly fainted, gave a grunt, and died.
WALTER:
    The nasty beast! What 'came of his remains?
OCEANA:
    The noble savage took them for his pains;
    He said by his pigs he'd early been forsaken,
    And so he'd eat the bear and save his bacon.   35
WALTER:
    And very pretty pork methinks he'll make;
    He's made, however, quite a large mistake:
    He'd orter kept him until he was fat —
    ———° knows perfectly how to manage that.
VAUGHAN (*without, left*):
    Where on earth's she got tew?   40

°Name of local hotel keeper.

OCEANA:

O my precious wig!
Here comes papa: I'll quickly hop the twig. (*Runs out*)

(*Enter Vaughan.*)

VAUGHAN:

Hello, young feller! what is this you're arter?
You haint' seed nuthin', hey you, of my darter?
A tarnal spry young critter did you see,   45
Pooty as paint, I swow, and just like me?

WALTER:

I scorn to lie, sir; and she has been here.

VAUGHAN:

The deuse she has! What made her disappear?

WALTER:

I love her, sir, sincerely: that's a fact.

VAUGHAN:

It's my belief, young feller, that you're cracked.   50
By tarnal jingo! here's a pretty fix.
You love my Oceana?

WALTER:

                                    Yes, like bricks.

VAUGHAN:

Then let me tell you, you confounded goose,
It ain't nohow the smallest sort of use;
I've gin her long ago to someone else.   55
So, you had best absquatulate, I guess.

WALTER:

I shall not stir.

VAUGHAN:

                    You won't?

WALTER:

                                    I won't! that's flat.

VAUGHAN:

I'll knock you into quite a small cocked hat.

(*Prepares to rush on him. Metamora, outside, exclaims, "Ugh!" Oceana rushes on, alarmed.*)

VAUGHAN:

Conglomeration! What on airth's the row?

OCEANA:
> O dearest father! walking home just now,　　　　　　　　60
> Thinking of nothing but the right *idee,*
> To cook the flapjacks you so like at tea,
> I saw a beast.

WALTER:
> 　　　　　　The brute!

OCEANA:
> 　　　　　　　　　　I softly crept;
> It was a weasel, and I thought he slept;
> I tried to catch it, but — O sounds of dread ——　　65

(Metamora, outside, "Ugh." Enter, right.)

METAMORA:
> Why this alarm? Don't fear; the critter's dead.

OCEANA:
> Dead!

METAMORA:
> As a herring. I knocked him on the head.
> White-livered cowards, let your cheeks grow red!
> He died like a Pollywog. He had to go,　　　　　　70
> Whether he liked the principle or no.
> His death you'll have to answer for; one more
> To the black list of injuries we bore,
> Since the first white man trod upon our ground,
> Rubbed out our footmarks, that now can't be found.　75

VAUGHAN:
> Come, that's unbusinesslike and rayther green;
> We bought these diggin's — how long has it been?
> Some hundred years, or thereabout, I guess.

METAMORA:
> Nothing! an acre or a little less.
> O, you're good buyers now, just as of old.　　　　　80
> Pale-faces, tremble! you may yet be sold.

VAUGHAN:
> Look here, my friend, you raise my ebenezer;
> And the probability is you'll catch a sneezer.

METAMORA:
> Thou ancient humbug, did Metamora puff
> A cloud of smoke, that blow would be enough　　　85
> To send thy soul from out its prison there!

Be calm, the Pollywog knows when to spare.
OCEANA:
Don't anger him.
VAUGHAN:
Bah! I don't care a fig.
OCEANA:
Think! he may scalp you.
VAUGHAN:
Can't — I wear a wig.
I say, you Injine, jest git up your steam   90
And start, or else you'll find this child a team.
METAMORA:
Old man, you've got the fire-water on your brain:
You've drowned your senses.
VAUGHAN:
Jingo! not a grain.
If you will fight, come on and mind your eye.
METAMORA:
Ha! Manito says it must be. Die!   95

(*Rushes on him. Oceana interposes.*)

OCEANA:
Majestic savage, spare, O spare my dad!
Or if you must take some one, take that lad.
WALTER:
No, sir! Emphatically I object to that.
METAMORA:
Metamora fights not, wars not with a rat.
The eagle, swooping through the upper sky,   100
Stoops not his mighty wing to catch a fly;
Nor can the red man's hatchet bend so low.
Metamora cannot see you, old man; go!
The spirit of revenge sits on my knife;
Yet, for this maiden's sake, I spare your life.   105
White squaw, approach! Don't tremble, for the storm
Is past, and Metamora's heart is warm.
Here, take this tail, plucked from a mongrel rooster.
OCEANA:
With pleasure, savage. Tell me, pray, what use, sir?
METAMORA:
Wear this, and wheresoever be your path,   110

'Twill save the bearer from the red man's wrath.

VAUGHAN:

Pooh! not a bit of it! it's all darned stuff!

METAMORA:

The Pollywog has said it. That's enough.

(*Exit.*)

VAUGHAN:

Jerusalem! but that ere red-skinned varmint
Has given us a pretty tightish sarmint.   115

(*Sees Walter pantomiming love to Oceana.*)

Come, none of that ere sort of telegraphin'!
Get along home, miss! I shan't stand no larfin'.
And you, sir! take your walking ticket too.
Hello! confound yeaour pictur! stop that, yeaou!

(*Separates them. Exit Walter, left, Oceana and Vaughan, right*)

Scene ii. — *Kitchen.*

Tapiokee and Child discovered.

Song, TAPIOKEE. Air, "O, slumber, my darling."

O, slumber, my pappoose! thy sire is not white;
And that injures your prospects a very great sight;
For the hills, and the dales, and the valleys you see,
They all were purloined, my dear pappoose, from thee.

O, slumber, my pappoose! the time will soon come   5
When thy rest shall be broken by very bad rum;
For, though in fair fighting the whites we beat down,
By a sling made of whiskey the red man is thrown.

TAPIOKEE:

Like evening, when the sun's last rays depart,
There's a deep gloom on Tapiokee's heart.
My husband is not here, nor do I know   10
What in the name of wonder keeps him so.
Sweet forest flower, why does your father stay?

CHILD:

Mamma, I do not know; but I should say
You needn't put yourself in such a stew.
He's using up those pale-faces a few. 15
And when I have seen a few more snows,
I can go slaying also, I suppose.

TAPIOKEE:

Chip of the ancient block, life of my life,
Mayst never be whittled by a Yankee's knife.
Hark! 'tis thy daddy's step; unbar the door; 20
I know it, though he's two rods off or more.
See to the venison pies and apple fritters,
And pour him out his tod of gin and bitters.

Enter Metamora.

Now, Pollywog, what news have you to tell? 25

METAMORA:

Don't bother, wife! I'm any thing but well.
I had a nap just now, and dreamed a dream.
O, how I wish it were what it did seem!
Methought the pale-faces were gathered all,
Unarmed, defenceless; on them I did fall. 30
Pile after pile of dead I sent to sleep,
Their red scalps streaming in a gory heap.
From the gray morning to the set of sun,
I killed and killed, till there was left but one
Of all the mighty host. The craven, he 35
Cried out while down upon his bended knee ——

TAPIOKEE:

What said the craven?

METAMORA:

      Why, what do you think?
He simply said, "Old fellow, let's take a drink."
With a loud yell the bonds of sleep I broke.

TAPIOKEE:

And then ——

METAMORA:

    Why, then, as a matter of course, I woke. 40

Enter Old Tar, with telescope.

TAR:

>Shiver my timbers, son of Massasoit,
>Blessed if I think your life is worth a doit.

METAMORA:

>Why do you borrow the pale-face's cheek?
>What makes the red man white? now, prythee, speak.

TAR:

>Splice my old pumps, you really take it cool! 45
>Weigh anchor and sheer off, you tarnal fool!
>There's a whole crowd of whites a-bearing down,
>Scouring each Indian settlement and town;
>They're steering here and on your very track!

METAMORA:

>The Pollywog will never turn his back. 50
>Say, where is Whiskee Toddi, skilled in talk?

TAR:

>Gone in the lager bier line in New York.
>He says it's blarney, talking in that way.
>He says you never give him aught to say.

(Drum, without.)

>Shiver my timbers! Do you hear that drum? 55

METAMORA:

>I hear it, and I answer, Let 'em come!
>Let the pale-faces enter. I'll stay here.
>With calumet and knife, I do not fear.

TAR:

>My eyes and limbs! but you're a pretty goose,
>To stay here when there ain't no sort of use. 60
>Such stupid conduct is what I call mush;
>So I'll cut painter now.

METAMORA:

>   Pray do, and brush.
>Good by, Old Tar.

TAR:

>   Well, Pollywog, good by.
>Take care of yourself; I've other fish to fry.   *(Exit.)*

(Drum and fife, outside.)

Enter Badenough, Worser, and soldiers; march down left.

BADENOUGH (*To soldiers*):
    Stand to your arms!
METAMORA:
                    But why *stand* to me?   65
WORSER:
    We're come to have a pleasant chat with thee,
    Old Philip.
METAMORA:
            What mean ye by Philip, you rude dogs?
    I'm Metamora, chief of the Pollywogs.
    My ears are open; what have you to say?
BADENOUGH:
    Our council's orders only we obey.   70
METAMORA:
    And what are they?
WORSER:
               Your presence they require;
    So, prythee, quickly leave your kitchen fire,
    And get a ticket for the railway car.
    What answer do you send them?
METAMORA:
                   I'll be thar.
BADENOUGH:
    The ticket office we will quickly show,   75
    If you will condescend to come.
METAMORA:
               I know.
WORSER:
    Don't make a muss; we can't return without you.
METAMORA:
    Pale-faces, Metamora's promise doubt you?
    For thirty winters I have breasted the cold wind,
    And unto those who've spoken to me kind   80
    I have been very yielding, like the willow,
    Drooping o'er the streamlet's gentle billow.
    You move with a single arm. Not so the rock
    That does the tempest's rage and lightning mock.
    Seek not by words the Pollywog to scare,   85
    When his heart says No. I will be there.

BADENOUGH:

 O gammon! But you'll come then by and by,
 And no mistake?

METAMORA:

     The Pollywog can't lie.

       (*Exeunt Badenough, Worser, and soldiers.*)

TAPIOKEE:

 Will Metamora brave the cruel law
 The pale-faces have made?

METAMORA:

      Wife, hold your jaw.   90
 Give me the knife my father bore when he
 Killed sheep for Keyzer in the Bowery.

      (*Exit Metamora, Tapiokee and child.*)

Scene III. — *Chamber.*

Centre doors, Table, with books, paper, pen, and ink. Chairs. Vaughan and Walter at table. Badenough, Worser, soldiers, etc., seated.

    Chorus, "Dan Tucker."

  We hardly can suppress our laughter;
  We know right well what we are after.
  Now, my friends, it's all *U P*
  With Metamora — he, he, he!

VAUGHAN:

 'Tis plain that savage chap hain't been to school.   5
 Who would have thought him such a tarnal fool?

BADENOUGH:

 He sucked our gammon in as slick as grease.

WORSER:

 I wish we had some more on 'em to fleece.

VAUGHAN:

 We ain't a-going to fleece 'em, understand;
 We'll do the handsome thing, and buy their land.   10
 Without a doubt he'll sell it for a trifle —
 A few beads, nails, a penknife, or a rifle.

BADENOUGH:

 Rifle's a good word. Hello, he's here!
 Of what shall we accuse him?

WORSER:

Never fear.
We'll cook his goose.   15

Enter Metamora.

METAMORA:
You've sent for me, and I've come.
If you've nothing to say, I may as well go hum.
What is it makes your old men look so glum?
And your young warriors grasp their weapons so,
As if they feared the onset of the foe?   20
Metamora does by no means like this fun.
Come, tell me what the Pollywog has done.

VAUGHAN:
Philip, 'tis thought to us that you don't cotton,
But rather like a possum you're complottin'
With some of them cantankerous Ingines   25
With us to kick up everlasting shines.

METAMORA:
The Pollywog can scarce believe his ears.
Do pale-faces counsel from their fears?
Well, I've got nothing more to say.

BADENOUGH:
In course we has.

WORSER:
So don't cut away.   30

METAMORA:
What is it?

BADENOUGH:
The thing we'd understand —
Why you put arms into each red man's hand.

METAMORA:
To shoot with. It is not so great a sin
As yours has been. Who gave my people gin?
Who was it changed the Indian's native hue,   35
With such vile stuff, making the red man blue?
The mountain rivulet is made impure
By the foul steam that rises from your door.

VAUGHAN:
Well, if you think sich things are really so,
Sell us your diggins right away, and go.   40

METAMORA:
Go whither, may I ask?

VAUGHAN:
To Jericho.

METAMORA:
I will not stir; for Metamora owns
This very lot, and here will lay his bones.

VAUGHAN:
Shall we dally with this pizin sarpint still?

METAMORA:
Your serpent hasn't lost its power to kill.   45

BADENOUGH:
This is all nonsense.

METAMORA:
I'm going.

VAUGHAN:
Hold!
There are some secrets that must yet be told.

METAMORA:
The Pollywog is listening.

VAUGHAN:
How died
Old Sassinger?

METAMORA:
Ha, ha! The fool was fried;
Mustard, peppered, salted, and put down: 50
So should a sassinger be served — done brown.

VAUGHAN:
Answer this question, savage, and be quick
About it.

METAMORA:
Go on.

VAUGHAN:
Who threw that last brick?

METAMORA:
Why do you ask me this? What gain you by it?

BADENOUGH:
We have a witness.   55

WORSER:
Yes, who saw you shy it.

BADENOUGH:

   A man well known, a first-class hatter's son,

   Bearing the name ——

WORSER:

              Of William Patterson.

BADENOUGH:

   He will not answer. Why, then, need we stay?

VAUGHAN:

   I really don't know what on airth to say.   60

METAMORA:

   Look at your book. Why, you don't know your part

   The Pollywog has got his own by heart.

VAUGHAN:

   Bring in the witness. He denies his acts.

Enter Anaconda.

Now tell us what you know of these ere facts.

METAMORA:

   Anaconda, are you the man — you know you are —   65

   I treated yesterday at Parker's bar?

   Brothers, can he speak words of truth to ye,

   Filled full of cocktails that he got from me?

VAUGHAN:

   In course he can, and will, I'll bet a hat.

METAMORA:

   Anaconda! — no; I will not call thee that.   70

   Squirt! say by these people you are led,

   Who've bought the sheep's tongue growing in thy head,

   And you have uttered a confounded lie!

   Well, goose, why don't you cackle? It is I

   Command it — Metamora, and thy king!   75

VAUGHAN:

   Hold on, I say! He shan't do no sich thing;

   In sich proceedings there ain't any sense.

   He's frightening the witness. Send him hence.

METAMORA:

   I'll do it. To the shades be thou a passenger!

   Black slave of the whites, go follow Sassinger!   80

(*Stabs Anaconda, who exits, right. Metamora rushes upstage. All in confusion.*)

White fools, beware! My knife has drunk the tide
Of treacherous blood, yet is not satisfied.
The spirits of the mighty Pollywog
Stretch out their cowhides long your race to flog.
And the big flood of the wild Indian's wrath,   85
Like Mississippi's, still shall swamp your path!
The war-whoop startle you from dreams at night,
And the red hatchet in the horrid light
Of blazing dwellings gleam! From east to west,
From the north to the south you never shall know rest,   90
But hear the cry of vengeance, feel the lash,
Till, for the lands you've stolen, you've paid the cash.
Ye chalked-faced humbugs, tremble from this hour!
I smite your nation and defy your power!

(*Throws hatchet in stage. Soldiers go down, cross front, and present muskets to Meta-mora, who seizes Vaughan and holds him forward as a shield. They fire.*)

ACT II, SCENE I. — *Wood.*

Enter Fitzfaddle, with a parasol over his head.

FITZFADDLE:
Dear me! what sultry weather 'tis for June!
I fear I soon should be a used-up coon.
Where is my love, the beauteous Oceana?
She cuts me in a most peculiar manner.
But that the thing's impossible, I'd say   5
There's probably a rival in the way.
It is not in the cards for me to fail.
Who could resist *cette magnifique coup d'œil?*

Enter Oceana.

Comment vous portez-vous ce jour, ma chere?
Je suis ravi de vous voir, by gar!   10
OCEANA:
Don't talk your foreign gibberish to me.
FITZFADDLE:
Don't call it gibberish, *ma belle amie;*
'Tis French, *ma chere,* a pretty tongue, and gay,
La langue du cœur, d'amour, et liberté.

OCEANA:

I don't know what you say. Give over, do. 15

FITZFADDLE:

Idole de ma vie! ah, je vous aime beaucoup.

Enter Vaughan.

VAUGHAN:

That's right, now; coo away, my turtle doves;
You match each other like a pair of gloves.

OCEANA:

They must be odd ones, then, papa, that's all,
For that "kid" don't agree with me at all. 20

FITZFADDLE:

O, *parlez* not so! *misérable moi!*
Vous êtes très cruelle, mademoiselle. Pourquoi?

VAUGHAN:

Eternal pickles upon sich a tongue!
If I know what he says, may I be hung!
Say, if you want Miss Oceana's hand, 25
Jest jerk a lingo we can understand.

FITZFADDLE:

Pardonnez-moi, mon père that is to be.

VAUGHAN:

Speak English, darn yer pictur!

FITZFADDLE:

                          Oui, sir-ee.

VAUGHAN:

Then do it quick!

OCEANA:

                "Nor leave the task to me."

VAUGHAN:

At once, then, children, let me join your hands. 30

OCEANA:

Forbear a moment; I forbid the banns.

VAUGHAN:

What for? By gracious, this is rather cool!

OCEANA:

Because I don't exactly like a fool.

FITZFADDLE:

Mort de ma vie! I mean that's rather rude.

OCEANA:

I'm glad you find it so; I meant you should.   35

FITZFADDLE:

Monsieur, that is, Sir, have I your consent?

VAUGHAN:

I told you so before.   [*Goes up and comes down right corner.*]

FITZFADDLE:

Then I'm content.

She shall be mine.

OCEANA:

She shan't!

FITZFADDLE:

Why, then, I swear

I must use violence! *Sacre tonnerre!*

OCEANA:

Is there no help? Walter, on thee I call.   40

Enter Walter.

WALTER:

Walter's beside thee, love. No need to bawl.

VAUGHAN:

Tear them asunder quickly! That's the way

I've seen the thing done often in a play.

WALTER:

My love, in vain I try thy grief to soothe.

OCEANA:

The course of true love never did run smooth.   45

(*Indian yell without.*)

Enter Metamora, Old Tar, and Indians.

METAMORA:

Down with them all! Scalp every mother's son!

OCEANA:

And serve 'em right! But what have the daughters done?

METAMORA:

Don't spare a soul, not e'en the squaw so pale.

OCEANA:

Stop! don't you recollect this rooster's tail?

I place it here upon my father's breast.   50

METAMORA:

Nuff sed. The Pollywog respects the past.
Away, and quit my sight! my rage shall cease.
But for that tail, you all were quite gone geese.
To save your lives is now, I know, absurd,
But Metamora never broke his word.   55

> (*Exeunt Walter, Vaughan, and Oceana. Business, and Metamora exit.*
> *Business of Fitzfaddle and Indians, after which all exeunt.*)

SCENE II. — *Front Wood.*

Enter Badenough and Worser, dragging in Tapiokee.

BADENOUGH:

Come, now, we'll shoot you if we don't obtain
Your name.

TAPIOKEE:

Poor Indian cannot help the pain,
But she can do what few can do among
Your white squaws.

WORSER:
             What's that?

TAPIOKEE:
                          She can hold her tongue.   5

BADENOUGH:

It's very easy for you to say that.
But that you won't I'm free to bet a hat.

TAPIOKEE:

Won't what?

BADENOUGH:
           Keep silent for a moment steady.

TAPIOKEE:

Done for a hat.

BADENOUGH:
             You've lost it, ma'am, already.

TAPIOKEE:

The white man is a fox in these abodes.   10

BADENOUGH:

I'll trouble you to name your hatter.

TAPIOKEE:

Rhoades.

BADENOUGH:

I'll stick you for a *V,* then, by and by.
But now to business, ma'am: prepare to die.

Enter Vaughan, Walter, and Fitzfaddle.

VAUGHAN:

Who are you talking to in that ere lingo?
It's Metamora's squaw, by tarnal jingo!   15
He spared our lives, and 'tis but right we should
Kill off his squaw to show our gratitude.

(*Tapiokee kneels to Fitzfaddle, who repulses her. Business.*)

Enter Metamora, with rifle, hurriedly.

METAMORA:

Hello, here! which of you has lived too long?
Pale-faces, this is coming it too strong.
One tear from Tapiokee, and, by thunder,   20
The axe shall hew your quivering limbs asunder.
One hair from Tapiokee's head, you'll find
The ashes of your bones upon the wind!
Ye lily-livered crew, go! quit my sight!
You'd best; the Pollywog is full of fight!   25

(*Exeunt all but Metamora and Tapiokee.*)

TAPIOKEE:

Worn with fatigue the Pollywog must be.
Shall Tapiokee make a cup of tea?

METAMORA:

No, my love, no; my nerves are too refined:
They cannot bear excitement of that kind.

Enter Old Tar.

Old Tar, my hearty, what have you got new?   30

OLD TAR:

Something that's pretty sartin to rile you:
You know Kantshine, the medicine man, who fills
Our hold with Indian Vegetable Pills!

METAMORA:

I do.

OLD TAR:

> He's in a most amazin' fright,
> The swob, from something that took place last night.   35
> He comes a-bearing down upon the swell,
> Just like a seventy-four, that same to tell.

Enter Kantshine.

METAMORA:

> Old hoss, have you been walking in your sleep?
> Or are you mesmerized? He's tight's a peep!

KANTSHINE:

> It's nothing of the sort; so there you're out.   40

METAMORA:

> Well, then, what makes you waddle so about?

KANTSHINE:

> The Smiths have with the Joneses met, and Brown,
> Jones, Black, and White, to pull the red man down.
> In point of fact, — and here my story ends, —
> We're flummuxed, and we haven't got no friends.   45

METAMORA:

> Flummuxed! Ha! why do you think this? Ho!

Enter Indians.

KANTSHINE:

> Why, last night, feeling sort of how-came-you-so,
> Considerably corned and rather fly,
> They in the barroom wouldn't let me lie;
> And ere I could a single sentence utter,   50
> They flung me headlong out into the gutter;
> And there I saw a poor benighted pig
> Food from the pavement trying for to dig,
> But couldn't come it. When the beast I saw,
> I thought of you, and bellowed out, *"Hi-yaw!"*   55
> He cut and ran, which tells me, without fail,
> The whites will win, the Pollywog turn tail.

METAMORA:

> And have you spread about this rigmarole?

KANTSHINE:

> I didn't do nothin' else.

METAMORA:

> You stupid fool!

Begone! you make the air unwholesome round   60
The Frog Pond.
KANTSHINE:
          Then blow me if I'm found
About these diggins long. My patience welts.
By Judas! I'll be off to catch some smelts.   (*Exit.*)
METAMORA:
Why do you hang your head? Is it for fear?
TAPIOKEE:
It's more than probable, I think, my dear.   65
METAMORA:
Say, is it your intention to show fight?
OLD TAR:
Well, then, I rather guess we won't tonight.
Since on life's voyage this 'ere child was shipped,
He hasn't seen no fun in getting whipped.
TAPIOKEE:
Can it be possible the Pollywog   70
Will scoot from danger like a ditch-born frog?
If you don't quickly rush upon the foe,
I swear to gracious, I myself will go,
And with my single arm strike thousands down,
Until the whites are done exceeding brown.   (*Exit.*)   75
METAMORA:
Rouse up, ye Pollywogs! for, like a coal,
A woman's words have kindled up my soul!
A burning heat, more terrible by far
Than blazing mountain or a lit cigar.
Go, warriors, and recollect the eye   80
Of a Howard Athenæum audience is on ye. Fly!

          (*Exeunt all but Metamora.*)

It's very probable you'd like to know
The reason why the Pollywog don't go
With his red brethren. Pray take notice, each,
He stops behind to have an exit speech.   85
And here it is: —   (*Takes stage.*)
Into the foe a feet or two I'll walk!
Death or my nation's glory! That's the talk.   (*Exit.*)

SCENE III. — *Landscape.*

Bridge across stage with return piece. Tapiokee and Child discovered.

Song, TAPIOKEE.

> Hush-a-by, baby, on the tree top;
> I've got no cradle, so thee I must rock;
> If the whites come, upon us they'll fall,
> Then down will go baby, mamma, and all.

TAPIOKEE:

Wake up! Good gracious me! I do declare!   5
In this last sleep, I've lost my son and heir.
Well, I must bear it calmly, I suppose.

CHILD:

Ma! Ma!

TAPIOKEE:

       Well, what?

CHILD:

            I want to scratch my nose.

Enter Metamora.

METAMORA:

My forest flower, why do you look so sad?

TAPIOKEE:

Alas! look there! No longer you're a dad.   10

METAMORA:

What! dead! The Pollywog is now bereft
Of all. There's no more of the same sort left.
If fate had not come first, I should have had,
With my own knife, to slay the gentle lad.

TAPIOKEE:

Do tell! What for?

METAMORA:

           To others we'll give place.   15
The Pollywogs have wriggled through their race.

Enter Fitzfaddle.

FITZFADDLE:

Nom du diable! I have lost my way.

TAPIOKEE:

That is the man insulted me today.

METAMORA:

Ha! the fierce spirit's howling for its prey!

FITZFADDLE:

Mon cher homme rouge, quel est le joli row?   20

METAMORA:

I have no time to listen to you now.

FITZFADDLE:

What have I done? You'll tell me, I suppose?

METAMORA:

Didn't you put your thumb up to your nose,
And tear your skirt away when she clung to it?

FITZFADDLE:

No, no, no.

METAMORA:

           No! Liar, I saw you do it!   25
Take your change of this.   (*Stabs him.*)

FITZFADDLE:

               Be quiet, do!
I'm settled. *Je suis un mouton perdu.*   (*Dies, left corner.*)

METAMORA:

Don't you feel honored, sir? You've lost your life,
And by no common weapon — Metamora's knife.

                   (*Noise without, "Follow, follow!"*)

Hark! the pale-faces come. My wife and I,   30
I have reason to suppose, must shortly die.
My Tapiokee, would you like to make
Vile pumpkin pies, or hominy, or bake
Innocent sheep to feed the appetites
Of the insatiate and carnivorous whites?   35

TAPIOKEE:

I rather guess I wouldn't. I'll tell why:
You've often told me never to say die.
If it amuses you my blood to shed,
Don't say another word, but go ahead.

(*Metamora stabs her; she falls and dies. Vaughan, Walter, Oceana, Badenough, Worser, Old Tar, Kantshine, soldiers, and Indians cross bridge from right and come down left.*)

VAUGHAN:

Philip, you're our captive. Nary bail.   40
Come, lads, just quick convey him to the jail.

Fitzfaddle dead! O, cry, you villain deep.

METAMORA:
Pooh! nonsense, sir. I did it in my sleep.

VAUGHAN:
Humbug! My friends, that gammon will not do.
Why don't you grab him now, you lazy crew?   45

METAMORA:
'Come one, come all! this rock shall fly
From its firm base as soon as I!'
Stay, stay! I find I've made a small mistake.
These lines are in the Lady of the Lake.

BADENOUGH:
Come, let us take you quickly to the jail.   50

METAMORA:
Metamora, pale-face, don't mean to turn tail.

WORSER:
Come and be hanged, then, right off, won't you?

METAMORA:
                                        No.

VAUGHAN:
Well, if the fool will neither stay nor go,
Let's shoot him in the cranium or the eye.

BADENOUGH:
Nuff sed.

METAMORA:
            The Pollywog don't fear to die.   55

(*Metamora goes up center, and takes his ground firmly. Badenough advances first, and snaps musket, then crosses to right corner. Worser does the same. At each shot, Metamora jumps and staggers as if shot. Vaughan goes up and snaps a pistol at him. Metamora jumps very high and falls, center. Badenough, Worser, and Vaughan go upstage, and shoot him with popguns.*)

VAUGHAN:
That's killed him.

METAMORA:
                Not quite, but near enough, I hope.
I feel it's almost time for me to slope.
The red man's fading out, and in his place
There comes a bigger, not a better, race.
Just as you've seen the squirming Pollywog   60
In course of time become a bloated frog.   (*Dies.*)

(*Burlesque combat by every body; all fall and die.*)

Chorus, "We're all nodding."

We're all dying, die, die, dying,
    We're all dying just like a flock of sheep.

Solo, Metamora.

You're all lying, lie, lie, lying,
    You're all lying; I wouldn't die so cheap.   65

METAMORA (*Rises*):
    Confound your skins, I will not die to please you.
TAPIOKEE (*Rises*):
    I shall get up too, if that is your game.
VAUGHAN (*Rises*):
    That's a good move, and so I'll do the same.

(*All rise.*)

METAMORA:
    And nothing now remains for us to do
    But make the usual appeal to you.   70
    Although they tell us money now is tight,
    Do pray accept our little bill tonight.
    You "*Pocahontas*" saved. I'm an implorer
    That you will do as much for "*Metamora.*"

FINALE.

Solo, Metamora.

If you would look out for pleasure,   75
    Come in here, each jolly, jolly dog,
And you'll find it without measure,
    To support the Pollywog.

Chorus.

Pollywog, Polly, Polly, Pollywog, etc.

Comic Dance.

TABLEAU

ANNA CORA OGDEN MOWATT

Fashion; or, Life in New York

>‹

Author of what is arguably the finest comedy of manners on the American stage at mid-nineteenth century, *Fashion; or, Life in New York* (1845), Anna Cora Ogden Mowatt (Ritchie) (1819–1870) was unusual in other respects. She was born in France, one of nine children of well-to-do parents; her father was a successful New York merchant. She returned with her family to New York in 1825. Proving herself to be something of a child prodigy, she read voraciously (all of Shakespeare, she said, by age ten); learned all the social graces; in 1834 secretly married James Mowatt, a lawyer twice her age; and a year later, at the age of sixteen, published an epic poem entitled *Pelayo; or, the Cavern of Cavadonga*. She continued to publish in numerous serials, often under assumed names, and ghost-wrote several books on wide-ranging topics. She undertook a sea voyage to Europe in 1837 as a cure for a bronchial ailment, and her observations of Americans aping European manners became the inspiration for *Fashion*. After her husband lost his fortune in 1841, Anna Mowatt began a career as a public reader and actress, becoming the first upper-class American woman to perform on the public stage. The success of her play *Fashion* allowed her to tour extensively, with her debut in June as a legitimate actress in *The Lady of Lyons* (as Pauline). James Mowatt died in 1851, and in 1854 she married William F. Ritchie, editor of the Richmond, Virginia, *Enquirer*. An unhappy marriage, apparently caused by differences over the slavery question, led her to live abroad after 1861. Mowatt wrote one other moderately successful play, *Armand, the Child of the People* (1847), as well as two accounts of theatrical life, *Autobiography of an Actress* (1854) and *Mimic Life; or, Before and Behind the Curtain* (1856).

FIGURE 4 *Enid Markey as Mrs. Tiffany and Will Geer as Adam Trueman in a 1959 off-Broadway revival of* Fashion.

↝ Fashion; or, Life in New York   *1845*

DRAMATIS PERSONAE

ADAM TRUEMAN, *a Farmer from Catteraugus*
COUNT JOLIMAITRE, *a fashionable European Importation*
COLONEL HOWARD, *an Officer in the U. S. Army*
MR. TIFFANY, *a New York Merchant*
T. TENNYSON TWINKLE, *a Modern Poet*
AUGUSTUS FOGG, *a Drawing-Room Appendage*
SNOBSON, *a rare species of Confidential Clerk*
ZEKE, *a colored Servant*
MRS. TIFFANY, *a Lady who imagines herself fashionable*
PRUDENCE, *a Maiden Lady of a certain age*
MILLINETTE, *a French Lady's Maid*
GERTRUDE, *a Governess*
SERAPHINA TIFFANY, *a Belle*
LADIES AND GENTLEMEN OF THE BALL-ROOM

ACT I

A splendid Drawing-Room in the House of Mrs. Tiffany. Open folding doors discov-ering a Conservatory. On either side glass windows down to the ground. Doors on right and left. Mirror, couches, ottomans, a table with albums, etc., beside it an arm-chair. Millinette dusting furniture, Zeke in a dashing livery, scarlet coat, etc.

ZEKE: Dere's a coat to take de eyes ob all Broadway! Ah! Missy, it am de fixins dat make de natural *born* gemman. A libery for ever! Dere's a pair ob insuppressibles to 'stonish de coloured population.

MILLINETTE: Oh, *oui*, Monsieur Zeke. (*Very politely*) I not *comprend* one word he say! (*Aside*)   5

ZEKE: I tell 'ee what, Missy, I'm 'stordinary glad to find dis a bery 'spectabul like situation! Now as you've made de acquaintance ob dis here family, and dere you've had a supernumerary advantage ob me — seeing dat I only receibed my appointment dis morning. What I wants to know is your publicated opinion, privately expressed, ob de domestic circle.   10

MILLINETTE: You mean vat *espèce*, vat kind of personnes are Monsieur and Madame Tiffany? Ah! Monsieur is not de same ting as Madame, — not at all.

ZEKE: Well, I s'pose he ain't altogether.

MILLINETTE: Monsieur is man of business, — Madame is lady of fashion.   15
Monsieur make the money, — Madame spend it. Monsieur nobody at all, — Madame everybody altogether. Ah! Monsieur Zeke, de money is

all dat is *necessaire* in dis country to make one lady of fashion. Oh! it is quite anoder ting in *la belle France!*

ZEKE: A bery lucifer explanation. Well, now we've disposed ob de heads of 20 de family, who come next?

MILLINETTE: First, dere is Mademoiselle Seraphina Tiffany. Mademoiselle is not at all one proper *personne.* Mademoiselle Seraphina is one coquette. Dat is not de mode in *la belle France;* de ladies, dere, never learn *la coquetrie* until dey do get one husband. 25

ZEKE: I tell 'ee what, Missy, I disreprobate dat proceeding altogeder!

MILLINETTE: Vait! I have not tell you all *la famille* yet. Dere is Ma'mselle Prudence — Madame's sister, one very *bizarre* personne. Den dere is Ma'mselle Gertrude, but she is not anybody at all; she only teach Mademoiselle Seraphina *la musique.* 30

ZEKE: Well, now, Missy, what's your own special defunctions?

MILLINETTE: I not understand, Monsieur Zeke.

ZEKE: Den I'll amplify. What's de nature ob your exclusive services?

MILLINETTE: *Ah, oui! je comprend.* I am Madame's *femme de chambre* — her lady's maid, Monsieur Zeke. I teach Madame *les modes de Paris,* and 35 Madame set de fashion for all New York. You see, Monsieur Zeke, dat it is me, *moi-même,* dat do lead de fashion for all de American *beau monde!*

ZEKE: Yah! yah! yah! I hab de idea by de heel. Well now, p'raps you can 'lustrify my officials?

MILLINETTE: Vat you will have to do? Oh! much tings, much tings. You 40 vait on de table, — you tend de door, — you clean de boots, — you run de errands, — you drive de carriage, — you rub de horses, — you take care of de flowers, — you carry de water, — you help cook de dinner, — you wash de dishes, — and den you always remember to do everyting I tell you to! 45

ZEKE: Wheugh, am dat *all?*

MILLINETTE: All I can tink of now. To-day is Madame's day of reception, and all her grand friends do make her one *petite* visit. You mind run fast ven de bell do ring.

ZEKE: Run? If it wasn't for dese superfluminous trimmings, I tell 'ee what, 50 Missy, I'd run —

MRS. TIFFANY (*Outside*): Millinette!

MILLINETTE: Here comes Madame! You better go, Monsieur Zeke.

ZEKE: Look ahea, Massa Zeke, doesn't dis open rich! (*Aside*)

(*Exit Zeke.*)

(*Enter Mrs. Tiffany right, dressed in the most extravagant height of fashion*)

MRS. TIFFANY: Is everything in order, Millinette? Ah! very elegant, very   55
elegant indeed! There is a *jenny-says-quoi* look about this furniture, — an
air of fashion and gentility perfectly bewitching. Is there not, Millinette?

MILLINETTE: Oh, *oui*, Madame!

MRS. TIFFANY: But where is Miss Seraphina? It is twelve o'clock; our visitors will be pouring in, and she has not made her appearance. But I hear   60
that nothing is more fashionable than to keep people waiting. — None
but vulgar persons pay any attention to punctuality. Is it not so, Millinette?

MILLINETTE: Quite *comme il faut*. — Great *personnes* always do make little *personnes* wait, Madame.

MRS. TIFFANY: This mode of receiving visitors only upon one specified day   65
of the week is a most convenient custom! It saves the trouble of keeping
the house continually in order and of being always dressed. I flatter myself that *I* was the first to introduce it amongst the New York *ee-light*. You
are quite sure that it is strictly a Parisian mode, Millinette?

MILLINETTE: Oh, *oui*, Madame; entirely *mode de Paris*.   70

MRS. TIFFANY: This girl is worth her weight in gold. (*Aside*) Millinette,
how do you say *arm-chair* in French?

MILLINETTE: *Fauteuil*, Madame.

MRS. TIFFANY: *Fo-tool!* That has a foreign — an out-of-the-wayish sound
that is perfectly charming — and so genteel! There is something about   75
our American words decidedly vulgar. *Fowtool!* how refined. *Fowtool!*
Arm-chair! what a difference!

MILLINETTE: Madame have one *charmante* pronunciation. *Fowtool!*
(*Mimicking aside*) Charmante, Madame!

MRS. TIFFANY: Do you think so, Millinette? Well, I believe I have. But a   80
woman of refinement and of fashion can always accommodate herself to
everything foreign! And a week's study of that invaluable work —
"French without a Master," has made me quite at home in the court language of Europe! But where is the new valet? I'm rather sorry that he is
black, but to obtain a white American for a domestic is almost impos-   85
sible; and they call this a free country! What did you say was the name of
this new servant, Millinette?

MILLINETTE: He do say his name is Monsieur Zeke.

MRS. TIFFANY: Ezekiel, I suppose. Zeke! Dear me, such a vulgar name will
compromise the dignity of the whole family. Can you not suggest some-   90
thing more aristocratic, Millinette? Something *French!*

MILLINETTE: Oh, *oui*, Madame; *Adolph* is one very fine name.

MRS. TIFFANY: A-dolph! Charming! Ring the bell, Millinette! (*Millinette
rings the bell.*) I will change his name immediately, besides giving him a

few directions. (*Enter Zeke, left. Mrs. Tiffany addresses him with great dignity.*) 95
Your name, I hear, is *Ezekiel*. — I consider it too plebeian an appellation
to be uttered in my presence. In future you are called A-dolph. Don't reply, — never interrupt me when I am speaking. A-dolph, as my guests
arrive, I desire that you will inquire the name of every person, and then
announce it in a loud, clear tone. *That* is the fashion in Paris. 100

(*Millinette retires up the stage.*)

ZEKE (*Speaking very loudly*):   Consider de office discharged, Missus.
MRS. TIFFANY: Silence! Your business is to obey and not to talk.
ZEKE: I'm dumb, Missus!
MRS. TIFFANY (*Pointing up stage*):   A-dolph, place that *fowtool* behind me.
ZEKE (*Looking about him*):   I habn't got dat far in de dictionary yet. No mat- 105
ter, a genus gets his learning by nature.

(*Takes up the table and places it behind Mrs. Tiffany, then expresses in dumb show
great satisfaction. Mrs. Tiffany, as she goes to sit, discovers the mistake.*)

MRS. TIFFANY: You dolt! Where have you lived not to know that *fowtool* is
the French for *arm-chair?* What ignorance! Leave the room this instant.

(*Mrs. Tiffany draws forward an arm-chair and sits. Millinette comes forward sup-
pressing her merriment at Zeke's mistake and removes the table.*)

ZEKE: Dem's de defects ob not having a libery education.

(*Exit Zeke.*)

(*Prudence peeps in.*)

PRUDENCE: I wonder if any of the fine folks have come yet. Not a soul, — 110
I knew they hadn't. There's Betsy all alone. (*Walks in*) Sister Betsy!
MRS. TIFFANY: Prudence! how many times have I desired you to call me
Elizabeth? Betsy is the height of vulgarity.
PRUDENCE: Oh! I forgot. Dear me, how spruce we do look here, to be sure,
— everything in first rate style now, Betsy. (*Mrs. Tiffany looks at her angrily.*) 115
Elizabeth, I mean. Who would have thought, when you and I were sit-
ting behind that little mahogany-coloured counter, in Canal Street, mak-
ing up flashy hats and caps —
MRS. TIFFANY: Prudence, what *do* you mean? Millinette, leave the room.
MILLINETTE: *Oui*, Madame. 120

(*Millinette pretends to arrange the books upon a side table, but lingers to listen.*)

PRUDENCE: But I always predicted it, — I always told you so, Betsy — I
always said you were destined to rise above your station!

MRS. TIFFANY: Prudence! Prudence! have I not told you that —

PRUDENCE: No, Betsy, it was *I* that told *you*, when we used to buy our silks
and ribbons of Mr. Antony Tiffany — *"talking Tony"* you know we used to   125
call him, and when you always put on the finest bonnet in our shop to go
to his, — and when you staid so long smiling and chattering with him, I
always told you that *something* would grow out of it — and didn't it?

MRS. TIFFANY: Millinette, send Seraphina here instantly. Leave the room.

MILLINETTE: *Oui*, Madame. So dis Americaine ladi of fashion vas one   130
milliner? Oh, vat a fine country for *les marchandes des modes!* I shall send
for all my relation by de next packet! (*Aside*)

(*Exit Millinette.*)

MRS. TIFFANY: Prudence! never let me hear you mention this subject
again. Forget what we *have* been, it is enough to remember that we *are* of
the *upper ten thousand!*   135

(*Prudence goes left and sits. Enter Seraphina, very extravagantly dressed.*)

MRS. TIFFANY: How bewitchingly you look, my dear! Does Millinette say
that that head-dress is strictly Parisian?

SERAPHINA: Oh yes, Mamma, all the rage! They call it a *lady's tarpaulin*,
and it is the exact pattern of one worn by the Princess Clementina at the
last court ball.   140

MRS. TIFFANY: Now, Seraphina, my dear, don't be too particular in your attentions to gentlemen not eligible. There is Count Jolimaitre, decidedly
the most fashionable foreigner in town, — and so refined, — so much
accustomed to associate with the first nobility in his own country that he
can hardly tolerate the vulgarity of Americans in general. You may de-   145
vote yourself to him. Mrs. Proudacre is dying to become acquainted with
him. By the by, if she or her daughters should happen to drop in, be sure
you don't introduce them to the Count. It is not the fashion in Paris to
introduce — Millinette told me so.

(*Enter Zeke.*)

ZEKE (*In a very loud voice*):   Mister T. Tennyson Twinkle!   150

MRS. TIFFANY: Show him up.   (*Exit Zeke.*)

PRUDENCE: I must be running away. (*Going*)

MRS. TIFFANY: Mr. T. Tennyson Twinkle — a very literary young man and
a sweet poet! It is all the rage to patronize poets! Quick, Seraphina, hand
me that magazine. — Mr. Twinkle writes for it.   155

(*Seraphina hands the magazine; Mrs. Tiffany seats herself in an arm-chair and opens
the book.*)

PRUDENCE (*Returning*):   There's Betsy trying to make out that reading without her spectacles. (*Takes a pair of spectacles out of her pocket and hands them to Mrs. Tiffany*) There, Betsy, I knew you were going to ask for them. Ah! they're a blessing when one is growing old!

MRS. TIFFANY: What do you mean, Prudence? A woman of fashion *never*   160
grows old! Age is always out of fashion.

PRUDENCE: Oh, dear! what a delightful thing it is to be fashionable. (*Exit Prudence. Mrs. Tiffany resumes her seat.*)

(*Enter Twinkle. He salutes Seraphina.*)

TWINKLE:
Fair Seraphina! The sun itself grows dim,
Unless you aid his light and shine on him!

SERAPHINA: Ah! Mr. Twinkle, there is no such thing as answering you.   165

TWINKLE (*Looks around and perceives Mrs. Tiffany*):   The "New Monthly Vernal Galaxy." Reading my verses, by all that's charming! Sensible woman! I won't interrupt her. (*Aside*)

MRS. TIFFANY (*Rising and coming forward*):   Ah! Mr. Twinkle, is that you? I was perfectly *abîmé* at the perusal of your very *distingué* verses.   170

TWINKLE: I am overwhelmed, Madam. Permit me. (*Taking the magazine*) Yes, they do read tolerably. And you must take into consideration, ladies, the rapidity with which they were written. Four minutes and a half by the stop watch! The true test of a poet is the *velocity* with which he composes. Really, they do look very prettily, and they read tolerably — *quite*   175
tolerably — *very* tolerably, — especially the first verse. (*Reads*) "To Seraphina T ——— ."

SERAPHINA: Oh! Mr. Twinkle!

TWINKLE (*Reads*):   "Around my heart" —

MRS. TIFFANY: How touching! Really, Mr. Twinkle, quite tender!   180

TWINKLE (*Recommencing*):   "Around my heart" —

MRS. TIFFANY: Oh, I must tell you, Mr. Twinkle! I heard the other day that poets were the aristocrats of literature. That's one reason I like them, for I do dote on all aristocracy!

TWINKLE: Oh, Madam, how flattering! Now pray lend me your ears!   185
(*Reads*)
"Around my heart thou weavest" —

SERAPHINA: That is such a *sweet* commencement, Mr. Twinkle!

TWINKLE (*Aside*):   I wish she wouldn't interrupt me! (*Reads*)
"Around my heart thou weavest a spell" —

MRS. TIFFANY: Beautiful! But excuse me one moment, while I say a word   190
to Seraphina! Don't be too affable, my dear! Poets are very ornamental

appendages to the drawing-room, but they are always as poor as their own verses. They don't make eligible husbands! (*Aside to Seraphina*)

TWINKLE (*Aside*): Confound their interruptions! My dear Madam, unless you pay the utmost attention, you cannot catch the ideas. Are you ready? 195 Well, now you shall hear it to the end! (*Reads*)
"Around my heart thou weavest a spell
"Whose" —

(*Enter Zeke.*)

ZEKE: Mister Augustus Fogg! A bery misty lookin' young gemman? (*Aside*)
MRS. TIFFANY: Show him up, A-dolph! (*Exit Zeke.*) 200
TWINKLE: This is too much!
SERAPHINA: Exquisite verses, Mr. Twinkle, — exquisite!
TWINKLE: Ah, lovely Seraphina! your smile of approval transports me to the summit of Olympus.
SERAPHINA: Then I must frown, for I would not send you so far away. 205
TWINKLE: Enchantress! It's all over with her. (*Aside*)

(*Retire up right and converse.*)

MRS. TIFFANY: Mr. Fogg belongs to one of our oldest families, — to be sure he is the most difficult person in the world to entertain, for he never takes the trouble to talk, and never notices anything or anybody, — but then I hear that nothing is considered so vulgar as to betray any emotion, 210 or to attempt to render oneself agreeable!

(*Enter Mr. Fogg, fashionably attired but in very dark clothes.*)

FOGG (*Bowing stiffly*): Mrs. Tiffany, your most obedient. Miss Seraphina, yours. How d'ye do, Twinkle?
MRS. TIFFANY: Mr. Fogg, how do you do? Fine weather, — delightful, isn't it? 215
FOGG: I am indifferent to weather, Madam.
MRS. TIFFANY: Been to the opera, Mr. Fogg? I hear that the *bow monde* make their *debutt* there every evening.
FOGG: I consider operas a bore, Madam.
SERAPHINA (*Advancing*): You must hear Mr. Twinkle's verses, Mr. Fogg! 220
FOGG: I am indifferent to verses, Miss Seraphina.
SERAPHINA: But Mr. Twinkle's verses are addressed to me!
TWINKLE: Now pay attention, Fogg! (*Reads*) —
"Around my heart thou weavest a spell
"Whose magic I" — 225

(*Enter Zeke.*)

ZEKE: Mister — No, he say he ain't no Mister —

TWINKLE:

"Around my heart thou weavest a spell

"Whose magic I can never tell!"

MRS. TIFFANY: Speak in a loud, clear tone, A-dolph!

TWINKLE: This is terrible!   230

ZEKE: Mister Count Jolly-made-her!

MRS. TIFFANY: Count Jolimaitre! Good gracious! Zeke, Zeke, —
A-dolph, I mean. — Dear me, what a mistake! (*Aside*) Set that chair out
of the way, — put that table back. Seraphina, my dear, are you all in order? Dear me! dear me! Your dress is so tumbled! (*Arranges her dress*) What   235
are you grinning at? (*To Zeke*) Beg the Count to *honour* us by walking up!
(*Exit Zeke.*) Seraphina, my dear (*Aside to her*) remember now what I told
you about the Count. He is a man of the highest, — good gracious! I am
so flurried; and nothing is so ungenteel as agitation! what will the Count
think! Mr. Twinkle, pray stand out of the way! Seraphina, my dear, place   240
yourself on my right! Mr. Fogg, the conservatory — beautiful flowers, —
pray amuse yourself in the conservatory.

FOGG: I am indifferent to flowers, Madam.

MRS. TIFFANY: Dear me! the man stands right in the way, — just where
the Count must make his *entray!* (*Aside*) Mr. Fogg, — pray —   245

(*Enter Count Jolimaitre, very dashingly dressed; he wears a moustache.*)

MRS. TIFFANY: Oh, Count, this unexpected honour —

SERAPHINA: Count, this inexpressible pleasure —

COUNT: Beg you won't mention it, Madam! Miss Seraphina, your most
devoted!

MRS. TIFFANY: What condescension! (*Aside*) Count, may I take the liberty   250
to introduce — Good gracious! I forgot. (*Aside*) Count, I was about to remark that we never introduce in America. All our fashions are foreign,
Count.

(*Twinkle, who has stepped forward to be introduced, shows great indignation.*)

COUNT: Excuse me, Madam, our fashions have grown antediluvian before
you Americans discover their existence. You are lamentably behind the   255
age — lamentably! 'Pon my honour, a foreigner of refinement finds great
difficulty in existing in this provincial atmosphere.

MRS. TIFFANY: How dreadful, Count! I am very much concerned. If there
is anything which I can do, Count —

SERAPHINA: Or I, Count, to render your situation less deplorable —   260

COUNT: Ah! I find but one redeeming charm in America — the superlative loveliness of the feminine portion of creation, — and the wealth of their obliging papas. (*Aside*)

MRS. TIFFANY: How flattering! Ah! Count, I am afraid you will turn the head of my simple girl here. She is a perfect child of nature, Count. 265

COUNT: Very possibly, for though you American women are quite charming, yet, demme, there's a deal of native rust to rub off!

MRS. TIFFANY: *Rust?* Good gracious, Count! where do you find any rust? (*Looking about the room*)

COUNT: How very unsophisticated!

MRS. TIFFANY: Count, I am so much ashamed, — I pray excuse me! Al- 270 though a lady of large fortune, and one, Count, who can boast of the highest connections, I blush to confess that I have never travelled, — while you, Count, I presume are at home in all the courts of Europe.

COUNT: *Courts?* Eh? Oh, yes, Madam, *very* true. I believe I am pretty well known in some of the courts of Europe — (*Aside*) police courts. In a 275 word, Madam, I had seen enough of civilized life — wanted to refresh myself by a sight of barbarous countries and customs — had my choice between the Sandwich Islands and New York — chose New York!

MRS. TIFFANY: How complimentary to our country! And, Count, I have no doubt you speak every conceivable language? You talk English like a 280 native.

COUNT: Eh, what? Like a native? Oh, ah, demme, yes, I am something of an Englishman. Passed one year and eight months with the Duke of Wellington, six months with Lord Brougham, two and a half with Count d'Orsay — knew them all more intimately than their best friends — no 285 heroes to me — hadn't a secret from me, I assure you, — *especially of the toilet.* (*Aside*)

MRS. TIFFANY: Think of that, my dear! Lord Wellington and Duke Broom! (*Aside to Seraphina*)

SERAPHINA: And only think of Count d'Orsay, Mamma! (*Aside to Mrs.* 290 *Tiffany*) I am so wild to see Count d'Orsay!

COUNT: Oh! a mere man milliner. Very little refinement out of Paris! Why, at the very last dinner given at Lord — Lord Knowswho, would you believe it, Madam, there was an individual present who wore a *black* cravat and took *soup twice!* 295

MRS. TIFFANY: How shocking! the sight of him would have spoilt my appetite! Think what a great man he must be, my dear, to despise lords and counts in that way. (*Aside to Seraphina*) I must leave them together. (*Aside*) Mr. Twinkle, your arm. I have some really very *foreign exotics* to show you.

TWINKLE: I fly at your command. I wish all her exotics were blooming in 300
their native soil! (*Aside, and glancing at the Count*)

MRS. TIFFANY: Mr. Fogg, will you accompany us? My conservatory is well
worthy a visit. It cost an immense sum of money.

FOGG: I am indifferent to conservatories, Madam; flowers are such a bore!

MRS. TIFFANY: I shall take no refusal. Conservatories are all the rage, — I 305
could not exist without mine! Let me show you, — let me show you.

(*Places her arm through Mr. Fogg's, without his consent. Exeunt Mrs. Tiffany, Fogg,
and Twinkle into the conservatory, where they are seen walking about.*)

SERAPHINA: America, then, has no charms for you, Count?

COUNT: Excuse me, — some exceptions. I find you, for instance, particularly charming! Can't say I admire your country. Ah! if you had ever
breathed the exhilarating air of Paris, ate creams at Tortoni's, dined at the 310
Café Royale, or if you had lived in London — felt at home at St. James's,
and every afternoon driven a couple of Lords and a Duchess through
Hyde Park, you would find America — where you have no kings, queens,
lords, nor ladies — insupportable!

SERAPHINA: Not while there was a Count in it! 315

(*Enter Zeke, very indignant.*)

ZEKE: Where's de Missus?

(*Enter Mrs. Tiffany, Fogg, and Twinkle, from the conservatory.*)

MRS. TIFFANY: Whom do you come to announce, A-dolph?

ZEKE: He said he wouldn't trust me — no, not eben wid so much as his
name; so I wouldn't trust him up stairs; den he ups wid *his stick* and I *cuts
mine.* 320

MRS. TIFFANY: Some of Mr. Tiffany's vulgar acquaintances. I shall die with
shame. (*Aside*) A-dolph, inform him that I am *not at home.* (*Exit Zeke.*) My
nerves are so shattered, I am ready to sink. Mr. Twinkle, that *fowtool,* if
you please!

TWINKLE: What? What do you wish, Madam? 325

MRS. TIFFANY: The ignorance of these Americans! (*Aside*) Count, may I
trouble you? That *fowtool,* if you please!

COUNT: She's not talking English, nor French, but I suppose it's American. (*Aside*)

TRUEMAN (*Outside*): Not at home! 330

ZEKE: No, Sar — Missus say she's not at home.

TRUEMAN: Out of the way, you grinning nigger!

(*Enter Adam Trueman, dressed as a farmer, a stout cane in his hand, his boots covered with dust. Zeke jumps out of his way as he enters. Exit Zeke.*)

TRUEMAN: Where's this woman that's not *at home* in her own house? May I be shot! if I wonder at it! I shouldn't think she'd ever feel *at home* in such a show-box as this! (*Looking round*)

MRS. TIFFANY: What a plebeian looking old farmer! I wonder who he is? (*Aside*) Sir — (*Advancing very agitatedly*) What do you mean, sir, by this *ow*-dacious conduct? How dare you intrude yourself into my parlor? Do you know who I am, sir? (*With great dignity*) You are in the presence of Mrs. Tiffany, sir!

TRUEMAN: Antony's wife, eh? Well now, I might have guessed that — ha! ha! ha! for I see you make it a point to carry half your husband's shop upon your back! No matter; that's being a good helpmate — for he carried the whole of it once in a pack on his own shoulders — now you bear a share!

MRS. TIFFANY: How dare you, you impertinent, *ow*dacious, ignorant old man! It's all an invention. You're talking of somebody else. What will the Count think! (*Aside*)

TRUEMAN: Why, I thought folks had better manners in the city! This is a civil welcome for your husband's old friend, and after my coming all the way from Catteraugus[1] to see you and yours! First a grinning nigger tricked out in scarlet regimentals —

MRS. TIFFANY: Let me tell you, sir, that liveries are all the fashion!

TRUEMAN: The fashion, are they? To make men wear the *badge of servitude* in a free land, — that's the fashion, is it? Hurrah for republican simplicity! I will venture to say now, that you have your coat-of-arms too!

MRS. TIFFANY: Certainly, sir; you can see it on the panels of my *voyture*.

TRUEMAN: Oh! no need of that. I know what your escutcheon must be! A bandbox *rampant*, with a bonnet *couchant*, and a pedlar's pack *passant!* Ha! ha! ha! that shows both houses united!

MRS. TIFFANY: Sir! You are most profoundly ignorant, — what do you mean by this insolence, sir? How shall I get rid of him? (*Aside*)

TRUEMAN (*Looking at Seraphina*):   I hope that is not Gertrude! (*Aside*)

MRS. TIFFANY: Sir, I'd have you know that — Seraphina, my child, walk with the gentlemen into the conservatory. (*Exeunt Seraphina, Twinkle, Fogg into conservatory.*) Count Jolimaitre, pray make due allowances for the errors of this rustic! I do assure you, Count — (*Whispers to him*)

[1] Catteraugus County is in western New York State, near Lake Erie and more than three hundred fifty miles from New York City.

TRUEMAN: Count! She calls that critter with a shoebrush over his mouth, Count! To look at him, I should have thought he was a tailor's walking advertisement! (*Aside*)   370

COUNT (*Addressing Trueman, whom he has been inspecting through his eye-glass*): Where did you say you belonged, my friend? Dug out of the ruins of Pompeii, eh?

TRUEMAN: I belong to a land in which I rejoice to find that you are a foreigner.

COUNT: What a barbarian! He doesn't see the honour I'm doing his country! Pray, Madam, is it one of the aboriginal inhabitants of the soil? To what tribe of Indians does he belong — the Pawnee or Choctaw? Does he carry a tomahawk?   375

TRUEMAN: Something quite as useful — do you see that? (*Shaking his stick. Count runs to right, behind Mrs. Tiffany.*)

MRS. TIFFANY: Oh, dear! I shall faint! Millinette! (*Approaching right*)   380 Millinette!

(*Enter Millinette, without advancing into the room.*)

MILLINETTE: *Oui*, Madame.

MRS. TIFFANY: A glass of water! (*Exit Millinette.*) Sir, (*Crossing to Trueman*) I am shocked at your plebeian conduct! This is a gentleman of the highest standing, sir! He is a *Count*, sir!   385

(*Enter Millinette, bearing a salver with a glass of water. In advancing towards Mrs. Tiffany, she passes in front of the Count, starts and screams. The Count, after a start of surprise, regains his composure, plays with his eye-glass, and looks perfectly unconcerned.*)

MRS. TIFFANY: What is the matter? What *is* the matter?

MILLINETTE: Noting, noting, — only — (*Looks at Count and turns away her eyes again*) only — noting at all!

TRUEMAN: Don't be afraid, girl! Why, did you never see a live Count before? He's tame — I dare say your mistress there leads him about by the   390 ears.

MRS. TIFFANY: This is too much! Millinette, send for Mr. Tiffany instantly! (*Crosses to Millinette, who is going*)

MILLINETTE: He just come in, Madame!

TRUEMAN: My old friend! Where is he? Take me to him — I long to have   395 one more hearty shake of the hand!

MRS. TIFFANY: Shake of the fist, you mean. (*Crosses to him*) If I don't make him shake his in your face, you low, *ow*dacious — no matter, we'll see.

Count, honour me by joining my daughter in the conservatory, I will return immediately.

400

(*Count bows and walks towards conservatory, Mrs. Tiffany following part of the way and then returning to Trueman.*)

TRUEMAN: What a Jezebel! These women always play the very devil with a man, and yet I don't believe such a damaged bale of goods as *that* (*Looking at Mrs. Tiffany*) has smothered the heart of little Antony!

MRS. TIFFANY: This way, sir, sal vous plait.   (*Exit, with great dignity.*)

TRUEMAN: *Sal vous plait.* Ha, ha, ha! We'll see what Fashion has done for   405
him.   (*Exit.*)

ACT II, SCENE I

Inner apartment of Mr. Tiffany's Counting-House. Mr. Tiffany seated at a desk looking over papers. Mr. Snobson on a high stool at another desk, with a pen behind his ear.

SNOBSON (*Rising, advances to the front of the stage, regards Tiffany and shrugs his shoulders*):   How the old boy frets and fumes over those papers, to be sure! He's working himself into a perfect fever — ex-actly, — therefore *bleeding's* the prescription! So here goes! (*Aside*) Mr. Tiffany, a word with you, if you please, sir?

TIFFANY (*Sitting still*):   Speak on, Mr. Snobson. I attend.   5

SNOBSON: What I have to say, sir, is a matter of the first importance to the credit of the concern — the *credit* of the concern, Mr. Tiffany!

TIFFANY: Proceed, Mr. Snobson.

SNOBSON: Sir, you've a handsome house — fine carriage — nigger in livery — feed on the fat of the land — everything first rate —   10

TIFFANY: Well, sir?

SNOBSON: My salary, Mr. Tiffany!

TIFFANY: It has been raised three times within the last year.

SNOBSON: Still it is insufficient for the necessities of an honest man, — mark me, an *honest* man, Mr. Tiffany.   15

TIFFANY (*Crossing*):   What a weapon he has made of that word! (*Aside*) Enough — another hundred shall be added. Does that content you?

SNOBSON: There is one other subject, which I have before mentioned, Mr. Tiffany, — your daughter, — what's the reason you can't let the folks at home know at once that I'm to be *the man?*   20

TIFFANY: Villain! And must the only seal upon this scoundrel's lips be placed there by the hand of my daughter? (*Aside*) Well, sir, it shall be as you desire.

SNOBSON: And Mrs. Tiffany shall be informed of your resolution?

TIFFANY: Yes.   25

SNOBSON: Enough said! That's the ticket! The CREDIT *of the concern's safe,* sir. (*Returns to his seat*)

TIFFANY: How low have I bowed to this insolent rascal! To rise himself, he mounts upon my shoulders, and unless I can shake him off he must crush me! (*Aside*)   30

(*Enter Trueman.*)

TRUEMAN: Here I am, Antony, man! I told you I'd pay you a visit in your money-making quarters. (*Looks around*) But it looks as dismal here as a cell in the State's prison!

TIFFANY (*Forcing a laugh*):   Ha, ha, ha! State's prison! You are so facetious! Ha, ha, ha!   35

TRUEMAN: Well, for the life of me I can't see anything so amusing in that! I should think the State's prison plaguy uncomfortable lodgings. And you laugh, man, as though you fancied yourself there already.

TIFFANY: Ha, ha, ha!

TRUEMAN (*Imitating him*):   Ha, ha, ha! What on earth do you mean by that   40
ill-sounding laugh, that has nothing of a laugh about it! This *fashion-worship* has made heathens and hypocrites of you all! *Deception* is your household God! A man laughs as if he were crying, and cries as if he were laughing in his sleeve. Everything is something else from what it seems to be. I have lived in your house only three days, and I've heard more lies   45
than were ever invented during a Presidential election! First your fine lady of a wife sends me word that she's not at home — I walk upstairs, and she takes good care that *I* shall not be *at home* — wants to turn me out of doors. Then *you* come in — take your old friend by the hand — whisper, the deuce knows what, in your wife's ear, and the tables are   50
turned in a tangent! Madam curtsies — says she's enchanted to see me — and orders her grinning nigger to show me a room.

TIFFANY: We were exceedingly happy to welcome you as our guest.

TRUEMAN: Happy? *You* happy? Ah! Antony! Antony! that hatchet face of yours, and those criss-cross furrows tell quite another story! It's many a   55
long day since you were *happy* at anything! You look as if you'd melted down your flesh into dollars, and mortgaged your soul in the bargain! Your warm heart has grown cold over your ledger — your light spirits heavy with calculation! You have traded away your youth — your hopes — your tastes for wealth! and now you *have* the wealth you coveted, what   60
does it profit you? Pleasure it cannot buy; for you have lost your *capacity* for enjoyment. Ease it will not bring; for the love of gain is never satis-

fied! It has made your counting-house a penitentiary, and your home a fashionable *museum* where there is no niche for you! You have spent so much time *ciphering* in the one, that you find yourself at last a very *cipher* in the other! See me, man! Seventy-two last August! — strong as a hickory and every whit as sound! 65

TIFFANY: I take the greatest pleasure in remarking your superiority, sir.

TRUEMAN: Bah! no man takes pleasure in remarking the superiority of another! Why the deuce can't you speak the truth, man? But it's not the *fashion,* I suppose! I have not seen one frank, open face since — no, no, I can't say that either, though lying *is* catching! There's that girl, Gertrude, who is trying to teach your daughter music — but Gertrude was bred in the country! 70

TIFFANY: A good girl; my wife and daughter find her very useful. 75

TRUEMAN: Useful? Well, I must say you have queer notions of *use!* — But come, cheer up, man! I'd rather see one of your old smiles, than know you'd realized another thousand! I hear you are making money on the true, American high-pressure system — better go slow and sure — the more steam, the greater danger of the boiler's bursting! All sound, I hope? Nothing rotten at the core? 80

TIFFANY: Oh, sound — quite sound!

TRUEMAN: Well, that's pleasant — though I must say you don't look very pleasant about it!

TIFFANY: My good friend, although I am solvent, I may say, perfectly solvent — yet you — the fact is, you can be of some assistance to me! 85

TRUEMAN: That's the *fact,* is it? I'm glad we've hit upon one *fact* at last! Well —

(*Snobson, who during this conversation has been employed in writing, but stops occasionally to listen, now gives vent to a dry, chuckling laugh.*)

TRUEMAN: Hey? What's that? Another of those deuced ill-sounding, city laughs! (*Sees Snobson*) Who's that perched up on the stool of repentance — eh, Antony? 90

SNOBSON: The old boy has missed his text there — *that's* the stool of repentance! (*Aside, and looking at Tiffany's seat*)

TIFFANY: One of my clerks — my confidential clerk!

TRUEMAN: Confidential? Why, he looks for all the world like a spy — the inquisitorial, hang-dog face — ugh! the sight of it makes my blood run cold! Come, (*Crosses*) let us talk over matters where this critter can't give us the benefit of his opinion! Antony, the next time you choose a confidential clerk, take one that carries his credentials in his face — those in his pocket are not worth much without! 95

100

(*Exeunt Trueman and Tiffany.*)

SNOBSON (*Jumping from his stool and advancing*):   The old prig has got the tin, or Tiff would never be so civil! All right — Tiff will work every shiner into the concern — all the better for me! Now I'll go and make love to Seraphina. The old woman needn't try to knock me down with any of her French lingo! Six months from to-day, if I ain't driving my two footmen 105 tandem, down Broadway — and as fashionable as Mrs. Tiffany herself, then I ain't the trump I thought I was! that's all. (*Looks at his watch*) Bless me! eleven o'clock, and I haven't had my julep yet? Snobson, I'm ashamed of you! (*Exit.*)

Scene II

The interior of a beautiful conservatory; a walk through the centre; stands of flower-pots in bloom; a couple of rustic seats. Gertrude, attired in white, with a white rose in her hair, watering the flowers. Colonel Howard, regarding her.

HOWARD: I am afraid you lead a sad life here, Miss Gertrude?

GERTRUDE (*Turning round gaily*):   What! amongst the flowers? (*Continues her occupation*)

HOWARD: No, amongst the thistles, with which Mrs. Tiffany surrounds you; the tempests, which her temper raises!

GERTRUDE: They never harm me. Flowers and herbs are excellent tutors. I 5 learn prudence from the reed, and bend until the storm has swept over me!

HOWARD: Admirable philosophy! But still this frigid atmosphere of fash-ion must be uncongenial to you? Accustomed to the pleasant compan-ionship of your kind friends in Geneva,[2] surely you must regret this cold 10 exchange?

GERTRUDE: Do you think so? Can you suppose that I could possibly pre-fer a ramble in the woods to a promenade in Broadway? A wreath of scented wild flowers to a bouquet of these sickly exotics? The odour of new-mown hay to the heated air of this crowded conservatory? Or can 1 you imagine that I could enjoy the quiet conversation of my Geneva friends, more than the edifying chit-chat of a fashionable drawing-room? But I see you think me totally destitute of taste?

HOWARD: You have a merry spirit to jest thus at your grievances!

[2] Geneva, New York, is a town in the Finger Lakes region of the state, about fifty miles west of Syracuse.

GERTRUDE: I have my *mania*, — as some wise person declares that all men   20
have, — and mine is a love of independence! In Geneva, my wants were
supplied by two kind old maiden ladies, upon whom I know not that I
have any claim. I had abilities, and desired to use them. I came here at my
own request; for here I am no longer *dependent! Voilà tout,* as Mrs. Tiffany
would say.   25

HOWARD: Believe me, I appreciate the confidence you repose in me!

GERTRUDE: Confidence! Truly, Colonel Howard, the *confidence* is entirely
on your part, in supposing that I confide that which I have no reason
to conceal! I think I informed you that Mrs. Tiffany only received visitors on her reception day — she is therefore not prepared to see you.   30
Zeke — Oh! I beg his pardon — Adolph made some mistake in admitting you.

HOWARD: Nay, Gertrude, it was not Mrs. Tiffany, nor Miss Tiffany, whom
I came to see; it — it was —

GERTRUDE: The conservatory perhaps? I will leave you to examine the   35
flowers at leisure! (*Crosses left*)

HOWARD: Gertrude — listen to me. If I only dared to give utterance to
what is hovering upon my lips! (*Aside*) Gertrude!

GERTRUDE: Colonel Howard!

HOWARD: Gertrude, I must — must —   40

GERTRUDE: Yes, indeed you *must,* must leave me! I think I hear somebody
coming — Mrs. Tiffany would not be well pleased to find you here —
pray, pray leave me — that door will lead you into the street. (*Hurries him
out through door, takes up her watering-pot, and commences watering flowers, tying up
branches, etc.*) What a strange being is man! Why should he hesitate to say
— nay, why should I prevent his saying, what I would most delight to   45
hear? Truly, man *is* strange — but woman is quite as incomprehensible!
(*Walks about gathering flowers*)

(*Enter Count Jolimaitre.*)

COUNT: There she is — the bewitching little creature! Mrs. Tiffany and
her daughter are out of ear-shot. I caught a glimpse of their feathers
floating down Broadway, not ten minutes ago. Just the opportunity I
have been looking for! Now for an engagement with this captivating   50
little piece of prudery! 'Pon my honour, I am almost afraid she will not
resist a *Count* long enough to give value to the conquest. (*Approaches her.*)
Ma belle petite, were you gathering roses for me?

GERTRUDE (*Starts on first perceiving him, but instantly regains her self-possession*):
The roses here, sir, are carefully guarded with thorns — if you have the
right to gather, pluck for yourself!   55

COUNT: Sharp as ever, little Gertrude! But now that we are alone, throw
off this frigidity, and be at your ease.

GERTRUDE: Permit me to *be alone*, sir, that I *may be* at my ease.

COUNT: Very good, *ma belle*, well said! (*Applauding her with his hands*) Never
yield too soon, even to a *title!* But, as the old girl may find her way back   60
before long, we may as well come to particulars at once. I love you; but
that you know already. (*Rubbing his eye-glass unconcernedly with his handkerchief*) Before long I shall make Mademoiselle Seraphina my wife, and, of
course, you shall remain in the family!

GERTRUDE (*Indignantly*):   Sir —   65

COUNT: 'Pon my honour you shall! In France we arrange these little matters without difficulty!

GERTRUDE: But I am an *American!* Your conduct proves that you are not
one! (*Going*)

COUNT (*Preventing her*):   Don't run away, my immaculate *petite Americaine!*   70
Demme, you've quite overlooked my condescension — the difference of
our stations — you a species of upper servant, an orphan — no friends.

(*Enter Trueman unperceived.*)

GERTRUDE: And therefore more entitled to the respect and protection of
every *true gentleman!* Had you been one, you would not have insulted me!

COUNT: My charming little orator, patriotism and declamation become   75
you particularly! (*Approaches her*) I feel quite tempted to taste —

TRUEMAN (*Thrusting him aside*):   An American hickory switch! (*Strikes him*)
Well, how do you like it?

COUNT: Old matter-of-fact! (*Aside*) Sir, how dare you?

TRUEMAN: My stick has answered that question!   80

GERTRUDE: Oh! now I am quite safe!

TRUEMAN: Safe! not a bit safer than before! All women would be safe, if
they knew how virtue became them! As for you, Mr. Count, what have
you to say for yourself? Come, speak out!

COUNT: Sir, — aw — aw — you don't understand these matters!   85

TRUEMAN: That's a fact! Not having had *your* experience, I don't believe I
do understand them!

COUNT: A piece of pleasantry — a mere joke —

TRUEMAN: A joke, was it? I'll show you a joke worth two of that! I'll teach
you the way we natives joke with a puppy who don't respect an honest   90
woman! (*Seizing him*)

COUNT: Oh! oh! demme — you old ruffian! let me go. What do you
mean?

TRUEMAN: Oh! a piece of pleasantry — a mere joke — very pleasant, isn't it?

(*Attempts to strike him again; Count struggles with him. Enter Mrs. Tiffany hastily, in her bonnet and shawl.*)

MRS. TIFFANY: What is the matter? I am perfectly *abîmé* with terror. Mr. 95
Trueman, what has happened?

TRUEMAN: Oh! we have been *joking!*

MRS. TIFFANY (*To Count, who is rearranging his dress*):   My *dear* Count, I did
not expect to find you here — how kind of you!

TRUEMAN: Your *dear* Count has been showing his *kindness* in a very *foreign* 100
manner. Too *foreign,* I think, he found it to be relished by an *unfashionable native!* What do you think of a puppy, who insults an innocent girl
all in the way of *kindness?* This Count of yours — this importation of —

COUNT: My dear Madam, demme, permit me to explain. It would be unbecoming — demme — particularly unbecoming of you — aw — aw — to 105
pay any attention to this ignorant person. (*Crosses to Trueman*) Anything that
he says concerning a man of my standing — aw — the truth is, Madam —

TRUEMAN: Let us have the truth, by all means, — if it is only for the nov-
elty's sake!

COUNT (*Turning his back to Trueman*):   You see, Madam, hoping to obtain a 110
few moments' private conversation with Miss Seraphina — with *Miss
Seraphina,* I say — and — aw — and knowing her passion for flowers, I
found my way to your very tasteful and *recherché* conservatory. (*Looks about
him approvingly*) *Very* beautifully arranged — does you great credit,
Madam! Here I encountered this young person. She was inclined to be 115
talkative; and I indulged her with — with a — aw — demme — a few
commonplaces! What passed between us was mere *harmless badinage* — on
my part. You, Madam, you — so conversant with our European manners — you are aware that when a man of fashion — that is, when a
woman — a man is bound — amongst noblemen, you know — 120

MRS. TIFFANY: I comprehend you perfectly — *parfittement,* my dear
Count.

COUNT: 'Pon my honour, that's very obliging of her. (*Aside*)

MRS. TIFFANY: I am shocked at the plebeian forwardness of this conceited
girl! 125

TRUEMAN (*Walking up to Count*):   Did you ever keep a reckoning of the lies
you tell in an hour?

MRS. TIFFANY: Mr. Trueman, I blush for you! (*Crosses to Trueman*)

TRUEMAN: Don't do that — you have no blushes to spare!

MRS. TIFFANY: It is a man of rank whom you are addressing, sir! 130

TRUEMAN: A rank villain, Mrs. Antony Tiffany! A *rich one* he would be,
had he as much *gold* as *brass!*

MRS. TIFFANY: Pray pardon him, Count; he knows nothing of *how ton!*

COUNT: Demme, he's beneath my notice. I tell you what, old fellow — (*Trueman raises his stick as Count approaches; the latter starts back*) the sight of him [135] discomposes me — aw — I feel quite uncomfortable — aw — let us join your charming daughter? I can't do you the honour to shoot you, sir, — (*To Trueman*) you are beneath me — a nobleman can't fight a commoner! Good-bye, old Truepenny! I — aw — I'm insensible to your insolence!

(*Exeunt Count and Mrs. Tiffany.*)

TRUEMAN: You won't be insensible to a cow-hide in spite of your nobility! [140] The next time he practises any of his foreign fashions on you, Gertrude, you'll see how I'll wake up his sensibilities!

GERTRUDE: I do not know what I should have done without you, sir.

TRUEMAN: Yes, you do — you know that you would have done well enough! Never tell a lie, girl! not even for the sake of pleasing an old man! [145] When you open your lips, let your heart speak! Never tell a lie! Let your face be the looking-glass of your soul — your heart its clock — while your tongue rings the hours! But the glass must be clear, the clock true, and then there's no fear but the tongue will do its duty in a woman's head!

GERTRUDE: You are very good, sir! [150]

TRUEMAN: That's as it may be! — How my heart warms towards her! (*Aside*) Gertrude, I hear that you have no mother?

GERTRUDE: Ah! no, sir; I wish I had.

TRUEMAN: So do I! Heaven knows, so do I! (*Aside, and with emotion*) And you have no father, Gertrude? [155]

GERTRUDE: No, sir — I often wish I had!

TRUEMAN (*Hurriedly*):   Don't do that, girl! don't do that! Wish you had a mother — but never wish that you had a father again! Perhaps the one you had did not deserve such a child!

(*Enter Prudence.*)

PRUDENCE: Seraphina is looking for you, Gertrude. [160]

GERTRUDE: I will go to her. (*Crosses*) Mr. Trueman, you will not permit me to thank you, but you cannot prevent my gratitude! (*Exit.*)

TRUEMAN (*Looking after her*):   If falsehood harbours there, I'll give up searching after truth!

(*Retires up the stage musingly, and commences examining the flowers.*)

PRUDENCE: What a nice old man he is, to be sure! I wish he would say [165] something! (*Aside. Walks after him, turning when he turns — after a pause*) Don't mind me, Mr. Trueman!

TRUEMAN: Mind you? Oh! no, don't be afraid (*Crosses*) — I wasn't minding you. Nobody seems to mind you much!

(*Continues walking and examining the flowers. Prudence follows.*)

PRUDENCE: Very pretty flowers, ain't they? Gertrude takes care of them.   170

TRUEMAN: Gertrude? So I hear — (*Advancing*) I suppose you can tell me now who this Gertrude —

PRUDENCE: Who she's in love with? I *knew* you were going to say that! I'll tell you all about it! Gertrude, she's in love with — Mr. Twinkle! and he's in love with her. And Seraphina, she's in love with Count Jolly — what-   175 d'ye-call-it: but Count Jolly don't take to her at all — but Colonel Howard — he's the man — he's desperate about her!

TRUEMAN: Why, you feminine newspaper! Howard in love with that quintessence of affectation! Howard — the only frank, straightforward fellow that I've met since — I'll tell him my mind on the subject! And   180 Gertrude hunting for happiness in a rhyming dictionary! The girl's a greater fool than I took her for! (*Crosses right*)

PRUDENCE: So she is — you see I know all about them!

TRUEMAN: I see you do! You've a wonderful knowledge — wonderful — of *other people's concerns!* It may do here, but take my word for it, in the   185 county of Catteraugus you'd get the name of a great *busy-body*. But perhaps you know that, too?

PRUDENCE: Oh! I always know what's coming. I feel it beforehand all over me. I knew something was going to happen the day you came here — and what's more I can always tell a married man from a single — I felt   190 right off that you were a bachelor!

TRUEMAN: Felt right off I was a bachelor, did you? you were sure of it — sure? — quite sure? (*Prudence assents delightedly.*) Then you felt wrong! — a bachelor and a widower are not the same thing!

PRUDENCE: Oh! but it all comes to the same thing — a widower's as good   195 as a bachelor any day! And besides, I knew that you were a farmer *right off.*

TRUEMAN: On the spot, eh? I suppose you saw cabbages and green peas growing out of my hat?

PRUDENCE: No, I didn't — but I knew all about you. And I knew — (*Look-*   200 *ing down and fidgeting with her apron*) — I knew you were for getting married soon! For last night I dreamt I saw your funeral going along the streets, and the mourners all dressed in white. And a funeral is a sure sign of a wedding, you know! (*Nudging him with her elbow*)

TRUEMAN (*Imitating her voice*):   Well, I can't say that I *know* any such thing!   205 you know! (*Nudging her back*)

PRUDENCE: Oh! it does, and there's no getting over it! For my part, I like
farmers — and I know all about setting hens and turkeys, and feeding
chickens, and laying eggs, and all that sort of thing!

TRUEMAN: May I be shot! if mistress newspaper is not putting in an ad-   210
vertisement for herself! This is your city mode of courting, I suppose, ha,
ha, ha! (*Aside*)

PRUDENCE: I've been west, a little; but I never was in the county of Catteraugus, myself.

TRUEMAN: Oh, you were not? And you have taken a particular fancy to go   215
there, eh?

PRUDENCE: Perhaps I shouldn't object —

TRUEMAN: Oh! — ah! — so I suppose. Now pay attention to what I am
going to say, for it is a matter of great importance to yourself.

PRUDENCE: Now it's coming — I know what he's going to say! (*Aside*)   220

TRUEMAN: The next time you want to tie a man for life to your apron-
strings, pick out one that don't come from the county of Catteraugus —
for green-horns are scarce in those parts, and modest women plenty!

(*Exit.*)

PRUDENCE: Now, who'd have thought he was going to say that! But I won't
give him up yet — I won't give him up.   (*Exit.*)   225

ACT III, SCENE I

Mrs. Tiffany's Parlor. Enter Mrs. Tiffany, followed by Mr. Tiffany.

TIFFANY: Your extravagance will ruin me, Mrs. Tiffany!

MRS. TIFFANY: And your stinginess will ruin me, Mr. Tiffany! It is totally
and *toot a fate* impossible to convince you of the necessity of *keeping up
appearances*. There is a certain display which every woman of fashion is
forced to make!   5

TIFFANY: And pray who made *you* a woman of fashion?

MRS. TIFFANY: What a vulgar question! All women of fashion, Mr.
Tiffany —

TIFFANY: In this land are *self-constituted*, like you, Madam — and *fashion*
is the cloak for more sins than charity ever covered! It was for *fashion's*   10
sake that you insisted upon my purchasing this expensive house — it was
for *fashion's* sake that you ran me in debt at every exorbitant upholsterer's
and extravagant furniture warehouse in the city — it was for *fashion's* sake
that you built that ruinous conservatory — hired more servants than
they have persons to wait upon — and dressed your footman like a har-   15
lequin!

MRS. TIFFANY: Mr. Tiffany, you are thoroughly plebeian, and insufferably *American,* in your grovelling ideas! And, pray, what was the occasion of these very *mal-ap-pro-pos* remarks? Merely because I requested a paltry fifty dollars to purchase a new style of head-dress — a *bijou* of an article   20 just introduced in France.

TIFFANY: Time was, Mrs. Tiffany, when you manufactured your own French head-dresses — took off their first gloss at the public balls, and then sold them to your shortest-sighted customers. And all you knew about France, or French either, was what you spelt out at the bottom of   25 your fashion-plates — but now you have grown so fashionable, forsooth, that you have forgotten how to speak your mother tongue!

MRS. TIFFANY: Mr. Tiffany, Mr. Tiffany! Nothing is more positively vulgarian — more *unaristocratic* than any allusion to the past!

TIFFANY: Why, I thought, my dear, that *aristocrats* lived principally upon   30 the past — and traded in the market of fashion with the bones of their ancestors for capital!

MRS. TIFFANY: Mr. Tiffany, such vulgar remarks are only suitable to the counting-house; in my drawing-room you should —

TIFFANY: Vary my sentiments with my locality, as you change your *manners* with your *dress!*   35

MRS. TIFFANY: Mr. Tiffany, I desire that you will purchase Count d'Orsay's "Science of Etiquette," and learn how to conduct yourself — especially before you appear at the grand ball, which I shall give on Friday!

TIFFANY: Confound your balls, Madam; they make *footballs* of my money,   40 while you dance away all that I am worth! A pretty time to give a ball when you know that I am on the very brink of bankruptcy!

MRS. TIFFANY: So much the greater reason that nobody should suspect your circumstances, or you would lose your credit at once. Just at this crisis a ball is absolutely *necessary* to save your reputation! There is Mrs.   45 Adolphus Dashaway — she gave the most splendid fête of the season — and I hear on very good authority that her husband has not paid his baker's bill in three months. Then there was Mrs. Honeywood —

TIFFANY: Gave a ball the night before her husband shot himself — perhaps you wish to drive me to follow his example? (*Crosses right*)   50

MRS. TIFFANY: Good gracious! Mr. Tiffany, how you talk! I beg you won't mention anything of the kind. I consider black the most unbecoming color. I'm sure I've done all that I could to gratify you. There is that vulgar old torment, Trueman, who gives one the lie fifty times a day — haven't I been very civil to him?   55

TIFFANY: Civil to his *wealth,* Mrs. Tiffany! I told you that he was a rich old farmer — the early friend of my father — my own benefactor — and that I had reason to think he might assist me in my present embarrassments. Your civility was *bought* — and like most of your *own* purchases has yet to be *paid* for.

MRS. TIFFANY: And will be, no doubt! The condescension of a woman of fashion should command any price. Mr. Trueman is insupportably indecorous — he has insulted Count Jolimaitre in the most outrageous manner. If the Count was not so deeply interested — so *abimé* with Seraphina, I am sure he would never honour us by his visits again!

TIFFANY: So much the better — he shall never marry my daughter! — I am resolved on that. Why, Madam, I am told there is in Paris a regular matrimonial stock company, who fit out indigent dandies for this market. How do I know but this fellow is one of its creatures, and that he has come here to increase its dividends by marrying a fortune?

MRS. TIFFANY: Nonsense, Mr. Tiffany. The Count, the most fashionable young man in all New York — the intimate friend of all the dukes and lords in Europe — not marry my daughter? Not permit Seraphina to become a Countess? Mr. Tiffany, you are out of your senses!

TIFFANY: That would not be very wonderful, considering how many years I have been united to you, my dear. Modern physicians pronounce lunacy infectious!

MRS. TIFFANY: Mr. Tiffany, he is a man of fashion —

TIFFANY: Fashion makes fools, but cannot *feed* them. By the bye, I have a request, — since you are bent upon ruining me by this ball, and there is no help for it, — I desire that you will send an invitation to my confidential clerk, Mr. Snobson.

MRS. TIFFANY: Mr. Snobson! Was there ever such an *you-nick* demand! Mr. Snobson would cut a pretty figure amongst my fashionable friends! I shall do no such thing, Mr. Tiffany.

TIFFANY: Then, Madam, the ball shall not take place. Have I not told you that I am in the power of this man? That there are circumstances which it is happy for you that you do not know — which you cannot comprehend, — but which render it essential that you should be civil to Mr. Snobson? Not you merely, but Seraphina also? He is a more appropriate match for her than your foreign favorite.

MRS. TIFFANY: A match for Seraphina, indeed! (*Crosses*) Mr. Tiffany, you are determined to make a *fow pas*.

TIFFANY: Mr. Snobson intends calling this morning. (*Crosses to left*)

MRS. TIFFANY: But, Mr. Tiffany, this is not reception day — my drawing-rooms are in the most terrible disorder —

TIFFANY: Mr. Snobson is not particular — he must be admitted.

(*Enter Zeke.*)

ZEKE: Mr. Snobson.

(*Enter Snobson; exit Zeke.*)

SNOBSON: How d'ye do, Marm? (*Crosses to center*) How are you? Mr. Tiffany, your most! —

MRS. TIFFANY (*Formally*):   Bung jure. Comment vow porte vow, Monsur Snobson?

SNOBSON: Oh, to be sure — very good of you — fine day.

MRS. TIFFANY (*Pointing to a chair with great dignity*):   Sassoyez vow, Monsur Snobson.

SNOBSON: I wonder what she's driving at? I ain't up to the fashionable lingo yet! (*Aside*) Eh? what? Speak a little louder, Marm?

MRS. TIFFANY: What ignorance! (*Aside*)

TIFFANY: I presume Mrs. Tiffany means that you are to take a seat.

SNOBSON: Ex-actly — very obliging of her — so I will. (*Sits*) No ceremony amongst friends, you know — and likely to be nearer — you understand? O.K., all correct. How *is* Seraphina?

MRS. TIFFANY: Miss Tiffany is not visible this morning. (*Retires up*)

SNOBSON: Not visible? (*Jumping up, crosses*) I suppose that's the English for can't see her? Mr. Tiffany, sir — (*Walking up to him*) what am I to understand by this *de-fal-ca-tion*, sir? I expected your word to be as good as your bond — beg pardon, sir — I mean *better* — considerably *better* — no humbug about it, sir.

TIFFANY: Have patience, Mr. Snobson. (*Rings bell*)

(*Enter Zeke.*)

Zeke, desire my daughter to come here.

MRS. TIFFANY (*Coming down centre*):   A-dolph — I say, A-dolph —

(*Zeke straightens himself and assumes foppish airs, as he turns to Mrs. Tiffany.*)

TIFFANY: Zeke.

ZEKE: Don't know any such nigga, Boss.

TIFFANY: Do as I bid you instantly, or off with your livery and quit the house!

ZEKE: Wheugh! I'se all dismission.   (*Exit.*)

MRS. TIFFANY: A-dolph, A-dolph! (*Calling after him*)

SNOBSON: I brought the old boy to his bearings, didn't I though! Pull that string, and he is sure to work right. (*Aside*) Don't make any stranger of me,

Marm — I'm quite at home. If you've got any odd jobs about the house   130
to do, I sha'n't miss you. I'll amuse myself with Seraphina when she
comes — we'll get along very cosily by ourselves.

MRS. TIFFANY: Permit me to inform you, Mr. Snobson, that a French
mother never leaves her daughter alone with a young man — she knows
your sex too well for that!   135

SNOBSON: Very *dis*-obliging of her — but as we're none French —

MRS. TIFFANY: You have yet to learn, Mr. Snobson, that the American *ee-light* — the aristocracy — the *how-ton* — as a matter of conscience,
scrupulously follow the foreign fashions.

SNOBSON: Not when they are foreign to their interests, Marm — for in-   140
stance — (*Enter Seraphina.*) There you are at last, eh, Miss? How d'ye do?
Ma said you weren't visible. Managed to get a peep at her, eh, Mr.
Tiffany?

SERAPHINA: I heard you were here, Mr. Snobson, and came without even
arranging my toilette; you will excuse my negligence?   145

SNOBSON: Of everything but *me*, Miss.

SERAPHINA: I shall never have to ask your pardon for *that*, Mr. Snobson.

MRS. TIFFANY: Seraphina — child — really —

(*As she is approaching Seraphina, Mr. Tiffany plants himself in front of his wife.*)

TIFFANY: Walk this way, Madam, if you please. To see that she fancies the
surly fellow takes a weight from my heart. (*Aside*)   150

MRS. TIFFANY: Mr. Tiffany, it is highly improper and not at all *distingué* to
leave a young girl —

(*Enter Zeke.*)

ZEKE: Mr. Count Jolly-made-her!

MRS. TIFFANY: Good gracious! The Count — Oh, dear! — Seraphina, run
and change your dress, — no, there's not time! A-dolph, admit him. (*Exit*   155
Zeke.) Mr. Snobson, get out of the way, will you? Mr. Tiffany, what are
you doing at home at this hour?

(*Enter Count Jolimaitre, ushered by Zeke.*)

ZEKE: Dat's de genuine article ob a gemman.   (*Aside. Exit.*)

MRS. TIFFANY: My dear Count, I am overjoyed at the very sight of you.

COUNT: Flattered myself you'd be glad to see me, Madam — knew it was   160
not your *jour de reception.*

MRS. TIFFANY: But for you, Count, all days —

COUNT: I thought so. Ah, Miss Tiffany, on my honour, you're looking
beautiful. (*Crosses to the right*)

SERAPHINA: Count, flattery from you — 165
SNOBSON: What? Eh? What's that you say?
SERAPHINA: Nothing but what etiquette requires. (*Aside to him*)
COUNT (*Regarding Mr. Tiffany through his eye-glass*):   Your worthy Papa, I believe? Sir, your most obedient.

(*Mr. Tiffany bows coldly; Count regards Snobson through his glass, shrugs his shoulders and turns away.*)

SNOBSON (*To Mrs. Tiffany*):   Introduce me, will you? I never knew a Count 170 in all my life — what a strange-looking animal!
MRS. TIFFANY: Mr. Snobson, it is not the fashion to introduce in France!
SNOBSON: But, Marm, we're in America. (*Mrs. Tiffany crosses to Count.*) The woman thinks she's somewhere else than where she is — she wants to make an *alibi*? (*Aside*) 175
MRS. TIFFANY: I hope that we shall have the pleasure of seeing you on Friday evening, Count?
COUNT: Really, Madam, my invitations — my engagements — so numerous — I can hardly answer for myself: and you Americans take offence so easily — 180
MRS. TIFFANY: But, Count, everybody expects you at our ball — you are the principal attraction —
SERAPHINA: Count, you *must* come!
COUNT: Since you insist — aw — aw — there's no resisting you, Miss Tiffany. 185
MRS. TIFFANY: I am so thankful. How can I repay your condescension. (*Count and Seraphina converse.*) Mr. Snobson, will you walk this way? — I have *such* a cactus in full bloom — remarkable flower! Mr. Tiffany, pray come here — I have something particular to say.
TIFFANY: Then speak out, my dear — I thought it was highly improper 190 just now to leave a girl with a young man? (*Aside to her*)
MRS. TIFFANY: Oh, but the Count, — that is different!
TIFFANY: I suppose you mean to say there's nothing of *the man* about him?

(*Enter Millinette with a scarf in her hand.*)

MILLINETTE: A-dolph tell me he vas here. (*Aside*) Pardon, Madame, I bring dis scarf for Mademoiselle. 195
MRS. TIFFANY: Very well, Millinette; you know best what is proper for her to wear.

(*Mr. and Mrs. Tiffany and Snobson retire up stage; she engages the attention of both gentlemen.*)

(*Millinette crosses towards Seraphina, gives the Count a threatening look, and commences arranging the scarf over Seraphina's shoulders.*)

MILLINETTE: Mademoiselle, *permettez-moi. Perfide!* (*Aside to Count*) If Mademoiselle vil stand *tranquille* one *petit moment.* (*Turns Seraphina's back to the Count, and pretends to arrange the scarf*) I must speak vid you to-day, or 200 I tell all — you find me at de foot of de stair ven you go. *Prends garde!* (*Aside to Count*)

SERAPHINA: What is that you say, Millinette?

MILLINETTE: Dis scarf make you so very beautiful, Mademoiselle, — *Je vous salue, mes dames.* (*Curtsies. Exit.*)

COUNT: Not a moment to lose! (*Aside*) Miss Tiffany, I have an unpleasant 205 — a particularly unpleasant piece of intelligence — you see, I have just received a letter from my friend the — aw — the Earl of Airshire; the truth is, the Earl's daughter — beg you won't mention it — has distinguished me by a tender *penchant.*

SERAPHINA: I understand — and they wish you to return and marry the 210 young lady; but surely you will not leave us, Count?

COUNT: If *you* bid me stay — I shouldn't have the conscience — I couldn't *afford* to tear myself away. I'm sure that's honest. (*Aside*)

SERAPHINA: Oh, Count!

COUNT: Say but one word — say that you shouldn't mind being made a 215 Countess — and I'll break with the Earl tomorrow.

SERAPHINA: Count, this surprise — but don't think of leaving the country, Count — we could not pass the time without you! I — yes, yes, Count — I do consent!

COUNT: I thought she would! (*Aside, while he embraces her*) Enchanted, rap- 220 ture, bliss, ecstasy, and all that sort of thing — words can't express it, but you understand. But it must be kept a secret — positively it *must!* If the rumour of our engagement were whispered abroad — the Earl's daughter — the delicacy of my situation, aw — you comprehend? It is even possible that our nuptials, my charming Miss Tiffany, *our nuptials* must 225 take place in private!

SERAPHINA: Oh, that is quite impossible!

COUNT: It's the latest fashion abroad — the very latest! Ah, I knew that would determine you. Can I depend on your secrecy?

SERAPHINA: Oh, yes! Believe me. 230

SNOBSON (*Coming forward in spite of Mrs. Tiffany's efforts to detain him*): Why, Seraphina, haven't you a word to throw to a dog?

TIFFANY: I shouldn't think she had after wasting so many upon a puppy. (*Aside*)

(*Enter Zeke, wearing a three-cornered hat.*)

ZEKE: Missus, de bran new carriage am below.

MRS. TIFFANY: Show it up, — I mean, — very well, A-dolph. (*Exit Zeke.*)   235
Count, my daughter and I are about to take an airing in our new *voyture*,
— will you honour us with your company?

COUNT: Madam, I — I have a most *pressing* engagement. A letter to write
to the *Earl of Airshire* — who is at present residing in the *Isle of Skye*. I
must bid you good-morning.   240

MRS. TIFFANY: Good-morning, Count.   (*Exit Count.*)

SNOBSON: I'm quite at leisure, (*Crosses to Mrs. Tiffany*) Marm. Books
balanced — ledger closed — nothing to do all the afternoon — I'm for
you.

MRS. TIFFANY (*Without noticing him*): Come, Seraphina, come!   245

(*As they are going, Snobson follows them.*)

SNOBSON: But, Marm — I was saying, Marm, I am quite at leisure — not
a thing to do; have I, Mr. Tiffany?

MRS. TIFFANY: Seraphina, child — your red shawl — remember — Mr.
Snobson, *bon swear!*   (*Exit, leading Seraphina.*)

SNOBSON: Swear! Mr. Tiffany, sir, am I to be fobbed off with a *bon swear?*   250
D —— n it, I will swear!

TIFFANY: Have patience, Mr. Snobson, if you will accompany me to the
counting-house —

SNOBSON: Don't count too much on me, sir. I'll make up no more accounts
until these are settled! I'll run down and jump into the carriage in spite   255
of her *bon swear.*   (*Exit.*)

TIFFANY: You'll jump into a hornet's nest, if you do! Mr. Snobson, Mr.
Snobson!   (*Exit after him.*)

SCENE II

Housekeeper's Room. Enter Millinette.

MILLINETTE: I have set dat *bête,* Adolph, to vatch for him. He say he
would come back so soon as Madame's *voiture* drive from de door. If he
not come — but he vill — he vill — he *bien étourdi,* but he have *bon
coeur.*

(*Enter Count.*)

COUNT: Ah! Millinette, my dear, you see what a good-natured dog I am to   5
fly at your bidding —

MILLINETTE: Fly? Ah! *trompeur!* Vat for you fly from Paris? Vat for you leave me — and I love you so much? Ven you sick — you almost die — did I not stay by you — take care of you — and you have no else friend? Vat for you leave Paris? 10

COUNT: Never allude to disagreeable subjects, *mon enfant!* I was forced by uncontrollable circumstances to fly to the land of liberty —

MILLINETTE: Vat you do vid all de money I give you? The last sou I had — did I not give you?

COUNT: I dare say you did, *ma petite* — wish you'd been better supplied! 15 (*Aside*) Don't ask any questions here — can't explain now — the next time we meet —

MILLINETTE: But, ah! ven shall ve meet — ven? You not deceive me, not any more.

COUNT: Deceive you! I'd rather deceive myself — I wish I could! I'd per- 20 suade myself you were once more washing linen in the Seine! (*Aside*)

MILLINETTE: I vil tell you ven we shall meet — On Friday night Madame give one grand ball — you come *sans doute* — den ven de supper is served — de Americans tink of noting else ven de supper come — den you steal out of de room, and you find me here — and you give me one 25 grand *explanation!*

(*Enter Gertrude, unperceived.*)

COUNT: Friday night — while supper is serving — *parole d'honneur* I will be here — I will explain every thing — my sudden departure from Paris — my — demme, my countship — every thing! Now let me go — if any of the family should discover us — 30

GERTRUDE (*Who during the last speech has gradually advanced*): They might dis- cover more than you think it advisable for them to know!

COUNT: The devil!

MILLINETTE: *Mon Dieu!* Mademoiselle Gertrude!

COUNT (*Recovering himself*): My dear Miss Gertrude, let me explain — aw — 35 aw — nothing is more natural than the situation in which you find me —

GERTRUDE: I am inclined to believe that, sir.

COUNT: Now — 'pon my honour, that's not fair. Here is Millinette will bear witness to what I am about to say —

GERTRUDE: Oh, I have not the slightest doubt of that, sir. 40

COUNT: You see, Millinette happened to be lady's-maid in the family of — of — the Duchess Chateau D'Espagne — and I chanced to be a par- ticular friend of the Duchess — *very particular* I assure you! Of course I saw Millinette, and she, demme, she saw me! Didn't you, Millinette?

MILLINETTE: Oh! *oui* — Mademoiselle, I knew him ver well.   45

COUNT: Well, it is a remarkable fact that — being in correspondence with this very Duchess — at this very time —

GERTRUDE: That is sufficient, sir — I am already so well acquainted with your extraordinary talents for improvisation, that I will not further tax your invention —   50

MILLINETTE: Ah! Mademoiselle Gertrude, do not betray us — have pity!

COUNT (*Assuming an air of dignity*):   Silence, Millinette! My word has been doubted — the word of a nobleman! I will inform my friend, Mrs. Tiffany, of this young person's audacity. (*Going*)

GERTRUDE: His own weapons alone can foil this villain! (*Aside*) Sir —   55
sir — Count! (*At the last word the Count turns.*) Perhaps, sir, the least said about this matter the better!

COUNT (*Delightedly*):   The least said? We won't say anything at all. She's coming round — couldn't resist me! (*Aside*) Charming Gertrude —

MILLINETTE: *Quoi?* Vat that you say?   60

COUNT: My sweet, adorable Millinette, hold your tongue, will you? (*Aside to her*)

MILLINETTE (*Aloud*):   No, I vill not! If you do look so from out your eyes at her again, I vill tell all!

COUNT: Oh, I never could manage two women at once, — jealousy makes the dear creatures so spiteful. The only valour is in flight. (*Aside*)   65
Miss Gertrude, I wish you good-morning. Millinette, *mon enfant, adieu.*
(*Exit.*)

MILLINETTE: But I have one word more to say. Stop! Stop! (*Exit after him.*)

GERTRUDE (*Musingly*):   Friday night, while supper is serving, he is to meet Millinette here and explain — what? This man is an impostor! His insulting me — his familiarity with Millinette — his whole conduct —   70
prove it. If I tell Mrs. Tiffany this, she will disbelieve me, and one word may place this so-called Count on his guard. To convince Seraphina would be equally difficult, and her rashness and infatuation may render her miserable for life. No — she shall be saved! I must devise some plan for opening their eyes. Truly, if I *cannot* invent one, I shall be the first   75
woman who was ever at a loss for a stratagem — especially to punish a villain or to shield a friend.   (*Exit.*)

ACT IV, SCENE I

Ballroom splendidly illuminated. A curtain hung at the further end. Mr. and Mrs. Tiffany, Seraphina, Gertrude, Fogg, Twinkle, Count, Snobson, Colonel Howard, a number of guests — some seated, some standing. As the curtain rises, a cotillion is danced; Gertrude dancing with Howard, Seraphina with Count.

COUNT (*Advancing with Seraphina to the front of the stage*): To-morrow then — to-morrow — I may salute you as my bride — demme, my Countess!

(*Enter Zeke with refreshments.*)

SERAPHINA: Yes, to-morrow.

(*As the Count is about to reply, Snobson thrusts himself in front of Seraphina.*)

SNOBSON: You said you'd dance with me, Miss — now take my fin, and we'll walk about and see what's going on.   5

(*Count raises his eye-glass, regards Snobson, and leads Seraphina away; Snobson follows, endeavouring to attract her attention, but encounters Zeke, bearing a waiter of refreshments; stops, helps himself, and puts some in his pockets.*)

Here's the treat! get my to-morrow's luncheon out of Tiff.

(*Enter Trueman, yawning and rubbing his eyes.*)

TRUEMAN: What a nap I've had, to be sure! (*Looks at his watch*) Eleven o'clock, as I'm alive! Just the time when country folks are comfortably *turned in,* and here your grand *turnout* has hardly begun yet! (*To Tiffany, who approaches*)

GERTRUDE (*Advancing*): I was just coming to look for you, Mr. Trueman. I   10
began to fancy that you were paying a visit to dream-land.

TRUEMAN: So I was child — so I was — and I saw a face — like yours — but brighter! — even brighter. (*To Tiffany*) There's a smile for you, man! It makes one feel that the world has something worth living for in it yet! Do you remember a smile like that, Antony? Ah! I see you don't — but I   15
do — I do! (*Much moved*)

HOWARD (*Advancing*): Good evening, Mr. Trueman. (*Offers his hand*)

TRUEMAN: That's right, man; give me your whole hand! When a man offers me the tips of his fingers, I know at once there's nothing in him worth seeking beyond his fingers' ends.   20

(*Trueman and Howard, Gertrude and Tiffany converse.*)

MRS. TIFFANY (*Advancing*): I'm in such a fidget lest that vulgar old fellow should disgrace us by some of his plebeian remarks! What it is to give a ball, when one is forced to invite vulgar people!

(*Mrs. Tiffany advances towards Trueman; Seraphina stands conversing flippantly with the gentlemen who surround her; amongst them is Twinkle, who, having taken a magazine from his pocket, is reading to her, much to the undisguised annoyance of Snobson.*)

Dear me, Mr. Trueman, you are very late — quite in the fashion, I declare!

TRUEMAN: Fashion! And pray what is *fashion*, Madam? An agreement between certain persons to live without using their souls! to substitute etiquette for virtue — decorum for purity — manners for morals! to affect a shame for the works of their Creator! and expend all their rapture upon the works of their tailors and dressmakers!

MRS. TIFFANY: You have the most *ow-tray* ideas, Mr. Trueman — quite rustic, and deplorably *American!* But pray walk this way. (*Mrs. Tiffany and Trueman go up stage.*)

COUNT (*Advancing to Gertrude, who stands centre, Howard a short distance behind her*): Miss Gertrude — no opportunity of speaking to you before — in demand, you know!

GERTRUDE: I have no choice, I must be civil to him. (*Aside*) What were you remarking, sir?

COUNT: Miss Gertrude — charming Ger — aw — aw — I never found it so difficult to speak to a woman before. (*Aside*)

GERTRUDE: Yes, a very charming ball — many beautiful faces here.

COUNT: Only one! — aw — aw — one — the fact is — (*Talks to her in dumb show*)

HOWARD: What could old Trueman have meant by saying she fancied that puppy of a Count — that paste-jewel thrust upon the little finger of society.

COUNT: Miss Gertrude — aw — 'pon my honour — you don't understand — really — aw — aw — will you dance the polka with me?

(*Gertrude bows and gives him her hand; he leads her to the set forming; Howard remains looking after them.*)

HOWARD: Going to dance with him, too! A few days ago she would hardly bow to him civilly — could old Trueman have had reasons for what he said? (*Retires*)

(*Dance, the polka; Seraphina, after having distributed her bouquet, vinaigrette and fan amongst the gentlemen, dances with Snobson.*)

PRUDENCE (*Peeping in, as dance concludes*):   I don't like dancing on Friday; something strange is always sure to happen! I'll be on the look out.

(*Remains peeping and concealing herself when any of the company approach*)

GERTRUDE (*Advancing hastily to center*):   They are preparing the supper —   50
now, if I can only dispose of Millinette while I unmask this insolent pre-
tender!   (*Exit.*)

PRUDENCE (*Peeping*):   What's that she said? It's coming!

(*Reenter Gertrude, bearing a small basket filled with bouquets; approaches Mrs.
Tiffany; they walk to the front of the stage.*)

GERTRUDE: Excuse me, Madam — I believe this is just the hour at which
you ordered supper?   55

MRS. TIFFANY: Well, what's that to you! So, you've been dancing with the
Count — how dare you dance with a nobleman — *you?*

GERTRUDE: I will answer that question half an hour hence. At present I
have something to propose, which I think will gratify you and please your
guests. I have heard that at the most elegant balls in Paris, it is custom-   60
ary —

MRS. TIFFANY: What? what?

GERTRUDE: To station a servant at the door with a basket of flowers. A
bouquet is then presented to every lady as she passes in — I prepared this
basket a short time ago. As the company walk in to supper, might not the   65
flowers be distributed to advantage?

MRS. TIFFANY: How *distingué!* You are a good creature, Gertrude — there,
run and hand the *bokettes* to them yourself! You shall have the whole
credit of the thing.

GERTRUDE: Caught in my own net! (*Aside*) But, Madam, I know so little of   70
fashions — Millinette, being French, herself will do it with so much
more grace. I am sure Millinette —

MRS. TIFFANY: So am I. She will do it a thousand times better than you —
there, go call her.

GERTRUDE (*Giving basket*):   But, Madam, pray order Millinette not to leave   75
her station till supper is ended — as the company pass out of the supper
room she may find that some of the ladies have been overlooked.

MRS. TIFFANY: That is true — very thoughtful of you, Gertrude. (*Exit
Gertrude.*) What a *recherché* idea!

(*Enter Millinette.*)

Here, Millinette, take this basket. Place yourself there, (*Center*) and dis- 80
tribute these *bokettes* as the company pass in to supper; but remember not
to stir from the spot until supper is over. It is a French fashion, you know,

Millinette. I am so delighted to be the first to introduce it — it will be all the rage in the *bowmonde!*

MILLINETTE: *Mon Dieu!* dis vill ruin all! (*Aside*) Madame, madame, let me   85
tell you, Madame, dat in France, in Paris, it is de custom to present *les* bouquets ven everybody first come — long before de supper. Dis would be *outré! barbare!* not at all *la mode!* Ven dey do come in, dat is de fashion in Paris!

MRS. TIFFANY: Dear me! Millinette, what is the difference? besides, I'd   90
have you to know that Americans always improve upon French fashions! here, take the basket, and let me see that you do it in the most *you-nick* and genteel manner.

(*Millinette poutingly takes the basket and retires up stage. A march. Curtain hung at the further end of the room is drawn back, and discloses a room, in the center of which stands a supper-table, beautifully decorated and illuminated; the company promenade two by two into the supper room; Millinette presents bouquets as they pass; Count leads Mrs. Tiffany.*)

TRUEMAN (*Encountering Fogg, who is hurrying alone to the supper room*):   Mr. Fogg, never mind the supper, man! Ha, ha, ha! Of course you are indif-   95
ferent to suppers!

FOGG: Indifferent! suppers — oh, ah — no, sir — suppers? no — no — I'm not indifferent to suppers. (*Hurries away towards table*)

TRUEMAN: Ha, ha, ha! Here's a new discovery I've made in the fashionable world! Fashion don't permit the critters to have *heads* or *hearts*, but it al-   100
lows them stomachs! (*To Tiffany, who advances*) So, it's not fashionable to *feel*, but it's fashionable to *feed*, eh, Antony? Ha, ha, ha!

(*Trueman and Tiffany retire towards supper room.*)

(*Enter Gertrude, followed by Zeke.*)

GERTRUDE: Zeke, go to the supper room instantly, — whisper to Count Jolimaitre that all is ready, and that he must keep his appointment with-out delay, — then watch him, and as he passes out of the room, place   105
yourself in front of Millinette in such a manner, that the Count cannot see her nor she him. Be sure that they do not see each other — everything depends upon that. (*Crosses to right*)

ZEKE: Missy, consider dat business brought to a scientific conclusion.

(*Exit into supper room. Exit Gertrude.*)

PRUDENCE (*Who has been listening*):   What can she want of the Count? I   110
always suspected that Gertrude, because she is so merry and busy! Mr. Trueman thinks so much of her, too, — I'll tell him this! There's

something wrong — but it all comes of giving a ball on a Friday! How astonished the dear old man will be when he finds out how much I know! (*Advances timidly towards the supper room*)

SCENE II

Housekeeper's room; dark stage; table, two chairs. Enter Gertrude, with a lighted candle in her hand.

GERTRUDE: So far the scheme prospers! and yet this imprudence — if I fail? Fail! to lack courage in a difficulty, or ingenuity in a dilemma, are not woman's failings!

(*Enter Zeke, with a napkin over his arm, and a bottle of champagne in his hand.*)

Well, Zeke — Adolph!

ZEKE: Dat's right, Missy; I feels just now as if dat was my legitimate title;   5
dis here's de stuff to make a nigger feel like a gemman!

GERTRUDE: But is he coming?

ZEKE: He's coming! (*Sound of a champagne cork heard*) Do you hear dat, Missy? Don't it put you all in a froth, and make you feel as light as a cork? Dere's nothing like the *union brand,* to wake up de harmonies ob de heart.   10
(*Drinks from bottle*)

GERTRUDE: Remember to keep watch upon the outside — do not stir from the spot; when I call you, come in quickly with a light — now, will you be gone!

ZEKE: I'm off, Missy, like a champagne cork wid de strings cut.   (*Exit.*)

GERTRUDE: I think I hear the Count's step. (*Crosses left; stage dark; she blows*   15
out candle.) Now, if I can but disguise my voice, and make the best of my French.

(*Enter Count.*)

COUNT: Millinette, where are you? How am I to see you in the dark?

GERTRUDE (*Imitating Millinette's voice in a whisper*):   Hush! *parle bas.*

COUNT: Come here and give me a kiss.   20

GERTRUDE: Non — non — (*Retreating, alarmed; Count follows.*) make haste, I must know all.

COUNT: You did not use to be so deuced particular.

ZEKE (*Without*):   No admission, gemman! Box office closed, tickets stopped!   25

TRUEMAN (*Without*):   Out of my way; do you want me to try if your head is as hard as my stick?

GERTRUDE: What shall I do? Ruined, ruined!

(*She stands with her hands clasped in speechless despair.*)

COUNT: Halloa! they are coming here, Millinette! Millinette, why don't
you speak? Where can I hide myself? (*Running about stage, feeling for a door*)   30
Where are all your closets? If I could only get out — or get in somewhere; may I be smothered in a clothes basket, if you ever catch me in
such a scrape again! (*His hand accidentally touches the knob of a door opening into
a closet.*) Fortune's favorite yet! I'm safe!

(*Gets into closet, and closes door. Enter Prudence, Trueman, Mrs. Tiffany, and Colonel
Howard, followed by Zeke, bearing a light.*)

PRUDENCE: Here they are, the Count and Gertrude! I told you so! (*Stops in*   35
surprise on seeing only Gertrude)
TRUEMAN: And you see what a lie you told!
MRS. TIFFANY: Prudence, how dare you create this disturbance in my
house? To suspect the Count, too — a nobleman!
HOWARD: My sweet Gertrude, this foolish old woman would —
PRUDENCE: Oh! you needn't talk — I heard her make the appointment —   40
I know he's here — or he's been here. I wonder if she hasn't hid him
away! (*Runs peeping about the room*)
TRUEMAN (*Following her angrily*):   You're what I call a confounded — trou-
blesome — meddling — old — prying — (*As he says the last word, Prudence
opens closet where the Count is concealed.*) Thunder and lightning!   45
PRUDENCE: I told you so!

(*They all stand aghast; Mrs. Tiffany, with her hands lifted in surprise and anger;
Trueman, clutching his stick; Howard, looking with an expression of bewildered horror
from the Count to Gertrude.*)

MRS. TIFFANY (*Shaking her fist at Gertrude*):   You depraved little minx! this is
the meaning of your dancing with the Count!
COUNT (*Stepping from the closet and advancing*):   I don't know what to make of
it! Millinette not here! Miss Gertrude — Oh! I see — a disguise — the   50
girl's desperate about me — the way with them all. (*Aside*)
TRUEMAN: I'm choking — I can't speak — Gertrude — no — no — it is
some horrid mistake! (*Partly aside, changes his tone suddenly*) The villain! I'll
hunt the truth out of him, if there's any in — (*Approaches Count threateningly*)
Do you see this stick? You made its first acquaintance a few days ago; it   55
is time you were better known to each other.

(*As Trueman attempts to seize him, Count escapes and shields himself behind Mrs.
Tiffany, Trueman following.*)

COUNT: You ruffian! would you strike a woman? — Madam — my dear
Madam — keep off that barbarous old man, and I will explain! Madam,
with — aw — your natural *bon gout* — aw — your fashionable refinement — aw — your — aw — your knowledge of *foreign customs* —   60

MRS. TIFFANY: Oh! Count, I hope it ain't a *foreign custom* for the nobility
to shut themselves up in the dark with young women? We think such
things *dreadful* in *America.*

COUNT: Demme — aw — hear what I have to say, Madam — I'll satisfy
all sides — I am perfectly innocent in this affair — 'pon my honour I   65
am! That young lady shall inform you that I am so herself! — can't
help it, sorry for her. Old matter-of-fact won't be convinced any other
way, — that club of his is so particularly unpleasant! (*Aside*) Madam, I
was summoned here *malgré moi*, and not knowing whom I was to meet
— Miss Gertrude, favour this company by saying whether or not you   70
directed — that — aw — aw — that coloured individual to conduct me
here?

GERTRUDE: Sir, you well know —

COUNT: A simple yes or no will suffice.

MRS. TIFFANY: Answer the Count's question instantly, Miss.   75

GERTRUDE: I did — but —

COUNT: You hear, Madam —

TRUEMAN: I won't believe it — I can't! Here, you nigger, stop rolling up
your eyes, and let us know whether she told you to bring that critter here?

ZEKE: I'se refuse to gib ebidence; dat's de device ob de skillfullest counsels   80
ob de day! Can't answer, Boss — neber git a word out ob dis child —
Yah! yah!   (*Exit.*)

GERTRUDE: Mrs. Tiffany, — Mr. Trueman, if you will but have patience —

TRUEMAN: Patience! Oh, Gertrude, you've taken from an old man something better and dearer than his patience — the one bright hope of nine-   85
teen years of self-denial — of nineteen years of —

(*Throws himself upon a chair, his head leaning on table*)

MRS. TIFFANY: Get out of my house, you *ow*dacious — you ruined — you
abimé young woman! You will corrupt all my family. Good gracious! don't
touch me, — don't come near me. Never let me see your face after to-
morrow. Pack. (*Goes up stage*)   90

HOWARD: Gertrude, I have striven to find some excuse for you — to doubt
— to disbelieve — but this is beyond all endurance!   (*Exit.*)

(*Enter Millinette in haste.*)

MILLINETTE: I could not come before — (*Stops in surprise at seeing the persons assembled*) *Mon Dieu!* Vat does dis mean?

COUNT: Hold your tongue, fool! You will ruin everything. I will explain to-morrow. (*Aside to her*) Mrs. Tiffany — Madam — my dear Madam, let me conduct you back to the ballroom. (*She takes his arm.*) You see I am quite innocent in this matter; a man of my standing, you know, — aw, aw — you comprehend the whole affair.

(*Exit Count leading Mrs. Tiffany.*)

MILLINETTE: I vill say to him von vord, I vill!   (*Exit.*)

GERTRUDE: Mr. Trueman, I beseech you — I insist upon being heard, — I claim it as a right!

TRUEMAN: Right? How dare you have the face, girl, to talk of rights? (*Comes down stage*) You had more rights than you thought for, but you have forfeited them all! All right to love, respect, protection, and to not a little else that you don't dream of. Go, go! I'll start for Catteraugus to-morrow, — I've seen enough of what fashion can do!   (*Exit.*)

PRUDENCE (*Wiping her eyes*):   Dear old man, how he takes on! I'll go and console him!   (*Exit.*)

GERTRUDE: This is too much! How heavy a penalty has my imprudence cost me! — his esteem, and that of one dearer — my home — my — (*Burst of lively music from ball-room*) They are dancing, and I — I should be weeping, if pride had not sealed up my tears.

(*She sinks into a chair. Band plays the polka behind till curtain falls.*)

ACT V

Mrs. Tiffany's Drawing-room — same scene as Act I. Gertrude seated at a table, with her head leaning on her hand; in the other hand she holds a pen. A sheet of paper and an inkstand before her.

GERTRUDE: How shall I write to them? What shall I say? Prevaricate I cannot — (*Rises and comes forward*) and yet if I write the truth — simple souls! how can they comprehend the motives for my conduct? Nay — the truly pure see no imaginary evil in others! It is only vice, that reflecting in its own image, suspects even the innocent. I have no time to lose — I must prepare them for my return. (*Resumes her seat and writes*) What a true pleasure there is in daring to be frank! (*After writing a few lines more, pauses*) Not so frank, either — there is one name that I cannot mention. Ah! that he should suspect — should despise me. (*Writes*)

(*Enter Trueman.*)

TRUEMAN: There she is! If this girl's soul had only been as fair as her face, — yet she dared to speak the truth, — I'll not forget that! A woman who refuses to tell a lie has one spark of heaven in her still. (*Approaches her*) Gertrude, (*Gertrude starts and looks up.*) what are you writing there? Plotting more mischief, eh, girl?

GERTRUDE: I was writing a few lines to some friends in Geneva.

TRUEMAN: The Wilsons, eh?

GERTRUDE (*Surprised, rising*):   Are you acquainted with them, sir?

TRUEMAN: I shouldn't wonder if I was. I suppose you have taken good care not to mention the dark room — that foreign puppy in the closet — the pleasant surprise — and all that sort of thing, eh?

GERTRUDE: I have no reason for concealment, sir! for I have done nothing of which I am ashamed!

TRUEMAN: Then I can't say much for your modesty.

GERTRUDE: I should not wish you to say more than I deserve.

TRUEMAN: There's a bold minx! (*Aside*)

GERTRUDE: Since my affairs seem to have excited your interest — I will not say *curiosity*, — perhaps you even feel a desire to inspect my correspondence? There, (*Handing the letter*) I pride myself upon my good nature, — you may like to take advantage of it?

TRUEMAN: With what an air she carries it off! (*Aside*) Take advantage of it? So I will. (*Reads*) What's this? "French chambermaid — Count — impostor — infatuation — Seraphina — Millinette — disguised myself — expose him." Thunder and lightning! I see it all! Come and kiss me, girl! (*Gertrude evinces surprise.*) No, no — I forgot — it won't do to come to that yet! She's a rare girl! I'm out of my senses with joy! I don't know what to do with myself! Tol, de rol, de rol, de ra! (*Capers and sings*)

GERTRUDE: What a remarkable old man! (*Aside*) Then you do me justice, Mr. Trueman?

TRUEMAN: I say I don't! Justice? You're above all dependence upon justice! Hurrah! I've found one true woman at last! *True?* (*Pauses thoughtfully*) Humph! I didn't think of that flaw! Plotting and manoeuvering — not much truth in that? An honest girl should be above stratagems!

GERTRUDE: But my *motive*, sir, was good.

TRUEMAN: That's not enough — your *actions* must be *good* as well as your

motives! Why could you not tell the silly girl that the man was an im- 45
postor?

GERTRUDE: I did inform her of my suspicions — she ridiculed them; the
plan I chose was an imprudent one, but I could not devise —

TRUEMAN: I hate devising! Give me a woman with the *firmness* to be
frank! But no matter — I had no right to look for an angel out of Par- 50
adise; and I am as happy — as happy as a lord! that is, ten times happier
than any lord ever was! Tol, de rol, de rol! Oh! you — you — I'll thrash
every fellow that says a word against you!

GERTRUDE: You will have plenty of employment then, sir, for I do not
know of one just now who would speak in my favour! 55

TRUEMAN: Not *one*, eh? Why, where's your dear Mr. Twinkle? I know all
about it — can't say that I admire your choice of a husband! But there's
no accounting for a girl's taste.

GERTRUDE: Mr. Twinkle! Indeed you are quite mistaken!

TRUEMAN: No — really? Then you're not taken with him, eh? 60

GERTRUDE: Not even with his rhymes.

TRUEMAN: Hang that old mother meddle-much! What a fool she has
made of me. And so you're quite free, and I may choose a husband for
you myself? Heart-whole, eh?

GERTRUDE: I — I trust there is nothing *unsound* about my heart. 65

TRUEMAN: There it is again. Don't prevaricate, girl! I tell you an *evasion* is
a *lie in contemplation,* and I hate lying! Out with the truth! Is your heart
free or not?

GERTRUDE: Nay, sir, since you *demand* an answer, permit *me* to demand by
what right you ask the question? 70

(*Enter Howard.*)

Colonel Howard here!

TRUEMAN: I'm out again! What's the Colonel to her? (*Retires up stage*)

HOWARD (*Crosses to her*): I have come, Gertrude, to bid you farewell. To-
morrow I resign my commission and leave this city, perhaps for ever. You,
Gertrude, it is you who have exiled me! After last evening — 75

TRUEMAN (*Coming forward to Howard*): What the plague have you got to say
about last evening?

HOWARD: Mr. Trueman!

TRUEMAN: What have you got to say about last evening? and what have
you to say to that little girl at all? It's Tiffany's precious daughter you're 80
in love with.

HOWARD: Miss Tiffany? Never! I never had the slightest pretension —

TRUEMAN: That lying old woman! But I'm glad of it! Oh! Ah! Um! (*Looking significantly at Gertrude and then at Howard*) I see how it is. So you don't choose to marry Seraphina, eh? Well, now, whom do you choose to marry? (*Glancing at Gertrude*) 85

HOWARD: I shall not marry at all!

TRUEMAN: You won't? (*Looking at them both again*) Why, you don't mean to say that you don't like — (*Points with his thumb to Gertrude*)

GERTRUDE: Mr. Trueman, I may have been wrong to boast of my good nature, but do not presume too far upon it. 90

HOWARD: You like frankness, Mr. Trueman, therefore I will speak plainly. I have long cherished a dream from which I was last night rudely awakened.

TRUEMAN: And that's what you call speaking plainly? Well, I differ with 95 you! But I can guess what you mean. Last night you suspected Gertrude there of — (*Angrily*) of what no man shall ever suspect her again while I'm above ground! You did her injustice, — it was a mistake! There, now that matter's settled. Go, and ask her to forgive you, — she's woman enough to do it! Go, go! 100

HOWARD: Mr. Trueman, you have forgotten to whom you dictate.

TRUEMAN: Then you won't do it? you won't ask her pardon?

HOWARD: Most undoubtedly I will not — not at any man's bidding. I must first know —

TRUEMAN: You won't do it? Then, if I don't give you a lesson in politeness — 105

HOWARD: It will be because you find me your *tutor* in the same science. I am not a man to brook an insult, Mr. Trueman! but we'll not quarrel in the presence of the lady. (*Crosses*)

TRUEMAN: Won't we? I don't know that — 110

GERTRUDE: Pray, Mr. Trueman — Colonel Howard, (*Crosses to center*) pray desist, Mr. Trueman, for my sake! (*Taking hold of his arm to hold him back*) Colonel Howard, if you will read this letter it will explain everything. (*Hands letter to Howard, who reads*)

TRUEMAN: He don't deserve an explanation! Didn't I tell him that it was a mistake? Refuse to beg your pardon! I'll teach him, I'll teach him! 115

HOWARD (*After reading*):   Gertrude, how I have wronged you!

TRUEMAN: Oh! you'll beg her pardon now? (*Between them*)

HOWARD: Hers, sir, and yours! Gertrude, I fear —

TRUEMAN: You needn't, — she'll forgive you. You don't know these women as well as I do, — they're always ready to pardon; it's their nature, 120 and they can't help it. Come along, I left Antony and his wife in the dining-room; we'll go and find them. I've a story of my own to tell! As for you, Colonel, you may follow. Come along, come along! (*Leads out Gertrude, followed by Howard*)

(*Enter Mr. and Mrs. Tiffany. Mr. Tiffany with a bundle of bills in his hand.*)

MRS. TIFFANY: I beg you won't mention the subject again, Mr. Tiffany. Nothing is more plebeian than a discussion upon economy — nothing more *ungenteel* than looking over and fretting over one's bills! 125

TIFFANY: Then I suppose, my dear, it is quite as ungenteel to *pay* one's bills?

MRS. TIFFANY: Certainly! I hear the *ee-light* never condescend to do anything of the kind. The honour of their invaluable patronage is sufficient for the persons they employ! 130

TIFFANY: *Patronage* then is a newly invented food upon which the working-classes fatten? What convenient appetites poor people must have! Now listen to what I am going to say. As soon as my daughter marries Mr. Snobson — 135

(*Enter Prudence, a three-cornered note in her hand.*)

PRUDENCE: Oh, dear! oh, dear! what shall we do? Such a misfortune! Such a disaster! Oh, dear! oh, dear!

MRS. TIFFANY: Prudence, you are the most tiresome creature! What *is* the matter?

PRUDENCE (*Pacing up and down the stage*):   Such a disgrace to the whole family! But I always expected it. Oh, dear! oh, dear! 140

MRS. TIFFANY (*Following her up and down the stage*):   What are you talking about, Prudence? Will you tell me what has happened?

PRUDENCE (*Still pacing, Mrs. Tiffany following*):   Oh! I can't, I can't! You'll feel so dreadfully! How could she do such a thing! But I expected nothing else! I never did, I never did! 145

MRS. TIFFANY (*Still following*):   Good gracious! what do you mean, Prudence? Tell me, will you tell me? I shall get into such a passion! What *is* the matter?

PRUDENCE (*Still pacing*):   Oh, Betsy, Betsy! That your daughter should have come to that! Dear me, dear me! 150

TIFFANY: Seraphina? Did you say Seraphina? What has happened to her? what has she done?

(*Following Prudence up and down the stage on the opposite side from Mrs. Tiffany*)

MRS. TIFFANY (*Still following*):   What *has* she done? What *has* she done?

PRUDENCE: Oh! something dreadful — dreadful — shocking!   155

TIFFANY (*Still following*):   Speak quickly and plainly — you torture me by
this delay, — Prudence, be calm and speak! What is it?

PRUDENCE (*Stopping*):   Zeke just told me — he carried her travelling trunk
himself — she gave him a whole dollar! Oh, my!

TIFFANY: Her trunk? where? where?   160

PRUDENCE: Round the corner!

MRS. TIFFANY: What did she want with her trunk? You are the most vex-
atious creature, Prudence! There is no bearing your ridiculous conduct!

PRUDENCE: Oh, you will have worse to bear — worse! Seraphina's gone!

TIFFANY: Gone! where?   165

PRUDENCE: Off! — eloped — eloped with the Count! Dear me, dear me!
I always told you she would!

TIFFANY: Then I am ruined! (*Stands with his face buried in his hands*)

MRS. TIFFANY: Oh, what a ridiculous girl! And she might have had such a
splendid wedding! What could have possessed her?   170

TIFFANY: The devil himself possessed her, for she has ruined me past all
redemption! Gone, Prudence, did you say gone? Are you *sure* they are
gone?

PRUDENCE: Didn't I tell you so! Just look at this note — one might know
by the very fold of it —   175

TIFFANY (*Snatching the note*):   Let me see it! (*Opens the note and reads*) "My
dear Ma, — When you receive this I shall be a *countess!* Isn't it a sweet
title? The Count and I were forced to be married privately, for reasons which I will explain in my next. You must pacify Pa, and put him
in a good humour before I come back, though now I'm to be a count-   180
ess I suppose I shouldn't care!" Undutiful huzzy! "We are going to
make a little excursion and will be back in a week. Your dutiful daughter — Seraphina." A man's curse is sure to spring up at his own hearth, —
here is mine! The sole curb upon that villain gone, I am wholly
in his power! Oh! the first downward step from honour — he who   185
takes it cannot pause in his mad descent and is sure to be hurried on to
ruin!

MRS. TIFFANY: Why, Mr. Tiffany, how you do take on! And I dare say to
elope was the most fashionable way after all!

(*Enter Trueman, leading Gertrude, and followed by Howard.*)

TRUEMAN: Where are all the folks? Here, Antony, you are the man I want.   190
We've been hunting for you all over the house. Why — what's the matter? There's a face for a thriving city merchant! Ah! Antony, you never
wore such a hang-dog look as that when you trotted about the country

with your pack upon your back! Your shoulders are no broader now — but they've a heavier load to carry — that's plain! 195

MRS. TIFFANY: Mr. Trueman, such allusions are highly improper! What would my daughter, *the Countess,* say!

GERTRUDE: The Countess? Oh! Madam!

MRS. TIFFANY: Yes, the Countess! My daughter Seraphina, the Countess *dee* Jolimaitre! What have you to say to that? No wonder you are surprised 200 after your *recherché, abimé* conduct! I have told you already, Miss Gertrude, that you were not a proper person to enjoy the inestimable advantages of my patronage. You are dismissed — do you understand? Discharged!

TRUEMAN: Have you done? Very well, it's my turn now. Antony, perhaps what I have to say don't concern you as much as some others — but I 205 want you to listen to me. You remember, Antony, (*His tone becomes serious.*) a blue-eyed, smiling girl —

TIFFANY: Your daughter, sir? I remember her well.

TRUEMAN: None ever saw her to forget her! Give me your hand, man. There — that will do! Now let me go on. I never coveted wealth — yet 210 twenty years ago I found myself the richest farmer in Catteraugus. This cursed money made my girl an object of speculation. Every idle fellow that wanted to feather his nest was sure to come courting Ruth. There was one — my heart misgave me the instant I laid eyes upon him — for he was a city chap, and not over-fond of the truth. But Ruth — ah! she 215 was too pure herself to look for guile! His fine words and his fair looks — the old story — she was taken with him — I said, "no" — but the girl liked her own way better than her old father's — girls always do! and one morning — the rascal robbed me — not of my money, — he would have been welcome to that — but of the only treasure I cherished — my 220 daughter!

TIFFANY: But you forgave her!

TRUEMAN: I did! I knew she would never forgive herself — that was punishment enough! The scoundrel thought he was marrying my gold with my daughter — he was mistaken! I took care that they should never 225 want; but that was all. She loved him — what will not woman love? The villain broke her heart — mine was tougher, or it wouldn't have stood what it did. A year after they were married, he forsook her! She came back to her old home — her old father! It couldn't last long — she pined — and pined — and — then — she died! Don't think me an old fool — 230 though I am one — for grieving won't bring her back. (*Bursts into tears*)

TIFFANY: It was a heavy loss.

TRUEMAN: So heavy that I should not have cared how soon I followed her, but for the child she left! As I pressed that child in my arms, I swore that

my unlucky wealth should never curse it, as it had cursed its mother! It   235
was all I had to love — but I sent it away — and the neighbors thought
it was dead. The girl was brought up tenderly but humbly by my wife's
relatives in Geneva. I had her taught true independence — she had
hands — capacities — and should use them! Money should never buy
her a husband! For I resolved not to claim her until she had made her   240
choice, and found the man who was willing to take her for herself alone.
She turned out a rare girl! and it's time her old grandfather claimed her.
Here he is to do it! And there stands Ruth's child! Old Adam's heiress!
Gertrude, Gertrude! — my child! (*Gertrude rushes into his arms.*)

PRUDENCE (*After a pause*):   Do tell; I want to know! But I knew it! I always   245
said Gertrude would turn out somebody, after all!

MRS. TIFFANY: Dear me! Gertrude an heiress! My dear Gertrude, I always
thought you a very charming girl — quite YOU-NICK — an heiress! I
must give her a ball! I'll introduce her into society myself — of course an
heiress must make a sensation! (*Aside*)   250

HOWARD: I am too bewildered even to wish her joy. Ah! there will be plenty
to do that now — but the gulf between us is wider than ever. (*Aside*)

TRUEMAN: Step forward, young man, and let us know what you are mut-
tering about. I said I would never claim her until she had found the man
who loved her for herself. I *have* claimed her — yet I never break my   255
word — I think I *have* found that man! and here he is. (*Strikes Howard on
the shoulder.*) Gertrude's yours! There — never say a word, man — don't
bore me with your thanks — you can cancel all obligations by making
that child happy! There — take her! — Well, girl, and what do you say?

GERTRUDE: That I rejoice too much at having found a parent for my first   260
act to be one of disobedience! (*Gives her hand to Howard*)

TRUEMAN: How very dutiful! and how disinterested!

(*Tiffany retires — and paces the stage, exhibiting great agitation.*)

PRUDENCE (*To Trueman*):   All the *single folks* are getting married!

TRUEMAN: No they are not. You and I are single folks, and we're not likely
to get married.   265

MRS. TIFFANY: My dear Mr. Trueman — my sweet Gertrude, when my
daughter, the Countess, returns, she will be delighted to hear of this
deenooment! I assure you that the Countess will be quite charmed!

GERTRUDE: The Countess? Pray, Madam, where *is* Seraphina?

MRS. TIFFANY: The Countess *dee* Jolimaitre, my dear, is at this moment on   270
her way to — to Washington! Where, after visiting all the fashionable
curiosities of the day — including the President — she will return to
grace her native city!

GERTRUDE: I hope you are only jesting, Madam? Seraphina is not married?

MRS. TIFFANY: Excuse me, my dear, my daughter had this morning the   275
honour of being united to the Count *dee* Jolimaitre!

GERTRUDE: Madam! He is an impostor!

MRS. TIFFANY: Good gracious! Gertrude, how can you talk in that disre-
spectful way of a man of rank? An heiress, my dear, should have better
manners! The Count —   280

(*Enter Millinette, crying.*)

MILLINETTE: Oh! Madame! I will tell everything — oh! dat monstre! He
break my heart!

MRS. TIFFANY: Millinette, what is the matter?

MILLINETTE: Oh! he promise to marry me — I love him much — and
now Zeke say he run away vid Mademoiselle Seraphina!   285

MRS. TIFFANY: What insolence! The girl is mad! Count Jolimaitre marry
my *femmy de chamber!*

MILLINETTE: Oh! Madame, he is not one Count, not at all! Dat is only de
title he go by in dis country. De foreigners always take de large title ven
dey do come here. His name *à Paris* vas Gustave Tread-mill. But he not   290
one Frenchman at all, but he do live one long time *à Paris.* First he live
vid Monsieur Vermicelle — dere he vas de head cook! Den he live vid
Monsieur Tire-nez, de barber! After dat he live vid Monsieur le Comte
Frippon-fin — and dere he vas le Comte's valet. Dere, now I tell
everyting, I feel one great deal better!   295

MRS. TIFFANY: Oh! good gracious! I shall faint! Not a Count! What will
everybody say? It's no such thing! I say he *is* a Count! One can see the
foreign *jenny says quoi* in his face! Don't you think I can tell a Count
when I see one? I say he *is* a Count!

(*Enter Snobson, his hat on — his hands thrust in his pocket — evidently a little intoxicated.*)

SNOBSON: I won't stand it! I say I won't!   300

TIFFANY (*Rushing up to him*):   Mr. Snobson, for heaven's sake — (*Aside*)

SNOBSON: Keep off. I'm a hard customer to get the better of! You'll see if I
don't come out strong!

TRUEMAN (*Quietly knocking off Snobson's hat with his stick*):   Where are your
manners, man?   305

SNOBSON: My business ain't with you, Catteraugus; you've waked up the
wrong passenger! — Now the way I'll put it into Tiff will be a caution.
I'll make him wince! That extra mint julep has put the true pluck in me.
Now for it! (*Aside*) Mr. Tiffany, sir — you needn't think to come over

me, sir — you'll have to get up a little earlier in the morning before you   310
do *that*, sir! I'd like to know, sir, how you came to assist your daughter in
running away with that foreign loafer? It was a downright swindle, sir.
After the conversation I and you had on that subject she wasn't your
property, sir.

TRUEMAN: What, Antony, is that the way your city clerk bullies his boss?   315

SNOBSON: You're drunk, Catteraugus — don't expose yourself — you're
drunk! Taken a little too much toddy, my old boy! Be quiet! I'll look after you, and they won't find it out. If you want to be busy, you may take
care of my *hat* — I feel so deuced weak in the chest, I don't think I *could*
pick it up myself. — Now to put the screws to Tiff. (*Aside*) Mr. Tiffany,   320
sir — you have broken your word, as no virtuous individual — no honourable member — of — the — com-mu-ni-ty —

TIFFANY: Have some pity, Mr. Snobson, I beseech you! I had nothing to
do with my daughter's elopement! I will agree to anything you desire —
your salary shall be doubled — trebled — (*Aside to him*)   325

SNOBSON (*Aloud*):   No you don't. No bribery and corruption.

TIFFANY: I implore you to be silent. You shall become partner of the concern, if you please — only do not speak. You are not yourself at this moment. (*Aside to him*)

SNOBSON: Ain't I though. I feel *twice* myself. I feel like two Snobsons   330
rolled into one, and I'm chock full of the spunk of a dozen! Now Mr.
Tiffany, sir —

TIFFANY: I shall go distracted! Mr. Snobson, if you have one spark of
manly feeling — (*Aside to him*)

TRUEMAN: Antony, why do you stand disputing with that drunken jack-   335
ass? Where's your nigger? Let him kick the critter out, and be of use for
once in his life.

SNOBSON: Better be quiet, Catteraugus. This ain't your hash, so keep your
spoon out of the dish. Don't expose yourself, old boy.

TRUEMAN: Turn him out, Antony!   340

SNOBSON: He daren't do it! Ain't I up to him? Ain't he in my power? Can't
I knock him into a cocked hat with a word? And now he's got my steam
up — I *will* do it!

TIFFANY (*Beseechingly*):   Mr. Snobson — my friend —

SNOBSON: It's no go — steam's up — and I don't stand at anything!   345

TRUEMAN: You won't *stand* here long unless you mend your manners —
you're not the first man I've *upset* because he didn't know his place.

SNOBSON: I know where Tiff's place is, and that's in the *State's Prison!* It's
bespoke already. He would have it! He wouldn't take pattern of me, and
behave like a gentleman! He's a *forger*, sir!   350

(*Tiffany throws himself into a chair in an attitude of despair; the others stand trans-fixed with astonishment.*)

He's been forging Dick Anderson's endorsements of his notes these ten months. He's got a couple in the bank that will send him to the wall any-how — if he can't make a raise. I took them there myself! Now you know what he's worth. I said I'd expose him, and I have done it!

MRS. TIFFANY: Get out of the house! You ugly, little, drunken brute, get   355
out! It's not true. Mr. Trueman, put him out; you have got a stick — put
him out!

(*Enter Seraphina, in her bonnet and shawl — a parasol in her hand.*)

SERAPHINA: I hope Zeke hasn't delivered my note. (*Stops in surprise at seeing
the persons assembled*)

MRS. TIFFANY: Oh, here is the Countess! (*Advances to embrace her*)

TIFFANY (*Starting from his seat, and seizing Seraphina violently by the arm*):   Are —   360
you — married?

SERAPHINA: Goodness, Pa, how you frighten me! No, I'm not married,
quite.

TIFFANY: Thank heaven.

MRS. TIFFANY (*Drawing Seraphina aside*):   What's the matter? Why did you   365
come back?

SERAPHINA: The clergyman wasn't at home — I came back for my jewels
— the Count said nobility couldn't get on without them.

TIFFANY: I may be saved yet! Seraphina, my child, you will not see me disgraced — ruined! I have been a kind father to you — at least I have tried   370
to be one — although your mother's extravagance made a *madman* of
me! The Count is an impostor — you seemed to like him — (*Pointing to
Snobson*) Heaven forgive me! (*Aside*) Marry *him* and save *me*. You, Mr.
Trueman, you will be my friend in this hour of extreme need — you will
advance the sum which I require — I pledge myself to return it. My wife   375
— my child — who will support them were I — the thought makes me
frantic! You will aid me? You had a child yourself.

TRUEMAN: But I did not *sell* her — it was her own doings. Shame on you,
Antony! Put a price on your own flesh and blood! Shame on such foul
traffic!
                                                                                    380
TIFFANY: Save me — I conjure you — for my father's sake.

TRUEMAN: For your *father's* SON's sake I will *not* aid you in becoming a
greater villain than you are!

GERTRUDE: Mr. Trueman, — Father, I should say — save him — do not
embitter our happiness by permitting this calamity to fall upon another —   385

TRUEMAN: Enough — I did not need your voice, child. I am going to settle this matter my own way.

(*Goes up to Snobson — who has seated himself and fallen asleep — tilts him out of the chair*)

SNOBSON (*Waking up*):   Eh? Where's the fire? Oh! it's you, Catteraugus.

TRUEMAN: If I comprehend aright, you have been for some time aware of your principal's forgeries?   390

(*As he says this, he beckons to Howard, who advances as witness.*)

SNOBSON: You've hit the nail, Catteraugus! Old chap saw that I was up to him six months ago; left off throwing dust into my eyes —

TRUEMAN: Oh, he did!

SNOBSON: Made no bones of forging Anderson's name at my elbow.

TRUEMAN: Forged at your elbow? You saw him do it?   395

SNOBSON: I did.

TRUEMAN: Repeatedly?

SNOBSON: Re-pea-ted-ly.

TRUEMAN: Then you, Rattlesnake, if he goes to the State's Prison, you'll take up your quarters there too. You are an accomplice, an *accessory!*   400

(*Trueman walks away and seats himself. Howard rejoins Gertrude. Snobson stands for some time bewildered.*)

SNOBSON: The deuce, so I am! I never thought of that! I must make myself scarce. I'll be off. Tiff, I say Tiff! (*Going up to him and speaking confidentially*) that drunken old rip has got us in his power. Let's give him the slip and be off. They want men of genius at the West, — we're sure to get on! You — you can set up for a writing-master, and teach copying *signatures;*   405 and I — I'll give lectures on *temperance!* You won't come, eh? Then I'm off without you. Good-bye, Catteraugus! Which is the way to California? (*Steals off*)

TRUEMAN: There's one debt your city owes me. And now let us see what other nuisances we can abate. Antony, I'm not given to preaching, there-   410 fore I shall not say much about what you have done. Your face speaks for itself, — the crime has brought its punishment along with it.

TIFFANY: Indeed it has, sir! In *one year* I have lived a *century* of misery.

TRUEMAN: I believe you, and upon one condition I will assist you —

TIFFANY: My friend — my first, ever kind friend, — only name it!   415

TRUEMAN: You must sell your house and all these gew-gaws, and bundle your wife and daughter off to the country. There let them learn economy, true independence, and home virtues, instead of foreign follies. As for yourself, continue your business — but let moderation, in future, be your counsellor, and let *honesty* be your confidential clerk.

TIFFANY: Mr. Trueman, you have made existence once more precious to me! My wife and daughter shall quit the city to-morrow, and —

PRUDENCE: It's all coming right! It's all coming right! We'll go to the county of Catteraugus. (*Walking up to Trueman*)

TRUEMAN: No, you won't — I make that a stipulation, Antony; keep clear of Catteraugus. None of your fashionable examples there!

(*Jolimaitre appears in the Conservatory and peeps into the room unperceived.*)

COUNT: What can detain Seraphina? We ought to be off!

MILLINETTE (*Turns round, perceives him, runs and forces him into the room*):   Here he is! Ah, Gustave, *mon cher* Gustave! I have you now and we never part no more. Don't frown, Gustave, don't frown —

TRUEMAN: Come forward, Mr. Count! and for the edification of fashion-able society confess that you're an impostor.

COUNT: An impostor? Why, you abominable old —

TRUEMAN: Oh, your feminine friend has told us all about it, the cook — the valet — barber, and all that sort of thing. Come, confess, and some-thing may be done for you.

COUNT: Well, then, I do confess I am no count; but really, ladies and gentlemen, I may recommend myself as the most capital cook.

MRS. TIFFANY: Oh, Seraphina!

SERAPHINA: Oh, Ma! (*They embrace and retire.*)

TRUEMAN: Promise me to call upon the whole circle of your fashionable acquaintances with your own advertisements and in your cook's attire, and I will set you up in business tomorrow. Better turn stomachs than turn heads!

MILLINETTE: But you will marry me?

COUNT: Give us your hand, Millinette! Sir, command me for the most del-icate *paté* — the daintiest *croquette à la royale* — the most transcendent *omelette soufflé* that ever issued from a French pastry-cook's oven. I hope you will pardon my conduct, but I heard that in America, where you pay homage to titles while you profess to scorn them — where *Fashion* makes the basest coin current — where you have no kings, no princes, no *nobility* —

TRUEMAN: Stop there! I object to your use of that word. When justice is found only among lawyers — health among physicians — and patrio-tism among politicians, *then* may you say that there is no *nobility* where there are no titles! But we *have* kings, princes, and nobles in abundance — of *Nature's stamp*, if not of *Fashion's* — we have honest men, warm-hearted and brave, and we have women — gentle, fair, and true, to whom no *title* could add *nobility*.

EPILOGUE

PRUDENCE:
I told you so! And now you hear and see.
I told you *Fashion* would the fashion be!

TRUEMAN:
Then both its point and moral I distrust.

COUNT:
Sir, is that liberal?

HOWARD:
Or is it just?

TRUEMAN:
The guilty have escaped!

TIFFANY:
Is, therefore, sin
Made charming? Ah! there's punishment within!
Guilt ever carries his own scourge along.

GERTRUDE:
Virtue her own reward!

TRUEMAN:
You're right, I'm wrong.

MRS. TIFFANY:
How we have been deceived!

PRUDENCE:
I told you so.

SERAPHINA:
To lose at once a title and a beau!

COUNT:
A count no more, I'm no more of *account*.

TRUEMAN:
But to a nobler title you may mount,
And be in time — who knows? — an honest man!

COUNT:
Eh, Millinette?

MILLINETTE:
                    Oh, *oui,* I know you can!
GERTRUDE (*To audience*):
    But, ere we close the scene, a word with you, —   15
    We charge you answer, — Is this picture true?
    Some little mercy to our efforts show,
    Then let the world your honest verdict know,
    Here let it see portrayed its ruling passion,
    And learn to prize at its just value — *Fashion.*   20

                    THE END

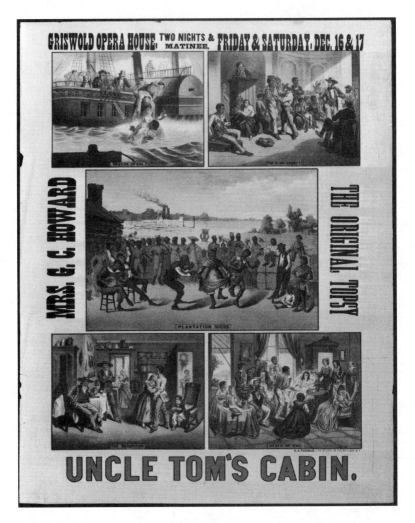

FIGURE 5 *Poster for* Uncle Tom's Cabin, *featuring the original Topsy, Mrs. George C. Howard.*

Uncle Tom's Cabin

><-

George L. Aiken (1830–1876), actor, playwright, and theater manager, was born in Boston, Massachusetts. The author of several plays, including *Helos the Helot* (1852), *Ups and Downs of New York Life* (1857), *The Doom of Deville* (1859), *Harry Blake* (1860), and *The Earl's Daughter* (1861), he is best known to scholars of the American theater for his adaptation of Harriet Beecher Stowe's novel *Uncle Tom's Cabin* (published in book form in March 1852). Aiken's effort, *Uncle Tom's Cabin; or, Life Among the Lowly* (written for production by the Howard family in Troy, New York, in September 1852, George C. Howard being Aiken's cousin), although the third adaptation, became the standard version after being combined in mid-November 1852 with Aiken's sequel, *The Death of Uncle Tom; or, the Religion of the Lowly*. The balance of Aiken's career was spent as an actor-playwright working largely for second-rate companies.

→ Uncle Tom's Cabin   1852

Based on the novel by Harriet Beecher Stowe.

DRAMATIS PERSONAE

UNCLE TOM	SAMBO
GEORGE HARRIS	QUIMBO
GEORGE SHELBY	DOCTOR
ST. CLARE	WAITER
PHINEAS FLETCHER	HARRY, *a child*
GUMPTION CUTE	EVA
MR. WILSON	ELIZA
DEACON PERRY	CASSY
SHELBY	MARIE
HALEY	OPHELIA
LEGREE	CHLOE
TOM LOKER	TOPSY
MARKS	

ACT I, SCENE I

Plain Chamber. Enter Eliza, meeting George.

ELIZA: Ah! George, is it you? Well, I am so glad you've come. (*George regards her mournfully.*) Why don't you smile, and ask after Harry?

GEORGE (*Bitterly.*):   I wish he'd never been born! I wish I'd never been born myself!

ELIZA (*Sinking her head upon his breast and weeping.*):   Oh George!   5

GEORGE: There now, Eliza, it's too bad for me to make you feel so. Oh! how I wish you had never seen me — you might have been happy!

ELIZA: George! George! how can you talk so? What dreadful thing has happened, or is going to happen? I'm sure we've been very happy till lately.

GEORGE: So we have, dear. But oh! I wish I'd never seen you, nor you me.   10

ELIZA: Oh, George! how can you?

GEORGE: Yes, Eliza, it's all misery! misery! The very life is burning out of me! I'm a poor, miserable, forlorn drudge! I shall only drag you down with me, that's all! What's the use of our trying to do anything — trying to know anything — trying to be anything? I wish I was dead!   1

ELIZA: Oh! now, dear George, that is really wicked. I know how you feel about losing your place in the factory, and you have a hard master; but pray be patient —

GEORGE: Patient! Haven't I been patient? Did I say a word when he came
and took me away — for no earthly reason — from the place where
everybody was kind to me? I'd paid him truly every cent of my earnings,
and they all say I worked well.

ELIZA: Well, it *is* dreadful; but, after all, he is your master, you know.

GEORGE: My master! And who made him my master? That's what I think
of. What right has he to me? I'm as much a man as he is. What right has
he to make a dray-horse of me? — to take me from things I can do better than he can, and put me to work that any horse can do? He tries to do
it; he says he'll bring me down and humble me, and he puts me to just the
hardest, meanest and dirtiest work, on purpose.

ELIZA: Oh, George! George! you frighten me. Why, I never heard you talk
so. I'm afraid you'll do something dreadful. I don't wonder at your feelings at all; but oh! do be careful — for my sake, for Harry's.

GEORGE: I have been careful, and I have been patient, but it's growing
worse and worse — flesh and blood can't bear it any longer. Every chance
he can get to insult and torment me he takes. He says that though I don't
say anything, he sees that I've got the devil in me, and he means to bring
it out; and one of these days it will come out, in a way that he won't like,
or I'm mistaken.

ELIZA: Well, I always thought that I must obey my master and mistress, or
I couldn't be a Christian.

GEORGE: There is some sense in it in your case. They have brought you up
like a child — fed you, clothed you and taught you, so that you have a
good education — that is some reason why they should claim you. But I
have been kicked and cuffed and sworn at, and what do I owe? I've paid
for all my keeping a hundred times over. I won't bear it — no, I *won't!*
Master will find out that I'm one whipping won't tame. My day will
come yet, if he don't look out!

ELIZA: What are you going to do? Oh! George, don't do anything wicked;
if you only trust in heaven and try to do right, it will deliver you.

GEORGE: Eliza, my heart's full of bitterness. I can't trust in heaven. Why
does it let things be so?

ELIZA: Oh, George! we must all have faith. Mistress says that when all
things go wrong to us, we must believe that heaven is doing the very best.

GEORGE: That's easy for people to say who are sitting on their sofas and
riding in their carriages; but let them be where I am — I guess it would
come some harder. I wish I could be good; but my heart burns and can't
be reconciled. You couldn't, in my place, you can't now, if I tell you all I've
got to say; you don't know the whole yet.

ELIZA: What do you mean?

GEORGE: Well, lately my master has been saying that he was a fool to let   60
me marry off the place — that he hates Mr. Shelby and all his tribe —
and he says he won't let me come here any more, and that I shall take a
wife and settle down on his place.

ELIZA: But you were married to *me* by the minister, as much as if you had
been a white man.   65

GEORGE: Don't you know I can't hold you for my wife if he chooses to part
us? That is why I wish I'd never seen you — it would have been better for
us both — it would have been better for our poor child if he had never
been born.

ELIZA: Oh! but my master is so kind.   70

GEORGE: Yes, but who knows? — he may die, and then Harry may be sold
to nobody knows who. What pleasure is it that he is handsome and smart
and bright? I tell you, Eliza, that a sword will pierce through your soul for
every good and pleasant thing your child is or has. It will make him
worth too much for you to keep.   75

ELIZA: Heaven forbid!

GEORGE: So, Eliza, my girl, bear up now, and good by, for I'm going.

ELIZA: Going, George! Going where?

GEORGE: To Canada; and when I'm there I'll buy you — that's all the hope
that's left us. You have a kind master, that won't refuse to sell you. I'll buy   80
you and the boy — heaven helping me, I will!

ELIZA: Oh, dreadful! If you should be taken?

GEORGE: I won't be taken, Eliza — I'll *die* first! I'll be free, or I'll die.

ELIZA: You will not kill yourself?

GEORGE: No need of that; they will kill me, fast enough. I will never go   85
down the river alive.

ELIZA: Oh, George! for my sake, do be careful. Don't lay hands on yourself, or anybody else. You are tempted too much, but don't. Go, if you
must, but go carefully, prudently, and pray heaven to help you!

GEORGE: Well, then Eliza, hear my plan. I'm going home quite resigned,   90
you understand, as if all was over. I've got some preparations made, and
there are those that will help me; and in the course of a few days I shall
be among the missing. Well, now, good by.

ELIZA: A moment — our boy.

GEORGE (*Choked with emotion.*):   True, I had forgotten him; one last look, and   95
then farewell!

ELIZA: And heaven grant it be not forever!   (*Exeunt.*)

Scene ii

A dining room. Table and chairs. Dessert, wine, etc., on table. Shelby and Haley discovered at table.

SHELBY: That is the way I should arrange the matter.

HALEY: I can't make trade that way — I positively can't, Mr. Shelby. (*Drinks.*)

SHELBY: Why, the fact is, Haley, Tom is an uncommon fellow! He is certainly worth that sum anywhere — steady, honest, capable, manages my whole farm like a clock!   5

HALEY: You mean honest, as niggers go. (*Fills glass.*)

SHELBY: No; I mean, really, Tom is a good, steady, sensible, pious fellow. He got religion at a camp-meeting, four years ago, and I believe he really *did* get it. I've trusted him since then, with everything I have — money, house, horses, and let him come and go round the country, and I always   10 found him true and square in everything.

HALEY: Some folks don't believe there is pious niggers, Shelby, but *I do.* I had a fellow, now, in this yer last lot I took to Orleans — 'twas as good as a meetin' now, really, to hear that critter pray; and he was quite gentle and quiet like. He fetched me a good sum, too, for I bought him cheap of a   15 man that was 'bliged to sell out, so I realized six hundred on him. Yes, I consider religion a valeyable thing in a nigger, when it's the genuine article and no mistake.

SHELBY: Well, Tom's got the real article, if ever a fellow had. Why last fall I let him go to Cincinnati alone, to do business for me and bring home   20 five hundred dollars. "Tom," says I to him, "I trust you, because I think you are a Christian — I know you wouldn't cheat." Tom comes back sure enough, I knew he would. Some low fellows, they say, said to him — "Tom, why don't you make tracks for Canada?" "Ah, master trusted me, and I couldn't," was his answer. They told me all about it. I am sorry to   25 part with Tom, I must say. You ought to let him cover the whole balance of the debt and you would, Haley, if you had any conscience.

HALEY: Well, I've got just as much conscience as any man in business can afford to keep, just a little, you know, to swear by, as twere; and then I'm ready to do anything in reason to 'blige friends, but this yer, you see, is a   30 leetle too hard on a fellow — a leetle too hard! (*Fills glass again.*)

SHELBY: Well, then, Haley, how will you trade?

HALEY: Well, haven't you a boy or a girl that you could throw in with Tom?

SHELBY: Hum! none that I could well spare; to tell the truth, it's only hard   35 necessity makes me willing to sell at all. I don't like parting with any of my hands, that's a fact. (*Harry runs in.*) Hulloa! Jim Crow! (*Throws a bunch of raisins towards him.*) Pick that up now! (*Harry does so.*)

HALEY: Bravo, little 'un! (*Throws an orange, which Harry catches. He sings and dances around the stage.*) Hurrah! Bravo! What a young 'un! That chap's   40
a case, I'll promise. Tell you what, Shelby, fling in that chap, and I'll settle the business. Come, now, if that ain't doing the thing up about the rightest!

(*Eliza enters. Starts on beholding Haley, and gazes fearfully at Harry, who runs and clings to her dress, showing the orange, etc.*)

SHELBY: Well, Eliza?
ELIZA: I was looking for Harry, please, sir.   45
SHELBY: Well, take him away, then.

(*Eliza grasps the child eagerly in her arms, and, casting another glance of apprehension at Haley, exits hastily.*)

HALEY: By Jupiter! there's an article, now. You might make your fortune on that ar gal in Orleans any day. I've seen over a thousand in my day, paid down for gals not a bit handsomer.
SHELBY: I don't want to make my fortune on her. Another glass of wine.   50
(*Fills the glasses.*)
HALEY (*Drinks and smacks his lips.*):   Capital wine — first chop. Come, how will you trade about the gal? What shall I say for her? What'll you take?
SHELBY: Mr. Haley, she is not to be sold. My wife wouldn't part with her for her weight in gold.
HALEY: Ay, ay! women always say such things, 'cause they hain't no sort of   55
calculation. Just show 'em how many watches, feathers and trinkets one's weight in gold would buy, and that alters the case, I reckon.
SHELBY: I tell you, Haley, this must not be spoken of — I say no, and I mean no.
HALEY: Well, you'll let me have the boy tho'; you must own that I have   60
come down pretty handsomely for him.
SHELBY: What on earth can you want with the child?
HALEY: Why, I've got a friend that's going into this yer branch of the business — wants to buy up handsome boys to raise for the market. Well, what do you say?   65
SHELBY: I'll think the matter over and talk with my wife.
HALEY: Oh, certainly, by all means; but I'm in a devil of a hurry and shall want to know as soon as possible, what I may depend on.

(*Rises and puts on his overcoat, which hangs on a chair. Takes hat and whip.*)

SHELBY: Well, call up this evening, between six and seven, and you shall
have my answer.   70
HALEY: All right. Take care of yourself, old boy!   (*Exit.*)
SHELBY: If anybody had ever told me that I should sell Tom to those rascally traders, I should never have believed it. Now it must come for aught
I see, and Eliza's child too. So much for being in debt, heigho! The fellow sees his advantage and means to push it.   (*Exit.*)   75

SCENE III

*Snowy landscape. Uncle Tom's Cabin. Snow on roof. Practicable door and window.
Dark stage. Music. Enter Eliza hastily, with Harry in her arms.*

ELIZA: My poor boy! they have sold you, but your mother will save you yet!

(*Goes to Cabin and taps on window. Aunt Chloe appears at window with a large
white night-cap on.*)

CHLOE: Good Lord! what's that? My sakes alive if it ain't Lizy! Get on
your clothes, old man, quick! I'm gwine to open the door.

(*The door opens and Chloe enters followed by Uncle Tom in his shirt sleeves holding a
tallow candle.*)

TOM (*Holding the light towards Eliza.*):   Lord bless you! I'm skeered to look at
ye, Lizy! Are ye tuck sick, or what's come over ye?   5
ELIZA: I'm running away, Uncle Tom and Aunt Chloe, carrying off my
child! Master sold him!
TOM & CHLOE: Sold him!
ELIZA: Yes, sold him! I crept into the closet by mistress' door tonight and
heard master tell mistress that he had sold my Harry and you, Uncle   10
Tom, both, to a trader, and that the man was to take possession to-
morrow.
CHLOE: The good lord have pity on us! Oh! it don't seem as if it was true.
What has he done that master should sell *him?*
ELIZA: He hasn't done anything — it isn't for that. Master don't want to   15
sell, and mistress — she's always good. I heard her plead and beg for us,
but he told her 'twas no use — that he was in this man's debt, and he had
got the power over him, and that if he did not pay him off clear, it would
end in his having to sell the place and all the people and move off.
CHLOE: Well, old man, why don't you run away, too? Will you wait to be   20
toted down the river, where they kill niggers with hard work and starving? I'd a heap rather die than go there, any day! There's time for ye, be

off with Lizy — you've got a pass to come and go any time. Come, bustle up, and I'll get your things together.

TOM: No, no — I ain't going. Let Eliza go — it's her right. I wouldn't be the one to say no — 'tain't in natur' for her to stay; but you heard what she said? If I must be sold, or all the people on the place, and everything go to rack, why, let me be sold. I s'pose I can bar it as well as any one. Mas'r always found me on the spot — he always will. I never have broken trust, nor used my pass no ways contrary to my word, and I never will. It's better for me to go alone, than to break up the place and sell all. Mas'r ain't to blame, and he'll take care of you and the poor little 'uns! (*Overcome.*)

CHLOE: Now, old man, what is you gwine to cry for? Does you want to break this old woman's heart? (*Crying.*)

ELIZA: I saw my husband only this afternoon, and I little knew then what was to come. He told me he was going to run away. Do try, if you can, to get word to him. Tell him how I went and why I went, and tell him I'm going to try and find Canada. You must give my love to him, and tell him if I never see him again on earth, I trust we shall meet in heaven!

TOM: Dat is right, Lizy, trust in the Lord — he is our best friend — our only comforter.

ELIZA: You won't go with me, Uncle Tom?

TOM: No; time was when I would, but the Lord's given me a work among these yer poor souls, and I'll stay with 'em and bear my cross with 'em till the end. It's different with you — it's more'n you could stand, and you'd better go if you can.

ELIZA: Uncle Tom, I'll try it!

TOM: Amen! The lord help ye!

(*Exit Eliza and Harry.*)

CHLOE: What is you gwine to do, old man! What's to become of you?

TOM (*Solemnly.*):   Him that saved Daniel in the den of lions — that saved the children in the fiery furnace — Him that walked on the sea and bade the winds be still — He's alive yet! and I've faith to believe he can deliver me.

CHLOE: You is right, old man.

TOM: The Lord is good unto all that trust him, Chloe.   (*Exeunt into cabin.*)

SCENE IV

Room in Tavern by the river side. A large window in flat, through which the river is seen, filled with floating ice. Moon light. Table and chairs brought on. Enter Phineas.

PHINEAS: Chaw me up into tobaccy ends! how in the name of all that's onpossible am I to get across that yer pesky river? It's a reg'lar blockade of ice! I promised Ruth to meet her to-night, and she'll be into my har if I don't come. (*Goes to window.*) Thar's a conglomerated prospect for a loveyer! What in creation's to be done? That thar river looks like a per-   5
miscuous ice-cream shop come to an awful state of friz. If I war on the adjacent bank, I wouldn't care a teetotal atom. Rile up, you old varmit, and shake the ice off your back!

(*Enter Eliza and Harry.*)

ELIZA: Courage, my boy — we have reached the river. Let it but roll be-tween us and our pursuers, and we are safe! (*Goes to window.*) Gracious   10
powers! the river is choked with cakes of ice!
PHINEAS: Holloa, gal! — what's the matter? You look kind of streaked.
ELIZA: Is there any ferry or boat that takes people over now?
PHINEAS: Well, I guess not; the boats have stopped running.
ELIZA (*In dismay.*): Stopped running?   15
PHINEAS: Maybe you're wanting to get over — anybody sick? Ye seem mighty anxious.
ELIZA: I — I — I've got a child that's very dangerous. I never heard of it till last night, and I've walked quite a distance to-day, in hopes to get to the ferry.   20
PHINEAS: Well, now, that's onlucky; I'm re'lly consarned for ye. Thar's a man, a piece down here, that's going over with some truck this evening, if he duss to; he'll be in here to supper to-night, so you'd better set down and wait. That's a smart little chap. Say, young'un, have a chaw tobaccy? (*Takes out a large plug and a bowie-knife.*)   25
ELIZA: No, no! not any for him.
PHINEAS: Oh! he don't use it, eh? Hain't come to it yet? Well, I have. (*Cuts off a large piece, and returns the plug and knife to pocket.*) What's the matter with the young 'un? He looks kind of white in the gills!
ELIZA: Poor fellow! he is not used to walking, and I've hurried him on so.
PHINEAS: Tuckered, eh? Well, there's a little room there, with a fire in it.   30
Take the baby in there, make yourself comfortable till that thar ferryman shows his countenance — I'll stand the damage.
ELIZA: How shall I thank you for such kindness to a stranger?
PHINEAS: Well, if you don't know how, why, don't try; that's the teeto-tal. Come, vamose! (*Exit, Eliza and Harry.*) Chaw me into sassage meat,   35
if that ain't a perpendicular fine gal! she's a reg'lar A No. 1 sort of female! How'n thunder am I to get across this refrigerated stream of water? I can't wait for that ferryman. (*Enter Marks.*) Halloa! what sort

of a critter's this? (*Advances.*) Say, stranger, will you have something to drink? 40

MARKS: You are excessively kind: I don't care if I do.

PHINEAS: Ah! he's a human. Holloa, thar! bring us a jug of whisky instantaneously, or expect to be teetotally chawed up! Squat yourself, stranger, and go in for enjoyment. (*They sit at table.*) Who are you, and what's your name? 45

MARKS: I am a lawyer, and my name is Marks.

PHINEAS: A land shark, eh? Well, I don't think no worse on you for that. The law is a kind of necessary evil; and it breeds lawyers just as an old stump does fungus. Ah! here's the whisky. (*Enter Waiter, with jug, and tumblers. Places them on table.*) Here, you — take that shin-plaster. (*Gives bill.*) I 50 don't want any change — thar's a gal stopping in that room — the balance will pay for her — d'ye hear? — vamose! (*Exit Waiter. Fills glass.*) Take hold, neighbor Marks — don't shirk the critter. Here's hoping your path of true love may never have an ice-choked river to cross! (*They drink.*)

MARKS: Want to cross the river, eh? 55

PHINEAS: Well, I do, stranger. Fact is, I'm in love with the teetotalist pretty girl, over on the Ohio side, that ever wore a Quaker bonnet. Take another swig, neighbor. (*Fills glasses, and they drink.*)

MARKS: A Quaker, eh?

PHINEAS: Yes — kind of strange, ain't it? The way of it was this: — I used 60 to own a grist of niggers — had 'em to work on my plantation, just below here. Well, stranger, do you know I fell in with that gal — of course I was considerably smashed — knocked into a pretty conglomerated heap — and I told her so. She said she wouldn't hear a word from me so long as I owned a nigger! 65

MARKS: You sold them, I suppose?

PHINEAS: You're teetotally wrong, neighbor. I gave them all their freedom, and told 'em to vamose!

MARKS: Ah! yes — very noble, I dare say, but rather expensive. This act won you your lady-love, eh? 70

PHINEAS: You're off the track again, neighbor. She felt kind of pleased about it, and smiled, and all that; but she said she could never be mine unless I turned Quaker! Thunder and earth! what do you think of that? You're a lawyer — come, now, what's your opinion? Don't you call it a knotty point? 75

MARKS: Most decidedly. Of course you refused.

PHINEAS: Teetotally; but she told me to think better of it, and come to-night and give her my final conclusion. Chaw me into mince meat, if I haven't made up my mind to do it!

MARKS: You astonish me!   80

PHINEAS: Well, you see, I can't get along without that gal; — she's sort of
fixed my flint, and I'm sure to hang fire without her. I know I shall make
a queer sort of Quaker, because you see, neighbor, I ain't precisely the
kind of material to make a Quaker out of.

MARKS: No, not exactly.   85

PHINEAS: Well, I can't stop no longer. I must try to get across that candav-
erous river some way. It's getting late — take care of yourself, neighbor
lawyer. I'm a teetotal victim to a pair of black eyes. Chaw me up to feed
hogs, if I'm not in a ruinatious state!   (*Exit.*)

MARKS: Queer genius, that, very! (*Enter Tom Loker.*) So you've come at last.   90

LOKER: Yes. (*Looks into jug.*) Empty! Waiter! more whisky!

(*Waiter enters, with jug, and removes the empty one. Enter Haley.*)

HALEY: By the land! if this yer ain't the nearest, now, to what I've heard
people call Providence! Why, Loker, how are ye?

LOKER: The devil! What brought you here, Haley?

HALEY (*Sitting, at table.*):   I say, Tom, this yer's the luckiest thing in the   95
world. I'm in a devil of a hobble, and you must help me out!

LOKER: Ugh! aw! like enough. A body may be pretty sure of that when
you're glad to see 'em, or can make something off of 'em. What's the
blow now?

HALEY: You've got a friend here — partner, perhaps?   100

LOKER: Yes, I have. Here, Marks — here's that ar fellow that I was with in
Natchez.

MARKS (*Grasping Haley's hand.*):   Shall be pleased with his acquaintance. Mr.
Haley, I believe?

HALEY: The same, sir. The fact is, gentlemen, this morning I bought a   105
young 'un of Shelby up above here. His mother got wind of it, and what
does she do but cut her lucky with him; and I'm afraid by this time that
she has crossed the river, for I tracked her to this very place.

MARKS: So, then, ye're fairly sewed up, ain't ye? He! he! he! it's neatly done,
too.   110

HALEY: This young 'un business makes lots of trouble in the trade.

MARKS: Now, Mr. Haley, what is it? Do you want us to undertake to catch
this gal?

HALEY: The gal's no matter of mine — she's Shelby's — it's only the boy.
I was a fool for buying the monkey.   115

LOKER: You're generally a fool!

MARKS: Come now, Loker, none of your huffs; you see, Mr. Haley's a-
puttin' us in a way of a good job. I reckon: just hold still — these yer

arrangements are my forte. This yer gal, Mr. Haley — how is she? what
is she? ·   120

(*Eliza appears, with Harry, listening.*)

HALEY: Well, white and handsome — well brought up. I'd have given
Shelby eight hundred or a thousand, and then made well on her.
MARKS: White and handsome — well brought up! Look here now, Loker,
a beautiful opening. We'll do a business here on our own account. We
does the catchin'; the boy, of course, goes to Mr. Haley — we takes the   125
gal to Orleans to speculate on. Ain't it beautiful? (*They confer together.*)
ELIZA: Powers of mercy, protect me! How shall I escape these human
bloodhounds? Ah! the window — the river of ice! That dark stream lies
between me and liberty! Surely the ice will bear my trifling weight. It is
my only chance of escape — better sink beneath the cold waters, with my   130
child locked in my arms, than have him torn from me and sold into
bondage. He sleeps upon my breast — Heaven, I put my trust in thee!
(*Gets out of window.*)
MARKS: Well, Tom Loker, what do you say?
LOKER: It'll do!

(*Strikes his hand violently on the table. Eliza screams. They all start to their feet. Eliza
disappears. Music, chord.*)

HALEY: By the land, there she is now! (*They all rush to the window.*)   135
MARKS: She's making for the river!
LOKER: Let's after her!

(*Music. They all leap through the window. Change.*)

SCENE V

Snow. Landscape. Music. Enter Eliza, with Harry, hurriedly.

ELIZA: They press upon my footsteps — the river is my only hope.
Heaven grant me strength to reach it, ere they overtake me! Courage, my
child! — we will be free — or perish! (*Rushes off. Music continued.*)

(*Enter Loker, Haley and Marks.*)

HALEY: We'll catch her yet; the river will stop her!
MARKS: No, it won't, for look! she has jumped upon the ice! She's a brave   5
gal, anyhow!
LOKER: She'll be drowned!
HALEY: Curse that young 'un! I shall lose him, after all.

LOKER: Come on, Marks, to the ferry!

HALEY: Aye, to the ferry! — a hundred dollars for a boat!   10

(*Music. They rush off.*)

SCENE VI

The entire depth of stage, representing the Ohio River filled with Floating Ice. Set bank on right and in front. Eliza appears, with Harry, on a cake of ice, and floats slowly across to left. Haley, Loker, and Marks, on bank right, observing. Phineas on opposite shore.

ACT II, SCENE I

A Handsome Parlor. Marie discovered reclining on a sofa.

MARIE (*Looking at a note.*):   What can possibly detain St. Clare? According to this note he should have been here a fortnight ago. (*Noise of carriage without.*) I do believe he has come at last.

(*Eva runs in.*)

EVA: Mamma! (*Throws her arms around Marie's neck, and kisses her.*)

MARIE: That will do — take care, child — don't you make my head ache!   5
(*Kisses her languidly.*)

(*Enter St. Clare, Ophelia, and Tom, nicely dressed.*)

ST. CLARE: Well, my dear Marie, here we are at last. The wanderers have arrived, you see. Allow me to present my cousin, Miss Ophelia, who is about to undertake the office of our housekeeper.

MARIE (*Rising to a sitting posture.*):   I am delighted to see you. How do you like the appearance of our city?   10

EVA (*Running to Ophelia.*):   Oh! is it not beautiful? My own darling home! — is it not beautiful?

OPHELIA: Yes, it is a pretty place, though it looks rather old and heathenish to me.

ST. CLARE: Tom, my boy, this seems to suit you?   15

TOM: Yes, mas'r, it looks about the right thing.

ST. CLARE: See here, Marie, I've brought you a coachman, at last, to order. I tell you, he is a regular hearse for blackness and sobriety, and will drive you like a funeral, if you wish. Open your eyes, now, and look at him. Now, don't say I never think about you when I'm gone.   20

MARIE: I know he'll get drunk.

ST. CLARE: Oh! no he won't. He's warranted a pious and sober article.

MARIE: Well, I hope he may turn out well; it's more than I expect, though.

ST. CLARE: Have you no curiosity to learn how and where I picked up Tom?   25

EVA: *Uncle* Tom, papa; that's his name.

ST. CLARE: Right, my little sunbeam!

TOM: Please, mas'r, that ain't no 'casion to say nothing bout me.

ST. CLARE: You are too modest, my modern Hannibal. Do you know, Marie, that our little Eva took a fancy to Uncle Tom — whom we met on   30
board the steamboat — and persuaded me to buy him.

MARIE: Ah! she is so odd.

ST. CLARE: As we approached the landing, a sudden rush of the passengers precipitated Eva into the water —

MARIE: Gracious heavens!   35

ST. CLARE: A man leaped into the river, and, as she rose to the surface of the water, grasped her in his arms, and held her up until she could be drawn on the boat again. Who was that man, Eva?

EVA: Uncle Tom! (*Runs to him. He lifts her in his arms. She kisses him.*)

TOM: The dear soul!   40

OPHELIA (*Astonished.*):   How shiftless!

ST. CLARE (*Overhearing her.*):   What's the matter now, pray?

OPHELIA: Well, I want to be kind to everybody, and I wouldn't have anything hurt, but as to kissing —

ST. CLARE: Niggers! that you're not up to, hey?   45

OPHELIA: Yes, that's it — how can she?

ST. CLARE: Oh! bless you, it's nothing when you are used to it!

OPHELIA: I could never be so shiftless!

EVA: Come with me, Uncle Tom, and I will show you about the house. (*Crosses with Tom.*)

TOM: Can I go mas'r?   50

ST. CLARE: Yes, Tom; she is your little mistress — your only duty will be to attend to her! (*Tom bows and exits.*)

MARIE: Eva, my dear!

EVA: Well, mamma?

MARIE: Do not exert yourself too much!   55

EVA: No, mamma! (*Runs out.*)

OPHELIA (*Lifting up her hands.*):   How shiftless!

(*St. Clare sits next to Marie on sofa. Ophelia next to St. Clare.*)

ST. CLARE: Well, what do you think of Uncle Tom, Marie?

MARIE: He is a perfect behemoth!

ST. CLARE: Come, now, Marie, be gracious, and say something pretty to a 60 fellow!

MARIE: You've been gone a fortnight beyond the time!

ST. CLARE: Well, you know I wrote you the reason.

MARIE: Such a short, cold letter!

ST. CLARE: Dear me! the mail was just going, and it had to be that or 65 nothing.

MARIE: That's just the way; always something to make your journeys long and letters short!

ST. CLARE: Look at this. (*Takes an elegant velvet case from his pocket.*) Here's a present I got for you in New York — a Daguerreotype of Eva and 70 myself.

MARIE (*Looks at it with a dissatisfied air.*): What made you sit in such an awkward position?

ST. CLARE: Well, the position may be a matter of opinion, but what do you think of the likeness? 75

MARIE (*Closing the case snappishly.*): If you don't think anything of my opinion in one case, I suppose you wouldn't in another.

OPHELIA (*Senteniously, aside.*): How shiftless!

ST. CLARE: Hang the woman! Come, Marie, what do you think of the likeness? Don't be nonsensical now. 80

MARIE: It's very inconsiderate of you, St. Clare, to insist on my talking and looking at things. You know I've been lying all day with the sick headache, and there's been such a tumult made ever since you came, I'm half dead!

OPHELIA: You're subject to the sick headache, ma'am? 85

MARIE: Yes, I'm a perfect martyr to it!

OPHELIA: Juniper-berry tea is good for sick head-ache; at least, Molly, Deacon Abraham Perry's wife, used to say so; and she was a great nurse.

ST. CLARE: I'll have the first juniper-berries that get ripe in our garden by the lake brought in for that especial purpose. Come, cousin, let us take a 90 stroll in the garden. Will you join us, Marie?

MARIE: I wonder how you can ask such a question, when you know how fragile I am. I shall retire to my chamber, and repose till dinner time.

(*Exit.*)

OPHELIA (*Looking after her.*): How shiftless! 95

ST. CLARE: Come, cousin! (*As he goes out.*) Look out for the babies! If I step upon anybody, let them mention it.

OPHELIA: Babies under foot! How shiftless! (*Exeunt.*)

SCENE II

A Garden. Tom discovered, seated on a bank, with Eva on his knee — his buttonholes are filled with flowers, and Eva is hanging a wreath around his neck. Music at opening of scene. Enter St. Clare and Ophelia, observing.

EVA: Oh, Tom! you look so funny.

TOM (*Sees St. Clare and puts Eva down.*):   I begs pardon, mas'r, but the young missis would do it. Look yer, I'm like the ox, mentioned in the good book, dressed for the sacrifice.

ST. CLARE: I say, what do you think, Pussy? Which do you like the best — to live as they do at your uncle's, up in Vermont, or to have a house-full of servants, as we do?

EVA: Oh! of course our way is the pleasantest.

ST. CLARE (*Patting her head.*):   Why so?

EVA: Because it makes so many more round you to love, you know.

OPHELIA: Now, that's just like Eva — just one of her odd speeches.

EVA: Is it an odd speech, papa?

ST. CLARE: Rather, as this world goes, Pussy. But where has my little Eva been?

EVA: Oh! I've been up in Tom's room, hearing him sing.

ST. CLARE: Hearing Tom sing, hey?

EVA: Oh, yes! he sings such beautiful things, about the new Jerusalem, and bright angels, and the land of Canaan.

ST. CLARE: I dare say; it's better than the opera, isn't it?

EVA: Yes; and he's going to teach them to me.

ST. CLARE: Singing lessons, hey? You are coming on.

EVA: Yes, he sings for me, and I read to him in my Bible, and he explains what it means. Come, Tom. (*She takes his hand and they exit.*)

ST. CLARE (*Aside.*):   Oh, Evangeline! Rightly named; hath not heaven made thee an evangel to me?

OPHELIA: How shiftless! How can you let her?

ST. CLARE: Why not?

OPHELIA: Why, I don't know; it seems so dreadful.

ST. CLARE: You would think no harm in a child's caressing a large dog even if he was black; but a creature that can think, reason and feel, and is immortal, you shudder at. Confess it, cousin. I know the feeling among some of you Northerners well enough. Not that there is a particle of virtue in our not having it, but custom with us does what Christianity ought to do: obliterates the feelings of personal prejudice. You loathe them as you would a snake or a toad, yet you are indignant at their wrongs. You would not have them abused but you don't want to have anything to do with them yourselves. Isn't that it?

OPHELIA: Well, cousin, there may be some truth in this.

ST. CLARE: What would the poor and lowly do without children? Your little child is your only true democrat. Tom, now, is a hero to Eva; his stories are wonders in her eyes; his songs and Methodist hymns are better than an opera, and the traps and little bits of trash in his pockets a mine of jewels, and he the most wonderful Tom that ever wore a black skin. This is one of the roses of Eden that the Lord has dropped down expressly for the poor and lowly, who get few enough of any other kind.

OPHELIA: It's strange, cousin; one might almost think you was a *professor*, to hear you talk.

ST. CLARE: A professor?

OPHELIA: Yes, a professor of religion.

ST. CLARE: Not at all; not a professor as you town folks have it, and, what is worse, I'm afraid, not a *practicer*, either.

OPHELIA: What makes you talk so, then?

ST. CLARE: Nothing is easier than talking. My forte lies in talking, and yours, cousin, lies in doing. And speaking of that puts me in mind that I have made a purchase for your department. There's the article now. Here, Topsy! (*Whistles.*)

(*Topsy runs on.*)

OPHELIA: Good gracious! what a heathenish, shiftless looking object! St. Clare, what in the world have you brought that thing here for?

ST. CLARE: For you to educate, to be sure, and train in the way she should go. I thought she was rather a funny specimen in the Jim Crow line. Here, Topsy, give us a song, and show us some of your dancing. (*Topsy sings a verse and dances a breakdown.*)

OPHELIA (*Paralyzed.*):   Well, of all things! If I ever saw the like!

ST. CLARE: (*Smothering a laugh.*):   Topsy, this is your new mistress — I'm going to give you up to her. See now that you behave yourself.

TOPSY: Yes, mas'r.

ST. CLARE: You're going to be good, Topsy, you understand?

TOPSY: Oh, yes, mas'r.

OPHELIA: Now, St. Clare, what upon earth is this for? Your house is so full of these plagues now, that a body can't set down their foot without treading on 'em. I get up in the morning and find one asleep behind the door, and see one black head poking out from under the table — one lying on the door mat, and they are moping and mowing and grinning between all the railings, and tumbling over the kitchen floor! What on earth did you want to bring this one for? 75

ST. CLARE: For you to educate — didn't I tell you? You're always preaching about educating, I thought I would make you a present of a fresh caught specimen, and let you try your hand on her and bring her up in the way she should go.

OPHELIA: I don't want her, I am sure; I have more to do with 'em now than 80 I want to.

ST. CLARE: That's you Christians, all over. You'll get up a society, and get some poor missionary to spend all his days among just such heathen; but let me see one of you that would take one into your house with you, and take the labor of their conversion upon yourselves. 85

OPHELIA: Well, I didn't think of it in that light. It might be a real missionary work. Well, I'll do what I can. (*Advances to Topsy.*) She's dreadful dirty and shiftless! How old are you, Topsy?

TOPSY: Dunno, missis.

OPHELIA: How shiftless! Don't know how old you are? Didn't anybody 90 ever tell you? Who was your mother?

TOPSY (*Grinning.*):   Never had none.

OPHELIA: Never had any mother? What do you mean? Where was you born?

TOPSY: Never was born. 95

OPHELIA: You musn't answer me in that way. I'm not playing with you. Tell me where you was born, and who your father and mother were?

TOPSY: Never was born, tell you; never had no father, nor mother, nor nothin'. I war raised by a speculator, with lots of others. Old Aunt Sue used to take car on us. 100

ST. CLARE: She speaks the truth, cousin. Speculators buy them up cheap, when they are little, and get them raised for the market.

OPHELIA: How long have you lived with your master and mistress?

TOPSY: Dunno, missis.

OPHELIA: How shiftless! Is it a year, or more, or less? 105

TOPSY: Dunno, missis.

ST. CLARE: She does not know what a year is: she don't even know her own age.

OPHELIA: Have you ever heard anything about heaven, Topsy? (*Topsy looks bewildered and grins.*) Do you know who made you? 110

TOPSY: Nobody, as I knows on, he, he, he! I spect I growed. Don't think nobody never made me.

OPHELIA: The shiftless heathen! What can you do? What did you do for your master and mistress?

TOPSY: Fetch water — and wash dishes — and rub knives — and wait on folks — and dance breakdowns. 115

OPHELIA: I shall break down, I'm afraid, in trying to make anything of you, you shiftless mortal!

ST. CLARE: You find virgin soil there, cousin; put in your own ideas — you won't find many to pull up. (*Exit, laughing.*) 120

OPHELIA (*Takes out her handkerchief. A pair of gloves falls. Topsy picks them up slyly and puts them in her sleeve.*): Follow me, you benighted innocent!

TOPSY: Yes, missis.

(*As Ophelia turns her back to her, she seizes the end of the ribbon she wears around her waist, and twitches it off. Ophelia turns and sees her as she is putting it in her other sleeve. Ophelia takes ribbon from her.*)

OPHELIA: What's this? You naughty, wicked girl, you've been stealing this?

TOPSY: Laws! why, that ar's missis' ribbon, a'nt it? How could it got caught in my sleeve? 125

OPHELIA: Topsy, you naughty girl, don't you tell me a lie — you stole that ribbon!

TOPSY: Missis, I declare for't, I didn't — never seed it till dis yer blessed minnit.

OPHELIA: Topsy, don't you know it's wicked to tell lies? 130

TOPSY: I never tells no lies, missis; it's just de truth I've been telling now and nothing else.

OPHELIA: Topsy, I shall have to whip you, if you tell lies so.

TOPSY: Laws, missis, if you's to whip all day, couldn't say no other way. I never seed dat ar — it must a got caught in my sleeve. (*Blubbers.*) 135

OPHELIA (*Seizes her by the shoulders.*): Don't you tell me that again, you barefaced fibber! (*Shakes her. The gloves fall on stage.*) There you, my gloves too — you outrageous young heathen! (*Picks them up.*) Will you tell me, now, you didn't steal the ribbon?

TOPSY: No, missis; stole de gloves, but didn't steal de ribbon. It was per- miskus. 140

OPHELIA: Why, you young reprobate!

TOPSY: Yes — I's knows I's wicked!

OPHELIA: Then you know you ought to be punished. (*Boxes her ears.*) What do you think of that? 145

TOPSY: He, he, he! De Lord, missus; dat wouldn't kill a 'skeeter. (*Runs off laughing, Ophelia follows indignantly.*)

SCENE III

The Tavern by the River. Table and chairs. Jug and glasses on table. On flat is a printed placard, headed: "Four Hundred Dollars Reward — Runaway — George Harris!" Phineas is discovered, seated at table.

PHINEAS: So yer I am; and a pretty business I've undertook to do. Find the husband of the gal that crossed the river on the ice two or three days ago. Ruth said I must do it, and I'll be teetotally chawed up if I don't do it. I see they've offered a reward for him, dead or alive. How in creation am I to find the varmint? He isn't likely to go round looking natural, with a full description of his hide and figure staring him in the face. (*Enter Mr. Wilson.*) I say, stranger, how are ye? (*Rises and comes forward.*)

WILSON: Well, I reckon.

PHINEAS: Any news? (*Takes out plug and knife.*)

WILSON: Not that I know of.

PHINEAS (*Cutting a piece of tobacco and offering it.*):   Chaw?

WILSON: No, thank ye — it don't agree with me.

PHINEAS: Don't, eh? (*Putting it in his own mouth.*) I never felt any the worse for it.

WILSON (*Sees placard.*):   What's that?

PHINEAS: Nigger advertised. (*Advances towards it and spits on it.*) There's my mind upon that.

WILSON: Why, now, stranger, what's that for?

PHINEAS: I'd do it all the same to the writer of that ar paper, if he was here. Any man that owns a boy like that, and can't find any better way of treating him, than branding him on the hand with the letter H, as that paper states, *deserves* to lose him. Such papers as this ar' a shame to old Kaintuck! that's my mind right out, if anybody wants to know.

WILSON: Well, now, that's a fact.

PHINEAS: I used to have a gang of boys, sir — that was before I fell in love — and I just told em: — "Boys," says I, "run now! Dig! put! jest when you want to. I never shall come to look after you!" That's the way I kept mine. Let 'em know they are free to run any time, and it jest stops their wanting to. It stands to reason it should. Treat 'em like men, and you'll have men's work.

WILSON: I think you are altogether right, friend, and this man described here is a fine fellow — no mistake about that. He worked for me some half dozen years in my bagging factory, and he was my best hand, sir. He is an ingenious fellow, too; he invented a machine for the cleaning of hemp — a really valuable affair; it's gone into use in several factories. His master holds the patent of it.

PHINEAS: I'll warrant ye; holds it, and makes money out of it, and then turns round and brands the boy in his right hand! If I had a fair chance, I'd mark him, I reckon, so that he'd carry it *one* while!

(*Enter George Harris, disguised.*)

GEORGE (*Speaking as he enters.*): Jim, see to the trunks. (*Sees Wilson.*) Ah! Mr. Wilson here? 40

WILSON: Bless my soul, can it be?

GEORGE (*Advances and grasps his hand.*): Mr. Wilson, I see you remember me Mr. Butler, of Oaklands. Shelby county.

WILSON: Ye — yes — yes — sir. 45

PHINEAS: Holloa! there's a screw loose here somewhere. That old gentlemen seems to be struck into a pretty considerable heap of astonishment. May I be teetotally chawed up! if I don't believe that's the identical man I'm arter. (*Crosses to George.*) How are ye, George Harris?

GEORGE (*Starting back and thrusting his hands into his breast.*): You know me? 50

PHINEAS: Ha, ha, ha! I rather conclude I do; but don't get riled, I an't a bloodhound in disguise.

GEORGE: How did you discover me?

PHINEAS: By a teetotal smart guess. You're the very man I want to see. Do you know I was sent after you? 55

GEORGE: Ah! by my master?

PHINEAS: No; by your wife.

GEORGE: My wife! Where is she?

PHINEAS: She's stopping with a Quaker family over on the Ohio side.

GEORGE: Then she is safe? 60

PHINEAS: Teetotally!

GEORGE: Conduct me to her.

PHINEAS: Just wait a brace of shakes and I'll do it. I've got to go and get the boat ready. 'Twon't take me but a minute — make yourself comfortable till I get back. Chaw me up! but this is what I call doing things in 65 short order. (*Exit.*)

WILSON: George!

GEORGE: Yes, George!

WILSON: I couldn't have thought it!

GEORGE: I am pretty well disguised, I fancy; you see I don't answer to the 70 advertisement at all.

WILSON: George, this is a dangerous game you are playing; I could not have advised you to it.

GEORGE: I can do it on my own responsibility.

WILSON: Well, George, I suppose you're running away — leaving your 75 lawful master, George, (I don't wonder at it) at the same time, I'm sorry, George, yes, decidedly. I think I must say that it's my duty to tell you so.

GEORGE: Why are you sorry, sir?

WILSON: Why to see you, as it were, setting yourself in opposition to the laws of your country.

GEORGE: *My* country! What country have *I*, but the grave? And I would to heaven that I was laid there!

WILSON: George, you've got a hard master, in fact he is — well, he conducts himself reprehensibly — I can't pretend to defend him. I'm sorry for you, now; it's a bad case — very bad; but we must all submit to the indications of providence. George, don't you see?

GEORGE: I wonder, Mr. Wilson, if the Indians should come and take you a prisoner away from your wife and children, and want to keep you all your life hoeing corn for them, if you'd think it your duty to abide in the condition in which you were called? I rather imagine that you'd think the first stray horse you could find an indication of providence, shouldn't you?

WILSON: Really, George, putting the case in that somewhat peculiar light — I don't know — under those circumstances — but what I might. But it seems to me you are running an awful risk. You can't hope to carry it out. If you're taken it will be worse with you than ever; they'll only abuse you, and half kill you, and sell you down river.

GEORGE: Mr. Wilson, I know all this. I *do* run a risk, but — (*Throws open coat and shows pistols and knife in his belt.*) There! I'm ready for them. Down South I never *will* go! no, if it comes to that, I can earn myself at least six feet of free soil — the first and last I shall ever own in Kentucky!

WILSON: Why, George, this state of mind is awful — it's getting really desperate. I'm concerned. Going to break the laws of your country?

GEORGE: My country again! Sir, I haven't any country any more than I have any father. I don't want anything of *your* country, except to be left alone — to go peaceably out of it; but if any man tries to stop me, let him take care, for I am desperate. I'll fight for my liberty, to the last breath I breathe! You say your fathers did it, if it was right for them, it is right for me!

WILSON (*Walking up and down and fanning his face with a large yellow silk handkerchief.*): Blast 'em all! Haven't I always said so — the infernal old cusses! Bless me! I hope I an't swearing now! Well, go ahead, George, go ahead. But be careful, my boy; don't shoot anybody, unless — well, you'd *better* not shoot — at least I wouldn't *hit* anybody, you know.

GEORGE: Only in self-defense.

WILSON: Well, well. (*Fumbling in his pocket.*) I suppose, perhaps, I an't following my judgment — hang it, I won't follow my judgment. So here, George. (*Takes out a pocket-book and offers George a roll of bills.*)

GEORGE: No, my kind, good sir, you've done a great deal for me, and this might get you into trouble. I have money enough, I hope, to take me as far as I need it.

WILSON: No; but you must, George. Money is a great help everywhere, can't have too much, if you get it honestly. Take it, *do* take it, *now* do, my boy!   120

GEORGE (*Taking the money.*):   On condition, sir, that I may repay it at some future time, I will.

WILSON: And now, George, how long are you going to travel in this way? Not long or far I hope? It's well carried on, but too bold.   125

GEORGE: Mr. Wilson, it is *so bold,* and this tavern is so near, that they will never think of it; they will look for me on ahead, and you yourself wouldn't know me.

WILSON: But the mark on your hand?

GEORGE (*Draws off his glove and shows scar.*):   That is a parting mark of Mr.   130 Harris' regard. Looks interesting, doesn't it? (*Puts on glove again.*)

WILSON: I declare, my very blood runs cold when I think of it — your condition and your risks!

GEORGE: Mine has run cold a good many years; at present, it's about up to the boiling point.   135

WILSON: George, something has brought you out wonderfully. You hold up your head, and move and speak like another man.

GEORGE (*Proudly.*):   Because I'm a *freeman!* Yes, sir; I've said "master" for the last time to any man. *I'm free!*

WILSON: Take care! You are not sure; you may be taken.   140

GEORGE: All men are free and equal *in the grave,* if it comes to that, Mr. Wilson.

(*Enter Phineas.*)

PHINEAS: Them's my sentiment, to a teetotal atom, and I don't care who knows it! Neighbor, the boat is ready, and the sooner we make tracks the better. I've seen some mysterious strangers lurking about these diggings,   145 so we'd better put.

GEORGE: Farewell, Mr. Wilson, and heaven reward you for the many kindnesses you have shown the poor fugitive!

WILSON (*Grasping his hand.*):   You're a brave fellow, George. I wish in my heart you were safe through, though — that's what I do.   150

PHINEAS: And ain't I the man of all creation to put him through, stranger? Chaw me up if I don't take him to his dear little wife, in the smallest possible quantity of time. Come, neighbor, let's vamose.

GEORGE: Farewell, Mr. Wilson.

WILSON: My best wishes go with you, George. (*Exit.*) 155

PHINEAS: You're a trump, old Slow-and-Easy.

GEORGE (*Looking off.*): Look! look!

PHINEAS: Consarn their picters, here they come! We can't get out of the house without their seeing us. We're teetotally treed!

GEORGE: Let us fight our way through them! 160

PHINEAS: No, that won't do; there are too many of them for a fair fight — we should be chawed up in no time. (*Looks round and sees trap door.*) Holloa! here's a cellar door. Just you step down here a few minutes, while I parley with them. (*Lifts trap.*)

GEORGE: I am resolved to perish sooner than surrender! (*Goes down trap.*) 165

PHINEAS: That's your sort! (*Closes trap and stands on it.*) Here they are!

(*Enter Haley, Marks, Loker and three Men.*)

HALEY: Say, stranger, you haven't seen a runaway darkey about these parts, eh?

PHINEAS: What kind of a darkey?

HALEY: A mulatto chap, almost as light-complexioned as a white man. 170

PHINEAS: Was he a pretty good-looking chap?

HALEY: Yes.

PHINEAS: Kind of tall?

HALEY: Yes.

PHINEAS: With brown hair? 175

HALEY: Yes.

PHINEAS: And dark eyes?

HALEY: Yes.

PHINEAS: Pretty well dressed?

HALEY: Yes. 180

PHINEAS: Scar on his right hand?

HALEY: Yes, yes.

PHINEAS: Well, I ain't seen him.

HALEY: Oh, bother! Come, boys, let's search the house. (*Exeunt.*)

PHINEAS: (*Raises trap.*) Now, then, neighbor George. (*George enters up trap.*) 185 Now's the time to cut your lucky.

GEORGE: Follow me, Phineas. (*Exit.*)

PHINEAS: In a brace of shakes. (*Is closing trap as Haley, Marks, Loker, etc., re-enter.*)

HALEY: Ah! he's down in the cellar. Follow me, boys! (*Thrusts Phineas aside, and rushes down trap, followed by the others. Phineas closes trap and stands on it.*)

PHINEAS: Chaw me up! but I've got 'em all in a trap. (*Knocking below.*) Be 190 quiet, you pesky varmints! (*Knocking.*) They're getting mighty oneasy.

(*Knocking.*) Will you be quiet, you savagerous critters! (*The trap is forced open. Haley and Marks appear. Phineas seizes a chair and stands over trap — picture.*) Down with you or I'll smash you into apple-fritters! (*Tableau — closed in.*)

SCENE IV

A Plain chamber.

TOPSY (*Without.*):   You go 'long. No more nigger dan you be! (*Enters, shouts and laughter without — looks off.*) You seem to think yourself white folks. You ain't nerry one — black *nor* white. I'd like to be one or turrer. Law! you niggers, does you know you's all sinners? Well, you is — everybody is. White folks is sinners too — Miss Feely says so — but I 'spects niggers is the biggest ones. But Lor! ye ain't any on ye up to me. I's so awful wicked there can't nobody do nothin' with me. I used to keep old missis a-swarin' at me ha' de time. I 'spects I's de wickedest critter in de world. (*Song and dance introduced. Enter Eva.*)

EVA: Oh, Topsy! Topsy! you have been very wrong again.

TOPSY: Well, I 'spects I have.

EVA: What makes you do so?

TOPSY: I dunno; I 'spects it's cause I's so wicked.

EVA: Why did you spoil Jane's earrings?

TOPSY: 'Cause she's so proud. She called me a little black imp, and turned up her pretty nose at me 'cause she is whiter than I am. I was gwine by her room, and I seed her coral earrings lying on de table, so I threw dem on de floor, and put my foot on 'em, and scrunches 'em all to little bits — he! he! he! I's so wicked.

EVA: Don't you know that was very wrong?

TOPSY: I don't car'! I despises dem what sets up for fine ladies, when dey ain't nothing but cream-colored niggers! Dere's Miss Rosa — she gives me lots of 'pertinent remarks. T'other night she was gwine to a ball. She put on a beau'ful dress dat missis give her — wid her har curled, all nice and pretty. She hab to go down de back stairs — dem am dark — and I puts a pail of hot water on dem, and she put her foot into it, and den she go tumbling to de bottom of de stairs, and de water go all ober her, and spile her dress, and scald her dreadful bad! He! he! he! I's so wicked!

EVA: Oh! how could you!

TOPSY: Don't dey despise me cause I don't know nothing? Don't dey laugh at me 'cause I'm brack, and dey ain't?

EVA: But you shouldn't mind them.

TOPSY: Well, I don't mind dem; but when dey are passing under my winder, I trows dirty water on 'em, and dat spiles der complexions.

EVA: What does make you so bad, Topsy? Why won't you try and be good? Don't you love anybody, Topsy?   35

TOPSY: Can't recommember.

EVA: But you love your father and mother?

TOPSY: Never had none, ye know, I telled ye that, Miss Eva.

EVA: Oh! I know; but hadn't you any brother, or sister, or aunt, or —

TOPSY: No, none on 'em — never had nothing nor nobody. I's brack — no   40
one loves me!

EVA: Oh! Topsy, I love you! (*Laying her hand on Topsy's shoulder.*) I love you because you haven't had any father, or mother, or friends. I love you, I want
you to be good. I wish you would try to be good for my sake. (*Topsy looks
astonished for a moment, and then bursts into tears.*) Only think of it, Topsy —   45
you can be one of those spirits bright Uncle Tom sings about!

TOPSY: Oh! dear Miss Eva — dear Miss Eva! I will try — I will try. I
never did care nothin' about it before.

EVA: If you try, you will succeed. Come with me. (*Crosses and takes Topsy's hand.*)

TOPSY: I will try; but den, I's so wicked!   50

(*Exit Eva followed by Topsy, crying.*)

SCENE V

Chamber. Enter George, Eliza and Harry.

GEORGE: At length, Eliza, after many wanderings, we are united.

ELIZA: Thanks to these generous Quakers, who have so kindly sheltered us.

GEORGE: Not forgetting our friend Phineas.

ELIZA: I do indeed owe him much. 'Twas he I met upon the icy river's
bank, after that fearful, but successful attempt, when I fled from the
slave-trader with my child in my arms.

GEORGE: It seems almost incredible that you could have crossed the river
on the ice.

ELIZA: Yes, I did. Heaven helping me, I crossed on the ice, for they were
behind me — right behind — and there was no other way.   1

GEORGE: But the ice was all in broken-up blocks, swinging and heaving up
and down in the water.

ELIZA: I know it was — I know it; I did not think I should get over, but I
did not care — I could but die if I did not! I leaped on the ice, but how I
got across I don't know; the first I remember, a man was helping me up
the bank — that man was Phineas.

GEORGE: My brave girl! you deserve your freedom — you have richly
earned it!

ELIZA: And when we get to Canada I can help you to work, and between
us we can find something to live on.   20

GEORGE: Yes, Eliza, so long as we have each other, and our boy. Oh, Eliza,
if these people only knew what a blessing it is for a man to feel that his
wife and child belong to *him!* I've often wondered to see men that could
call their wives and children *their own,* fretting and worrying about anything else. Why, I feel rich and strong, though we have nothing but our   25
bare hands. If they will only let me alone now, I will be satisfied —
thankful!

ELIZA: But we are not quite out of danger; we are not yet in Canada.

GEORGE: True, but it seems as if I smelt the free air, and it makes me strong!

(*Enter Phineas, dressed as a Quaker.*)

PHINEAS (*With a snuffle.*):   Verily, friends, how is it with thee? — hum!   30

GEORGE: Why, Phineas, what means this metamorphosis?

PHINEAS: I've become a Quaker, that's the meaning on't.

GEORGE: What — you?

PHINEAS: Teetotally! I was driven to it by a strong argument, composed of
a pair of sparkling eyes, rosy cheeks, and pouting lips. Them lips would   35
persuade a man to assassinate his grandmother! (*Assumes the Quaker tone
again.*) Verily, George, I have discovered something of importance to the
interests of thee and thy party, and it were well for thee to hear it.

GEORGE: Keep us not in suspense!

PHINEAS: Well, after I left you on the road, I stopped at a little, lone tav-   40
ern, just below here. Well, I was tired with hard driving, and after my
supper I stretched myself down on a pile of bags in the corner, and pulled
a buffalo hide over me — and what does I do but get fast asleep.

GEORGE: With one ear open, Phineas?

PHINEAS: No, I slept ears and all for an hour or two, for I was pretty well   45
tired; but when I came to myself a little, I found that there were some
men in the room, sitting round a table, drinking and talking; and I
thought, before I made much muster, I'd just see what they were up to,
especially as I heard them say something about the Quakers. Then I listened with both ears and found they were talking about you. So I kept   50
quiet, and heard them lay off all their plans. They've got a right notion of
the track we are going to-night, and they'll be down after us, six or eight
strong. So, now, what's to be done?

ELIZA: What *shall* we do, George?

GEORGE: I know what I shall do! (*Takes out pistols.*)   55

PHINEAS: Ay-ay, thou seest, Eliza, how it will work — pistols — phitz —
poppers!

ELIZA: I see; but I pray it come not to that!

GEORGE: I don't want to involve any one with or for me. If you will lend me your vehicle, and direct me, I will drive alone to the next stand.   60

PHINEAS: Ah! well, friend, but thee'll need a driver for all that. Thee's quite welcome to do all the fighting thee knows; but I know a thing or two about the road that thee doesn't.

GEORGE: But I don't want to involve you.

PHINEAS: Involve me! Why, chaw me — that is to say — when thee does   65
involve me, please to let me know.

ELIZA: Phineas is a wise and skillful man. You will do well, George, to abide by his judgment. And, oh! George, be not hasty with these — young blood is hot! (*Laying her hand on pistols.*)

GEORGE: I will attack no man. All I ask of this country is to be left alone,   70
and I will go out peaceably. But I'll fight to the last breath before they shall take from me my wife and son! Can you blame me?

PHINEAS: Mortal man cannot blame thee, neighbor George! Flesh and blood could not do otherwise. Woe unto the world because of offenses, but woe unto them through whom the offense cometh! That's gospel, teetotally!   75

GEORGE: Would not even you, sir, do the same, in my place?

PHINEAS: I pray that I be not tried; the flesh is weak — but I think my flesh would be pretty tolerably strong in such a case; I ain't sure, friend George, that I shouldn't hold a fellow for thee, if thee had any accounts to settle with him.   80

ELIZA: Heaven grant we be not tempted.

PHINEAS: But if we are tempted too much, why, consarn 'em! let them look out, that's all.

GEORGE: It's quite plain you was not born for a Quaker. The old nature has its way in you pretty strong yet.   85

PHINEAS: Well, I reckon you are pretty teetotally right.

GEORGE: Had we not better hasten our flight?

PHINEAS: Well, I rather conclude we had; we're full two hours ahead of them, if they start at the time they planned; so let's vamose.   (*Exeunt.*)

Scene vi

A Rocky Pass in the Hills. Large set rock and platform.

PHINEAS (*Without.*):   Out with you in a twinkling, every one, and up into these rocks with me! run *now*, if you *ever* did run! (*Music. Phineas enters, with Harry in his arms. George supporting Eliza.*) Come up here; this is one of our old hunting dens. Come up. (*They ascend the rock.*) Well, here we are.

Let 'em get us if they can. Whoever comes here has to walk single file be- 5
tween those two rocks, in fair range of your pistols — d'ye see?

GEORGE: I do see. And now, as this affair is mine, let me take all the risk,
and do all the fighting.

PHINEAS: Thee's quite welcome to do the fighting, George; but I may have
the fun of looking on, I suppose. But see, these fellows are kind of debat- 10
ing down there, and looking up, like hens when they are going to fly up
onto the roost. Hadn't thee better give 'em a word of advice, before they
come up, just to tell 'em handsomely they'll be shot if they do.

(*Loker, Marks, and three Men enter.*)

MARKS: Well, Tom, your coons are fairly treed.

LOKER: Yes, I see 'em go up right here; and here's a path — I'm for going 15
right up. They can't jump down in a hurry, and it won't take long to fer-
ret 'em out.

MARKS: But, Tom, they might fire at us from behind the rocks. That would
be ugly, you know.

LOKER: Ugh! always for saving your skin, Marks. No danger, niggers are 20
too plaguy scared!

MARKS: I don't know why I shouldn't save my skin, it's the best I've got;
and niggers do fight like the devil sometimes.

GEORGE (*Rising on the rock.*):   Gentlemen, who are you down there and what
do you want? 25

LOKER: We want a party of runaway niggers. One George and Eliza Harris, and their son. We've got the officers here, and a warrant to take 'em
too. D'ye hear? An't you George Harris, that belonged to Mr. Harris, of
Shelby county, Kentucky?

GEORGE: I am George Harris. A Mr. Harris, of Kentucky, did call me his 30
property. But now I'm a freeman, standing on heaven's free soil! My wife
and child I claim as mine. We have arms to defend ourselves and we
mean to do it. You can come up if you like, but the first one that comes
within range of our bullets is a dead man!

MARKS: Oh, come — come, young man, this ar no kind of talk at all for 35
you. You see we're officers of justice. We've got the law on our side, and
the power and so forth; so you'd better give up peaceably, you see — for
you'll certainly have to give up at last.

GEORGE: I know very well that you've got the law on your side, and the
power; but you haven't got us. We are standing here as free as you are, and 40
by the great power that made us, we'll fight for our liberty till we die!
(*During this, Marks draws a pistol, and when he concludes fires at him. Eliza
screams.*) It's nothing, Eliza; I am unhurt.

PHINEAS (*Drawing George down.*):   Thee'd better keep out of sight with thy speechifying; they're teetotal mean scamps.

LOKER: What did you do that for, Marks?   45

MARKS: You see, you get jist as much for him dead as alive in Kentucky.

GEORGE: Now, Phineas, the first man that advances I fire at; you take the second and so on. It won't do to waste two shots on one.

PHINEAS: But what if you don't hit?

GEORGE: I'll try my best.   50

PHINEAS: Creation! chaw me up if there a'nt stuff in you!

MARKS: I think I must have hit some on'em. I heard a squeal.

LOKER: I'm going right up for one. I never was afraid of niggers, and I an't a going to be now. Who goes after me?

(*Music. Loker dashes up the rock. George fires. He staggers for a moment, then springs to the top. Phineas seizes him. A struggle.*)

PHINEAS: Friend, thee is not wanted here! (*Throws Loker over the rock.*)   55

MARKS (*Retreating.*):   Lord help us — they're perfect devils!

(*Music. Marks and Party run off. George and Eliza kneel in an attitude of thanksgiving, with the Child between them. Phineas stands over them exulting. Tableau.*)

ACT III, SCENE I

Chamber. Enter St. Clare, followed by Tom.

ST. CLARE (*Giving money and papers to Tom.*):   There, Tom, are the bills, and the money to liquidate them.

TOM: Yes, mas'r.

ST. CLARE: Well, Tom, what are you waiting for? Isn't all right there?   5

TOM: I'm 'fraid not, mas'r.

ST. CLARE: Why, Tom, what's the matter? You look as solemn as a judge.

TOM: I feel very bad, mas'r. I allays have thought that mas'r would be good to everybody.

ST. CLARE: Well, Tom, haven't I been? Come, now, what do you want? There's something you haven't got, I suppose, and this is the preface.   10

TOM: Mas'r allays been good to me. I haven't nothing to complain of on that head; but there is one that mas'r isn't good to.

ST. CLARE: Why, Tom, what's got into you? Speak out — what do you mean?

TOM: Last night, between one and two, I thought so. I studied upon the matter then — mas'r isn't good to *himself.*   15

ST. CLARE: Ah! now I understand; you allude to the state in which I came
home last night. Well, to tell the truth, I *was* slightly elevated — a little
more champagne on board than I could comfortably carry. That's all,
isn't it?   20

TOM (*Deeply affected — clasping his hands and weeping.*):   All! Oh! my dear
young mas'r, I'm 'fraid it will be *loss of all — all*, body and soul. The good
book says "it biteth like a serpent and stingeth like an adder," my dear
mas'r.

ST. CLARE: You poor, silly fool! I'm not worth crying over.   25

TOM: Oh, mas'r! I implore you to think of it before it gets too late.

ST. CLARE: Well, I won't go to any more of their cursed nonsense, Tom —
on my honor, I won't. I don't know why I haven't stopped long ago; I've
always despised *it,* and myself for it. So now, Tom, wipe up your eyes and
go about your errands.   30

TOM: Bless you, mas'r. I feel much better now. You have taken a load from
poor Tom's heart. Bless you!

ST. CLARE: Come, come, no blessings; I'm not so wonderfully good, now.
There, I'll pledge my honor to you, Tom, you don't see me so again. (*Exit
Tom.*) I'll keep my faith with him, too.   35

OPHELIA (*Without.*):   Come along, you shiftless mortal!

ST. CLARE: What new witchcraft has Topsy been brewing? That commotion is of her raising, I'll be bound.

(*Enter Ophelia, dragging in Topsy.*)

OPHELIA: Come here now; I will tell your master.

ST. CLARE: What's the matter now?   40

OPHELIA: The matter is that I cannot be plagued with this girl any longer.
It's past all bearing; flesh and blood cannot endure it. Here I locked her
up and gave her a hymn to study; and what does she do but spy out where
I put my key, and has gone to my bureau, and got a bonnet-trimming and
cut it all to pieces to make dolls' jackets! I never saw anything like it in   45
my life!

ST. CLARE: What have you done to her?

OPHELIA: What have I done? What haven't I done? Your wife says I ought
to have her whipped till she couldn't stand.

ST. CLARE: I don't doubt it. Tell me of the lovely rule of woman. I never   50
saw above a dozen women that wouldn't half kill a horse or servant, either, if they had their own way with them — let alone a man.

OPHELIA: I am sure, St. Clare, I don't know what to do. I've taught and
taught — I've talked till I'm tired; I've whipped her, I've punished her in
every way I could think of, and still she's just what she was at first.   55

ST. CLARE: Come here, Tops, you monkey! (*Topsy crosses to St. Clare, grinning.*) What makes you behave so?

TOPSY: 'Spects it's my wicked heart — Miss Feely says so.

ST. CLARE: Don't you see how much Miss Ophelia has done for you? She says she has done everything she can think of. 60

TOPSY: Lord, yes, mas'r! old missis used to say so, too. She whipped me a heap harder, and used to pull my ha'r, and knock my head agin the door; but it didn't do me no good. I 'spects if they's to pull every spear of ha'r out o' my head, it wouldn't do no good neither — I's so wicked! Laws! I's nothin' but a nigger, no ways! (*Goes up.*) 65

OPHELIA: Well, I shall have to give her up; I can't have that trouble any longer.

ST. CLARE: I'd like to ask you one question.

OPHELIA: What is it?

ST. CLARE: Why, if your doctrine is not strong enough to save one heathen 70 child, that you can have at home here, all to yourself, what's the use of sending one or two poor missionaries off with it among thousands of just such? I suppose this girl is a fair sample of what thousands of your heathen are.

OPHELIA: I'm sure I don't know; I never saw such a girl as this. 75

ST. CLARE: What makes you so bad, Tops? Why won't you try and be good? Don't you love any one, Topsy?

TOPSY (*Comes down.*): Dunno nothing 'bout love; I loves candy and sich, that's all.

OPHELIA: But, Topsy, if you'd only try to be good, you might. 80

TOPSY: Couldn't never be nothing but a nigger, if I was ever so good. If I could be skinned and come white, I'd try then.

ST. CLARE: People can love you, if you are black, Topsy. Miss Ophelia would love you, if you were good. (*Topsy laughs.*) Don't you think so?

TOPSY: No, she can't b'ar me, 'cause I'm a nigger — she'd's soon have a 85 toad touch her. There can't nobody love niggers, and niggers can't do nothin'! I don't car'! (*Whistles.*)

ST. CLARE: Silence, you incorrigible imp, and begone!

TOPSY: He! he! he! didn't get much out of dis chile! (*Exit.*)

OPHELIA: I've always had a prejudice against negroes, and it's a fact — I never 90 could bear to have that child touch me, but I didn't think she knew it.

ST. CLARE: Trust any child to find that out, there's no keeping it from them. But I believe all the trying in the world to benefit a child, and all the substantial favors you can do them, will never excite one emotion of gratitude, while that feeling of repugnance remains in the heart. It's a 95 queer kind of a fact, but so it is.

OPHELIA: I don't know how I can help it — they are disagreeable to me, this girl in particular. How can I help feeling so?

ST. CLARE: Eva does, it seems.

OPHELIA: Well, she's so loving. I wish I was like her. She might teach me a lesson. 100

ST. CLARE: It would not be the first time a little child had been used to instruct an old disciple, if it were so. Come, let us seek Eva, in her favorite bower by the lake.

OPHELIA: Why, the dew is falling, she mustn't be out there. She is unwell, I know. 105

ST. CLARE: Don't be croaking, cousin — I hate it.

OPHELIA: But she has that cough.

ST. CLARE: Oh, nonsense, of that cough — it is not anything. She has taken a little cold, perhaps. 110

OPHELIA: Well, that was just the way Eliza Jane was taken — and Ellen —

ST. CLARE: Oh, stop these hobgoblin, nurse legends. You old hands get so wise, that a child cannot cough or sneeze, but you see desperation and ruin at hand. Only take care of the child, keep her from the night air, and don't let her play too hard, and she'll do well enough.   (*Exeunt.*) 115

Scene II

The flat represents the lake. The rays of the setting sun tinge the waters with gold. A large tree. Beneath this a grassy bank, on which Eva and Tom are seated side by side. Eva has a Bible open on her lap. Music.

TOM: Read dat passage again, please, Miss Eva?

EVA (*Reading.*): "And I saw a sea of glass, mingled with fire." (*Stopping suddenly and pointing to lake.*) Tom, there it is!

TOM: What, Miss Eva?

EVA: Don't you see there? There's a "sea of glass mingled with fire." 5

TOM: True enough, Miss Eva. (*Sings.*)
Oh, had I the wings of the morning,
I'd fly away to Canaan's shore;
Bright angels should convey me home,
To the New Jerusalem. 10

EVA: Where do you suppose New Jerusalem is, Uncle Tom?

TOM: Oh, up in the clouds, Miss Eva.

EVA: Then I think I see it. Look in those clouds, they look like great gates of pearl; and you can see beyond them — far, far off — it's all gold! Tom, sing about "spirits bright." 15

TOM (*Sings.*):
  I see a band of spirits bright,
  That taste the glories there;
  They are all robed in spotless white,
  And conquering palms they bear.
EVA: Uncle Tom, I've seen *them*.
TOM: To be sure you have; you are one of them yourself. You are the brightest spirit I ever saw.
EVA: They come to me sometimes in my sleep — those spirits bright —
  They are all robed in spotless white,
  And conquering palms they bear.
  Uncle Tom, I'm going there.
TOM: Where, Miss Eva?
EVA (*Pointing to the sky.*): I'm going *there*, to the spirits bright, Tom; I'm going before long.
TOM: It's jest no use tryin' to keep Miss Eva here; I've allays said so. She's got the Lord's mark in her forehead. She wasn't never like a child that's to live — there was always something deep in her eyes. (*Rises and comes forward. Eva also comes forward, leaving Bible on bank.*)

(*Enter St. Clare.*)

ST. CLARE: Ah! my little pussy, you look as blooming as a rose! You are better now-a-days, are you not?
EVA: Papa, I've had things I wanted to say to you a great while. I want to say them now, before I get weaker.
ST. CLARE: Nay, this is an idle fear, Eva; you know you grow stronger every day.
EVA: It's all no use, papa, to keep it to myself any longer. The time is coming that I am going to leave you, I am going, and never to come back.
ST. CLARE: Oh, now, my dear little Eva! you've got nervous and low spirited; you mustn't indulge such gloomy thoughts.
EVA: No, papa, don't deceive yourself, I am *not* any better; I know it perfectly well, and I am going before long. I am not nervous — I am not low spirited. If it were not for you, papa, and my friends, I should be perfectly happy. I want to go — I long to go!
ST. CLARE: Why, dear child, what has made your poor little heart so sad? You have everything to make you happy that could be given you.
EVA: I had rather be in heaven! There are a great many things here that makes me sad — that seem dreadful to me; I had rather be there; but I don't want to leave you — it almost breaks my heart!
ST. CLARE: What makes you sad, and what seems dreadful, Eva?

EVA: I feel sad for our poor people; they love me dearly, and they are all good and kind to me. I wish, papa, they were all *free!*

ST. CLARE: Why, Eva, child, don't you think they are well enough off now?   55

EVA (*Not heeding the question.*):   Papa, isn't there a way to have slaves made free? When I am dead, papa, then you will think of me and do it for my sake?

ST. CLARE: When you are dead, Eva? Oh, child, don't talk to me so. You are all I have on earth!   60

EVA: Papa, these poor creatures love their children as much as you do me. Tom loves his children. Oh, do something for them!

ST. CLARE: There, there, darling; only don't distress yourself, and don't talk of dying, and I will do anything you wish.

EVA: And promise me, dear father, that Tom shall have his freedom as   65 soon as — (*Hesitating.*) — I am gone!

ST. CLARE: Yes, dear, I will do anything in the world — anything you could ask me to. There, Tom, take her to her chamber, this evening air is too chill for her. (*Music. Kisses her. Tom takes Eva in his arms, and exits. Gazing mournfully after Eva.*) Has there ever been a child like Eva? Yes, there has   70 been; but their names are always on grave-stones, and their sweet smiles, their heavenly eyes, their singular words and ways, are among the buried treasures of yearning hearts. It is as if heaven had an especial band of angels, whose office it is to sojourn for a season here, and endear to them the wayward human heart, that they might bear it upward with them in   75 their homeward flight. When you see that deep, spiritual light in the eye when the little soul reveals itself in words sweeter and wiser than the ordinary words of children, hope not to retain that child; for the seal of heaven is on it, and the light of immortality looks out from its eyes!

(*Music. Exit.*)   80

SCENE III

A corridor. Proscenium doors on. Music. Enter Tom, he listens at door and then lies down. Enter Ophelia, with candle.

OPHELIA: Uncle Tom, what alive have you taken to sleeping anywhere and everywhere, like a dog, for? I thought you were one of the orderly sort, that liked to lie in bed in a Christian way.

TOM (*Rises. Mysteriously.*):   I do, Miss Feely, I do, but now —

OPHELIA: Well, what now?   5

TOM: We mustn't speak loud; Mas'r St. Clare won't hear on't; but Miss Feely, you know there must be somebody watchin' for the bridegroom.

OPHELIA: What do you mean, Tom?

TOM: You know it says in Scripture, "At midnight there was a great cry made, behold, the bridegroom cometh!" That's what I'm spectin' now, every night, Miss Feely, and I couldn't sleep out of hearing, noways. 10

OPHELIA: Why, Uncle Tom, what makes you think so?

TOM: Miss Eva, she talks to me. The Lord, he sends his messenger in the soul. I must be thar, Miss Feely; for when that ar blessed child goes into the kingdom, they'll open the door so wide, we'll all get a look in at the glory! 15

OPHELIA: Uncle Tom, did Miss Eva say she felt more unwell than usual to-night?

TOM: No; but she told me she was coming nearer — thar's them that tells it to the child, Miss Feely. It's the angels — it's the trumpet sound afore the break o' day! 20

OPHELIA: Heaven grant your fears be vain! Come in, Tom. (*Exeunt.*)

SCENE IV

Eva's Chamber. Eva discovered on a couch. A table stands near the couch with a lamp on it. The light shines upon Eva's face, which is very pale. Scene half dark. Uncle Tom is kneeling near the foot of the couch, Ophelia stands at the head, St. Clare at back. Scene opens to plaintive music. After a strain enter Marie, hastily.

MARIE: St. Clare! Cousin! Oh! what is the matter now?

ST. CLARE (*Hoarsely.*): Hush! she is dying!

MARIE (*Sinking on her knees, beside Tom.*): Dying!

ST. CLARE: Oh! if she would only wake and speak once more. (*Bending over Eva.*) Eva, darling! (*Eva uncloses her eyes, smiles, raises her head and tries to speak.*) Do you know me, Eva? 5

EVA (*Throwing her arms feebly about his neck.*): Dear papa. (*Her arms drop and she sinks back.*)

ST. CLARE: Oh heaven! this is dreadful! Oh! Tom, my boy, it is killing me!

TOM: Look at her, mas'r. (*Points to Eva.*)

ST. CLARE (*A pause.*): She does not hear. Oh Eva! tell us what you see. What is it? 10

EVA (*Feebly smiling.*): Oh! love! joy! peace! (*Dies.*)

TOM: Oh! bless the Lord! it's over, dear mas'r, it's over.

ST. CLARE (*Sinking on his knees.*): Farewell, beloved child! the bright eternal doors have closed after thee. We shall see thy sweet face no more. Oh! woe for them who watched thy entrance into heaven when they shall wake and find only the cold, gray sky of daily life and thou gone forever. (*Solemn music, slow curtain.*) 15

Act iv, Scene i

A street in New Orleans. Enter Gumption Cute, meeting Marks.

CUTE: How do ye dew?

MARKS: How are you?

CUTE: Well, now, squire, it's a fact that I am dead broke and busted up.

MARKS: You have been speculating, I suppose!

CUTE: That's just it and nothing shorter.   5

MARKS: You have had poor success, you say?

CUTE: Tarnation bad, now I tell you. You see I came to this part of the country to make my fortune.

MARKS: And you did not do it?

CUTE: Scarcely. The first thing I tried my hand at was keeping school. I   10
opened an academy for the instruction of youth in the various branches
of orthography, geography, and other graphies.

MARKS: Did you succeed in getting any pupils?

CUTE: Oh, lots on 'em! and a pretty set of dunces they were too. After the
first quarter, I called on the repectable parents of the juveniles, and re- 15
quested them to fork over. To which they politely answered — don't you
wish you may get it?

MARKS: What did you do then?

CUTE: Well, I kind of pulled up stakes and left those diggins. Well then I
went into Spiritual Rappings for a living. That paid pretty well for a   20
short time, till I met with an accident.

MARKS: An accident?

CUTE: Yes; a tall Yahoo called on me one day, and wanted me to summon
the spirit of his mother — which, of course, I did. He asked me about a
dozen questions which I answered to his satisfaction. At last he wanted   25
to know what she died of — I said, Cholera. You never did see a critter
so riled as he was. "Look yere, stranger," said he, "it's my opinion that
you're a pesky humbug! for my mother was blown up in a *Steamboat!*"
with that he left the premises. The next day the people furnished me
with a conveyance, and I rode out of town.   30

MARKS: Rode out of town?

CUTE: Yes; on a rail!

MARKS: I suppose you gave up the spirits, after that?

CUTE: Well, I reckon I did; it had such an effect on my spirits.

MARKS: It's a wonder they didn't tar and feather you.   35

CUTE: There was some mention made of that, but when they said *feathers*,
I felt as if I had wings and flew away.

MARKS: You cut and run?

CUTE: Yes; I didn't like their company and I cut it. Well, after that I let myself out as an overseer on a cotton plantation. I made a pretty good thing 40
of that, though it was dreadful trying to my feelings to flog the darkies;
but I got used to it after a while, and then I used to lather 'em like Jehu.
Well, the proprietor got the fever and ague and shook himself out of
town. The place and all the fixings were sold at auction and I found myself adrift once more. 45

MARKS: What are you doing at present?

CUTE: I'm in search of a rich relation of mine.

MARKS: A rich relation?

CUTE: Yes, a Miss Ophelia St. Clare. You see, a niece of hers married one
of my second cousins — that's how I came to be a relation of hers. She 50
came on here from Vermont to be housekeeper to a cousin of hers, of the
same name.

MARKS: I know him well.

CUTE: The deuce you do! — well, that's lucky.

MARKS: Yes, he lives in this city. 55

CUTE: Say, you just point out the locality, and I'll give him a call.

MARKS: Stop a bit. Suppose you shouldn't be able to raise the wind in that
quarter, what have you thought of doing?

CUTE: Well, nothing particular.

MARKS: How should you like to enter into a nice, profitable business — 60
one that pays well?

CUTE: That's just about my measure — it would suit me to a hair. What
is it?

MARKS: Nigger catching.

CUTE: Catching niggers! What on airth do you mean? 65

MARKS: Why, when there's a large reward offered for a runaway darkey, we
goes after him, catches him, and gets the reward.

CUTE: Yes, that's all right so far — but s'pose there ain't no reward offered?

MARKS: Why, then we catches the darkey on our own account, sells him,
and pockets the proceeds. 70

CUTE: By chowder, that ain't a bad speculation!

MARKS: What do you say? I want a partner. You see, I lost my partner last
year, up in Ohio — he was a powerful fellow.

CUTE: Lost him! How did you lose him?

MARKS: Well, you see, Tom and I — his name was Tom Loker — Tom 75
and I were after a mulatto chap, called George Harris, that run away
from Kentucky. We traced him though the greater part of Ohio, and

came up with him near the Pennsylvania line. He took refuge among
some rocks, and showed fight.

CUTE: Oh! then runaway darkies show fight, do they? 80

MARKS: Sometimes. Well, Tom — like a headstrong fool as he was —
rushed up the rocks, and a Quaker chap, who was helping this George
Harris, threw him over the cliff.

CUTE: Was he killed?

MARKS: Well, I didn't stop to find out. Seeing that the darkies were 85
stronger than I thought, I made tracks for a safe place.

CUTE: And what became of this George Harris?

MARKS: Oh! he and his wife and child got away safe into Canada. You see,
they will get away sometimes though it isn't very often. Now what do you
say? You are just the figure for a fighting partner. Is it a bargain? 90

CUTE: Well, I rather calculate our teams won't hitch, no how. By chowder,
I hain't no idea of setting myself up as a target for darkies to fire at —
that's a speculation that don't suit my constitution.

MARKS: You're afraid, then?

CUTE: No, I ain't, it's against my principles. 95

MARKS: Your principles — how so?

CUTE: Because my principles are to keep a sharp lookout for No. 1. I
shouldn't feel wholesome if a darkie was to throw me over that cliff to
look after Tom Loker. (*Exeunt arm-in-arm.*)

SCENE II

Gothic Chamber. Slow music. St. Clare discovered, seated on sofa. Tom at left.

ST. CLARE: Oh! Tom, my boy, the whole world is as empty as an egg shell.

TOM: I know it, mas'r, I know it. But oh! if mas'r could look up — up
where our dear Miss Eva is —

ST. CLARE: Ah, Tom! I do look up; but the trouble is, I don't see anything
when I do. I wish I could. It seems to be given to children and poor, hon- 5
est fellows like you, to see what we cannot. How comes it?

TOM: Thou hast hid from the wise and prudent, and revealed unto babes;
even so, Father, for so it seemed good in thy sight.

ST. CLARE: Tom, I don't believe — I've got the habit of doubting — I want
to believe and I cannot. 10

TOM: Dear mas'r, pray to the good Lord: "Lord, I believe; help thou my
unbelief."

ST. CLARE: Who knows anything about anything? Was all that beautiful
love and faith only one of the ever-shifting phases of human feeling,

having nothing real to rest on, passing away with the little breath? And is there no more Eva — nothing?

TOM: Oh! dear mas'r, there is. I know it; I'm sure of it. Do, do, dear mas'r, believe it!

ST. CLARE: How do you know there is, Tom? You never saw the Lord.

TOM: Felt Him in my soul, mas'r — feel Him now! Oh, mas'r! when I was sold away from my old woman and the children, I was jest a'most broken up — I felt as if there warn't nothing left — and then the Lord stood by me, and He says, "Fear not, Tom," and He brings light and joy into a poor fellow's soul — makes all peace; and I's so happy, and loves everybody, and feels willin' to be jest where the Lord wants to put me. I know it couldn't come from me, 'cause I's a poor, complaining creature — it comes from above, and I know He's willin' to do for mas'r.

ST. CLARE: (*Grasping Tom's hand.*): Tom, you love me!

TOM: I's willin' to lay down my life this blessed day for you.

ST. CLARE (*Sadly.*): Poor, foolish fellow! I'm not worth the love of one good, honest heart like yours.

TOM: Oh, mas'r! there's more than me loves you — the blessed Saviour loves you.

ST. CLARE: How do you know that, Tom?

TOM: The love of the Saviour passeth knowledge.

ST. CLARE (*Turns away.*): Singular! that the story of a man who lived and died eighteen hundred years ago can affect people so yet. But He was no man. (*Rises.*) No man ever had such long and living power. Oh! that I could believe what my mother taught me, and pray as I did when I was a boy! But, Tom, all this time I have forgotten why I sent for you. I'm going to make a freeman of you so have your trunk packed, and get ready to set out for Kentucky.

TOM (*Joyfully.*): Bless the Lord!

ST. CLARE (*Dryly.*): You haven't had such very bad times here, that you need be in such a rapture, Tom.

TOM: No, no, mas'r, 'tain't that; it's being a *freeman* — that's what I'm joyin' for.

ST. CLARE: Why, Tom, don't you think, for your own part, you've been better off than to be free?

TOM: No, *indeed*, Mas'r St. Clare — no, indeed!

ST. CLARE: Why, Tom, you couldn't possibly have earned, by your work, such clothes and such living as I have given you.

TOM: I know all that, Mas'r St. Clare — mas'r's been too good; but I'd rather have poor clothes, poor house, poor everything, and have 'em

mine, than have the best, if they belong to somebody else. I had *so,* mas'r;   55
I think it's natur', mas'r.

ST. CLARE: I suppose so, Tom; and you'll be going off and leaving me in a
month or so — though why you shouldn't no mortal knows.

TOM: Not while mas'r is in trouble. I'll stay with mas'r as long as he wants
me, so as I can be any use.   60

ST. CLARE (*Sadly.*):   Not while I'm in trouble, Tom? And when will my trouble be over?

TOM: When you are a believer.

ST. CLARE: And you really mean to stay by me till that day comes? (*Smiling
and laying his hand on Tom's shoulder.*) Ah, Tom! I won't keep you till that day.   65
Go home to your wife and children, and give my love to all.

TOM: I's faith to think that day will come — the Lord has a work for
mas'r.

ST. CLARE: A work, hey? Well, now, Tom, give me your views on what sort
of a work it is — let's hear.   70

TOM: Why, even a poor fellow like me has a work; and Mas'r St. Clare,
that has larnin', and riches, and friends, how much he might do for the
Lord.

ST. CLARE: Tom, you seem to think the Lord needs a great deal done for
him.   75

TOM: We does for him when we does for his creatures.

ST. CLARE: Good theology, Tom. Thank you, my boy; I like to hear you
talk. But go now, Tom, and leave me alone. (*Exit Tom.*) That faithful fellow's words have excited a train of thoughts that almost bear me, on the
strong tide of faith and feeling, to the gates of that heaven I so vividly   80
conceive. They seem to bring me nearer to Eva.

OPHELIA (*Outside.*):   What are you doing there, you limb of Satan? You've
been stealing something, I'll be bound.

(*Ophelia drags in Topsy.*)

TOPSY: You go 'long, Miss Feely, 'tain't none o' your business.

ST. CLARE: Heyday! what is all this commotion?   85

OPHELIA: She's been stealing.

TOPSY (*Sobbing.*):   I hadn't neither.

OPHELIA: What have you got in your bosom?

TOPSY: I've got my hand dar.

OPHELIA: But what have you got in your hand?   90

TOPSY: Nuffin'.

OPHELIA: That's a fib, Topsy.

TOPSY: Well, I 'spects it is.

OPHELIA: Give it to me, whatever it is.

TOPSY: It's mine — I hope I may die this bressed minute, if it don't belong   95
to me.

OPHELIA: Topsy, I order you to give me that article; don't let me have to
ask you again. (*Topsy reluctantly takes the foot of an old stocking from her bosom and
hands it to Ophelia.*) Sakes alive! what is all this? (*Takes from it a lock of hair, and
a small book, with a bit of crape twisted around it.*)

TOPSY: Dat's a lock of ha'r dat Miss Eva give me — she cut if from her   100
own beau'ful head herself.

ST. CLARE (*Takes book.*): Why did you wrap *this* (*Pointing to crape.*) around the
book?

TOPSY: 'Cause — 'cause — 'cause 'twas Miss Eva's. Oh! don't take 'em
away, please! (*Sits down on stage, and, putting her apron over her head, begins to sob   105
vehemently.*)

OPHELIA: Come, come, don't cry; you shall have them.

TOPSY (*Jumps up joyfully and takes them.*): I wants to keep 'em, 'cause dey
makes me good; I ain't half so wicked as I used to was. (*Runs off.*)

ST. CLARE: I really think you can make something of that girl. Any mind
that is capable of a *real sorrow* is capable of good. You must try and do   110
something with her.

OPHELIA: The child has improved very much; I have great hopes of her.

ST. CLARE: I believe I'll go down the street, a few moments, and hear the
news.

OPHELIA: Shall I call Tom to attend you?   115

ST. CLARE: No, I shall be back in an hour.   (*Exit.*)

OPHELIA: He's got an excellent heart, but then he's so dreadful shiftless!
(*Exit.*)

SCENE III

Front Chamber. Enter Topsy.

TOPSY: Dar's somethin' de matter wid me — I isn't a bit like myself. I
haven't done anything wrong since poor Miss Eva went up in de skies
and left us. When I's gwine to do anything wicked, I tinks of her, and
somehow I can't do it. I's getting to be good, dat's a fact. I 'spects when I's
dead I shall be turned into a little brack angel.   5

(*Enter Ophelia.*)

OPHELIA: Topsy, I've been looking for you; I've got something very particular to say to you.

TOPSY: Does you want me to say the catechism?

OPHELIA: No, not now. 10

TOPSY (*Aside.*):   Golly! dat's one comfort.

OPHELIA: Now, Topsy, I want you to try and understand what I am going to say to you.

TOPSY: Yes, missis, I'll open my ears drefful wide.

OPHELIA: Mr. St. Clare has given you to me, Topsy.

TOPSY: Den I b'longs to you, don't I? Golly! I thought I always belong to 15
you.

OPHELIA: Not till to-day have I received any authority to call you my property.

TOPSY: I's your property, am I? Well, if you say so, I 'spects I am.

OPHELIA: Topsy, I can give you your liberty. 20

TOPSY: My liberty?

OPHELIA: Yes, Topsy.

TOPSY: Has you got 'um with you?

OPHELIA: I have, Topsy.

TOPSY: Is it clothes or wittles? 25

OPHELIA: How shiftless! Don't you know what your liberty is, Topsy?

TOPSY: How should I know when I never seed 'um?

OPHELIA: Topsy, I am going to leave this place; I am going many miles away — to my own home in Vermont.

TOPSY: Den what's to become of dis chile? 30

OPHELIA: If you wish to go, I will take you with me.

TOPSY: Miss Feely, I doesn't want to leave you no how, I loves you I does.

OPHELIA: Then you shall share my home for the rest of your days. Come, Topsy.

TOPSY: Stop, Miss Feely; does dey hab any oberseers in Varmount? 35

OPHELIA: No, Topsy.

TOPSY: Nor cotton plantations, nor sugar factories, nor darkies, nor whipping nor nothing?

OPHELIA: No, Topsy.

TOPSY: By Golly! de quicker you is gwine de better den. 40

(*Enter Tom, hastily.*)

TOM: Oh, Miss Feely! Miss Feely!

OPHELIA: Gracious me, Tom! what's the matter?

TOM: Oh, Mas'r St. Clare! Mas'r St. Clare!

OPHELIA: Well, Tom, well?

TOM: They've just brought him home and I do believe he's killed? 45

OPHELIA: Killed?

TOPSY: Oh dear! what's to become of de poor darkies now?

TOM: He's dreadful weak. It's just as much as he can do to speak. He wanted me to call you.

OPHELIA: My poor cousin! Who would have thought of it? Don't say a 50 word to his wife, Tom; the danger may not be so great as you think; it would only distress her. Come with me; you may be able to afford some assistance.   (*Exeunt.*)

SCENE IV

Handsome Chamber. St. Clare discovered seated on sofa. Ophelia, Tom and Topsy are clustered around him. Doctor back of sofa feeling his pulse. Scene opens to slow music.

ST. CLARE (*Raising himself feebly.*):   Tom — poor fellow!

TOM: Well, mas'r?

ST. CLARE: I have received my death wound.

TOM: Oh, no, no, mas'r!

ST. CLARE: I feel that I am dying — Tom, pray!   5

TOM (*Sinking on his knees.*):   I do, pray, mas'r! I do pray!

ST. CLARE (*After a pause.*):   Tom, one thing preys upon my mind — I have forgotten to sign your freedom papers. What will become of you when I am gone?

TOM: Don't think of that, mas'r.   10

ST. CLARE: I was wrong, Tom, very wrong, to neglect it. I may be the cause of much suffering to you hereafter. Marie, my wife — she — oh! —

OPHELIA: His mind is wandering.

ST. CLARE (*Energetically.*):   No! it is coming *home* at last! (*Sinks back.*) At last! at last! Eva, I come! (*Dies. Music — slow curtain.*)   15

ACT V, SCENE I

An Auction Mart. Uncle Tom and Emmeline at back. Adolf, Skeggs, Marks, Mann, and various spectators discovered. Marks and Mann come forward.

MARKS: Hulloa, Alf! what brings you here?

MANN: Well, I was wanting a valet, and I heard that St. Clare's valet was going; I thought I'd just look at them.

MARKS: Catch me ever buying any of St. Clare's people. Spoiled niggers every one — impudent as the devil.   5

MANN: Never fear that; if I get 'em, I'll soon have their airs out of them — they'll soon find that they've another kind of master to deal with than St. Clare. 'Pon my word, I'll buy that fellow — I like the shape of him. (*Pointing to Adolf.*)

MARKS: You'll find it'll take all you've got to keep him — he's deucedly ex- *10*
travagant.

MANN: Yes, but my lord will find that he *can't* be extravagant with *me.* Just
let him be sent to the calaboose a few times, and thoroughly dressed
down, I'll tell you if it don't bring him to a sense of his ways. Oh! I'll reform him, up hill and down, you'll see. I'll buy him; that's flat.

(*Enter Legree, he goes up and looks at Adolf, whose boots are nicely blacked.*)

LEGREE: A nigger with his boots blacked — bah! (*Spits on them.*) Holloa, *15*
you! (*To Tom.*) Let's see your teeth. (*Seizes Tom by the jaw and opens his mouth.*)
Strip up your sleeve and show your muscle. (*Tom does so.*) Where was you
raised?

TOM: In Kintuck, mas'r.

LEGREE: What have you done? *20*

TOM: Had care of mas'r's farm.

LEGREE: That's a likely story. (*Turns to Emmeline.*) You're a nice-looking girl
enough. How old are you? (*Grasps her arm.*)

EMMELINE (*Shrieking.*): Ah! you hurt me.

SKEGGS: Stop that, you minx! No whimpering here. The sale is going to be- *25*
gin. (*Mounts the rostrum.*) Gentlemen, the next article I shall offer you to-day
is Adolf, late valet to Mr. St. Clare. How much am I offered? (*Various bids
are made. Adolf is knocked down to Mann for eight hundred dollars.*) Gentlemen, I now offer a prime article — the quadroon girl, Emmeline, only fifteen years of age, warranted in every respect. (*Business as before. Emmeline is* *30*
sold to Legree for one thousand dollars.) Now, I shall close to-day's sale by offering you the valuable article known as Uncle Tom, the most useful nigger
ever raised. Gentlemen in want of an overseer, now is the time to bid.

(*Business as before. Tom is sold to Legree for twelve hundred dollars.*)

LEGREE: Now look here, you two belong to me. (*Tom and Emmeline sink on
their knees.*)

TOM: Heaven help us, then! *35*

(*Music. Legree stands over them exulting. Picture — closed in.*)

SCENE II

The Garden of Miss Ophelia's House in Vermont. Enter Ophelia and Deacon Perry.

DEACON: Miss Ophelia, allow me to offer you my congratulations upon
your safe arrival in your native place. I hope it is your intention to pass
the remainder of your days with us?

OPHELIA: Well, Deacon, I have come here with that express purpose.

DEACON: I presume you were not over-pleased with the South?   5

OPHELIA: Well, to tell you the truth, Deacon, I wasn't; I liked the country very well, but the people there are so dreadful shiftless.

DEACON: The result, I presume, of living in a warm climate.

OPHELIA: Well, Deacon, what is the news among you all here?

DEACON: Well, we live on in the same even jog-trot pace. Nothing of any   10
consequence has happened — Oh! I forgot. (*Takes out handkerchief.*) I've lost my wife; my Molly has left me. (*Wipes his eyes.*)

OPHELIA: Poor soul! I pity you, Deacon.

DEACON: Thank you. You perceive I bear my loss with resignation.

OPHELIA: How you must miss her tongue!   15

DEACON: Molly certainly was fond of talking. She always would have the last word — heigho!

OPHELIA: What was her complaint, Deacon?

DEACON: A mild and soothing one, Miss Ophelia: she had a severe attack of the lockjaw.   20

OPHELIA: Dreadful!

DEACON: Wasn't it? When she found she couldn't use her tongue, she took it so much to heart that it struck to her stomach and killed her. Poor dear! Excuse my handkerchief; she's been dead only eighteen months.

OPHELIA: Why, Deacon, by this time you ought to be setting your cap for   25
another wife.

DEACON: Do you think so, Miss Ophelia?

OPHELIA: I don't see why you shouldn't — you are still a good-looking man, Deacon.

DEACON: Ah! well, I think I do wear well — in fact, I may say remarkably   30
well. It has been observed to me before.

OPHELIA: And you are not much over fifty?

DEACON: Just turned of forty, I assure you.

OPHELIA: Hale and hearty?

DEACON: Health excellent — look at my eye! Strong as a lion — look at   35
my arm!! A No. 1 constitution — look at my leg!!!

OPHELIA: Have you no thoughts of choosing another partner?

DEACON: Well, to tell you the truth, I have.

OPHELIA: Who is she?

DEACON: She is not far distant. (*Looks at Ophelia in an anguishing manner.*) I   40
have her in my eye at this present moment.

OPHELIA (*Aside.*):   Really, I believe he's going to pop. Why, surely, Deacon, you don't mean to —

DEACON: Yes, Miss Ophelia, I do mean; and believe me, when I say — (*Looking off.*) The Lord be good to us, but I believe there is the devil   45 coming!

(*Topsy runs on, with bouquet. She is now dressed very neatly.*)

TOPSY: Miss Feely, here is some flowers dat I hab been gathering for you. (*Gives bouquet.*)

OPHELIA: That's a good child.

DEACON: Miss Ophelia, who is this young person?

OPHELIA: She is my daughter.   50

DEACON (*Aside.*):   Her daughter! Then she must have married a colored man off South. I was not aware that you had been married, Miss Ophelia?

OPHELIA: Married! Sakes alive! what made you think I had been married?

DEACON: Good gracious, I'm getting confused. Didn't I understand you to say that this — somewhat tanned — young lady was your daughter?   55

OPHELIA: Only by adoption. She is my adopted daughter.

DEACON: O — oh! (*Aside.*) I breathe again.

TOPSY: By Golly! dat old man's eyes stick out of 'um head dre'ful. Guess he never seed anything like me afore.

OPHELIA: Deacon, won't you step into the house and refresh yourself after   60 your walk?

DEACON: I accept your polite invitation. (*Offers his arm.*) Allow me.

OPHELIA: As gallant as ever, Deacon. I declare, you grow younger every day.

DEACON: You can never grow old, madam.   65

OPHELIA: Ah, you flatterer!   (*Exeunt.*)

TOPSY: Dar dey go, like an old goose and gander. Guess dat ole gemble-mun feels kind of confectionary — rather sweet on my old missis. By Golly! she's been dre'ful kind to me ever since I come away from de South; and I loves her, I does, 'cause she takes such car' on me and gives   70 me dese fine clothes. I tries to be good too, and I's gettin 'long 'mazin' fast. I's not so wicked as I used to was. (*Looks out.*) Holloa! dar's some one comin' here. I wonder what he wants now. (*Retires, observing.*)

(*Enter Gumption Cute, very shabby, a small bundle, on a stick, over his shoulder.*)

CUTE: By chowder, here I am again. Phew, it's a pretty considerable tall piece of walking between here and New Orleans, not to mention   75 the wear of shoe-leather. I guess I'm about done up. If this streak of bad luck lasts much longer, I'll borrow sixpence to buy a rope, and hang myself right straight up! When I went to call on Miss Ophelia, I swow

if I didn't find out that she had left for Vermont; so I kind of con- 80
cluded to make tracks in that direction myself and as I didn't have any
money left, why I had to foot it, and here I am in old Varmount once
more. They told me Miss Ophelia lived up here. I wonder if she will remember the relationship. (*Sees Topsy.*) By chowder, there's a darkey. Look
here, Charcoal!

TOPSY (*Comes forward.*):   My name isn't Charcoal — it's Topsy.   85

CUTE: Oh! your name is Topsy, is it, you juvenile specimen of Day & Martin?

TOPSY: Tell you I don't know nothin' 'bout Day & Martin. I's Topsy and I
belong to Miss Feely St. Clare.

CUTE: I'm much obleeged to you, you small extract of Japan, for your in-   90
formation. So Miss Ophelia lives up there in the white house, does she?

TOPSY: Well, she don't do nothin' else.

CUTE: Well, then, just locomote your pins.

TOPSY: What — what's dat?

CUTE: Walk your chalks!   95

TOPSY: By Golly! dere ain't no chalk 'bout me.

CUTE: Move your trotters.

TOPSY: How you does spoke! What you mean by trotters?

CUTE: Why, your feet, Stove Polish.

TOPSY: What does you want me to move my feet for?   100

CUTE: To tell your mistress, you ebony angel, that a gentleman wishes to
see her.

TOPSY: Does you call yourself a gentleman! By Golly! you look more like
a scar'crow.

CUTE: Now look here, you Charcoal, don't you be sassy. I'm a gentleman   105
in distress; a done-up speculator; one that has seen better days — long
time ago — and better clothes too, by chowder! My creditors are like my
boots — they've no soles. I'm a victim to circumstances. I've been
through much and survived it. I've taken walking exercise for the benefit
of my health; but as I was trying to live on air at the same time, it was a   110
losing speculation, 'cause it gave me such a dreadful appetite.

TOPSY: Golly! you look as if you could eat an ox, horns and all.

CUTE: Well, I calculate I could, if he was roasted — it's a speculation I
should like to engage in. I have returned like the fellow that run away in
Scripture; and if anybody's got a fatted calf they want to kill, all they got   115
to do is to fetch him along. Do you know, Charcoal, that your mistress is
a relation of mine?

TOPSY: Is she your uncle?

CUTE: No, no, not quite so near as that. My second cousin married her niece.

TOPSY: And does you want to see Miss Feely? 120

CUTE: I do. I have come to seek a home beneath her roof, and take care of all the spare change she don't want to use.

TOPSY: Den just you follow me, mas'r.

CUTE: Stop! By chowder, I've got a great idee. Say, you Day & Martin, how should you like to enter into a speculation? 125

TOPSY: Golly! I doesn't know what a spec — spec — cu — what-do-you-call-'um am.

CUTE: Well, now, I calculate I've hit upon about the right thing. Why should I degrade the manly dignity of the Cutes by becoming a beggar — expose myself to the chance of receiving the cold shoulder as a 130 poor relation? By chowder, my blood biles as I think of it! Topsy, you can make my fortune, and your own, too. I've an idee in my head that is worth a million of dollars.

TOPSY: Golly! is your head worth dat? Guess you wouldn't bring dat out South for de whole of you. 135

CUTE: Don't you be too severe, now, Charcoal; I'm a man of genius. Did you ever hear of Barnum?

TOPSY: Barnum! Barnum! Does he live out South?

CUTE: No, he lives in New York. Do you know how he made his fortin?

TOPSY: What is him fortin, hey? Is it something he wears? 140

CUTE: Chowder, how green you are!

TOPSY (*Indignantly.*): Sar, I hab you to know I's not green; I's brack.

CUTE: To be sure you are, Day & Martin. I calculate, when a person says another has a fortune, he means he's got plenty of money, Charcoal.

TOPSY: And did he make the money? 145

CUTE: Sartin sure, and no mistake.

TOPSY: Golly! now I thought money always growed.

CUTE: Oh, git out! You are too cute — you are cuterer than I am — and I'm Cute by name and cute by nature. Well, as I was saying, Barnum made his money by exhibiting a *woolly* horse; now wouldn't it be an all- 150 fired speculation to show you as the woolly gal?

TOPSY: You want to make a sight of me?

CUTE: I'll give you half the receipts, by chowder!

TOPSY: Should I have to leave Miss Feely?

CUTE: To be sure you would. 155

TOPSY: Den you hab to get a woolly gal somewhere else, Mas'r Cute. (*Runs off.*)

CUTE: There's another speculation gone to smash, by chowder! (*Exit.*)

SCENE III

A Rude Chamber. Tom is discovered, in old clothes, seated on a stool. He holds in his hand a paper containing a curl of Eva's hair. The scene opens to the symphony of "Old Folks at Home."

TOM: I have come to de dark places; I's going through de vale of shadows. My heart sinks at times and feels just like a big lump of lead. Den it gits up in my throat and chokes me till de tears roll out of my eyes; den I take out dis curl of little Miss Eva's hair, and the sight of it brings calm to my mind and I feels strong again. (*Kisses the curl and puts it in his breast — takes out a silver dollar, which is suspended around his neck by a string.*) Dere's de bright silver dollar dat Mas'r George Shelby gave me the day I was sold away from old Kentuck, and I've kept it ever since. Mas'r George must have grown to be a man by this time. I wonder if I shall ever see him again. 5

(*Song. "Old Folks at Home." Enter Legree, Emmeline, Sambo and Quimbo.*)

LEGREE: Shut up, you black cuss! Did you think I wanted any of your infernal howling? (*Turns to Emmeline.*) We're home. (*Emmeline shrinks from him. He takes hold of her ear.*) You didn't ever wear earrings? 10

EMMELINE (*Trembling.*):   No, master.

LEGREE: Well, I'll give you a pair, if you're a good girl. You needn't be so frightened; I don't mean to make you work very hard. You'll have fine times with me and live like a lady; only be a good girl. 15

EMMELINE: My soul sickens as his eyes gaze upon me. His touch makes my very flesh creep.

LEGREE (*Turns to Tom, and points to Sambo and Quimbo.*):   Ye see what ye'd get if ye'd try to run off. These yer boys have been raised to track niggers and they'd just as soon chaw one on ye up as eat their suppers; so mind yourself. (*To Emmeline.*) Come, mistress, you go in here with me. (*Taking Emmeline's hand, and leading her off.*) 20

EMMELINE (*Withdrawing her hand, and shrinking back.*):   No, no! let me work in the fields; I don't want to be a lady.

LEGREE: Oh! you're going to be contrary, are you? I'll soon take all that out of you. 25

EMMELINE: Kill me, if you will.

LEGREE: Oh! you want to be killed, do you? Now come here, you Tom, you see I told you I didn't buy you jest for the common work; I mean to promote you and make a driver of you, and to-night ye may jest as well begin to get yer hand in. Now ye jest take this yer gal, and flog her; ye've seen enough on't to know how. 30

TOM: I beg mas'r's pardon — hopes mas'r won't set me at that. It's what I a'nt used to — never did, and can't do — no way possible.

LEGREE: Ye'll larn a pretty smart chance of things ye never did know be- 35 fore I've done with ye. (*Strikes Tom with whip, three blows. Music chord each blow.*) There! now will ye tell me ye can't do it?

TOM: Yes, mas'r! I'm willing to work night and day, and work while there's life and breath in me; but this yer thing I can't feel it right to do, and, mas'r, I *never* shall do it, *never!* 40

LEGREE: What! ye black beast! tell *me* ye don't think it right to do what I tell ye! What have any of you cussed cattle to do with thinking what's right? I'll put a stop to it. Why, what do ye think ye are? May be ye think yer a gentleman, master Tom, to be telling your master what's right and what a'nt! So you pretend it's wrong to flog the gal? 45

TOM: I think so, mas'r; 'twould be downright cruel, and it's what I never will do, mas'r. If you mean to kill me, kill me; but as to raising my hand agin any one here, I never shall — I'll die first!

LEGREE: Well, here's a pious dog at last, let down among us sinners — pow- erful holy critter he must be. Here, you rascal! you make believe to be so 50 pious, didn't you never read out of your Bible, "Servants, obey your mas- ters"? An't I your master? Didn't I pay twelve hundred dollars, cash, for all there is inside your cussed old black shell? An't you mine, body and soul?

TOM: No, no! My soul a'nt yours, mas'r; you haven't bought it — ye can't buy it; it's been bought and paid for by one that is able to keep it, and you 55 can't harm it!

LEGREE: I can't? we'll see, we'll see! Here, Sambo! Quimbo! give this dog such a breaking in as he won't get over this month!

EMMELINE: Oh, no! you will not be so cruel — have some mercy! (*Clings to Tom.*)

LEGREE: Mercy? you won't find any in this shop! Away with the black cuss! 60 Flog him within an inch of his life!

(*Music. Sambo and Quimbo seize Tom and drag him up stage. Legree seizes Emme- line, and throws her round. She falls on her knees, with her hands lifted in supplication. Legree raises his whip, as if to strike Tom. Picture closed in.*)

SCENE IV

Plain Chamber. Enter Ophelia, followed by Topsy.

OPHELIA: A person inquiring for me, did you say, Topsy?

TOPSY: Yes, missis.

OPHELIA: What kind of a looking man is he?

TOPSY: By golly! he's very queer looking man? anyway; and den he talks so dre'ful funny. What does you think? — yah! yah! he wanted to 'zibite me as de woolly gal! yah! yah!

OPHELIA: Oh! I understand. Some cute Yankee, who wants to purchase you, to make a show of — the heartless wretch!

TOPSY: Dat's just him, missis; dat's just his name. He tole me dat it was Cute — Mr. Cute Speculashum — dat's him.

OPHELIA: What did you say to him, Topsy?

TOPSY: Well, I didn't say much, it was brief and to the point — I tole him I wouldn't leave you, Miss Feely, no how.

OPHELIA: That's right, Topsy; you know you are very comfortable here — you wouldn't fare quite so well if you went away among strangers.

TOPSY: By golly! I know dat; you takes care on me, and makes me good. I don't steal any now, and I don't swar, and I don't dance breakdowns. Oh! I isn't so wicked as I used to was.

OPHELIA: That's right, Topsy; now show the gentleman, or whatever he is, up.

TOPSY: By golly! I guess he won't make much out of Miss Feely. (*Crosses and exits.*)

OPHELIA: I wonder who this person can be? Perhaps it is some old acquaintance, who has heard of my arrival, and who comes on a social visit.

(*Enter Cute.*)

CUTE: Aunt, how do ye do? Well, I swan, the sight of you is good for weak eyes. (*Offers his hand.*)

OPHELIA (*Coldly drawing back.*):   Really, sir, I can't say that I ever had the pleasure of seeing you before.

CUTE: Well, it's a fact that you never did. You see I never happened to be in your neighborhood afore now. Of course you've heard of me? I'm one of the Cutes — Gumption Cute, the first and only son of Josiah and Maria Cute, of Oniontown, on the Onion river in the north part of this ere State of Varmount.

OPHELIA: Can't say I ever heard the name before.

CUTE: Well then, I calculate your memory must be a little ricketty. I'm a relation of yours.

OPHELIA: A relation of mine! Why, I never heard of any Cutes in our family.

CUTE: Well, I shouldn't wonder if you never did. Don't you remember your niece, Mary?

OPHELIA: Of course I do. What a shiftless question!

CUTE: Well, you see my second cousin, Abijah Blake, married her. So you   40
see that makes me a relation of yours.

OPHELIA: Rather a distant one, I should say.

CUTE: By chowder! I'm *near* enough, just at present.

OPHELIA: Well, you certainly are a sort of connection of mine.

CUTE: Yes, kind of sort of.   45

OPHELIA: And of course you are welcome to my house, as long as you wish
to make it your home.

CUTE: By chowder! I'm booked for the next six months — this isn't a bad
speculation.

OPHELIA: I hope you left all your folks well at home?   50

CUTE: Well, yes, they're pretty comfortably disposed of. Father and
mother's dead, and Uncle Josh has gone to California. I am the only representative of the Cutes left.

OPHELIA: There doesn't seem to be a great deal of *you* left. I declare, you
are positively in rags.   55

CUTE: Well, you see, the fact is, I've been speculating — trying to get
banknotes — specie-rags, as they say — but I calculate I've turned out
rags of another sort.

OPHELIA: I'm sorry for your ill luck, but I am afraid you have been shiftless.   60

CUTE: By chowder! I've done all that a fellow could do. You see, somehow,
everything I take hold of kind of bursts up.

OPHELIA: Well, well, perhaps you'll do better for the future; make yourself
at home. I have got to see to some house-hold matters, so excuse me for
a short time. (*Aside.*) Impudent and shiftless.   (*Exit.*)   65

CUTE: By chowder! I rather guess that this speculation will hitch. She's a
good-natured old critter; I reckon I'll be a son to her while she lives, and
take care of her valuables arter she's a defunct departed. I wonder if they
keep the vittles in this ere room? Guess not. I've got extensive accommo-
dations for all sorts of eatables. I'm a regular vacuum, throughout —   70
pockets and all. I'm chuck full of emptiness. (*Looks out.*) Holloa! who's this
elderly individual coming up stairs? He looks like a compound essence of
starch and dignity. I wonder if he isn't another relation of mine. I should
like a rich old fellow now for an uncle.

(*Enter Deacon Perry.*)

DEACON: Ha! a stranger here!   75

CUTE: How d'ye do?

DEACON: You are a friend to Miss Ophelia, I presume?

CUTE: Well, I rather calculate that I am a leetle more than a friend.

DEACON (*Aside.*):   Bless me! what can he mean by those mysterious words? Can he be her — no I don't think he can. She said she wasn't — well, at all events, it's very suspicious.   80

CUTE: The old fellow seems kind of stuck up.

DEACON: You are a particular friend to Miss Ophelia, you say?

CUTE: Well, I calculate I am.

DEACON: Bound to her by any tender tie?   85

CUTE: It's something more than a tie — it's a regular double-twisted knot.

DEACON: Ah! just as I suspected. (*Aside.*) Might I inquire the nature of that tie?[1]

CUTE: Well, it's the natural tie of relationship.

DEACON: A relation — what relation?   90

CUTE: Why, you see, my second cousin, Abijah Blake, married her niece, Mary.

DEACON: Oh! is that all?

CUTE: By chowder, ain't that enough?

DEACON: Then you are not her husband?   95

CUTE: To be sure I ain't. What put that ere idee into your cranium?

DEACON (*Shaking him vigorously by the hand.*):   My dear sir, I'm delighted to see you.

CUTE: Holloa! you ain't going slightly insane, are you?

DEACON: No, no fear of that; I'm only happy, that's all.   100

CUTE: I wonder if he's been taking a nipper?

DEACON: As you are a relation of Miss Ophelia's, I think it proper that I should make you my confidant; in fact, let you into a little scheme that I have lately conceived.

CUTE: Is it a speculation?   105

DEACON: Well, it is, just at present; but I trust before many hours to make it a surety.

CUTE: By chowder! I hope it won't serve you the way my speculations have served me. But fire away, old boy, and give us the prospectus.

DEACON: Well, then, my young friend, I have been thinking, ever since   110 Miss Ophelia returned to Vermont, that she was just the person to fill the place of my lamented Molly.

CUTE: Say, you, you couldn't tell us who your lamented Molly was, could you?

---

[1] The sense of this line suggests that the aside should come at the beginning, and the question should be addressed to Cute.

DEACON: Why, the late Mrs. Perry, to be sure.   115
CUTE: Oh! then the lamented Molly was your wife?
DEACON: She was.
CUTE: And now you wish to marry Miss Ophelia?
DEACON: Exactly.
CUTE (*Aside.*):   Consarn this old porpoise! if I let him do that he'll Jew me   120
   out of my living. By chowder! I'll put a spoke in his wheel.
DEACON: Well, what do you say? will you intercede for me with your aunt?
CUTE: No! bust me up if I do!
DEACON: No?
CUTE: No, I tell you. I forbid the bans. Now, ain't you a purty individual,   125
   to talk about getting married, you old superannuated Methuselah specimen of humanity! Why, you've got one foot in etarnity already, and
   t'other ain't fit to stand on. Go home and go to bed! have your head
   shaved, and send for a lawyer to make your will, leave your property to
   your heirs — if you hain't got any, why leave it to me — I'll take care of   130
   it, and charge nothing for the trouble.
DEACON: Really, sir, this language to one of my standing, is highly indecorous — it's more, sir, than I feel willing to endure, sir. I shall expect an ex-
   planation, sir.
CUTE: Now, you see, old gouty toes, you're losing your temper.   135
DEACON: Sir, I'm a deacon; I never lost my temper in all my life, sir.
CUTE: Now, you see, you're getting excited; you had better go; we can't
   have a disturbance here!
DEACON: No, sir! I shall not go, sir! I shall not go until I have seen Miss
   Ophelia. I wish to know if she will countenance this insult.   140
CUTE: Now keep cool, old stick-in-the-mud! Draw it mild, old timber-toes!
DEACON: Damn it all, sir, what —
CUTE: Oh! only think, now, what would people say to hear a deacon
   swearing like a trooper?
DEACON: Sir — I — you — this is too much, sir.   145
CUTE: Well, now, I calculate that's just about my opinion, so we'll have no
   more of it. Get out of this! start your boots, or by chowder! I'll pitch you
   from one end of the stairs to the other.

(*Enter Ophelia.*)

OPHELIA: Hoity toity! What's the meaning of all these loud words?
CUTE: Well, you see, Aunt —   ⎫
                                       ⎬ (*Together.*)   150
DEACON: Miss Ophelia, I beg —   ⎭
CUTE: Now, look here, you just hush your yap! How can I fix up matters if
   you keep jabbering?

OPHELIA: Silence! for shame, Mr. Cute. Is that the way you speak to the
deacon?   155

CUTE: Darn the deacon!

OPHELIA: Deacon Perry, what is all this?

DEACON: Madam, a few words will explain everything. Hearing from this
person that he was your nephew, I ventured to tell him that I cherished
hopes of making you my wife, whereupon he flew into a violent passion,   160
and ordered me out of the house.

OPHELIA: Does this house belong to you or me, Mr. Cute?

CUTE: Well, to you, I reckon.

OPHELIA: Then how dare you give orders in it?

CUTE: Well, I calculated that you wouldn't care about marrying old half-a- 165
century there.

OPHELIA: That's enough; I will marry him; and as for you, (*Points.*) get out.

CUTE: Get out?

OPHELIA: Yes; the sooner the better.

CUTE: Darned if I don't serve him out first though.   170

(*Music. Cute makes a dash at Deacon, who gets behind Ophelia. Topsy enters, with a
broom and beats Cute around stage. Ophelia faints in Deacon's arms. Cute falls, and
Topsy butts him kneeling over him. Quick drop.*)

ACT VI, SCENE I

*Dark landscape. An old, roofless shed. Tom is discovered in shed, lying on some old cot-
ton bagging. Cassy kneels by his side, holding a cup to his lips.*

CASSY: Drink all ye want. I knew how it would be. It isn't the first time I've
been out in the night, carrying water to such as you.

TOM (*Returning cup.*): Thank you, missis.

CASSY: Don't call me missis. I'm a miserable slave like yourself — a lower
one than you can ever be! It's no use, my poor fellow, this you've been try-   5
ing to do. You were a brave fellow. You had the right on your side; but it's
all in vain for you to struggle. You are in the Devil's hands; he is the
strongest, and you must give up.

TOM: Oh! how can I give up?

CASSY: You see *you* don't know anything about it; I do. Here you are, on a   10
lone plantation, ten miles from any other, in the swamps; not a white person here who could testify, if you were burned alive. There's no law here
that can do you, or any of us, the least good; and this man! there's no
earthly thing that he is not bad enough to do. I could make one's hair
rise, and their teeth chatter, if I should only tell what I've seen and been   15

knowing to here; and it's no use resisting! Did I *want* to live with him? Wasn't I a woman delicately bred? and he! — Father in Heaven! what was he and is he? And yet I've lived with him these five years, and cursed every moment of my life, night and day.

TOM: Oh heaven! have you quite forgot us poor critters?   20

CASSY: And what are these miserable low dogs you work with, that you should suffer on their account? Every one of them would turn against you the first time they get a chance. They are all of them as low and cruel to each other as they can be; there's no use in your suffering to keep from hurting them?   25

TOM: What made 'em cruel? If I give out I shall get used to it and grow, little by little, just like 'em. No, no, Missis, I've lost everything, wife, and children, and home, and a kind master, and he would have set me free if he'd only lived a day longer — I've lost everything in *this* world, and now I can't lose heaven, too: no I can't get to be wicked besides all.   30

CASSY: But it can't be that He will lay sin to our account; he won't charge it to us when we are forced to it; he'll charge it to them that drove us to it. Can I do anything more for you? Shall I give you some more water?

TOM: Oh missis! I wish you'd go to Him who can give you living waters!

CASSY: Go to him! Where is he? Who is he?   35

TOM: Our Heavenly Father!

CASSY: I used to see the picture of him, over the altar, when I was a girl but *he isn't here!* there's nothing here but sin, and long, long despair! There, there, don't talk any more, my poor fellow. Try to sleep, if you can. I must hasten back, lest my absence be noted. Think of me when I am gone,   40 Uncle Tom, and pray, pray for me.

(*Music. Exit Cassy. Tom sinks back to sleep.*)

SCENE II

Street in New Orleans. Enter George Shelby.

GEORGE: At length my mission of mercy is nearly finished, I have reached my journey's end. I have now but to find the house of Mr. St. Clare, re-purchase old Uncle Tom, and convey him back to his wife and children, in old Kentucky. Some one approaches; he may, perhaps, be able to give me the information I require. I will accost him. (*Enter Marks.*) Pray, sir,   5 can you tell me where Mr. St. Clare dwells?

MARKS: Where I don't think you'll be in a hurry to seek him.

GEORGE: And where is that?

MARKS: In the grave!

GEORGE: Stay, sir! you may be able to give me some information concern-   10
ing Mr. St. Clare.

MARKS: I beg pardon, sir, I am a lawyer; I can't afford to *give* anything.

GEORGE: But you would have no objections to selling it?

MARKS: Not the slightest.

GEORGE: What do you value it at?   15

MARKS: Well, say five dollars, that's reasonable.

GEORGE: There they are. (*Gives money.*) Now answer me to the best of your
ability. Has the death of St. Clare caused his slaves to be sold?

MARKS: It has.

GEORGE: How were they sold?   20

MARKS: At auction — they went dirt cheap.

GEORGE: How were they bought — all in one lot?

MARKS: No, they went to different bidders.

GEORGE: Was you present at the sale?

MARKS: I was.   25

GEORGE: Do you remember seeing a negro among them called Tom?

MARKS: What, Uncle Tom?

GEORGE: The same — who bought him?

MARKS: A Mr. Legree.

GEORGE: Where is his plantation?   30

MARKS: Up in Louisiana, on the Red River; but a man never could find it,
unless he had been there before.

GEORGE: Who could I get to direct me there?

MARKS: Well, stranger, I don't know of any one just at present 'cept myself,
could find it for you; it's such an out-of-the-way sort of hole; and if you   35
are a mind to come down handsomely, why, I'll do it.

GEORGE: The reward shall be ample.

MARKS: Enough said, stranger; let's take the steamboat at once.   (*Exeunt.*)

Scene III

A Rough Chamber. Enter Legree. Sits.

LEGREE: Plague on that Sambo, to kick up this yer row between Tom and
the new hands. (*Cassy steals on and stands behind him.*) The fellow won't be fit
to work for a week now, right in the press of the season.

CASSY: Yes, just like you.

LEGREE: Hah! you she-devil! you've come back, have you? (*Rises.*)

CASSY: Yes, I have; come to have my own way, too.

LEGREE: You lie, you jade! I'll be up to my word. Either behave yourself or stay down in the quarters and fare and work with the rest.

CASSY: I'd rather, ten thousand times, live in the dirtiest hole at the quarters, than be under your hoof! 10

LEGREE: But you are under my hoof, for all that, that's one comfort; so sit down here and listen to reason. (*Grasps her wrist.*)

CASSY: Simon Legree, take care! (*Legree lets go his hold.*) You're afraid of me, Simon, and you've reason to be; for I've got the Devil in me!

LEGREE: I believe to my soul you have. After all, Cassy, why can't you be 15 friends with me, as you used to?

CASSY (*Bitterly.*): Used to!

LEGREE: I wish, Cassy, you'd behave yourself decently.

CASSY: *You* talk about behaving decently! and what have you been doing? You haven't even sense enough to keep from spoiling one of your best 20 hands, right in the most pressing season, just for your devilish temper.

LEGREE: I was a fool, it's fact, to let any such brangle come up. Now when Tom set up his will he had to be broke in.

CASSY: You'll never break *him* in.

LEGREE: Won't I? I'd like to know if I won't? He'd be the first nigger that 25 ever come it round me! I'll break every bone in his body but he shall give up. (*Enter Sambo, with a paper in his hand, stands bowing.*) What's that, you dog?

SAMBO: It's a witch thing, mas'r.

LEGREE: A what?

SAMBO: Something that niggers gits from witches. Keep 'em from feeling 30 when they's flogged. He had it tied round his neck with a black string.

(*Legree takes the paper and opens it. A silver dollar drops on the stage, and a long curl of light hair twines around his finger.*)

LEGREE: Damnation. (*Stamping and writhing, as if the hair burned him.*) Where did this come from? Take it off! burn it up! burn it up! (*Throws the curl* 35 *away.*) What did you bring it to me for?

SAMBO (*Trembling.*): I beg pardon, mas'r; I thought you would like to see um.

LEGREE: Don't you bring me any more of your devilish things. (*Shakes his fist at Sambo who runs off. Legree kicks the dollar after him.*) Blast it! where did he get that? If it didn't look just like — whoo! I thought I'd forgot that. Curse me 40 if I think there's any such thing as forgetting anything, any how.

CASSY: What is the matter with you, Legree? What is there in a simple curl of fair hair to appall a man like you — you who are familiar with every form of cruelty.

LEGREE: Cassy, to-night the past has been recalled to me — the past that I have so long and vainly striven to forget.   45

CASSY: Has aught on this earth power to move a soul like thine?

LEGREE: Yes, for hard and reprobate as I now seem, there has been a time when I have been rocked on the bosom of a mother, cradled with prayers and pious hymns, my now seared brow bedewed with the waters of holy baptism.   50

CASSY (*Aside.*):   What sweet memories of childhood can thus soften down that heart of iron?

LEGREE: In early childhood a fair-haired woman has led me, at the sound of Sabbath bells, to worship and to pray. Born of a hard-tempered sire, on whom that gentle woman had wasted a world of unvalued love, I fol- 55 lowed in the steps of my father. Boisterous, unruly and tyrannical, I despised all her counsel, and would have none of her reproof, and, at an early age, broke from her to seek my fortunes on the sea. I never came home but once after that; and then my mother, with the yearning of a heart that must love something, and had nothing else to love, clung to 60 me, and sought with passionate prayers and entreaties to win me from a life of sin.

CASSY: That was your day of grace, Legree; then good angels called you, and mercy held you by the hand.

LEGREE: My heart inly relented; there was a conflict, but sin got the vic- 65 tory, and I set all the force of my rough nature against the conviction of my conscience. I drank and swore, was wilder and more brutal than ever. And one night, when my mother, in the last agony of her despair, knelt at my feet, I spurned her from me, threw her senseless on the floor, and with brutal curses fled to my ship.   70

CASSY: Then the fiend took thee for his own.

LEGREE: The next I heard of my mother was one night while I was carousing among drunken companions. A letter was put in my hands. I opened it, and a lock of long, curling hair fell from it, and twined about my fingers, even as that lock twined but now. The letter told me that my mother 75 was dead, and that dying she blest and forgave me! (*Buries his face in his hands.*)

CASSY: Why did you not even then renounce your evil ways?

LEGREE: There is a dread, unhallowed necromancy of evil, that turns things sweetest and holiest to phantoms of horror and afright. That pale, loving mother, — her dying prayers, her forgiving love, — wrought in 80 my demoniac heart of sin only as a damning sentence, bringing with it a fearful looking for of judgment and fiery indignation.

CASSY: And yet you would not strive to avert the doom that threatened you.

LEGREE: I burned the lock of hair and I burned the letter; and when I saw them hissing and crackling in the flame, inly shuddered as I thought of everlasting fires! I tried to drink and revel, and swear away the memory; but often in the deep night, whose solemn stillness arraigns the soul in forced communion with itself, I have seen that pale mother rising by my bed-side, and felt the soft twining of that hair around my fingers, 'till the cold sweat would roll down my face, and I would spring from my bed in horror — horror! (*Falls in chair — After a pause.*) What the devil ails me? Large drops of sweat stand on my forehead, and my heart beats heavy and thick with fear. I thought I saw something white rising and glimmering in the gloom before me, and it seemed to bear my mother's face! I know one thing; I'll let that fellow Tom alone, after this. What did I want with his cussed paper? I believe I am bewitched sure enough! I've been shivering and sweating ever since! Where did he get that hair? It couldn't have been that! I *burn'd* that up, I know I did! It would be a joke if hair could rise from the dead! I'll have Sambo and Quimbo up here to sing and dance one of their dances, and keep off these horrid notions. Here, Sambo! Quimbo!   (*Exit.*)

CASSY: Yes, Legree, that golden tress was charmed; each hair had in it a spell of terror and remorse for thee, and was used by a mightier power to bind thy cruel hands from inflicting uttermost evil on the helpless!

(*Exit.*)

SCENE IV

Street. Enter Marks meeting Cute, who enters dressed in an old faded uniform.

MARKS: By the land, stranger, but it strikes me that I've seen you somewhere before.

CUTE: By chowder! do you know now, that's just what I was going to say?

MARKS: Isn't your name Cute?

CUTE: You're right, I calculate. Yours is Marks, I reckon.

MARKS: Just so.

CUTE: Well, I swow, I'm glad to see you. (*They shake hands.*) How's your wholesome?

MARKS: Hearty as ever. Well, who would have thought of ever seeing you again. Why, I thought you was in Vermont?

CUTE: Well, so I was. You see I went there after that rich relation of mine — but the speculation didn't turn out well.

MARKS: How so?

CUTE: Why, you see, she took a shine to an old fellow — Deacon Abraham Perry — and married him.

MARKS: Oh, that rather put your nose out of joint in that quarter.

CUTE: Busted me right up, I tell you. The Deacon did the hand-some thing though, he said if I would leave the neighborhood and go out South again, he'd stand the damage. I calculate I didn't give him much time to change his mind, and so, you see, here I am again.   20

MARKS: What are you doing in that soldier rig?

CUTE: Oh, this is my sign.

MARKS: Your sign?

CUTE: Yes; you see, I'm engaged just at present in an all-fired good specu-lation, I'm a Fillibusterow.   25

MARKS: A what?

CUTE: A Fillubusterow! Don't you know what that is? It's Spanish for Cuban Volunteer; and means a chap that goes the whole perker for glory and all that ere sort of thing.

MARKS: Oh! you've joined the order of the Lone Star!   30

CUTE: You've hit it. You see I bought this uniform at a second hand cloth-ing store, I puts it on and goes to a benevolent individual and I says to him, — appealing to his feelings, — I'm one of the fellows that went to Cuba and got massacred by the bloody Spaniards. I'm in a destitute con-dition — give me a trifle to pay my passage back, so I can whop the   35 tyrannical cusses and avenge my brave fellow soger what got slewed there.

MARKS: How pathetic!

CUTE: I tell you it works up the feelings of benevolent individuals dread-fully. It draws tears from their eyes and money from their pockets. By   40 chowder! one old chap gave me a hundred dollars to help on the cause.

MARKS: I admire a genius like yours.

CUTE: But I say, what are you up to?

MARKS: I am the traveling companion of a young gentleman by the name of Shelby, who is going to the plantation of a Mr. Legree of the Red   45 River, to buy an old darkey who used to belong to his father.

CUTE: Legree — Legree? Well, now, I calculate I've heard that ere name afore.

MARKS: Do you remember that man who drew a bowie knife on you in New Orleans?   50

CUTE: By chowder! I remember the circumstance just as well as if it was yesterday; but I can't say that I recollect much about the man, for you see I was in something of a hurry about that time and didn't stop to take a good look at him.

MARKS: Well, that man was this same Mr. Legree.   55

CUTE: Do you know, now, I should like to pay that critter off!

MARKS: Then I'll give you an opportunity.

CUTE: Chowder! how will you do that?

MARKS: Do you remember the gentleman that interfered between you and Legree?   60

CUTE: Yes — well?

MARKS: He received the blow that was intended for you, and died from the effects of it. So, you see, Legree is a murderer, and we are only witnesses of the deed. His life is in our hands.

CUTE: Let's have him right up and make him dance on nothing to the   65 tune of Yandee Doodle!

MARKS: Stop a bit. Don't you see a chance for a profitable speculation?

CUTE: A speculation! Fire away, don't be bashful, I'm the man for a speculation.

MARKS: I have made a deposition to the Governor of the state on all the   70 particulars of that affair at Orleans.

CUTE: What did you do that for?

MARKS: To get a warrant for his arrest.

CUTE: Oh! and have you got it?

MARKS: Yes; here it is. (*Takes out paper.*)   75

CUTE: Well, now, I don't see how you are going to make anything by that bit of paper?

MARKS: But I do. I shall say to Legree, I have got a warrant against you for murder; my friend, Mr. Cute, and myself are the only witnesses who can appear against you. Give us a thousand dollars, and we will tear the war-   80 rant and be silent.

CUTE: Then Mr. Legree forks over a thousand dollars, and your friend Cute pockets five hundred of it, is that the calculation?

MARKS: If you will join me in the undertaking.

CUTE: I'll do it, by chowder!   85

MARKS: Your hand to bind the bargain.

CUTE: I'll stick by you thro' thick and thin.

MARKS: Enough said.

CUTE: Then shake. (*They shake hands.*)

MARKS: But I say, Cute, he may be contrary and show fight.   90

CUTE: Never mind, we've got the law on our side, and we're bound to stir him up. If he don't come down handsomely we'll present him with a neck-tie made of hemp!

MARKS: I declare you're getting spunky.

CUTE: Well, I reckon, I am. Let's go and have something to drink. Tell   95 you what, Marks, if we don't get *him,* we'll have his hide, by chowder! (*Exeunt, arm-in-arm.*)

SCENE V

Rough Chamber. Enter Legree, followed by Sambo.

LEGREE: Go and send Cassy to me.

SAMBO: Yes, mas'r.   (*Exit.*)

LEGREE: Curse the woman! she's got a temper worse than the devil; I shall
do her an injury one of these days, if she isn't careful. (*Re-enter Sambo,
frightened.*) What's the matter with you, you black scoundrel?   5

SAMBO: S'help me, mas'r, she isn't dere.

LEGREE: I suppose she's about the house somewhere?

SAMBO: No, she isn't, mas'r; I's been all over de house and I can't find nothing of her nor Emmeline.

LEGREE: Bolted, by the Lord! Call out the dogs! saddle my horse. Stop! are   10
you sure they really have gone?

SAMBO: Yes, mas'r; I's been in every room 'cept the haunted garret and dey
wouldn't go dere.

LEGREE: I have it! Now, Sambo, you jest go and walk that Tom up here,
right away! (*Exit Sambo.*) The old cuss is at the bottom of this yer whole   15
matter; and I'll have it out of his infernal black hide, or I'll know the reason why! I *hate* him — I *hate* him! And isn't he *mine?* Can't I do what I
like with him? Who's to hinder, I wonder? (*Tom is dragged on by Sambo and
Quimbo, Legree grimly confronting Tom.*) Well, Tom, do you know I've made
up my mind to *kill* you?   20

TOM: It's very likely, Mas'r.

LEGREE: I — *have* — *done* — *just* — *that* — *thing*, Tom, unless you'll tell
me what do you know about these yer gals? (*Tom is silent.*) D'ye hear?
Speak!

TOM: I han't got anything to tell, mas'r.   25

LEGREE: Do you dare to tell me, you old black rascal, you don't know?
Speak! Do you know anything?

TOM: I know, mas'r; but I can't tell anything. *I can die!*

LEGREE: Hark ye, Tom! ye think, 'cause I have let you off before, I don't
mean what I say; but, this time, I have made *up my mind*, and counted the   30
cost. You've always stood it out agin me; now, I'll *conquer ye or kill ye!* one
or t'other. I'll count every drop of blood there is in you, and take 'em, one
by one, 'till ye give up!

TOM: Mas'r, if you was sick, or in trouble, or dying, and I could save you,
I'd *give* you my heart's blood; and, if taking every drop of blood in this   35
poor old body would save your precious soul, I'd give 'em freely. Do the
worst you can, my troubles will be over soon; but if you don't repent yours
won't never end.

(*Legree strikes Tom down with the butt of his whip.*)

LEGREE: How do you like that?

SAMBO: He's most gone, mas'r! [40]

TOM (*Rises feebly on his hands.*):   There an't no more you can do. I forgive you with all my soul. (*Sinks back, and is carried off by Sambo and Quimbo.*)

LEGREE: I believe he's done for finally. Well, his mouth is shut up at last — that's one comfort. (*Enter George Shelby, Marks and Cute.*) Strangers! Well what do you want? [45]

GEORGE: I understand that you bought in New Orleans a negro named Tom?

LEGREE: Yes, I did buy such a fellow, and a devil of a bargain I had of it, too! I believe he's trying to die, but I don't know as he'll make it out.

GEORGE: Where is he? Let me see him? [50]

SAMBO: Dere he is. (*Points to Tom.*)

LEGREE: How dare you speak? (*Drives Sambo and Quimbo off. George exits.*)

CUTE: Now's the time to nab him.

MARKS: How are you, Mr. Legree?

LEGREE: What the devil brought you here? [55]

MARKS: This little bit of paper. I arrest you for the murder of Mr. St. Clare. What do you say to that?

LEGREE: This is my answer! (*Makes a blow at Marks, who dodges, and Cute receives the blow — he cries out and runs off, Marks fires at Legree, and follows Cute.*) I am hit! — the game's up! (*Falls dead. Quimbo and Sambo return and carry him off laughing.*)

(*George Shelby enters, supporting Tom. Music. They advance to front and Tom falls.*)

GEORGE: Oh! dear Uncle Tom! do wake — do speak once more! look up! Here's Master George — your own little Master George. Don't you know me? [60]

TOM (*Opening his eyes and speaking in a feeble tone.*):   Mas'r George! Bless de Lord! it's all I wanted! They hav'n't forgot me! It warms my soul; it does my old heart good! Now I shall die content! [65]

GEORGE: You shan't die! you mustn't die, nor think of it. I have come to buy you, and take you home.

TOM: Oh, Mas'r George, you're too late. The Lord has bought me, and is going to take me home.

GEORGE: Oh! don't die. It will kill me — it will break my heart to think [70] what you have suffered, poor, poor fellow!

TOM: Don't call me, poor fellow! I *have* been poor fellow; but that's all past and gone now. I'm right in the door, going into glory! Oh, Mas'r George!

Heaven has come! I've got the victory, the Lord has given it to me! Glory be to His name! (*Dies.*)   75

(*Solemn music. George covers Uncle Tom with his cloak, and kneels over him. Clouds work on and conceal them, and then work off.*)

SCENE VI

Gorgeous clouds, tinted with sunlight. Eva, robed in white, is discovered on the back of a milk-white dove, with expanded wings, as if just soaring upward. Her hands are extended in benediction over St. Clare and Uncle Tom who are kneeling and gazing up to her. Expressive music. Slow curtain.

END

DION BOUCICAULT

The Poor of New York

><

The prolific and theatrically active Dion (Dionysus) Lardner Boucicault (Boursiquot) (1820–1890) was born in Dublin. He worked as an actor and playwright in England in the mid-1830s and early 1840s, lived in France during the late 1840s, then returned to England, where he married his second wife, actress Agnes Robertson, in 1853. Boucicault finally came to America in 1853, where he lived until 1860, and again from 1870 to 1890. Prior to his arrival in the United States, Boucicault had authored at least twenty-two plays, including the successful *London Assurance* (1841); by the time he returned to England in 1860, he had added thirty titles to his canon. In all, he has been credited with as many as two hundred plays. Boucicault also established a reputation in the 1850s as a theater manager in New Orleans; Washington, D.C.; and New York. In 1856 he was responsible for the enactment of a U.S. copyright law that gave playwrights, "along with the right to present and publish the said composition, the sole right to act, perform or represent the same." Among the numerous plays he wrote while in America were *The Poor of New York* (1857), adapted from *Les Pauvres de Paris* by Brisbarre and Nus; *The Octoroon* (1859), one of the most effective melodramas of the period on racism; and *Dot* (1859), an adaptation of *The Cricket on the Hearth*. Boucicault is also important for his Irish plays: *The Colleen Bawn* (1860), *Arrah na Pogue* (1865), *The O'Dowd* (1873), and *The Shaughraun* (1874). In 1874 he wrote the Civil War play *Belle Lamar*, and in 1865, for actor Joseph Jefferson, a version of *Rip Van Winkle*. During the last years of his life, as tastes changed, Boucicault's popularity waned.

The Poor of New York

DRAMATIS PERSONAE

CAPTAIN FAIRWEATHER	DANIELS
GIDEON BLOODGOOD	EDWARDS
BADGER	MRS. FAIRWEATHER
MARK LIVINGSTONE	MRS. PUFFY
PAUL	ALIDA
PUFFY	LUCY
DAN	

SCENE: *The first act occurs during the Commercial Panic of 1837. The remainder of the drama takes place during the Panic of 1857.*

ACT I

THE PANIC OF 1837

The private office of a banking house in New York; door at back, leading to the Bank; Door leading to a side street; Gideon Bloodgood seated, at desk.

(*Enter Edwards, with a sheet of paper.*)

EDWARDS: The stock list, sir; — second board of brokers.
BLOODGOOD (*Rising eagerly.*): Let me see it. Tell the cashier to close the Bank on the stroke of three, and dismiss the clerks. (*Reads.*)

(*Exit Edwards.*)

So — as I expected, every stock is down further still, and my last effort to retrieve my fortune has plunged me into utter ruin? (*Crushes up the paper.*)   5
To-morrow, my drafts to the amount of eighty thousand dollars will be protested. Tomorrow, yonder street, now so still, will be filled with a howling multitude, for the house of Bloodgood, the Banker, will fail, and in its fall will crush hundreds, thousands, who have their fortunes laid up here.   10

(*Re-enter Edwards.*)

FIGURE 6 *Act V, scene II of* The Poor of New York. *Apartment building set on fire by Bloodgood in order to destroy incriminating papers hidden within. For a description of the fire effects, see the introduction.*

EDWARDS: Here are the keys of the safe sir, and the vault. (*Leaves keys on desk and shows a check to Bloodgood.*) The building committee of St. Peter's new church have applied for your donation. It is a thousand dollars.

BLOODGOOD: Pay it. (*Exit Edwards.*) To-morrow, New York will ring from Union Square to the Battery with the news — "Bloodgood has absconded" — but to-morrow I shall be safe on board the packet for Liverpool — all is prepared for my flight with my only care in life, my only hope — my darling child — her fortune is secure — (*Rises.*) The affair will blow over; Bloodgood's bankruptcy will soon be forgotten in the whirl of New York trade, but Alida, my dear Alida will be safe from want.

(*Re-enter Edwards.*)

EDWARDS: Here, sir, are the drafts on the Bank of England, 70,000 dollars. (*Hands papers to Bloodgood, who places them in his pocketbook.*)

BLOODGOOD: Are the clerks all gone?

EDWARDS: All, sir, except Mr. Badger.

BLOODGOOD: Badger! the most negligent of all! That is strange.

EDWARDS: His entries are behindhand, he says, and he is balancing his books.

BLOODGOOD: Desire him to come to me. (*Sits. Exit Edwards.*)

(*Enter Badger, smoking cigar.*)

BADGER: You have asked for me.

BLOODGOOD: Yes; you are strangely attentive to business to-day, Mr. Badger.

BADGER: Everything has a beginning.

BLOODGOOD: Then you will please begin to-morrow.

BADGER: To-morrow! no sir, my business must be done to-day. *Carpe diem* — make most of to-day — that's my philosophy.

BLOODGOOD: Mr. Badger, Philosophy is not a virtue in a banker's clerk.

BADGER: Think not?

BLOODGOOD (*Impatiently.*):   Neither philosophy nor impertinence. You are discharged from my employment.

BADGER: Pardon me! I do not catch the precise word.

BLOODGOOD (*Sternly.*):   Go, sir, go! I discharge you.

BADGER: Go! — discharge me? I am still more in the dark, I can understand my services not being required in a house that goes on, but where the house is ready to burst up the formality of telling a clerk he is discharged, does seem to me an unnecessary luxury.

BLOODGOOD (*Troubled.*):   I do not understand you, sir.

BADGER (*Seating himself on a desk, deliberately dangling his legs.*): No! well I'll dot my i's and cross my t's and make myself plain to the meanest capacity. In business there are two ways of getting rich, one hard, slow and troublous: this is called labor; — 50

BLOODGOOD: Sir!

BADGER: Allow me to finish. The other easy, quick and demanding nothing but a pliant conscience and a daring mind — is now pleasantly denominated financiering — but when New York was honest, it was called fraudulent bankruptcy, that was before you and I were born. 55

BLOODGOOD: What do you mean?

BADGER: I mean that for more than two years I have watched your business transactions; when you thought me idle, my eyes were everywhere: in your books, in your safe, in your vaults; if you doubt me question me about your operations for the last three months. 60

BLOODGOOD: This is infamous!

BADGER: That is precisely the word I used when I came to the end of your books.

EDWARDS (*Outside.*): This way, sir.

(*Enter Edwards, with Captain Fairweather.*)

BLOODGOOD (*To Badger, in alarm.*): Not a word.

BADGER: All right. 65

EDWARDS (*Introducing Captain Fairweather.*): This is Mr. Bloodgood.

CAPTAIN: Glad to see you, sir. You will pardon my intruding at an hour when the bank, I am told, is closed.

BLOODGOOD: I am at your service, sir. 70

(*He makes a sign for Badger to retire, but the latter remains.*)

BADGER (*To Captain.*): You may speak, sir; Mr. Bloodgood has no secrets from me. I am in his confidence.

CAPTAIN (*Sits.*): I am a sea-captain, in the India Trade. My voyages are of the longest, and thus I am obliged to leave my wife and two children almost at the mercy of circumstances. I was spending a happy month with my 75 darlings at a little cozy place I have at Yonkers while my ship was loading, when this infernal commercial squall set in — all my fortune, 100,000 dollars, the fruits of thirty years' hard toil — was invested in the United States Bank — it was the livelihood of my wife — the food of my little children — I hurried to my brokers and sold out. I saved myself just in time. 80

BLOODGOOD: I admire your promptitude.

CAPTAIN: To-morrow I sail for China; for the last three weeks I have worried my brains to think how I should bestow my money — to-day I bethought me of your house — the oldest in New York — your name stands beyond suspicion, and if I leave this money in your hands, I can sleep nightly with the happy assurance that whatever happens to me, my dearest ones are safe.   85

BADGER: You may pull your nightcap over your ears with that established conviction.

CAPTAIN: Now, I know your bank is closed, but if you will accept this money as a special deposit, I will write to you how I desire it to be in-   90
vested hereafter.

BLOODGOOD (*Pensive.*):   You have a family?

CAPTAIN: Don't talk of them — tears of joy come into my eyes whenever I think of those children — and my dear wife, the patient, devoted companion of the old sailor, whose loving voice murmurs each evening a   95
prayer for those who are on the sea; and my children, sir, two little angels; one a fair little thing — we call her Lucy — she is the youngest — all red and white like a little bundle of flowers; and my eldest — my son Paul — we named him after Paul Jones — a sailor's whim; well, sir, when the ship is creaking and groaning under my feet, when the squall drives the   100
hail and sleet across my face, amidst the thunder, I only hear three voices — through the gloom I can see only three faces, pressed together like three angels waiting for me in heaven, and that heaven is my home. But, how I do talk, sir — forgetting that these things can't interest you.

BLOODGOOD: They do, more than you imagine. I, too, have a child — only   105
one — a motherless child!

CAPTAIN: Ain't it good to speak of the little beings? Don't it fill the heart like a draught of sweet water? My darling torments, here is their fortune — I have it in my hand — it is here — I have snatched it from the waves; I have won it across the tempest; I have labored, wrestled, and suf-   110
fered for it; but it seemed nothing, for it was for them. Take it, sir. (*He hands [him] a pocketbook.*) In this pocketbook you will find one hundred thousand dollars. May I take your receipt and at once depart for my vessel?

BADGER (*Aside.*):   This is getting positively interesting.

BLOODGOOD: Your confidence flatters me. You desire to place this money   115
with me as a special deposit?

CAPTAIN: If you please. Will you see that the amount is correct?

BLOODGOOD (*Counting.*):   Mr. Badger, prepare the receipt.

BADGER (*Writing.*):   "New York, 13th of December, 1837. Received, on special deposit, from ———— " (*To Captain.*) Your name, sir?   120

CAPTAIN: Captain Fairweather, of the ship Paul and Lucy, of New York.

BADGER (*Writing.*):   Captain Fairweather, of the ship —

BLOODGOOD: One hundred thousand dollars — quite correct.

BADGER (*Handing receipt to Bloodgood, and watching him closely as he takes the pen.*): Please sign the receipt. (*Aside.*) His hand does not tremble, not a muscle moves. What a magnificent robber! 125

BLOODGOOD (*To Captain.*): Here is your receipt.

CAPTAIN: A thousand thanks. Now I am relieved of all trouble.

BADGER (*Aside.*): That's true.

CAPTAIN: I must return in haste to the Astor House, where I dine with my owners at four — I fear I am late. Good-day, Mr. Bloodgood. 130

BLOODGOOD: Good-day Captain, and a prosperous voyage to you. (*Exit Captain Fairweather. Badger opens ledger.*) What are you doing, Mr. Badger?

BADGER: I am going to enter that special deposit in the ledger.

BLOODGOOD: Mr. Badger!

BADGER: Mr. Bloodgood! 135

BLOODGOOD (*Brings him down.*): I have been deceived in you. I confess I did not know your value.

BADGER (*Modestly.*): Patience and perseverance, sir, tells in the long run.

BLOODGOOD: Here are one thousand dollars — I present them to you for your past services. 140

BADGER (*Takes the money, and walks over to the ledger on the desk, which he closes significantly.*): And for the present service?

BLOODGOOD: What do you mean?

BADGER: My meaning is as clear as Croton. I thought you were going to fail — I see I was wrong — you are going to abscond.

BLOODGOOD: Mr. Badger! this language — 145

BADGER: This deposit is special; you dare not use it in your business; your creditors cannot touch it — ergo, you mean to make a raise, and there's but one way — absconsion! absquatulation.

BLOODGOOD (*Smiling.*): It is possible that this evening I may take a little walk out of town. 150

BADGER: In a steamboat?

BLOODGOOD: Meet me at Peck Slip, at five o'clock, and I will hand you double the sum I gave you.

BADGER (*Aside.*): In all three thousand dollars.

(*Re-enter Edwards.*)

EDWARDS: Your daughter, sir; Miss Alida is in the carriage at the door and is screaming to be admitted. 155

BLOODGOOD: Tell the nurse to pacify her for a few moments.

EDWARDS: She dare not, sir; Miss Alida has torn nurse's face in a fearful manner already. (*Exit.*)

BADGER: Dear, high-spirited child! If she is so gentle now, what will she be when she is twenty, and her nails are fully developed? 160

BLOODGOOD (*Takes hat.*): I will return immediately. (*Exit.*)

BADGER (*Following Bloodgood with his eyes.*): Oh, nature, wonderful mistress! Keep close to your daughter, Bloodgood, for she is your master! Ruin, pillage, rob fifty families to make her rich with their misery, happy in their 165 tears. I watched him as he received the fortune of that noble old sailor — not a blink — his heart of iron never quailed, but in this heart of iron there is a straw, a weakness by which it may be cracked, and that weakness is his own child — children! They are the devil in disguise. I have not got any except my passions, my vices — a large family of spoilt and ungrate- 170 ful little devils, who threaten their loving father with a prison.

EDWARDS (*Outside.*): I tell you, sir, he is not in.

CAPTAIN (*Outside.*): Let me pass I say. (*He enters very much agitated.*) Where is he? Where is he?

BADGER (*Surprised.*): What is the matter, sir? 175

CAPTAIN: Mr. Bloodgood — I must see him — speak to him this instant. Do you not hear me?

BADGER: But —

CAPTAIN: He has not gone.

BADGER: Sir — 180

CAPTAIN: Ah! he is here!

(*Re-enter Bloodgood.*)

BLOODGOOD: What is the meaning of this.

CAPTAIN: Ah! you — it is you — (*Trying to restrain his emotion.*) Sir, I have changed my mind; here is your receipt; have the goodness to return me the deposit I — I — left with you. 185

BLOODGOOD: Sir!

CAPTAIN: I have another investment for this sum, and I — beg you to re-store it to me.

BLOODGOOD: Restore it! you have a very strange way, sir, of demanding what is due to you. 190

CAPTAIN: It is true; pardon me but I have told you it is all I possess. It is the fortune of my wife, of my children, of my brave Paul, and my dear little Lucy. It is their future happiness, their life! Listen, sir; I will be frank with you. Just now, on returning to my hotel, I found the owners of my ship waiting dinner for me, well, they were speaking as merchants 195 will speak of each other — your name was mentioned — I listened — and they said — It makes me tremble even now — they said there were rumors abroad to-day that your house was in peril.

BLOODGOOD: I attach no importance, sir, to idle talk.

CAPTAIN: But I attach importance to it, sir. How can I leave the city with   200
this suspicion on my mind that perhaps I have compromised the future
of my family.

BLOODGOOD: Sir!

CAPTAIN: Take back your receipt, and return me my money.

BLOODGOOD: You know sir, that it is after banking hours. Return to-   205
morrow.

CAPTAIN: No. You received my deposit after banking hours.

BLOODGOOD: I am not a paying teller, to count out money.

CAPTAIN: You did not say so, when you counted it in.

(*Enter Edwards.*)

EDWARDS: The driver says you will be late for the —   210

BLOODGOOD (*Trying to stop him.*):   That will do.   (*Exit Edwards.*)

CAPTAIN: What did he say? (*Runs to the window.*) A carriage at the door —

BADGER (*Aside.*):   Things are getting complicated here.

CAPTAIN: Yes — I see it all. He is going to fly with the fortunes and savings of his dupes! (*Tearing his cravat.*) Ah! I shall choke! (*Furiously to Blood-*   215
good.) But I am here, villain, I am here in time.

BLOODGOOD: Sir.

CAPTAIN: To-morrow, you said — return to-morrow — but to-morrow
you will be gone. (*Precipitates himself on Bloodgood.*) My money, my money. I
will have it this instant! Do not speak a word, it is useless, I will not lis-   220
ten to you. My money, or I will kill you as a coward should be killed,
Robber! Thief!

BADGER (*Aside.*):   Hi!hi! This is worth fifty cents — reserved seats extra.

BLOODGOOD (*Disengaging himself.*):   Enough of this scandal. You shall have
your money back again.   225

CAPTAIN: Give it me — ah! — (*In pain.*) My head! (*To Bloodgood.*) Be
quick, give it to me, and let me go. (*Staggering and putting his hands to face.*)
My God! what is this strange feeling which overcomes me.

BADGER: He is falling, what's the matter of him?

(*Captain falls in chair.*)

BLOODGOOD: His face is purple. (*Takes pocketbook and commences to count out*   230
money.)

(*Soft music to end of act.*)

CAPTAIN: I am suffocating; some air. I cannot see; everything is black before my eyes. Am I dying? O, no, no! it cannot be, I will not die. I must

see them again. Some water — quick! Come to me — my wife — my
children! Where are they that I cannot fold them in my arms! (*He looks
strangely and fearfully into the face of Bloodgood for an instant, and then breaks into a
loud sob.*) Oh, my children — my poor, poor, little children! (*After some con-*   235
vulsive efforts to speak his eyes become fixed.)

BLOODGOOD (*Distracted.*):   Some one run for help. Badger, a doctor quick.

BADGER (*Standing over Captain.*):   All right, sir, I have studied medicine —
that is how I learned most of my loose habits. (*Examines the Captain's pulse
and eyes.*) It is useless sir. He is dead.

BLOODGOOD (*Horrified.*):   Dead! (*Bloodgood's attitude is one of extreme horror. This*   240
*position gradually relaxes as he begins to see the advantages that will result from the
Captain's death.*) Can it be possible?

BADGER (*Tearing open the Captain's vest. The receipt falls on the ground.*):   His heart
has ceased to beat — congestion in all its diagnostics.

BLOODGOOD: Dead!

BADGER: Apoplexy — the symptoms well developed — the causes nat-   245
ural, overexcitement and sudden emotion.

BLOODGOOD (*Relaxing into an attitude of cunning.*):   Dead!

BADGER: You are spared the agony of counting out his money.

BLOODGOOD: Dead!

BADGER (*Sees receipt on ground.*):   Ha! here is the receipt! Signed by Blood-   250
good. As a general rule never destroy a receipt — there is no knowing
when it may yet prove useful. (*Picks it up, and puts it in his pocket.*)

Tableau.

(*A lapse of twenty years is supposed to intervene between the first and second acts.*)

ACT II

THE PANIC OF 1857

SCENE I

The Park, near Tammany Hall.

(*Enter Livingstone.*)

LIVINGSTONE: Eight o'clock in the morning! For the last hour I have been
hovering round Chatham street — I wanted to sell my overcoat to some
enterprising Israelite, but I could not muster the courage to enter one of
those dens. Can I realize the fact? Three months ago, I stood there the
fashionable Mark Livingstone, owner of the Waterwitch yacht, one of   5

the original stock-holders in the Academy of Music, and now, burst up, sold out, and reduced to breakfast off this coat. (*Feels in pocket.*) What do I feel? a gold dollar — undiscovered in the Raglan of other days! (*Withdraws his hand.*) No; 'tis a five-cent piece!

(*Enter Puffy, with a hot-potato arrangement.*)

PUFFY: Past eight o'clock! I am late this morning.   10

LIVINGSTONE: I wonder what that fellow has in his tin volcano — it smells well. Ha! what are those funny things? Ah!

PUFFY: Sweet potatoes, sir.

LIVINGSTONE: Indeed! (*Aside.*) If the Union Club saw me — (*Looks around.*) No; I am incog — hunger cries aloud. Here goes.   15

PUFFY: Why, bless me, if it ain't Mr. Livingstone!

LIVINGSTONE: The devil! He knows me — I dare not eat a morsel.

PUFFY: I'm Puffy, sir; the baker that was — in Broadway — served you sir, and your good father afore you.

LIVINGSTONE: Oh, Puffy — ah, true. (*Aside.*) I wonder if I owe him any-   20
thing.

PUFFY: Down in the world now, sir — over speculated like the rest on 'em. I expanded on a new-fangled oven, that was to bake enough bread in six hours to supply to the whole United States — got done brown in it my-self — subsided into Bowery — expanded again on woffles, caught a   25
second time — obliged to contract into a twelve foot front on Division street. Mrs. P. tends the indoor trade — I do a locomotive business in potatoes, and we let our second floor. My son Dan sleeps with George Washington No. 4, while Mrs. P. and I make out under the counter; Mrs. P., bein' wide, objects some, but I says — says I, "My dear, everybody   30
must contract themselves in these here hard times."

LIVINGSTONE: So you are poor now, are you? (*Takes a potato, playfully.*)

PUFFY: Yes sir; I ain't ashamed to own it — for I hurt nobody but myself. Take a little salt, sir. But, Lord bless you, sir, poverty don't come amiss to me — I've got no pride to support. Now, there's my lodgers —   35

LIVINGSTONE: Ah, your second floor.

PUFFY: A widow lady and her two grown children — poor as mice, but proud, sir — they was grand folks once; you can see that by the way they try to hide it. Mrs. Fairweather is a —

LIVINGSTONE: Fairweather — the widow of a sea captain, who died here   40
in New York twenty years ago.

PUFFY: Do you know my lodgers?

LIVINGSTONE: Three months ago, they lived in Brooklyn — Paul had a clerkship in the Navy Yard.

PUFFY: But when the panic set in, the United States government con-   45
tracted — it paid off a number of employees, and Mr. Paul was discharged.

LIVINGSTONE: They are reduced to poverty and I did not know it. — No,
how could I. (*Aside.*) Since my ruin I have avoided them. (*Aloud.*) And
Lucy — I mean Miss Fairweather? —   50

PUFFY: She works at a milliner's in Broadway — bless her sweet face and
kind smile — me and my wife, we could bake ourselves into bread afore
she and they should come to want; and as for my boy Dan — talk of going through fire and water for her — he does that every night for nothing. Why, sir, you can't say "Lucy," but a big tear will come up in his eye   55
as big as a cartwheel, and then he'll let out an almighty cuss, that sounds
like a thousand o' brick.

(*Enter Paul and Mrs. Fairweather, dressed in black.*)

LIVINGSTONE: Oh! (*In confusion, hides the potato in his pocket, and hums an air as
she walks away. Aside.*) I wonder if they know me.

MRS. FAIRWEATHER: Ah, Mr. Puffy.   60

PUFFY: What, my second floor. Mrs. Fairweather — good morning, Mr.
Paul; I hope no misfortune has happened — you are dressed in mourning.

MRS. FAIRWEATHER: This is the anniversary of my poor husband's death;
this day, twenty years ago, he was taken away from us — we keep it sacred to his memory.   65

PAUL: It was a fatal day for us. When my father left home he had 100,000
dollars on his person — when he was found lying dead on the sidewalk
of Liberty street, he was robbed of all.

MRS. FAIRWEATHER: From that hour misfortune has tracked us — we
have lost our friends.   70

PUFFY: Friends — that reminds me — why where is Mr. Livingstone —
there's his coat —

PAUL: Livingstone!

PUFFY: We were talking of you, when you came up. He slipped away.

(*Re-enter Livingstone.*)

LIVINGSTONE: I think I dropped my coat. (*Recognizing them.*) Paul — am I   75
mistaken?

MRS. FAIRWEATHER: No, Mr. Livingstone.

PAUL: Good morning, sir.

LIVINGSTONE: Sir! — Mr. Livingstone — have I offended you?

PAUL: We could not expect you to descend to visit us in our poor lodging.   80

MRS. FAIRWEATHER: We cannot afford the pleasure of your society.

LIVINGSTONE: Let me assure you that I was ignorant of your misfortune — and if I have not called — it was because — a — because —
(*Aside.*) What shall I say. (*Aloud.*) — I have been absent from the city; —
may I ask how is your sister?   85

PAUL: My sister Lucy is now employed in a millinery store in Broadway —
she sees you pass the door every day.

LIVINGSTONE (*Aside.*):   The devil — I must confess my ruin, or appear a
contemptible scoundrel.

PAUL: Livingstone — I cannot conceal my feelings, we were schoolmates   90
together — and I must speak out.

LIVINGSTONE (*Aside.*):   I know what's coming.

PAUL: I'm a blunt New York boy, and have something of the old bluff
sailor's blood in my veins — so pardon me if I tell you that you have be-
haved badly to my sister Lucy.   95

LIVINGSTONE: For many months I was a daily visitor at your house — I
loved your sister.

PAUL: You asked me for Lucy's hand — I gave it, because I loved you as a
brother — not because you were rich.

LIVINGSTONE (*Aside.*):   To retrieve my fortunes so that I might marry — I   100
speculated in stocks and lost all I possessed. To enrich Lucy and her family, I involved myself in utter ruin.

PAUL: The next day I lost my clerkship — we were reduced to poverty, and
you disappeared.

LIVINGSTONE: I can't stand it — I will confess all — let me sacrifice every   105
feeling but Lucy's love and your esteem —

MRS. FAIRWEATHER: Beware, Mr. Livingstone, how you seek to renew our
acquaintance; recollect my daughter earns a pittance behind a counter —
I take in work, and Paul now seeks the poorest means of earning an hon-
est crust of bread.   110

LIVINGSTONE: And what would you say if I were not better off than yourselves — if I too were poor — if I —

PUFFY: You, poor, you who own a square mile of New York?

(*Enter Bloodgood.*)

LIVINGSTONE: Mr. Bloodgood!

BLOODGOOD: Ah, Livingstone — why do you not call to see us? You   115
know our address — Madison square — my daughter Alida will be delighted. — By the way — I have some paper of yours at the bank, it
comes due to-day — ten thousand dollars, I think — you bank at the
Chemical?

LIVINGSTONE: Yes, I do — that is did, — bank there.   120

BLOODGOOD: Why don't you bank with me, a rich and careless fellow like you — with a large account.

LIVINGSTONE: Yes — I — (*Aside.*) He is cutting the ground from under my feet.

PAUL: Mr. Bloodgood — pardon me, sir, but I was about to call on you to-day to solicit employment. 125

BLOODGOOD: I'm full, sir, — indeed I think of reducing salaries, everybody is doing so.

LIVINGSTONE: But you are making thousands a week?

BLOODGOOD: That is no reason that I should not take advantage of the times — (*Recognizing Puffy.*) Ah, Mr. Puffy, that note of yours. 130

PUFFY: Oh, Lord! (*Aside.*) It is the note Mrs. Fairweather gave me for her rent.

BLOODGOOD: My patience is worn out.

PUFFY: It's all right sir. 135

BLOODGOOD: Take care it is.   (*Exit.*)

PUFFY: There goes the hardest cuss that ever went to law.

LIVINGSTONE: Paul — my dear friend — will you believe me — my feelings are the same towards you — nay more tender, more sincere than ever — but there are circumstances I cannot explain. 140

MRS. FAIRWEATHER: Mr. Livingstone, say no more — we ask no explanation.

LIVINGSTONE: But I ask something — let me visit you — let me return to the place that I once held in your hearts.

PUFFY: 219 Division street — Puffy, Baker. Dinner at half past one — come to-day, sir — do, sir. 145

PAUL: We cannot refuse you.

MRS. FAIRWEATHER: I will go to Lucy's store and let her know. Ah! Mr. Livingstone — she has never confessed that she loved you — but you will find her cheek paler than it used to be.   (*Exit.*) 150

PAUL: And now to hunt for work — to go from office to office pleading for employment — to be met always with the same answer — "we are full" — or "we are discharging hands" — Livingstone, I begin to envy the common laborer who has no fears, no care, beyond his food and shelter — I am beginning to lose my pity for the poor.

LIVINGSTONE: The poor! — whom do you call the poor? Do you know them? do you see them? They are more frequently found under a black coat than under a red shirt. The poor man is the clerk with a family, forced to maintain a decent suit of clothes, paid for out of the hunger of his children. The poor man is the artist who is obliged to pledge the tools of his trade to buy medicines for his sick wife. The lawyer who, craving 160 for employment, buttons up his thin paletot to hide his shirtless breast. These needy wretches are poorer than the poor, for they are obliged to conceal their poverty with the false mask of content — smoking a cigar to disguise their hunger — they drag from their pockets their last quarter, to cast it with studied carelessness, to the beggar, whose mattress at   165 home is lined with gold. These are the most miserable of the Poor of New York.

(*A small crowd has assembled round Livingstone during this speech; they take him for an orator; one of them takes down what he says on tablets.*)

(*Enter Policeman.*)

PUFFY AND CROWD: Bravo — Bravo — Hurrah — get on the bench!
POLICEMAN: Come — I say — this won't do.
LIVINGSTONE: What have I done.   170
POLICEMAN: No stumping to the population allowed in the Park.
LIVINGSTONE: Stumping!!
REPORTER: Oblige me with your name, sir, for the Herald.
LIVINGSTONE: Oh! (*Rushes off, followed by Paul.*)

SCENE II

Exterior of Bloodgood's Bank, Nassau Street.

(*Enter Bloodgood.*)

BLOODGOOD (*Looking at papers.*):   Four per cent a month — ha! if this panic do but last, I shall double my fortune! Twenty years ago this very month — ay, this very day — I stood in yonder bank, a ruined man. Shall I never forget that night — when I and my accomplice carried out the body of the old sailor and laid it there. (*Points.*) I never pass the spot   5 without a shudder. But his money — that founded my new fortune.

(*Enter Alida.*)

Alida, my dear child, what brings you to this part of the city?
ALIDA: I want two thousand dollars.
BLOODGOOD: My dearest child, I gave you five hundred last week.
ALIDA: Pooh! what's five hundred? You made ten thousand in Michigan   10 Southern last week — I heard you tell Mr. Jacob Little so.
BLOODGOOD: But —
ALIDA: Come, don't stand fooling about it; go in and get the money — I must have it.
BLOODGOOD: Well, my darling, if you must. Will you step in?   15

ALIDA: Not I. I'm not going into your dirty bank. I've seen all your clerks — they're not worth looking at.

BLOODGOOD: I'll go and fetch it.   (*Exit.*)

ALIDA: This is positively the last time I will submit to this extortion. (*Opens a letter and reads.*) "My adored Alida — I fly to your exquisite feet; I am the most wretched of men. Last night, at Hall's I lost two thousand dollars — it must be paid before twelve o'clock. Oh, my queen! My angel! Invent some excuse to get this money from your father, and meet me at Maillard's at half-past eleven. When shall we meet again alone, in that box at the opera, where I can press my lips to your superb eyes, and twine my hands in your magnificent hair? *Addio carissima!* The Duke of Calcavella." I wonder if he showed that to any of his friends before he sent it!

(*Re-enter Bloodgood, followed by Puffy.*)

BLOODGOOD: I tell you, sir, it must be paid. I have given you plenty of time.

PUFFY: You gave me the time necessary for you to obtain execution in the Marine Court.

BLOODGOOD: Alida, my love, there is a draft for the money. (*Gives her notes. She takes them.*) And now, will you do me a favor? Do not be seen about so much, in public, with that foreign Duke.

ALIDA: I never ask you for a draft but you always give me a pill to take with it.

BLOODGOOD: I don't like him.

ALIDA: I do — bye-bye.   (*Exit.*)

BLOODGOOD: How grand she looks! That girl possesses my whole heart.

PUFFY: Reserve a little for me, sir. This here note, it was give to me by my 2d floor in payment for rent. It's as good as gold, sir — when they are able to pay it. I'd sooner have it —

BLOODGOOD: My Puffy, you are the worst kind of man; you are a weak honest fool. You are always failing — always the dupe of some new swindler.

PUFFY: Lord love you, sir! if you was to see the folks you call swindlers — the kindest, purest, 2d floor as ever drew God's breath. I told them that this note was all right — for if they know'd I was put about, along of it, I believe they'd sell the clothes off their backs to pay it.

BLOODGOOD (*Aside.*):   This fellow is a fool. But I see, if I levy execution the note will be paid. (*Aloud.*) Very good, Mr. Puffy. I will see about it.

PUFFY: You will! I knew it — there — when folks says you're a hard man — I says — no — no mor'n a rich man's got to be.

BLOODGOOD: Very good. (*Aside.*) I'll put an execution on his house at once. (*Aloud.*) Good morning, Mr. Puffy.   (*Exit.*)

PUFFY: Good morning, sir. So, I'm floated off that mud bank. Lord! if he   55
had seized my goods and closed me up — I'd never a dared to look Mrs.
Fairweather in the face agin.   (*Exit.*)

Scene III

*The interior of Puffy's house. A poor but neat room — window at back. Mrs. Fair-
weather is arranging dinner.*

(*Enter Lucy, with a box.*)

LUCY: My dear mother.

MRS. FAIRWEATHER: My darling Lucy. Ah, your eye is bright again. The
thought of seeing Mark Livingstone has revived your smile.

LUCY: I have seen him. He and Paul called at Madame Victorine's.

MRS. FAIRWEATHER: Is your work over, Lucy, already?   5

LUCY: What we expected has arrived, mother. This dress is the last I shall
receive from Madame Victorine — she is discharging her hands.

MRS. FAIRWEATHER: More misfortunes — and Paul has not been able to
obtain employment.

(*A knock. Enter Mrs. Puffy.*)

MRS. PUFFY: May I come in? it's only Mrs. Puffy. I've been over the oven   10
for two hours! Knowing you had company — I've got a pigeon pie —
such a pie — um — oo — mutton kidneys in it — and hard biled
eggs — love ye! — then I've got a chicken, done up a way of my own! I'll
get on a clean gown and serve it up myself.

MRS. FAIRWEATHER: But my dear Mrs. Puffy — really we did not mean to   15
incur any expense —

MRS. PUFFY: Expense! why, wasn't them pigeons goin' to waste — they was
shot by Dan — and we can't abide pigeons, neither Puffy nor I. Then the
rooster was running round — always raisn' hereafter early in the
mornin' — a noosance, it was —   20

(*Enter Dan.*)

DAN: Beg pardon, ladies — I just stepped in —

LUCY: Good day, Dan.

DAN: Day, Miss! — (*Aside to Mrs. Puffy.*) Oh! mother, ain't she pootty this
morning.

MRS. PUFFY (*Smoothing her hair.*):   What have you got there, Dan'el?   25

DAN: When I was paying the man for them birds — (*Mrs. Puffy kicks
him.*) — Creation! mother — you're like the stocks — you can't move

a'thout crushin' somebody — well, he'd got this here pair o' boots ornder his arm — why, ses I, if ever der was a foot created small enough to go into them thar, it is Miss Lucy's — so I brought them for you to look at. 30

LUCY: They are too dear for me, Dan, pray give them back.

DAN: Well, ye see — the man has kinder gone, Miss — he said he'd call again — some time next fall —

MRS. FAIRWEATHER: Dan — Mrs. Puffy — you are good, kind, dear souls — when the friends of our better days have deserted us — when the 35 rich will scarcely deign to remember us — you, without any design, but with the goodness of God in your hearts — without any hope but that of hiding your kindness, you help me. Give me your hands — I owe you too much already — but you must bestow on us no more out of your poverty. 40

MRS. PUFFY: Lord, Mrs! just as if me and Puffy could bestow anything — and what's Dan fit for?

DAN: Yes — what's I'm fit for?

MRS. FAIRWEATHER: Well, I will accept your dinner to-day on one condition — that you will all dine with us. 45

MRS. PUFFY: Oh — my! Dine with up-town folks!

LUCY: Yes indeed, Dan, you must.

DAN: Lord, miss! I sent no account at dinin' with folks — I take my food on the fust pile of bricks, anyhow.

MRS. PUFFY: I'm accustomed to mine standin', behind the counter. 50

DAN: We never set down to it, square out — except on Sundays.

MRS. PUFFY: Then it don't seem natural — we never eat, each of us is employed a-helping of the other.

DAN: I'll fix it! Father, and mother, and I, will all wait on you.

LUCY (*Laughing.*):   That's one way of dining together, certainly. 55

(*Enter Paul and Livingstone.*)

LIVINGSTONE: Here we are. Why, what a comfortable little cage this is!

DAN: Let me take your coat and hat, sir.

LIVINGSTONE: Thank you. (*Exit Dan and Mrs. Puffy.*) How like the old times, eh, Lucy? (*Sits by her.*)

MRS. FAIRWEATHER (*Aside to Paul.*):   Well, Paul, have you obtained employ- 60 ment?

PAUL: No, mother; but Livingstone is rich — he must have influence, and he will assist me.

MRS. FAIRWEATHER: Heaven help us! I fear that the worst is not come.

PAUL: Nonsense, mother — cheer up! Is there anything you have con- 65 cealed from me?

MRS. FAIRWEATHER: No — nothing you need know. (*Aside.*) If he knew that for five weeks we have been subsisting on the charity of these poor people.

(*Enter Mrs. Puffy with a pie, followed by Dan with a roast chicken and Puffy, loaded with plates and various articles of dinner service.*)

MRS. PUFFY: Here it is.   70

LUCY: Stay — we must lay more covers; help me, Paul.

LIVINGSTONE: Let me assist you. (*They join another table to the first.*)

MRS. FAIRWEATHER: Mr. and Mrs. Puffy and Dan dine with us.

PAUL: Bravo!

LIVINGSTONE: Hail Columbia! (*Dan begins dancing about.*)

LUCY: Why, Dan — what's the matter?   75

DAN: Oh, nothing, miss.

LUCY: How red your face is!

DAN: Don't mind, miss.

MRS. PUFFY: Oh Lord! I forgot that dish; it has been in the oven for an hour.

DAN: It ain't at all hot. (*Paul touches it and jumps away.*) It's got to burn into   80
the bone afore George Washington No. 4[1] gives in.

(*Lays down the plate — they all sit.*)

PUFFY: Now, this is agreeable — I have not felt so happy since I started
my forty horse power oven.

LIVINGSTONE: This pie is magnificent. (*Mrs. Puffy rises.*)

MRS. PUFFY: Oh, sir, you make me feel good.   85

DAN (*Holding the table*):   Mother can't express her feelings without upsetting
the table.

(*Enter two Sheriff's Officers.*)

PAUL: What persons are these?

PUFFY: What do you want?

FIRST SHERIFF'S OFFICER: I am the Deputy Sheriff — I come at the suit of   90
Gideon Bloodgood, against Susan Fairweather and Jonas Puffy —
amount of debt and costs, one hundred and fifty dollars.

PAUL: My mother!

PUFFY: He said he would see about it — Oh, Mrs. Fairweather — I hope
you will forgive me — I couldn't help it.   95

DEPUTY SHERIFF: I do not want to distress you; Mr. Livingstone will perhaps pay the debt — or give me his check.

PAUL: Livingstone!

---

[1] A fire engine. In the nineteenth century they were frequently named.

LIVINGSTONE *(After a pause.)*:   I cannot help you. Yes, I will rather appear what I am a ruined man, than seem a contemptible one — I am penniless,   100
broken — for weeks I have been so — but I never felt poverty till now.

Tableau.

ACT III

A Room in the house of Gideon Bloodgood; the furniture and ornaments are in a style of exaggerated richness, white satin and gold. Bloodgood is discovered writing at a table on one side, Alida seated reading a newspaper on the other.

BLOODGOOD: What are you reading?

ALIDA: The New York *Herald.*

BLOODGOOD: You seem interested in it?

ALIDA: Very. Shall I read aloud?

BLOODGOOD: Do. *(Goes on writing.)*   5

ALIDA *(Reads.)*:   "Wall street is a perch, on which a row of human vultures sit, whetting their beaks, ready to fight over the carcass of a dying enterprise. Amongst these birds of prey, the most vulturous is perhaps Gid Bloodgood. This popular financier made his fortune in the lottery business. He then dabbled a little in the slave trade, as the Paraquita case   10
proved, — last week by a speculation in flour he made fifty thousand dollars, this operation raised the price of bread four cents a loaf, and now there are a thousand people starving in the hovels of New York — we nominate Gid for Congress, expense to be paid by the admiring crowd — send round the hat." Father! *(Rises.)* Are you not rich?   15

BLOODGOOD: Why do you ask?

ALIDA: Because people say that riches are worshipped in New York, that wealth alone graduates society. This is false, for I am young, handsome and your heiress — yet I am refused admission into the best families here whose intimacy I have sought.   20

BLOODGOOD: Refused admission! Is not Fifth Avenue open to you?

ALIDA: Fifth Avenue! that jest is stale. Fifth Avenue is a shop where the richest fortunes are displayed like the dry goods in Stewart's windows, and like them, too, are changed daily. But why do we not visit those families at whose names all men and all journals bow with respect, the Liv-   25
ingstones, the Astors, Van Renssalaers. Father, these families receive men less rich than you — and honor many girls who don't dress as well as I do, nor keep a carriage.

BLOODGOOD: Is not the Duke of Calcavella at my feet?

ALIDA: The Duke de Calcavella is an adventurer to whom you lend 30
money, who escorts me to my box at the opera that he may get in free.

BLOODGOOD: You minx, you know you love him.

ALIDA: I am not speaking of love — but of marriage.

BLOODGOOD: Marriage!

ALIDA: Yes, marriage! This society in New York which has shut its doors 35
against me, it is from amongst these families that I have resolved to
choose a husband.

BLOODGOOD (*Rising.*): Alida, do you already yearn to leave me? For you
alone I have hoarded my wealth — men have thought me miserly, when I
have had but one treasure in the world and that was you, my only child. To 40
the rest of my fellow creatures I have been cold and calculating, because in
you alone was buried all the love my heart could feel — my fortune, take
it, gratify your caprices — take it all, but leave me your affection.

ALIDA: You talk as if I were still a child.

BLOODGOOD: I would to God you were! Oh, Alida, if you knew how fear- 45
ful a thing it is for a man like me to lose the only thing in the world that
ties him to it!

ALIDA: Do you wish me to marry the Duke de Calcavella?

BLOODGOOD: A *roué*, a gambler! Heaven forbid!

ALIDA: Besides, they say he has a wife in Italy. 50

BLOODGOOD: I shall forbid him the house.

ALIDA: No, you won't.

BLOODGOOD: His reputation will compromise yours.

ALIDA: Judge my nature by your own — I may blush from anger — never
from shame. 55

(*Enter Edwards.*)

EDWARDS: Mr. Mark Livingstone.

ALIDA: Livingstone! This is the first time that name has ever been an-
nounced in this house.

BLOODGOOD: He comes on business. Tell Mr. Livingstone I cannot see
him. Beg him to call at my office to-morrow. 60

ALIDA: Show him up.

BLOODGOOD: Alida!

ALIDA (*Sharply to Edwards.*): Do you hear me?

BLOODGOOD: This is tyranny — I — I — (*In a rage to Edwards.*) Well,
blockhead, why do you stand staring there? Don't you hear the order? 65
Show him up. (*Exit Edwards.*)

ALIDA: Livingstone!

(*Enter Mark Livingstone.*)

LIVINGSTONE: Mr. Bloodgood — Miss Bloodgood — (*Bows.*) I am most fortunate to find you at home.

ALIDA: I trust that Mrs. Livingstone your mother, and Miss Livingstone your sister, are well? 70

LIVINGSTONE (*Coldly.*):   I thank you. (*Gaily.*) Allow me to assure you that you were the belle of the opera last night.

ALIDA: Yet you did not flatter me with your presence in our box.

LIVINGSTONE: You noticed my absence! You render me the happiest and proudest member of my club. 75

ALIDA: By the way, papa, I thought you were going to be a member of the Union.

LIVINGSTONE: Ahem! (*An awkward silence.*) He was black-balled last week.

BLOODGOOD: I think, Mr. Livingstone you have some business with me. 80

ALIDA: Am I in the way?

LIVINGSTONE: Not at all — the fact is, Miss Bloodgood — my business can be explained in three words.

BLOODGOOD: Indeed!

LIVINGSTONE: I am ruined. 85

ALIDA: Ruined!

LIVINGSTONE: My father lived in those days when fancy stocks were unknown, and consequently was in a position to leave me with a handsome fortune. I spent it — extravagantly — foolishly. My mother, who loves me "not wisely but too well," heard that my name was pledged for a large 90 amount, — Mr. Bloodgood held my paper — she sold out all her fortune without my knowledge, and rescued my credit from dishonor.

BLOODGOOD: Allow me to observe, I think she acted honorably, but foolishly.

LIVINGSTONE (*Bows to Bloodgood.*):   She shared my father's ideas on these 95 matters; well (*Turns to Alida.*) finding I was such good pay, your father lent me a further sum of money, with which I speculated in stocks to recover my mother's loss — I bulled the market — lost — borrowed more — the crisis came — I lost again — until I found myself ruined.

BLOODGOOD (*Rising.*):   Mr. Livingstone, I anticipate the object of your 100 present visit — you desire some accommodation — I regret that it is out of my power to accord it. If you had applied to me a few days earlier I might have been able to — but — a — at the present moment it is quite impossible.

LIVINGSTONE (*Aside.*):   Impossible — the usual expression — I am familiar 105 with it. (*Rising — aloud.*) I regret exceedingly that I did not fall on that more fortunate moment to which you allude — a thousand pardons for my untimely demand —

BLOODGOOD: I hope you believe I am sincere when I say —

LIVINGSTONE: Oh! I am sure of it. Accept my thanks — good morning, Miss Bloodgood.

BLOODGOOD (*Ringing the bell.*):   I trust you will not be put to serious inconvenience.

LIVINGSTONE: Oh, no. (*Aside.*) A revolver will relieve me of every difficulty. (*Aloud.*) Good day, Mr. Bloodgood.   (*Exit.*)

BLOODGOOD: I like his impudence! To come to me for assistance! Let him seek it of his aristocratic friends — his club associates who blackballed me last week.

ALIDA (*Who has been seated writing at table.*):   Father, come here.

BLOODGOOD: What is it?

ALIDA: I am writing a letter which I wish you to sign.

BLOODGOOD: To whom?

ALIDA: To Mr. Livingstone.

BLOODGOOD: To Livingstone!

ALIDA: Read it.

BLOODGOOD (*Reads.*):   "My dear sir, give yourself no further anxiety about your debt to me; I will see that your notes are paid — and if the loan of ten thousand dollars will serve you, I beg to hold that amount at your service, to be repaid at your convenience. Yours truly." (*Throwing down letter.*) I will write nothing of the kind.

ALIDA: You are mistaken — you will write nothing else.

BLOODGOOD: With what object?

ALIDA: I want to make a purchase.

BLOODGOOD: Of what?

ALIDA: Of a husband — a husband who is a gentleman — and through whom I can gain that position you cannot with all your wealth obtain — you see — the thing is cheap — there's the pen. (*She rings a bell.*)

BLOODGOOD: Is your mind so set on this ambition?

ALIDA: If it cost half your fortune. (*Bloodgood signs.*)

(*Enter Edwards.*)

(*To servant.*) Deliver this letter immediately.

EDWARDS (*Takes the letter and is going out, when he runs against Badger, who is cooly entering.*):   I have told you already that my master is not to be seen.

BADGER: So you did — but you see how mistaken you were. There he is — I can see him distinctly.

BLOODGOOD: Badger! (*To Edwards.*) You may go, Edwards.

BADGER (*To Edwards.*):   James — get out.   145

BLOODGOOD: What can he want here?

BADGER: Respected Gideon, excuse my not calling more promptly, but since my return from California, this is my first appearance in fashionable society.   150

ALIDA (*Proudly.*):   Who is this fellow?

BADGER: Ah, Alida, how is the little tootles? You forget me.

ALIDA: How can I recollect every begging imposter who importunes my father.

BADGER: Charming! The same as ever — changed in form, but the heart, my dear Gideon, the same ever, is hard and dry as a biscuit.   155

ALIDA: Father, give this wretch a dollar and let him go.

BADGER: Hullo! Miss Bloodgood, when I hand round the hat it is time enough to put something in it. Gideon, ring and send that girl of yours to her nurse.

ALIDA: Is this fellow mad?   160

BLOODGOOD: Hush! my dear!

ALIDA: Speak out your business — I am familiar with all my father's affairs.

BADGER: All? I doubt it.

(*Enter Edwards, followed by Lucy.*)

EDWARDS: This way, Miss. (*To Alida.*) Here is your dress maker.   165

ALIDA (*Eyeing Lucy.*):   Ha! you are the young person I met this morning walking with Mr. Livingstone?

LUCY: Yes, Madam.

ALIDA: Hum! follow me, and let me see if you can attend on ladies as diligently as you do on gentlemen.   (*Exeunt Alida and Lucy.*)   170

BLOODGOOD (*Looking inquiringly at Badger.*):   So you are here again. I thought you were dead.

BADGER: No; here I am — like a bad shilling, come back again. I've been all over the world since we parted twenty years ago. Your 3,000 dollars lasted me for some months in California. Believe me, had I known that   175 instead of absconding, you remained in New York, I would have hastened back again ten years ago, to share your revived fortunes.

BLOODGOOD: I am at a loss to understand your allusions, sir — nor do I know the object of your return to this city. We have plenty of such persons as you in New York.   180

BADGER: The merchants of San Francisco did not think so, for they subscribed to send me home.

BLOODGOOD: What do you mean?

BADGER: I mean the Vigilance Committee.

BLOODGOOD: What do you intend to do here?

BADGER: Reduced in circumstance and without character, the only resource left to me is to start a bank.

BLOODGOOD: Well, Mr. Badger; I cannot see in what way these things can affect me!

BADGER: Can't you? Ahem! Do you ever read the Sunday papers?

BLOODGOOD: Never.

BADGER: I've got a romance ready for one of them — allow me to give you a sketch of it.

BLOODGOOD: Sir —

BADGER: The scene opens in a bank on Nassau street. Twenty years ago a very respectable old sea captain, one winter's night, makes a special deposit of one hundred thousand dollars — nobody present but the banker and one clerk. The old captain takes a receipt and goes on his way rejoicing — but, lo! and behold you! — in half an hour he returns — having ascertained a fact or two, he demands his money back, but while receiving it he is seized by a fit of apoplexy, and he dies on the spot. End of Chapter One.

BLOODGOOD: Indeed, Mr. Badger, your romance is quite original.

BADGER: Ain't it! never heard it before, did you? — no! Good! Chapter Two. (*Pointedly.*) The banker and his clerk carried the body out on the sidewalk, where it was discovered, and the next day the Coroner's Jury returned a verdict accordingly. The clerk receiving 3,000 dollars hush money left for parts unknown. The banker remained in New York, and on the profits of this plunder established a colossal fortune. End of Part No. 1 — to be continued in our next.

BLOODGOOD: And what do you suppose such a romance will be worth?

BADGER: I've come to you to know.

BLOODGOOD: I am no judge of that.

BADGER: Ain't you? — well — in Part No. 2, I propose to relate that this history is true in every particular, and I shall advertise for the heirs of the dead man.

BLOODGOOD: Ha! you know his name then?

BADGER: Yes, but I see you don't. I wrote the acknowledgement which you signed — you had not even the curiosity then to read the name of your victim.

BLOODGOOD: Really, Mr. Badger, I am at a loss to understand you. Do you mean to insinuate that this romance applies in any way to me?

BADGER: It has a distant reference.

BLOODGOOD: Your memory is luxurious — perhaps it can furnish some better evidence of this wonderful story than the word of a convict ejected   225
from California as a precaution of public safety.

BADGER: You are right — my word is not worth much.

BLOODGOOD: I fear not.

BADGER: But the receipt, signed by you, is worth a great deal.

BLOODGOOD (*Starting.*):   Ha! you lie!   230

BADGER: Let us proceed with my romance. When the banker and his clerk searched for the receipt, they could not find it — a circumstance which only astonished one of the villains — because the clerk had picked up the document and secured it in his pocket. I don't mean to insinuate that this applies in any way to you.   235

BLOODGOOD: Villain!

BADGER: Moral: As a general rule, never destroy receipts — it is no knowing when they may not prove useful.

BLOODGOOD: Were it so, this receipt is of no value in your hands — the heirs of the dead man can alone establish a claim.   240

BADGER (*Rising.*):   That's the point — calculate the chance of my finding them, and let me know what it is worth.

BLOODGOOD: What do you demand?

BADGER: Five thousand dollars.

BLOODGOOD: Five thousand devils!   245

BADGER: You refuse?

BLOODGOOD: I defy you — find the heir if you can.

(*Enter Edwards.*)

EDWARDS: Mr. Paul Fairweather!

(*Enter Paul. Badger starts, then falls laughing in a chair.*)

BLOODGOOD: Your business, sir, with me.

PAUL: Oh, pardon me, Mr. Bloodgood — but the officers have seized the   250
furniture of our landlord — of your tenant — for a debt owed by my mother. I come to ask your mercy — utter ruin awaits two poor families.

BADGER: Oh, Supreme Justice! there is the creditor, and there is the debtor.

PAUL: My mother — my sister — I plead for them, not for myself.   255

BLOODGOOD: I have waited long enough.

BADGER (*Rising.*):   So have I. (*To Paul.*) Have you no friends or relations to help you?

PAUL: None, sir: My father is dead.

(*Bloodgood returns to his table.*)

BLOODGOOD: Enough of this. (*Rings the bell.*)   260

BADGER: Not quite; I feel interested in this young gentlemen — don't you?

BLOODGOOD: Not at all; therefore my servant will show you both out — so you may talk this matter over elsewhere.

BADGER (*To Paul.*):   Your name is familiar to me — was your father in   265 trade?

PAUL: He was a sea captain.

BADGER: Ah! he died nobly in some storm, I suppose — the last to leave his ship?

PAUL: No, sir, he died miserably! Twenty years ago, his body was found on   270 the side walk on Liberty street, where he fell dead by apoplexy.

BLOODGOOD (*Rising.*):   Ah!

(*Enter Edwards.*)

BADGER: James, show us out — we'll talk over this matter elsewhere.

BLOODGOOD: No — you — you can remain. Leave us, Edwards.

BADGER: Ah, I told you that the young man was quite interesting.   275 Alphonse, get out.

(*Exit Edwards.*)

BLOODGOOD: My dear Mr. Badger, I think we have a little business to settle together?

BADGER: Yes, my dear Gideon. (*Aside to him.*) Stocks have gone up — I want fifty thousand dollars for that receipt.   280

BLOODGOOD: Fifty thousand!

BADGER (*Aside.*):   You see the effect of good news on the market — quite astonishing; ain't it.

BLOODGOOD: If you will step down to the dining-room, you will find lunch ready — refresh yourself, while I see what can be done for this   285 young man.

BADGER (*Aside.*):   What are you up to? You want to fix him — to try some game to euchre me. Go it! I've got the receipt; you're on the hook — take out all the line you want. (*Calls.*) Ho! without there!

(*Enter Edwards.*)

Maximilian, vamos! Show me to the banquetting-hall.   290

(Exit, with Edwards.)

BLOODGOOD: Your situation interests me; but surely, at your age — you can find employment.

PAUL: Alas, sir, in these times, it is impossible. I would work, yes, at any kind of labor — submit to anything, if I could save my mother and sister from want.   295

BLOODGOOD: Control your feelings; perhaps I can aid you.

PAUL: Oh, sir, I little expected to find in you a benefactor.

BLOODGOOD: My correspondents at Rio Janeiro require a book-keeper — are you prepared to accept this situation? But there is a condition attached to this employment that may not suit you — you must start by   300 the vessel which sails to-morrow.

PAUL: To-morrow!

BLOODGOOD: I will hand you a thousand dollars in advance of salary, to provide for your mother and sister; they had better leave this city until they can follow you. You hesitate.   305

PAUL: Oh, sir, 'tis my gratitude that renders me silent.

BLOODGOOD: You accept? the terms are two thousand dollars a year.

PAUL *(Seizing his hand.)*:   Mr. Bloodgood, the prayers of a family whom you have made happy, will prosper your life. God bless you, sir! I speak not for myself, but for those still more dear to me.   310

BLOODGOOD: Call again in an hour, when your papers of introduction and the money shall be ready.

PAUL: Farewell, sir. I can scarcely believe my good fortune.   *(Exit.)*

BLOODGOOD: So, now to secure Badger. *(Sitting down and writing.)* He must, at any risk, be prevented from communicating with the mother and   315 daughter until they can be sent into some obscure retreat. I doubt that he is in possession of this receipt, *(Rings a bell)* but I will take an assurance about that. *(Rings.)*

(Enter Lucy.)

LUCY: I will do my best, miss, to please you. Oh, let me hasten from this house!   320

(Enter Mark Livingstone.)

LIVINGSTONE: Lucy!

LUCY: Mark!

LIVINGSTONE: What brings you here?

LUCY: What brings the poor into the saloons of the rich?

(*Enter Alida, unseen by the others.*)

ALIDA (*Aside.*):   Mr. Livingstone here, and with this girl!   325

LIVINGSTONE: My dear Lucy, I have news, bright news, that will light up a smile in your eyes — I am once more rich. But before I relate my good fortune, let me hear from you the consent to share it.

LUCY: What do you mean?

LIVINGSTONE: I mean, dearest one, that I love you — I love you with all   330
my reckless, foolish, worthless heart.

ALIDA (*Advancing.*):   Mr. Livingstone, my father is waiting for you in his study.

LIVINGSTONE: A thousand pardons, Miss Bloodgood; I was not aware — excuse me. (*Aside.*) I wonder if she overheard me. (*To Lucy.*) I will see you again this evening.   (*Exit.*)   335

ALIDA (*To Lucy, who is going.*):   Stay; one word with you. Mr. Livingstone loves you? Do not deny it, I have overheard you.

LUCY: Well, Miss Bloodgood, I have no account to render you in this matter.

ALIDA: I beg your pardon — he is to be my husband.

LUCY: Your husband?   340

ALIDA: Be quiet and listen. Mr. Livingstone is ruined — my father has come to his aid; but one word from me, and the hand, extended to save him from destruction, will be withdrawn.

LUCY: But you will not speak that word?

ALIDA: That depends —   345

LUCY: On what? his acceptance of your hand? he does not love you.

ALIDA: That is not the question.

LUCY: You have overheard that he loves *me*.

ALIDA: That is no concern of mine.

LUCY: And you will coldly buy this man for a husband, knowing that you   350
condemn him to eternal misery!

ALIDA: You are candid, but not complimentary. Let us hope that in time he will forget you, and learn to endure me.

LUCY: Oh, you do not love him. I see, it is his name you require to cover the shame which stains your father's, and which all his wealth cannot   355
conceal. Thank Heaven! his love for me will preserve him from such a cowardly scheme.

ALIDA: I will make him rich. What would you make him?

LUCY: I would make him happy.

ALIDA: Will you give him up?   360

LUCY: Never!

ALIDA: Be it so.

(*Re-enter Livingstone.*)

LIVINGSTONE: Lucy, dear Lucy, do you see that lady? — she is my guardian angel. To her I owe my good fortune — Mr. Bloodgood has told me all, and see, this letter is in her own handwriting; now, let me 365 confess, Miss Bloodgood, that had I not been thus rescued from ruin, I had no other resource but a Colt's revolver.

LUCY: Mark!

LIVINGSTONE: Yes, Lucy — I had resolved I could not endure the shame and despair which beset me on all sides. But let us not talk of such mad- 370 ness — let us only remember that I owe her my life.

ALIDA (*Aside.*):   And I intend to claim the debt.

LIVINGSTONE: More than my life — I owe to her all that happiness which you will bestow upon me.

LUCY: Me! me! — Mark! — No, it is impossible. 375

LIVINGSTONE: Impossible!

LUCY: I cannot be your wife.

LIVINGSTONE: What mean you, Lucy?

LUCY (*With supreme effort.*):   I — I do not love you.

LIVINGSTONE: You jest, Lucy — yet, no — there are tears in your eyes. 380

LUCY (*Looking away.*):   Did I ever tell you that I loved you?

LIVINGSTONE: No, it is true — but your manner, your looks, I thought —

LUCY: You are not angry with me, are you?

LIVINGSTONE: I love you too sincerely for that, and believe me I will never intrude again on your family, where my presence now can only produce 385 pain and restraint; may I hope, however, that you will retain enough kindness towards me, as to persuade your mother to accept my friend-ship? It will soothe the anguish you have innocently inflicted, if your family will permit me to assist them. Have you the generosity to make this atonement? I know it will pain you all — but you owe it to me. (*Lucy* 390 *falls, weeping, in a chair.*) Pardon me, Miss Bloodgood. Farewell, Lucy. (*To Alida.*) I take my leave.   (*Exit.*)

ALIDA: He has gone — you may dry your eyes.

LUCY: Oh! I know what starvation is — I have met want face-to-face, and I have saved him from that terrible extremity. 395

ALIDA: He offered you money; I should prefer that my husband should not have pecuniary relations with you — at least, not at present — so, as you are in want — here is some assistance. (*Offers her purse to Lucy.*)

LUCY (*Rising.*):   You insult me, Miss Bloodgood.

ALIDA: How can an offer of money insult anybody? 400

LUCY: You thought I sold my heart — no — I gave it. Keep your gold, it would soil my poverty; you have made two fellow-beings unhappy for life — God forgive you! (*Exit.*)

(*Re-enter Bloodgood.*)

BLOODGOOD: What is the matter, Alida?

(*Re-enter Badger.*)

BADGER: Your cook is perfect, your wine choice. (*He pockets the napkins.*)   405
Well, now suppose we do a little business.

BLOODGOOD (*Rings bell.*):   It is time we began to understand each other.

(*Enter Edwards.*)

Has that letter been delivered?

(*Edwards bows, and at a sign from Bloodgood, exits.*)

BADGER: Do you wish to enter into particulars in the presence of this charming creature?   410

BLOODGOOD: Her presence will not affect our business.

(*Re-enter Edwards, and two Police Officers.*)

BADGER: Just as you please. What proposition have you to make?

BLOODGOOD: I propose to give you into custody for an attempt to extort money by threats and intimidation.

FIRST POLICEMAN: You are our prisoner.   415

BADGER: Arrested!

BLOODGOOD: Let him be searched; on his person will be found a receipt signed by me which he purloined from my desk yonder.

BADGER: Well played, my dear Gideon, but, knowing the character of the society into which I was venturing, I left the dear document safe at   420
home. Good morning, Gid — Miss Bloodgood, yours. General — Colonel — take care of me. (*Goes [off] with Policemen.*)

ACT IV, SCENE I

Union Square — Night. The snow falls.

(*Puffy discovered, with a pan of roasting chestnuts. Paul crouches in a corner of the street.*)

PUFFY: Lord! how cold it is. I can't sell my chestnuts. I thought if I posted myself just there, so as to catch the grand folks as they go to the opera, they might fancy to take in a pocket-full, to eat during the performance.

(*Enter Dan, with two trunks on his shoulder, followed by a Gentleman.*)

DAN: There is the hotel. I'll wait here while you see if you can get a room.

(*Exit Gentleman, into hotel.*)

PUFFY: Dan, my boy, what cheer?   5
DAN: This is the first job I've had to-day.
PUFFY: I've not taken a cent.
DAN: Have you been home to dinner?
PUFFY: No; I took a chestnut. There wasn't more than enough for the old
woman and you, so I dined out.   10
DAN: I wasn't hungry much, so I boried a bit o' 'bacca.
PUFFY: Then the old woman had all the dinner, that's some comfort —
one of us had a good meal to-day.
DAN: I don't know, father — she's just ugly enough to go and put it by for
our supper.   15

(*Enter Mrs. Puffy, with a tin can.*)

PUFFY: Here she is.
MRS. PUFFY: Ain't you a nice pair? For five mortal hours I've been carryin'
this dinner up and down Broadway.
DAN: I told you so.
MRS. PUFFY: You thought to give old mother the slip, you undootiful   20
villin — but I've found ye both. Come, here's your suppers — I've kept it
warm under my cloak.
PUFFY: Lay the table on the gentleman's trunk.
DAN (*Looking into the tin can.*):   A splendid lump of bread, and a chunk of
beef!   25
PUFFY: Small feed for three human beings.
DAN: Here goes.
PUFFY: Stay, Dan. (*Placing his hands over the bread.*) God bless us, and pity the
Poor of New York. Now I'll share the food in three.
DAN (*Pointing to Paul.*):   Father, that cuss in the corner there looks kinder   30
bad — suppose you have the food in four.
MRS. PUFFY: I don't want more. Give him mine — I ain't at all cold.
DAN: Mother, there's a tear on the end of your nose — let me break it off.
MRS. PUFFY: Get out.
DAN (*Takes a piece of bread, and goes to Paul.*):   Hello, stranger! He's asleep.   35
MRS. PUFFY: Then don't wake him. Leave the bread in his lap. (*Dan places
the bread, softly, beside Paul, and rejoins the party — they eat.*)

(*Enter a Gentleman, followed by Badger.*)

BADGER (*Very ragged, with some opera books in one hand, and boxes of matches in the other.*):   Book of the opera, sir? take a book, sir — they will charge you double inside. Well, buy a box of lucifers — a hundred for three cents. (*Dodging in front of him to prevent him passing.*) Genuine Pollak's — try one. (*Exit Gentleman — Badger changes his tone, and calls after him.*) If you're short of 40
cash, I'll lend you a shilling. He wants all he has got to pay his omnibus. Jerusha! ain't it cold! Tum-iddy-tum-iddy-tum. (*Performs a short dance, while he hums a banjo melody.*) I could play the banjo on my stomach, while all my shivering anatomy would supply the bones.

(*Enter Mrs. Fairweather.*)

MRS. FAIRWEATHER: I cannot return to our miserable home without food 45
for my children. Each morning, we separate in search of work, in search of food, only to meet again at night — their poor faces thin with hunger. (*She clasps her hands in anguish.*) Ah! what's here? yes, this remains — it is gold!

BADGER (*Overhearing her last word.*):   Gold! Book of the opera, ma'am? 50

MRS. FAIRWEATHER: Tell me, friend, where can I buy a loaf of bread at this hour?

BADGER: There's a saloon open in the 4th Avenue. (*Aside.*) Gold — she said gold.

MRS. FAIRWEATHER: Will they accept this pledge for some food? (*Shows a* 55
ring to Badger.)

BADGER (*Eagerly.*):   Let me see it. (*Looks around.*)

MRS. FAIRWEATHER: It is my wedding ring.

(*Badger examines it by the light of the Druggist's window.*)

BADGER (*Aside.*):   I can easily make off with it. (*Rubs his nose with the ring while he considers.*)

MRS. FAIRWEATHER: My children are starving — I must part with it to buy them bread. 60

BADGER (*Whistles — hesitates — and returns the ring.*):   Go along, go buy your children food, start, and don't show that ring to anybody else. You deserve to lose it for showing it to such a blackguard as I am.

(*Exit Mrs. Fairweather.*)

(*Enter Bloodgood.*)

BLOODGOOD: What's the time? The opera must be nearly over. (*Looks at his watch by the light of the Druggist's window.*)

BADGER: Book of the opera, sir — only authorized edition. (*Recognizing* 65
him.) Bloodgood!

BLOODGOOD: Badger! (*They advance. Bloodgood puts his hand into the breast of his coat.*)

BADGER: Ah, my dear Gideon — (*Suddenly.*) Take your hand out of your breast — come! none of that — I've a knife up my sleeve that would rip you up like a dried codfish before you could cock that revolver you have 70 there so handy.

BLOODGOOD (*Withdrawing his hand.*):   You are mistaken.

BADGER: Oh, no! I am not. I have not been ten years in California for nothing — you were just thinking that you could blow out my brains, and swear that I was trying to garrote you. 75

BLOODGOOD: What do you want?

BADGER: I want your life — but legally. A week ago, I came out of prison — you had removed the Fairweather family — I could not find a trace of them but I found the receipt where I had concealed it. Tomorrow I shall place it in the hands of the District Attorney with my confession 80 of our murder of the Sea Captain.

BLOODGOOD: Murder —

BADGER: Only think what a fine wood cut for the Police Gazette we shall make, carrying out the dead body between us.

BLOODGOOD: Demon! 85

BADGER: There will be a correct plan of your back office in the Herald — headed — the Bloodgood Tragedy.

BLOODGOOD: Come to my house to-morrow, and bring that document with you.

BADGER: No, sir — ee! once caught twice shy. You owe a call. Come to my 90 house to-night — and alone.

BLOODGOOD: Where do you live?

BADGER: Nineteen and a half Cross Street, Five Points — fifth floor back — my name is on the door in chalk.

BLOODGOOD: In an hour I will be there. 95

BADGER: In an hour. Don't forget to present my compliments to your charming daughter — sweet creature! the image of her father — how I should like to write something in her album. (*Exit Bloodgood. Enter two Gentlemen from Hotel — they talk. Cries.*) Here's lucifers — three cents a hundred. (*Gentlemen shake hands and separate. Following one off.*) Here's 100 this miscellaneous stock of lumber, just imported from Germany, to be sold out — an alarming sacrifice, in consequence of the present state of the money market. (*Exit importuning the gentleman, who tries to escape.*)

PUFFY: Come mother, we must get home —

MRS. PUFFY: Dan, have you seen nothing of poor Mrs. Fairweather and 105
her children?

DAN: No, mother — I can't find out where they have gone to — I guess
they've quit New York.

MRS. PUFFY: God help them — wherever they are!

PUFFY: Come, mother. 110

(*Music — Puffy and Mrs. Puffy go out — Dan goes up and speaks with a gentleman.*)

(*Enter Lucy.*)

LUCY: This is the place. The sisters of charity in Houston Street told me
that I might find work at this address. (*Reads paper.*) 14th Street. Oh,
Heaven! be merciful to me, this is my last hope. (*Exit.*)

(*Paul rises and comes forward.*)

PAUL: My limbs are powerless. How long have I slept there? — another
long day has passed — I have crept round the hotels — the wharves — 115
I have begged for work — but they laughed at my poor thin form —
the remnant of better days hung in tatters about me — and I was
thrust from the door, by stronger wretches than I. To-day I applied to
get employment as a waiter in a hotel — but no, I looked too miserable.
Oh, my mother! my poor mother! my dear sister! were it not for you, I 120
would lie down here and die where I was born, in the streets of New
York.

DAN: All right, sir — to the Brevoort House. Here, you lazy cuss, shoulder
this trunk, and earn a quarter —

(*Enter a Porter.*)

PAUL: Yes — oh, gladly! — 125

PORTER: It's myself will do that same. (*Paul and the Porter seize the trunk.*)
Lave yer hoult — you dandy chap wid the black coat.

PAUL: He called to me.

PORTER: It is the likes of you — that ud be takin' the bread out of the
mouths of honest folks. 130

PAUL: God help me! I have not tasted bread for two days.

PORTER: The Lord save us! why didn't ye say so? — take the trunk and
welkim. (*Paul trying to lift it. Exit Dan.*)

GENTLEMAN: Come along, quick! (*Exit Gentleman.*)

PAUL (*Unable to lift it, staggers back.*): I — I — can't — I am too weak from 135
hunger.

PORTER: Look at this, my jewel. (*Tossing the trunk on his shoulder.*) That's the way of — id — all right, yer honor! (*Exit Porter.*)

PAUL (*Falling against the lamp-post in despair, on his knees.*):   Oh, God — you who have refused to me the force to earn my bread, give me the resigna-   140 tion to bear your will.

(*Re-enter Lucy.*)

LUCY: The lady was from home — they told me to call next week — oh, could I see some kindly face — I would beg, yes — I would ask alms.

(*Enter a Gentleman.*)

Sir — pardon me — would you —
GENTLEMAN: Eh?   145
LUCY (*Stammering.*):   I — I — I —
GENTLEMAN: What do you want?
LUCY (*Faintly.*):   The — the — Bowery — if — if — you please —
GENTLEMAN: Just turn to the right and keep straight on.   (*Exit.*)
LUCY: Oh coward! coward! — I have not the courage to beg.   150

(*Enter Mrs. Fairweather.*)

MRS. FAIRWEATHER: They refused to take my ring — they said I had stolen it — they drove me from the house. To what have I come! — to beg in the streets — yes, for them, for my children!
PAUL (*Rising.*):   Let me return to our home — perhaps Mother or Lucy may have found work.   155
MRS. FAIRWEATHER: Sir! sir! — In the name of your mother — help my poor children.
LUCY (*Covering her face with one hand, and holding out the other.*):   For pity's sake — give me the price of —
PAUL: Mother!!   160
LUCY: My Brother!   } (*Together*)
MRS. FAIRWEATHER: My Son!
PAUL: Oh, mother! my own Lucy! my heart is broken! (*They embrace.*) Have you concealed from me the extent of your misery?
MRS. FAIRWEATHER: My son! my poor children! I cannot see you die of   165 hunger and cold!
PAUL: Take Lucy home, mother — and I will bring you food.
MRS. FAIRWEATHER: Paul, promise me that nothing will tempt you to a dishonorable act.
PAUL: Do not fear, mother; the wretched have always one resource — they   170 can die! Do not weep, Lucy — in an hour I will be with you. (*Exeunt Lucy*

and Mrs. Fairweather.) I will go and await the crowd as they leave the Academy of Music — amongst them Heaven will inspire some Christian heart to aid me.

SCENE II

The vestibule of the Academy of Music.

(*Enter Alida and Livingstone. Music within.*)

ALIDA: How strange that my father has not returned.

LIVINGSTONE: Allow me to look for the carriage.

ALIDA: I will remain here. (*Exit Livingstone.*) At last I have won the husband I desire. He is entangled in my father's debt; in one month hence I shall be Livingstone's wife. Our box is now crowded with the first people 5 in New York. — The dear Duke still makes love to me — to which Livingstone appears indifferent — so much the better — once Mrs. Livingstone he may do as he likes and so will I.

(*Enter Paul.*)

PAUL: Ah 'tis she — Alida Bloodgood.

ALIDA: I wonder they permit such vagabonds to hang about the opera. 10

(*Re-enter Livingstone.*)

LIVINGSTONE: The carriage is ready — (*Recognizing Paul.*) Paul!

PAUL: Livingstone!

LIVINGSTONE: Great heaven! In what condition do I find you.

PAUL: We are poor — we are starving.

ALIDA: Give the poor fellow a dollar, and send him away. 15

LIVINGSTONE: My dear Alida, you do not know — this is a school fellow — an old friend —

ALIDA: I know that you are keeping me in the cold — ah! I see the Duke of Calcavella on the steps yonder, smoking a cigar. He will see me home, don't let me take you from your old friend.   (*Exit.*) 20

LIVINGSTONE (*Aside.*):   Cold — heartless girl! (*Aloud.*) Come, Paul, come quickly, bring me to where I shall find your mother — your sister — stay, let me first go home, and get money, I will meet you at your lodgings — where do you live?

PAUL: Number nineteen and a half Cross Street — Five Points — I will 25 wait for you at the door.

LIVINGSTONE: In less than an hour I shall be there.   (*Exeunt.*)

SCENE III

No. 19½ Cross Street — Five Points. Two adjoining attic rooms: that of Badger, that of the Fairweather family. Music. Lucy is seated and Mrs. Fairweather is kneeling.

LUCY: Surely an hour has passed and Paul has not returned.

MRS. FAIRWEATHER: Oh, merciful father! protect my poor children.

(*Enter Badger in his attic with his box of matches. He scrapes several which do not light. Mrs. Fairweather rises and goes to window.*)

BADGER: One hundred matches like that for one cent. (*Lighting one.*) Oh, lucky chance! here's one that condescends. (*Lights a candle in a bottle.*)

MRS. FAIRWEATHER: Day after day goes by — no hope — the future   5
worse than the present — dark — dark. Oh! this load of wretchedness is too much to bear.

LUCY: The candle is going out.

MRS. FAIRWEATHER: So much the better, I shall not be able to see your
tears. (*Lucy rests her face on her hands.*)   10

BADGER (*Taking a bottle from his pocket.*):   There's the concentrated essence of comfort — the poor man's plaster for the inside.

LUCY (*Aside.*):   Is there no way to end this misery? None but death.

BADGER (*Taking from pocket a slice of bread and meat wrapped in a bit of newspaper.*):
Here's my supper. (*Addressing an imaginary servant.*) James, lay the table —
spread the table cloth. — "Yes sa" — (*Places the newspaper over the table.*) It's   15
cold here, there's a draught in this room, somewhere. — James, champagne. Thank you, James. (*Drinks and eats.*)

MRS. FAIRWEATHER (*Aside, coming down.*):   If Paul had only Lucy to support, they might live — why should I prolong my life only to hasten theirs.

BADGER: The draught comes from — (*Examining the wall.*) — yes there are   20
great chinks in the wall — I must see my landlord and solicit repairs. A new family moved into the next room, yesterday; I wonder who they are?

LUCY: The wretched always have one resource — they can die!

BADGER (*At his table eating — he has taken the blanket from his bed and wrapped it about his shoulders.*):   Now let us do a little business. James, turn up the
gas. Yes sa! — (*He snuffs out the candle with his fingers.*) Thank you. Ahem!   25
James, Bloodgood is coming for the receipt bequeathed to me by the old sailor. What price shall we set upon it, James?

LUCY (*Aside.*):   When I am gone, there will be one mouth less to feed —
Paul will have but one care to provide for.

MRS. FAIRWEATHER (*Aside.*):   In this room, we had some charcoal — there   30
is enough left to bestow on me an easy death.   (*Mrs. Fairweather exits.*)

BADGER: I think $50,000 would be the figure — Oh, what a prospect opens before me — 50,000 dollars — I should resume specie payments.

LUCY (*Looks into room.*):   What is mother doing? ah, she is lighting the pan of charcoal on which we prepare our food — ah! — the thought! — could I induce her to leave me alone. Hem. — The deadly fumes of that fuel will bestow on me an easy death.

MRS. FAIRWEATHER (*Re-enters.*):   It is there — now, now, while I have the courage of despair.

BADGER: 50,000 dollars! I'll have a pair of fast trotters, and dine at Delmonico's. James, more champagne. (*Takes a drink from bottle.*) Thank you —

LUCY & MRS. FAIRWEATHER (*Together.*):   Mother — Lucy.

LUCY: Dear mother — I have just thought of a friend — a — a — fellow work girl, from whom I may get assistance —

MRS. FAIRWEATHER: Go, then, my child — yes — go at once.

LUCY: I fear to go alone. Come with me, you can wait at the corner of the street until I come out.

MRS. FAIRWEATHER (*Putting on her bonnet. Aside.*):   When she is out of sight, I can return and accomplish my purpose.

LUCY (*Casting a cloak over her head. Aside.*):   I will come back by another way.

MRS. FAIRWEATHER: Come, Lucy.

LUCY: I am ready, mother. (*Aside.*) She does not think that we are about to part forever.

MRS. FAIRWEATHER (*Aside.*):   My poor child!

LUCY: Kiss me — mother, for my heart is cold. (*They embrace.*)

BADGER (*Cogitating.*):   50,000 dollars! I'll have a box at Grace Church and a pew at the opera.

LUCY: Mother, I am ready.   (*Exeunt.*)

BADGER (*Finding his bottle empty.*):   What's the news? Let us consult my table cloth. What journal have we here. (*Reads.*) "Chevalier Greely has got a new hat." — It's the *Herald* — What's here? — (*Reads*) "You lie — villainy — you lie, and you know it." No! it's the *Tribune.*

(*Enter Bloodgood.*)

BLOODGOOD: Ah, Mr. Badger.

BADGER: Please wipe your feet, before you come in — my carpet is new. I am glad to see you. Take a seat upon the sofa. (*Pointing to bed.*)

BLOODGOOD: Come, sir; to business. You have the receipt with you, I suppose?

BADGER: You know I've got it, or you would not have come.

BLOODGOOD: How much do you want for it?

BADGER: Stay a moment. Let us see. You have had for twenty years in your   70
possession, the sum of $100,000, the profits of one robbery — well, at
eight per cent, this sum would be doubled.

BLOODGOOD: Let me see the document, and then we can estimate its
value.

BADGER (*Drawing receipt from pocket.*):   Here it is.   75

BLOODGOOD (*Springing towards him.*):   Let me have it.

BADGER: Hands off!

BLOODGOOD (*Drawing pistol.*):   That paper, give it me, or I'll blow your
brains out!

BADGER (*Edging slowly towards the bed.*):   Ah! that's your calculation.   80

BLOODGOOD: Now you are in my power.

BADGER: It's an old dodge, but ineffective. Come, no violence — I'll give
you the paper.

BLOODGOOD: A bullet is a good argument.

BADGER (*Drawing from beneath his pillow, two enormous pistols.*):   A brace of bul-   85
lets are better still!

BLOODGOOD: Damnation!

BADGER: Derringer's self-cocking. Drop your hand, or I'll blow you into
pi. — So, you took me for a fool: — that's where you made a mistake. I
took you for a thorough rascal, that's where I did *not* make a mistake.   90
Now, to business.

BLOODGOOD (*Surlily.*):   How much do you want?

BADGER: Fifty thousand dollars!

BLOODGOOD: Be it so.

BADGER: In gold, or Chemicals.   95

BLOODGOOD: Very well. To-morrow —

BADGER: No — to-night.

BLOODGOOD: To-night!

BADGER: Yes; I wish to purchase a brown stone house on the avenue early
in the morning.   100

BLOODGOOD: Come with me to my house in Madison Square.

BADGER: No, thank you. I'll expect you here in an hour with the money.

BLOODGOOD (*Aside.*):   He has me in his power — I must yield. (*Aloud.*) I
will return, then, in an hour.

BADGER: Let me light you out. Mind the bannister — don't break your   105
precious neck, at least, not to-night. No, go in front, will you? I prefer it.

BLOODGOOD: What for?

BADGER (*With pistol and candle.*):   A fancy of mine — a want of confidence.
A want of confidence, in fact, pervades the community.   (*Exeunt.*)

(*Re-enter Lucy.*)

LUCY: I took a cross street, and ran rapidly home. Now I am alone; the   110
fumes of the charcoal will soon fill this small room. They say it is an easy
death — but let me not hesitate — let me sleep the long sleep where
there are no more tears, no more suffering.   (*Exit into closet.*)

(*Re-enter Badger.*)

BADGER: So! that is settled. I hope he will be cautious and escape the gar-
roters. James, my chibouque. (*Takes his pipe.*)   115

(*Re-enter Mrs. Fairweather.*)

MRS. FAIRWEATHER: Poor Lucy! I dared not look back upon her as we
parted forever. Despair hastened my steps. My poor children! I have
given you all I had, and now I hope my wretched life will serve you in
your terrible need. Come, courage; let me prevent the fresh air from entering. (*Takes bits of linen and stops window and door.*)   120

BADGER (*Snuffing.*):   I smell charcoal — burning charcoal — where can it
come from?

MRS. FAIRWEATHER: Now let me stop the door.

BADGER (*Smoking.*):   It's very odd; I've a queer feeling in my head; let me lie
down awhile. (*Lies on his bed.*)   125

(*Enter Lucy, with a brazier of charcoal, alight.*)

MRS. FAIRWEATHER: That's done. (*Going towards closet, and meeting Lucy.*)
Now the hour has come.

LUCY: The moment has arrived. (*Sets down the brazier.*)

MRS. FAIRWEATHER: Lucy!

LUCY: Mother!   130

MRS. FAIRWEATHER: My child, what is this? For what purpose are you
here?

LUCY: And you, mother, why have you fastened those apertures so closely?
Like me, you wish to die!

MRS. FAIRWEATHER: No, no, you shall not die! my darling child — you are   135
young — life is before you — hope — happiness.

LUCY: The future! what is it? The man I love will soon wed another. I have
no future, and the present is a torture.

MRS. FAIRWEATHER: Hush, my child, hush!

LUCY: Is it not better to die thus, than by either grief or hunger?   140

MRS. FAIRWEATHER (*Falling in a chair.*):   Already my senses fail me. Lucy my
child, live, live!

LUCY (*Falls at her feet.*):   No; let us die together — thus, mother — as often as I knelt to you as a child, let me pray for those we love.

MRS. FAIRWEATHER: Oh, merciful Judge in heaven, forgive us — forgive 145 my child — and let — your anger fall — on me — alone —

LUCY: God bless my dear brother — and you my dear Mark, may — you be — hap — (*Murmurs the rest of the prayer.*)

BADGER: It's very cold! I feel quite sleepy. I must not go to sleep. (*Sings in a low voice.*) "Oh, down in ole Virginny." 150

PAUL (*Without, knocking.*):   Mother, open the door, why is the door locked? Mother, mother! Open, mother, open! (*Knocks violently. Mrs. Fairweather, arising, tries to reach the door, but cannot, and falls. Paul bursts open the door and enters with Livingstone; they start back — Livingstone breaks the window, and Paul runs to his mother.*) Too late! too late! They have committed suicide!

LIVINGSTONE: They live still. Quick, bear them outside into the air. (*Carries Lucy out while Paul assists his mother into the next room.*)

BADGER (*Starting up.*):   How hot it is here — I cannot breath. Have I drunk 155 too much? Nonsense! I could drink a dozen such bottles. Let me try my legs a bit — where's the door? I can't see it — my head spins round — come, Badger, no nonsense now. God! I'm suffocating! Am I going to die, to die like that old sea captain? (*Tears off his cravat.*) Justice of Heaven! I am strangling. Help! Help! Bloodgood will return and find me helpless, 160 then he will rob me of the receipt, as I robbed the old sailor — I know him of old — he is capable of it, but he shall not have it! There in its nook, if I have the strength to reach it — it is safe — safe. (*Drags himself along the floor, lifts up a loose board, puts the receipt beneath it and falls exhausted.*) There!

PAUL (*Entering the room.*):   I heard smothered cries for help — they came 165 from this floor.   (*Exit.*)

(*Enter Bloodgood.*)

BLOODGOOD: Here I am, Badger. (*Starts back, suffocated.*) What a suffocating atmosphere! where is he? ha! is he intoxicated?

PAUL (*Entering room.*):   Perhaps the cry came from here, dead?

BLOODGOOD: Paul Fairweather! 170

PAUL: Gideon Bloodgood!

BADGER (*Raising his head.*):   What names were those? Both of them! Together, here! (*To Paul.*) Listen — while I yet have breath to speak — listen! Twenty years ago, that man robbed your father of $100,000!

PAUL: Robbed! 175

BLOODGOOD: Scoundrel!

BADGER: I've got the proofs.

PAUL: The proofs?

BADGER: I have 'em safe — you'll find 'em — th — ah — (*Falls backward insensible; Paul and Bloodgood stand aghast.*)

ACT V, SCENE I

Brooklyn Heights, overlooking the city of New York and its harbors. The stage is occupied by a neat garden, on a natural terrace of the heights — a frame cottage stands, prettily built — a table with breakfast laid, at which Mrs. Fairweather and Paul are seated.

(*Enter Mrs. Puffy, from the cottage, with a teapot.*)

MRS. PUFFY: There's the tea. Bless me, how hot it is to-day! Who would think that we were in the month of February? (*Sits.*)

MRS. FAIRWEATHER: Your husband is late to breakfast.

PAUL: Here he comes.

(*Enter Puffy, gaily.*)

PUFFY: How is everybody? and above everybody, how is Miss Lucy this morning? (*Sits at table.*)   5

MRS. FAIRWEATHER: Poor child! her recovery is slow — the fever has abated, but she is still very weak.

PAUL: Her life is saved, for a whole month she hovered over the grave.

PUFFY: But how is it we never see Mr. Livingstone? Our benefactor is like Santa Claus — he showers benefits and blessings on us all, yet never shows us his face.   10

MRS. FAIRWEATHER: He brought us back to this, our old home — he obtained employment for Paul in the Navy Yard.

PUFFY: He set me up again in my patent oven, and got me a government contract for Navy biscuit.   15

MRS. PUFFY: He is made of the finest flour that heaven ever put into human baking; he'll die of over-bigness of the heart.

MRS. FAIRWEATHER: That's a disease hereditary in your family.

PAUL (*Rising.*):   I will tell you why Livingstone avoids our gratitude. Because my sister Lucy refused his love — because he has sold his hand to Alida Bloodgood — and he has given us the purchase money.   20

PUFFY: And amongst those who have served us, don't let us forget poor Badger.

(*Enter Badger, behind.*)

BADGER: They are talking of me. 25

MRS. FAIRWEATHER (*Rising.*): Forget him! Forget the man who watched Lucy during her illness, with more than the tenderness of a brother! A woman never can forget anyone who has been kind to her children.

MRS. PUFFY: Them's my sentiments to a hair.

BADGER: You shan't have cause to change them. 30

PAUL: Badger!

BADGER: Congratulate me. I have been appointed to the police. The commissioners wanted a special service to lay on to Wall Street's savagery, it seems has concentrated there, and we want to catch a big offender.

MRS. PUFFY: They all go to Europe. 35

PUFFY: That accounts for the drain of specie.

(*Mr. and Mrs. Puffy take off the breakfast table.*)

MRS. FAIRWEATHER: I will tell Lucy that her nurse has come. (*Exit into cottage.*)

PAUL: Now, Badger, the news.

BADGER: Bad, sir. To-night. Mr. Livingstone is to be married to Alida Bloodgood. 40

PAUL: What shall I do? I dare not accuse Bloodgood of this robbery, unless you can produce the proofs — and perhaps the wretch has discovered and destroyed them.

BADGER: I think not. When I recovered from the effects of the charcoal, the day after my suffocation, I started for my lodging — I found the 45 house shut up, guarded by a servant of Bloodgood's — the banker had bought the place. But I had concealed the document too cunningly; he has not found it.

PAUL: But knowing this man to be a felon, whom we may be able at any hour to unmask, can we allow Livingstone to marry his daughter? 50

(*Enter Livingstone.*)

LIVINGSTONE: Paul, I have come to bid you farewell, and to see Lucy for the last time —

(*Enter Lucy.*)

LUCY: For the last time, why so — (*Paul and Badger run to assist her forward.*)

LIVINGSTONE: Lucy, dear Lucy.

BADGER: Now take care — sit down —

LUCY: Ah, my good kind nurse. (*She sits.*) You are always by my side.

BADGER: Always ready with a dose of nasty medicine, ain't I — well now I've got another dose ready — do you see this noble kind heart, Lucy; it

looks through two honest blue eyes into your face — well tell me what
you see there — 60
LUCY: Why do you ask me? (*Troubled.*)
BADGER: Don't turn your eyes away — the time has come when deception
is a crime, Lucy — look in his face and confess the infernal scheme by
which Alida Bloodgood compelled you to renounce your love.
LIVINGSTONE: Alida! 65
LUCY: Has she betrayed me —
BADGER: No! you betrayed yourself — one night in the ravings of your
fever, when I held your hands in the paroxysm of your frenzy, I heard
the cries that came from your poor wounded heart; shall I repeat the
scene. 70
LUCY (*Hiding her face in her hands.*): No, no.
LIVINGSTONE: Paul, is this true? have I been deceived?
PAUL: You have — Lucy confessed to me this infamous bargain, extorted
from her by Alida Bloodgood; and to save you from ruin, she sacrificed
her love — 75
LIVINGSTONE: Lucy! dear Lucy, look up. It was for your sake alone that I
accepted this hated union — to save you and yours from poverty — but
whisper one word, tell me that ruin of fortune is better than ruin of the
heart. (*Lucy falls upon his neck.*)
BADGER: Hail Columbia! I know a grand party at Madison Square that 80
will cave in to-night — hi! — I shall be there to congratulate that sweet
girl.

(*Enter Dan.*)

DAN: Mother! mother! where's my hat, quick, there's a fire in New York.
(*He runs into the house and re-enters with a telescope, looks off toward the city.*)
BADGER: Yes, and there is a fire here too, but one we don't want to put
out — 85
PAUL: Now Mark, I can confess to you that documents exist — proofs of
felony against Bloodgood, which may at any moment consign him to the
State Prison and transfer to our family his ill-gotten wealth.
LIVINGSTONE: Proofs of felony?
DAN: The fire is in Chatham Street. 90
PAUL: Twenty years ago he robbed my father of 100,000 dollars.
BADGER: And I was his accomplice in the act; we shared the plunder be-
tween us —
DAN: No it isn't in Chatham Street — I see it plainly — it is in Cross
Street, Five Points. 95
BADGER (*Starting.*): Cross Street — where, where — (*Runs up.*)

LIVINGSTONE: But if these proofs — these documents exist, where are they?

DAN: It is the tenement house two doors from the corner.

BADGER: Damnation! it is our old lodging! you ask where are these proofs,   100 these documents? they are yonder, in the burning house — fired by Bloodgood to destroy the papers he could not find — curses on him!

(*Enter Mrs. Puffy, with Dan's hat.*)

MRS. PUFFY: Here's your hat, Dan.

BADGER: Quick! Dan, my son — for our lives! Dan! the fortunes of Lucy and Paul and the old woman are all in that burning house.   105

(*Dan begins to thrust his trousers into his boots. Enter Mrs. Fairweather and Puffy.*)

BADGER: I mean to save it or perish in the flames.

DAN: Count me in. (*They run out.*)

Tableau

SCENE II

Stage dark. The exterior of the tenement house, No. 19½ Cross Street, Five Points — the shutters of all the windows are closed. A light is seen through the round holes in the shutters of the upper windows — presently a flame rises — it is extinguished — then revives. The light is seen to descend as the bearer of it passes down the staircase, the door opens cautiously — Bloodgood, disguised, appears — he looks round — closes the door again — locks it.

BLOODGOOD: In a few hours this accursed house will be in ruins. The receipt is concealed there — and it will be consumed in the flames. (*The glow of fire is seen to spread from room to room.*) Now Badger — do your worst — I am safe!   (*Exit.*)

(*The house is gradually enveloped in fire, a cry outside is heard "Fi-er!" "Fi-er!" It is taken up by other voices more distant. The tocsin sounds — other churches take up the alarm — bells of Engines are heard. Enter a crowd of persons. Enter Badger, without coat or hat — he tries the door — finds it fast; seizes a bar of iron and dashes in the ground-floor window, the interior is seen in flames. Enter Dan.*)

DAN (*Seeing Badger climbing into the window.*): Stop! Stop! (*Badger leaps in and*   5 *disappears. Shouts from the mob; Dan leaps in — another shout, Dan leaps out again black and burned, staggers forward and seems overcome by the heat and smoke. The shutters of the garret fall and discover Badger in the upper floor. Another cry from the crowd, a loud crash is heard, Badger disappears as if falling with the inside of the building. The shutters of the windows fall away, and the inside of the house is seen, gutted by the fire; a cry of horror is uttered by the mob. Badger drags himself from the ruins, and falls across the sill of the lower window. Dan and two of the mob run to help him forward but recoil before the heat; at length they succeed in rescuing his body — which lies center stage. Livingstone, Paul, and Puffy, rush on. Dan kneels over Badger and extinguishes the fire which clings to parts of his clothes.)*

SCENE III

The Drawing-Room in Bloodgood's mansion, in Madison Square — illuminated. Music within.

(Enter Bloodgood.)

BLOODGOOD: The evidence of my crime is destroyed — no power on earth can reveal the past. *(Enter Alida, dressed as a bride.)* My dearest child, tonight you will leave this roof; but from this home in your father's heart, none can displace you.

ALIDA: Oh, dear papa, do take care of my flounces — you men pat one about as if a dress was put on only to be rumpled.   5

BLOODGOOD: The rooms below are full of company. Has Livingstone arrived?

ALIDA: I did not inquire. The duke is there, looking the picture of misery, while all my female friends pretend to congratulate me — but I know   10 they are dying with envy and spite.

BLOODGOOD: And do these feelings constitute the happiest day of your life? Alida, have you no heart?

ALIDA: Yes, father, I have a heart — but it is like yours. It is an iron safe in which are kept the secrets of the past.   15

(Enter Edwards.)

EDWARDS: The clergyman is robed, sir, and ready to perform the ceremony.

BLOODGOOD: Let the bridesmaids attend Miss Bloodgood. *(The curtains are raised, and the Bridesmaids enter. Bloodgood goes up and off, and immediately returns with the bridal party.)* Welcome, my kind friends. *(Alida speaks aside with the duke.)* Your presence fills me with pride and joy — but where is the bridegroom? Has no one seen my son-in-law?   20

EDWARDS *(Announcing.)*:   Mr. Mark Livingstone.

(*Enter Livingstone.*)

BLOODGOOD: Ah! at last. What a strange costume for a bridegroom.

ALIDA (*Turns, and views Livingstone.*):   Had I not good reasons to be assured of your sincerity, Mr. Livingstone, your appearance would lead me to believe that you looked upon this marriage as a jest, or a masquerade.   25

LIVINGSTONE: As you say, Miss Bloodgood, it is a masquerade — but it is one where more than one mask must fall.

BLOODGOOD (*Aside.*):   What does he mean?

ALIDA: You speak in a tone of menace. May —

BLOODGOOD: Perhaps I had better see Mr. Livingstone alone — he may   30
be under some misapprehension.

LIVINGSTONE: I am under none, sir — although I believe you may be; and what I have to say and do, demands no concealment. I come here to decline the hand of your daughter. (*Movement amongst the crowd.*)

BLOODGOOD: You must explain this public insult.   35

LIVINGSTONE: I am here to do so, but I do not owe this explanation to you; I owe it to myself, and those friends I see here, whose presence under your roof is a tribute to the name I bear. My friends, I found myself in this man's debt; he held in pledge all I possessed — all but my name; that name he wanted to shelter the infamy in which his own was covered, and   40
I was vile enough to sell it.

BLOODGOOD: Go on, sir; go on.

LIVINGSTONE: With your leave, I will.

ALIDA: These matters you were fully acquainted with, I presume, when you sought my hand.   45

LIVINGSTONE: But I was not acquainted with the contents of these letters — written by you, to the Duke of Calcavella.

BLOODGOOD: Dare you insinuate that they contain evidence derogatory to the honor of my child?

LIVINGSTONE: No, sir; but I think Miss Bloodgood will agree with me,   50
that the sentiments expressed in these letters entitle her to the hand of the duke rather than to mine. (*He hands letters to Alida.*)

ALIDA: Let him go, father.

LIVINGSTONE: Not yet. You forget that my friends here are assembled to witness a marriage, and all we require is a bride.   55

BLOODGOOD: Yes; a bride who can pay your debts.

(*Enter Paul, Lucy, and Mrs. Fairweather.*)

PAUL: No, sir; a bride who can place the hand of a pure and loving maiden in that of a good and honest man.

BLOODGOOD: How dare you intrude in this house?

PAUL: Because it is mine; because your whole fortune will scarcely serve   60
to pay the debt you owe the widow and the children of Adam Fairweather!

BLOODGOOD: Is my house to be invaded by beggars like these! Edwards
send for the police. Is there no law in New York for ruffians?

(*Enter Badger, in the uniform of an officer of police.*)

BADGER: Yes, plenty — and here's the police.   65

BLOODGOOD: Badger!

BADGER: What's left of him.

BLOODGOOD (*Wildly.*):   Is this a conspiracy to ruin me?

BADGER: That's it. We began it twenty years ago; we've been hatching it
ever since; we let you build up a fortune; we tempted you to become an   70
incendiary; we led you on from misdemeanor to felony — and that's
what I want you for.

BLOODGOOD: What do you mean?

BADGER: My meaning is set forth very clearly in an affidavit, on which the
Recorder, at this very late hour for business, issued this warrant for your   75
arrest.

(*Enter two Policemen. Alida falls in a chair.*)

BLOODGOOD: Incendiary! Dare you charge a man of my standing in this
city, with such a crime, without any cause?

BADGER: Cause! you wanted to burn up this receipt, which I was just in
time to rescue from the flames!   80

BLOODGOOD (*Drawing a knife.*):   Fiend! you escaped the flames here — now
go to those hereafter!

BADGER: Hollo! (*Disarms Bloodgood and slips a pair of handcuffs on him.*)
Gideon — my dear Gideon — don't lose your temper. (*Throws him back,
manacled, on the sofa.*)

PAUL: Miss Bloodgood, let me lead you from this room.   85

ALIDA (*Rises, and crosses to her father.*):   Father.

BLOODGOOD: Alida, my child.

ALIDA: Is this true? (*A pause.*) It is — I read it in your quailing eye — on
your paling lips. And it was for this that you raised me to the envied position of the rich man's heiress — for this you roused my pride — for this   90
you decked me in jewels — to be the felon's daughter. Farewell.

BLOODGOOD: Alida — my child — my child — it was for you alone I
sinned — do not leave me.

ALIDA: What should I do in this city? can I earn my bread? what am I fit

for — with your tainted name and my own sad heart? (*Throws down her* 95
bride's coronet.) I am fit for the same fate as yours — infamy.   (*Exit.*)

BADGER: Duke, you had better see that lady out. (*Exit Duke.*) Gideon, my
dear, allow me to introduce you to two friends of mine, who are anxious
to make your acquaintance.

BLOODGOOD: Take me away; I have lost my child — my Alida; take me 100
away; hide me from all the world.

PAUL: Stay! Mr. Bloodgood, in the midst of your crime there was one
virtue; you loved your child; even now your heart deplores her ruin —
not your own. Badger, give me that receipt. (*Takes the receipt from Badger.*)
Do you acknowledge this paper to be genuine? 105

BLOODGOOD: I do.

PAUL (*Tears it.*):   I have no charge against you. Let him be released. Restore
to me my fortune, and take the rest; go, follow your child; save her from
ruin, and live a better life.

BLOODGOOD: I cannot answer you as I would. (*Turns aside in tears and goes out* 110
with Policemen and Badger, who releases Bloodgood.)

LIVINGSTONE: That was nobly done, Paul. Now my friends, since all is
prepared for my marriage let the ceremony proceed.

MRS. FAIRWEATHER: But where is Mrs. Puffy?

BADGER: Here they are, outside, but they won't come in.

PAUL: Why not? 115

BADGER: They are afraid of walking on the carpets.

LIVINGSTONE: Bring them in.

BADGER: That's soon done.   (*Exit.*)

MRS. FAIRWEATHER: Poor, good, kind people — the first to share our sorrow, the last to claim a part in our joy. 120

(*Enter Badger and Dan — Puffy and one Policeman — Mrs. Puffy and the other Po-*
liceman.)

BADGER: They wouldn't come — I was obliged to take 'em in custody.

DAN: Oh! mother, where's this?

MRS. PUFFY: I'm walkin' on a feather bed.

PUFFY: He wouldn't let me wipe my shoes.

LIVINGSTONE: Come in — these carpets have never been trodden by more 125
honest feet, these mirrors have never reflected kinder faces — come in —
breathe the air here — you will purify it.

MRS. PUFFY: Oh, Dan, what grand folks — ain't they?

DAN: Canvass backs every one on 'em.

LIVINGSTONE: And now, Lucy, I claim your hand. (*Music inside.*) All is 130
ready for the ceremony.

BADGER: You have seen the dark side of life — you can appreciate your fortune, for you have learned the value of wealth.

MRS. FAIRWEATHER: No, we have learned the value of poverty. (*Gives her hand to Puffy.*) It opens the heart. 135

PAUL (*To the public.*): Is this true? have the sufferings we have depicted in this mimic scene, touched your hearts, and caused a tear of sympathy to fill your eyes? If so, extend to us your hands.

MRS. FAIRWEATHER: No, not to us — but when you leave this place, as you return to your homes, should you see some poor creatures, extend your 140 hands to them, and the blessings that will follow you on your way will be the most grateful tribute you can pay to the Poor of New York.

END

FIGURE 7 *Cover of an advertising herald for* Shore Acres, *showing James A. Herne, center, and vignettes of scenes from the play.*

JAMES A. HERNE

Shore Acres

⊁⊱

Actor, playwright, and manager James A. Herne (1839–1901) was born Aherne; he changed his name to coincide with a playbill misspelling. Herne became the "apostle of simplicity" in his dramaturgy and the best example of an American playwright conscious of fostering realism at the turn of the century. His theater career began as an actor in 1854, and he spent some twenty years traveling and working as actor and manager in many locales (New York; Washington, D.C.; Baltimore; Philadelphia; Montreal; Salt Lake City). In the 1870s he became a stage manager in California; met David Belasco, with whom he collaborated on early plays; and married in 1878 his second wife, actress Katherine Corcoran, who became the inspiration for and collaborator in his subsequent work. With Belasco he wrote his first important play, *Chums,* renamed *Hearts of Oak* in 1880 (he bought the rights from Belasco and ultimately made a fortune from the play). Original plays that followed include: *The Minute Men of 1774–75* (1886); *Drifting Apart* (1888; originally called *Mary, the Fisherman's Child*); *Margaret Fleming* (1891), historically his most important play; *My Colleen* (1891); *Shore Acres* (1892), his greatest commercial success and an acting vehicle for both Hernes; *The Reverend Griffith Davenport,* based on a novel by Helen Gardner, and *Sag Harbor* (both 1899). In 1897 Herne articulated his credo as a literary craftsman in "Art for Truth's Sake in the Drama" in the magazine *Arena.* Herne's daughter Chrystal, who first appeared in her father's plays, became a moderately successful actress.

→ Shore Acres   *1892*

A Comedy in Four Acts

DRAMATIS PERSONAE

MARTIN BERRY, *owner of "Shore Acres" and keeper of Berry Light*
NATHAN'L BERRY, *"Uncle Nat," his elder brother*
JOEL GATES, *a grass widower*
JOSIAH BLAKE, *postmaster and storekeeper*
SAM WARREN, *a young physician*
CAPTAIN BEN HUTCHINS, *skipper of the "Liddy Ann"*

DR. LEONARD	IKE RICHARDS
SQUIRE ANDREWS	LEM CONANT
TIM HAYES	ABE HIGGINS
YOUNG NAT BERRY	STEVE BAILEY

"Kinder work around"

DAVE BURGESS	THE MAIL CARRIER
GABE KILPATRICK	
BILL HODGEKINS	

Fishermen, crew of the "Liddy Ann"

BOB BERRY	MARY BERRY
ANN BERRY, *Martin's wife*	MILLIE BERRY
HELEN BERRY, *Martin's daughter*	MANDY GATES
LIDDY ANN NYE	BOB LEONARD
MRS. ANDREWS	SIS LEONARD
MRS. LEONARD	
PERLEY, *Mrs. Berry's hired girl*	

The twins (BOB LEONARD, SIS LEONARD)

ACT I: *View of "Shore Acres Farm," near Bar Harbor. "Hayin' Time."*
ACT II: *The Berry farmhouse kitchen. "The Silver Weddin'."*
ACT III: *Scene I. Interior of Berry Lighthouse. "Havin' an Understandin'."*
          Scene II. Exterior of Berry Lighthouse. "The 'Liddy Ann' in a Sou'easter."
ACT IV: *Same as Act II. Fifteen months later. "Me an' the Children."*
TIME: 1891.
PLACE: *Berry, on Frenchman's Bay, near Bar Harbor, on the coast of Maine.*

ACT I

"HAYIN' TIME"

View of "Shore Acres Farm," near Bar Harbor.

Frenchman's Bay, with Mount Desert Island and its range of grandly picturesque hills in the distance. Away off to the right are the stately Schoodac Mountains, veiled in mist.

On the right of the stage, at the back, on a rocky bluff dotted with dwarf pines, and overlooking the bay, is Berry Light. It is separated from the farmhouse by a shady road, which runs across the stage from left to right. The farmhouse, on the right, is barely visible, being hidden in a profusion of shrubs and flowers. Trees overhang the roof; a white-washed fence divides the door yard from the road. Several shining milk pails are hanging on the fence, and on one of the palings hangs a small weather-beaten mail bag; near it hangs a battered tin horn. The door yard is filled with old-fashioned flowers.

To the left of the stage is an old barn, its doors open, its littered yard enclosed by a rail fence. A dove cote is built into the peak of its gabled roof, and doves come and go leisurely.

Outside the fence, at the upper end, is a pump, beneath which is a trough filled with water. Against the lower end of the fence lies a plough. Trees overhang the roof of the barn, and join those overhanging the house from the other side. At right center is a gnarled old tree, and beneath it is a bench. Down left, below the fence, is a wheelbarrow.

At the rise of the curtain, and until the act is well in progress, the wind gently sways the foliage with a slight rustling sound. Birds sing, and flit to and fro. The sound of multitudinous insects is the one distinct note of the scene. The bay is calm, quiet, and in the distance a catboat is occasionally seen sailing lazily, appearing and disappearing among the islands. A tiny steam launch appears once, about the middle of the act, and is seen no more. A mowing machine is heard at work in the distance off left. It stops, turns, goes on again, while the voice of the driver is heard guiding his horses, with "Whoa! Stiddy! Get up! Whoa Bill! (All this must be very distant.)

At the rise of curtain, Millie, a little girl about four years old, is sitting down left near the plough, playing in the sand with clam shells and pieces of old crockery. She wears a quaint little calico dress, and has a small white flannel shawl around her shoulders, crossed in front and tied behind her back. Her shoes are very dusty, her little hands are dirty.

On the road, off stage to the right, a horse and wagon can be heard driving up and stopping outside; and presently the Mail Carrier appears, with a mail bag and a basket of groceries. He is a kindly-looking man of middle age, wearing a linen duster, driving gloves and a straw hat. He goes to the bag hanging on the fence, takes two letters from it, and puts in a newspaper wrapped for mailing. He drops the letters into his own bag, and places the basket of groceries beside the fence.

MAIL CARRIER (*Putting his hands to his mouth, calls*): Whoop! Whoop! Whoop!

At his call, Millie leaves her play and runs to him. They are evidently good friends.

MILLIE: Hello!

MAIL CARRIER: Hello, Millie! I swan I'm afeared I've fergot yeh this mornin'.

MILLIE: Oh! Hev yeh?

MAIL CARRIER: Well, not quite. (*Feels in his coat pocket, gets out a piece of candy as if it were the usual thing, and gives it to her*)

MILLIE (*Pleased*): Thank yeh.

5

MAIL CARRIER: Hain't yeh got a kiss fer me?

MILLIE: I guess so. (*Lifts up her face; he kisses her*)   10

MAIL CARRIER: I'll bring yeh a bigger piece to-morry. Good-bye. (*He goes off right, and is heard driving away*)

Millie nibbles the candy as she watches him out of sight, then she resumes her play.

After the mail wagon drives away, Helen enters, left, followed by Uncle Nat. Helen is a girl of seventeen, with a frank yet thoughtful manner, indicating a girl of advanced ideas. She has golden-red hair and brown eyes; she is picturesquely dressed, and wears a sunbonnet. She carries a small pail full of berries, and a tin cup hangs from a crooked finger.

Uncle Nat is a man of sixty, and his large sturdy frame shows signs of toil. His eyes, of a faded blue-gray, have the far seeing look common to sailors. He wears his yellow-white hair rather long, and he is clean-shaven save for the tippet of straw-white beard that seems to grow up from his chest and to form a sort of frame for his benevolent, weather-beaten old face. Uncle Nat is of the soil, yet there is an inherent poise and dignity about him that are typical of the men who have mastered their environment. He has great cheerfulness and much sly, quiet humor. He wears overalls of a faded blue, a blue checked jumper, beneath which one glimpses a red flannel shirt, and on his head is a farmer's much-battered wide straw hat. His sleeves are rolled back, and he carries a pitchfork in his hand.

As the scene progresses, one is impressed by the frank comradeship between the old man and the girl. On his part there is tenderness, and a deep interest in her problems; there is admiration too for her fine spirit of independence. Helen shows a suppressed feeling of bitterness as she talks. She is high-spirited and proud, yet simple and direct. They pause a little above center as they talk.

HELEN (*Talking as she enters*):   Yes, I know, Uncle Nat, perhaps I oughtn't. But Father makes me mad when he talks as he does about Sam.

UNCLE NAT (*Soothingly*):   Well, now, things'll come out all right ef you'll only hev patience. You're young, so's Sam. I told 'im so t'other day. Sez I,   15
"Sam Warren," sez I, "you hain't got a mite o' sense," I sez.

HELEN (*In the same manner*):   Father says — if he catches me speaking to him again, he'll —

UNCLE NAT: You mustn't let 'm ketch yeh! (*Chuckles*) Law sakes, ef I couldn't spark a fellah athout my father ketchin' me at it, I'd bag my head.   20

HELEN (*With gentle reproach*):   I can't bear deceit —

UNCLE NAT: Neither kin I, but what yeh goin' to do about it — give Sam up?

HELEN (*Determinedly*):   No! (*She crosses to the right, and sits on the bench under the tree, and says with an undercurrent of defiance*) I'll never give him up — I'll leave home first.   25

UNCLE NAT (*Teasingly*):   Oh, Nell! You wouldn't hev spunk enough fer that.

HELEN (*Half smiling, then thoughtfully*):   Wouldn't I —

UNCLE NAT: No sirree! (*Crosses to the left and places the pitchfork against the fence*)

HELEN: You'll see — it'll be his own fault if I do. (*Rising and going toward him*) Uncle Nat, if you were my father, would you —   30

UNCLE NAT (*Wistfully, with a tender cadence in his voice*):   Ef I was yer father, Nell? Ef I was yer father, I'm afeard I'd let you do jes' about's you'd a mind to. Allus *did* seem es ef you was my baby anyway, an' I'd give the two eyes out'n my head to see you an' Sam happy. But I ain't yer father, Nell — I ain't yer father. (*The last with a regretful sigh*)   35

HELEN (*Softly*):   I sometimes wish you were.

UNCLE NAT (*Goes to her and places his hands affectionately on her shoulders*):   Now, hol' on! Thet ain't right. No sirree! Thet ain't right, an' you know it.

HELEN: Father's changed. (*Leaves him and goes slowly back to the bench*) He never takes me on his knee any more. (*With a slight shade of resentment*)   40

UNCLE NAT (*Smiling, and looking at her admiringly*):   You're gittin' too heavy I guess.

HELEN: No, it isn't that. Mother's noticed it, and she feels pretty bad about it too, although she pretends not to see it.

UNCLE NAT: Of course she dooze. She ain't a-goin to see no changes in a man   45
she's been married to nigh on to twenty-five year, not ef she kin help it.

HELEN (*Rises, and as she does so she sees Mr. Blake's buggy, which is supposedly standing off stage, right. Immediately her whole manner changes, and she says with an impatient tone in her voice*):   There's Mr. Blake's buggy again! (*Shrugging her shoulders*) He's here about all the time lately.

UNCLE NAT (*Rather seriously*):   He *is* here pooty consid'ble, ain't he? What's he after I wonder?   50

HELEN (*Resentfully*):   Principally — me.

UNCLE NAT (*Surprised, but rather amused*):   He ain't!

HELEN (*With finality*):   Yes he is. Father wants me to marry him.

UNCLE NAT (*Frightened*):   He don't!

HELEN (*In the same manner*):   Yes, he does. Mr. Blake told me as much the   55
other day.

UNCLE NAT: My! My! Thet's too bad. I swan thet's too bad. I'm afeared yer father don't understand yeh, Helen. Has he said anythin' to yeh about 't himself?

HELEN (*Still standing by the bench*):   No, not yet — but he will, and then —   60
well — (*Half savagely*) He'll find out I'm not Mother —

UNCLE NAT: Tut — tut — tut — there yeh go — Thet's yer father all over again — thet's yer father all over again.

Joel Gates drifts into the farmyard from the road, left. Little Mandy drifts in after him. Gates is dressed in dark overalls, with suspenders, a soiled white shirt, no vest, and an old drab soft hat. He carries a scythe, the snath under his left arm, the blade to the ground with the point off to the left, and he has a whetstone in his right hand. He looks as if life had battered him mercilessly. He is small and slight, his face weather-washed, kindly; his keen little eyes seem to be as a child's with a question in them, always asking "What is it all about anyhow! — I d'know!" He is never seen without Mandy. Her whole little personality is part of his; the nondescript, faded clothing, the rhythm of movement. The faraway look in the old face is repeated in the apple-blossom beauty of the child. He rarely addresses her or seems aware of her presence.

GATES (*In a drawl*):   Good day, Nathan'l.

UNCLE NAT: Hello, Joel!   65

GATES (*Talking as he walks across the stage toward the right*):   Why ain't yeh in th' hay field?

UNCLE NAT: Ben there good part th' mornin'. Who be you a-cuttin' fer t'day, Joel?

GATES: Simm'ns. Jes' got done. Goin' t' cut m'own now. Can't afford to   70 lose this weather.

UNCLE NAT: No; too good weather to lose, an' no mistake.

Gates is about to exit, with Mandy behind him, when he stops abruptly near the bench. Mandy pauses also.

GATES: Oh, Nathan'l! Will yeh lend me yer gun fer a day 'r two?

UNCLE NAT (*Reluctantly*):   Yes — I guess'o. What fer? (*Coming down center*)

GATES: There's a fox 'r suthin' a-playin' ol' Nick with my chicklings.   75

UNCLE NAT: Thet so? Helen, git me ol' Uncle Sam'l, will yeh? She's a-standin' in her corner in the kitchen. (*Helen goes into the house*) Hello, Mandy! (*Chuckles*) How d'yeh do? — You ben in the hay field too? (*The child nods*) By George — you're a great haymaker. I'll tell you what — when you git a scythe inter yer hands th' grasshoppers is got to jump   80 over the fence an' no mistake, ain't they, Joel? (*Chuckles*) Will yeh shake hands with me? (*Urging the child kindly*)

GATES: Go on — shake hands.

Mandy shyly creeps behind her father.

UNCLE NAT: Bashful, ain't she?

GATES (*Reaching around to where the child stands behind him, and pressing her closer to him*):   Yes — she's a shy sort o' critter. Don't never seem t' want t' play   85 with nobody nor nothin' but me.

UNCLE NAT: She's a-growin' ain't she — growin' jes' like a weed. My — my! How like her mother she dooze look, don't she?

GATES (*With a break in his voice and a catch in his breath, placing his hand on her head and looking at her*):   Yeh. Gits to look more an' more like her every day in the week.   90

UNCLE NAT (*Hesitatingly, as if loth to arouse unhappy memories*):   I suppose — yeh hain't never heerd nothin' of her — sence — hev yeh, Joel?

GATES (*Out of the depths of pitiful memories*):   No — nothin'. (*With a great sigh*)

Helen returns with the gun and crosses to Uncle Nat. Gates also crosses to Uncle Nat, leaving Mandy in front of the bench. After Helen gives Uncle Nat the gun, she goes over to Millie, who has been playing in the sand, all unconscious of things that have been going on about her, and sits down beside her and plays with her. Mandy timidly sits on the edge of the bench; she watches her father intently with a look of trust and affectionate content which one sees in a dearly loved dog when near his master.

The attitude of Gates and Uncle Nat in the episode of the gun is that of two boys gloating over a treasure.

UNCLE NAT: Well — here's ol' Uncle Sam'l. Take good keer of 'r. I set a good deal o' store by Sam'l. (*He hands Gates the gun*)   95

GATES (*Putting the stone in his pocket, laying down his scythe and taking the gun*):   Is she — eh — ludded?

UNCLE NAT: Yes, I allus keep 'r ludded.

GATES: Doos she — eh — kick?

UNCLE NAT: She never kicked me, d'know what she might do to a feller   100 she didn't like.

GATES (*Handling the gun with pride, as though it were a great privilege, his eyes travelling the length of it admiringly, and then looking at Uncle Nat with his face aglow*):   Fit all through the war with 'r, didn't yeh?

UNCLE NAT: Yeh.

GATES: Sixth Maine?

UNCLE NAT (*His hands clasped behind him, shoulders thrown back, his head high in the air, teeters to and fro on his heels and toes*):   Yeh — Sixth Maine, Company A.   105 Her 'n me's tramped a good many miles together, one way 'nother. (*His voice is quiet and his face tense with memories*)

GATES (*In an awed hushed voice*):   Did yeh ever — kill a rebel 'th her?

UNCLE NAT (*In a matter-of-fact tone*):   Don't know. I used t' jes' p'int 'er, shet both my eyes 'n let 'r do her own work.

GATES (*Reflectively*):   I guess thet's 'bout as good a way as any fer me t'kill   110 thet 'ere fox. (*He is fussing with the gun and unconsciously aims it at Uncle Nat*)

UNCLE NAT (*Taking hold of the gun and pushing it aside*):   Hol' on, yeh danged ol' fool — Didn't I jes tell yeh she was ludded?

GATES: What yer skeered of? I wa'n't a-goin' to pull the trigger — I was only jes' aimin' 'r.   115

UNCLE NAT: Well, aim 'r at somebody else.

GATES: There ain't nobody else handy.

UNCLE NAT: I swan thet's too bad.

GATES: Well, good day. (*Takes up the scythe, and puts the gun over his shoulder*) I'll bring 'r back safe an' sound. 120

> *Gates goes off right. Mandy quietly slips from the bench and slowly drifts after him. Uncle Nat attracts her attention by playfully snapping his fingers at her, and she turns and shows quite a little interest in his kindly friendliness. She passes on, her eyes fixed wonderingly upon him. Uncle Nat is amused and chuckles. After they go off, he seats himself on the bench under the tree.*

HELEN: Oh, Uncle Nat! Have you and Sam done anything more about your back pension?

UNCLE NAT: Well, Sam got me t' sign some papers over at the Squire's t'other day — but — I d'want him to do nothin' about my back pension. (*With mock indignation*) What do you an' him take me fur? One o' them 'ere pension grabbers? 125

HELEN (*Going up left*): Well, Sam says you're entitled to it, and he's going to try and get it for you too.

UNCLE NAT: Sam says lots o' things asides his prayers, don't he, Nell?

HELEN (*Pausing and leaning over the fence*): I guess he does. (*They laugh together softly with amused understanding*) 130

UNCLE NAT: Where yeh goin'?

HELEN: Oh, I don't know. Just for a stroll. (*And much occupied with her problems, she disappears down the road to the left*)

UNCLE NAT (*Rises from the bench a little stiffly, as if checked by a slight rheumatic twinge, goes down left and gets the wheelbarrow. He starts off as if he might be going to get fodder for the noon meal of the animals, when he notices Millie and says jovially*): Well, Millie, d'yeh want a ride?

MILLIE (*Dropping her play and brushing off her frock, eagerly*): Yes.

UNCLE NAT: Well, climb into the kerridge an' don't keep the ol' hoss waitin'. Yeh know how to git into a kerridge? 135

MILLIE: Yes. (*She sits on the edge of the wheelbarrow*)

UNCLE NAT: Well, I don't know whether yeh do or not. Take a back seat. (*He tips the wheelbarrow gently so that she slides into the back of it. She is a bit startled for a moment*) You see, I knew yeh didn't know how to git into a kerridge. The fust thing yeh know this ol' hoss'll kick up and knock the dashboard out, an' spill yeh all over the place, an' yeh won't like thet a bit. (*He wheels her off, right*) 140

> *Blake enters from the barn. He is a man of forty years; he has black hair, and his side-whiskers are close cut. The rest of his face is cleanly shaven. He is dressed in a gray*

business suit, "store made"; the coat is a single-breasted frock, very slightly cutaway, buttoned with one button at the breast. He wears a white laundered shirt, and a rather high standing collar with a black ready-made tie. His hat is a silk one, old, but not battered, brown at the edges of the crown and brim. His shoes have been home-polished, but are dusty. He has drab castor gloves, not new; he carries a buggy whip, an old white one. He has a black silk ribbon watch guard around his neck, and a gold watch. He is portly and well-to-do, but jovial. He is rather good-looking, and has the air of a contented, cheerful businessman, shrewd, but not cunning or mean; he is always smiling. He passes through the gate of the barnyard, and goes right center.

He is followed by Martin, a heavy robust man of fifty. He is slow and deliberate in manner and speech. His face and hands are weather-beaten, his hair is sandy-gray and cropped, and he has a short stubby beard. He wears pepper-and-salt trousers tucked into his boots, a black vest, and an open, white, home-made and home-laundered shirt with collar attached. His shirt sleeves are rolled up a trifle, showing red flannel beneath. He has a black silk sailor handkerchief, and a black soft hat, well worn. He carries a jack-knife in his right hand, and is opening and shutting the blade with his thumb as he walks along, "clicking" it. His left hand is behind his back, and his head is down, as if in deep thought. He stops inside the rail fence.

At the same time enters from the house, Perley, the "hired girl," a strong muscular girl of about twenty, in a calico dress, with her sleeves rolled up to her shoulders, showing her red powerful arms. She pays no attention to Blake or Martin, and goes to the mail bag, takes it down, takes out the paper, crosses over and gives it to Martin, who mechanically looks at the address as if he knew what it was, as it is a regularly "subscribed for" paper. She crosses back to the basket of provisions, puts the bag into the basket, stands with her back to the men, with her hands on her hips, and looks up and down the road for a moment. She then takes up the basket and goes into the house.

The dialogue between Martin and Blake has gone on right through the action, from the moment they entered.

BLAKE: No, sirree. I tell yeh, Martin, the day o' sentiment's gone. We're livin' in a practical age. Any man's liable to go to bed poor 'n wake up a milli'naire. Ef I'd had a friend to give me such a boost and such advice's 145
I've given you I'd hev owned half the State o' Maine, I believe.

MARTIN (*At the lower end of the fence, and facing the audience; putting the paper in the watch pocket of his vest*): Why, yeh see's I told yeh, Mother left the place to me 'n Nathan'l, an' we sort o' promised 'er we'd never sell it an —

BLAKE: Sentiment! All sentiment! Any man thet'll hang on to an old farm 150
jes' 'cause — (*Goes to the pump, takes the cup and pumps water into it*) he sort o' promised his dead mother he'd never sell it, ain't got no business to live in this bustlin', go-ahead, money-makin', devil-take-the-hindermost day of ours — (*Drinks*) thet's all I've go to say. (*Laughs. Pours the balance of the water into the trough, replaces the cup, and wipes his mouth*)

MARTIN (*Casually*): P'r'aps you never sot much store b'your mother, Mr. 155
Blake.

BLAKE: I never hed no mother — thet is not to speak of. You know all about thet as well as I do. (*He returns to Martin*)

MARTIN: Thet mus' be the reason yeh can't understand —

BLAKE (*Patronizingly*): I kin understand this. (*Leaning with his back to the fence,* 160 *both elbows on the top rail*) "Shore Acres" is a good enough farm as Maine farms go — yeh manage by hard work to make a livin' fer yerself an' family —

MARTIN (*Defensively, nodding his head at Blake*): A good — comfortable — livin'! (*He puts his foot upon the middle rail*) 165

BLAKE (*Admitting the correction good-naturedly*): A good comfortable livin'! (*Switching the whip up and down*)

MARTIN (*With quiet dignity*): An' pay my debts.

BLAKE: An' pay — your debts.

MARTIN (*Complacently*): Don't owe no man nothin', an' kin sleep nights.

BLAKE (*Patronizingly, agreeing with him*): From sundown to cockcrow — I 170 ain't a-goin' to dispute thet, thet's a-l-l right. Well, now, you happen to hev a hundred an' sixty rod, more or less, of about the sightliest shore front to be found on the coast. Yeh didn't know thet till I told yeh, did yeh?

MARTIN: No, I didn't. (*Climbs up, sits on the rail fence, facing the house, and sticks* 175 *the knife into the rail between his legs*)

BLAKE: Well! This shore front makes your land val'able. (*Turning and putting his foot on the bottom rail*) Not to plant potatoes in — but to build summer cottages on. I tell yeh, the boom's a-comin' here jes' as sure as you're born. (*Carried away by his own enthusiasm*) Bar Harbor's got s' high, yeh can't touch a foot of it — not by coverin' it with gold dollars. This has 180 got to be the next p'int. (*Goes to the bench, right, and sits down.*)

MARTIN (*He is impressed by Blake's enthusiasm, but there is caution in his immediate response*): Seems so — the way you put matters.

BLAKE: Seems so? 'Tis so. You pool your land in with mine — (*He talks with a confident, good-natured, yet shrewd business air. He lays out a plan on the grass with the end of his whip.*) We'll lay out quarter-acre lots, cut avenoos, plant trees, build a driveway to the shore, hang on to all the shore front an' cor- 185 ner lots — sell every one o' the others, see!!! They'll build on em' an' that'll double the value of ours — see! — they'll have to pay the heft o' the taxes 'cause they've built; we'll be taxed light 'cause we didn't — see?

MARTIN (*In the same manner*): I d'know as I jes' see.

BLAKE (*Confidentially*): If we can get holt of half a dozen just the right sort 190 o' fellahs — city fellahs — yeh know — fellahs that hev got inflooance to bring folks down here — we can afford to give 'em each an inside lot, here an' there, provided they'll guarantee to build, lay out their grounds, an' help to make the place attractive. That'll give us a kind of starter — see? (*Chuckles.*)   195

MARTIN (*Warming a bit at Blake's confident statements*):   Seems es ef that wouldn't be a bad idee.

BLAKE: *Bad* idee? It's *the* idee! (*Rising and going to Martin, confidentially*) Let me show you —

He takes a notebook from his pocket, and begins to show Martin some calculations he has jotted down. They become so absorbed in this that they do not notice Gates, who enters right, followed by Mandy.

GATES (*Smiling ingratiatingly*):   How d' do? (*If encouraged he would stop, but they* 200 *merely nod*) I hear you fellahs is a'goin' to boom things here 'n the spring. (*He goes quite close to Blake and Martin, who are deep in discussion. He tries to peer over their shoulders, and raises his voice as if they were deaf*) Is thet so thet Jordan Ma'sh's[1] comin' down here to go inter business? (*He pauses, inviting a response; again braces up a bit and makes another effort, now in a manner implying that he is doing them a great favor*) I wouldn't mind sellin' thet seven acre o' mine — ef I thought I could git rich out 'n it.   205

Blake looks over his shoulder as if a puff of wind or something had disturbed him, then pointedly resumes his talk with Martin. Gates is crestfallen, and turns away.

GATES: Gosh! How some folks kin get stuck up 's soon as they git a little mite rich — I never see — (*He shuffles off left, with mingled dignity and resentment, followed by Mandy*)

BLAKE: I tell yeh, Martin, I've got the scheme! You go in with me an' in less than a year I'll make you so rich you can live in Bangor. Move your mother's remains up there, an' have 'em buried in one o' them fine   210 cemet'ries, an' put a handsome stun over her as you'd ought to do.

MARTIN: Nathan'l an' me 's ben savin' up fer a stun. I guess we've got most enough now to git one — money's scurse with us — we don't see much *real* cash.

BLAKE: I'll tell you what I'll do. I'll take a mortgage on the farm for the   215 money to start you — an' you kin sell the lots.

MARTIN (*Hesitatingly*):   I'll talk to Nathan'l an' Ann.

BLAKE: Talk to 'em — of course — but don't let 'em talk you out of the scheme. There's a good deal of sentiment in Nathan'l.

---

[1] Jordan Marsh — a Boston department store.

MARTIN: It'd make me pooty rich, wouldn't it?   220

BLAKE: Rich? Well, I guess. Yeh wouldn't hev to be borrowin' nobody else's chaise to go to meetin' in.

MARTIN: Seems es though it hed ought to be done, don't it? Yet it seems a kind o' pity to —

BLAKE: To get rich, eh? (*Laughs*) Say, look a-here! Honest now — wouldn't   225
you like to live better 'n you do? Now Honest Injun, wouldn't yeh?

MARTIN (*A bit warmed by Blake's suggestions*):   I suppose I would.

BLAKE: Of course yeh would, an' yeh'd like to have your family live better. Helen'd ought to hev a real good syminerry eddication — she's worth it, she's a bright han'some girl — she'd ought to be a bookkeeper or suthin'.   230
(*Complacently*) I was a-tellin' her t'other day 'bout your a-wantin' her 'n me to git married, an' —

MARTIN (*Showing interest*):   What'd she say?

Blake purses his lips and shakes his head dubiously.

MARTIN: Did yeh offer her the piannah, as I told yeh to?

BLAKE: Y-e-s —   235

MARTIN (*Nonplussed*):   I thought she'd 'a'jumped at the piannah. She's so fond o' music.

BLAKE: I offered her everything I could think of. I offered to build her a house an' let her paint an' paper it any way she'd a mind to.

MARTIN (*Pondering*):   I guess I'd better talk to her myself. She giner'ly does   240
what I tell her to.

BLAKE: Yes, but you see girls are beginning to think they've a right to marry who they please.

MARTIN (*With pride in Helen, and pride in his own power to control her*):   Not *my* girl.   245

BLAKE (*Going right, with a shade of resentment*):   I'm afraid I'll never git very close to her so long 's young Doc Warren's around.

MARTIN (*Angrily*):   Doc Warren! — She don't keep company along o' him no more? (*As if in doubt*)

BLAKE: Don't she?   250

MARTIN: I guess not. I told her I didn't want she should — thet's allus ben enough.

BLAKE: Them free thinkers is hard to git shut of. They're dangerous to young folks' religion.

MARTIN: Helen's ben riz a stric' Babtis' — I guess she'll stay so; she's a   255
pious girl.

BLAKE: Them's the wust when they do change. Sam Warren was *raised* respectable enough. His father and mother were Presbyterians.

MARTIN (*His memory carries him into the past, and a smile creeps into his face as he answers patronizingly*):   Ol' man Warren was a good-natured honest ol' soul an' all thet — but I never thought he had any too much sense.   260

BLAKE: No! If he had he wouldn't have worked himself to a skeleton tryin' to make a doctor out of his boy. (*Laughs*)

MARTIN (*Nodding his head wisely*):   The mother had a good deal to do with thet, I guess.

BLAKE: Six o' one an' half a dozen o' the other. What she said was law with   265 the ol' man and what he said was gospel with her. They thought the sun jes rose an' sot in their Sam, an' now look at 'im. First he read Emanuel Swedenborg, an' he was a red-hot Swedenborgian — then he got hold of Spencer an' Darwin an' a lot o' them kind o' lunatics an' began to study frogs an' bugs an' things. (*He laughs. Martin laughs too, but not so heartily as*   270 *Blake does*) Why, sir! One mornin', a spell ago, as I was goin' to Ellsworth, I seed him a-settin' on his hunkers in the middle of the rud, watchin' a lot of ants runnin' in an' out of a hole. (*Both roar with laughter at this*) D'yeh remember thet free lecture he gave with the magic lantern in the schoolhouse, on evolution 's he called it?   275

MARTIN: Yes, some of 'em wanted to tar an' feather 'im thet time.

BLAKE: Oh! Pshaw! That wouldn't 'a'done! (*A slight pause*) Now he's come out as a home-a-pathic physician — (*Laughs*) He ain't a doctor — he's a pheesycian — goes around wantin' to cure sick folks with sugar shot — by George! (*Both laugh heartily*)   280

MARTIN: L'see — ain't he a-tendin' ol' Mis' Swazy now?

BLAKE (*Carelessly*):   Yep! Doc Leonard give her up, an' they had to have him. (*Starts to go off right, then stops*) Oh, I'm goin' to git rid o' all my hawgs. I'd like you to have them two shoats, they're beauties!

MARTIN (*Preoccupied*):   I guess I've got all I want.   285

BLAKE: Well, think over thet there land business. If you want to get rich, now's your chance — if you don't, I can't help it. Good day! (*Martin nods*) Good hay weather. (*Scans the sky*)

MARTIN: Fust-rate.

BLAKE (*As he goes off right*):   Most through?   290

MARTIN: Finish this week ef the weather holds.

BLAKE (*Outside*):   Good day!

MARTIN: Good day! (*He looks after Blake, then slowly and thoughtfully enters the barn, head down, hands behind his back*)

Helen's voice is heard off left. She talks as she enters; she has an arm around Young Nat, a handsome boy of fourteen. He is an errand boy in Blake's store. He wears knickerbockers, and a cap with no visor. He has the air of being spoiled and thoroughly selfish. Helen's manner toward him is one of amused and affectionate tolerance.

HELEN (*Laughing indulgently*):   La, Nat! What good would my marrying Mr. Blake do you?   295

YOUNG NAT: Lots o' good. You could coax money out o' him, an' give it to me.

HELEN (*Shocked*):   Oh! Nat Berry! (*Shakes her finger at him*) Would you take that kind of money?

YOUNG NAT: I'd take any kind o' money. 'Tain't no worse than weighin' yer   300
hand with the sugar, is it?

HELEN (*As if talking to a child, placing her hands to his face*):   Well, Natty dear —

YOUNG NAT (*Pushing her hands away*):   Don't call me Natty. Gosh, don't I hate thet! Mother makes me so 'shamed every time she comes up to   305
Blake's. This is the last suit o' knickerbockers she gits on me. Gosh, wouldn't I have lots o' things ef you'd marry ol' Blake! (*Putting his arms around her, coaxingly*) Say, Nell, will yeh? Marry ol' Blake — do. Jes' this once an' I'll never ask you again. Will you? I'll do as much fer you some day! Will you?   310

HELEN: No, I won't! I don't want to marry Mr. Blake.

YOUNG NAT (*Reproachfully; going right*):   Ain't you selfish!

HELEN: Aren't you selfish!

YOUNG NAT: You'd marry Doc Warren mighty quick ef Father'd let you.

HELEN (*Smiling proudly*):   I guess I would.   315

Sam Warren enters by the road, right, at the back. He is tall, handsome and manly, with an open honest face, and a frank manner. He stands for a moment, leaning over the fence, listening to Young Nat with an amused smile.

YOUNG NAT (*Coming toward Helen*):   Hands like a blacksmith, poor's Job, proud as a peacock an' — (*With awe*) don't believe there's any Hell.

HELEN (*Quietly smiling*):   Well, neither do I.

YOUNG NAT: O-O-O-h! — Nell Berry! I'll tell yer father, an' then you'll find out!   320

Sam comes down and takes Young Nat by the ear and twists it playfully. Young Nat howls.

SAM: What do *you* think about it, Nat?

YOUNG NAT (*Crying*):   Ouch! L' go my ear!

HELEN (*Going to Young Nat and folding him in her arms*):   Ah!

YOUNG NAT: An' you let go of me, too. (*Pushing her away and going up center*)

HELEN: Sam! You've hurt him. You're too rough. Don't cry, Nat.   325

SAM: I didn't mean to hurt him, Nell. He's more mad than hurt I guess, aren't you, Nat?

YOUNG NAT (*Crying*):   None of yer business! I'll get even with you fer this some day, you see if I don't! I wish I was big enough, I'd show you whether there's any Hell or not, you great big blacksmith, pickin' on a lit-   330
tle fellah like me! (*He goes off left, crying*)

Sam laughs and crosses to right center, watching him.

HELEN (*With gentle reproach*):   You shouldn't tease Nat so, Sam. You know he doesn't like you. (*She sits beneath the tree on the bench, right. She is vibrating with content and happiness in the presence of the man she loves*)

SAM (*Sits down on the plough lying against the barnyard fence*):   That seems to be a general complaint around these parts. A fellow that knows some things   335
his great-great-grandfather didn't know is an object of suspicion here. (*As he talks, he picks up a handful of sand and lets it slip through his fingers*)

HELEN (*Smiling*):   Well, what are you going to do about it?

SAM (*Cheerily*):   Keep right on knowing. Just as long as they build printing offices, we've got to know, that's all there is about that.

HELEN: I'm afraid — (*Laughs softly*) *my* reading is going to get me into   340
trouble.

SAM: How so?

HELEN (*Still amused*):   Why, the other day I was trying to tell Father something about evolution and "The Descent of Man," but he got mad and wouldn't listen.   345

SAM (*Laughing*):   Family pride! You know, Nell, there are lots of people who wouldn't be happy in this world if they couldn't look forward to a burning lake in the next. (*Takes a book out of his pocket and carelessly flips over the pages, looking at her as he talks*)

HELEN: Kind of sad, isn't it?

SAM: Oh! I don't know! They take a heap of comfort preparing to keep out   350
of it, I suppose.

HELEN (*Seeing the book in Sam's hand, rises and goes toward him*):   What book's that? (*Trying to read the title on the cover*)

SAM (*Rising*):   "A Hazard of New Fortunes."[2]

HELEN: Have you read it?   355

SAM: Yes.

HELEN (*Eagerly reaching for it*):   May I read it?

---

[2] An 1890 novel by William Dean Howells that examines the lack of causality in human affairs.

SAM: Yes, I brought it for you. (*He gives her the book*)

Helen delightedly takes the book and begins eagerly scanning the pages as she turns and goes back to the bench under the tree, speaking as she goes.

HELEN: I've been longing for this book. I read a fine article about it in the Boston paper. (*Sits down and looks at Sam with a joyous smile*) Thank you ever so much, Sam. 360

SAM (*Pointing to the book*):   That's a book you won't have to hide. Your father'll listen to that. If he was a speculating man, now, it would do him good.

HELEN (*Turning the leaves of the book, and pausing here and there at a page as something interesting catches her eye*):   How's poor old Mrs. Swazy getting along? 365

SAM (*In a matter-of-fact way*):   First-rate. She'll pull through this time.

As the scene progresses, Sam moves about restlessly, as though preoccupied with something. He is never far away from Helen and always has his eyes and attention focused upon her.

HELEN (*Looking up at him with awe and wonder*):   Oh! Sam! After they'd all given her up — (*Proudly but ingenuously*) Well, they'll have to acknowledge that you're a great physician now.

SAM (*Laughs*):   Great fiddlesticks! Why, the folks around here wouldn't let me doctor a sick kitten if they could help it. 370

HELEN: Why, you'll get the credit of this!

SAM: Yes! Me and the Lord! (*Laughs*) I'm satisfied so long as the old lady gets well. (*Helen is still sitting on the bench, glancing over the book, a look of contentment and happiness upon her face. Sam, who has been leaning against the barnyard fence, goes to her thoughtfully, his whole manner changed. He stands slightly above her to the left, puts one foot on the bench, leans on his knee and bends over her, and says in a rather quiet tense voice*) Nell — I want to tell you something. 375

HELEN (*Without looking up, says gaily as Sam pauses*):   Something good, I hope.

SAM (*In the same manner*):   Don't I always tell you good things?

HELEN (*With a teasing little laugh, looking up at him over her shoulder*):   Most — always, Sam!

SAM (*Quietly, looking down into her eyes*):   I'm going away. 380

HELEN (*Seems stunned. The joy passes out of her face; her eyes are still upon him, but all the happiness is gone from them. The book drops from her hands and falls to the ground. She slowly slides along the bench away from him as though to study him better. She is pale and frightened, and in a dry voice with a low cry of pain, she says*):   Oh! — Sam! (*Then, feeling it cannot be true, she leans toward him and adds in a very appealing voice*) Honest?

SAM (*Quietly*): Honest. What's the use of my staying here? (*Sits down left of Helen*) Nobody'll speak to me except Nathan'l — and your mother — and you. (*Putting his arm around her*)

HELEN (*Drawing away from him, endeavoring to overcome her emotion*): Don't, Sam — Please don't.

SAM (*With a dry laugh*): And *you're* half afraid to.

HELEN (*Brokenly*): No! I'm not afraid — only you know — Father says —

SAM (*In the same manner*): I know — they all say it. Blake says I've got dynamite in my boots. Just because I can't believe as they do — they won't any of 'em look at me if they can help it. So I'm going out West, where a fellow can *believe* as he likes and *talk* as he likes —

HELEN (*With awe, her eyes upon him*): To — *Chicago?*

SAM (*Amused*): Oh no-o! A fellow may *believe* what he likes in Chicago, but he mustn't *say* too much about it. I'm going a-w-a-y out West. Montana — or somewhere out that way.

HELEN (*Innocently, in a pathetic voice*): Oh my! I'll never get so far as that, will I?

SAM (*Not heeding her, rising and walking up center*): I want to get where I can sprout a new idea without being *sat* on.

HELEN (*In a crushed voice*): Yes, of course — you're right.

SAM: Where I won't be hampered by dead men's laws and dead men's creeds.

HELEN (*Turning to him in a chiding manner*): Why, you don't blame Father for believing as *his* father believed, do you?

SAM: No. But I *do* blame him for sitting down on me just because I can't believe the same way. I tell you, Nell — (*He picks up a pebble*) one world at a time is good enough for me; and I've made up my mind that I'm going to *live* while I'm in this one — (*He throws the pebble as far as he can reach, watching its flight*) and I'm going to do something more than practice medicine in Berry. Sitting around, waiting for patients — (*Rather contemptuously*) such as old Mrs. Swazy. (*He puts his hands in his pockets and turns down center*)

HELEN (*Getting up from the bench and going to him, center*): Yes. But — what's going to become of *me?*

Sam goes to her with arms outstretched, and enfolds her lovingly.

SAM (*Tenderly*): You! You're going to stay right here with your mother till I get started. Then I'm coming back to get you and take you out there and show those western fellows a *real* Yankee girl. (*Amused*) You know, Nell, the newspapers used to print pictures of them with pants on and a stovepipe hat!

HELEN (*Making a pitiful effort to be cheerful*):   Yes! But they don't do that now, Sam.

SAM: No, they do *not* do that now. You girls have come to stay, there's no getting around that fact, and we cranks are going to help you stay here.   425 (*He notices the book lying on the ground*) Let me show you something in that book.

They walk over to the bench, Sam's arm remains about Helen. She sits down, he picks up the book and sits at her left, and they both become deeply absorbed in reading.

MARTIN (*Enters from the barn, leading a horse by the halter to water him at the trough.*[3] *His head is bent and he is in deep thought, pondering upon the idea of getting rich which Blake has suggested to him. He does not see Helen and Sam until he turns to re-enter the barn. When his eyes rest upon them, so content and absorbed in each other, he pauses amazed, and his face flames with bitter resentment. He is unable to speak for a moment, then he blurts out harshly*):   Sam Warren, hain't yeh got no more pride than to come where yeh ain't wanted?

Sam and Helen start in surprise. Helen shyly draws away from Sam.

SAM (*Looks up with a very affable air and says pleasantly and respectfully*):   Hello,   430 Mr. Berry! Yes sir, I have.

MARTIN (*In the same manner*):   Well, what yeh doin' here, then?

SAM (*Looking at Helen slyly as if it were a good joke*):   I thought — I *was* wanted.

MARTIN (*Taking a menacing step toward him*):   Didn't I tell yeh yeh wa'n't?

SAM (*Smiling, but rather reluctantly*):   Yes sir, — *you* did!   435

Sam plays this scene very quietly, never losing his temper; plays it as if something else of more immediate importance were on his mind.
  The scene throughout is pitched in a quick staccato, which reaches its height in Helen's cry of terror as the two men clinch. Then there is a pause, and the rest of the scene, until Martin leaves the stage, is completed in tense low tones that are portentous of trouble. There is active hate on Martin's part. Sam's attitude is one of simple manly poise.

MARTIN: Well, ain't thet enough?

SAM (*Pleasantly*):   Yes, I suppose it is — but I thought that — maybe you'd like to know — (*Rises and goes toward him*)

MARTIN (*Goaded by Sam's manner, fiercely*):   I don't want to know nothin'! An' I don't want *her* to know nothin' thet I don't want her to know! (*Indicat-*   440 *ing Helen with a nod of his head*)

---

[3] If it is not convenient to have a horse, Martin can come in with two heavy stable buckets, one in each hand, which he fills with water from the trough. [Herne's note]

SAM (*Making another effort to conciliate him*):   Why you see, Mr. Berry — you can't help —

MARTIN (*Breaking in and shouting at him*):   I'm a-bringin' up my family! An' I don't want no interference from you — nor Darwin — nor any o' the rest o' the breed! (*With a passionate sweep of his arm. He half turns as if to go*)   445

SAM (*Smiling*):   Darwin's dead, Mr. Berry —

MARTIN (*Turning and interrupting, resentfully*):   Them *books* ain't dead.

SAM (*Very positive and very much satisfied with his statement*):   No! "Them books" are going to be pretty hard to kill.

MARTIN (*Sharply, turning to Helen, who is still seated on the bench*):   What book's   450 thet yeh got there now? (*Indicating the book with a wrathful toss of his arm*)

HELEN (*Very gently*):   One of Sam's books, Father.

MARTIN (*Glaring at Sam*):   Well, give it right straight back to Sam. I don't want nothin' to do with *him* nor his books.

SAM (*Kindly, correcting him*):   It *is* my book, Mr. Berry, but it was written by   455 a man —

MARTIN (*His temper rising steadily, flashes at him*):   I won't hev yeh a-bringin' them books here! A-learnin' my daughter a pack o' lies, about me an' my parents a-comin' from monkeys —

SAM (*His eyes twinkling with suppressed amusement, answers soothingly*):   La bless   460 you, Mr. Berry! That was ages ago!

MARTIN (*Is goaded to the extreme by Sam's manner*):   I don't care how long ago it was, I won't hev it flung in my children's faces.

HELEN (*Is much distressed by her father's bitter temper, and she suddenly attempts to calm him, and approaches Martin, who has been standing near the barnyard gate. She timidly holds out the book to him, and says pleadingly*):   Father, I wish you'd let me read you this little bit —   465

MARTIN (*With ugly stubbornness, checks her with a sweep of his arm, as though pushing away some harmful or noxious thing*):   I don't want to hear it. I read *The Bangor Whig*, an' *The Agriculturist*, an' the Bible, an' thet's enough. There ain't no lies in *them*.

SAM (*Ironically*):   No, especially in *The Bangor Whig!*

Here the staccato changes to a deep ominous murmur.

MARTIN (*Peering at Sam through half-closed lids, mutters*):   I'm skeered of a man   470 thet ain't got no religion.

SAM (*With quiet assurance*):   But, Mr. Berry, I *have* got a religion.

MARTIN (*Doubtfully, in the same manner*):   What is it?

SAM (*His manner becoming serious, in a voice warm with feeling, pointing off with a sweep of his arm*):   Do you hear those insects singing?

MARTIN (*Rather puzzled, mumbles*):   Yes — I hear 'em!   475

SAM (*Seriously and calmly*):   Well, that's their religion, and I reckon mine's just about the same thing.

MARTIN (*With supreme disgust and contempt in his voice and manner*):   Oh! Good Lord! (*He starts for the barn with the horse*)

HELEN (*With tender appeal, swiftly following him*):   Father, why won't you ever   480
let Sam tell you —

Martin, goaded to the breaking point, turns upon Helen, dropping the halter and allowing the horse to go into the barn.

MARTIN (*Hardly able to control his rage*):   Look a-here, Nell! I've had all the words I'm goin' to hev with *you* — (*Shaking his closed fist threateningly*) But by the Eternal, I ain't a-goin' to hev thet fellah a-comin' here preachin' his infidelity to my family. (*Frantic with rage, he now says more*   485
than he intends to, deliberately and fiercely) If you *want* him, you *take* him, an' clear out!

Sam approaches quickly, intensely moved by what Martin has said.

SAM: Do you mean that, Mr. Berry?

HELEN (*Her head high in the air, her whole attitude one of noble defiance*):   I will! (*As though accepting the challenge*)

MARTIN (*Looks at Helen, quite broken, all the fire of his passion in ashes, and murmurs thickly*):   Yeh won't?   490

HELEN (*Proudly, her eyes full of burning tears, her voice vibrating with emotion*):   Won't I? You'll see whether I will or not! (*There is a challenge in her voice too*)

SAM (*Moving toward Martin, intensely excited by his words*):   Mr. Berry — if you'll say that again —

MARTIN (*Springs at Sam and clutches him by the throat*):   Damn you!

SAM (*Swiftly seizes Martin's wrist with his left hand, drawing back his right hand to strike*):   Damn you!   495

HELEN (*With a cry of terror, covering her face with her hands, calls out appealingly*):   Oh! Sam — don't!

The sound of Helen's voice brings both men to their senses, and they relax their hold upon each other. They stand silent for a moment, both a little ashamed.

MARTIN (*In a heartbroken manner*):   D'yeh mean to steal my child from me?

SAM (*Quietly, adjusting his collar*):   I'm not going to *steal* her, Mr. Berry — I'm going out West to *earn* her!

MARTIN (*Speaking through his teeth, vehemently*):   Sam Warren, I hated you   500
afore — but *now* you've shamed me afore my own child. Git off'n my farm an' don't yeh never set foot on't agin — (*Quiet low and passionately*) It's dangerous fer both of us.

Martin wearily drags himself into the barn.

> *Helen stands dazed and heartbroken. Sam leans against the fence, his hands in his pockets, his head bent, deep in thought. There is a moment's pause.*

> *Ann[4] bustles cheerily out of the house. She is a woman of forty-five, handsome in a wholesome, motherly way. She is dressed in a freshly laundered, becoming calico dress, and her sleeves are rolled up beyond the elbows, showing a pair of shapely arms. She is quick and energetic in all her movements. To her, home is the most desirable place in the world, and she rules it with all the skill and love of a typical American housewife. Her manner is pleasant and happy. She is always smiling and always sees the best side of everything. Nothing disturbs her; she meets all the problems of her daily life with a quiet and unobtrusive efficiency.*

ANN: Well Helen, I was jes' a-wonderin' what'd become o' you. Sam Warren! I hup Martin hain't seen yeh; I say, hain't seen yeh. 505

SAM: Yes, he has —

ANN: Didn't he hev a tantrum; I say, a tantrum!

HELEN (*Concealing her true feelings, listlessly*): No, mother, he didn't say much — not as much as —

ANN: I want to know! Well, there must ha' ben sumpthin' powerful on his 510 mind; I say, on his mind.

SAM: I guess there is now, if there wasn't before. (*Sadly*)

ANN: Well, Nell, blow the horn. Dinner's all sot an' I don't want it to git cold. Sorry I can't ask yeh to stop, Sam; I say, I'm sorry I can't ask yeh to stop. (*She goes into the house*) 515

SAM: Thank you, I don't think I'd enjoy the meal. (*Helen and he look at each other, her eyes fill with tears*)

> *Helen goes up to the fence, picks up the horn hanging there and blows it twice. Then she turns back to Sam, letting the horn slip from her hand to the ground.*

SAM (*Slowly*): Well, Nell, I suppose you and I might just as well say good-bye now as any time —

HELEN (*Again quite overcome at the thought of parting with him, holds out her hand, which he takes*): Good-bye Sam. (*Cries*)

SAM (*Very tenderly*): Good-bye Nell. (*Draws her to him*) Don't cry! I don't 520 know how soon I'll get away, but just as soon as I can I will. I'll try to see you before I go — if not — I'll —

HELEN (*Pleadingly*): You can't take me with you, can you, Sam?

SAM (*Wistfully*): No, Nell, I can't. I haven't got money enough. I ought to

---

[4] Ann begins all her speeches slowly, increasing in rapidity as she progresses. She is in the habit of repeating the final words of all her speeches emphatically, as though the person she were addressing had not heard her. [Herne's note]

have a hundred dollars more than I've got to get away myself. (*Medita-*   525
tively) I wonder if Blake'd lend me a hundred dollars.

HELEN (*Still struggling with her tears*):   I wouldn't ask him — he'd only refuse
you. (*She breaks down and clings to Sam like a child*) It's going to be awful lonesome —

SAM (*Deeply moved*):   I know — it's going to be pretty lonesome for me too.   530
There, now — (*Taking both her hands in his*) I thought this was going to
be one of those partings without tears — (*Trying to cheer her up*) nor
promises — nothing but just confidence.

HELEN (*Making an effort to overcome her grief*):   All right — Sam. (*Lifting her
head and taking a deep breath to get hold of herself, bravely but still with a slight break
in her voice*) If I don't see you before you go, good-bye. (*Goes to the house, as*   535
if to go inside, stops at the door, and turns as though struck by a sudden thought) I
don't think you'd better come here again, Sam. I don't want to quarrel
with Father if I can help it — (*With a note of fatality*) I'll have to some day
I know — but I want to avoid it just as long as I can. (*She smiles and tries to
brave it out, but it is plain that she is silently crying*)

SAM (*Stands a moment, looking at her tenderly and longingly, as though loth to leave her.
He cannot control his own feelings. He turns away abruptly as he says*):   Good-   540
bye, Nell, keep up your courage, my girl. And remember, it isn't as though
it was forever, you know. (*He goes off right above the house*)

HELEN (*Her eyes follow him off*):   Good-bye, Sam. (*Waves her hand as if in response to him and calls after him*) Take good care of yourself, won't yeh?

SAM (*Speaking off stage, as though from a little distance*):   I'll take care of myself,   545
you take care of yourself.

Helen turns slowly away and drags herself, broken and weary, into the house.
    *There is a brief pause, then Mary Berry, a lively girl of about 10, comes running
from the road, left, into the yard. She has a little bunch of wild flowers in her hand. She
is skipping gaily, and just as she is about to enter the house, Bob Berry, a sturdy little
fellow of about 8 years with rosy cheeks and dancing eyes, runs on excitedly from the left,
with his schoolbooks tied in a strap.*

BOB: Mary, Mary, take my books in the house, I'm goin' in swimmin'.

He throws the books into her hands and runs off right, above the house.

MARY (*Calling after him*):   Bob Berry, if you go in swimmin' I'll tell yer Ma.
BOB (*In the distance, off right*):   Tell if yeh want to — ol' tattle tale.
MARY (*Running into the house*):   Ma, Ma, Bob's goin' in swimmin' —   550

*Ike Richards, Lem Conant, Abe Higgins, and Steve Bailey, farmhands, enter from the
left. With them is Tim Hayes, the hired man, a good-natured, red-headed Irishman.
They are playing with an old football, laughing and scuffling in a friendly way.*

Gates, with Mandy in his wake, follows the men on and watches them, keenly interested.

GATES: Give me a kick.

TIM (*Good-naturedly*): Let the ould man have a kick.

The others jeer at this.

ABE: He can't kick it, he's too old.

GATES (*Enraged*): Too old, am I? You jes' see. (*Gates seizes the ball and gives it a tremendous kick which sends it flying down the road. The men cheer him derisively. Gates picks up a chip and puts it on his shoulder*)

GATES (*To Abe, assuming a defiant attitude*): If I'm too old, you jes' knock this chip off'n my shoulder. 555

Abe hesitates, but the other men urge him on, at last forcing him into the fight. He and Gates have a brief rough-and-tumble wrestling match, which ends when Gates ducks Abe in the water trough.

The men greet Abe's defeat with shouts of laughter, and he hurries somewhat sheepishly into the house, followed by the others. Gates looks after them, wagging his head triumphantly.

GATES (*Calling after them*): Too old, am I? They don't build houses like they used to. An' they don't make boys like they used to, nuther! (*With an air of high satisfaction he goes off, down the road, lower right, followed by Mandy*)

Enter Uncle Nat along the road, upper right, wheeling Millie in the barrow. Millie has a line through the rod of the barrow, and is pretending to drive.

UNCLE NAT (*Talking as he enters*): An' after that they lived in peace and died in Greece, an' was buried in a pot of honey. 560

MILLIE: What's the else of it, Uncle Nat?

UNCLE NAT: There ain't no else to it. Besides, this hoss don't do 'nother stroke of work till he gets his oats. (*He wheels the barrow down stage below the bench, right*)

MILLIE (*Climbing out*): Wait till I unhitch yeh —

UNCLE NAT: This is a new-fangled hoss. He can hitch himself up and unhitch himself, and currycomb himself and get his own oats, an' — (*Uncle Nat goes to the trough and starts to wash his hands*) 565

MILLIE (*Following him up to the trough*): Hossy want a drink?

UNCLE NAT: No — hossy don't want a drink. Hossy wants to wash his hands so thet he can set down to the table like a clean respect'ble hoss. (*Millie splashes water in his face. He staggers back, pretending to be drenched and shaking the wet off*) Is thet what yeh call givin' hossy a drink? 570

MILLIE (*Chuckling*): Yep.

UNCLE NAT: Well, the fust thing yeh know, this hoss'll duck yeh in the hoss trough.

MILLIE: No he won't.

UNCLE NAT: Won't he? You jes' see if he won't. (*He talks to Millie in the man-*   575
ner of one child talking to another) You can't throw water in a hossy's face without makin' him mad no more than yeh can give a elephant a chaw o' terbacker without makin' *him* mad. Did yeh ever give a elephant a chaw o' terbacker?

MILLIE: No!   580

UNCLE NAT: Well, don't yeh try it, cause I knowed a boy in a circus once that give a elephant a chaw o' terbacker, an' he didn't see thet boy agin fer more n' a hundred years. But he jes' remembered it an' he blew water all over him. I tell yeh, elephants has got good memories — (*Uncle Nat takes a clean bandanna handkerchief out of his pocket and wipes his hands. He is about to en-ter the house, when he is stopped by the voice of Martin, who comes from the barn and pauses outside the barnyard gate*)

Millie resumes her play in the sand.

MARTIN (*Casually*):   Nathan'l.   585

UNCLE NAT (*Kindly*):   Hello, Martin.

MARTIN: Be yeh hungry?

UNCLE NAT (*Still mechanically wiping his hands*):   Not powerful, but able to git away with my rayshuns 'thout no coaxin' I guess. Why? (*Taking a step to-ward Martin*)

MARTIN (*Still casually*):   'Cause I'd like to talk to yeh — (*Studying his face*   590
closely) an' I d'know's I'll hev a better chance.

UNCLE NAT (*Cheerily; putting his handkerchief back in his pocket*):   I d'know's yeh will, Martin. (*He moves a few steps down right; Martin is up left center near the barnyard*)

MARTIN (*Hesitates, picks up a stick, takes out a jackknife and whittles it, looking intently at the stick and walking down a few steps toward Uncle Nat. He seems rather to dread saying what is on his mind. Uncle Nat looks at him furtively; this unusual request puz-zles him; he is apprehensive that it is of Helen and Blake that his brother wishes to talk, and a look of disapproval sweeps into his eyes. His face grows a bit stern, but his man-ner is kindly and attentive. After a pause Martin blurts out abruptly*):   Mr. Blake's been here.   595

UNCLE NAT (*Gazes at him curiously, looks off right as if he could still see Blake's buggy there, picks up a straw and chews it, and says carelessly*):   Hez' 'e? (*Seats himself on the wheelbarrow*)

MARTIN (*Seating himself on the stable bucket, which he has turned bottom upward*): Yes. He argues that we'd ought to cut the farm up into buildin' lots.

UNCLE NAT (*Is dazed by this. It is so sudden and unexpected that he scarcely gets its full meaning, as he murmurs in a low tense voice*):   Dooze 'e?

MARTIN: Y-e-s. He says there's a boom a-comin' an' the land's too val'able to work.   600

UNCLE NAT (*Murmurs mechanically*):   Dooze — 'e — ?

MARTIN: Yes. He wants I should pool in with him, an' build cottages an' sell 'em at a hundred per cent more'n they cost, an' git's rich's Jay Gould.[5]

UNCLE NAT (*Slowly it comes to him that his brother is saying "Sell the farm." He grows cold — there is a heavy painful lump where his heart was beating a moment ago. His eyes grow dim and tired — there is no sunshine — no more music in the day. Sell the farm — the dear fields with all their slopes and undulations, the great old silver birches guarding the orchard from the pastures, the gnarled oaks along the rocky shore. He knows in a thousand aspects this old farm, summer and winter, always affable and friendly to him, and it is here he has learned to know God and love him. He answers casually enough in a tone of wonderment*):   I want t' know 'f he dooze. (*A moment's pause*) Where d's he talk o' beginnin'?   605

MARTIN (*Blurting out half defiantly, half shamefacedly*):   Out there at th' north end o' the shore front — an' work back t' his line.

UNCLE NAT (*The numbness passes and there is a tingling in his veins. Tense set lines come into his face and his voice grows vital. He talks with his usual clear cadence and gentle rhythm*):   Yeh don't mean up yonder? (*Pointing with his thumb over his shoulder, right. Martin looks up and nods*) Not up at the ol' pastur'?

MARTIN (*Slowly*):   Y-e-s —   610

UNCLE NAT (*In a tense voice*):   Dooze 'e calk'late to take in the knoll thet looks out t'Al'gator Reef?

MARTIN (*As before*):   Y-e-s — I s'pose he — dooze.

UNCLE NAT (*Rising, speaking quietly, but with a quiver of smothered feeling in his voice*):   Did yeh tell him — 'bout — Mother's bein' buried there — ?

MARTIN (*Sulkily*):   He knows all 'bout thet jes' as well as you do.   615

UNCLE NAT (*With significance, but very simply*):   Dooze. Well — what's he calk'late to do with Mother?

MARTIN: He advises puttin' on her in a cimitery up to Bangor.

UNCLE NAT (*A deprecating shadowy smile flits across his face; he shakes his head slowly and replies*):   She'd never sleep comfort'ble in no cimitery, Martin — Mother wouldn't.   620

MARTIN: Blake says thet's the choice bit o' the hull pa'sell.

UNCLE NAT (*Gently persuasive*):   Then who's got so good a right to it as Mother has? Yeh don't begrutch it to her, do yeh, Martin?

---

[5] Jay Gould (1836–1892) was a U.S. financier who made a fortune in railroad investments.

MARTIN: I don't begrutch nothin'. Only, Blake says folks ain't a-goin' to pay fancy prices fer lots 'thout they hev their pick.   625

UNCLE NAT (*Gently reproachful*):   D'ye think any fancy price had ought to buy Mother's grave, Martin?

MARTIN: Thet's sent'ment!

UNCLE NAT (*As though rebuked*):   Is it?

MARTIN: Yes, it is — Blake says —   630

UNCLE NAT (*Nodding his head, with a little sad half-smile*):   Dooze — well — (*He sighs*) P'r'aps 'tis — (*There is a pause; then, as though a flood of memories had suddenly rushed over him*) You don't rec'llect much about Father — de yeh, Martin?

MARTIN: No.   635

UNCLE NAT: You was so young — (*His eyes look far off down the years, and he tells the story simply and directly and the clear cadence and soft rhythm are like the colors in a picture*) a baby a'most, the evenin' him an' Si Leech was lost tryin' to save the crew o' thet 'ere brig — thet went to pieces on the reef yonder. (*Indicates over his shoulder with a nod of his head*)

MARTIN (*Under the spell of Uncle Nat's mood, is touched, and replies very gently*):   No. Mother'n you never seemed to care to talk much about thet.   640

UNCLE NAT: Mother an' me seen the hull thing from the p'int o' thet 'ere knoll — (*With a slight indication of his head over his shoulder*) After it was all over she sent me hum — told me to take care o' you — said thet I needn't come back — thet she'd stay there an' wait fer him. 'Taw'n't no use t'argy with Mother, y'know, an' so I went. I put you in yer cradle an' sot down   645 alongside o' yeh. I d'know as I ever passed jes' sich a night — seemed s'kinder l-o-n-g. (*Pause*) Jes' as soon as it was light enough to see — I went back to find out what'd come o' her — I didn't know but what she might hev — but she hadn't — she was there — jes' where I left her — I don't believe she'd moved an inch the hull night. It had been a-rainin' —   650 (*Pause*) Her eyes was sot in her head and starin' right out to sea — ef I'd 'a' met her any other place but there, I swear I wouldn't 'a' know'd 'r. I took her by the hand to sort o' coax 'r away. "Nathan'l," she says, "when I die — I want yeh should bury me right here on this spot — so's ef Father ever *dooze* come back — he'll find me waitin' fer him." I hed to turn   655 'round an' look at 'er — her voice sounded so kinder strange — seemed as ef it come from way off somewheres. (*Pause*) She lived a good many years after thet — but I don't believe she ever missed a day 'thout goin' over t' thet knoll. I allus sort o' imagined she wa'n't never jes' right in her head after thet night. (*Uncle Nat is lost in memories for a moment. Then catching   660 his breath and pulling himself together, he continues*) Well, Martin, there she is.

We buried her there at last — you an' me did. I d'know, but seems to me — ef I was you — I'd kinder hate to sell thet fer a buildin' lot. Thet is, I'd want to be pooty partic'lar who I sold it to.

MARTIN (*In the manner of a spoiled child, closing his knife with a sharp click*):   I'm 665 tired o' lightkeepin'.

UNCLE NAT (*Warmly, with quick understanding*):   I don't blame yeh. Why didn't yeh say thet afore? Yeh needn't do it no longer. Tim an' me kin take keer o' the light jes' as well's not. I only sort o' hang onto it 'cause Father had it put there, an' the Gover'ment named it after him — he used to think 670 so much o' that.

MARTIN (*Defending himself*):   You *give* me your interest in the farm anyhow — made it all over to me the day I was married.

UNCLE NAT (*Warmly, with a fine spirit of conciliation*):   I know it an' I hain't never regretted it. I ain't a-regrettin' of it now. 675

MARTIN (*Peevishly*):   You seem to kind o' shameface me for wantin' to sell it.

UNCLE NAT: Didn't mean to, Martin — it's only nat'ral thet I should feel kind o' bad to see the ol' place cut up — but law sakes! Who'm I thet I should set my face agin improvements I'd like to know? (*Laughs*) You've got a wife, an' children, an' a family, an' all thet. Mr. Blake mus' be right. 680 So go 'head an' build, an' git rich, an' move up to Boston ef yeh want to. Only, Martin — don't sell thet. (*Indicating over his shoulder, right, with his head*) Leave me thet, an' I'll build on't an' stay an' take keer o' th' light, as long's I kin — an' after thet — why — well, after thet — yeh kin put both on us in a cimitery ef yeh hev a mind to. 685

His voice trails off into silence. Martin stands downcast. Uncle Nat remains immovable, self-hypnotized by the recital of his story — somehow all the sting of it has passed and he is at peace. He is still contemplating the remote days of his boyhood, and he stands there picking a bit of string into fine shreds too deeply absorbed to be aware of the life about him.

Millie is lying asleep on the sand.
Ann enters briskly from the house.

ANN: Sakes alive! Martin Berry, ain't you a-comin' to yer dinner today? I say today? (*Goes up center and looks off right*)

MARTIN (*Slowly, starting toward house*):   Yes, I was jest a-comin'. (*As he crosses to the house, he says very gently*) Nathan'l, dinner's waitin'. (*He goes slowly and thoughtfully into the house*)

ANN (*Looking up the road and calling*):   Bob — B-o-b! Bob B-e-r-r-y — 690 Come out o' thet water — Come to yer dinner! — Yer back'll be all blistered! (*She sees Millie lying asleep and goes down to her*) Bless thet child, she's clean fagged out! Come to Ma, precious. (*She takes Millie tenderly in her arms*) Come Nathan'l, your dinner'll be stun cold. I say stun cold. (*She goes into the house with the child*)

Uncle Nat stands deep in meditation.

The Curtain descends slowly.

ACT II

"THE SILVER WEDDIN' "

The Berry farmhouse kitchen.

A quaint old New England farmhouse kitchen of the better class, used partly as a living room. There is a large window center, full of pots of growing flowers. Beneath the window is a table upon which Helen places cups and saucers and from which she serves tea during the dinner. To the right of the window is a wooden sink with an old-fashioned hand pump, and there is a large stove to the left of the window, upon which a kettle is boiling and pots are stewing. Behind it is a woodbox. On the shelf back of the stove stands an old-fashioned cuckoo clock.

A sturdy old open stairway is against the left wall, and at the back of it is a row of pegs, where hang Uncle Nat's old army coat and cap, and Helen's jacket and tam-o'-shanter. There is a door leading to the woodhouse to the left of the stove. Standing parallel to the stairs is a long dining table, covered with a white linen cloth. Against the side of the stairs is a heavy old-fashioned mahogany sideboard, from which Helen later takes small articles, such as tumblers and salt-and-pepper holders. At the foot of the stairs a door opens into the sitting room. There is a worktable, right, below the sink, covered with material for making bread, and on it are several loaves of bread fresh from the oven. Below the worktable is a door leading outside. To the right, between the door and the sink, is an alcove where stands a large old-fashioned dresser, holding dishes, pans, and various kitchen furnishings, also several large pies.

At the rise of the curtain, Ann, Helen, and Perley are in the midst of extensive preparations for dinner. Millie is down right, by a chair, making doll's bread, very intent on her work. Ann is hot and flustered. She is dressed in an old-fashioned black silk dress, open at the neck, with a white lace collar. The skirt is pinned up, showing a white petticoat underneath trimmed with home-made lace, and there is a big white apron over all. Perley is cool and unconcerned. Mary and Bob, with aprons over their best clothes, are sitting on the stairs, polishing spoons and forks. Helen is setting the table. She is dressed daintily in a simple muslin frock, and also wears a large apron to protect her dress. She is grave and thoughtful; the memory of the encounter with her father is still sharp upon her. She moves about, doing her work with swift deft touches.

ANN (*At the stove, stirring the cranberry sauce*):   Sakes alive! I hup another silver weddin' won't come in this house in a hurry; I say, in a hurry. (*She goes to the table, and starts sharpening a carving knife, preparatory to cutting a large loaf of bread which is on the table*)

HELEN (*At the foot of the table, as she finishes placing the knives and forks*): Ma, I've arranged all the presents on the center table. (*Smiling. She is very tender and sympathetic in her attitude toward her mother*) The sitting room looks like a jewelry store. (*She goes to the sideboard, left, and takes from it a glass jar holding teaspoons, and places it on the center of the table*)

MARY: Oh, let's go'n see! (*Runs off into the sitting room*)

BOB: Yes, let's do. (*Follows Mary*)

HELEN: Aren't you proud of them, Mother?

ANN (*Seriously*): Helen, you know what the Bible says about pride's one day havin' a fall. No, I ain't proud. (*Turning and coming down slowly toward the center of the stage, absentmindedly drawing the carving knife across the steel as she talks*) Of course, it's nice to be so remembered by everybody, an' there's a good many nice presents there — some I ben a-wishin' fer. But I think I value yourn an' the young uns' an' Nathan'l's an' Martin's the best o' the lot. Not thet I ain't grateful, but, somehow, the nearer — (*Fills up, hastily brushes away a tear with the back of her hand, and turns to the stove to hide her emotion. Lifts the griddle and pokes the fire*) How like the Ol' Harry this fire dooze burn! Seems es ef everythin' went agin me today; I say, today. (*Calls*) Tim! (*To Perley, sharply*) Tell Tim I want him. (*Puts the griddle back on the stove, and closes the damper*)

Perley goes down to the door, right, opens it, and calls Tim, each time in a different and higher key.

PERLEY: T-i-m — T-i-m — T-i-i-m-m —

TIM (*Outside, in the distance*): More power to ye, but it's the foine loongs ye have in ye! Fwat is it?

PERLEY: Mis' Berry wants y-o-u. (*Goes back to her work*)

ANN (*To Perley, handing her a saucepan of potatoes*): Mash them 'taters; I say, mash them 'taters.

Perley gets the potato masher, takes the pan of potatoes to the sink, peels and mashes them, adding butter, salt, and a little milk.
Tim appears at the door in his shirt sleeves.

TIM: Fwat is it, ye Andhrewscoggin' mermaid, ye? (*He starts to come into the room*)

ANN (*Stopping him, peremptorily*): Scrape yer feet, Tim Hayes, an' don't track the hull cow shed over my clean floor; I say, clean floor. (*She is standing near the window, center*)

TIM (*Wipes his feet on the door mat, and speaks ingratiatingly*): Yis ma'am. I will ma'am. Fwat can I do for ye?

ANN: I want you should split me a handful of fine wood; this 'ere fire's actin' like the very Ol' Nick today; I say, today.

Tim goes into the woodhouse, and reappears almost immediately with a handful of small wood which he gives to Ann, who puts a few pieces on the fire. He returns to the woodhouse and during the next scene he is heard splitting wood.

PERLEY (*Who has now finished mashing the potatoes; speaking through Tim's business*):
What yeh want I should do 'th these 'ere 'taters?

ANN: Put 'em in a veg'table dish an' set 'em in the ov'n to brown; I say, to brown.   35

Perley puts the potatoes into a vegetable dish, smooths them over, shakes two or three spots of pepper on them, and puts them in the oven. She takes plenty of time over this.

Ann stirs the cranberries, tastes them, lifts up the kettle and sets it back, and puts the griddle on the hole.

Uncle Nat appears at the top of the stairs, dressed in a new "store" suit. He looks very important and proud, and glances down expecting all eyes to be upon him, but nobody notices him. He comes down a few steps. His new boots hurt him, and he pauses and bends his feet on the toes, as if to ease the boots, murmuring to himself "Gosh, but these shoes do hurt!" He straightens up, comes down a few more steps, and again eases his right boot and, making a wry face, he slips his foot partly out of the boot, and finishes the descent limping, but with a comfortable sense of relief. When he is well toward the left center of the stage, he stands, anxious to be noticed.

UNCLE NAT (*In a jubilant tone*):   Well, Helen, I got 'em on!

HELEN (*Coming down to his left, and speaking delightedly*):   Oh Uncle Nat! Ma, look! Isn't he sweet?

ANN (*Stops in her work at the table in front of the window, and comes down right of him*):   Well Nathan'l, how nice you do look; I say, look.

Perley comes forward a few steps and gazes at him admiringly.

UNCLE NAT: How do they fit me?   40

ANN: Jes' es ef they was made —

HELEN (*More critically*):   Turn round, Uncle Nat. (*He does so with an air of great importance, and is very happy over the impression he is creating, for it is many a long day since he had a new suit of clothes. Helen smooths the back of his coat down with her hand*) The waist might be a trifle longer. Don't you think so, Ma?

ANN (*Inspecting him carefully with her arms on her hips*):   Oh! Do you think so? Seems to me's ef 'twas meant to be jes' thet way. (*Goes back to the stove*) I say,   45
jes' thet way.

HELEN: Well, maybe it was. (*A pause. She returns to her work at the table*)

UNCLE NAT (*Fingering his vest*):   Helen, there's a button come off this vest a'ready. I guess they're jes' stuck on. I wish you'd sew 'em on with thread, by 'n' by.   50

HELEN: All right, Uncle Nat, good strong thread.

UNCLE NAT (*With a complete change of manner, full of businesslike importance*): Well, how be yeh gettin' along — I hope yeh hain't sp'ilt nothin' sense I ben away. Helen, will you get me my apron. (*He takes off his coat and places it carefully over the back of a chair, and comes down center. Helen gets him a woman's checked apron*) I want you should tie it in a bowknot so that when the company comes, I can get it off handy. (*He stands with arms outstretched; Helen ties the apron around him just beneath his shoulders. He pushes it down*) Not too high-waisted, not too high-waisted. (*He pushes his foot back into the boot and limps to the stove*) How's the ol' cranberries gettin' on? (*Slight pause*) Who sot these cranberries on the back of the stove? (*Looks around at them all accusingly*) Don't yeh know nothin' in this house, or don't yeh? (*Lifts up the saucepan and puts it on the front of the stove. Tastes the cranberries, and says reproachfully*) Oh Ma, I'm sorry yeh put more sugar in the cranberries, yeh got 'em too sweet. I had 'em jes' right when I left 'em. (*Nobody answers*) Ma, did you put any more sugar in them cranberries?

ANN (*Busy at the table, right, speaking over her shoulder*): I didn't put no more sugar in 'em.

UNCLE NAT: Well, somebody has. Helen, did you put any more sugar in them cranberries?

HELEN: No, Uncle Nat.

UNCLE NAT: Well, somebody did. (*Turning to Perley in an accusing manner*) Perley, did you put any more sugar in them cranberries?

PERLEY (*A little resentfully, drawling*): I hain't teched 'em.

UNCLE NAT (*Testily, imitating her drawl*): Well, *some*body's teched 'em. Cranberries couldn't walk off the stove and get into the sugar bucket by themselves.

PERLEY: They wuz a-scorchin', an, I sot 'em back, thet's all I done.

UNCLE NAT (*In disgust*): Well I wish you'd let 'em alone. I'd ruther have I don't know what around me than a lot of women when I'm a-cookin' of a dinner. (*Taking the saucepan off the stove, and setting it in the sink*) Nell, dish out them cranberries and set 'em t' cool some place 'r other, will yeh?

HELEN: Yes, in a minute. (*Gets a preserve dish from the alcove, dishes out the berries, and sets them on the table at the window*)

Bob runs on from the sitting room.

BOB: Ma, can we play store with the presents?

ANN: Yes, play with 'em all you like, but don't break any of 'em; I say, don't break any of 'em.

BOB: Oh, we won't break 'em. (*Runs off*) Mary! Mary! Ma says we can play with 'em.

UNCLE NAT (*With happy expectancy*): Now, les' see how the ol' turkey's a-gettin' on. (*Goes over to the stove, sees the damper is shut, and says indignantly*) Now in the name of common sense, who shut up thet damper! (*Opens the damper with a jerk*)

ANN: Yeh must 'a' done it yerself.   90

UNCLE NAT: Upon my word, a man can't leave a stove out of his hands five minutes without somebody a-foolin' with it. (*He opens the oven door and looks at the turkey, his face aglow with admiration. They all stand around him, very much interested*) By George, ain't he a beauty? (*In a grieved tone*) Who turned him on his back? I had him on his side.

HELEN: You want him to brown all over, don't you?   95

UNCLE NAT: See here, who's cookin' this turkey, you or me? (*Smacking his lips*) Get the platter, he's done. Ef he stays in there any longer, he'll be burned to a crisp. (*Helen gets a platter from the dresser*) Ma, you get me a dish-towel.

Ann gives him a dishtowel. All is bustle and excitement as he lifts out the dripping pan, and sets it on top of the stove. Uncle Nat is left and the women are right of the stove.

Tim comes in from the woodhouse with an armful of wood, both large and small pieces, which he dumps into the woodbox, afterward brushing the chips which cling to his sleeve into the box. He stands and looks admiringly at the turkey.

UNCLE NAT (*Glowing with pride*):   What do you think of thet for a turkey, eh   100
Tim?

TIM: As they say in ould Ireland, that's a burrd!

He goes over to Perley, who stands near the sink, right, throws his arm around her, and hugs her roughly and quickly. She hits him with a dishcloth, and he runs out down right, laughing, followed by Perley hitting the air with the dishcloth, trying to reach him. After he goes, she returns coolly to her work at the sink. This byplay is unnoticed by the others, who are intent on the turkey.

UNCLE NAT (*To Ann and Helen, chuckling; speaking through Tim's business*):   I wonder what they call a turkey in Ireland, a critter? Give me a large fork. (*Helen gives him one*) Now a big spoon (*Ann gives him one*)   105

ANN (*As Uncle Nat starts to lift the turkey out with the fork and spoon*):   Be careful. Don't stick the fork into the turkey; ef you break the skin, the juice'll all run out; I say, run out.

HELEN: Be careful, Uncle Nat, don't drop him.

UNCLE NAT (*Puts the turkey back in the pan, turns from one woman to the other, and says with gentle exasperation*):   Say, if you can find anythin' to do about the   110
house, I wish you'd go an' do it an' leave me alone. Yeh've got me s' nervous, I don't know whether I'm standin' on my head or my heels. (*Gets the turkey into the platter, and says joyously*) There he is! Now put him in the oven

to keep warm, while I make the gravy. (*Proceeds to stir the gravy in the dripping pan*) Nell, pour a little water in there, careful now. (*She pours some into the pan from the tea kettle*) Thet's enough. Thet'll do — Thet'll do! (*He pushes the kettle spout up*) 115

HELEN (*Protesting*):   Why, Uncle Nat, you won't have half gravy enough! (*Attempts to pour more in*) Ma, I wish you'd look at this!

UNCLE NAT (*Turning to Ann*):   Ma, you attend to your own business.

While Uncle Nat is talking to Ann, Helen pours more water into the pan. Uncle Nat turns and sees her doing it, and he pushes the spout up and burns his finger. Helen drops the kettle on the stove.

UNCLE NAT: Now you've done it, Nell! You've got enough gravy to sail a boat in. (*Blowing his scalded fingers*) 120

HELEN: Well, you want to thicken it with some flour, don't you? Here! (*She takes the dredging box and sifts in the flour*)

UNCLE NAT (*Making the best of it, stirs in the flour as she sifts*):   Thet'll do — Thet'll do — Thet'll do! Do you want to make a paste of it? Oh, Nell, don't put so much in, you've got it all full o' lumps now. (*Unconsciously blowing his scalded fingers, holding them up in the air, and then again blowing them*) 125

HELEN: All right, Uncle Nat. Make the gravy yourself. (*She returns to her work*)

UNCLE NAT (*After a slight pause. He is now stirring the gravy*):   Now gimme the giblets, an' I'll stir 'em in an' make the giblet sass. (*There is no answer. He speaks a little louder*) I say, some one o' yeh gimme the giblets, an' I'll make the giblet sass. (*The three women stop in their work and look at one another, as if to say "What are we going to do now?"*) Come, hurry up! (*A pause, Uncle Nat blows his fingers*) Gimme the giblets I tell you! (*Silence. Helen crosses over to Perley. Uncle Nat gets impatient*) Will yeh gimme the giblets, Ma? 130

ANN: I don't know where they be.

UNCLE NAT: They're in the choppin' tray, wherever you stuck it. 135

ANN (*Holding up the empty chopping tray, and showing it to him*):   No they ain't nuther; I say, nuther.

UNCLE NAT (*As he continues to stir the gravy*):   Well, they was there. What yeh done with 'em?

ANN: I hain't done nothin' with 'em. 140

UNCLE NAT (*Getting testy again*):   Well, somebody's done suthin' with 'em. (*Turning to Helen*) Hev you seen 'em, Nell?

HELEN: No, Uncle Nat.

UNCLE NAT: Well, somebody's seen 'em. (*Turning to Perley, accusingly*) Perley, hev you been a-monkeyin' with them giblets? 145

PERLEY (*Who has been trying to escape observation by violently scouring a pan at the sink, blurts out*):   I fed 'em to the chickings.

UNCLE NAT (*Dropping the spoon with utter exasperation*):   Well, of all the durn gawks I ever see you beat all! Thet ends the dinner! No giblet sass. Me a-settin' down fer half an hour a-choppin' giblets fer you to feed to the chickings. Perley, yeh're a nateral born gawk.   150

ANN (*Crossing to the table*):   Oh, Nathan'l, give me a hand with this table, will yeh?

UNCLE NAT (*Going to the lower end of the table*):   What yeh want to do with it, Ma?

ANN: Oh, jes' set it out a piece from the stair.   155

UNCLE NAT (*As they move the table slightly toward center*):   Be keerful, Ma, it fell down last Washin'ton's birthday. (*Crossing to the window and looking out*) Looks a leetle like a shower. I hope it won't keep any of the company away.

ANN: Oh, I guess not. They ain't nuther sugar nor salt; I say, nuther sugar   160 nor salt.

Millie by this time has made all the dough into little loaves on a tin plate, and she now takes the plate to Ann. She has managed to get herself pretty well messed up with flour.

MILLIE: Mama, please bake this for dolly'n me.

ANN: Powers above! Look at thet child! What'n the name of all possessed hev yeh been a-doin' with yerself? I say, a-doin' with yerself?

MILLIE: Makin' bwead for dolly'n me.   165

ANN (*Smiling indulgently*):   Well, I should say you hed. Nathan'l, tend to thet baby; I say, thet baby. (*She takes the plate of dough from Millie*)

During the following scene, Ann, Helen and Perley busy themselves with the dinner things.

UNCLE NAT: Yes, ef I didn't tend to her, I'd like to know who would. (*Crosses to the sink, takes a clean towel, and pumps water on one end of it. He then goes center to Millie*) Upon my word, Millie, this is too bad. Here's company a-comin' and you think we've got nothin' to do but run after you young uns every   170 five minutes of the day. We put yeh all three this mornin' — why didn't yeh stay put? Mussy, mussy, mussy, what a dirty child!

MILLIE: That ain't dirt, it's bwead.

UNCLE NAT (*Getting down on his knees, and beginning to clean her hands with the wet end of the towel*):   Well, it's mighty dirty bread. Who'd yeh 'spose'd eat bread from such dirty hands as those? Who you makin' bread fer?   175

MILLIE: Dolly.

UNCLE NAT (*Drying her hands*):   Well, it's a good thing that dolly's only got one eye. She'd never eat bread from such dirty hands, not unless you kept it on the blind side of her. (*Washing her face*) My sakes alive, why, you'd scare all Mama's visitors out o' th' house with such a dirty face.   180

MILLIE (*Talking through the towel*):   Bob's got a false face.

UNCLE NAT: What's that?

MILLIE: Bob's got a false face.

UNCLE NAT (*Drying her face*):   Hez he?

MILLIE: Yes. (*Talking through the towel*) I wish you'd buy me a false face, will   185
yeh, Uncle Nat?

UNCLE NAT: You don't want no false face, you want yer own sweet pooty little clean face. (*Kisses her*) Now shake yer frock. (*She shakes it in his face*) Don't shake it in my face. Stand over there and shake it.

MILLIE: Ain't I a nice clean child now, Uncle Nat?   190

UNCLE NAT: You're the nicest cleanest child in the hull State of Maine.

As Uncle Nat finishes making Millie tidy, the noise of approaching wagons is heard in the distance, and now all the guests except Blake arrive outside, amid great bustle and laughter, as if they had finished the journey in a race. Instantly all is excitement indoors.

UNCLE NAT: Hello, Ann, here they be! (*Crosses up left*) Helen, take my apron off. (*She does so. Uncle Nat puts on his coat quickly, and hurries off, right, leaving the door open. He is heard greeting the guests outside*)

ANN: Mussy on me, an' I ain't fit to be seen to a nigger clambake; I say, clambake! (*She takes her apron off. Helen unpins her dress, and smooths it down*)   195

Helen and Perley go to the window. Bob and Mary run in from the sitting room. Millie goes to the door, right.

CAPTAIN BEN (*Outside*):   Hello, Nathan'l — Many happy returns o' the day!

UNCLE NAT (*Outside*):   Don't git things mixed, Cap'n. This ain't *my* fun'ral. (*All laugh*) Step right in. Tim an' me'll take care o' the hosses.

All the guests enter together, laughing and talking. Captain Ben Hutchins comes first. He is a jolly man of about fifty, half farmer, half skipper, with iron-gray hair and a full beard; he wears a blue suit with brass buttons and a peaked cap. He is accompanied by Liddy Ann Nye, a motherly widow in half-mourning. They are followed by Squire Andrews, a very tall, wiry, distinguished-looking man about seventy-five. He is well-preserved, and has very gray hair and a pink face. He is very deaf, and carries a tin ear-trumpet which has seen much service. With him is Mrs. Andrews, a tall woman with white hair; she is dressed in good taste. The Doctor, Mrs. Leonard, and the Twins enter last. The Doctor is a genial country physician. His wife is a trifle overdressed; as her husband is a professional man, she feels a bit above the farmers' wives. The Twins are nicely dressed; the boy is in knickerbockers, and the little girl wears a white dress, trimmed with lace. The Doctor and the boy take off their hats as they enter. All the guests scrape their feet on the mat. They all speak at once.

DOCTOR: Many happy returns of the day, Mrs. Berry!

MRS. LEONARD: Returns of the day, Mrs. Berry, I'm sure.   200

SQUIRE ANDREWS: Many happy returns of the day, Mis' Berry!

MRS. ANDREWS: I wish you many happy returns of the day.

CAPTAIN BEN: May ye live another twenty-five years, an' invite us all agin.

MRS. NYE: Well, Ann, I swan yeh look younger'n yeh did twenty-five years
ago, an' no wonder!   205

As they speak, they are all endeavoring to shake Ann by the hand.

ANN (*Shaking hands with them all, excited and happy*):   Don't come near me, if
you don't want to get yer clothes spattered. This ol' stove sputters like I
d'know what today. I'm greasier'n a pig. I'm 'bleeged t'yeh all fer comin';
I say, fer comin'.

CAPTAIN BEN: Oh! Ketch any of us missin' one o' *your* dinners! (*All laugh*) I   210
was tellin' Mis' Nye that ef I had a cook like you aboard the "Liddy Ann,"
I'd stay t' sea the year 'round. (*Laughs*)

MRS. ANDREWS: The boot's on the other leg. We're obleeged to *you* fer
askin' of us.

SQUIRE ANDREWS (*With the horn at his ear*):   What do you say?   215

MRS. ANDREWS (*Through the trumpet*):   I said Mis' Berry's lookin' well.

SQUIRE ANDREWS: Oh yes — she allus looks well.

ANN: Well, ef you'll all step into the settin' room an' lay off yer things, I'll
run upstairs an' try to make the *bride* presentable.

ALL (*Laughing*):   Certainly, certainly, by all means! (*They all go off through the*   220
door leading to the sitting room)

ANN: Children, take the twins in an' show 'em the presents, an' let 'em look
at yer noo red albyum. (*She goes upstairs, followed by Perley*)

Bob and Mary, one on each side of the Twins, lead them by the hand in the direction of
the sitting room. The Doctor, who is going out last, is stopped by Millie, who has a di-
lapidated doll, with no clothes, no hair, one eye, one arm and half a leg gone, in her
arms.

MILLIE: Tan 'oo ture my dolly, Doctor?

DOCTOR: Cure your dolly? I guess so. What appears to be the matter with
her? (*Taking the doll, and entering into the mood of the child*)   225

MILLIE: She's sick.

DOCTOR: Sick! (*Looking the doll over*) I should say she was. What's come of
her other eye?

MILLIE: She swallowed it, an' it's down in her little tummick.

DOCTOR: Is *that* so? My, my! She *is* in a bad way. Well, come along, and   230
let's see what we can do for her. (*He goes out after the others, leading Millie*)

During this scene, Helen has been busying herself with the table, putting on the bread, butter, cranberry sauce, etc.

Martin and Blake enter through the door, right. Blake is in his best black suit, and Martin is dressed in his Sunday clothes.

MARTIN (*Speaking as he comes in*): Where's Ma, Helen? (*Crosses over to the row of pegs at the back of the stairs and hangs up his hat*)

HELEN (*Coldly*): She'll be here in a minute. (*Shows that she and her father have not been on the best of terms since the quarrel with Sam. She is not rude, however*)

As Blake notices Helen's manner, he draws back and pretends to be wiping his feet on the doormat, so as not to hear what passes. He does not enter the room until Martin crosses the stage for his exit.

MARTIN (*Pauses, and looks at Helen*): Hain't you got over the sulks yet?

HELEN: I'm not in any sulks, but I can't laugh when you stick pins in me.   235
(*She crosses over to the stove, kneels down, opens the oven door, and looks at the turkey*)

MARTIN: I don't want to stick pins into yeh, Nell. You give up Sam Warren, an' you an' me'll never have a word.

HELEN (*Speaking over her shoulder and temporarily stopping her work, trying to hide her feelings*): He'll not trouble any of us much longer, I guess.

MARTIN (*Pleased*): Hev yeh forbid him a-seein' of yeh?

HELEN: *You* have, haven't you?   240

MARTIN: Yes.

HELEN: Well?

MARTIN: An' ef he knows when he's well off, he'll do as I say. Company's come, I see.

HELEN (*Rising*): Yes, they're in the sitting room.   245

MARTIN (*As he goes out, left*): Come along, Mr. Blake.

BLAKE: I'll be there in a minute.

MARTIN (*As he reaches the sitting room, he is heard saying genially*): Be yeh all here?

THE GUESTS (*Outside*): Many happy returns of the day!   250

BLAKE (*Whose eyes have been fixed on Helen from the moment he entered*): Well, Helen!

HELEN (*Pleasantly, but distantly*): How do you do, Mr. Blake.

During this scene, Helen goes to the sideboard, gets the tumblers and salt cellars, and begins arranging them on the table. She is at the left of the table; Blake stands right center.

BLAKE: I suppose you'll be hevin' a silver weddin' of your own one o' these days, eh?   255

HELEN (*Carelessly*): I don't know, I'm sure.

BLAKE: Did Sam tell yeh about wantin' to borry a hundred dollars o' me?

HELEN (*Interested for the first time*):   No. When?

BLAKE: Yesterday afternoon.

HELEN (*Eagerly*):   Did you lend it to him?   260

BLAKE: No, but I told him I'd give him a thousand if he'd pick a fuss with you, clear out, an' promise never to come back.

HELEN (*Smiling scornfully*):   What'd he say?

BLAKE (*Pauses deprecatingly*):   Said he'd — see me in Hell fust.

HELEN: H'm! (*As if to say "I knew he'd say just that." She turns and busies herself near the head of the table*)   265

CAPTAIN BEN (*Outside*):   I said fifty fathom.

THE GUESTS (*Outside*):   Oh! We didn't understand yeh, Cap'n Ben.

BLAKE (*Insinuatingly*):   Has yer father said anything to yeh about me *lately*?

HELEN (*With a bitter little laugh*):   No, he doesn't say much to me *lately* about anything, or anybody.   270

BLAKE: Well! I've got the biggest scheme fer gettin' him an' me rich! I'll tell you what I'll do with you.

HELEN (*Proudly*):   I don't want you should do anything with me, Mr. Blake. (*Crosses to the dresser, right*)

BLAKE: Your father's set his mind on you an' me gettin' married, y'know.

HELEN: My father had better mind his own business. (*She picks up a pie and wipes the under part of the plate with a dishtowel*)   275

BLAKE: His *own* business! Great Scott! D'yeh mean to say it ain't his business who his daughter marries?

HELEN: That's just exactly what I mean to say. (*Crosses to the table, left, with the pie and sets it on the table*)

BLAKE (*Gives a long low whistle*):   Well, Sam Warren *has* filled your head with his new-fangled ideas, an' *no* mistake.   280

HELEN (*Filling up with tears*):   Never mind Sam Warren, Mr. Blake. I can talk for myself.

BLAKE: That's just why I think s'much of you. Helen, I'm goin' to be awful rich. I'll give you half of every dollar I make for the next twenty years, if you'll marry me.   285

HELEN (*Kindly, but with finality*):   No, Mr. Blake, I can't marry you. (*She is left of the table; Blake is right, close to the table*)

BLAKE (*Wistfully*):   Too old, I suppose?

HELEN (*Sighing heavily*):   No, it's not that. That wouldn't make any difference to *me.*

BLAKE: Too orthodox? (*With large generosity*) You needn't go to meetin' if you don't want to. You can read all the novels you've a mind to. (*Beaming and enthusiastic, with a warm spirit of sacrifice*) I'll read *them books* with you.   290

HELEN (*With a hopeless little laugh*): Oh, Mr. Blake, you don't understand me. (*Crosses to the sink, taking off her apron*)

BLAKE (*Intensely*): No, nor you me. I never set my mind on a thing yet I didn't get. 295

HELEN (*Scornfully*): I'm afraid you've done it this time, Mr. Blake. (*Gives her apron a vigorous and emphatic shake as she hangs it up on a peg by the sink*)

BLAKE: No, I haven't. I'm goin' to have you, Helen, or die a-tryin'. (*She turns and looks at him; he continues quickly*) Nothin' *underhand* though — nothin' underhand.

HELEN (*With a scornful toss of her head*): I should hope not. (*There is a note of de-* 300 *fiance in her voice*)

Uncle Nat enters through the door, right.

UNCLE NAT: Helen — (*She runs to him and he says in a tense whisper*) Sam's out there by the wood pile. He's got the money an' —

HELEN (*Joyously*): Got the hundred dollars? Where did he get it?

UNCLE NAT (*Evading the question*): He wants to see you — (*Helen starts to go past him out the door. He stops her*) Not thet way. Slip out through the wood- 305 house. (*Helen runs out through the woodhouse door, left*)

BLAKE (*Suspecting something, starts to go to the window as Helen crosses outside*): What's the matter? Anything wrong?

Uncle Nat stands between Blake and the window, picks up an apron, and shakes it in his face.

UNCLE NAT: Helen's speckled pullet's fell inter the rain barrel.

BLAKE: Oh! I hope she ain't drowned. (*Trying to see through the window*)

UNCLE NAT: No, she ain't drownded, but she's awful wet. 310

Ann comes down the stairs, all freshened up, followed by Perley.

ANN (*Speaking as she comes down*): Well, be we all ready, Perley?

PERLEY: Yes'm. (*Puts the potatoes on the table*)

ANN: Well, let's have 'em in, Nathan'l.

UNCLE NAT: All right. You put the turkey on the table, an' I'll hev 'em in in three shakes of a lamb's tail. 315

Uncle Nat goes into the sitting room. As he is supposed to open the sitting room door, a loud laugh is heard.
    Ann puts the turkey on the table.

UNCLE NAT (*Outside*): Come, dinner's all sot, an' fetch three or four chairs with you.

ANN (*For the first time seeing Blake, who has been standing at the window, his hands behind his back*):   Good afternoon, Mr. Blake. I was 'feared you couldn't git here, yeh're such a busy man.

BLAKE (*Coming down to the table*):   I'd drop business anytime to eat one o' *your* dinners, Mrs. Berry.   320

ANN: Well, I d'know whether the turkey sp'iled or not. Nathan'l's so fussy; I say, so fussy.

All the guests enter, laughing and chatting. Captain Ben, the Doctor and Martin carrying chairs. Uncle Nat is also carrying a chair, and is laughing heartily at some remark that has just been made. The guests stand around expectantly, waiting for Ann to seat them. Martin goes to the head of the table and begins to carve the turkey. The children come on leading the Twins, in the same manner as they went off.

CAPTAIN BEN (*As he enters*):   It's the pootiest kind of a trip this time o' year.

MARTIN: How long'll you be gone this time?   325

CAPTAIN BEN: 'Bout six weeks to two months.

UNCLE NAT: When d'ye sail, Cap'n Ben?

CAPTAIN BEN: T'night — fust o' the tide.

UNCLE NAT: I've a durn good notion t' go with yeh. D'yeh want any more hands?   330

CAPTAIN BEN: Yep, come on, Nathan'l. I'll give you a berth, ten dollars, an' found.

ANN: Oh, fer pity's sake, don't take him till I get these dishes washed.

MARTIN: Where'll yeh set us, Ma?

ANN (*Who has been standing at the upper end of the table on Martin's right, recollecting herself*):   Oh! Mr. Blake — (*He does not answer. She calls again*) Mr. Blake!   335

BLAKE (*Who has been at the window lost in thought, his arms folded behind him, his head bent*):   Eh? Oh, I beg pardon.

As Ann indicates each place, the guest acknowledges it with a little bow preparatory to taking his or her seat.

ANN (*Indicating Blake's place at her right*):   Set there please. I suppose I'd ought to make a speech — Mis' Nye — (*Indicates her place at Martin's left, at the upper end of the table*) to thank yeh all — Doctor — (*Indicates his place left of Mrs. Nye*) for yer pooty presents — Mis' Leonard — (*Indicates her place left of the*   340 *Doctor*) but I never made a speech except once — Cap'n Ben — (*Indicates his place left of Mrs. Leonard*) 'n thet was twenty-five years ago — Mis' Andrews — (*Indicates her place right of Blake*) an' then all I said was "yes" — (*All laugh. She shouts*) Squire — Squire — (*He takes his place next to his wife*) I tell Martin thet ef I do live with him twenty-five years longer — the chil-   345 dren 'll hev t' wait —

BOB (*Stamping his foot*):   Oh gosh! I wish you'd never hev any company —
we allus hev t' wait! (*Goes off left, leading Sis Leonard by the hand, followed by
Mary leading Bob Leonard. Uncle Nat half follows them off, motioning them to be
quiet*)

ANN: — it'll only be 'count of the presents. (*All laugh*) Well, set by.

*All busy themselves at the table, and do not see Helen, who enters, right, crying. She
comes to Uncle Nat, who draws her to the center of the stage.*

HELEN (*Softly*):   He *is* going tonight, Uncle Nat.   350

UNCLE NAT (*Tensely and quietly, soothing her*):   There, don't let 'em see you
cryin'. It'll all come right some day. You wait on the table. (*Turning to Ann
and covering up his concern for Helen with a cheery manner*) Where be yeh a-goin'
to put me, Ma?

By this time everybody is seated.

ANN (*Pointing*):   Oh, you're down at the foot o' the class. (*All laugh*)   355

UNCLE NAT: Allus was at the foot of the class — (*Laughs, and sits down*)

Millie enters through the door, right, with her apron full of clam shells.

MILLIE (*Dropping the shells on the floor*):   Where's my place, Mama?

MRS. NYE: Bless the darlin'!

CAPTAIN BEN (*Gets up and offers his chair with mock ceremony*):   Sit right down
here, I'll wait.   360

MRS. ANDREWS (*Nudging the Squire*):   Look at thet child.

SQUIRE ANDREWS: Yes — I will —

The above exclamations are simultaneous, and all are laughing.

ANN: My blossom! Come to Ma, precious.

*Millie goes to her; Ann takes her on her lap, wipes her face and hands with a napkin,
and puts her in her high chair, which Perley has brought to the table.
    Martin has gone on carving. Blake has tucked his napkin in his neck, diamond-wise,
and spread the ends all over his chest. The Doctor and Mrs. Leonard have placed their
napkins in their laps. Mrs. Nye has laid hers beside her place. Mrs. Andrews fastens the
Squire's napkin around his neck. Uncle Nat sticks his in the breast of his vest like a handkerchief. All are laughing and chatting, then suddenly Martin taps on the table with the
handle of his knife. They all pause instantly, and there is silence as they bow their heads
in prayer. This must be done in a perfunctory manner, but in all seriousness.*

MARTIN (*Quickly*):   Now sing out what kind uv a j'int yeh'll hev.

The Squire remains with his head on the table; Uncle Nat shakes him.

UNCLE NAT: Squire, Squire! (*The Squire looks up and places his hand to his ear*)   365
Meetin's out.

MRS. ANDREWS: I'll hev secon' j'int, an' the Squire 'll hev a bit o' the breast. (*Mrs. Andrews has the Squire's plate*)

SQUIRE ANDREWS (*Puts his hand to his ear*):   Hey? — What?

MRS. ANDREWS: I said you'd hev a bit o' the breast.

MRS. NYE: I'll hev a wing.   370

CAPTAIN BEN (*Heartily*):   Gimme anything so's it's turkey.

BLAKE: I've no particular choice.

UNCLE NAT (*After all the others have spoken*):   Neither hev I. I'll hev the part that went over the fence last, ef nob'dy else *wants* it.

Martin helps rapidly. Ann serves the cranberry sauce. Perley and Helen pass the vegetables, bread, and butter. They all eat heartily.

CAPTAIN BEN (*With his mouth full*):   Now thet's what I call turkey.   375

UNCLE NAT: Thet's what we cooked her fer, Cap'n Ben. Ann, don't be so stingy with yer ol' cranberry sass. (*Passes his plate.*)

ANN (*As she helps Uncle Nat to cranberry sauce*):   Well, yeh can pass up again. There's plenty more in the sass dish.

UNCLE NAT: I only said that to be polite.   380

MARTIN: Now, folks, don't be bashful. It costs jes' the same whether yeh eat 'r not.

All laugh, except the Squire, who is busy eating.
    Joel Gates appears in the doorway, carrying Uncle Nat's gun, with Mandy beside him. He stands there and cranes his neck to look over at the table, his eyes gloating over the food. No one notices him. They are all intent upon their food.

UNCLE NAT: I don't believe the Squire heard a word of it. Squire, did you hear what Martin said?

SQUIRE ANDREWS (*With his hand back of his ear*):   Eh?   385

UNCLE NAT: He said it costs jes' the same whether yeh eat or not.

SQUIRE ANDREWS: Oh, we'll eat a lot.

UNCLE NAT: No, no — Not lot.

GATES (*Still standing at the doorway, ingratiatingly*):   How d' do?

UNCLE NAT (*Looking up and seeing him for the first time*):   Hello, Joel!   390

MARTIN (*With hearty hospitality*):   Hello, Joel — jes' in time. Set by an' hev some dinner with us.

All the guests greet Gates.

GATES (*Steps over the threshold, glowing at the invitation, followed by Mandy*):   I didn't know yeh hed comp'ny.

ANN: Perley, set 'm a chair; I say, a chair. (*Perley starts to get a chair for him*)   395

GATES (*Protestingly, to Perley*):   No! No! (*Apologetically, to all the guests*) I ain't fit to set down with comp'ny, I ben workin' round the barn. I jes' fetched back yer gun, Nathan'l.

HELEN: I'll take her, Mr. Gates.

GATES (*As he hands her the gun*):   Be careful, Hel'n, she's ludded.   400

Helen sets the gun in the corner by the sink.

UNCLE NAT (*Casually*):   Did yeh manage to kill thet there fox, Joel?

GATES: I found out 't wa'n't a fox. (*Very much interested in the turkey and the guests' enjoyment of it*)

UNCLE NAT: Thet so. What was it?

GATES: 'Twas a skunk.

A murmur of amusement goes around the table. Gates starts to go.

MARTIN: Set down an' hev some turkey.   405

GATES (*Deprecatingly, looking at the table longingly*):   No, I'm too s'iled. Ef I'd 'a' knowed you was hevin' turkey — I mean comp'ny, I'd 'a' cleaned myself up a bit.

UNCLE NAT (*While eating*):   Now thet yeh be here, let Ma fix some on a plate to take hum with yeh.   410

ANN: Yes. Here, Martin, give him this, you can fix yerself some more. (*Holds Martin's plate; Martin fills it*)

UNCLE NAT (*To the child*):   Mandy, you come here an' git a piece of Ma Berry's pie.

GATES (*To the child, who hesitates and looks up at him inquiringly*):   Go 'n git it, ef yeh want to.   415

Mandy goes to Uncle Nat, who gives her a huge piece of pie. She returns to her father, holding the pie with both hands, her face in a glow of wonder.

ANN (*Giving Helen a plate piled high with food*):   Helen, pass this to Mr. Gates.

GATES (*As Helen gives him the plate*):   Thank yeh, thank yeh. I'll jes' step inter the woodhouse an' eat it, then I kin hand the plate back.

MARTIN: No, set down there, ef yeh won't come to the table. Hel'n give 'im a chair.   420

Helen places a chair, center. Her manner is very gentle and kind.

GATES: *Thank* yeh.

Helen gets Millie's small rocking-chair for Mandy. She sits down in it, and slowly rocks to and fro, and for the first time a look of childish joy appears on her face.

Gates settles himself in the chair carefully, with his knees drawn together and his toes resting on a rung, so as to make a table of his lap. With his shoulders hunched, he attacks the overflowing plate and becomes absorbed in the food. He eats as if he had been saving himself for this meal, and feeds the child generously with dainty morsels.

Meantime, the talk at the table continues.

DOCTOR: Oh! By the way, Mr. Blake, did you buy the Swazy place?

BLAKE: Yes.

CAPTAIN BEN: L'see, how many acres is there in thet place?

BLAKE: Eighty odd.   425

MARTIN: What'd yeh hev to pay fer it, if it's a fair question?

BLAKE: Paid enough fer it — they knew I had to hev it.

UNCLE NAT: They ain't givin' land away nowadays, be they, Mr. Blake?

DOCTOR (*To Perley*):   Will you give me another cup of tea, please? (*She takes his cup and fills it from the teapot on the stove*) I'd like to sell you that ma'sh of   430
mine, Mr. Blake.

BLAKE: How much shore front hev yeh got there?

DOCTOR: Sixty-seven rod.

BLAKE: What'll yeh take fer it?

DOCTOR: Well, I'm asking twenty-five hundred dollars for it.   435

BLAKE: Good Heavens! You hev sot it up. I'll give yeh a thousand fer it, half cash.

DOCTOR: The Squire's offered me more than *that* for it.

BLAKE (*Astonished*):   The Squire! What's he want with it?

SQUIRE ANDREWS (*Hearing this*):   Thet's my business. You don't s'pose you're   440
goin' to be the only one to git rich out'n the boom, do yeh?

BLAKE: I *started* it.

SQUIRE ANDREWS: Columbus discovered Americky, but he don't *own* it.
(*All laugh. The Squire looks round the table, well satisfied*)

UNCLE NAT (*Laughing uproariously, to the Squire on his left*):   Squire, thet's the best thing yeh ever said in yer life — I say thet's the best — (*Pauses, as he   445
realizes the Squire is paying no attention, but is busily eating*) Yeh didn't know yeh said it, did yeh? (*The Squire still pays no attention. Uncle Nat turns to the rest of the company*) He didn't hear himself say it. (*All laugh*)

CAPTAIN BEN: So the Squire's got the fever too, eh?

SQUIRE ANDREWS: Yes, an' got it bad — see — (*Pulls out an oil paper map of   450
his farm, laid off in lots, unfolds it, and shows it to the company*)

BLAKE: By George, he's got the start of all of us.

GATES (*Picking gingerly on a drumstick*):   Mr. Blake, I'd like t' sell yeh thet seven acre o' mine. I got a great view there. Yeh kin see fer fifty mile round, ef yer eyesight's good enough.

BLAKE: What d'yeh want fer it?   455

GATES (*Very importantly*):   Well, it's sort o' got round thet I sot a price. I told Gabe Kilpatrick, and he says I'd ought to git ten 'r fifteen thousand dollars for it. (*All laugh*) Gabe says it'd make a great buildin' site fer Vanderbilt 'r Rockenfeeder 'r any 'o them far-seein' fellers. (*All laugh*)

ANN: Oh, Martin, thet man thet was here to see yeh yesterday was here 460
agin today — who is he?

MARTIN (*Speaking slowly and unwillingly*):   His name's Beardsley.

UNCLE NAT (*Cheerfully and unsuspiciously*):   What is he, Martin?

MARTIN (*Ponderously*):   Surveyor!

UNCLE NAT: *Surveyor?* 465

MARTIN: Surveyor for this 'ere new geruntee land an' improv'ment company.

CAPTAIN BEN: Martin, will yeh gimme jes' a leetle taste more o' thet stuffin'? (*Passes his plate, Martin helps him*)

ANN (*For the first time a little uneasy*):   What's he want here, Martin? 470

MARTIN (*As if forced to a stand, defiantly*):   He's goin' to survey the farm.

ANN (*Gulping down her food*):   Survey it! What fer? I say, what fer?

MARTIN (*In desperation*):   I'm goin' to cut it up into buildin' lots, ef yeh must know. (*The guests stop eating*)

Ann is quite overcome at this news. She swiftly moves her chair out from the table, and stares at Martin in consternation.

MARTIN (*With forced change of tone*):   Hev another wing, Mis' Nye. 475

MRS. NYE (*Soothingly*):   Hain't et what I got on my plate yit, Martin.

A damper now falls on the party.

ANN (*Passionately*):   Martin Berry, you ain't a-goin' to sell the farm, be yeh? I say, be yeh?

MARTIN (*Stubbornly*):   You heerd what I said, didn't yeh?

ANN: Yes — I heerd yeh, but I can't *believe* yeh. 480

MARTIN: It's *mine*, ain't it?

ANN (*Brokenly*):   Yes, I s'pose 'tis.

MARTIN: Well, hain't I got a right to do what I like with my own?

ANN: I d'know's you got any right to turn me an' the children out o' house 'n hum. 485

Gates gently rises and gives his empty plate to Helen, a look of apprehension on his face. He tiptoes from the room through the door, right, followed by Mandy.
Uncle Nat gets up and places his chair in a corner, left, and crosses to right center.

MARTIN: Thet's sentiment — I ain't a-goin' to turn yeh out o' nothin'. I'm a-goin' to move yeh all up to Bangor — I'm a-goin' to git rich.

ANN (*Rising and folding her arms, her head in the air, proudly and defiantly*):   You won't move *me* up to Bangor, not ef you git as rich as Methuselum.

MARTIN: I'll leave it to Mr. Blake ef I —   490

BLAKE: I must say I think Martin's scheme's a —

ANN (*Still with spirit, but with a break in her voice*):   I don't allow's Mr. Blake's got any right to jedge atween you an' me in this: I say, in this.

MARTIN (*Rising, and striking his fist on the table, angrily*):   Look a-here! I'm goin' to git rich in spite o' yeh. Doctor, will yeh hev another piece o' the   495 breast? I ain't a-goin' to be browbeat.

DOCTOR: No, thank you.

MARTIN (*In a great temper by this time*):   Fust Nathan'l tries it an' then you must set up a —

UNCLE NAT (*Very tensely, but quietly*):   I hain't never browbeat yeh, Martin —   500 I only ast yeh to leave me thet little piece up yonder.

MARTIN: I won't leave yeh nothin'! I'm durned ef I don't sell the hull thing, humstead, graveyard an' every dum —

Young Nat enters through the door, right, out of breath and greatly agitated.

YOUNG NAT: Mr. Blake — Mr. Blake — Mr. Blake — (*Breathes fast*) You're wanted up at the store. (*All are listening*) There's been a package o' money   505 took out o' the safe.

BLAKE (*Swinging around in his chair so as to face Young Nat, and resting his arms on the back as he talks*):   A package o' money! What sort of a package?

YOUNG NAT: A hundred-dollar package.

Helen, who is standing a little above right center, listens intently.

BLAKE: Who's been in the store today, thet yeh know of?

YOUNG NAT (*Breathlessly*):   Well, there was Mis' Peasley's hired girl, but she   510 didn't take it. Joe Bennett — Dan Nourse — Sam Warren — (*Draws out Sam Warren's name significantly*)

BLAKE (*Quickly*):   Sam Warren! By George! (*Hitting the back of his chair with his hand*) He stole it.

HELEN (*With suppressed anger and shame*):   Oh, Mr. Blake!

BLAKE (*To Uncle Nat, with a significant look*):   Thet's the speckled pullet thet   515 fell into the rain barrel! (*To the others*) He hed to hev a hundred dollars to go out West with. (*All the guests except Captain Ben nod their heads as if to say "That's so, that's bad."*) He tried to borry it o' *me*. I wouldn't lend it to him, an' so he *stole* it. (*The guests all nod "That's it."*)

HELEN (*Coming down swiftly to right center, quietly but determinedly*):   You lie!   520

MARTIN (*Who is still at the head of the table*):   Helen! (*A slight pause*) How dast you call Mr. Blake a liar?

HELEN (*Her voice quivering with indignation*):   How *dare he* call Dr. Warren a
thief?

BLAKE (*A little angrily*):   He *is* a —   525

HELEN (*Fiercely*):   You're a —

MARTIN (*In a low tense tone, approaching her angrily with his hand clenched and partly
lifted*):   Helen, if you say that agin, I swear I'll —

Ann turns around with her back to the table, and starts crying into her apron.

UNCLE NAT (*Who has been standing with his fingers to his lips, trembling, fearful of
Martin's anger, goes between them and lays his hand on Martin's shoulder*):   Martin! Don't do nothin' thet yeh'll be sorry fer all the days o' yer life.

*All the guests have risen, rather embarrassed, but fascinated by this scene, and are
standing at their places around the table. Mrs. Andrews explains to the Squire through
the ear trumpet.*

MARTIN (*Shaking Uncle Nat's hand off*):   Take yer hand off'n me. I tell yeh I   530
won't be browbeat by you, an' I won't hev *her* (*With an angry gesture toward
Helen*) insult my friends.

HELEN (*Her voice trembling with unshed tears of rage, her face flushed with angry excitement*):   He insulted *me*, and if Sam Warren doesn't *thrash* him before
night, it'll be because I can't make him do it, that's all.

*Helen, during this scene, shows she is the modern girl and has the temper inherited from
her father. Mrs. Berry is the old-fashioned, submissive wife, awed and frightened at
Helen's daring to oppose her father.*

BLAKE (*Losing his temper*):   He'll be in the lockup before night, if I can put   535
him there. (*Picks up his hat and cane from the table by the window*)

MARTIN (*Turning and picking up the gun from the corner by the sink, and rushing over
to Blake with it*):   That's the thing to do. Git a warrant fer him an' ef he
raises his hand to yeh — you — *shoot* — him.

*Uncle Nat has been standing at one side, his kind old face white and drawn with an-
guish. He now comes forward and interposes.*

UNCLE NAT: Hol' on, Martin! Uncle Sam'l's mine — an' she wa'n't never
made fer *murderin'* folks. (*Quietly, but with authority, he takes the gun and puts*   540
it back in the corner by the sink)

BLAKE (*Shaking his cane, a very heavy one, threateningly*):   This'll do me!

HELEN (*Dominating the whole situation, in a low voice quivering with contempt, to
Blake*):   Oh! You *coward!* (*Turning to her father*) Father, Sam's going away
today. (*With tremendous authority*) You'd better let him go if you know when
you're well off.

MARTIN (*Taking her tone, tauntingly*):   You'd better not interfere if you know   545
when *you're* well off. I s'pose you'd like to go with him?

HELEN (*Throwing her head proudly in the air*):   Yes — I would.

MARTIN (*Beside himself*):   By God! If I lay my hands on him, I'll kill him.

HELEN: If you dare lay a finger on him, I'll — (*Springs toward Martin as she
speaks, with hands clenched. Uncle Nat catches her and puts his hand over her mouth.
The tension is broken, and Helen bursts into tears, her head resting on Uncle Nat's
breast*)

   *The guests now quietly leave the room, one by one, by the door left. Mrs. Nye takes Mil-
lie's hand and follows the others.*

     *Perley, during all this, has gone on clearing away the table as if nothing had hap-
pened, only occasionally glancing in the direction of Helen and Martin. She now goes
into the woodhouse, taking the platter with the turkey on it, as if to have her dinner
there.*

MARTIN (*Crossing to the door, right, as he speaks*):   You'll find out that I've got   550
something to say about what you'll do and what you won't do! Who
you'll marry and who you won't marry! (*He starts to go out. Young Nat blocks
his way, and he pushes him roughly outside*) Come along, Mr. Blake! (*Blake passes
out ahead of Martin, who turns and gives a last fierce fling at Helen*) You're not of
age yet, my lady. I'll show Sam Warren thet ef my grandfathers *was* mon-   555
keys, they wa'n't thieves. (*He goes out*)

   *As Helen hears their receding footsteps, she runs to the window, and watches them out
of sight. She is in a bitter, angry mood, and tears fill her eyes.*

     Uncle Nat sinks wearily and despondently into a chair, left center.

     *Ann is still standing with her back to the audience, crying into her apron. She is
dazed and broken.*

UNCLE NAT: Well, Ann, it seems es ef our turkey'd come to a sort of an on-
timely *end*, hain't she?

   *Helen leaves the window, takes a cup and saucer from the table, goes to the stove, pours
out a cup of tea and comes down stage, slowly and listlessly, and seats herself left of the
table. She mechanically reaches well across the table for the milk and sugar, stirs the tea,
sips it, and nibbles a crust of bread.*

ANN (*Turning, her voice tremulous with tears*):   Oh, Nathan'l, I'm so 'shamed. I'll
never look a neighbor in the face agin. Twenty-five years married, an'   560
nothin' like this ever happened afore. (*Begins to cry*) To think o' the dinner
all sp'iled after me cookin' myself hoarse over it. (*Starts toward the sitting
room door*) It's enough to provoke a saint out of Heaven; I say, a saint out
of Heaven. (*She goes off into the sitting room*)

UNCLE NAT (*In a quick decisive voice*):   Well, Helen, I guess Sam'd better git 565
right away from here jes' 's quick's he kin.

HELEN (*Frightened, quickly, in an awed whisper*):   Do you think he took the
money, Uncle Nat?

UNCLE NAT (*Rising and going center*):   'Tain't thet, but there'll be trouble ef
him an' Martin comes together. (*He takes off his coat, doubles it up, and throws* 570
*it in a chair, and begins to clear the table, first gathering the napkins, then the knives
and forks, as he talks*)

HELEN: He *has* got a hundred dollars, y'know.

UNCLE NAT (*Continuing with his work at the table*):   I know thet. (*Reluctantly*) I
let him hev the biggest part of it myself.

HELEN (*Amazed*):   You?

UNCLE NAT: It's the money me 'n Martin's ben a-savin' up to buy a tomb- 575
stun fer Mother.

HELEN (*Rising, and striking the table with her fist*):   Then he shan't stir —
one — single — step. (*Determined, her eyes flashing*)

UNCLE NAT (*Dropping the knives and forks he has in his hand and leaning over the
table, appealingly*):   I beg of yeh, Nell — git him away from here. There'll
be murder ef yeh don't! (*Crosses to the right with two chairs*) 580

HELEN: I don't *care*. They *shan't* call him a thief.

UNCLE NAT (*Stops and turns*):   Now — now — Haven't they called 'im
everything they could lay their tongues to a'ready? Don't yeh see thet I
dasn't tell Martin I let Sam hev thet money? (*Puts the chairs down and goes
back to the table*) Don't yeh see thet it won't do fer Martin an' *me* to come 585
together? (*Taps the table with his forefinger*) Things hes gone too fur now.

HELEN: That's so — he's not to go. He's got to pay that money back.

UNCLE NAT (*Under the stress of deep conflict and emotion, half turns away from the table
with the napkins in his hands; then he turns around again and drops the napkins back
on the table*):   Yes, but he's jes' as pig-headed as any of the rest of us, an' if
he knowed the money was Martin's he wouldn't tech a cent of it, not with
a forty-foot pole. He'd want to stay right here an' fight it out — I'm 590
'feared. (*Picks up a chair and goes toward right center with it*)

HELEN (*With quick decision*):   He mustn't do that. I'd go with him if it weren't
for Mother.

UNCLE NAT (*Putting down the chair and, turning around amazed and awed, whispers
quickly*):   Would yeh, Nell? (*He comes back to the table*) 595

HELEN (*Bitterly*):   This'll never be a home to me any more.

UNCLE NAT (*Taking another chair and going to the window*):   It'll never be a hum
to anybody any more, Nell. It's goin' to be all cut up into buildin' lots anyway.

HELEN (*By this time she has worked her way round to the foot of the table. She now goes to Uncle Nat*):   If it weren't for Mother, I wouldn't stay here another minute. (*Appealingly*) Would you blame me, Uncle Nat?   600

UNCLE NAT (*Down left, goes to her and they meet center. He says tenderly*):   How could I blame yeh, Helen? Things'll never be the same here agin, an' Sam'd be all upsot out there athout you — an' you'd never be satisfied here athout him. (*With gentle insinuation*) Now would yeh? He might get goin' to the dogs out there, an' then yeh'd worry — an' blame yerself —   605 an' — (*Persuasively*) I d'know — seems to me — 's ef —

HELEN (*Taking fire from his suggestion, is all eagerness and determination*):   How can we get away? They'd see us on the train.

UNCLE NAT (*Considering*):   Oh, you mustn't go by no train. I'll drive yeh over as far as Ellsworth, an' —   610

At this moment, Captain Ben passes the window. Uncle Nat glances up and sees him, over his shoulder. He is struck by a sudden idea and goes toward the window and calls.

UNCLE NAT: Oh, Cap'n Ben! — Cap'n Ben! (*As Uncle Nat calls, Captain Ben turns and stands leaning on the windowsill, looking into the room*) When did yeh say yeh was a-goin' t' sail?

CAPTAIN BEN: 'Bout an hour'r so — ef it don't come on to blow — looks kinder as ef we *might* git a sou'easter afore mornin'. (*Turns and starts to go,*   615 *scanning the sky*)

UNCLE NAT (*Stopping him again in a voice of hushed anxiety*):   Cap'n Ben! (*Captain Ben again pauses, and looks at Uncle Nat*) Helen an' Sam's ben a-thinkin' o' takin' a trip down the coast fer quite a spell — (*Looks and nods at him significantly*) Would you mind droppin' 'em at St. Andrews's 'r somewheres along there?   620

CAPTAIN BEN (*Taken aback for a moment, then, comprehending the situation, answers with bluff heartiness*):   No, plenty o' room an' plenty o' grub aboard.

UNCLE NAT: Kin they go aboard now an' be stowed away somewheres?

CAPTAIN BEN: Yes, I guess so. Nell, yeh kin come right along with me now in my buggy. (*He leaves the window and continues off, right*)

During this scene, Helen has been standing tense as she begins to realize the significance of Uncle Nat's talk with Captain Ben. Now she turns and darts toward the pegs beside the woodhouse door, where hang her jacket and tam-o'-shanter. She pulls the cap quickly on her head, thrusts her arms into the sleeves of her jacket, and dashes swiftly to the door, right. Uncle Nat checks her flight.

UNCLE NAT: Helen! — Helen!   625

HELEN (*Stopping*):   What is it, Uncle Nat?

There is a moment's pause as they both stand looking at each other. Then Helen comes slowly back.

UNCLE NAT (*Significantly, taking a plain little silver ring off his finger*):   Thet's my mother's weddin' ring. You give it to Sam, an' tell 'im to use it the fust chance he gits. (*He takes her hand, puts the ring into it, and folds her fingers around it*) Now run along. Cap'n Ben's a-waitin'. (*He pushes her gently toward the*   630 *door, and goes quickly to the table as though to hide his emotion*)

Helen walks slowly to the door, looking at the ring. She stops, and a sudden sense of loss seizes her. She turns, and, with a cry, goes back to Uncle Nat.

HELEN: Oh, Uncle Nat, I don't believe I *can* leave you and Mother — not even for him. (*Flings herself into his arms and bursts into tears*)

UNCLE NAT (*Folding her in his arms, his voice shaking with tears*):   There now, don't talk l'k thet — Don't yeh start me a-cryin', 'cause ef yeh do, I'm afeared I won't let yeh go. (*As he talks, he turns and moves with her very slowly*   635 *toward the door. His tone is the soothing one he would use to a child*) Now, see here. Tonight's my watch at the light, an' when you an' Sam an' Cap'n Ben an' all on yeh is a-sailin' down the harbor, a-singin' an' a-laughin' an' enj'yin' yerselves — jes' as yeh git to the light, you look over there an' sez you to Sam, sez you — There's ol' Uncle Nat's eye, sez you — He's a-winkin' an'   640 a-blinkin' an' a-thinkin' of us, sez you.

HELEN: Good-bye, Uncle Nat.

UNCLE NAT: No! We ain't a-goin' t' say good-bye; we're jes' a-goin' to say good afternoon, thet's all! (*Tries to laugh*) P'r'aps I'll come out there and see yeh one o' these days.   645

HELEN (*Who has been comforted by Uncle Nat's words, laughs at him almost joyously through her tears*):   Oh! — Will you, Uncle Nat?

UNCLE NAT (*His face taking on a look of longing, with something of renunciation*):   I said — p'r'aps — (*A pause*) In thet there palace o' yourn yeh used to talk s'much about when yeh was little. Remember when yeh was little how yeh used to say thet when yeh growed up, yeh'd marry a prince an' live in   650 a gol' palace, an' I was to come an' see yeh, an' yeh was to dress me all up in silks, an' satins, an' di'monds, an' velvets —

He half laughs, half cries, kisses her, almost pushes her out of the door, closes the door and bursts into tears, leaning his two arms on the door and burying his face in them.

Curtain

ACT III, SCENE I

"HAVIN' AN UNDERSTANDIN'"

Interior of Berry Lighthouse.

The room is octagonal in shape, with walls of whitewashed stone, and its chief feature is an iron stairway leading to the tower above. This stairway starts well down left, then makes a turn, and extends up and across the back wall. There are small windows at intervals along the stairway. Beneath the stairs, about center, is a small, high, barred window, through which a terrific storm is seen raging. At intervals waves dash against the window.

The entrance to the lighthouse is through a door on the right; it is made of heavy planks, and has a large latch and a heavy, old-fashioned lock. (Note: This door must be framed and set so as to slam with force.)

The whole room has an oily look and smell. On a shelf to the right of the window, about eighteen inches from the floor, is an oil barrel with a brass cock; beside it are some oil cans and a brass gallon measure for filling the lighthouse lamps. There is a brass pan on the floor beneath the barrel to catch the drip. Beside it is a wooden bucket. There is a shears for trimming the lamps on the floor at the foot of the stairway, and near it lies a coil of life-saving rope. A ship's glass, a sou'wester, an oilskin coat, and a pair of oilskin overalls hang on pegs on the wall, left. Leaning against the wall are oars and a boat hook. Several unlighted lanterns are standing about the floor.

The light from above shines down on the room.

At the rise of the curtain rain is heard falling in torrents outside. The wind howls, lightning flashes, and thunder crashes at intervals.

Uncle Nat is discovered down left sweeping the floor. He has the dirt in a little heap and is getting it into a shovel with a broom. His actions are mechanical and his manner is preoccupied. He has on his working clothes and his trousers are tucked into high boots.

Martin enters hurriedly from the right. He wears oilskins and carries a lighted lantern. He is pale and excited. As he opens the door, the rain, wind, and thunder can be heard outside. He slams the door behind him; puts the lantern on the floor, right; and stands a picture of excited anger.

MARTIN (*Standing down right*):   Helen's gone!

UNCLE NAT (*Who has looked up over his shoulder as Martin entered, and then immediately resumed his work, quietly says*):   Y-e-s.

MARTIN: Along with Sam Warren. (*Uncle Nat looks up, concludes not to speak and continues his work*) Did you know she was a-goin'?

UNCLE NAT (*Without looking up*):   Yeh.

MARTIN: Why didn't yeh tell me?

UNCLE NAT (*Has got all the dirt on the shovel by this time; now he empties it into the bucket, right, sweeping off the shovel so that no dust will remain on it. He speaks as he does this*):   'Cause yeh didn't desarve to be told!

5

MARTIN (*Striking a clenched fist against his open palm*):   I'm her father, ain't I?

UNCLE NAT (*Drily as he hangs the shovel against the wall*):   Yeh didn't act's ef yeh was, today.

MARTIN (*Who is still standing down right*):   Then yeh blame me?

UNCLE NAT (*Quietly*):   Well, I ain't a-goin' to lie about it, Martin. (*He hangs up the broom*)

MARTIN: An' yeh uphold her?

UNCLE NAT: Yeh didn't know your own child, Martin thet's all. Ef yeh hed yeh'd 'a' knowed thet yeh might jest's well 'a' stuck thet there gaft (*Points to the boat hook*) inter her heart as to hev said what yeh did 'bout Sam Warren. (*He knocks on the oil barrel to see how much it contains*)

MARTIN (*With concentrated bitterness*):   He's a thief.

UNCLE NAT: Tut! Tut! Tut! He ain't. An' you know it jes' as well 's I do. (*He takes up the pan from beneath the barrel, pours the drippings into an oil can, wipes the pan with a bunch of waste, then wipes the cock of the barrel*) Yeh unly said it 'cos yeh was crazy, crazier'n a loon. I knowed she wouldn't stay here long after thet. Yeh see, she ain't me, Martin — she's young, an' — (*Slight pause*)

MARTIN: Where's Tim?

UNCLE NAT: Tim went to Ells'orth this evenin', hain't got back yit.

MARTIN: How'd they go?

UNCLE NAT: 'Long o' the mail. (*Crosses to the window, wipes the pane and peers out at the storm*)

MARTIN: I said how'd *they* go?

UNCLE NAT: Oh! Cap'n Ben took 'em in the "Liddy Ann."

MARTIN (*Still standing right*):   What time'd they start?

UNCLE NAT (*Up center near the window*):   Fust o' the ebb.

MARTIN (*Slowly and with hate*):   I hope they sink afore ever they pass the light.

UNCLE NAT (*Quietly, turning and looking at Martin*):   I wouldn't say thet if I was you, Martin — (*There is a brilliant flash of lightning followed by a loud crash of thunder. Uncle Nat nods toward the window, indicating the storm, and adds*) You mought git yer wish.

MARTIN (*As before*):   I mean ev'ry word I say. She's *disgraced* me.

UNCLE NAT (*Never losing his tone of patient gentleness*):   You've disgraced yourself, Martin, I guess. (*He is wiping the things on the bench with the waste*)

MARTIN (*Slowly, through his teeth*):   Be they married?

UNCLE NAT: No!

MARTIN (*With a sneer*):   Humph!

UNCLE NAT: Not — yit.

MARTIN (*Bitterly*):   An' never will be.

UNCLE NAT (*With quiet confidence; he is down left*):   Oh yes, they will. (*Thunder*   45
and lightning) Ef they ever live to git to any place. Helen ain't a-goin' to
forgit thet she's got a mother an' sisters — an' —

MARTIN (*Going to him left, and laughing derisively*):   You're tryin' to make me
believe 'twas me that made her go — d'ye think I'm blind? She went
'cause she hed to go to hide suthin' wuss from her mother 'n me; she went   50
'cause she couldn't 'a' held up 'r head much longer here — she's —

UNCLE NAT (*Dropping his work and turning on him and for the first time showing deep
feeling*):   Martin, don't yeh dare say it! Fer ef yeh do, I swear I'll strangle
yeh right where yeh stand. (*The light from the tower grows dim*)

Note: This must be worked very gradually.

MARTIN (*Stubbornly standing his ground*):   It's true an' you know it. Thet's why
yeh hurried 'em away.   55

UNCLE NAT (*Making a movement as though to spring at Martin's throat, shrieks
hoarsely*):   Martin, you've got to take thet back! (*The light in the tower flick-
ers and goes almost out. There is the distant sound of a ship's gun*)

UNCLE NAT (*With a sudden change of manner, in a quick, startled voice, as he glances up
at the light*):   Good land, what's the matter with the light? (*He crosses down
right, and picks up the lighted lantern which Martin placed there on his entrance,
speaking as he does so*) Tim's fergot to trim thet lamp, sure's you're born.
(*Lantern in hand, he turns to go up the stairs. At the same moment Martin seizes the
boat hook, and stands in front of the stairs, barring Uncle Nat's way*)

MARTIN (*Hoarsely, but determined*):   Yeh shan't go up them stairs.

UNCLE NAT (*Paralyzed with horror*):   Martin!   60

The ship's gun is heard again; it is nearer this time.

MARTIN (*In cold and measured tones*):   I say yeh shan't go up them stairs.

Again the gun sounds outside.

UNCLE NAT (*Almost beside himself*):   Why, Martin! — Thet's the "Liddy
Ann"! (*The gun is heard once more*) Thet's her gun!

MARTIN (*Stolid, quiet, intense*):   I know it.

UNCLE NAT (*With a cry of protest and unbelief*):   She'll go to pieces on the reef!   65

MARTIN (*Grimly*):   Let her go.

UNCLE NAT (*Half crazed*):   Yes — but — Helen'll go with 'er! (*He starts for the
stairs*)

MARTIN (*Stopping him*):   Keep away, Nathan'l. I tell yeh thet light ain't
a-goin' to be lit.

UNCLE NAT (*Frantically pleading, his voice broken with emotion*):   Martin, f'r   70
God's sake, list'n to *me!*

MARTIN (*Doggedly*):   I won't listen to nothin'.

UNCLE NAT (*Walking firmly over to him, speaking as he does so*):   You've *got* to listen. (*Martin makes an angry movement*) I say — you've got to listen! We've
got to hev an understandin' right here and now. (*Martin submits sullenly, and*   75
*Uncle Nat continues to talk in hurried, nervous tones, pacing up and down the space
between Martin and the door, like a caged lion, rolling and unrolling the sleeves of his
red flannel shirt*) I've ben playin' secon' fiddle to you long enough, Martin
Berry, ever sence yeh was born. When yeh was a baby I walked the floor
with yeh, an' sung yeh t' sleep night after night. At school I fit yer battles
fer yeh, an' once I saved yer life.

The gun is heard outside.

MARTIN: Yeh needn't throw thet in my face.   80

UNCLE NAT: I hain't a-throwin' it in yer face. I only want yeh not to forgit
to remember it, thet's all. (*He goes to the window and peers out*)

MARTIN (*Doggedly*):   I know all about thet, I tell yeh.

UNCLE NAT: Do yeh? Well, then I'll tell yeh somethin' yeh didn't know.
(*Walks over and deliberately faces him, and says emphatically*) Did you ever know   85
thet I might 'a' married your wife Ann?

MARTIN (*Raising the boat hook, making a step toward him, white with rage, almost
shrieks*):   W-h-a-t?

UNCLE NAT (*Hurried, tense, and almost hysterical*):   Hol' on — I ain't through
yit. I thought more o' her than ever a miser did o' money. But when I see
thet you liked her too — I jes' went off t' the war — an' I let yeh hev her!   90
(*Taps Martin's chest with his forefinger*) An' thet's sumpthin' yeh didn't know
all about — wa'n't it, Martin Berry? (*The gun is heard outside*) But thet's neither here nor there — her child is out there — my child by rights! (*With
sudden sublime conviction, almost heaven-inspired*) Martin, thet light hez got to
be lit! (*With an angry snarl*) I give yeh the mother, but I'm damned ef I'm   95
a-goin' to let yeh murder the child! Come away from them stairs, Martin — come away from them stairs, I say!

*Uncle Nat seizes Martin, and the two men have a quick struggle. Then Uncle Nat with
almost superhuman strength throws Martin the whole length of the room. Martin is
dazed; he reels and staggers like a drunken man toward the door by which he entered,
and blindly gropes his way out into the storm.*

   *Uncle Nat seizes the lantern and starts to crawl up the stairs. It is hard work to
climb them; the excitement has been too much for him. He gets up a few steps, then slips
down again; he crawls up again on hands and knees, and once more slips down. He
makes still another effort, falters, staggers, and, with a heartbreaking cry, falls and rolls
down the stairs.*

UNCLE NAT: God help me! I hain't got the strength!

The thunder crashes, the sea roars, the lightning flashes.
The stage darkens as the light above goes completely out.

SCENE II

"THE 'LIDDY ANN' IN A SOU'EASTER"

Exterior of Berry Lighthouse.

NOTE: *The storm noises are well worked up before the scene opens. The stage is completely dark, as is the front of the theatre.*

An expanse of wild, storm-tossed waves, with the lighthouse, a dark, shadowy bulk, rising from the rocky coast on the left. The rain is pouring in torrents, the thunder roars, the lightning flashes. The boom of a ship's gun is heard above the din of the storm, and in the darkness, the "Liddy Ann," sloop-rigged and under reefed jib, makes her way slowly through the heavy seas, from right to left. She is off her course and perilously near the rocks. At intervals her gun booms and she sends up distress signals. The figures of Captain Ben, Dave Burgess, Gabe Kilpatrick, and Bill Hodgekins, as well as Sam and Helen, can be dimly discerned on board. The shouts of Captain Ben giving orders, and the replies of the crew are drowned by the noise of the storm.

For a few moments the "Liddy Ann" tosses helplessly in the darkness. Then a tiny light appears in the lowest window of the lighthouse. For a second it wavers, then slowly it rises from window to window, as Uncle Nat climbs the stairs to the tower. In another moment the light in the tower blazes forth, showing the "Liddy Ann" her course. A shout of relief goes up from those on the boat, and the "Liddy Ann" makes her way safely past the rocks.

ACT IV

"ME AN' THE CHILDREN"

The scene is the same as in Act II. It is fifteen months later.

Snow is falling heavily outside. The wind is howling; a little drift of snow can be seen on the window sash. A fire burns briskly in the stove and everything has the appearance of the day's work being over. The leaves of the table are folded, and a red checked cloth covers the table on which is a lighted lamp. The tea kettle is singing on the fire. Uncle Nat's gun is in its place in the corner by the sink, and his old army coat and cap are hanging on the pegs under the stairs, as in Act II. There is a large rocking chair up right, and a small one stands above the table, left. At the rise of the curtain, Young Nat is seated reading a book at the upper end of the table; he now wears long trousers instead of knickerbockers. From time to time he turns a page but instantly resumes his position to preserve the idea that he is very intent on the story before him. His elbows are resting on the table at either side of the book and his head is supported by both hands.

Martin is seated on a chair, which is tilted back against the wall below the door, right. On his knees lies a blueprint map of his farm, which has been surveyed and laid off in lots. He is very dejected and in deep thought. Without realizing it, he is grieving over the absence of his daughter, filled with bitter remorse for having driven her out of her home.

Ann is sitting at the right of the table, mending stockings. She wears a warm-colored woolen dress, with a white embroidered collar, and a crisp white apron.

Uncle Nat and Perley are preparing the Children for bed. Uncle Nat is seated, center, and Perley stands beside him. Uncle Nat is just finishing buttoning up Millie's nightdress, while Perley is helping Mary.

The Children all have nightdresses and worsted slippers on, and their clothes are lying in little heaps, one in front of each child, as though they had just stepped out of them. Millie's hair is in curl papers. Mary's hair is braided and tied. The children's night-dresses are made of Canton flannel, with legs and arms, covering them from the neck to the ankles, and they button at the back, Mary's and Bob's straight up and down, and Millie's with a little fall behind to let down.

Uncle Nat, Perley, and the Children are having a great deal of fun as the curtain goes up.

YOUNG NAT (*Looking up from his book, as though continuing a conversation*): I tell yeh there ain't no Santy Claus! It's y'r father and mother!

MILLIE: They is too a Santy Claus, ain't they, Uncle Nat?

UNCLE NAT: Of course there is. See here, Nat, you jest read your book. When a boy gits too big to know there ain't no Santy Claus, he ought to   5 know enough to keep his thumb out'n the Christmas puddin'.

Young Nat laughs and resumes his reading.

MILLIE: Did yeh ever see him, Uncle Nat?

UNCLE NAT: See'm? Yes, sir, I seen him — lots o' times.

BOB (*Smiling*): When was it, Uncle Nat? (*The Children surround Uncle Nat, scenting a story*)

UNCLE NAT: It was a g-r-e-a-t many years ago, when I was a little boy, not   10 near so big's as you be, Bob.

MILLIE: Was you ever as big as Bob?

UNCLE NAT: Yes, sir, an' bigger. I was as big as you be once, an' once I was as little as Mis' Pearce's new baby. (*The Children all laugh*)

MILLIE: An' didn't have no more hair on yer head?   15

UNCLE NAT (*Chuckling*): I hain't got much more now. (*The Children all laugh*)

ANN (*Looking up from her mending*): Now young uns, hang up yer stockin's an' go to bed, I say go to bed. (*The Children, all excitement, prepare to hang up their stockings*)

BOB: I'm goin' to hang up my pants.

UNCLE NAT: You give me a piece of string an' I'll tie up one leg an' you tie   20
up t'other, an' thet way we'll get done quicker. (*Bob ties up one leg, Uncle Nat the other*)

MILLIE (*Watching enviously*):   I wish I wore pants.

UNCLE NAT: Do yeh, Millie? Well yeh may yit afore yeh die. Don't you get
discouraged. Things is comin' your way mighty fast. I tell you what you
do. You give me yer petticoat and I'll tie up the skirt and make as good a   25
bag as Bob's pants. That'll beat yer stockin's.

The Children all agree to this enthusiastically.

ANN (*While Uncle Nat is busy tying Millie's petticoat*):   Mary, ain't you goin' to
hang up yourn?

MARY: Yes, Mother. (*With a smile*) But I'm afeard I won't get anything.

*The Children remove some towels which have been hanging on a line at the back of the
stove, to make room for their stockings.*

UNCLE NAT: Now come on, git some pins. Bob, you get some clothespins.   30
(*They rush to Ann, who gives them pins*) We'll hang Millie in the middle —
jes' like a fiddle. Gimme a couple o' them pins, Mary. Bob, you go over
there — (*Hanging Bob's knickerbockers on the line right*) You got the clothespins, Bob? (*Bob rushes into the woodhouse, and comes back with two clothespins.
Uncle Nat fastens his knickerbockers to the line with them*) Mary, where'll you   35
go? — oh, over here — (*He hangs Mary's stocking, left*)

*During this scene Perley has lighted a candle and stands waiting to show the Children
to bed. Ann watches Uncle Nat and the Children with amused interest.*

UNCLE NAT: Nat, ain't you goin' to hang up?

YOUNG NAT: Naw! 'Cause I know there ain't no Santy Claus.

MILLIE (*Crossing to him and almost crying*):   They is too, Nat Berry — you
won't go to heaven ef you say thet.   40

UNCLE NAT: He won't go to heaven at all ef he don't say his prayers. Come
now, gether up yer duds an' be off to bed.

*The Children all pick up their clothes and shoes. Mary and Bob say "Good night"
and kiss their Uncle Nat, then their father, who is moody, and their mother last. She
kisses them tenderly. They go upstairs. Perley stands at the foot of the stairs, lighting
them up.*

MILLIE (*To Uncle Nat, who picks her up in his arms, clothes and all*):   I wish you'd
sleep with me tonight, Uncle Nat.

UNCLE NAT: Oh! My suz! I couldn't git inter *your* bed — be yeh skeered?   45

MILLIE: Jes' a 'ittle teeny might. (*Hides her head in his neck*)

UNCLE NAT: No, yeh ain't nuther. Yeh jes' want t' git me to try to git my long legs inter thet trundle bed o' yourn (*Puts her down*) and then kick me out on the floor like yeh did las' Sunday mornin'. But yeh ain't a-goin' to do it tomorry mornin'. (*Spanks her playfully*) Go 'long with yeh, yeh little   50 hypocrite.

MILLIE (*Goes over and stands by her father demurely, with her clothes under her arm*): Good night, Papa. (*Martin picks her up by her elbows, takes her in his arms, and kisses her, quite tenderly, and unconsciously lets the map fall to the floor, where it lies unobserved. Then he sets Millie down and becomes once more lost in his thoughts. Millie moves a few steps away from Martin, then turns and looks at him and says softly and shyly*) I wish you a Merry Kiss'mus. (*Martin makes no response, and Millie turns to Uncle Nat lingeringly, as though loth to go to bed*) I wish it was   55 mornin' so's I could see what's in my petticoat.

UNCLE NAT (*Dogmatically*):   Oh! Yeh do — do yeh? Tell yeh what yeh do, Millie. Yeh go to bed an' sleep till mornin' and then t'will be mornin' in the mornin'.

MILLIE (*Going over to her mother*):   Good night, Mama. (*Kisses her*)

ANN: Good night, I say good night. (*Bends over and kisses her tenderly*)   60

MILLIE (*Full of Old Nick*):   Good night, Uncle Nat. (*Going to him*)

UNCLE NAT: Good night.

MILLIE: Sleep tight.

UNCLE NAT: Go t' bed, yeh little baggage yeh! Be yeh going to bed 'r not? (*Shoos her away*)

MILLIE (*Goes to the foot of stairs, and stops suddenly*):   Oh! Uncle Nat?   65

UNCLE NAT: What is it?

MILLIE (*In a mysterious whisper*):   Look what's behind yeh!

UNCLE NAT (*Entering into her play*):   Oh, I'm skeered to look — what is it?

MILLIE (*In the same manner*):   Santy Claus!

UNCLE NAT (*Pretending to be frightened, jumps*):   Where? (*Millie laughs*) Ain't   70 yeh 'shamed to skeer me like that — I've a good mind to — (*He runs after her, she runs and laughs*)

MILLIE: Yeh can't ketch me! (*Laughs and runs around the table. Bob and Mary appear at the top of the stairs laughing and say "Run, Millie, quick, Millie!" Uncle Nat pretends he can't catch Millie*)

UNCLE NAT (*At last catching Millie by the waist of her nightdress at the back, and carrying her as he would a carpet bag. She laughs very heartily all through the scene*): Now, my young lady, I've got yeh and I'll see whether yeh'll got to bed or not! (*Carries her upstairs triumphantly, followed by Perley with the candle. He is heard talking all the way up the stairs; Millie is laughing*) I bet I'll put yeh to   75 bed — or I'll know the reason why. (*Uncle Nat, Perley, and the Children go off through the door at the top of the stairs, and their voices die away in the distance*)

ANN (*Calling after them*):   I swan, Nathan'l, you're wuss 'n the young uns —
I say wuss 'n the young uns! (*Gets up and goes to the window and looks out at the
storm*) Mussy on me, what a night! I pity anybody thet's got to be out on
sech a night as this. (*She turns from the window, and notices Martin, who sits*   80
brooding) Martin, ain't you well — I say ain't you well?

MARTIN (*Gloomily, not crossly*):   Oh yes, I s'pose I'm well enough.

ANN (*Crosses to him and smooths his hair*):   Yeh worry too much — 'tain't a mite
o' use to worry. I wish you'd take some o' thet pikrey — I know it'd do you
good — I say I know it'd do you good.   85

MARTIN: I d'want n-o — pik-rey. Pikrey won't do me no good.

ANN (*Goes back to the table and resumes her work*):   Thet's jes' what Cap'n Ben
Hutchins said last spring. But Liddy Ann managed to git some on't inter
his vittels right along athout his knowin' of it an' it cured him. He was
mad's a hornet when he found it out. I've half a mind to try it — I say to   90
try it.

MARTIN (*In the same manner*):   Don't you put no pikrey inter my vittels if you
know when you're well off.

ANN (*Gently, with placid confidence and assurance*):   Well, Martin, jes' as soon as
you sell a few o' them lots yeh got laid off, — yeh said yeh was goin' to   95
sell a couple a hundred of 'em in the spring, didn't yeh? I say didn't yeh?
(*Absorbed in her mending*)

MARTIN (*As if evading the question*):   I said I *hoped* I'd sell some on 'em in the
spring.

ANN (*Gently*):   Well I sh'd hope so, now thet you've cut the farm all up inter
griddle cakes. Well soon's yeh do — I'm goin' to hev yeh go up t' Boston   100
an' see a *reel* doctor. Not but what Dr. Leonard's good enough, but now
thet we're goin' to get rich, we kin afford a little better one. You ain't right
an' I know it — I say, an' I know it. (*There is a tremendous burst of laughter from
upstairs. Then Uncle Nat comes flying down, followed by all the clothes, shoes, etc. the
Children had carried up. He half falls, and lands sitting on the bottom step. The Children all appear at the top of the stairs with Perley, laughing. Martin jumps. Ann gives
a scream and rises*) Mussy on me — I tho't 'twas an earthquake! I say an
earthquake! What in time's the matter with yeh?   105

UNCLE NAT (*Looking up with an apologetic air*):   Me'n the children hevin' a
little fun, thet's all.

ANN: I should think yeh was. (*She crosses over to the stairs and calls up to the Children*) Ef I come up there 'th my slipper I'll give you suthin' to cut up
about. Go to bed this minute, every man jack o' yeh, an' don't let me hear   110
another word out o' yeh this night. (*As Ann speaks there is a dead silence and the
Children all sneak away on tiptoe*) Perley, come and git these duds. I say git
these duds. (*Perley comes down and gathers up the clothes and goes off with them up-*

stairs. Ann sits down to her darning again, and for the first time observes Young Nat) Nat Berry, ben't you goin' to bed tonight?

YOUNG NAT (*Absorbed in his book; without looking up*):   Jes's soon's I finish this 115 chapter. The Black Ranger's got the girl in his power an' Walter Danforth's on his trail.

ANN: Le'see. (*She seizes the book and becomes absorbed in it. Young Nat thrums on the table; he is impatient, but polite; finally he falls into a reverie over what he has been reading*)

During the talk between Young Nat and his mother, Uncle Nat slowly rises from the stairs. Now he goes up stage and peers out of the window, speaking as he does so.

UNCLE NAT: By George — we'll hev sleighin' tomorry an' *no* mistake, ef this keeps on! (*He comes down stage and addresses the rest of the speech directly to* 120 *Martin, who pays no attention to him. Uncle Nat takes a chair and sits a little to the right of center. He lifts his left leg with his hands to cross it over his right, but a rheumatic twinge stops him. He tries a second time, and succeeds in crossing his legs; his hands are clasped over his knee. His half-furtive glances at Martin, now and then, are full of affection and sympathy. The desire to engage his brother's attention is the persistent note of his mood, and Martin's rebuffs only act as a stimulus to his efforts. Now he looks expectantly at Martin, who continues to ignore him. Then he becomes interested in his shoe as he detects a broken place in it. He examines it carefully, and runs his finger over it. There is a slight pause and again he resumes his efforts to break down his brother's sullen resentment. There is an intimate tone in his voice as he remarks*) I hain't seen sech a storm — not sence I d'know when. Not sence thet *big* snowstorm we had 'way back in '59. (*He looks at Martin's blank face as if for confirmation, but there is no response*) Thet *was* a snowstorm! Couldn't see no fences n'r nothin'. Mail didn't git along here fer more'n a week. (*He looks* 125 *at Martin as before. The same forbidding mask meets his inviting smile. He shakes his foot meditatively as if to gain sympathy from it; then he gives a long sigh*) Ol' Sam Hutchins was a-haulin' wood, an' got snowed in, an' when they dug him out he was friz stiffer'n a poker, a-settin' right on his lud. (*A pause. He steals a quick, inquiring glance at his brother's immobile face, then with the manner of one who finds himself in pleasant company, he remarks with fine unction*) I kinder like to see snow on Christmas. It kinder — I d'know — seems kinder sorter 130 more Christmassier — somehow. (*He gives another glance at the unresponsive Martin, then he rises. He leans heavily on his right foot, then he moves the foot up and down, his shoe creaking loudly as he does so. He goes up to the window and looks out once more at the storm*) Phew! Ain't she a-comin' down! The ol' woman up in the sky's pluckin' her geese tonight fur all she's worth an' no mistake. (*He comes down, sees the map Martin has dropped, and picks it up. He handles it as though it were something precious. He looks at it a moment, and then bends his eyes upon his brother in a fine pride, as having in this map achieved a rare and wonderful thing. Then he seats himself in the same chair as before and looks over the map)* Treemont Str — eet. (*Tracing the map with his forefinger*) Corn — hill Str — eet. (*With a glance of pride at Martin*) Wash — in' — ton Str — eet. (*There is* 135 *a long pause, then Uncle Nat glances about the room*) 'Y George, Washin'ton Street's a-goin' to run right straight through the kitchen here, ain't she? (*He looks at Martin, who, for the first time meets Uncle Nat's eye, and shifts uneasily in his chair*) Haw — thorne Av — en — oo. (*He traces the map with his forefinger. Martin casts impatient furtive glances at him from under his eyebrows; then he gets up and goes toward Uncle Nat*) Hawthorne Avenoo begins at the northeast end o' the ol' barn an' runs due east to — 140

MARTIN (*Quietly taking the map from him, folding it up and putting it in the breast pocket of his coat*):   Ef you hain't got nuthin' better t' do than to set there a-devilin' me, I'd advise you to go to bed. (*He returns to his chair and lapses into his former mood*)

Uncle Nat and Ann exchange glances of wonderment and pleasure at the thought of Martin's having spoken to Uncle Nat. It is a big moment for them. Ann catches her breath and a look of surprise and delight crosses her face. She starts to speak, but Uncle Nat motions her to be quiet by putting his right hand over his lips and waving his left hand at her for additional emphasis. Then he rises and takes a few steps toward Martin. His face is illumined and quivers with joy, he speaks feelingly.

UNCLE NAT: Martin — thet's the fust word you've spoke to me in over fifteen months. (*Martin remains stolid and silent. Uncle Nat continues half sadly, half jokingly*) Don't you think I've wore black fer you long enough? (*Wistfully*) 145 Say, Martin, let's you and me shake hands and wish each other Merry Christmas tomorry jes' like we used to — when we was boys together — will yeh?

MARTIN: I don't care nuthin' 'bout Christmas — one day's good another t' me. 150

UNCLE NAT (*Gently*):   'Twa'n't allus so.

MARTIN: Well it's so now. Merry Christmas — Humph! I'd like t'know what I've got to be merry about.

UNCLE NAT: Yeh've got *me* — ef yeh'll hev me —

MARTIN (*Significantly*):   Humph! 155

UNCLE NAT: You've got Ann. (*Martin looks up. Uncle Nat continues quickly as if he should not have said that*) You've got the children.

MARTIN (*Half bitterly*):   Yes, till they git big enough to be some help, then they'll clear out an' leave me as their sister did.

UNCLE NAT (*Very gently*):   Now — now — now — Helen didn't clear out an' 160 leave *you*. She never'd 'a' gone ef you hadn't 'a' — said what yeh said about —

MARTIN (*Murmurs almost inaudibly*): There now.

UNCLE NAT (*Finishing the sentence under his breath*): Sam Warren.

MARTIN: I don't want to git inter no argument 'th you tonight! I know what I done an' I know what *she* done.

UNCLE NAT: Yeh never will let me tell yeh nothin'.

MARTIN: I don't want to *know* nothin' —

UNCLE NAT (*With a quizzical smile*): Well — yeh come pooty nigh a-knowin' of it. I never see a man s' fond o' huggin' a sore thumb 's you be. (*With a complete change of tone*) Will yeh help me to fill the children's stockin's?

MARTIN (*Half softening*): I hain't got nothin' to put in 'em.

UNCLE NAT: Well, I hain't got much, but what I hev got 's a-goin' in. Come, Ma, let's you and me play Santa Claus, then I'll go to bed. (*Ann makes no reply. Uncle Nat sees that she is absorbed in her book, chuckles, and decides to leave her alone. He passes Young Nat, flicking him on the shoulder with his handkerchief as he does so, and says*) Nat, come out in the woodhouse and lend 's a hand here, will yeh?

Uncle Nat goes off into the woodhouse. Young Nat gives his mother an impatient look, then shrugs his shoulders resignedly and follows Uncle Nat off. They return almost immediately, carrying between them a large woodbasket containing a lot of bundles, which they place down center. Uncle Nat sits in the same chair as before, Young Nat kneels at his left, and they begin to undo the presents. There are dolls, slates, picture books, big candy canes, a sleigh, a pair of skates, mittens, comforters, and any quantity of cheap toys, also a new dress pattern. As the things begin to reveal themselves, Martin is interested in spite of himself.

YOUNG NAT (*With a note of triumph in his voice*): I *told* yeh 't was yer father an' mother all the time.

UNCLE NAT (*Continuing with his work*): Did yeh? Well, yeh didn't know's much as yeh thought yeh did, old smarty. It ain't yer father an' mother *this* time — it's yer Uncle Nat, by George! (*They both laugh*)

MARTIN: I hope yeh hain't been a-runnin' yerself in debt agin fer them children.

UNCLE NAT: No, I hain't run in debt this time. I paid spot cash *this time*. Thet's how I got such good bargains. (*Shows a harlequin with a string to make it jump*) Jes' look at thet now fer five cents. (*Pulls the string and laughs*) It's wuth more'n thet to see Millie pull the string jes' once. (*Chuckling*)

MARTIN: I didn't know yeh had any money by yeh.

UNCLE NAT: I hadn't. I got Blake t' cash my pension warrant. (*He says this without making any boast of it*)

MARTIN: An' spent the hull on't on the young uns as usual, I s'pose.

UNCLE NAT (*Still busy with the things; in a matter-of-fact tone*): Yep!

MARTIN: *Eight dollars* on sech foolishness — it's wicked.

UNCLE NAT (*For the first time stopping his work and looking up*): Say, what d'yeh s'pose I stood up to be shot at fer thirteen dollars a month fer, ef it wa'n't t' hev a little fun on my income? Think I'm a-carryin' around this bullet in my shoulder all these years f'r nuthin'? Not much, Johnny Roach! (*Goes back to his work*) 195

MARTIN (*Gently*): Yeh might 'a' bought yerself an overcut —

UNCLE NAT: Overcut — such weather as this? (*Holding up a candy cane*) Not while candy canes is a-sellin' b'low cost. What's the matter with the one I've got?

MARTIN: Thet ol' army cut? It's patched from one end to t'other. 200

UNCLE NAT: Thet makes it all the warmer. (*With humor*) 'Sides, yeh mustn't never despise a man jes' 'cause he wears a ragged cut.

ANN (*Slamming the book shut with a sense of supreme satisfaction*): There! Ef ever a mean, contemptible houn' got his jest deserts thet Black Ranger got his'n — I say thet Black Ranger got his'n. Walter Danforth jes' — 205

YOUNG NAT (*With loud protest*): Oh, *Mother,* don't tell! I want to read it myself. (*Goes back to the table, sits down, and resumes reading*)

ANN: I swan ef I didn't forgit it was Christmas Eve — an' all about the stockin's. Nat Berry — don't you ever bring another one o' them books inside these doors when I've got work to do. (*Jumps up and begins helping Uncle Nat*) Ain't thet a pooty dolly — I say a pooty dolly! 210

They now proceed to fill the Children's clothes, and hang things on the outside of them. There must be enough stuff to pack them. At the same time footsteps are heard on the porch outside, there is a stamping of feet as if to knock off the snow, and Blake enters. The snow drifts in as he opens the door and the wind howls. He is covered with snow and well muffled up. Martin, who has been half interested in the business of the Christmas presents, rises. Ann and Uncle Nat stop in their work. Young Nat looks up from his reading. Uncle Nat takes the empty basket and puts it back in the woodhouse.

BLAKE: Too blizzardy to stop to knock. By George, what a night! I hain't seen such a storm since I dunno when. (*He is about to shake the snow from his clothing when Ann stops him*)

ANN: Don't shake it off on my clean floor, Mr. Blake. Nathan'l, git a broom.

Uncle Nat gets the broom, takes Blake up stage and sweeps the snow from his clothes, as the dialogue continues.

Perley comes downstairs with the lighted candle and puts it on the table. Then she crosses over to help with the presents.

BLAKE: Didn't think I'd ever git here — by George. The snow's waist deep — (*To Uncle Nat*) Thank yeh, thet'll do I guess. 215

UNCLE NAT (*Hanging up the broom*): Set down by the fire an' warm yerself. (*He places a chair for Blake*) Ef yer feet are cold stick 'em in the oven an' toast 'em a bit.

BLAKE: I'll thaw out my back first. (*Stands in front of the stove with his coat tails drawn apart and warms his back. Uncle Nat and Ann resume their work, Perley helping them. Blake observes them a moment in silence*) Well, y're at it I see. (*He watches them with a tinge of sadness in his face*)

UNCLE NAT: Yep! Christmas only comes oncet a year, y'know, in this family.

ANN (*Displaying the dress pattern*): Thet's a-goin' to make Millie an awful pooty dress. Nathan'l, what was thet a yard?

UNCLE NAT: I d'know — I never ask no prices.

ANN (*Contemplating the dress pattern*): Won't Millie be proud o' thet! I'll have it made up jes' 's stylish 's kin be. (*Puts it in Millie's skirt, or beneath it*) I say jes 's stylish 's kin be.

UNCLE NAT: I heerd yeh — I *heerd* yeh —

BLAKE: By George, Martin, I'd give all I'm wuth in the world to hev jes' *one* stockin' a-hangin' in my chimney corner tonight.

ANN: You'd ought t' got married long ago, Mr. Blake.

BLAKE: I never saw but one girl wuth *hevin'* and she wouldn't hev *me*. (*Sighing.*) I'll never git married now.

ANN: It must be kinder lunsome athout no children nor nothin', specially at Christmas. I say at Christmas.

BLAKE: I never noticed how lunsome it was till I see you a-fillin' them stockin's. I've ben s' busy all my life makin' *money* I hain't hed time to git lunsome. Now I'm gittin' old, I begin to see thet p'r'aps I might — (*He shakes off his retrospective mood*) Oh, Martin! (*He sets a chair down stage in front of Martin, sits astride it, and leans his hands on the back. They talk in low tones while Ann, Perley, and Uncle Nat continue their work. Blake's tone now is tense and low*) Did you hear about the Land Company's bustin'?

MARTIN (*Alarmed*): Bustin'? What? When? How? (*He starts to rise. Blake motions him back in his chair and hushes him*)

BLAKE (*As if discharging a disagreeable duty*): Sh! Yes sir, busted cleaner'n a whistle. Opposition fellers done it. They've bought up Lemoine, an' thrown it on the Boston market way down. Got a lot of Boston big bugs goin' to build there soon's the weather breaks.

MARTIN: Then *your* boom's over?

BLAKE: Yes, for five years anyway. (*Apologetically*) Folks ain't a-goin' to come here when they can go to Lemoine for the same money'r less.

MARTIN (*With finality*): An' I'm ruined.

BLAKE (*Really sorry*):   Looks thet way — now — I'm sorry to say.

MARTIN (*Slowly*):   With my farm mortgaged to you for fifteen hundred dollars, an' the money spent in cuttin' it up inter buildin' lots. (*Blake drums on the back of the chair with his fingers. Martin rises as if to spring at him and says between his teeth but in a low tone*) Damn you — I —   255

BLAKE (*Quieting him in the same way as before*):   Hol' on. (*Points to Ann and Uncle Nat*) Yeh don't want them t' know, do yeh?

MARTIN (*Sinking back in his chair and covering his face with his hands*):   No, not tonight, don't tell 'em tonight.

Helen and Sam appear at the window. Helen has a baby in her arms. Uncle Nat looks up, sees them, gives a start.

UNCLE NAT: Oh! My! (*They cross the window and disappear*)   260

ANN: What in time is the matter with you?

Blake looks up, Martin does not stir.

UNCLE NAT: A tech of rheumatiz I guess. (*Rubs his shoulder*)

ANN: La! You sot my heart right in my mouth.

Blake resumes his former attitude. Uncle Nat whispers in Ann's ear. She starts to scream, and he claps his hand over her mouth then he motions her toward the woodhouse door. Ann runs out. Perley comes over to Uncle Nat to find out what is the matter. He whispers to her also; she gives a little scream and he claps his hand over her mouth and cautions her to be quiet. Uncle Nat goes out through the woodhouse door, followed by Perley. All this is unobserved by Blake and Martin.

BLAKE (*In an undertone to Martin; this can just be heard by the audience*):   Don't worry, Martin, mebbe things'll come out all right.   265

Martin shakes his head without looking up.

BLAKE: All yeh've got to do is to keep up the interest — y'know.

MARTIN (*Without looking up*):   Interest — how'm I goin' t' pay interest an' the farm all cut up?

BLAKE: I know, it's goin' to be a tough job. You'll hev to begin all over agin — seed down the avenoos — cut down the shade trees — an' plow   270 up the hotel site.

Enter Uncle Nat from the woodhouse, carrying a baby, and followed by Ann. Martin and Blake are so absorbed in their talk that they do not see them.

MARTIN: I wish you'd ben struck dumb afore ever you come here to set us all by the ears with y'r blame land scheme — I hain't had a minute's peace sence you fust put it inter my head.

BLAKE (*Good-naturedly*):   Thet's right, blame me. *Blame me.*   275

MARTIN (*Flaming up in bitterness*):   Who else *should* I blame? Ef it hadn't 'a' ben fer you, I'd 'a' ben satisfied as I was. (*Uncle Nat comes to center and Ann takes the baby, takes the shawl from around it and hands it back to Uncle Nat, who comes slowly down center*) Helen'd never left hum ef it hadn't 'a' ben fer you — (*Raising his head aloft*) I wish I was dead. I'm ashamed to look my wife an' children in the face. (*Just at this moment he sees Uncle Nat, who has been   280 drawing near, the baby in his arms. Martin rises, and pauses, startled*) What's thet — ?

UNCLE NAT (*Beaming, his voice almost choking with joy*):   Kinder sorter looks like a baby — don't it — ?

MARTIN (*Puzzled*):   Whose is it?   285

UNCLE NAT (*Looking down at the baby and rocking it back and forth in his arms*):   I d'know's I jes know!

MARTIN (*Looks all round the room*):   Where'd it come from?

UNCLE NAT: I got it — out on the doorstep jes' now.

MARTIN: Well, put it right straight back on the doorstep — I ain't the   290 poor-master.

UNCLE NAT: This baby ain't lookin' fer no poorhouse — this baby's goin' to stay right here.

MARTIN: There's too many babies here now.

UNCLE NAT: No there ain't nuther. Yeh can't hev too many babies in a   295 home. (*He crosses and sits in chair center, and rocks the baby in his arms*)

BLAKE (*Hungrily, coming forward*):   Give it to me. By George, I'll take it!

ANN (*Coming down to Martin, and speaking gently, her voice full of tears*):   Martin, won't yeh guess whose baby this is?

MARTIN: I ain't a-guessin' babies.   300

ANN (*Twining her arms around his neck*):   Guess this one, jes' fer me, Martin. Jes' as a sort of a Christmas present.

MARTIN (*Looks at her earnestly, then says softly*):   Taint — Nell's — ?

ANN (*Drops her eyes to the floor, afraid of how he will take her answer*):   Yes — It's poor Nell's.   305

MARTIN (*In a fierce loud whisper*):   Poor Nell's? Yeh don't mean to say thet he didn't marry her?

Uncle Nat draws the baby close to his breast as if to shield it from even that thought.

ANN: Oh yes, Martin, he married her.

MARTIN (*Misinterpreting her words and her action, aghast, slowly, in a loud whisper*):   You don't mean to say she's *dead?*

ANN: No, Martin, she ain't dead.   310

MARTIN (*After a pause*):   Where is she?

ANN (*Points to the woodhouse*): Out there.

*Martin looks from Ann to Uncle Nat, and back to Ann. Then he walks slowly up stage
toward the woodhouse. At the door he pauses, hesitates, and finally says*

MARTIN: Nathan'l — be keerful — don't drop that baby. (*He goes slowly out
through the woodhouse door*)

*Uncle Nat, still seated, continues to rock the baby back and forth. Ann looks down into
the baby's face. Blake goes to the stove and stands with his back to it, and his coat tails
parted behind him, absorbed in thought.*

UNCLE NAT (*As Martin goes out, with quiet, sly humor*): I've held you many a
time an' I never dropped *you*. (*Pause*) Well, Ma, I s'pose you're awful   315
proud 'cause you're a gran'mother. (*Reflectively*) Seems only the day 'afore
yist'day since Nell was a baby herself.

*The woodhouse door opens and Martin enters slowly, leading Helen by the hand. She
looks dazed, but very happy to be back in her home. They are followed by Sam, now a
bearded handsome man who appears to be perfectly happy and gratified that Helen's
wish to bring her baby home has been fulfilled. Sam has returned from the West a prosperous, successful man; they are both well dressed and have an air of achievement. Perley follows Sam into the room, her face beaming with joy. There is a long pause;
everybody's eyes are on Martin and Helen. He leads her proudly and slowly down the
stage before he speaks.*

MARTIN: Nell — my girl — I'm glad to see yeh back, thet's all I got to say.

*It is with difficulty that Martin can get these words out. Tears are in his eyes and voice.
He kisses her. Blake has been standing spellbound, and now he blows his nose to hide his
emotion. Helen creeps into her father's embrace, puts her arms around his neck, and looks
pleadingly first at him and then at Sam, as though to say "Father, haven't you got a
word for Sam?" Martin's gaze follows hers and he sees Sam. Helen draws away a little
and Martin moves toward Sam. Ann goes to Helen and puts her arms about her; both
women are tense, expectantly waiting to see what Martin will do.*

MARTIN (*Making a big effort to conquer his pride*): Sam, I don't b'lieve I acted
jes's a father ought to hev acted towards Nell, an' I didn't treat you quite   320
right I know — I — (*Hesitantly stretches out his hand which Sam takes in a hearty
grasp, and the two men shake hands*)

Ann and Helen, in great relief, embrace each other joyously.

SAM (*In a big warmhearted manner*): Oh! That's all right, Mr. Berry! You
didn't quite understand me, that's all.

MARTIN (*Introspectively*): Thet must 'a' ben it, I didn't understand yeh. (*Then
with a complete change of manner Martin turns briskly to Uncle Nat, who is still*

*seated in the chair nursing the baby, and in an almost boyish manner, says to him with
an air of ownership*) Give me thet baby! 325

*During the scene Helen and Sam go up left center to Young Nat and greet him affec-
tionately. He proudly displays his long trousers. Then they turn to Perley, who stands
above the table and greet her warmly. She helps Helen off with her things, also takes
Sam's hat and coat and hangs them up on the pegs beside the woodhouse door.*

UNCLE NAT (*Imperturbably*):   No sir, this baby goes right straight back on the
doorstep where it come from —

MARTIN: Give me that baby I tell yeh —

UNCLE NAT (*Rocking the baby in his arms*):   No sir! there's too many babies
here now. This ain't no poorhouse. 330

MARTIN: You give me thet baby.

UNCLE NAT (*Getting up and handing him the baby*):   All right — take y'r ol'
baby — I'm durned ef I don't hev a baby o' my own one o' these days —
yeh see ef I don't — an' then I'm durned ef I'll lend her to any of yeh —
(*He goes up stage*)

*During the next scene, Ann goes up stage, pokes the fire, and puts the kettle, which is on
the back of the stove, in one of the front holes, where it at once begins to sing; she bustles
about, gets the teapot and makes some tea. Martin is standing center, holding the baby
in his arms, with Sam on one side and Helen on the other.*

MARTIN (*Looking down at the baby*):   How old is it? 335

HELEN: Three months last Sunday.

MARTIN: Thet so? (*Looking down at it and smiling proudly*) It's a pooty baby. (*A
pause*) What is it?

SAM (*Proudly*):   Boy!

MARTIN: Thet so? (*Glancing up*) H-h-hev — yeh — named him yit? 340

HELEN: Sam calls him Martin.

MARTIN: Thet so! (*Calls to Uncle Nat, full of pride*) Nathan'l, he's a boy an' his
name's Martin.

UNCLE NAT: Oh! Good Lord! I knowed all 'bout thet long ago. (*Sits in the
rocking-chair*)

MARTIN: Thet so — I thought I was tellin' yeh news. 345

UNCLE NAT: Yeh wa'n't tellin' me no news, was he, Nell?

HELEN: No, indeed.

MARTIN: Gimme that rockin' chair.

UNCLE NAT (*Getting up from the rocking chair and placing it in the middle of the stage*):
Give him the rockin' chair — he's a grandfather. He owns the *house* now —

*Martin seats himself in the rocking chair with the baby on his knee. Uncle Nat sits in
the chair down right formerly occupied by Martin.*

ANN (*Bringing the pot of tea and cups and saucers over to the table*):   Here, Hel'n,   350
you an' Sam drink this cup o' tea.

> *Helen and Sam sit down at the table, Sam at the upper end and Helen on his right.*
> *Young Nat is seated on the left of the table. During the preceding scene, Blake has been*
> *hovering on the outskirts of the group, forgotten for the moment by all, profoundly*
> *moved at what is taking place. He now musters up his courage to speak to Sam.*

BLAKE: Dr. Warren! Oh, Dr. Warren!

SAM (*Rises and goes to him*):   Hello, Mr. Blake. Helen, here's Mr. Blake.

HELEN (*Bows pleasantly*):   Why, how do you do, Mr. Blake?

BLAKE: Oh, I'm feeling pretty good for an old man. (*Turning to Sam*) Dr.   355
Warren, I'm awfully ashamed of the part I had in drivin' you away. It was
small potatoes an' few in a hill.

SAM (*With the same hearty manner in which he spoke to Martin*):   Oh, that's all
right, Mr. Blake. You folks around here didn't understand fellows like
me, that's all.   360

BLAKE: Well, I'm ashamed of it all the same. (*He crosses to Helen*) Helen — I
mean Mrs. Warren — will you shake hands with me?

HELEN: Why certainly, Mr. Blake. (*They shake hands*) Oh, by the way, Mr.
Blake, did you ever find out who stole your hundred dollars that time?

> *All listen.*

BLAKE (*Ashamed*):   Well to tell the truth it never *was* stole.   365

ALL: What!

HELEN (*Amazed*):   Never was stolen?

BLAKE: No! We found it stuck away in the back part o' the safe — among
a lot of papers.

YOUNG NAT (*Rising and standing left below the table, half grinning and half ashamed,*
with a sort of bravado):   That was some o' *my* work. I hid it there.   370

HELEN: You — ?

ANN: You — what fer — I say what fer?

YOUNG NAT (*Half crying*):   I wanted to git even with Sam Warren fer pullin'
my ear — I heerd him ask Mr. Blake fer a hundred dollars an' I hid the
package. I was sorry the minute I done it and I'd 'a' told long ago only I   375
was afraid of a lickin'.

ANN: Well, I swan to goodness ef you ain't wuss'n the Black Ranger —
I say wuss'n the Black Ranger! G' long up to bed this minute an' not
a doughnut nor a mouthful o' pie do you git fer a week — I say fer a
week!   380

YOUNG NAT (*Picking up his book, and taking the candle which Perley hands him, cry-*
ing):   I won't stay here after to-morry — you see if I do — I'll go out

West an' be a cowboy 'r somethin' — you see if I don't! (*He stamps upstairs in a rage*)

ANN (*Calling after him*): Gimme thet book — I say gimme thet book!

YOUNG NAT (*At the top of the stairs, throws the book, which almost strikes Perley*): Take yer ol' book! I don't want it! (*He trumps off, banging the door*)

ANN: Perley — put thet book in the fire. (*Perley picks up the book, starts to the* 385 *stove with it, opens it, becomes absorbed in it, backs to the small rocking chair above the table, sits down, and reads it*) Martin Berry, be you a-goin' to let thet boy go out West an' be a cowboy or somethin' — I say or somethin'? (*Her voice rises in an angry shriek*)

UNCLE NAT (*Who is still seated down right*): You set him to milkin' ol' Brindle to-morry — she'll knock all the cowboy out'n him.

They all laugh.

BLAKE: Meanness is like a kickin' gun, ain't it? A feller never knows when 390 it's goin' to knock him over.

MARTIN (*Curiously*): Ef it's a fair question, Sam, where did yeh git the hundred dollars yeh went away with?

SAM (*Pointing to Uncle Nat*): Didn't he ever tell you?

UNCLE NAT: I let him hev ninety-two dollars an' eight cents of it. 395

MARTIN (*Surprised*): Where'd *you* get it?

UNCLE NAT: I borrowed the ninety-two dollars. Borrowed it off'n you an' me an' Mother. I knowed Mother wouldn't mind waitin' a month or two longer an' — it's all paid back long ago, Martin. It's in the ol' bean pot in the pantry there. (*To Blake*) Mr. Blake, thet was the speckled pullet thet 400 fell into the rain barrel thet time.

BLAKE: Well, I don't know as it's goin' to do any good to stand here callin' ourselves hard names. Martin, I wish you'd let me hold thet baby jes' a minute.

Sam leans over to Helen as if to say "Don't let him, he might drop it."

MARTIN: No, *sir* — 405

ANN: Be keerful, you ain't used to handlin' babies, Mr. Blake, I say babies.

BLAKE: I suppose I could learn, same's the rest of yeh, if I had a chance, couldn't I? (*He takes the baby carefully in his arms, and looks lovingly at it*) Mrs. Warren, I hope you won't bias me with the Junior here — I feel's if me an' the Junior was goin' to be great cronies. (*Leans over the baby*) Look here, if 410 they're mean to you here, you jes' come up to Blake's an' yeh can hev all the candy an' apples an' crackers yeh can lug off.

UNCLE NAT (*With concern*): See here, Blake, you mustn't go to feedin' thet baby on green apples up to thet store —

BLAKE (*To Helen, a little wistfully*):   I suppose I can come over an' see him   415
once in a while?

HELEN: Certainly!

BLAKE: Thank yeh. (*He looks at her. Ann comes and takes the baby. A knock is heard at the door, right*)

ANN: Come in — I say, come in.

Enter Gates and Mandy, both muffled up to their chins in worn, ragged garments, and covered with snow. Mandy's eyes instantly fall on the presents hanging by the stove, and throughout the scene she continues to stare wistfully at them.

GATES (*Speaking as he enters*):   How d'do? (*He sees Helen and Sam, and his tone*   420
changes to one of surprise) Why, how' d'do? I'd no idee *you'd* got back. Ef I'd
'a' knowed thet, I'd ben over afore — (*He sees Ann with the baby in her arms*) What's thet?

ANN: A baby — what'd yeh suppose 'twas? (*She crosses down left and seats herself in a low chair by the sitting room door, rocking the baby on her knees. Uncle Nat goes back to his work with the presents*)

GATES (*Confusedly*):   I wa'n't supposin' nothin'. I hadn't heerd any rumors   425
afloat 'bout your havin' — (*The mistake dawns upon the characters, who look from one to the other and burst into a laugh, not sudden, but gradual. Gates is nonplussed*)
Uh — whose is it?

HELEN: Mine.

GATES: *Yourn?* Well, who'd ever 'a' thought o' *your* havin' a baby? I tell yeh
what, Nathan'l, thet West *is* a growin' country an' *no* mistake! (*To Ann*) I   430
jes' come over to see ef I could leave Mandy here a spell tomorry — I got
a job over t' Pearce's thet's *got* to be done tomorry, an' they got measles
over there an' I'm skeered to take'r with me —

ANN: What'n the name o' common sense'd yer want to fetch'r out such a
night's this fur? D'yeh want to kill'r — I say kill'r?   435

GATES: Kill'r? Gosh, I guess *not*. (*He pats Mandy lovingly*) She wouldn't stay
t'hum.

ANN: Lunsome I guess, I say lunsome.

GATES: I guess'o — she's allus lunsome. Seems lunsomer Christmasses
than any other time.   440

ANN: Let'r stay here now. She can sleep with the children, I say with the
children.

GATES: Want to, Mandy? (*She looks up at him, he leans down to her and she whispers in his ear. With an apologetic smile*) Says she'd ruther sleep with me.

ANN: Well, she mustn't be lunsome tomorry — she must come over an'   445
spend this Christmas with us —

UNCLE NAT (*Coming down from the stove, where he has been working with the presents, with a doll which he gives to Mandy*):   Here's a dolly fer yeh, Mandy. This's goin' t'be the jolliest Christmas we've had fer many a year.

MARTIN (*Suddenly remembering*):   An' the last one we'll ever hev in this ol'   450
house.

SAM: The last — I hope not.

HELEN (*At the same time*):   Why, Father, what do you mean?

Uncle Nat looks at Martin in amazement.

MARTIN: My durn land boom's busted.

ANN (*Looking over at him full of sympathy*):   An' thet's what's been a-worryin' of
yeh! Poor Martin, I say poor Martin!   455

All the faces change; all are silent for a moment.

GATES (*To Blake*):   Is thet *so?*

BLAKE (*Earnestly and sympathetically*):   That's 'bout so.

GATES: Then yeh ain't a-goin' t'build thet there Opperry House?

BLAKE: Well — no — not right off — I guess.

GATES: Sorry. I'd like t'seen thet Opperry House. Them plans was beauti-   460
ful. Knocks me out'n a job too — (*Chuckles*) I guess I got 'bout th' unly
farm in the county thet hain't ben surveyed 'r cut up fer sumpthin' 'r
other.

*Uncle Nat places a chair for him, right center. Gates sits with Mandy standing between
his knees. Uncle Nat goes back to his work.*

MARTIN: Hel'n, I'm poorer'n I was the day I come into the world. Blake
owns "Shore Acres" now — or will by spring when his mortgage comes   465
due.

SAM: How much is it mortgaged for, Mr. Berry?

BLAKE: All it's wuth.

ANN: Fifteen hundred dollars!

MARTIN: It'd take me ten years to lift it.   470

GATES (*Shakes his head*):   Yeh couldn't do it in ten year. (*Reflectively*) No *sir* —
fifteen hundred dollars!

*During the above scene Sam has been talking to Helen in a whisper, unheard by the au-
dience.*

SAM: Nell, what d'you say if we mortgage our home and lend the money
to your father?

HELEN (*Delighted*):   Of course — that's the thing to do —   475

SAM: We may lose it —

HELEN: No we won't — and if we do we're young — we'll get another.

SAM: Shall I tell him — ?

HELEN: Yes.

SAM: All right, here goes. (*Aloud*) Father — I mean Mr. Berry — we can   480
help you *some*. We can reduce the principal a little and keep up the interest for you. Nell and I have scraped a little home together out there. We'd
hate to lose it, but we'll borrow what we can on it and —

MARTIN (*Deeply moved*): No — you shan't do thet — let the ol' place go —

SAM: Come out West with us and make a fresh start.   485

HELEN (*Eagerly*): Oh yes, Father — do!

MARTIN: No, I'm 'feared I hain't got spunk enough. I'll stay here. Mother'n the children an' Nathan'l can go ef they've a mind to —

ANN (*Her voice breaking*): Martin Berry, I didn't marry yeh to leave yeh. I'll
stay right here with yeh. We'll live in the lighthouse ef we hev to, I say ef   490
we hev to.

UNCLE NAT (*In a gentle drawl*): Well, ef you think yeh're a-goin' to get red o'
me — yeh're mighty much mistaken. Mother allus told me to watch out
fer yeh, an' now by George thet yeh're gettin' into yer secon' childhood,
I'm a-goin' to do it —   495

SAM: Mr. Blake won't foreclose — will you, Mr. Blake?

BLAKE (*Regretfully*): I'm sorry, but it's out o' my hands. I'm as bad off as
Martin is. I've bought, and mortgaged, and borrowed on everything I
had — I can't realize fifty cents on the dollar. I'm simply land poor. Interest a-eatin' me up, principal a-comin' due — I don't know which way   500
to turn. My lawyers advise me to make an assignment the first o' the year.
Well, I guess I'll be a-joggin' along hum —

UNCLE NAT: What's yer hurry, Mr. Blake?

BLAKE (*With a big sigh*): Well — it's a-gettin' late — an' I don't feel jes' right
somehow — (*He gets into his coat and hat, Uncle Nat helping him*)   505

HELEN: Better let Sam prescribe for you, Mr. Blake.

BLAKE (*Glancing at her and then at the baby, says gently*): He *has* — that's what
ails me I guess.

SAM: I can fetch you around all right, Mr. Blake.

BLAKE (*Hunting in his coat pockets for his gloves, and laughing in an effort to assume his
old, cheery manner*): What with, sugar shot? No, by George, I hain't got t'   510
thet yet — (*He pulls out his gloves, and with them a letter postmarked and stamped,
and addressed to Nathaniel Berry*) Oh, Nathan'l, here's a letter come for you
this evenin'. It's postmarked Washington, D.C. Weather bein' so bad I
thought I'd bring it over.

UNCLE NAT (*Taking letter, mildly surprised and interested*):   Much obleeged, but   515
I dunno who'd write me from Washin'ton.

ANN: The Pres'dent mebbe, wishin' yeh a Merry Christmas.

GATES: Yes! The Pres'dent ginerally wishes everybody a Merry Christmas — specially ef it's a-comin' on election time.

UNCLE NAT (*Turning the letter over and over*):   Nell, would you mind a-readin'   520
this? Your eyes is younger'n mine. (*Gives her the letter*)

HELEN (*Opens the letter and reads it aloud. The letter is written on a letter sheet with
a small printed heading, such as is used by attorneys at law, not a commercial letter-
head*):   "Washington, D.C., December 18, 1892. Nathaniel Berry Es-
quire, Berry, Maine. Sir: Dr. Samuel Warren of Trinidad, Colorado, some
months ago commissioned us to present your claim to back pension. We
are pleased to inform you that our efforts on your behalf have been suc-   525
cessful and that your claim amounting to $1,768.92 has been finally al-
lowed. We have this day written Dr. Warren. Awaiting your further
pleasure, we are, Very truly yours, Higgins and Wells, Attorneys at law."
Oh! Uncle Nat!

There is a general murmur of amazement.

UNCLE NAT (*Who is standing beside Helen*):   Well, I won't tech it. I d'want   530
no back pension, an' I don't want nothin' to do with no durn lawyers. A
pension grabber's next thing to a bounty jumper, an' I'll be jiggered ef I
tech it.

ANN (*Still sitting down left with the baby*):   Why not? I say why not?

UNCLE NAT: 'Cause I never fit fer no back pension. I fit — 'Cause — (*He*   535
*catches Ann's eye and stops. Ann looks at him significantly, and then at Martin, who
sits, the picture of dejection. Uncle Nat glances around at the others, and reads the same
implication in all their eyes. He wavers and finishes lamely*) 'Cause I fit.

ANN: Yeh airned it — didn't yeh? I say yeh airned it?

SAM: You know there's a good deal of difference between earning a pension and grabbing a pension.

GATES: Oh! My — yes — heaps. Seems to me — ef I was you — (*No one*   540
pays any attention to Gates and his voice trails off into silence)

UNCLE NAT: Thet's so — I didn't think o' thet. Le's see — (*His face is illu-*
mined with a rarely beautiful smile) Tomorry's Christmas, ain't it? Ma, I hain't
made you a *reel* Christmas present — not sence the day you was married,
hev I?

ANN (*Smiling at him*):   Thet wa'n't Christmas.   545

UNCLE NAT (*Chuckling*):   Jes' as good — wa'n't it? I'll tell yeh what I'll do —
ef Martin'll make the place over to you — I'll take the back pension.

MARTIN (*Broken and greatly touched by Uncle Nat's generosity*):   I'd know as I've got a right to say either yes or no. I'll do whatever you and Mother wants I should. I hain't got a word to say. 550

UNCLE NAT (*Going to Martin and clapping him on the back*):   Yeh don't need to say another word, Martin, not another blessed word. (*Turning to Helen*) Helen, git me ol' Uncle Sam'l. Say, Martin, Uncle Sam'l's the gal thet won the pension, an' she's the feller thet ought to hev it. (*Helen brings the gun down to Uncle Nat, who is standing center. He takes it and speaks to it affectionately, half crying, half laughing*) Well, ol' gal, yeh've got yer deserts at last. Yeh 555 not only saved the Union, but, by Gosh, yeh've saved this hull family! (*Still holding the gun, Uncle Nat starts to go through the Manual of Arms, while Gates watches him and imitates him*) Attention! (*He comes stiffly to attention. Gates does the same*) Shoulder-r-r Arms! (*He brings the gun to his shoulder. Gates pretends to do the same thing*) Carr-r-r-y Arms! Pre-e-sent Arms!

As Uncle Nat starts to present arms, the gun goes off suddenly. It must be loaded so as to make a great smoke and not too much noise. There is a movement of general excitement and panic. Helen's first thought is for her baby, and she rushes over to Ann and takes it in her arms. Gates picks up Mandy, heels in the air, and head down, and rushes to the door, right, as if to save her anyway. He stands frantically pawing the door in the attempt to find the latch and escape with Mandy out of harm's way, giving frightened little gasps as he does so. As the smoke clears away, the others all gather around Uncle Nat, who explains that the explosion was an accident. They are all excitedly talking and laughing, and completely oblivious of Gates, who, as the panic dies down, comes to his senses and turns his attention to Mandy. She is completely enveloped in her wraps and he has some difficulty in getting her right side up. When he finally discovers her feet, he sets her on the ground, frees her head from its wrappings, smooths her hair, feels her body to assure himself that no bones are broken, kisses her, and croons over her. Uncle Nat, still holding the gun, comes down to him, and starts to explain, but, at his approach Gates has another attack of fright, and seizing Mandy, he starts to back toward the door, waving Uncle Nat away.

UNCLE NAT (*Laughing*):   That's the fust time Uncle Sam'l ever kicked me! 560

GATES (*Putting his fingers in his ears*):   Gosh, that deefened me! (*Then, as if to test his hearing, he cries*) Oh! Oh! Oh!

Everyone laughs. They have all recovered their spirits as readily as they became depressed.

BLAKE (*Who has got to the door by this time*):   Well, good night. (*He goes out.*)

GATES (*Who is still nervous*):   I go your way a piece, Mr. Blake. (*He hurries after Blake, dragging Mandy with him. Uncle Nat shows them out, closes the door and locks it after them*)

ALL (*Calling after them*):   Good night, good night. 565

ANN: Come now, it's bedtime, I say bedtime.

There is a general movement. Uncle Nat puts the gun away, then he turns and begins the task of locking up for the night, plodding slowly and methodically about the room. Perley lights a candle, and goes upstairs and off. Ann lights a candle which she leaves on the table for Uncle Nat, and picks up the lamp. She and Helen move toward the door down left.

HELEN: Yes — I'm pretty tired. Shall we sleep in my old room?

ANN: O' course.

HELEN (*As she goes off left*):   Are all the children well?

ANN (*Following Helen off*):   You'd 'a' thought so if you'd seen'm trainin'   570
around here this evenin' (*Outside*) with Nathan'l.

Sam and Martin come down left, following Ann and Helen. Martin has his arm around Sam's shoulders.

MARTIN: So you're a-doin' well out there, eh Sam?

SAM: First rate. That's the country for a young man.

MARTIN: I s'pose 'tis. Chicago must be a great city.

SAM: A wonderful city. Why don't you come out for the World's Fair?[6] (*He*   575
goes off through the door lower left. Martin pauses at the door, turns, and looks at Uncle Nat)

MARTIN (*In a low voice*):   Nathan'l. (*Uncle Nat looks up*) Yeh never told Ann about that night in the lighthouse — did yeh?

UNCLE NAT (*Coming down a few steps toward him; in a deep whisper*):   I never told her nothin'.

MARTIN (*After a pause*):   She'd ought to 'a' had you. 'Twan't jes' right some-   580
how — (*He goes slowly off, lower left, closing the door*)

Uncle Nat stands looking after Martin, his face lighted up by an inner glow of peace and happiness. His thoughts are reflected in his face, but not a word is spoken. The scene is played in absolute silence.

He sinks into the rocking chair close by with a sigh of content and satisfaction. He settles himself comfortably, with his chin resting in his right hand as he thinks.

UNCLE NAT (*He thinks this*):   Well, everythin's all right again. (*He nods his head approvingly*) I wonder how long Nell 'n' Sam's a-goin' to stay? A month 'r two anyway. (*Then a soft, tender smile creeps slowly into his face at the thought of the baby*) Bless thet baby! I wonder what the young uns'll say in the mornin'?   585
It'll be better'n a circus here when Millie sees thet baby. (*He chuckles softly*

[6] The Chicago World's Columbian Exposition, designed to celebrate the four hundredth anniversary of Christopher Columbus's discovery of America, opened in May of 1893 and closed at the end of October.

at the thought. Then suddenly he scans the door, wondering if he locked it. He rises slowly, easing himself on the arms of the chair, and plods to the door; he tries the lock, then tucks the doormat snugly against the sill to keep the snow from drifting in. Then he goes to the window, rubs the pane to clear the frost from it and peers out) Gracious! What a night! *(He stoops down, and looks up to find the lighthouse beacon. He nods his head)* Ol' Berry's all right — Tim's there. *(As he turns from the window, shrugging his shoulders and shivering a little)* Snow'll be ten foot deep in the mornin'. *(He goes to the stove and sets the kettle back, lifts one of the lids and looks at the fire. A thought strikes him)* By George, it's a-goin' to be pooty hard work to git the ol' farm inter shape again! *(He shuts the damper)* Well, hard work never skeered me — *(He goes to the woodhouse door and fastens the bolt. Coming down to the table he picks up the candle which Ann left there for him and starts to go up the stairs. At the foot he pauses, then he moves down to the door, softly pushes it open, and stands there for a moment looking off. He smiles to himself as he thinks)* I wonder what the young uns'll say in the mornin'? *(For a moment he is lost in thought; his right arm slowly relaxes. Then he turns and starts to climb slowly up the stairs, his heavy footfalls echoing through the empty room. The wind howls outside; the sharp snow tinkles rhythmically upon the windowpane. The stage darkens slightly. He reaches the top of the stairs and goes off, closing the door after him. The stage is left in darkness except for the firelight flickering through the chinks of the stove. The cuckoo clock strikes twelve, and the curtain slowly descends.)*

590

595

FINIS

Secret Service

———————————————— >⥊< ————————————————

Wililam Hooker Gillette (1853–1937) was born into a prominent Hartford, Connecticut, family, the son of an early abolitionist, supporter of the temperance movement, and U.S. Senator. Gillette, who grew up in an atmosphere of learning (though his theatrical leanings were not encouraged), left home at the age of twenty for a career on the stage and became a well-respected and successful actor, often performing in his own plays in parts tailored to suit him. He also became an articulate spokesperson for his cool, understated approach to acting, most fully developed in a lecture published in 1913 as *The Illusion of the First Time in Acting*. As an actor he is remembered for roles in his two most successful plays: the Civil War spy melodrama *Secret Service* (1895), in which he played Thorne/Dumont; and *Sherlock Holmes* (1899), in which he played the title role over thirteen hundred times. Gillette's first full-length play was *The Professor* (1879). Other notable plays include *Esmeralda* (1881), *The Private Secretary* (1884), *Held by the Enemy* (1886), *A Legal Wreck* (1888), *All the Comforts of Home* (1890), *Too Much Johnson* (1894), *Clarice* (1905), and *Electricity* (1910). In 1929–30 Gillette undertook a farewell tour of *Sherlock Holmes*. Shortly after its conclusion in May, he received honorary degrees from Columbia and Yale universities and Trinity and Dartmouth colleges. Gillette continued acting until 1936, appearing that year in a tour of Austin Strong's *Three Wise Fools*. From 1932–36 he worked on his last play, *The Crown Prince of the Incas*, never completed. A lasting monument to Gillette is the home he designed and built on a hill overlooking the Connecticut River near Hadlyme, Connecticut. Known as Gillette's Castle, this imposing twenty-four-room structure, based on medieval design, is now part of the Gillette State Park and is open to the public.

→ # Secret Service 1895

A romance of the Southern Confederacy

A drama in four acts

First produced in its original form, under the title of *The Secret Service,* at the Broad Street Theatre, Philadelphia, on May 13, 1895, with the following cast:

CAPTAIN RALPH CHALLONER	Maurice Barrymore
MR. BENTON ARRELSFORD	William Harcourt
MAJOR GENERAL RANDOLPH	H. B. Bradley
WILFRED VARNEY	Edwin Arden
DR. HORACE GARNET	R. F. McClannin
HENRY DUMONT	M. L. Alsop
JONAS	T. E. Jackson
LILLIAN VARNEY	Mary Hampton
CAROLINE MITFORD	Odette Tyler
MRS. GENERAL VARNEY	Ida Vernon
MARTHA	Alice Leigh
ELEANOR FAIRFAX	Elaine Eillson
MISS KITTRIDGE	Lulu Hopper
MISS FARRINGTON	Meta Brittain

The production was unsuccessful and was immediately withdrawn. After radical revision, it was produced at the Garrick Theatre, New York, on October 5, 1896, with the following cast:

GENERAL NELSON RANDOLPH	Joseph Brennan
MRS. GENERAL VARNEY	Ida Waterman
EDITH VARNEY	Amy Busby
WILFRED VARNEY	Walter Thomas
CAROLINE MITFORD	Odette Tyler
LEWIS DUMONT/CAPTAIN THORNE	William Gillette
HENRY DUMONT	M. L. Alsop
MR. BENTON ARRELSFORD	Campbell Gollan
MISS KITTRIDGE	Meta Brittain
LIEUTENANT MAXWELL	Francis Neilson
MARTHA	Alice Leigh
JONAS	H. D. James
LIEUTENANT FORAY	William B. Smith

◄ FIGURE 8 *William Gillette in* Secret Service.

LIEUTENANT ALLISON	Louis Duval
SERGEANT WILSON	I. N. Drew
SERGEANT ELLINGTON	Henry Wilton
CORPORAL MATSON	H. A. Murey
CAVALRY ORDERLY	
ARTILLERY ORDERLY	
HOSPITAL MESSENGER	
FIRST WAR DEPT. MESSENGER	
SECOND WAR DEPT. MESSENGER	
THIRD WAR DEPT. MESSENGER	
FOURTH WAR DEPT. MESSENGER	
TELEGRAPH OFFICE MESSENGER A	
TELEGRAPH OFFICE MESSENGER B	
EDDINGER	

SCENE: *An evening in Richmond during the war of the rebellion at a time when the Northern forces were entrenched before the city and endeavoring by all possible means to break down the defenses and capture the Confederate capital. While no special effort has been made in the direction of historical accuracy, the City of Richmond at the time set forth in* Secret Service *was in a state of the utmost excitement and confusion. Wounded and dying were being brought in from the defenses by the car-load. Churches, libraries and public buildings were converted into hospitals. Owing to the scarcity of surgeons and medical attendants women and even young girls assisted at the dressing of wounds and nursed the sufferers day and night. Other women were occupied sewing coarse and heavy sand bags for the strengthening of the fortifications. Strict military discipline was impossible. Courts martial if held at all were composed of any available material, even private citizens serving if necessary. Troops were being hurried in from the South and no careful scrutiny was attempted. This made it possible for many Northern secret service men to enter the city and remain there in various disguises. In the midst of this trouble a brave attempt at gaiety was kept up — chiefly by the young people in a desperate endeavor to distract their minds from the terrible situation. There were dances and "starvation parties," so called because of the necessarily limited fare provided and the booming of the great siege guns often sounded above the strains of a dreamy waltz or the lively beat of a polka.*

ACT I

Drawing-room in General Varney's house — Franklin Street — Richmond. Eight o'clock. Richly furnished. Southern characteristics. Fire-place on left side. Wide doors or arch up left set diagonally open to a front hall. Portieres on these doors or arch to draw, completely closing opening. Stairway seen through these doors or arch, in the hall, at back, ascending from a landing a few steps high back of center of opening, and rise off to the left. Entrance to street off left below stairs. Entrance to dining room and kitchen off right below stairs. Both of these openings are back of double doors or arch up left center. Wide door at center opening to a back parlor which is being used for women who come there to sew and work for hospitals. Two double French windows on right side, one up stage set oblique, and one down, both opening to a wide veranda. Shrubbery, etc., beyond the veranda and vines, etc., on balustrade and posts of veranda — which must be in line of sight for whole house outside the upper of these two windows. Both these windows are "French" extending down to floor, and to open and close on hinges. They also have curtains or draperies which can easily be drawn to cover them. Below window down right a writing desk and chair. Between these windows stand a pedestal and vase of flowers to be knocked over by Thorne in Act IV. Chair near pedestal — chair and cabinet right of center door against wall. Table left of center door against wall with lamp and vase of flowers. Couch down right center. Table and two chairs left center. Chair each side of the fireplace. Hall seat in hall. Pedestal and statue on landing in hall. Dark or nearly dark outside windows with strong moonlight effect. Lights on in hall and in room up center, but not glaring — light in the room itself full on but shaded so that it gives subdued effect. No fire in fireplace. Portieres on both windows closed at rise. Windows closed at rise. As curtain rises low distant boom of cannonading rolls in distance and quiets down — then is heard again. Miss Kittridge, one of the women who is sewing for the hospitals, enters from the center doors. Stops, listens to the sound of cannon — with worried look — crosses to window and looks out. Flashes on her face, then turns and goes toward table at left. She gathers up pieces of cloth and linen rags that are on the table, looks toward window again, then takes them off at center door, closing the door carefully after her. Sounds of a heavy door closing outside left. Enter at door up left Wilfred Varney, a boy of about sixteen — impetuous — Southern — black-eyed — dark hair. He is fairly well dressed, but in a suit that has evidently been worn some time. Dark shade. He comes rapidly into the room looking about. Goes to door up center, opens it a little way and looks off. Closes it. Goes to window. Throws open portieres and windows and looks anxiously off. Red flashes on backing. Distant boom and low thunder of cannon. Enter Martha, a negro servant, coming from door at foot of stairs. Wilfred turning sees her, and crosses toward her.

WILFRED: Where's mother?

MARTHA: She's up staars with Mars Howard sah.

WILFRED: Ah've got to see 'er!

MARTHA: Mars Howard he's putty bad dis ebenin' — Ah dunno's she'd want to leave 'im. — Ah'll go up an' see what she says. (*Exit door up left and up the stairway.*)   5

(*Wilfred left alone, moves restlessly about, especially when low rumble of distant cannon is heard. Effect of passing artillery in the street outside. On hearing it he hurries to the window and looks out, continuing to do so while the sounds of the passing guns, horses and men are heard. While he is at the window Mrs. Varney enters, coming down the stairway and on at door up left. She is quiet, pale, with white or nearly white hair and a rather young face. Her dress is black and though rich, is plain. Not in the least "dressy" or fashionable. In manner she is calm and self-possessed. She pauses and looks at Wilfred a moment. He turns and sees her. Martha follows her down and exits door at foot of stairway.*)

WILFRED (*Goes toward her.*):   Howard isn't worse is he?

MRS. VARNEY: Ah'm afraid so.

WILFRED: Anything Ah can do?

MRS. VARNEY (*Shakes head.*):   No — no. — We can only wait — and hope. (*Wilfred walks away a little as if he could not quite say the thing on his mind.*) Ah'm thankful there's a lull in the cannonading. Do they know why it stopped? (*boom of cannon — a low distant rumble*)

WILFRED: It hasn't stopped altogether — don't you hear?

MRS. VARNEY: Yes, but compared to what it was yesterday — you know it shook the house — and Howard suffered dreadfully!

WILFRED (*Suddenly facing her*):   So did I mother! (*low boom of cannon*)

MRS. VARNEY: You!

WILFRED: When Ah hear those guns and know the fighting's on, it makes me —

MRS. VARNEY (*Goes toward table left center, interrupting quickly.*):   Yes, yes — we all suffered — we all suffered, dear! (*Sits right of table.*)

WILFRED: Mother, Ah want to speak to you! You may not like it but you must listen — you must let me — (*Goes toward her.*)

MRS. VARNEY (*Motioning so that he stops; slight pause. She soon speaks in a low voice. She takes his hand in a motherly way.*):   I know — what it is.

WILFRED: Ah can't stay back here any longer! It's worse than being shot to pieces! Ah can't do it mother! (*Mrs. Varney looks steadily into Wilfred's face but says nothing. Soon she turns away a little as if she felt tears coming into her eyes.*) Why don't you speak?

MRS. VARNEY (*turning to him with a faint attempt to smile*):   Ah don't know what to say.

WILFRED: Say you won't mind if Ah go down there and help 'em!

MRS. VARNEY: It wouldn't be true!

WILFRED: I can't stay here!

MRS. VARNEY: You're so young Wilfred!

WILFRED: No younger than Tom Kittridge — no younger than Ell Stuart — nor cousin Stephen — nor hundreds of the fellows fighting down there! — See mother — they've called for all over nineteen — that was weeks ago! The eighteen call may be out any minute — the next one after that takes me! Do I want to stay back here till they order me out! Ah should think not! (*Walks about, stops and speaks to Mrs. Varney.*) If Ah was hit with a shell an' had to stay it would be different! But Ah can't stand this — Ah can't do it mother!

MRS. VARNEY (*rising and going to him*):   I'll write to your father.

WILFRED: Why that'll take forever! You don't know where his Division is — They change 'em every day! I can't wait for you to write.

MRS. VARNEY (*Shakes head and speaks finally.*):   I couldn't let you go without his   45
consent! You must be patient! (*Wilfred starts slowly toward door with head lowered in disappointment, — but not ill-naturedly. Mrs. Varney looks yearningly after
him a moment as he moves away, then goes toward him.*) Wilfred! (*Wilfred turns
and meets her and she holds him and smooths his hair a little with her hand.*) Don't
feel bad that you have to stay here with your mother a little longer!

WILFRED: Aw — It isn't that!   50

MRS. VARNEY: My darling boy — I know it! You want to fight for your
country — and I'm proud of you! I want my sons to do their duty! But
with your father commanding a brigade at the front and one boy lying
wounded — perhaps mortally — (*Pause — Mrs. Varney moves away a few
steps.*)

WILFRED (*After pause — goes to her.*):   Well you'll write to father tonight,   55
won't you?

MRS. VARNEY: Yes — yes!

(*Door bell is heard ringing in distant part of the house. Wilfred and Mrs. Varney both
listen. Martha crosses outside door up left from right, on her way to open the front door.
Heavy sound of door off left. In a moment she returns and appears at door up left.*)

MARTHA: Hit's one o' de men fum de hossiple ma'am. (*Wilfred hurries to door
and exits to see the Messenger.*)

MRS. VARNEY: We've just sent all the bandages we have.

MARTHA: He says de's all used up, an' two more trains juss come in   60
crowded full o' wounded sojers — an' mos' all of 'em dreful bad!

MRS. VARNEY: Is Miss Kittridge here yet?

MARTHA: Yaas'm.

MRS. VARNEY: Ask her if they've got enough to send. Even if it's only a
little, let them have it. What they need most is bandages.   65

MARTHA (*crossing toward door up center*):   Yaas'm. (*Exits. Mrs. Varney goes toward
the door up left, stops near the door.*)

MRS. VARNEY: Oh — (*beckoning*) Come in. (*She moves toward center. Messenger
appears at the door. He is a crippled soldier in battered Confederate uniform. His arm
is in a sling.*) What hospital did you come from?

MESSENGER (*Remains up near door left.*):   The Winder ma'am.

MRS. VARNEY: Have you been to St. Paul's? You know the ladies are work-   70
ing there tonight.

MESSENGER: Yes — but they hain't a-workin' for the hospitals, ma'am —
they're making sandbags for the fortifications.

MRS. VARNEY: Well, I hope we can give you something.

MISS KITTRIDGE (*Enters at door up center bringing a small bundle of lint, etc.*):
This is all there is now. (*Hands package to the Messenger.*) If you'll come back   75

in an hour, we'll have more for you. (*Messenger takes package and exits door left. Sound of front door closing outside.*) We're all going to stay tonight, Miss Varney. There's so many more wounded come in it won't do to stop now.

MRS. VARNEY (*on sofa*):   No, no — we mustn't stop.

MISS KITTRIDGE: Is — is your son — is there any change?   80

MRS. VARNEY: Ah'm afraid the fever's increasing.

MISS KITTRIDGE: Has the Surgeon seen him this evening?

MRS. VARNEY: No — oh, no! (*shaking her head*) We couldn't ask him to come twice — with so many waiting for him at the hospital.

MISS KITTRIDGE: But they couldn't refuse you Mrs. Varney! There's that   85
man going right back to the hospital! I'll call him and send word that — (*starting toward the door*)

MRS. VARNEY: No, no — I can't let you! (*Rises.*)

MISS KITTRIDGE: Not for — your own son?

MRS. VARNEY: Think how many sons must be entirely neglected to visit
mine twice! (*Sound of door outside left. Enter Edith Varney, a light quick entrance,*   90
coming from outside — hat in hand as if just taking it off as she enters.) Edith dear!
How late you are! You must be tired out!

EDITH: Ah'm not tired at all! Besides, I haven't been at the hospital all day.
Good-bye, Miss Kittridge! I want to tell Mama something.

MISS KITTRIDGE: O dear! I'll get out of hearing right quick!   (*Exit.*)   95

EDITH (*up to door lightly and calling after Kittridge*):   I hope you don't mind.

MISS KITTRIDGE: Mercy, no!

(*Edith closes the door and goes to Mrs. Varney, taking her down stage to chair right of
table. Mrs. Varney sits in chair and Edith on stool close to her in front of table.*)

EDITH: Mama — what do you think? What do you think?

MRS. VARNEY: What is it, dear?

EDITH: Ah've been to see the President!   100

MRS. VARNEY: What — Mr. Davis!

EDITH: Yes! An' Ah asked him for an appointment for Captain Thorne for
the War Department Telegraph Service — an' he gave it to me — a Special Commission! Appointing him to duty here in Richmond — a very
important position — so now he won't have to be sent back to the   105
front — an' it'll be doing his duty just the same.

MRS. VARNEY: But Edith — you don't —

EDITH: Yes it will, Mama! The President told me they needed a man who
understood telegraphing and who was of high enough rank to take
charge of the Service! And you know Cap'n Thorne is an expert! Since   110
he's been here in Richmond he's helped 'em in the telegraph office very
often — Lieutenant Foray told me so! (*Mrs. Varney slowly rises and moves*

away — slight pause.) Now, Mama, Ah feel you're going to scold — an' you mustn't because it's all fixed, an' the commission'll be sent over here in a few minutes — just as soon as it can be made out! An' the next time he comes Ah'm to hand it to him myself. 115

MRS. VARNEY: He's coming this evening.

EDITH (*Looks at Mrs. Varney an instant before speaking — then in low voice*):   How do you know?

MRS. VARNEY (*going back of table*):   This note came half an hour ago. (*about to* 120 *hand note from table to Edith, who sees note and anticipates her action, picking it up and going quickly right with it*)

EDITH: Has it been here — all this time? (*Opens envelope eagerly, and reads note.*)

MRS. VARNEY (*after a moment*):   You see what he says? This'll be his last call. — He's got his orders to leave. (*Sits right of table left center.*)

EDITH (*Sits on sofa.*):   Why, it's too ridiculous! Just as if the commission from the President wouldn't supersede everything? It puts him at the 125 head of the Telegraph Service! He'll be in the command of the Department! — He says — (*glancing at note*) good-bye call does he! All the better — it'll be that much more of a surprise! (*rising and going toward Mrs. Varney*) Now Mama, don't you breathe — Ah want to tell him myself!

MRS. VARNEY: But Edith dear — Ah don't quite approve of your going to 130 the President about this.

EDITH (*changing from light manner to earnestness*):   But listen, Mama — Ah couldn't go to the War Department people — Mr. Arrelsford's there in one of the offices — and ever since Ah refused him you know how he's treated me! — (*slight deprecatory motion from Mrs. Varney*) If Ah'd applied for 135 the appointment there he'd have had it refused — and he'd have got them to order Cap'n Thorne away right off — Ah know he would — and — (*Stands motionless as she thinks of it.*) That's where his orders to go came from!

MRS. VARNEY: But my dear — 140

EDITH: It is, Mama! (*slight pause*) Isn't it lucky I got that commission today!

(*Door bell rings in distant part of the house. Jonas goes across hall to the door up left. Mrs. Varney moves up stage a little waiting to see who it is. Edith listening. Heavy sound of door off left. Jonas enters at the door up left.*)

JONAS (*coming to Mrs. Varney*):   It's a officer, ma'am. He says he's fum de President — an — (*Hands a card to Mrs. Varney.*) he's got ter see Miss Edith pussonully.

EDITH (*low voice*):   It's come, Mama! 145

MRS. VARNEY (*Rises and goes up center.*):   Ask the gentleman in. (*Hands card to Edith. Jonas exits left.*)

EDITH (*overjoyed but keeping voice low*):   It's the Commission!

MRS. VARNEY (*low voice*):   Do you know who it is?

EDITH: No! But he's from the President — it must be that!

(*Enter Jonas at door up left. He comes on a little bowing someone in. Enter Lt. Maxwell at door up left. He is a very dashing young officer, handsome, polite and dressed in a showy and perfectly fitting uniform. Jonas exits. Mrs. Varney advances a little.*)

LT. MAXWELL: Good evening. (*Bows; Mrs. Varney and Edith bow slightly. To*   150
Mrs. Varney) Have Ah the honah of addressing Miss Varney?

MRS. VARNEY: I am Mrs. Varney, sir. (*emphasizing "Mrs." a little*)

LT. MAXWELL (*bowing to Mrs. Varney*):   Madam — Ah'm very much afraid
this looks like an intrusion on my part, but Ah come from the President
and he desires me to see Miss Varney personally!   155

MRS. VARNEY: Anyone from the President could not be otherwise than
welcome. This is my daughter. (*indicating Edith*)

(*Lt. Maxwell bows to Edith and she returns the salutation. He then walks across to her, taking a large brown envelope from his belt.*)

LT. MAXWELL: Miss Varney, the President directed me to deliver this into
your hands — with his compliments. (*handing it to Edith*) He is glad to be
able to do this not only at your request, but as a special favor to your fa-   160
ther, General Varney.

EDITH (*taking envelope*):   Oh, thank you!

MRS. VARNEY: Won't you be seated, Lieutenant?

EDITH: O yes — do! (*Holds envelope pressed very tight against her side.*)

LT. MAXWELL: Nothing would please me so much, ladies — but Ah have   165
to be back at the President's house right away. Ah'm on duty this
evening. — Would you mind writing me off a line or two, Miss
Varney — just to say you have the communication?

EDITH: Why certainly — (*Takes a step or two toward desk at right.*) You want a
receipt — I — (*Turns and crosses toward door up left.*) I'll go upstairs to my   170
desk — it won't take a moment! (*Turns at door.*) And — could I put in
how much I thank him for his kindness?

LT. MAXWELL: Ah'm sure he'd be more than pleased! (*Edith exits and hastens
up the stairway.*)

MRS. VARNEY (*moving forward slowly*):   We haven't heard so much cannonading today, Lieutenant. Do they know what it means?   175

LT. MAXWELL (*going forward with Mrs. Varney*):   Ah don't think they're quite
positive, ma'am, but they can't help lookin' for a violent attack to follow.

MRS. VARNEY: I don't see why it should quiet down before an assault!

LT. MAXWELL: It might be some signal, ma'am, or it might be they're moving their batteries to open on a special point of attack. They're tryin' ev'ry way to break through our defenses, you know. 180

(*Door bell rings in distant part of house.*)

MRS. VARNEY: It's very discouraging! (*Seats herself at table.*) We can't seem to drive them back this time!

LT. MAXWELL: We're holding 'em where they are though! They'll never get in unless they do it by some scurvy trick — that's where the danger lies! 185

(*Heavy sound of door off left.*)

EDITH (*Enters, coming lightly and quickly down the stairway, with a note in her hand, and without the official envelope, which she has left in her room.*):   Is Lieutenant Maxwell — (*seeing him down stage with Mrs. Varney and going across toward them*) O yes!

(*Jonas enters at door up left as Edith reaches up center, showing in Captain Thorne.*)

JONAS (*low voice*):   Will you jess kinely step dis way, suh!

(*Mrs. Varney rises and moves down in front of and then up left of table. Maxwell turns and meets Edith up right center.*)

EDITH (*meeting Maxwell*):   I didn't know but you — (*She stops — hearing Jonas and quickly turns, looking off left.*) Oh! — Captain Thorne! 190

(*Enter Captain Thorne at door up left meeting and shaking hands with Edith. Thorne is dressed as a Confederate Captain of Artillery. [His uniform] is somewhat worn and soiled. Lt. Maxwell turned and moved up a little on Edith's entrance, remaining a little right of center. Jonas exits left.*)

EDITH (*giving Thorne her hand briefly*):   We were expecting you! — Here's Captain Thorne, Mama!

(*Mrs. Varney moves up left center meeting Thorne and shaking hands with him graciously. — Edith turns away and goes to Lt. Maxwell. Thorne and Mrs. Varney move up center near small table and converse.*)

EDITH: I wasn't so very long writing it, was I lieutenant? (*She hands him the note.*)

LT. MAXWELL: Ah've never seen a quicker piece of work, Miss Varney. 195 (*putting note in belt or pocket*) When you want a clerkship ovah at the Government offices you must shorely let me know!

EDITH (*smilingly*):   You'd better not commit yourself — Ah might take you at your word!

LT. MAXWELL: Nothing would please me so much Ah'm sure! All you've 200
got to do is just to apply!

EDITH: Lots of the girls are doing it — they have to, to live! Aren't there a
good many where you are?

LT. MAXWELL: Well we don't have so many as they do over at the Treasury.
Ah believe there are more ladies there than men! 205

MRS. VARNEY (*Comes down a little.*):   Perhaps you gentlemen have met! (*glancing toward Maxwell*)

(*Thorne shakes head a little and steps forward, looking at Maxwell.*)

MRS. VARNEY: Cap'n Thorne — Lieutenant Maxwell.

THORNE (*slight inclination of head*):   Lieutenant.

LT. MAXWELL (*returning bow pleasantly*):   I haven't had the pleasure —
though Ah've heard the Cap'n's name mentioned several times! 210

THORNE: Yes? (*Mrs. Varney and Edith are looking at Maxwell.*)

LT. MAXWELL (*as if it were rather amusing*):   In fact Cap'n, there's a gentleman
in one of our offices who seems mighty anxious to pick a fight with you!

(*Edith is suddenly serious and a look of apprehension spreads over Mrs. Varney's face.*)

THORNE (*easily*):   Pick a fight! Really! Why what office is that, Lieutenant?

LT. MAXWELL (*slightly annoyed*):   The War Office, sir! 215

THORNE: Dear, dear! Ah didn't suppose you had anybody in the War Office who wanted to fight!

LT. MAXWELL (*almost angry*):   An' why not, sir?

THORNE (*easily*):   Well if he did he'd hardly be in an office would he — at a
time like this? 220

LT. MAXWELL (*trying to be light again*):   Ah'd better not tell him that,
Cap'n — he'd certainly insist on havin' you out!

THORNE (*moving down with Mrs. Varney*):   That would be too bad — to interfere with the gentleman's office hours! (*Thorne and Mrs. Varney move
down near table — in conversation.*)

LT. MAXWELL (*to Edith*):   He doesn't believe it, Miss Varney, — but it's certainly true, an' I dare say you know who the — 225

EDITH (*quickly interrupting Maxwell — low voice*):   Please don't Lieutenant! —
I — (*an apprehensive glance toward Thorne*) I'd rather not — (*with a slight catch
of breath*) — talk about it!

LT. MAXWELL (*after short pause of surprise*):   Yes, of course! — Ah didn't know 230
there was any —

EDITH (*interrupting again, with attempt to turn it off*):   Yes! (*a rather nervous effort
to laugh lightly*) — You know there's always the weather to fall back on!

LT. MAXWELL (*picking it up easily*):   Yes — Ah should say so! An' mighty bad weather too — most of the time!   235

EDITH (*laughingly*):   Yes — isn't it! (*They laugh a little and go on talking and laughing to themselves, moving toward right upper window for a moment and soon move across toward door up left as if Maxwell were going.*)

MRS. VARNEY (*back of table with Thorne*):   From your note Captain Thorne, I suppose you're leaving us soon. Your orders have come.

THORNE: Yes — Mrs. Varney, they have. — Ah'm afraid this'll be my last call.   240

MRS. VARNEY: Isn't it rather sudden? It seems to me they ought to give you a little time.

THORNE: Ah well (*slight smile*) we have to be ready for anything, you know!

MRS. VARNEY (*with a sigh*):   Yes — I know! — It's been a great pleasure to have you drop in on us while you were here. We shall quite miss your   245 visits.

THORNE (*a slight formality in manner*):   Thank you. I shall never forget what they've been to me.

(*Maxwell is taking leave of Edith up center.*)

EDITH: Lieutenant Maxwell is going, Mama!

MRS. VARNEY: So soon! Excuse me a moment, Captain! (*Goes hurriedly toward*   250 *Maxwell — Thorne goes near mantel.*) Ah'm right sorry to have you hurry away, Lieutenant. We shall hope for the pleasure of seeing you again.

LT. MAXWELL: Ah shall certainly call, Mrs. Varney — if you'll allow me. — Cap'n! (*saluting Thorne from near the door up left*)

THORNE (*turning from mantel; half salute*):   Lieutenant!   255

LT. MAXWELL: Miss Varney! Mrs. Varney! (*Bowing to each. Exits. Mrs. Varney follows Maxwell off at door up left — speaking as she goes.*)

MRS. VARNEY: Now remember Lieutenant, you're to come sometime when duty doesn't call you away so soon!

(*Edith turns and moves slowly to table up center on Maxwell's exit.*)

LT. MAXWELL (*outside — voice getting more distant*):   Trust me to attend to that, Mrs. Varney.   260

(*Heavy sound of door off left*)

THORNE (*moving toward Edith who is up center near small table*):   Shall I see Mrs. Varney again?

EDITH (*getting a rose from vase on table*):   Oh yes — you'll see her again! — But not just now.

THORNE: I haven't long to stay.   265

EDITH (*down center a little*):   Well — do you know — Ah think you have more time than you really think you have! It would be odd if it came out that way — wouldn't it? (*playing with flower in her hand*)

THORNE: Yes — but it won't come out that way.

EDITH: Yes — but you — (*She stops as Thorne is taking the rose from her hand —*   270 *which she was holding up in an absent way as she talked. Thorne at the same time holds the hand she had it in. She lets go of the rose and draws away her hand.*)

EDITH (*a little embarrassed*):   You know — you can sit down if you want to! (*indicating chair at left of table*)

THORNE: Yes — I see.

EDITH (*Sits at right of table.*):   You'd better! — Oh, I've a great many things to say!

THORNE: Oh — you have!   275

EDITH (*Nodding — her left hand is on the table.*):   Yes.

THORNE: I have only one.

EDITH (*looking up at him*):   And — that is — ?

THORNE (*taking her left hand in both of his*):   Good-bye.

EDITH: But Ah don't really think you'll have to say it!   280

THORNE (*looking tenderly down at her*):   I know I will!

EDITH (*low voice — more serious*):   Then it'll be because you want to!

THORNE (*quickly*):   No! It will be — because I must.

EDITH (*rising slowly and looking at him a little mischievously as she does so*):   Oh — because you must! (*Thorne nods a little. Edith walks toward center thinking*   285 *whether to tell him or not. He watches her. She suddenly turns back and goes again to table left center.*) You don't know some things I do!

THORNE (*laughing a little at first*):   Ah think that's more than likely, Miss Varney! (*Goes to left of table.*) Would you mind telling me a few so Ah can somewhat approach you in that respect?

EDITH (*seriously*):   Ah wouldn't mind telling you one, and that is, it's very   290 wrong for you to think of leaving Richmond yet!

THORNE: Ah — but you don't —

EDITH (*Sits in chair right of table, breaking in quickly.*):   Oh, yes, Ah do!

THORNE (*Sits in chair left of table, looking up at her amused.*):   Well — what?

EDITH: Whatever you were going to say! Most likely it was that there's   295 something or other Ah don't know about! — But Ah know this — (*looking away front — eyes lowered a little*) you were sent here only a few weeks ago to recover from a very bad wound — (*Thorne looks down and [a] little front quickly.*) — and you haven't nearly had time for it yet!

THORNE (*as if amused*):   Ha, ha — yes. (*looking up at Edith with usual expression*)   300 Ah do look as if the next high wind would blow me away, don't I?

EDITH (*turning to him earnestly — half rising*):   No matter how you look, you ought not — Oh — (*rising fully and turning away from him*) You're just making fun of it, like you always do! (*Goes up center, turns to Thorne again.*) No matter! You can make all the fun you like, but the whole thing is settled, and you aren't going away at all!   305

(*Thorne has risen when Edith did.*)

THORNE: Oh — Ah'm not!

EDITH: No!

THORNE: Well, that's quite a change for me! (*Puts hat on table and moves up near Edith going back of table.*) Perhaps you wouldn't mind telling me what I am going to do?   310

EDITH (*turning to him*):   Ah wouldn't mind at all — an' it's this — you see, Ah've been to the — (*Hesitates.*) Now! Ah'm almost afraid to tell you!

THORNE (*near Edith*):   Don't tell me Miss Varney — because it's really true. I've got my order — I'm leaving tonight.   315

(*Edith looks at Thorne an instant — then turns and goes right and sits on couch, looking at him from there.*)

EDITH (*after an instant*):   Where — to the front?

EDITH (*Moves over to Edith.*):   We can't always tell where orders'll take us. (*Sits on the couch beside her.*)

EDITH: But listen! Supposing there were other orders — from a higher authority — appointing you to duty here?

THORNE (*eyes lowered before him*):   It wouldn't make any difference.   320

EDITH (*sudden alarm*):   You don't — you don't mean you'd go — in spite of them? (*Thorne raises his eyes to hers in slight surprise and looks at her an instant. Then he nods affirmatively.*) But if it proved your first order was a mistake — and — (*In her earnestness she makes a little motion with her left hand within his reach.*)

THORNE (*taking her hand in his*):   It wasn't a mistake (*Hesitates, looks up in her face   325 an instant — then releasing her hand rises and moves up a little standing faced up toward window.*)

EDITH (*After watching Thorne until he is motionless, rises and comes up to him with a new apprehension.*):   Is it — something dangerous?

THORNE (*turning to Edith and speaking lightly*):   Oh, well — (*slight laugh*) enough to make it interesting!

EDITH (*low voice*):   Don't be angry if I ask you again about your orders — I must know!   330

THORNE: Why?

EDITH: No matter — tell me!

THORNE: I can't do that Miss Varney.

EDITH: You needn't! Ah know! (*Thorne with a sudden apprehensive glance to front; looks back at her once.*) They're sending you on some mission where death is almost certain. They'll sacrifice your life because they know you are fearless and will do anything! There's a chance for you to stay here and be just as much use — and Ah'm going to ask you to do this! It isn't your life alone — there are other lives to think of — that's why I ask you! — It may not sound well — but — you see — 335 340

THORNE (*catching her hands passionately*): Ah my — (*suddenly recovering and partly turning away — not, however, releasing her hands*) No no! — You shan't have this against me too!

EDITH: Against you! Why? Why? What do you mean? Why is it against you? 345

THORNE (*holding her hands close*): Because I must go — my business is elsewhere — I ought never to have seen you or spoken to you — but I had to come to this house — and you were here — and how could I help it? Oh — I couldn't — for my whole — it's only you in the — (*Stops, releases her hands, and turns blindly right. Then, as if to go left, speaks.*) Your mother — I'll say good-bye to her! 350

EDITH (*going quickly in his way*): No! — You must listen! They need you here in Richmond! — The President told me so himself! — Your orders are to stay! You are given a Special Commission on the War Department Telegraph service, and you — 355

THORNE (*quickly, decisively, but in subdued voice*): No! No! I won't take it! I couldn't take it Miss Varney!

EDITH: You'll do that much for me!

THORNE (*holding her hands*): It's for you that I'll do nothing of the kind! If you ever think of me again remember I refused it! 360

EDITH (*breaking into Thorne's last few words*): You can't refuse! It's the President's request — it's his order! (*leaving him and going toward door*) Please wait a minute! I left it upstairs and you'll see —

THORNE: No! Don't get it! (*following her*) Don't get it! I won't look at it!

EDITH (*Stops and turns*): But I want you to see what it is! It puts you at the head of everything! You have entire control! When you see it Ah know you'll accept! Please wait!   (*Exits at door up left and runs up the stairway.*) 365

THORNE (*as she goes*): Miss Varney — I can't —

EDITH (*as she goes*): Oh yes you can!

(*Thorne stands looking off after Edith for an instant. Then turns and hurries down to table and seizing his hat, starts rapidly up toward door up left as if to go. As Thorne starts down for hat sound of heavy door outside left, closing with a bang. Enter at door up left Caroline Mitford, skipping in lightly, crossing back of Thorne to up center. She is breathless from having run across the street. Her dress is made of what is supposed to have been a great grandmother's wedding gown as light and pretty as possible, with a touch of the old-fashioned in cut and pattern. She is very young and attractive.)*

CAROLINE (*Comes quickly on — stops abruptly.*):   Oh! — Good evening!   370
THORNE (*mechanical salute*):   Miss Mitford! (*Turns and looks up the stairs.*)
CAROLINE (*saluting*):   Yes of co'se — Ah forgot! — How lucky this is! You're just the very person Ah wanted to see! (*going toward couch*) Ah'll tell you all about it in just a minute! Goodness me! (*Sits.*) Ah'm all out o' breath — just runnin' ovah from our house! (*Devotes herself to breathing for* 375 *an instant.*)
THORNE (*going quickly down to her*):   Miss Mitford — would you do something for me?
CAROLINE: Why of co'se Ah would!
THORNE (*rapidly*):   Thank you very much! — Tell Miss Varney when she comes down — Just say good-night for me and tell her I've gone!   380
CAROLINE (*pretending astonishment*):   Why Ah wouldn't do such a thing for the wide, wide world! It would be a wicked dreadful lie — because you won't be gone!
THORNE: I'm sorry you look at it that way — Good-night Miss Mitford! (*Turns to go.*)
CAROLINE (*jumping to her feet and coming round on his left between him and the door*): No no! — You don't seem to understand! Ah've got something to say to   385 you!
THORNE (*hurriedly*):   Yes — but some other time — (*trying to go*)
CAROLINE (*detaining him*):   No no no! — Wait! (*Thorne stops.*) There isn't any other time! It's tonight! — We're going to have a starvation party!
THORNE: Good heavens — another of those things!   390
CAROLINE: Yes — we are! It's goin' to be ovah at mah house this time! Now we'll expect you in half an hour. (*her fingers up to emphasize the time*)
THORNE: Thank you, Miss Mitford, but I can't come! (*indicating off*) I've got to be —
CAROLINE (*interrupting*):   N — n — n — (*until she quiets him*) Now that   395 wouldn't do at all! You went to Mamie Jones's! Would you treat me like that?
THORNE: Mamie Jones — that was last week Thursday — (*Caroline trying to stop him with "now — now — now!" etc.*) Her mother — (*Caroline louder with "now — now!" Thorne raises his voice above the din.*) Her mother —   400

(*As Caroline is still going on he gives it up and looks front in despair.*)

CAROLINE (*when quiet has come, very distinctly*):   Now there isn't any use o' talkin'!

THORNE (*Nods.*):   Yes I see that!

CAROLINE: Didn't you promise to obey when Ah gave orders? Well, these are orders! 405

THORNE (*turning to her for a last attempt*):   Yes, but this time —

CAROLINE: This time is just the same as all the other times only worse! (*Turns away and goes to back of table left center and picks up flowers; Thorne turns and goes a little way toward up right center as if discouraged. Caroline speaks without turning.*) Besides that, she expects it.

(*Thorne turns at once and looks across at Caroline.*)

THORNE: What did you say? (*Moves toward her.*)

CAROLINE (*smelling a flower daintily, facing front*):   Ah say — she expects it — 410 that's all!

THORNE: Who do you mean?

CAROLINE (*Turns and looks at him.*):   Who?

THORNE (*assent*):   Um-hm!

CAROLINE (*innocently*):   Who expects you? 415

THORNE (*assent again*):   Ah ha!

CAROLINE: Why, Edith of co'se! Who did you s'pose Ah was talkin' about all this time?

THORNE: Oh! She expects me to — (*gesture up toward door left*)

CAROLINE: Why of co'se she does! Just to take her ovah! — Goodness me! 420 You needn't stay if you don't want to! Now Ah'll go an' tell her you're waiting — that's what Ah'll do. (*Starts up toward stairs, stops and turns at door.*) You won't go now?

THORNE: If she expects it Miss Mitford (*moving up toward her*), I'll wait an' take her over — but I can't stay a minute! 425

CAROLINE: Well Ah thought you'd come to your senses some time or other! You don't seem to quite realize what you've got to do! — See here, Mr. Captain — (*bringing him down center a little with her, on her right*) Was she most ready?

THORNE: Well — e — how do I — how — 430

CAROLINE: What dress did she have on?

THORNE: Dress?

CAROLINE: Oh, you men! Why she's only got two!

THORNE (*relieved*):   Yes — well then very likely this was one of them, Miss Mitford! 435

CAROLINE (*starting up toward door*):   Oh, no mattah — Ah'm going up anyway! (*Thorne moves up center as Caroline goes up left center. Caroline stops near door*

and turns to Thorne.) Cap'n Thorne — you can wait out there on the veranda! (*pointing to window up right*)

THORNE (*Glances where she points — then to her.*):   I know — but if I wait right   440
here she'll —

CAROLINE (*majestically*):   Those are orders! (*Thorne looks at her an instant —
then salutes and wheels about making complete turn to right and starts toward the
window. Caroline is watching him admiringly. As Thorne reaches right center*) It's
cooler outside you know!

THORNE (*turning to her and standing in stiff military attitude*):   Pardon me, Miss   445
Mitford — orders never have to be explained!

CAROLINE: That's right — I take back the explanation! (*taking one step to her
right as she gives odd little salute*)

THORNE (*with deferential salute in slight imitation of hers — but with step to his left*):
That's right Miss Mitford — take it back! (*Turns and is reaching to pull aside
curtains of window with right hand.*)

CAROLINE: And — oh yes! — Cap'n!

(*Thorne turns to her again questioningly — right hand still holding curtain behind
him.*)

CAROLINE (*a peremptory order*):   Smoke!   450

(*For an instant Thorne does not understand. Then he sees it and relapses at once into
easy manner, stepping forward a little and feeling with right hand in coat front for
cigar — turning somewhat to front.*)

THORNE: Oh — ha — ha — (*smiling*) you mean one of those Nashville
sto —

CAROLINE: Silence sir! (*Thorne looks at her quickly.*) Orders never have to be
explained!

THORNE (*with salute*):   Right again Miss Mitford — orders never have to be   455
explained! (*Exits at window up right.*)

CAROLINE (*Looks admiringly after Thorne.*):   He's splendid! If Wilfred was
only like that! (*Thinks.*) But then — our engagement's broken off anyway
so what's the diff! — Only — if he was like that — Ah'd — no! Ah don't
think Ah'd — (*Shakes head.*)   460

(*Enter Mrs. Varney at door left. Caroline does not notice her until she comes near, then
breaks off in middle of sentence and goes right on in same breath.*)

Why how dy do!

MRS. VARNEY: Why Caroline dear! What are you talking about all to yourself?

CAROLINE (*confused*):   Oh — just — Ah was just saying you know —

that — why Ah don't know — Ah don't really know what Ah was goin' 465
to — e — Do you think it's goin' to rain?

MRS. VARNEY: Dear me, child — I haven't thought about it! — Why what
have you got on? Is that a new dress?

CAROLINE: New dress! Well Ah should think so! These are my great
grandmother's mother's weddin' clothes! Aren't they just the most beau- 470
tiest you ever saw! Just in the nick of time too! Ah was on my very last
rags, an' Ah didn't know what to do — an' Mama gave me a key and told
me to open an old horsehair trunk in the garret — an' Ah did — and
these were in it! (*Takes a dance step or two, holding dress out.*) Just in time for
the starvation party tonight! Ran ovah here to show it to Edith — where 475
is she?

MRS. VARNEY: She won't be over tonight, I'm afraid. (*Crosses to right center.*)

CAROLINE: Oh yes she will!

MRS. VARNEY: But I've just come down dear!

CAROLINE: Yes — but Ah'm just going *up* dear! 480

(*Caroline turns and runs quickly up the stairs and off. Mrs. Varney alone a moment.
After a little she moves down front in thought. She turns to desk and prepares to write
a letter. Suddenly Caroline races down the stairs again and runs lightly on at door up
left. Mrs. Varney looks up surprised. Caroline hurries across toward window as if going
out.*)

MRS. VARNEY: You see Caroline, it was no use!

CAROLINE (*turning*):   No use! (*Comes down in front of couch near Mrs. Varney.*)

MRS. VARNEY: Why you don't mean — in this short time —

CAROLINE: Goodness me! Ah didn't stop to argue with her — Ah just told
her! 485

MRS. VARNEY: Told her what, child!

CAROLINE: Why — that Cap'n Thorne was waitin' for her out yere on the
v'randah!

MRS. VARNEY: She isn't going is she?

CAROLINE: Well, Ah wouldn't like to say for sure (*moving nearer Mrs. Varney* 490
and lower voice) but you just watch which dress she has on when she comes
down! Now Ah'll go out there an' tell him she'll be down in a minute —
then the whole thing's finished up all round! Ah have more trouble getting people fixed so they can come to my party than it would take to run
a blockade into Savannah every fifteen minutes! (*Goes around couch and runs* 495
off at window up right.)

(*Mrs. Varney looks after Caroline with a smile for a moment, and then taking some paper and envelopes in her hand, rises, and moves as if to go to door up left. Enter Wilfred
at door up left, coming in as if he wished to avoid being seen, and looking off up stair-*

way as he enters. He carries a package under his coat, which is done up in a paper loosely. He turns quickly seeing Mrs. Varney and makes a very slight movement as if to conceal the package he carries. He stands looking at her.)

MRS. VARNEY: What have you got there Wilfred?

WILFRED: Here? (*Brings out package.*) O — it's only — (*Looks at her a little guiltily.*) Have you written that letter yet?

MRS. VARNEY: No dear — I've been too busy. But I'm going to do it right now. (*Goes across to door at left. Near the door she glances round a little anxiously at* 500 *Wilfred. He is looking at her. Then she exits and goes up the stairs.*)

(*Wilfred turns away after she has gone. Glances round room, goes down to table left center and begins to undo the package cautiously. He has hardly got the paper loosened — just enough to enable audience to see that it contains a pair of military trousers — when Caroline appears at window.*)

CAROLINE (*speaking off at window right*):   Those are orders Cap'n — an' orders never have to be explained!

(*Wilfred hurriedly stuffs the trousers inside his coat and buttons it over them.*)

THORNE (*outside, at a little distance*):   Perfectly right Miss Mitford!

(*Caroline enters through window, closing it after her, but does not close portieres. Wilfred is about to start toward down left. Caroline turning from window sees Wilfred.*)

CAROLINE: Good evening Mr. Varney.

WILFRED (*coldly*):   Good evening Miss Mitford! (*Both now start rapidly toward* 505 *door up left but as it brings them toward each other they stop simultaneously in order to avoid meeting.*)

CAROLINE: Excuse me — Ah'm in a hurry!

WILFRED: That's plain enough! (*Looks at her.*) Another party Ah reckon!

CAROLINE: You reckon perfectly correct — it is another party!

WILFRED: Dancing!

CAROLINE (*Speaks emphatically*):   What of it? What's the matter with danc- 510 ing Ah'd like to know?

WILFRED: Nothing's the matter with it — if you want to *do* it!

CAROLINE: Well Ah want to *do* it fast enough if that's all you mean! (*Turns away.*)

WILFRED: But I must say it's a pretty way to carry on — with the sound of the cannon not six miles away! 515

(*Wilfred is dead in earnest not only in this scene but in all his scenes.*)

CAROLINE (*Turns back to him.*):   What do you want us to do? Sit down and cry about it? — That would do a heap o' good now wouldn't it?

WILFRED: Oh — I haven't time to talk about it! (*Starts to go.*)

CAROLINE: Well it was you who started out to talk about it — Ah'm right sure Ah didn't! 520

WILFRED (*After glance to see that no one is near, turns on her.*): Oh — you needn't try to fool me! Ah know well enough how you've been carrying on since our engagement was broken off! Half a dozen officers proposing to you — a dozen for all Ah know!

CAROLINE: What difference does it make? Ah haven't got to marry 'em 525 have I?

WILFRED: Well — (*twist of head*) it isn't very nice to go on like that Ah must say — proposals by the wholesale! (*turning away*)

CAROLINE: Goodness gracious — what's the use of talking to me about it? *They're* the ones that propose — *Ah* don't! 530

WILFRED (*turning on her*): Well what do you let 'em do it for?

CAROLINE: How can Ah help it?

WILFRED: Ho! (*sneer*) Any girl can help it! You helped it with me all right!

CAROLINE: Well, that was different! (*a queer look at him*)

WILFRED: And ever since you threw me ovah — 535

CAROLINE (*indignantly*): Oh! — Ah *didn't* throw you ovah — you just *went* ovah! (*Turns away a little.*)

WILFRED: Well, Ah went over because you walked off alone with Major Sillsby that night we were at Drury's Bluff an' encouraged him to propose — (*Caroline looks round in wrath.*) Yes — encouraged him! 540

CAROLINE: Of co'se Ah did! Ah didn't want 'im hangin' round forever did Ah? That's the on'y way to finish 'em off!

WILFRED: You want to finish too many of 'em off! Nearly every officer in the 17th Virginyah Ah'll be sworn!

CAROLINE: What do you want me to do — string a placard round my neck 545 saying "No proposals received here — apply at the office!" Would that make you feel any better?

WILFRED (*throwing it off with pretended carelessness*): Oh, it doesn't make any difference to me what you do!

CAROLINE: Well if it doesn't make any difference to you, it doesn't even 550 make as much as that to me! (*Turns and sits on left end of couch.*)

WILFRED (*turning on her again*): Oh — it doesn't! Ah think it *does* though! You looked as if you enjoyed it pretty well while the 3rd Virginyah was in the city!

CAROLINE: Enjoyed it! Ah should think Ah did! (*jumping up*) Ah just love 555 every one of 'em! They're on their way to the front! They're going to fight for us — an' — an' die for us — an' Ah love 'em. (*Turns away.*)

WILFRED: Well why don't you accept one of 'em an' have done with it!

CAROLINE: How do you know but what Ah'm going to?

WILFRED (*Goes toward her a little.*):   Ah suppose it'll be one of those smart young fellows with a cavalry uniform!

CAROLINE: It'll be *some* kind of a uniform! It won't be anyone that stays in Richmond — Ah can tell you that!

WILFRED (*After looking at her — unable for a moment to speak — looks round room helplessly, then speaks in a low voice.*):   Now I see what it was! I had to stay in Richmond — an' so you —

CAROLINE (*in front of couch*):   Well — (*looking down, playing with something with her foot*) that made a heap o' difference! (*Looks up — different tone.*) Why Ah was the on'y girl on Franklin Street that didn't have a — a — someone she was engaged to at the front! The on'y one! Just think what it was — to be out of it like that! (*Wilfred simply looks at her.*) Why you've no idea what Ah suffered! Besides, it's our — our duty to help all we can!

WILFRED (*hoarsely*):   Help! (*thinking of his trousers*)

CAROLINE: Yes — help! There aren't many things we girls can do — Ah know that well enough! But Colonel Woodbridge — he's one o' Morgan's men you know — well he told Mollie Pickens that the boys fight *twice* as well when they have a — a sweetheart at home! (*Wilfred glances about quickly.*)

WILFRED: He said that did he?

CAROLINE: Yes — an' if we can make 'em fight twice as well — why we just ought to do it — that's all! We girls can't do much but we can do something!

WILFRED (*Short pause — He makes an absentminded motion of feeling the package under his arm.*):   You're in earnest are you?

CAROLINE: Earnest!

WILFRED: You really want to help — all you can!

CAROLINE: Well Ah should think so!

WILFRED: An' if Ah was — (*Glances around cautiously.*) If I was going to join the army would you help me?

CAROLINE (*looking front and down; slight embarrassment*):   Why of co'se Ah would — if it was anything Ah could do!

WILFRED (*earnestly — quite near her*):   Oh it's something you can do all right — Ah'm sure o' that!

CAROLINE (*hardly daring to look up*):   What is it?

WILFRED (*unrolling a pair of old gray army trousers, taking them from under his coat so that they spread before her on cue*):   Cut these off! (*Short pause; Caroline looking at trousers. Wilfred looks at her; soon goes on very earnestly holding them before his own legs to measure.*) They're about twice too long! All you got to do is to cut 'em off about there — an' sew the ends so they won't ravel out!

CAROLINE (*the idea beginning to dawn on her*):   Why they're for the Army! (*tak-*   595
ing trousers and hugging them to her — legs hanging down)

WILFRED: Sh! — Don't speak so loud for heaven's sake! (*a glance back as if
afraid of being overheard*) Ah've got a jacket here, too! (*Shows her a small army
coat.*) Nearly a fit — came from the hospital — Johnny Seldon wore it —
he won't want it any more you know — an' he was just about my size!

CAROLINE (*low voice*):   No — he won't want it any more. (*Stands thinking.*)   600

WILFRED (*after a slight pause*):   Well! — Ah thought you said you wanted to
help!

CAROLINE (*quickly*):   Oh yes — Ah do! Ah do!

WILFRED: Well go on — what are you waiting for?

CAROLINE (*near end of couch*):   Yes! Yes! (*Hurriedly drops on knees on floor and takes*   605
hold, spreading trousers out exactly and patting them smooth.) This is the place
isn't it? (*pointing to near the knees*)

WILFRED: No — not up there — Here! (*indicating about three inches from the
bottom of the trouser leg*)

CAROLINE: Oh yes! Ah see! (*Hurriedly snatches pins from her dress; puts one in
mouth and one in place Wilfred indicates — all very rapid and earnest. Takes hold of
other leg of trousers, speaking as if pin in mouth — innocently and without looking
up.*) The other one just the same? (*A musical rise to voice at end of this. Wilfred*   610
does not deign to reply. Caroline hearing nothing looks up at him.) Oh yes, o' co'se!
(*She quickly puts pin in other leg of trousers.*)

(*From trouser business Caroline's demeanor toward Wilfred is entirely changed. It is
because he is going to join the army.*)

(*Caroline on floor with trousers and coat takes hold of the work with enthusiasm.*) Do
you see any scissors around anywhere? (*Wilfred dashes about looking on tables,
after putting jacket on end of couch.*) This won't never tear — (*trying to tear off
trousers' leg*) — for all Ah can do!   615

WILFRED (*First looking on table down left center and picking up paper jacket was
wrapped in. He gets a work-basket from table up center and quickly brings it.*):
There must be some in here! (*Hands the scissors out of the basket to Caroline. As
she reaches up from her position on the floor to take them, she looks in Wilfred's face an
instant — then quickly down to work again. Then she works with head down. Wilfred
leaves wrapping paper up stage out of the way.*)

CAROLINE (*slight pause — on her knees near couch; low voice, not looking up at him*):
When are you goin' to wear 'em?

WILFRED: When they're cut off!

CAROLINE (*Looks up at him; thread or scissors in mouth.*):   You mean — you're
really —   620

WILFRED: Um hm! (*assent*)

CAROLINE: But your mother —

WILFRED: She knows it.

CAROLINE: Oh!

WILFRED: She's going to write the General tonight. 625

CAROLINE: But how about if he won't let you?

WILFRED (*with boyish determination, but keeping voice down*): Ah'll go just the same!

CAROLINE (*Suddenly jumps to her feet dropping everything on the floor and catches his hand.*): Oh Ah'm *so* glad! Why it makes another thing of it! When Ah said that about staying in Richmond Ah didn't know! Oh, Ah do want to 630 help all I can!

WILFRED (*who has been regarding her burst of enthusiasm rather coldly*): You do!

CAROLINE: Indeed — indeed Ah do!

WILFRED: Then cut those off for Heaven's sake!

CAROLINE: Oh yes! (*She catches up trousers, jacket, etc., and sits quickly on couch and* 635 *excitedly paws them over.*) Where shall Ah cut 'em?

WILFRED: The same place — Ah haven't grown any!

CAROLINE: Dear me — Ah don't know where it was!

WILFRED: You stuck some pins in!

CAROLINE (*finding pins*): Oh yes — here they are! (*seizing the trousers and go-* 640 *ing to work, soon cutting off one of the trousers' legs*)

WILFRED: That's it!

CAROLINE: When did you say she was going to write?

WILFRED: Tonight.

CAROLINE (*looking up with distrust*): She doesn't want you to go does she?

WILFRED: Ah don't reckon she does — very much! 645

CAROLINE: She'll tell him not to let you!

WILFRED (*Looks at her with wide open eyes.*): No!

CAROLINE: That's the way they always do!

WILFRED: The devil!

CAROLINE: Ah should think so! 650

WILFRED: What can Ah do!

CAROLINE: Write to him yourself.

WILFRED: Good idea!

CAROLINE: Then you can just tell him what you like!

WILFRED: Ah'll tell him Ah *can't* stay here! 655

CAROLINE (*excitedly rising, letting the jacket fall on floor*): Tell him you're com- ing anyhow!

WILFRED: Ah will!

CAROLINE: Whether he says so or not!

WILFRED: Then he'll say so, won't he? 660

CAROLINE: O' co'se he will — there ain't anything else to say!

WILFRED: Ah'll do it! (*Starts to go up left; stops and goes back to Caroline.*) Say — you're pretty good! (*Catching one of Caroline's hands impulsively. Caroline looks down at work in her hand.*) Ah'll go upstairs an' write it now! (*Starts toward door. Caroline watches him. He turns back and she looks quickly down at her work again.*) Finish those things as soon as you can an' leave 'em here — in the hall closet! (*indicating outside left*)   665

CAROLINE (*nodding her head*):   Yes!

WILFRED: An' don't let anyone see 'em whatever you do!

CAROLINE (*shaking her head*):   No!

(*Wilfred hurries off at door up left. Caroline looks after him with expression of ecstasy — lapsing into dreaminess as she turns to front. Suddenly bethinks herself with a start and a little "O" and slipping down on floor near chair she goes excitedly to work on the trousers, cutting at the other leg with violence and rapidly, getting it nearly cut through so that later it dangles by a few threads. Suddenly she stops work and listens. Then with great haste she gathers up all the things she can, leaving the jacket however where it fell, and jumps to her feet with them in her arms, hugging the confused bundle close against her and hastily tucking in portions that hang out so that Mrs. Varney won't see what it is.*)

MRS. VARNEY (*Enters from up left coming down the stairway and into the room.*): Oh — you haven't gone yet!   670

CAROLINE: Not quite! I mean not yet! It doesn't begin for an hour you know!

MRS. VARNEY: What doesn't begin?

CAROLINE: The party!

MRS. VARNEY: Oh — then you have plenty of time! (*turning as if to go up center*)

CAROLINE (*hastening across toward door left with her arms full of things*):   Yes — but Ah'll have to go now sure enough! (*She drops the scissors.*)   675

MRS. VARNEY (*turning*):   You dropped your scissors dear!

CAROLINE: Oh! (*coming back for them*) I — I thought I heard something! (*In picking them up she lets the cut-off end of a trouser leg fall but does not notice it and goes toward door up left.*)

MRS. VARNEY (*coming down stage*):   What are you making, Caroline?

CAROLINE (*turning near door*):   Oh — Ah was just altering a dress, that's all!   680 (*turning to go*)

MRS. VARNEY (*stooping and picking up the piece of trouser leg*):   Here, Carrie! — you dropped a — a — (*Looks at it.*)

CAROLINE (*hurrying to Mrs. Varney and snatching the piece — stuffing it in with rest*): Oh yes! — (*Looks at Mrs. Varney an instant. The other piece of trouser leg is hang-*

ing by its shred in full sight.) That — that was one of the sleeves! (*Turns and hurries off at door up left and exits door below stairway.*)

(*Mrs. Varney after a moment turns and goes toward door up center. Seeing something on the couch she stops and goes to pick it up. On coming to it she finds the little gray soldier's jacket left by Caroline in her hasty scramble. Mrs. Varney stoops and picks it up and stands looking at it facing front. After a brief pause the loud sound of hurried opening of front door outside left and tramp of heavy feet on the floor is heard. Mrs. Varney looks up and across left, letting the coat fall on the couch. Enter Mr. Benton Arrelsford up left, a tall fine looking Southern man of about thirty-five or forty dressed in citizen's clothes — black frock coat — rather distinguished appearance. He is seen outside door up left hurriedly placing a guard of Confederate soldiers at doors outside up left, also at foot of stairs, and at any other exit in sight. Mrs. Varney, much surprised, moves toward door left. Mr. Arrelsford at the same time and as noiselessly as possible, hastens into the room.*)

MRS. VARNEY: Mr. Arrelsford! (*Goes toward center, up a little.*)   685

ARRELSFORD (*Comes quickly across to Mrs. Varney. Speaks in a low voice and rapidly.*): Ah was obliged to come in without ceremony, Mrs. Varney. You'll understand when I tell you what it is!

MRS. VARNEY: And those men — (*Motions toward guards.*)

ARRELSFORD: They're on guard at the doors out there!

MRS. VARNEY (*low voice*):   On guard! — You mean —   690

ARRELSFORD: Ah'm very much afraid we've got to put you to a little inconvenience, Mrs. Varney! (*Glances about cautiously. Mrs. Varney stands astonished.*) Is there anybody in that room? (*pointing to door up center*)

MRS. VARNEY: Yes — a number of ladies sewing for the hospitals.

ARRELSFORD: Kindly come this way a little. (*going down stage with Mrs. Varney*) One of your servants has got himself into trouble, Mrs. Varney, an' we're compelled to have him watched!   695

MRS. VARNEY: What kind of trouble?

ARRELSFORD (*low voice*):   Pretty serious, ma'am! That's the way it looks now! — You've got an old white-haired niggah here —   700

MRS. VARNEY: You mean Jonas?

ARRELSFORD: Ah believe that's his name!

MRS. VARNEY: You suspect him of something!

ARRELSFORD (*keeping voice down*):   We don't suspect — we *know* what he's done! (*Glances round before going on.*) He's been down in the Libby Prison 705 under pretense of selling something to the Yankees we've got in there, an' he now has on his person a written communication from one of them which he intends to deliver to some Yankee agent here in Richmond! (*Goes around in front of table and up near door up left center.*)

MRS. VARNEY (*motionless a second looking at Arrelsford but soon recovers*):   Send for the man! (*starting to move up stage and toward left*) Let us see if this —   710

ARRELSFORD (*quickly stopping her*):   No! Not yet! (*Glances quickly round at doors and windows — then speaks in lowered voice but with great intensity and clearness.*) Ah've got to get that paper! If he's alarmed he'll destroy it! Ah've got to have it! It'll give us the clue to one o' their cursed plots! They've been right close on this town for months — trying to break down our defenses and get in on us. This is some rascally game they're at to weaken us from the   715 inside! Two weeks ago we got word from our agents that we keep over there in the Yankee lines telling us that two brothers — Lewis and Henry Dumont — have been under Secret Service orders to do some rascally piece of work here in Richmond. We had close descriptions of these fellows but we've never been able to lay our hands on 'em till last night!   720

MRS. VARNEY (*near Arrelsford, intense whisper*):   You've got them?

ARRELSFORD (*low voice but intense*):   We've got one o' them! An' it won't take long to run down the othah!

MRS. VARNEY: The one — the one you caught — was he here in Richmond?   725

ARRELSFORD: No — he was brought in last night with a lot o' men we captured making a raid.

MRS. VARNEY: Taken prisoner!

ARRELSFORD (*Nods affirmatively, glances round.*):   Let himself be taken! That's one of their tricks for getting through our lines when they want to bring   730 a message or give some signal.

MRS. VARNEY: You mean, they get into Libby Prison?

ARRELSFORD: Yes! Damn them! (*this oath indistinctly between his teeth*) But we were on the lookout for this man and we spotted him pretty quick. I gave orders not to search him or to take away his clothes but to put him in   735 with the others and keep the closest watch on him that was ever kept on a man! We knew from his coming in that his brother must be here in the city and he'd send a message to him the first chance he got.

MRS. VARNEY: But Jonas! How could he —

ARRELSFORD: Easy enough! He comes down to Libby to sell goubers to   740 the prisoners — we let 'im pass — he fools around awhile until he gets a chance to brush against this man Dumont — we're watching an' we see a bit of paper pass between 'em! The old rascal's got that paper now ma'am, an' besides these men in heah I've got a dozen more on the outside watching him through the windows! (*Turns and moves up, glancing off*   745 *left with some anxiety.*)

MRS. VARNEY (*After slight pause, turns and speaks in intense but subdued voice, almost a whisper.*):   The man he gives it to! *He's* the one you want!

ARRELSFORD (*approaching her quickly, low voice but intense*):   Yes! But I can't
wait long! If the Niggah sees a man or hears a sound he'll destroy it before we can jump in on 'im — an' I must have that paper! (*Strides quickly
up, Mrs. Varney following a step or two; speaks off up left in low but sharp voice.*)
Corporal!   750

(*Enter Corporal at door up left; he salutes and stands.*)

How is it now?
CORPORAL (*low voice*):   All quiet sir!

(*Arrelsford and Mrs. Varney face each other.*)

ARRELSFORD (*low, intense*):   It won't do to wait — I've got to get that paper!
It's the key to the game they're trying to play against us!
MRS. VARNEY (*half whisper*):   No no! The man he's going to give it to! Get   755
him!
ARRELSFORD: That paper might give us a clue! If not I'll make the niggah
tell! Damn it — I'll shoot it out of him! (*Turns to Corporal.*) How quick
can you get at him from that door! (*pointing off up left*)
CORPORAL (*no salute, low voice*):   It's through a hallway — and across the   760
dining-room.
ARRELSFORD: Well, take two men and —
MRS. VARNEY (*interrupting, touching Arrelsford to stop him*):   Why not keep your
men out of sight and let me send for him — here?
ARRELSFORD (*after a second's thought*):   That's better! We'll get 'im in here!   765
While you're talking to him they can nab him from behind! (*Turns to Cor-
poral.*) You heard?
CORPORAL: Yes, sir.
ARRELSFORD: Keep your men out of sight — get 'em back there in the
hall — an' while we're making him talk send a man down each side and   770
pin him! Hold 'im stiff! He mustn't destroy any paper he's got!

(*Corporal salutes and exits with men off left. Mrs. Varney turns to Arrelsford, who is
well up center, with her hand on the bell rope.*)

MRS. VARNEY: Now, Mr. Arrelsford?
ARRELSFORD: Yes.

(*Mrs. Varney rings the bell. Short pause. Enter Martha at door up left. She stands in
the doorway.*)

MRS. VARNEY (*near mantel*):   Is there anyone I can send to the hospital,
Martha?   775
MARTHA: Luther's out yere, ma'am.
MRS. VARNEY: Luther? (*Considers.*) No — he's too small. I don't want a boy.

MARTHA: Jonas is here, mam — if you want him.

MRS. VARNEY: Oh, Jonas — yes! Tell 'im to come in here right away.

MARTHA: Yaas'm. (*Exit.*)   780

(*Mrs. Varney crosses and sits on couch. Arrelsford waits up center. Old Jonas appears at the door up left coming from door below stairs. He is a thick-set gray-haired old negro. He comes a few steps into the room. Mrs. Varney looks at Jonas and he at her — at first he is entirely unsuspecting, but in a moment, seeing Arrelsford standing up center his eyes shift about restlessly for an instant.*)

MRS. VARNEY: Jonas —

JONAS: Yes ma'am.

MRS. VARNEY: Have you any idea why I sent for you?

JONAS: Ah heers you was wantin' to sen' me to de hossiple ma'am.

(*Corporal and Men enter behind Jonas.*)

MRS. VARNEY: Oh — then Martha told you.   785

(*Corporal motions to Men and they instantly step forward — one on each side of Jonas, and stand motionless.*)

JONAS: Waal she didn't ezzackly say whut you — (*Sees man each side of him and stops in the midst of his speech. He does not start, but is frozen with terror. Stands motionless. Expression of face scarcely changes. Soon he lowers his eyes and then begins stealthily to get his right hand toward his inside breast pocket.*)

(*Corporal gives a sharp order. The men instantly seize Jonas. Corporal quickly feels in his pocket. Jonas struggles desperately but in an instant the Corporal has the paper which he hands — with a salute — to Arrelsford. Mrs. Varney rises as men seize Jonas.*)

ARRELSFORD: See if there's anything more!

CORPORAL (*Quickly searches Jonas. Men still holding him, raising his arms above his head, etc. After the search Men release Jonas and stand guard one on each side of him. Corporal salutes.*):   That's all sir.

ARRELSFORD (*Turns to lamp on table up center, opening the paper as he does so, while Corporal is searching Jonas. Mrs. Varney watches him intently. Arrelsford reads the paper quickly and at once wheels round on Jonas, speaks in low voice but sharp and telling.*):   Who was this for? (*Jonas stands silent.*) If you don't tell it's going to be mighty bad for you! (*Jonas stands silent looking at Arrelsford, who, after   790 pause, turns to Mrs. Varney.*) I'm right sorry ma'am, but it looks like we've got to shoot 'im! (*Eyeing Jonas; goes down center.*) Corporal! (*Motions him to approach — Corporal steps to Arrelsford on salute; Arrelsford speaks in low voice.*) Take him outside and get it out of him! String him up till he talks! You understand! (*Corporal salutes and is about to turn.*) Here! (*Corporal turns to Arrelsford   795 *on salute; Arrelsford glances toward window at right and back left.*) Go down on that side — back of the house! (*pointing left*) And keep it quiet! Nobody must know of this! Not a soul!

(*Corporal salutes again, goes up to Men, and gives an order. Men turn on order and march Jonas off at door up left, all very quick with military precision. Corporal goes with them. Arrelsford stands watching exit until they are gone and the sound of the closing of heavy front door is heard, then turns to Mrs. Varney. They keep voices down to nearly a whisper in the following scene, but with utmost force and intensity.*)

MRS. VARNEY (*indicating paper in his hand*):   Was there anything in that —
ARRELSFORD (*near Mrs. Varney*):   We've got the trick they want to play!   800
MRS. VARNEY: But not the man — not the man who is to play it!
ARRELSFORD: I didn't say that!
MRS. VARNEY: There's a clue?
ARRELSFORD: There *is* a clue!
MRS. VARNEY: Will it answer? Do you know who —   805
ARRELSFORD: As plain as if we had his name!
MRS. VARNEY: Thank God! (*Motionless an instant, then extends her hand for the paper.*) Let me see it! (*Arrelsford momentary hesitation — then hands her the paper, which she looks at and then reads aloud.*) "ATTACK TONIGHT — PLAN 3 — USE TELEGRAPH" — (*slight motion or sound from Arrelsford*   810
to quiet her and a quick glance round) What does it mean?
ARRELSFORD (*Takes paper.*):   They attack tonight! — The place where they strike is indicated by "Plan 3." (*finger on the words on paper*)
MRS. VARNEY: Plan three?
ARRELSFORD: He knows what they mean by that! It's arranged before-   815
hand!
MRS. VARNEY: And — the last — the last there! (*quick look at paper*) "Use Telegraph"?
ARRELSFORD: He's to use our War Department Telegraph Lines to send some false order and weaken that position — the one they indicate by   820
"Plan Three" — so they can break through and come down on the city!
MRS. VARNEY: Oh! (*pause, then suddenly*) But the one — the man who is to do this — there's nothing about *him!*
ARRELSFORD: There *is* something about him!
MRS. VARNEY (*rapidly — almost run together*):   What? Where? I don't see it!   825
ARRELSFORD: "Use Telegraph!" (*The two stand looking at one another.*) We know every man on the Telegraph Service — and every man of them's true! But there's some who want to get into that service that we don't know quite so well!
MRS. VARNEY: He would be one!   830

ARRELSFORD: There aren't so very many! (*These speeches given suggestively —
with slight pause after each.*) It isn't every man that's an expert! — The niggah brought this paper to your house, Mrs. Varney?

MRS. VARNEY: My — (*Hesitates, beginning to realize.*)

ARRELSFORD: For more than a month your daughter has been working to   835
get an appointment for someone on the Telegraph Service — perhaps *she*
could give us some idea —

(*A moment's pause, the two looking at one another, then suddenly Mrs. Varney turns
and hurries to window up right and quickly pulls curtains together, turning and facing
back to Arrelsford at same instant.*)

IS HE THERE? (*Mrs. Varney nods affirmatively and comes toward Arrelsford.*)
Could he hear what we said?

MRS. VARNEY (*Shakes head negatively.*):   He's at the further end! (*Arrelsford   840
glances at windows nervously; Mrs. Varney, after a pause, speaks in low voice.*) You
have a description you say!

ARRELSFORD: Yes — at the office.

MRS. VARNEY: Then this man — this Captain Thorne —

ARRELSFORD (*with vehemence*):   There *is* no Captain Thorne! This fellow   845
you have in your house is Lewis Dumont! (*short pause*)

MRS. VARNEY: You mean — he came here to —

ARRELSFORD (*with vindictive fury breaking through in spite of himself — yet voice subdued almost to a sharp whisper*):   He came to this town — he came to this
house — knowing your position and the influence of your name — for
the sole purpose of getting some hold on our Department Telegraph line!   850
He's corrupted your servants — he's thick with the men in the telegraph
office — what he hasn't done God A'mighty knows! But Washington
ain't the only place where there's a Secret Service! We've got one here in
Richmond! Oh — (*a shake of his head*) two can play at that game — an it's
my move now! (*Goes up right center a few steps.*)   855

(*Enter Edith Varney running rapidly down stairway and calling out excitedly as she
comes. She wears a white dress and has in her hand the large official envelope which she
took upstairs in earlier scene. Arrelsford goes toward windows up right.*)

EDITH: Mama! Mama! — Quick Mama! (*Mrs. Varney hurries toward door up
left to meet her. Arrelsford turns in surprise looking toward door.*) Under my window — in the bushes — they're hurting someone frightfully! Ah'm sure
they are! Oh — come! (*starting toward door to lead the way; Mrs. Varney stands
looking at Edith, who stops surprised that she does not follow.*) If you aren't coming   860
Ah'll go myself! (*turning to go*)

MRS. VARNEY: Wait, Edith! (*Edith stops and turns back to Mrs. Varney.*) I must tell you something — it'll be a terrible shock I'm afraid! (*Edith goes toward Mrs. Varney, Arrelsford turns away a little — standing near right center watching window.*) A man we trusted as a friend has shown himself a treacherous conspirator against us! 865

EDITH (*after a slight pause — low voice*):   Who? (*Pause. Mrs. Varney cannot bring herself to speak the name. After a slight pause, in the same low voice*) Who is it?

ARRELSFORD (*swinging round on her; low voice but with vindictiveness*):   It is the gentleman, Miss Varney, whose attentions you have been pleased to accept in the place of mine! 870

(*Short pause. Edith looking at Arrelsford, white and motionless. Then she turns her face appealing to her mother; Mrs. Varney nods slowly in affirmation. Edith puts the envelope with Commission in belt or bosom of dress in an absent manner.*)

EDITH (*low voice*):   Is it Mr. Arrelsford who makes this accusation?

ARRELSFORD (*breaking out hotly but keeping voice down*):   Yes, since you wish to know! From the first I've had my suspicions that this — (*Stops on seeing Edith's move toward the window up right.*)

(*Edith turns on "Since you wish to know" and goes quickly toward the window. Arrelsford steps before her; speaks rapidly in low voice.*)

Where are you going?

EDITH (*low voice*):   For Captain Thorne. 875

ARRELSFORD (*low voice*):   Not now!

EDITH (*turning with flashing indignation on Arrelsford; low voice*):   Mr. Arrelsford, if this is something you're afraid to say to him — don't you *dare* say it to me!

ARRELSFORD (*indignantly; low voice*):   Miss Varney, if you — 880

MRS. VARNEY (*interrupting quickly, low voice*):   Edith, he has good reason for not meeting Captain Thorne now!

EDITH (*turning quickly to Mrs. Varney*):   Ah should think he had! The man who said that to his face wouldn't live to speak again!

MRS. VARNEY: My dear, you don't — 885

EDITH: Mama — this man has left his desk in the War Department so that he can have the pleasure of persecuting me! He's never attempted anything in the active service before! And when I ask him to face the man he accuses he turns like a coward!

ARRELSFORD (*angrily, but keeping his voice subdued*):   Mrs. Varney, if she thinks — 890

EDITH (*low voice*):   I think nothing! I know a man of Captain Thorne's character is above suspicion!

ARRELSFORD (*low voice*):   His character! Ha ha! (*a sneer*) Where did he come
from? — Who is he?

EDITH: Who are you?   895

ARRELSFORD: That's not the question.

EDITH (*low voice*):   Neither is it the question who is he! If it were I'd answer
it — I'd tell you he's a soldier who has fought and been wounded for his
country!

ARRELSFORD (*low voice but incisive*):   We're not so sure of that!   900

EDITH (*after a pause of indignation*):   He brought us letters from General
Stonewall Jackson and —

ARRELSFORD (*quick and sharp*):   General Jackson was killed before his letter
was presented!

EDITH: What does that signify if he wrote it?   905

ARRELSFORD: Nothing — *if* he wrote it!

EDITH: Mr. Arrelsford, if you mean — (*Mrs. Varney goes to Edith putting her
hands on Edith's arm.*)

MRS. VARNEY (*low voice*):   Listen Edith! They have proofs of a conspiracy on
our Government Telegraph Lines. (*Arrelsford says "Sh" and goes to window up
right; Edith turns from Arrelsford and looks before her, listening on mention of "Telegraph Lines"; Mrs. Varney leads Edith a little left of center.*) Two men in the   910
Northern Secret Service have been sent here to do this work. One is in
Libby Prison. Our old Jonas went there today — secretly took a message
from him and brought it here — to the other! (*Edith turns toward Mrs. Varney sharply.*) We've just had Jonas in here and found that paper on him!

(*Arrelsford comes down right looking off through curtains of windows.*)

EDITH (*rapidly, desperately, in low voice*):   But he hasn't said it was for —   915

(*Dull heavy sound of front door closing outside left.*)

ARRELSFORD (*low voice but incisively*):   Not yet — but he will! (*Edith looks at
him not comprehending; enter Corporal at door up left who stands on salute; Ladies
turn to him, Edith breathless with anxiety, Mrs. Varney calm but intent. Arrelsford
goes to Corporal and speaks in low voice.*) Well, what does he say?

CORPORAL (*low voice*):   Nothing sir — he won't speak!

ARRELSFORD (*sharply, but voice subdued*):   What have you done?

CORPORAL: Strung him up three times and —   920

ARRELSFORD (*enraged but keeping his voice down*):   Well string him up again! If
he won't speak shoot it out of him! Kill the dog! (*Comes blindly down left;
Corporal salutes and exits; Arrelsford turns to Ladies and goes back of table, gets hat
from table.*) We don't need the niggah's evidence — there's enough without it!

EDITH (*low voice*):   There's nothing!   925

ARRELSFORD (*at table, low voice*):   By twelve o'clock tonight you'll have all the proof you want!

EDITH: There's no proof at all!

ARRELSFORD: I'll show it to you at the telegraph office! Do you dare go with me?   930

EDITH (*low voice*):   Dare! (*Moves toward him.*) I *will* go with you!

ARRELSFORD (*low voice*):   I'll call for you in half an hour! (*Goes up toward left door.*)

EDITH: Wait! — what are you going to do?

ARRELSFORD (*Comes down back of table; low voice but incisive*):   I'm going to let him get this paper! He'll know what they want him to do — and then 935 we'll see him try to do it!

EDITH: You're going to spy on him — hound him like a criminal!

ARRELSFORD: I'm going to prove what he is!

EDITH (*low voice*):   Then prove it openly! Prove it at once! It's a shame to let a suspicion like that rest on an honorable man! Let him come in here 940 and —

ARRELSFORD (*low voice*):   Impossible!

EDITH (*low voice*):   Then do something else but do it now! (*Turning away a little, speaks desperately.*) We must know that he is — that he's innocent! We must know that! (*a thought; turns to Arrelsford.*) You say the prisoner in 945 Libby is his brother — that's what you said — his brother! Bring him here! Go to the prison and bring that man here!

ARRELSFORD (*speaking across table, subdued exclamation*):   What!

EDITH: Let them meet! Bring them face to face! Then you can see whether —   950

ARRELSFORD (*low voice, speaks rapidly*):   You mean — bring them together here?

EDITH: Yes!

ARRELSFORD: As if the prisoner was trying to escape?

EDITH: Any way you like — but end it!   955

ARRELSFORD: When?

EDITH: Now!

ARRELSFORD (*after instant's thought*):   I'm willing to try that! — Can you keep him here? (*with a motion toward windows*)

EDITH (*scarcely more than a movement of lips*):   Yes.   960

ARRELSFORD: It won't be more than half an hour. Be out there on the veranda. When I tap on the glass bring him into this room and leave him alone!

EDITH (*hardly more than nod and a whisper*):   Yes. (*Turns away toward front.*)

ARRELSFORD (*Goes rapidly toward door up left, stops and turns near door.*): I rely on   965
you Miss Varney to give him no hint or sign that we suspect —

(*Mrs. Varney and Edith both turn indignantly on him, Mrs. Varney with slight exclamation.*)

EDITH (*interrupting Arrelsford*): Mr. Arrelsford!

(*Arrelsford stands an instant — then bows stiffly and exits at door up left. Edith
stands where she was as if stunned. Mrs. Varney looks after Arrelsford, then turns to
Edith.*)

EDITH (*after pause, not looking round, nearly whisper*): Mama! (*Reaches out her
hand as if feeling for help or support; Mrs. Varney comes to Edith and takes her hand.*)
Mama!

MRS. VARNEY (*low voice*): I'm here, Edith!   970

EDITH (*pause, Edith thinking of something, her eyes wide open, staring vacantly before
her and holding tight to Mrs. Varney's hand*): Do you think — do you
think — that could be what he meant? (*Mrs. Varney looking intently at Edith*)
The Commission I got for him — this afternoon.

MRS. VARNEY (*low voice*): Yes — yes!

EDITH: The Commission you know — from the President — for the —   975
for the Telegraph Service! He — he — refused to take it!

MRS. VARNEY: Refused!

EDITH (*nodding a little, hardly able to speak*): He said — he said it was for me
that he could not!

MRS. VARNEY: It's true then!   980

EDITH (*turning quickly to her and trying to stop her by putting her hand over her mouth,
speaking rapidly, breathlessly, yet not in a loud voice*): No no! Don't say it!

MRS. VARNEY (*putting Edith's hand away*): Yes!

EDITH: Oh, no!

MRS. VARNEY: Infamous traitor! They ought to lash him through the
streets of Richmond!   985

EDITH (*impulsively trying to stop Mrs. Varney*): No Mama! No — no — no!
(*She stops — a moment's pause, she realizes the truth; speaks in almost a whisper.*)
Yes — yes — (*Stops, pauses, stands erect, looks about, motions Mrs. Varney to go.*)

(*Mrs. Varney turns quietly and leaves the room, going out at the door up left. Edith
stands supporting herself without knowing that she does so — one hand on a table or
back of chair. Soon coming to herself she turns and goes toward the window up right.
When near center she stops. Stands there a moment looking toward the window. Then
brushes her hand quickly across her eyes and takes the President's Commission from the
bosom of dress. She looks at it as if thinking, folds it slowly and puts it back again, and
then walks to the window, throws aside the curtains and pushes it open. Captain*)

Thorne, outside at some distance, makes sound with chair as though he rose and pushed or set it back and the sound of his footsteps outside approaching briskly follows at once. Edith moves back away from the window and near table and stands there looking at the window. After footsteps and after Edith is motionless, Captain Thorne walks briskly and unsuspiciously into the room at window up right, glancing about as he does so — not seeing Edith until he is a little way in. Upon seeing her he stops an instant where he is, and then goes directly across to her and is about to take her hand as he speaks.)

THORNE: Miss Varney —

EDITH (*as she snatches her hand away and shrinks back slightly; breathless*):   No — don't touch me! (*A second's pause; she recovers almost instantly.*) Oh — it was   990
you! (*smiling as if at her own stupidity*) Why how perfectly absurd I am! (*crossing in front of Thorne lightly and going to window at up right*) Ah'm sure Ah ought to be ashamed of myself! (*Turns to him.*) Do come out a minute — on the veranda — Ah want to talk to you about a whole lot o' things! There's half an hour yet before the party! (*turning to go*) Isn't it a lovely   995
night! (*Exits at the window up right with forced gaiety of manner disappearing in the darkness.*) Oh, come along!

(*Thorne stands looking at Edith when she first speaks. As she crosses he is looking down a little but looks slowly up toward front and turns a little after her cross, looking at her as she stands for a moment in the window. After her exit he slowly turns toward front and his eyes glance about and down once as he weighs the chances.*)

EDITH (*after brief pause for above, calling gaily from outside, not too near the window*): Oh, Cap'n Thorne!

(*Thorne turns quickly looking off right again; hesitates an instant; makes up his mind; walks rapidly to window — a slight hesitating there, without stopping. Exits at window.*)

Act II

The same room as in Act I; strong moonlight outside both windows at right. Portieres are closed at both windows. Nine o'clock. Mrs. Varney discovered seated at desk down right. She is not busy with anything but sits watching that no one goes out to the veranda. Sound of closing of door outside left; enter Miss Kittridge at door up center, which stands ajar as if she had recently come out.

MRS. VARNEY: Was it the same man?

MISS KITTRIDGE: No; they sent another one this time.

MRS. VARNEY: Did you have anything ready?

MISS KITTRIDGE: Oh yes — Ah gave 'em quite a lot. We've all been at the bandages — that's what they need most. (*Mrs. Varney rises; seems preoccupied; goes across to left and looks off. Miss Kittridge watches her rather anxiously a moment.*) Did you want anything, Mrs. Varney?

MRS. VARNEY (*turning*): No — I — nothing, thank you. (*Miss Kittridge is turning to go but stops when Mrs. Varney speaks again. Mrs. Varney goes nearer to Miss Kittridge.*) Perhaps it would be just as well if any of the ladies want to go, to let them out the other way. You can open the door into the dining-room. We're expecting someone here on important business.

MISS KITTRIDGE: Ah'll see to it, Mrs. Varney.

MRS. VARNEY: Thank you. (*Exit Miss Kittridge at door up center. Mrs. Varney stands a moment, then goes down left and rings bell, crosses to right center, going back of table, then goes slowly up center, waiting. Enter Martha at door up left from door right of stairway.*) Did Miss Caroline go home?

MARTHA (*near door*): No'm. She's been out yere in de kitchen fur a while.

MRS. VARNEY: In the kitchen!

MARTHA: Yaas'm.

MRS. VARNEY: What is she doing?

MARTHA: She's been mostly sewin' and behavin' mighty strange and sumfin a great deal o' de time. Ah bleeve she's gittin' ready to go home now.

MRS. VARNEY: Ask her to come here a moment.

MARTHA: Yaas'm. (*Turns and exits up left. Mrs. Varney waits a little, then goes forward a few steps. Enter Caroline at left door from door right of stairway. She comes into the room trying to look very innocent.*)

MRS. VARNEY: Caroline — (*Caroline goes down center with Mrs. Varney. She is expecting to hear something said about the sewing she has been doing.*) Are you in a hurry to get home? Because if you can wait a few minutes while I go upstairs to Howard it'll be a great help.

CAROLINE (*looking around in some doubt*): You want me to — just wait? Is that all?

MRS. VARNEY: I — (*Hesitates a little.*) — I don't want anyone to go out on the veranda just now. (*Caroline looks toward veranda.*) Edith's there — with —

CAROLINE (*suddenly comprehending*): Oh yes! (*Glances toward windows.*) Ah know how that is — Ah'll attend to it! (*Crosses to up right center.*)

MRS. VARNEY: Just while I'm upstairs — it won't be long! (*Goes to door left and turns.*) Be careful won't you dear! (*Exit and up the stairway.*)

CAROLINE: Careful! Well Ah should think so! As if Ah didn't know enough for that! (*Goes toward window up right and pauses. Her face is radiant with the imagined romance of the situation; peeps out slyly through curtains. After a moment she turns, an idea having occurred to her, and quickly rolls the couch up across before the window, kneels on it with her back to the audience, and tries to peep through curtains. Enter Wilfred door up left, coming in cautiously and if he had been watching for an opportunity. He stops just within the door and looks back up stairway. He has on trousers which Caroline fixed for him and also the jacket. Caroline rises and turns from the couch and sees Wilfred, startled at first. He turns to her; she stands adoring him in his uniform, which, though showing strange folds and awkwardness at the bottom of the trousers from being cut off and sewed by an amateur, do not appear grotesque or laughable.)*

CAROLINE (*subdued exclamation, seeing Wilfred in uniform*):   Oh!

WILFRED (*low voice, speaking across from door*):   Mother isn't anywhere around is she?

CAROLINE (*coming to center*):   She — she just went upstairs.

WILFRED (*down a little*):   Ah'm not running away — but if she saw me with these things on she might feel funny.

CAROLINE (*half to herself*):   She might not feel so very funny!

WILFRED: Well — you know — (*going over to desk down right and taking papers and letters from pockets*) how it is with a feller's mother. (*Caroline nods; Wilfred hurriedly searches for letter among others, feeling in different pockets, so that he speaks without much thinking what he says.*) Other people don't care — but mothers — well — they're different.

CAROLINE (*Speaks absently*):   Yes — other people don't care! (*Moves toward up left, the thought of Wilfred actually going giving her a slight sinking of the heart at which she herself is surprised.*)

WILFRED: Ah've written that letter to the General! — Here it is — on'y Ah've got to end it off some way! (*Pulls a chair sideways to desk and half sits, intent on finishing the letter; prepares pen and runs hand into his hair impetuously.*) Ah'm not going to say "Your loving son" or any such rubbish as that! It would be an almighty let-down! Ah *love* him of course — but this isn't that kind of a letter! (*pointing out writing on letter and speaking as if he supposed Caroline was at his shoulder*) Ah've been telling him — (*Looking round sees that Caroline is standing at a considerable distance looking at him.*) — What's the matter?

CAROLINE: Nothing — !

WILFRED: Ah thought you wanted to help!

CAROLINE (*quickly*):   Oh yes — Ah do! Ah do! (*Goes to Wilfred at desk; he looks in her face an instant, followed by a pause; then Caroline stammeringly asks*) The — the (*indicating his trousers by a little gesture*) — are they how you wanted 'em?

WILFRED: What?

CAROLINE: Those things. (*pointing to trousers*)

WILFRED (*Glances at legs.*):   Oh — they're all right! Fine! — Now about this letter — tell me what you think! (*turning to letter again*)

CAROLINE: Tell me what you said!

WILFRED: Want to hear it?

CAROLINE: Ah've got to haven't I? How could Ah help you if I didn't know what it was all about!

WILFRED: You're pretty good! (*Looks at her briefly.*) You *will* help me won't you? (*catching hold of her hand as she stands near him*)

CAROLINE: Oh' co'se Ah will — (*After an instant's pause draws hand away from him.*) about the letter!

WILFRED: That's what I mean! — It's mighty important you know! Everything depends on it!

CAROLINE: Well Ah should think so! (*Gets chair from between windows and pulls it near Wilfred on his left and sits looking over the letter while he reads   showing deep interest.*)

WILFRED: Ah just gave it to him strong!

CAROLINE: That's the *way* to give it to him!

WILFRED: You can't fool round with *him* much! He means business! But he'll find out Ah mean business too!

CAROLINE: That's right — everybody means business! — What did you say?

WILFRED: Ah said this! (*Reads letter.*) "General Ransom Varney — Commanding Division Army of the Northern Virginia — Dear Papa — This is to notify you that Ah want you to let me come right now! If you don't Ah'll come anyhow — that's all! The eighteen call is out — the seventeen comes next an' Ah'm not going to wait for it! Do you think Ah'm a damned coward? Tom Kittridge has gone! He was killed yesterday at Cold Harbor. Billy Fisher has gone. So has Cousin Stephen and he ain't sixteen. He lied about his age but Ah don't want to do that unless you make me. Answer this right now or not at all!"

CAROLINE: That's splendid!

WILFRED: Do you think so?

CAROLINE: Why it's just the thing!

WILFRED: But how'm Ah going to end it?

CAROLINE: Just end it!

WILFRED: How?

CAROLINE: Sign your name.

WILFRED: Nothing else?

CAROLINE: What else is there?

WILFRED: Just "Wilfred"?

CAROLINE: O'co'se!

WILFRED (*Looks at her an instant then turns suddenly to desk and writes his name.*): That's the thing! (*Holds it up.*) Will the rest of it do?

CAROLINE: Do! Ah should think so! (*rising*) Ah wish he had it now! (*Goes*   105
toward center.)

WILFRED (*rising*):   So do I! — It might take two or three days! (*Moves*
toward Caroline.) Ah can't wait that long! Why the Seventeen call
might — (*Stops; thinks frowningly.*)

CAROLINE (*suddenly turning*):   Ah'll tell you what to do! — Telegraph! (*Wil-*
fred looks at her — she at him. After an instant he glances at the letter.)

WILFRED: Whew! (*a whistle*) Ah haven't got money enough for that!   110

CAROLINE: 'Twon't take so very much!

WILFRED: Do you know what they're charging now? Over seven dollars a
word!

CAROLINE: Let 'em charge! We can cut it down so there's only a few words
an' it means just the same! (*They both go at the letter each holding it on his or her*   115
side.) The address won't cost a thing!

WILFRED: Won't it?

CAROLINE: No! They never do! There's a heap o' money saved right now!
We can use that to pay for the rest! (*Wilfred looks at her a little puzzled.*)
What comes next? (*Both look over the letter.*)   120

WILFRED: "Dear Papa" —

CAROLINE: Leave that out! (*Both scratch at it with pens or pencils.*)

WILFRED: Ah didn't care much for it anyway!

CAROLINE: He knew it before.

WILFRED: Ah'm glad it's out!   125

CAROLINE: So'm I! What's next? (*reading*) "This — is — to — notify —
you — that — Ah — want — you — to — let — me — come —
right — now." We might leave out that last "to."

WILFRED *and* CAROLINE (*reciting it off together experimentally to see how it reads*
without the "to"):   "Ah — want — you — let — me — come — right —
now." (*after instant's thought both shake heads.*)   130

WILFRED: No!

CAROLINE: No!

WILFRED: It doesn't sound right.

CAROLINE: That's only a little word anyhow!

WILFRED: So it is. What's after that? (*Both eagerly look at letter.*)   135

CAROLINE: Wait — here it is! (*Reads.*) "If — you — don't — Ah'll —
come — anyhow — that's — all." (*They consider.*)

WILFRED: We might leave out "that's all."

CAROLINE (*quickly*):   No! Don't leave that out! It's very important. It doesn't
seem so but it is! It shows — (*Hesitates.*) Well — it shows that's all there   140
is about it! That one thing might convince him!

WILFRED: We've got to leave out something!

CAROLINE: Yes — but not that! Perhaps there's something in the next! (*Reads.*) "The — eighteen — call — is — out — " That's got to stay!
WILFRED (*Reads.*):   "The — seventeen — comes — next."   145
CAROLINE: That's got to stay!
WILFRED (*shaking head*):   Yes!
CAROLINE (*taking it up*):   "Ah'm — not — going — to — wait — for — it!" (*shaking head without looking up*) No! No!
WILFRED (*shaking head*):   No!   150
CAROLINE: We'll find something in just a minute! (*reading*) "Do — you — think — Ah'm — a — damned — coward!" (*Both look up from the letter simultaneously and gaze at each other in silence for an instant.*)
WILFRED (*after pause*):   We might leave out the —
CAROLINE (*breaking in on him with almost a scream*):   No no! (*They again regard each other.*)
WILFRED: That "damn"'s going to cost us seven dollars and a half!   155
CAROLINE: It's worth it! Why it's the best thing you've got in the whole thing! Your papa's a general in the army! He'll *understand* that! What's next? Ah know there's something now.
WILFRED (*Reads*):   "Tom — Kittridge — has — gone. He — was — killed — yesterday — at — Cold — Harbor."   160
CAROLINE (*slight change in tone, a little lower*):   Leave out that about his (*very slight catch of breath*) about his being killed.
WILFRED (*looking at her*):   But he was!
CAROLINE (*suddenly very quiet*):   Ah know he was — but you haven't got to tell him the news — have you?   165
WILFRED: That's so! (*They both cross off the words.*)
CAROLINE (*becoming cheerful again*):   How does it read now? (*both looking over the letter*)
WILFRED: It reads just the same — except that about Tom Kittridge.
CAROLINE (*looking at Wilfred astonished*):   Just the same! After all this work!

(*They look at one another rather astounded for an instant, then suddenly turn to the letter again and study over it earnestly. Sound of door bell in distant part of house. Soon after Martha crosses outside left coming from door right of stairway to go to door. Sound of door off left. A moment later she is seen going up the stairway carrying a large envelope. Wilfred and Caroline are so absorbed in work that they do not observe the bell or Martha's movements.*)

CAROLINE (*looking up from letter*):   Everything else has *got* to stay!   170
WILFRED: Then we can't telegraph — it would take hundreds of dollars!
CAROLINE (*with determination*):   Yes we can! (*Wilfred looks at her; she takes the letter.*) Ah'll send it! (*backing up a little toward door up left*)

WILFRED: How can you —

CAROLINE: Never you mind! 175

WILFRED (*Follows her up a little.*): See here! (*taking hold of letter*) Ah'm not going to have you spending money!

CAROLINE: Ha! There's no danger! Ah haven't got any to spend!

WILFRED (*Releases hold on letter.*): Then what are you going to do?

CAROLINE (*turning up toward door up left with letter*): Oh — Ah know! (*Turns* 180 *toward Wilfred.*) Ah reckon Douglass Stafford'll send it for me!

WILFRED (*quickly to her*): No he won't! (*They face each other; Caroline surprised.*)

CAROLINE: What's the reason he won't?

WILFRED (*slight pause*): If he wants to send it for *me* he can — but he won't send it for *you!* 185

CAROLINE: What do you care s'long as he sends it?

WILFRED (*looking at Caroline — slight change of tone — softer*): Well — Ah care! That's enough! (*They look at each other, then both lower eyes, looking in different directions.*)

CAROLINE: Oh, well — if you feel like that about it — ! (*Turns away.*)

WILFRED (*eyes lowered*): That's the way Ah feel! (*Pause; Wilfred looks up at* 190 *her — goes down toward her.*) You — you won't give up the idea of helping me because I feel like that — will you?

CAROLINE (*impulsively, with start and turn toward Wilfred*): Mercy no — Ah'll help you all I can! (*Wilfred impulsively takes her hand as if in gratitude and so quick that she draws it away and goes on with only a slight break.*) About the 195 letter!

WILFRED: That's what Ah mean! (*They stand an instant, Caroline looking down, Wilfred at her.*)

CAROLINE (*suddenly turning toward desk*): Ah'm going to see if we can't leave out something else! (*Sits at desk; Wilfred goes near her and stands looking over her, intent on the letter.*)

(*Enter Mrs. Varney, coming down the stairway and into the room at door up left. She has an open letter in her hand. She also brings a belt and cap rolled up together. She pauses at the door and motions someone who is outside left to come in. Martha follows her down and exits through door right of stairway. Enter an orderly up left just from his horse after a long ride. Dusty, faded and bloody uniform; yellow stripes; face sunburned and grim. He stands near the door waiting, without effort to be precise or formal, but nevertheless being entirely soldierly. Mrs. Varney waits until he enters.*)

MRS. VARNEY (*Comes down center a little.*): Wilfred! (*Wilfred and Caroline turn* 200 *quickly. They both stare motionless for a moment.*) Here's a letter from your father. He sent it by the orderly. (*Wilfred moves a step or two toward Mrs. Varney and stands looking at her. Caroline slowly rises with her eyes on Mrs. Varney, who*

speaks calmly but with the measured quietness of one who is controlling herself.) He
tells me — (*Stops a little but it is only her voice that falls; she does not break down or
show emotion; holds letter toward Wilfred.*) You read it!   205

(*Wilfred, after glance at Caroline, steps quickly to Mrs. Varney and takes the letter.
Reads it — Mrs. Varney looking away a little as he does so. Caroline's eyes upon Wilfred as he reads. The Orderly faced to right on obliqued line of door. Wilfred finishes very
soon. He glances at the Orderly, then hands the letter to his mother as he steps across to
him.*)

WILFRED (*standing before the Orderly*):   The General says Ah'm going back
with you!
ORDERLY (*saluting*):   His orders, sir!
WILFRED: When do we start?
ORDERLY: Soon as you can sir — Ah'm waiting!   210
WILFRED: We'll make it right now! (*Turns and walks quickly to his mother.*)
You won't mind, mother.

(*Mrs. Varney does not speak, but quietly strokes the hair back from his forehead with a
trembling hand — and only once. She then hands him the belt that has seen service and
the cap that is old and worn.*)

MRS. VARNEY (*low voice*):   Your brother wanted you to take these — I told
him you were going; (*Wilfred takes them; puts on the belt at once.*) He says he
can get another belt — when he wants it. You're to have his blankets   215
too — Ah'll get them. (*Crosses Wilfred and goes off at door up left and off to left
going back of orderly.*)
WILFRED (*finishing adjusting the belt; Caroline motionless but now looking down at the
floor; Wilfred suppresses excitement.*):   Fits as if it was made for me! (*to Orderly*) Ah'll be with you in a jiffy! (*Goes to Caroline.*) We won't have to send
that now — (*indicating letter*) will we? (*Caroline shakes her head a little without
looking up — then slowly raises hand in which she has the letter and holds it out to
him, her eyes still on the floor. Wilfred takes the letter mechanically and keeps it in his
hand during the next few lines, tearing it up absent-mindedly.*) You're pretty   220
good — to help me like you did! You can help me again if you — if you
want to! (*Caroline raises her eyes and looks at him.*) Ah'd like to fight twice as
well if — (*Hesitates. Caroline looks at him an instant longer and then looks down
without speaking.*) Good-bye! (*Wilfred holds out his hand. Caroline puts her hand
in his without looking at him.*) Perhaps you'll write to me about — about   225
helping me fight twice as well! Ah wouldn't mind if you telegraphed!
That is — if you telegraphed that you would! (*Slight pause. Wilfred holding
Caroline's hand boyishly; Caroline looking down. Wilfred tries to say something but
can't find the words. Enter Mrs. Varney at door up left; Wilfred hears her and turns —
leaving Caroline and meeting his mother near center. She brings an army blanket*

rolled and tied. Wilfred takes it and slings it over his shoulder.) Good-bye mother! (*Kisses her rather hurriedly; Mrs. Varney stands passive.*) You won't mind, will you. (*Crosses at once to Orderly with eagerness and enthusiasm.*) Ready sir! (*salut-* 230 *ing; Orderly turns and marches off at door up left, Wilfred following.*)

(*The opening and closing of the door outside is heard, and then it is still. Mrs. Varney is the first to move. She turns and walks slowly up a few steps, her back to the audience, but with no visible emotion. It is as if her eyes filled with tears and she turned away. When she stops, Caroline moves a little, her eyes still down, walking slowly across toward door left, but not with emphasized deliberation. Mrs. Varney hears her going and turns in time to speak just before she reaches the door.*)

MRS. VARNEY: Going, dear? (*Caroline nods her head a little without looking around.*) Oh yes! (*Speaks with a shade of forced cheerfulness.*) Your party, of course! You ought to be there! (*Caroline stops and speaks back into the room without looking at Mrs. Varney.*)

CAROLINE (*subdued voice; with a sad little shake of head*): There won't — (*Shakes head again a little.*) There won't be any party tonight. (*Exit door left.*) 235

MRS. VARNEY (*After an instant's wait starts toward door up left.*): Caroline! Stop a moment! (*at door*) I don't want you to go home alone! (*Goes down left and rings the bell.*)

CAROLINE (*outside*): Oh Ah don't mind!

(*Sounds of front door and heavy steps of men outside, up left. Mrs. Varney goes up left, looks off and then retires back a little into the room. Enter Arrelsford and two soldiers at the door up left. He motions men to stand at the door and goes quickly to Mrs. Varney.*)

ARRELSFORD (*low voice*): Is he — ? (*a motion toward window at right*)

MRS. VARNEY (*hardly above a whisper*): Yes! (*Glances round toward window.*) 240

(*Enter Caroline at door up left from off left.*)

CAROLINE: Oh Mrs. Varney — there's a heap o' soldiers out yere! You don't reckon anything's the mattah do you?

(*Enter Martha at door up left from door right of stairway. Arrelsford goes back to Mrs. Varney to window up right, looks through curtains.*)

MRS. VARNEY (*hastening to Caroline*): Sh! — No — there's nothing the mat-ter! Martha, I want you to go home with Miss Mitford — at once! (*urg-ing Caroline off*) Good night dear! (*kissing her*) 245

CAROLINE: Good night! (*Looks up in Mrs. Varney's face.*) You don't reckon she could go with me to — (*Hesitates.*) somewhere else, do you?

MRS. VARNEY: Why where do you want to go?

CAROLINE: Just to — just to the telegraph office!

(*Arrelsford turns sharply and looks at Caroline from window.*)

MRS. VARNEY: Now! At this time of night!   250
CAROLINE: Ah've got to! Oh, it's very important business!

(*Arrelsford watching Caroline*)

MRS. VARNEY: Of course, then Martha must go with you! Good night!
CAROLINE: Good night! (*Exit Caroline and Martha at door up left and off.*)
MRS. VARNEY (*calling off to Martha*):   Martha, don't leave her an instant!
MARTHA: No'm — Ah'll take care! (*heavy sound of door outside up left*)   255
ARRELSFORD (*going up center quickly — low, sharp voice*):   What is she going to
   do at the telegraph office?
MRS. VARNEY (*going down left center a little; low voice*):   I've no idea!
ARRELSFORD: Has she had any conversation with him? (*Motions toward
   right.*)
MRS. VARNEY: Why — they were talking together here — early this   260
   evening! But it isn't possible she could —
ARRELSFORD: Anything is possible! (*Goes over to Corporal at up left quickly, pass-
   ing back of Mrs. Varney, who moves up to right center as he crosses.*) Have Eddinger
   follow that girl! Don't let any dispatch go out until I see it! Make no mistake about that! (*Corporal exits with salute at door up left; brief pause; Arrelsford*   265
   turns to Mrs. Varney.) Are they both out there? (*Motions toward window.*)
MRS. VARNEY (*glance back at right first*):   Yes! Did you bring the man from
   Libby Prison?
ARRELSFORD: The guard's holding him in the street. When we get Thorne
   in here alone I'll have him brought up to that window (*pointing*) an'   270
   shoved into the room!

(*Corporal reappears at the door and waits for further orders. Arrelsford and Mrs. Varney continue in low tones.*)

MRS. VARNEY: Where shall I —
ARRELSFORD: Out there (*pointing up left and going toward door a little*) where
   you can get a view of this room!
MRS. VARNEY: But if he sees me —   275
ARRELSFORD: He won't if it's dark in the hall! (*Turns to Corporal and gives order in low distinct voice.*) Shut off those lights out there! (*indicating lights outside the door or archway up left. Corporal exits; lights off.*) We can close these
   curtains can't we?
MRS. VARNEY: Yes. (*Arrelsford draws curtains at door up left.*)   280
ARRELSFORD: I don't want much light in here! (*indicating drawing-room. Corporal and Men exit up left. Arrelsford goes to table up left center and turns gas or lamp*

down; Mrs. Varney turns down lamp on desk — stage in half light. Arrelsford carefully moves couch away from window up right and opens portieres of window, and then speaks almost in a whisper.) Now open those curtains! Carefully! Don't attract attention! (*indicating window down right*)

(*Mrs. Varney very quietly draws back the curtains to window down right — moonlight through the window covers as much of stage as possible, as well as backing up right.*)

ARRELSFORD (*moving over to up left center and speaking across to Mrs. Varney after lights are down*): Are those women in there yet? (*indicating door up center*)

MRS. VARNEY: Yes.   285

ARRELSFORD: Where's the key? (*Mrs. Varney moves noiselessly to the door.*) Is it on the inside? (*Mrs. Varney turns and nods affirmatively.*) Lock the door!

(*Mrs. Varney turns the key as noiselessly as possible. Edith suddenly appears at window up right coming on quickly and closing the windows after her. Mrs. Varney and Arrelsford both turn and stand looking at her. Edith turns to them and stands an instant.*)

EDITH (*going toward Mrs. Varney with hand stretched out — very low voice — but breathlessly and with intensity*): Mama! (*Mrs. Varney hurries forward with her center; Arrelsford remains up left center looking on.*) I want to speak to you!

ARRELSFORD (*low tone, stepping forward*): We can't wait!   290

EDITH: You must! (*Arrelsford moves back protestingly. Edith turns to Mrs. Varney — almost a whisper*) I can't — I can't do it! Oh — let me go!

MRS. VARNEY (*very low voice*): Edith! You were the one who —

EDITH (*almost a whisper*): I was sure then!

MRS. VARNEY: Has he confessed?   295

EDITH (*quickly*): No no! (*glance toward Arrelsford*)

ARRELSFORD (*low voice — sharp*): Don't speak so loud!

MRS. VARNEY (*low voice*): What is it Edith — You must tell me!

EDITH (*almost a whisper*): Mama — he loves me! (*breathless with emotion*) — Yes — and I — Oh — let someone else do it!   300

MRS. VARNEY: You don't mean that you — (*Arrelsford comes forward quickly.*)

EDITH (*seeing Arrelsford approach and crossing to him*): No no! Not now! Not now!

MRS. VARNEY: More reason now than ever!

ARRELSFORD: We *must* go on!   305

EDITH (*turning desperately upon Arrelsford in low voice*): Why are you doing this?

ARRELSFORD: Because I please!

EDITH (*low voice but with force*): You never pleased before! Hundreds of suspicious cases have come up — hundreds of men have been run down —   310 but you preferred to sit at your desk in the War Department.

MRS. VARNEY: Edith!

ARRELSFORD: We won't discuss that now!

EDITH: No — we'll end it! I'll have nothing more to do with the affair!

ARRELSFORD: You won't! 315

MRS. VARNEY: You won't!

EDITH: Nothing at all! — Nothing! — Nothing!

ARRELSFORD (*low voice but with vehemence*): At your own suggestion Miss Varney, I agreed to a plan by which we could criminate this friend of yours — or establish his innocence. At the critical moment — when 320 everything's ready you propose to withdraw — making it a failure and perhaps allowing him to escape altogether!

MRS. VARNEY: You mustn't do this Edith!

EDITH (*desperately*): He's there! The man is there — at the further end of the veranda! What more do you want of me! 325

ARRELSFORD (*low voice, sharp, intense*): Call 'im into this room! If anyone else should do it he'd suspect! He'd be on his guard!

EDITH (*after pause*): Very well — I'll call 'im into this room. (*Moves as if to do so.*)

ARRELSFORD: One thing more! I want 'im to have this paper! (*holding out paper taken from Jonas in Act I*) Tell 'im where it came from — tell 'im the 330 old niggah got it from a prisoner in Libby!

EDITH (*quietly*): Why am I to do that?

ARRELSFORD (*low but very strong*): Why not? If he's innocent where's the harm? If not — if he's in this plot — the message on that paper will send 'im to the telegraph office tonight and that's just where we want him! 335

EDITH: I never promised that!

ARRELSFORD (*hard sharp voice though subdued*): Do you still believe him innocent?

EDITH (*pause; slowly raises her head erect, looks Arrelsford full in the face; almost whisper*): I still — believe him — innocent!

ARRELSFORD: Then why are you afraid to give him this? (*indicating paper*) 340

(*Pause. Edith turns to Arrelsford, stretches out her hand and takes the paper from him. She pauses a moment. Arrelsford and Mrs. Varney watch her. She turns and moves up a few steps toward the window; stops and stands listening; noise of chair off right.*)

EDITH: Captain Thorne's coming.

ARRELSFORD (*going to door up left and holding curtain back*): This way Mrs. Varney! Quick! Quick! (*Arrelsford and Mrs. Varney hasten off at the door up left, closing portieres after them.*)

(*Edith moves and stands near table. Sound of Thorne's footsteps on veranda outside windows. Edith slowly turns toward the window and stands looking at it with a fas-*

cinated dread. Thorne opens the window and enters at once, coming a few steps into the room, when he stops and stands an instant looking at Edith as she looks strangely at him. Then he goes to her.)

THORNE (*low voice, near Edith*):   Is anything the matter?

EDITH (*slightly shakes her head before speaking; nearly a whisper*):   Oh *no!*   345

THORNE: You've been away such a long time!

EDITH: Only a few minutes!

THORNE: Only a few years.

EDITH (*easier*):   Oh — if that's a few years — (*turning away front a little*) what a lot of time there is!   350

THORNE: No. — There's only tonight!

EDITH (*turning to him; a breathless interrogation*):   What!

THORNE (*taking her hands*):   There's only tonight and you in the world! — Oh — see what I've been doing! I came here determined not to tell you I love you — and for the last half hour I've been telling you nothing else!   355 Ah, my darling — there's only tonight and you!

EDITH (*suddenly moving back a little from him; nearly a breathless whisper*):   No no — you mustn't! (*a quick apprehensive glance around down toward left and back; speaks very quickly, as if afraid she would be overheard*) — not now! (*Stands turned away from Thorne.*)

(*Thorne holds position he was in an instant. Then moves back slightly, and as she is looking front he darts a quick suspicious glance toward curtains up left and instantly back to her. Edith moves forward a little, Thorne slowly releasing her hand. — After looking at her there an instant Thorne darts another swift glance — this time toward the window up right and the same instant back to her again.*)

THORNE (*low voice, from where he stands, above her*):   Don't mind what I said   360 Miss Varney — I must have forgotten myself. (*brief pause; steps down to her*) Believe me I came to make a friendly call and — and say good-bye. (*bowing slightly*) Permit me to do so now. (*Turns up at once and walks toward door up left.*)

EDITH (*quickly across to right center as Thorne goes up*):   Oh! — Cap'n Thorne! (*This is timed to stop him just before he reaches the closed portieres of door up left. Thorne turns and looks at Edith — moonlight across from window right on him. Edith tries to be natural, but her lightness somewhat forced.*) Before you go I —   365 (*slight quiver in her voice*) — I wanted to ask your advice about something! (*Stands turned a little to front.*)

THORNE (*Looks at her motionless an instant longer, then turns his head slowly toward the portieres on his left; turns back to Edith again and at once moves down to her.*):   Yes?

EDITH: What do you think this means? (*Holds the piece of paper out toward him but avoids looking in his face.*)

THORNE (*stepping quickly to her and taking the paper easily*):   Why, what is it? (*a half-glance at the paper as he takes it*)

EDITH: It's a — (*Hesitates slightly; recovers at once and looks up at him brightly.*) That's what I want you to tell me. 370

THORNE (*looking at the paper*):   Oh — you don't know!

EDITH (*shaking head slightly*):   No. (*Stands waiting, eyes averted. Thorne glances quickly at her an instant on peculiar tone of "no".*)

THORNE (*looking again at the paper*):   A note from someone?

EDITH: It might be. 375

THORNE (*glancing about*):   Well, it's pretty dark here! (*Glances toward low-turned lamp on desk; crosses to it.*) If you'll excuse me I'll turn up this lamp a little more — (*going to desk*) then we can see what it is. (*Turns up lamp.*) There we are! (*Looks at paper; as soon as he sees it, looks front quickly showing that he recognizes it, without a start; slow turn to Edith, then looks at the paper again — reads as if with difficulty.*) "Attack . . . tonight" — There's something about 380 "Attack tonight" — (*Turns to Edith.*) Could you make out what it was?

(*Edith shakes head negatively. Her lips move, but she cannot speak. She turns away. Thorne looks at her a second, then a slow turn of head, looking up stage, then turns to examine the paper again.*)

"Attack . . . tonight . . . plan . . . three." (*Looks up front as if considering; repeats.*) Plan three! (*considering again, slight laugh*) Well — this thing must be a puzzle of some kind, Miss Varney. (*turning to her*)

EDITH (*slowly, strained voice, as if forcing herself*):   It was taken from a Yankee 385 prisoner!

THORNE (*instantly coming from former easy attitude into one showing interest and surprise; looks at Edith*):   So! Yankee prisoner eh? (*While speaking he is instinctively holding paper in right hand as if to look at it again when he finishes speaking to Edith.*)

EDITH: Yes — down in Libby! — He gave it to one of our servants — old Jonas!

THORNE (*Turns quickly to paper.*):   Why here! This might be something — 390 (*Looks again at the paper.*) "Attack tonight — plan three — use Telegraph —" (*second's pause; he looks up front*) Use Telegraph! (*Turns quickly to Edith and goes toward her.*) This might be something important Miss Varney! Looks like a plot on our Department Telegraph Lines! Who did Jonas give it to? 395

EDITH: No one!

THORNE: Well — how — how —

EDITH: We took it away from him!

THORNE: Oh! (*long "Oh" of "How could you!" Starting at once as if to cross above Edith to left*) That was a mistake!   400

EDITH (*detaining him; speaks rapidly, almost a whisper*): What are you going to do?

THORNE (*strong; determined*): Find that nigger and make him tell who this paper was for — he's the man we want! (*crossing back of her to left and up toward door*)

EDITH (*turning quickly to him*): Cap'n Thorne — they've lied about you!

THORNE (*wheeling round like a flash and coming down quickly to her*): Lied about   405
me! What do you mean? (*seizing her hands and looking in her face to read what it is*)

EDITH (*quick, breathless, very low, almost whisper*): Don't be angry — I didn't think it would be like this!

THORNE (*with great force*): Yes — but what have you done?

EDITH (*breaking loose from him and crossing to left*): No! (*almost a quick cry spoken   410
close on his speech*)

THORNE (*as she crosses before him, trying to detain her*): But I must know!

(*Heavy sound of door outside left and of steps and voices in the hall — "Here! This way!" etc.*)

CORPORAL (*off left, speaking outside door*): This way! Look out on that side will you?

(*Thorne stands near center listening.*)

EDITH: Oh! (*going rapidly up left*) — I don't want to be here! (*Exits door up left and goes up stairs out of the way of the soldiers; Thorne instantly backs away, drawing revolver and stands ready for attack from up left.*)

(*Enter at once on exit of Edith, Corporal with two Men at door up left. They cross rapidly toward window up right — Corporal leading, carrying a lighted lantern. Thorne, seeing Corporal, at once breaks position and moves across towards up center as Men cross, watching Corporal, who is up right center.*)

CORPORAL (*near window*): Out here! Look out now!   415

(*Men exit at window up right.*)

THORNE (*quick on Corporal's speech so as to stop him*): What is it Corporal? (*putting revolver back into holster*)

(*Thorne stands up center in moonlight from window facing Corporal.*)

CORPORAL (*turning and saluting*): Prisoner sir — broke out o' Libby! We've run him down the street — he turned in here somewhere! If he comes in that way would you be good enough to let us know! (*pointing to the window down right*)

THORNE: Go on, Corporal! (*Starts across to window.*) I'll look out for this window! (*Exit Corporal window up right.*)   420

(*Thorne strides rapidly to window down right, pushes curtain back each side and stands within the window looking out. Right hand on revolver, left hand holding curtains back. Moonlight on through windows across stage. Dead pause for an instant. Suddenly two men who crossed with Corporal appear at window up right holding Henry Dumont. With a sudden movement they force him on through the window and disappear quickly outside. Dumont stands where he landed, looking back through window not comprehending what is going on. He gives a quick glance about the room. Dumont wears uniform of United States Cavalry, worn with service. He is pale as from lack of food — but not emaciated or ill. Thorne down right standing motionless near window waiting — Dumont up right center, holding position he struck on entrance. Enough light on him to show the blue United States uniform. After a second's pause Dumont turns from the window and looks slowly about the room, taking in the various points like a caged animal, turning his head very slowly as he looks one way and another. Soon he moves a few steps down and pauses. Turns and makes out a doorway up left, and after a glance round, he walks rapidly toward it. Just before he reaches the door there is a slight sound outside, and the blades of two or three bayonets come down into position through the curtains, showing at the door and barring his exit. He stops on seeing the bayonets. Slight click of bayonets striking together as they come into position. Light outside window right strikes across blades of bayonets. On noise of bayonets, Thorne turns quickly and moves a few steps into the room, trying to see who is there. He sees Dumont and stands looking across at him. Bayonets withdrawn at once after they are shown. Dumont turns from the door and begins to move slowly down stage at left, along the wall. Just as he is coming around table down left toward center he sees Thorne and stops dead. Both men motionless, their eyes upon each other. Dumont makes a start as if to escape through window up right, moving across toward it.*)

THORNE (*quick and loud order as Dumont starts toward window*):   Halt — You're a prisoner!

(*Dumont, after instant's hesitation on Thorne's order, starts rapidly toward window up right. Thorne heads him off, meeting him and seizes him.*)

THORNE: Halt! I say!

(*The two men struggle together, moving quickly down stage very close to front — getting as far as possible from those who are watching them.*)

THORNE (*loud voice, as they struggle down stage*):   Here's your man Corporal!   425
What are you doing there?

DUMONT (*when down as far as possible — holding Thorne motionless an instant and hissing out between his teeth, without pause or inflection on words*):   ATTACK

TONIGHT — PLAN   THREE — TELEGRAPH — DO   YOU GET IT?

THORNE (*quick*):   YES!

430

(*This dialogue in capitals shot at each other with great force and rapidity — and so low that people outside door could not hear.*)

DUMONT (*low voice, almost whisper*):   They're watching us! Shoot me in the leg!

THORNE (*holding Dumont motionless*):   No no! I can't do that!

DUMONT: You must!

THORNE: I can't shoot my own brother!

435

DUMONT: It's the only way to throw 'em off the scent!

THORNE: Well I won't do it anyhow!

DUMONT: If you won't do it I will! Give me that revolver! (*pushing left arm out to get revolver*)

THORNE (*holding Dumont's arm back motionless*):   No no Harry! You'll hurt yourself!

440

DUMONT (*beginning to struggle to get revolver*):   I don't care! Let me have it!

(*They struggle quickly and move into light from window down right.*)

THORNE (*calling out as he struggles with Dumont*):   Here's your man Corporal! What's the matter with you!

DUMONT (*holding Thorne motionless in light and trying to get at his revolver*):   Give me that gun!

445

THORNE (*as Dumont holds him and is just getting revolver; loud, aspirated, sharp*):   Look out Harry! You'll hurt yourself! (*Gets his right hand on revolver to hold it; Dumont manages with his left to wrench Thorne's hand loose from the revolver and hold it up while he seizes the weapon with his right hand and pulls it out of the holster. At the same time he shoves Thorne off.*)

THORNE: Look out! (*as Dumont throws him off and attempts to fire the gun at himself. Before Thorne can recover and turn Dumont fires. There is a quick sharp scream from ladies outside left. Dumont with a groan, staggers down toward center and falls mortally wounded holding the revolver in his hand until he is down and then releasing it, so that Thorne can find it near.*) Harry — you've shot yourself! (*on shot and scream; instantly dives for the revolver and gets it, coming up on same motion with it in right hand and stands in careless attitude just over Dumont's body. Men's voices heard outside up left; Arrelsford gives an order.*)

(*Enter Arrelsford and Men from door up left, followed by Edith, Mrs. Varney and Miss Kittridge. Enter Corporal and men from the window up right. Arrelsford runs at once to table up center and turns up lamp. Others stand on tableau — Mrs. Varney and Edith at left, Miss Kittridge up left; Men in doorway and up right center near window.*)

ARRELSFORD, MRS. VARNEY, EDITH, MISS KITTRIDGE, CORPORAL, MEN (*as they enter*): Where is he! What has he done! He's shot the man! This way now! etc. (*Exclamations stop at once on lights on.*)　　　　450

THORNE (*with careless swing of revolver across him toward center as he brings it up to put back into holster — as the people stop quiet*): There's your prisoner Corporal — look out for him! (*Stands putting revolver back into holster.*)

ACT III

The War Department Telegraph Office. Ten o'clock. A plain and somewhat battered and grimy room on the second floor of a public building; stained and smoky walls. Large windows — the glass covered with grime and cobwebs. Plaster off walls and ceiling in some places. All this from neglect — not from bombardment. It is a room which was formerly somewhat handsome. Moldings and stucco-work broken and discolored. Very large and high door or double doors up right center obliqued. This door opens to a corridor showing plain corridor-backing of a public building. This door must lead off well to right so that it shall not interfere with window showing up left center. Three wide French windows up left and left center oblique[d] a little, with balcony outside extending right and left and showing several massive white columns, bases at balcony and extending up out of sight as if for several stories above. Backing of windows showing night view of city roofs and buildings as from height of second floor. Large disused fireplace with elaborate marble mantel in bad repair and very dirty on right side behind telegraph tables. Door up center opening to cupboard with shelves on which are Battery Jars and Telegraph Office truck of various kinds. Room lighted by gas on right above right telegraph table, several burners branching from a main pipe and all to turn on and off easily by means of one cock in main pipe, just above the telegraph table. Show evening through window up left — dark, with lights of buildings very faint and distant, keeping general effect outside window of darkness. (Moonlight at window on the massive white columns and the characters who go out on the balcony.) Corridor outside door up right center not strongly illuminated. In the room itself fair light but not brilliant. Plain, solid table with telegraph instruments down right center. Another table with instruments along wall at right side. Table down right braced to look as if fastened securely to the floor. Also see that wire connections are properly made from all the instruments in the room to wires running up the wall on right side, thence across along ceiling to up left and out through broken panes in upper part of windows up left. This large bunch of wires leading out, in plain sight, is most important. Large office clock over mantel set at 10 o'clock at opening and to run during the Act. Two instruments A. and D. on table right center — A. is at right end of table and is only one used at that table, D. being for safety. B. and C. on long table against fireplace. B. is at lower end of table, C. at upper end; one chair at table down right center. Two chairs at table right. One chair up center. No sound of cannonading in this Act. At opening there are two Operators at work, one at table down right center, one at table on right side. They are in old gray uniform, but in shirt sleeves. Coats are hung up or thrown on chairs one *side. Busy click-effects of instruments. After first continued clicking for a moment there are occasional pauses. Messengers [1] and [2] near door up right center. Messenger 3 in front of door center talking to Messenger 4. Messenger 2 is looking out of middle window over left.*

SECOND OPERATOR (LT. ALLISON) (*at table right, instrument B., finishing writing a dispatch*): Ready here! (*Messenger [1] steps quickly forward and takes dispatch.*) Department! The Secretary must have it tonight! (*Messenger salutes and exits quickly at door up right with dispatch. Short pause. Other Messenger standing on attention.*)

FIRST OPERATOR (LT. FORAY) (*at table down right center, instrument A.*): Ready here! (*Messenger [2] steps quickly down and takes dispatch from Lt. Foray.*) To the President — General Watson — marked private! (*Messenger [2] salutes and off quickly door up right.*) 5

(*Lt. Allison at right moves to another instrument when it begins to click and answers call.*)

MESSENGER 1 (*Enters hurriedly at door up right and comes down to table right center with dispatch.*): Major Bridgman!

LT. FORAY (*looking up from work*): Bridgman! Where's that?

MESSENGER 1 (*Glances at dispatch.*): Longstreet's Corp.

LT. FORAY: That's yours, Allison. (*Resumes work.*)

(*Lt. Allison holds out hand for dispatch. Messenger 1 gives it to him and exits at door up right. [Lt.] Allison sends message on instrument B. Sound of band of music in distance increasing very gradually. Messengers [go to] windows left and look out but glance now and then at operators.*)

MESSENGER 2 (*opening center window and looking out*): What's that going up Main Street? 10

MESSENGER 3 (*Looks out.*): Richmond Grays!

MESSENGERS 2 and 4: No!

(*All look out through middle window up left.*)

MESSENGER 2: That's what they are sure enough!

MESSENGER 3: They're sending 'em down the river! 15

MESSENGER 2: Not tonight!

MESSENGER 4: Seems like they was, though!

MESSENGER 3: I didn't reckon they'd send the Grays out without there was something going on!

MESSENGER 4: How do you know but what there is? 20

MESSENGER 2: Tonight! Why good God! It's as quiet as a tomb!

MESSENGER 4: Ah reckon that's what's worrying 'em! It's so damned unusual!

(*Sound of band gradually dies away. Before music dies away, Lt. Foray finishes a dispatch and calls.*)

LT. FORAY: Ready here! (*Messenger 3 down to him and takes dispatch.*) Department — from General Lee — duplicate to the President!   25

(*Messenger 3 salutes and exits quickly up right. Enter an Orderly, door up right; goes quickly down to Lt. Foray. Messengers 2 and 4 stand, talking near windows left.*)

ORDERLY (*Salutes.*):   The Secretary wants to know if there's anything from General Lee come in tonight?

LT. FORAY: Just sent one over an' a duplicate went out to the President.

ORDERLY: The President's with the Cabinet yet — he didn't go home! They want an operator right quick to take down a cipher.   30

LT. FORAY (*calling out to Lt. Allison*):   Got anything on, Charlie?

LT. ALLISON: Not right now!

LT. FORAY: Well go over to the Department — they want to take down a cipher.

(*Lt. Allison gets coat and exits door up right, putting coat on as he goes, followed by the Orderly who came for him. Door up right is opened from outside by a couple of Young Officers in showy and untarnished uniforms, who stand in most polite attitudes waiting for a lady to pass in. Lt. Foray very busy writing at table right center, taking message from instrument A. but stops this message for Caroline scene.*)

FIRST YOUNG OFFICER: Right this way, Miss Mitford!   35

SECOND YOUNG OFFICER: Allow me, Miss Mitford! This is the Department Telegraph office!

(*Enter at the door up right Caroline. The young officers follow her in. Martha enters after the officers, and waits near door well up stage.*)

CAROLINE (*Coming down center, speaks in rather subdued manner and without vivacity, as if her mind were upon what she came for.*):   Thank you!

FIRST YOUNG OFFICER: Ah'm afraid you've gone back on the Army, Miss Mitford!   40

CAROLINE (*Looks at First Young Officer questioningly*):   Gone where?

SECOND YOUNG OFFICER: Seems like we ought to a' got a salute as you went by!

CAROLINE: Oh yes! (*Salutes in perfunctory and absent-minded manner and turns away glancing about room and moving down a step or two.*) Good evening! (*nodding to one of the Messengers waiting up left*)   45

MESSENGER 2 (*touching cap and stepping quickly to Caroline*):   Good evening, Miss Mitford! Could we do anything for you in the office tonight?

(Messenger [1] remains up near upper window left.)

CAROLINE: Ah want to send a telegram!

(The three officers stand looking at Caroline quieted for a moment by her serious tone.)

SECOND YOUNG OFFICER: Ah'm afraid you've been havin' bad news, Miss Mitford?

CAROLINE: No — *(shaking her head)* no!

FIRST YOUNG OFFICER: Maybe some friend o' yours has gone down to the front!

CAROLINE *(beginning to be interested)*: Well — supposing he had — would you call that bad news?

FIRST YOUNG OFFICER: Well Ah didn't know as you'd exactly like to —

CAROLINE: Then let me tell you — as you didn't know — that *all* my friends go down to the front!

SECOND YOUNG OFFICER: I hope not *all* Miss Mitford!

CAROLINE: Yes — all! If they didn't they wouldn't *be* my friends.

FIRST YOUNG OFFICER: But some of us are obliged to stay back here to take care of you.

CAROLINE: Well there's altogether too many trying to take care of me! You're all discharged! *(Crosses to down left.)*

(Messenger 3 enters door up right center and joins Messenger 4 up left center near upper window. Officers fall back a little, looking rather foolish but entirely good-natured.)

SECOND YOUNG OFFICER: If we're really discharged Miss Mitford, looks like we'd have to go!

FIRST YOUNG OFFICER: Yes — but we're mighty sorry to see you in such bad spirits Miss Mitford!

SECOND YOUNG OFFICER *and* MESSENGER 2: Yes indeed we are, Miss Mitford!

CAROLINE *(turning)*: Would you like to put me in real good spirits?

FIRST YOUNG OFFICER: Would we!

SECOND YOUNG OFFICER: You try us once!

MESSENGER 2: Ah reckon there ain't anything we'd like bettah!

CAROLINE: Then Ah'll tell you *just* what to do! *(They listen eagerly.)* Start out this very night and never stop till you get to where my friends are — lying in trenches and ditches and earthworks between us and the Yankee guns!

SECOND YOUNG OFFICER, FIRST YOUNG OFFICER, MESSENGER 2 *(remonstrating)*: But really, Miss — you don't mean —

CAROLINE: Fight Yankees a few days and lie in ditches a few nights till 80
those uniforms you've got on look like they'd been some *use* to somebody!
If you're so anxious to do something for me, *that's* what you can do! (*turning away*) It's the only thing Ah want!

(*The Young Officers stand rather discouraged an instant.*)

LT. FORAY (*business*): Ready here! (*Messenger 3 steps quickly down to him.*) Department! Commissary General's office! (*Messenger 3 salutes, takes dispatch* 85
*and exits up right center. Messenger 2 returns to Messenger 4 during this, and stands
with him near window up left center.*)

(*Messenger [1] enters quickly at door up right center and comes down to Lt. Foray,
handing him a dispatch and at once makes his exit by same door. First and Second
Young Officers exit dejectedly after Messenger.*)

CAROLINE (*going across with determined air near Lt. Foray when she sees an opportunity*): *Oh* Lieutenant Foray!

LT. FORAY (*Turns and rises quickly with half salute. Caroline gives a little attempt at a
military salute.*): I beg your pardon, Miss! (*Grabs at his coat which is on a chair
near at right and hastily starts to put it on.*) I didn't know —

CAROLINE (*remonstrating*): No no — don't! Ah don't mind. You see — Ah
came on business! 90

LT. FORAY (*Puts on coat.*): Want to send something out?

CAROLINE: Yes!

LT. FORAY (*going to her*): 'Fraid we can't do anything for you here! This is the
War Department, Miss.

CAROLINE: Ah know that — but it's the on'y way to send, an' Ah — (*sud-* 95
den loud click of instrument on instrument B. Lt. Foray turns and listens.)

LT. FORAY (*crossing back of table right center*): Excuse me a minute, won't you?
(*going to instrument on lower table right and answering; writing down message, etc.*)

CAROLINE: Yes — Ah will. (*a trifle disconcerted, stands uneasily*)

LT. FORAY: Ready here! (*Messenger 2 down quickly to table*) Department! Quick
as you can — they're waiting for it! (*Messenger 2 takes dispatch, salutes, and
exits. Lt. Foray rises and crosses to Caroline.*) Now what was it you wanted us to 100
do, Miss?

CAROLINE: Just to (*short gasp*) to send a telegram.

LT. FORAY: I reckon it's private business?

CAROLINE (*looking at him with wide open eyes*): Ye — yes! It's — private!

LT. FORAY: Then you'll have to get an order from some one in the depart- 105
ment. (*Goes down to back of table right center and picks up papers.*)

CAROLINE: That's what Ah thought (*taking out a paper*) so Ah got it. (*Hands
it to him.*)

LT. FORAY (*glancing at paper*): Oh — Major Selwin!

CAROLINE: Yes — he — he's one of my —

LT. FORAY: It's all right then! (*Instrument B. calls. He quickly picks up a small sheet of paper and a pen and places them on table near Caroline and pushes chair up with almost the same movement.*) You can write it here Miss. 110

CAROLINE: Thank you. (*Sits at table — looks at paper — picks out sheet — smooths it out and writes, pausing an instant to think once or twice and a nervous glance toward Lt. Foray, who returns to table and answers call and sits, taking down dispatch hurriedly. Martha standing motionless up stage, waiting — her eyes fixed on the telegraph instruments. Caroline starts and draws away suspiciously on loud click of instrument A. near her; moves over to left side of table, looking suspiciously at the instrument — puts pen in mouth — gets ink on tongue — makes wry face. She carefully folds up her dispatch when she has written it, and turns down a corner. Lt. Foray when nearly through, motions to Messenger 4.*)

LT. FORAY (*still writing, speaks hurriedly*): Here! (*Messenger 4 comes down quickly.*) Department! Try to get it before the President goes! (*handing Messenger 4 dispatch, who salutes and exits. Lt. Foray rising, to Caroline*) Is that ready yet, Miss? 115

CAROLINE (*rising, hesitating*): Yes, but I — (*Finally starts to hand it to him.*) Of course you've — (*Hesitates.*) You've got to take it!

LT. FORAY (*brief puzzled look at her*): Yes, of course.

(*She hands him the dispatch. He at once opens it.*)

CAROLINE (*sharp scream*): Oh! (*Quickly seizes the paper out of his hand. They stand looking at one another.*) Ah didn't tell you to *read* it! 120

LT. FORAY (*after look at her*): What did you want?

CAROLINE: Ah want you to *send* it!

LT. FORAY: How am I going to send it if I don't read it!

CAROLINE (*after looking at him in consternation*): Do — you — mean — to — say — 125

LT. FORAY: I've got to spell out every word! Didn't you know that!

CAROLINE (*sadly, and shaking her head from side to side*): Oh — Ah must have — but Ah — (*Pauses trying to think what to do.*)

LT. FORAY: Would there be any harm in my — 130

CAROLINE (*turning on him with sudden vehemence*): Why Ah wouldn't have you see it for worlds! My gracious! (*Soon opens the dispatch and looks at it.*)

LT. FORAY (*good-naturedly*): Is it as bad as all that!

CAROLINE: Bad! It isn't bad at all! On'y — Ah only don't want it to get out all over the town — that's all. 135

LT. FORAY: It won't ever get out from this office, Miss. (*Caroline looks steadfastly at Lt. Foray.*) We wouldn't be allowed to mention anything outside!

CAROLINE (*doubtful look at him*):   You wouldn't!

LT. FORAY: No Miss. All sorts of private stuff goes through here.

CAROLINE (*with new hope*):   Does it?   140

LT. FORAY: Every day! Now if that's anything important —

CAROLINE (*impulsively*):   O yes — it's — (*recovering herself*) — it is!

LT. FORAY: Then I reckon you'd better trust it to me.

CAROLINE (*Looks at him for a moment.*):   Ye — yes — Ah reckon Ah had!
(*Hesitatingly hands him her telegram.*)

(*Lt. Foray takes the paper and at once turns away to the table as if to go to business of
sending it on instrument B.*)

CAROLINE (*quickly*):   Oh stop! (*Lt. Foray turns and looks at her from table.*) Wait   145
till I — (*going up stage toward door hurriedly*) Ah don't want to be here —
while you *spell out every word!* Ah couldn't stand *that!*

(*Lt. Foray stands good-naturedly waiting. Caroline takes hold of Martha to start out
of door with her. Enter Eddinger — a private in a gray uniform — at door up right.
Caroline and Martha stand back out of his way. He glances at them and at once goes
down to Lt. Foray, salutes and hands him a written order and crosses to left center,
wheels and stands at attention. Lt. Foray looks at the order, glances at Eddinger, then
at Caroline. Caroline and Martha move as if to go out at door up right.*)

LT. FORAY: Wait a minute, please! (*standing near table down right. Caroline and
Martha stop and turn toward him.*) Are you Miss Mitford?

CAROLINE: Yes — Ah'm Miss Mitford!   150

LT. FORAY: I don't understand this! Here's an order just come in to hold
back any dispatch you give us.

CAROLINE (*after looking speechless at him a moment*):   Hold back any — hold
back —

LT. FORAY: Yes Miss. And that ain't the worst of it!   155

CAROLINE: Wh — what else is there? (*Comes down a little way looking at Lt.
Foray with open eyes; Martha remains near door.*)

LT. FORAY: This man has orders to take it back with him. (*slight pause*)

CAROLINE: Take it back with him? Take what back with him?

LT. FORAY: Your dispatch Miss. (*Caroline simply opens mouth and slowly draws in
her breath.*) There must be some mistake, but that's what the order says.   160

CAROLINE (*with unnatural calmness*):   And where does it say to take it back to?

LT. FORAY (*Looks at the order.*):   The name is Arrelsford! (*brief pause*)

CAROLINE: The order is for that man (*indicating Eddinger*) to take my dispatch back to Mr. Arrelsford?

LT. FORAY: Yes Miss.   165

CAROLINE: An' does it say anything in there about what Ah'm goin' to be doin' in the meantime?

LT. FORAY: No.

CAROLINE: That's too bad!

LT. FORAY: I'm right sorry this has occurred Miss, and —   170

CAROLINE: Oh — (*shaking head*) there isn't any occasion for your feeling sorry — because it hasn't occurred! And besides that it isn't goin' to occur! (*becoming excited*) When it does you can go aroun' bein' sorry all you like! Have you got the faintest idea that Ah'm goin' to let him take my telegram away with him and show it to that man! Do you suppose —   175

MARTHA (*coming forward a step and breaking in in a voice like a siren*): No, sir! You ain't a goin' ter do it — you can be right sure you ain't!

LT. FORAY: But what can I do, Miss?

CAROLINE (*advancing*): You can either send it or hand it back to me — that's what you can do!   180

MARTHA (*calling out*): Yes suh — that's the very best thing you can do! An' the sooner you do it the quicker it'll be done — Ah kin tell you that right now!

LT. FORAY: But this man has come here with orders to —

CAROLINE (*going defiantly to Eddinger and facing him*): Well, this man can go   185 straight back and report to Mr. Arrelsford that he was unable to carry out his orders! (*defiant attitude toward Eddinger*) That's what he can do!

MARTHA (*now thoroughly roused and coming to a sense of her responsibility*): Let 'im take it! Let 'im take it ef he wants to so pow'fle bad! Just let the other one there give it to him — an' then see 'im try an' git out through this do'   190 with it! (*standing solidly before door up right center with folded arms and ominously shaking head; talks and mumbles on half to herself*) Ah want to see him go by! Ah'm just a' waitin' fur a sight o' him gittin' past dis do'! That's what ah'm waitin' fur! (*Goes on talking half to herself, quieting down gradually.*) Ah'd like to know what they s'pose it was Ah come'd round yere for anyway — these   195 men with their orders an' fussin' an' —

LT. FORAY (*down right when quiet is restored*): Miss Mitford, if I was to give this dispatch back to you now it would get me into a heap o' trouble.

CAROLINE (*looking at him*): What kind of trouble?

LT. FORAY: Might be put in prison — might be shot!   200

CAROLINE: You mean they might —

LT. FORAY: Sure to do one or the other!

CAROLINE: Just for givin' it back to me?

LT. FORAY: That's all.

CAROLINE (*after looking silently at him for a moment*): Then you'll have to keep it!   205

LT. FORAY (*sincerely, after a pause*): Thank you Miss Mitford!

CAROLINE (*a sigh, reconciling herself to the situation*): Very well — that's understood! You don't give it back to me — an' you can't give it to him — so nobody's disobeying any orders at all! (*going up and getting a chair from up center and bringing it forward*) And that's the way it stands! (*Banging chair down to emphasize her words close to Eddinger and directly between him and Lt. Foray, then plumps herself down on the chair and facing right, looks unconcerned.*) Ah reckon Ah can stay as long as he can! (*half to herself*) Ah haven't got much to do!

LT. FORAY: But Miss Mitford —

CAROLINE: Now there ain't any good o' talkin'! If you've got any telegraphin' to do, you better do it. Ah won't disturb you!

(*Rapid steps heard in corridor outside. Enter Arrelsford door up right coming in hurriedly, somewhat flushed and excited. He looks hastily about, and goes at once toward Lt. Foray.*)

ARRELSFORD: What's this! Didn't he get here in time?

LT. FORAY: Are you Mr. Arrelsford?

ARRELSFORD: Yes. (*sharp glance at Caroline*) Are you holding back a dispatch?

LT. FORAY: Yes sir.

ARRELSFORD: Why didn't he bring it?

LT. FORAY: Well Miss Mitford — (*Hesitates, with a motion toward Caroline.*)

ARRELSFORD (*comprehending*): Oh! (*Crosses back of Caroline and Eddinger to left.*) Eddinger! (*Eddinger wheels to left facing him.*) Report back to Corporal Matson. Tell him to send a surgeon to the prisoner who was wounded at General Varney's house — if he isn't dead by this time! (*Moves over to left as Eddinger goes up; Caroline turns and looks at him on hearing "prisoner," rising at same time and pushing chair back up center. Eddinger salutes and exits quickly up right center. Arrelsford turns and starts toward Lt. Foray.*) Let me see what that dispatch —

(*Lt. Foray stands right with Caroline's dispatch in his hand. Caroline steps quickly in front of Arrelsford, who stops in some surprise at her sudden move.*)

CAROLINE (*facing Arrelsford*): Ah expect you think you're going to get my telegram an' read it?

ARRELSFORD: I certainly intend to do so!

CAROLINE: Well there's a great big disappointment loomin' up right in front of you!

ARRELSFORD (*with suspicion*): So! You've been trying to send out something you don't want us to see!

CAROLINE: What if Ah have?

ARRELSFORD: Just this! You won't send it — and I'll see it! (*about to pass Caroline*) This is a case where — (*Caroline steps in front of Arrelsford again so that he has to stop.*)

CAROLINE: This is a case where you ain't goin' to read my private writin'. (*Stands looking at him with blazing eyes.*)

ARRELSFORD: Lieutenant — I have an order here putting me in charge!   240
Bring that dispatch to me!

(*Lt. Foray about to move toward Arrelsford; Martha suddenly steps down in front of Lt. Foray with ponderous tread and stands facing him.*)

MARTHA: Mistah Lieutenant can stay juss about whar he is! (*brief pause*)

ARRELSFORD (*to Lt. Foray*):   Is that Miss Mitford's dispatch?

LT. FORAY: Yes sir!

ARRELSFORD: Read it! (*Caroline turns with a gasp of horror. Martha turns in slow*   245
anger. Lt. Foray stands surprised for an instant.) Read it out!

CAROLINE: You shan't do such a thing! You have no right to read a private telegram —

MARTHA (*speaking with Caroline*):   No sah! He ain't no business to read her letters — none whatsomever!   250

ARRELSFORD (*angrily*):   Silence! (*Caroline and Martha stop talking.*) If you in-terfere any further with the business of this office I'll have you both put under arrest! (*to Lt. Foray*) Read that dispatch!

(*Caroline gasps breathless at Arrelsford — then turns and buries her face on Martha's shoulder sobbing.*)

LT. FORAY (*Reads with some difficulty.*):   "Forgive me — Wilfred darling — please — forgive me and I will help you all I can."   255

ARRELSFORD: That dispatch can't go! (*Turns and moves left a few steps.*)

CAROLINE (*turning and facing Arrelsford, almost calm with anger*):   That dispatch can go! An' that dispatch will go! (*Arrelsford turns and looks at Caroline; Martha moves up on right side ready to exit, standing well up center and turning toward Arrelsford.*) Ah know someone whose orders even you are bound to · respect and someone who'll come here with me an' see that you do it!   260

ARRELSFORD: I can show good and sufficient reasons for what I do!

CAROLINE: Well you'll have to show good and sufficienter reasons than you've shown to me — Ah can tell you that, Mr. Arrelsford!

ARRELSFORD: I give my reasons to my superiors, Miss Mitford!

CAROLINE: Then you'll have to go 'round givin' 'em to everybody in Rich-   265
mond, Mr. Arrelsford! (*Saying which Caroline makes a deep curtsey and turns and sweeps out through door up right followed in the same spirit by Martha who turns at the door and also makes a profound curtsey to Arrelsford, going off haughtily.*)

(*Lt. Foray sits down at table right center and begins to write. Arrelsford looks after Caroline an instant and then goes rapidly over to Lt. Foray.*)

ARRELSFORD: Let me see that dispatch!

LT. FORAY (*slight doubt*):   You said you had an order, sir.

ARRELSFORD (*impatiently*):   Yes — yes! (*Throws order down on telegraph table.*) Don't waste time!   270

(*Lt. Foray picks up order and looks closely at it for an instant.*)

LT. FORAY: Department order sir?

ARRELSFORD (*assenting shortly*):   Yes.

LT. FORAY: I suppose you're Mr. Arrelsford all right?

ARRELSFORD: Of course!

LT. FORAY: We have to be pretty careful sir! (*Hands him Caroline's telegram and*   275
goes on writing. Arrelsford takes it eagerly and reads it; thinks an instant.)

ARRELSFORD: Did she seem nervous or excited when she handed this in?

LT. FORAY: She certainly did!

ARRELSFORD: Anxious not to have it seen?

LT. FORAY: Anxious! I should say so! She didn't want me to see it!

ARRELSFORD: We've got a case on here and she's mixed up in it!   280

LT. FORAY: But that dispatch is to young Varney — the General's son!

ARRELSFORD: So much the worse! It's one of the ugliest affairs we ever had! I had them put me on it and I've got it down pretty close! (*going across left*) We'll end it right here in this office inside of thirty minutes!

(*Enter a Private at door up right. He comes down at once to Arrelsford.*)

ARRELSFORD (*turning to him*):   Well, what is it?   285

PRIVATE: The lady's here sir!

ARRELSFORD: Where is she?

PRIVATE: Waiting down below — at the front entrance.

ARRELSFORD: Did she come alone?

PRIVATE: Yes sir.   290

ARRELSFORD: Show her the way up. (*Private salutes and exits; Arrelsford comes to Lt. Foray.*) I suppose you've got a revolver there? (*Lt. Foray brings up revolver in matter-of-fact way from beneath his table and puts it on table, resuming business of writing, etc.*) I'd rather handle this thing myself — but I might call on you. Be ready — that's all!

LT. FORAY: Yes sir.   295

ARRELSFORD: Obey any orders you get an' send out all dispatches unless I stop you.

LT. FORAY: Very well, sir.

(*Door up right is opened by the Private last on, and Edith is shown in. Arrelsford meets her. Private exits.*)

EDITH (*in a low voice but under control*):   I — I've accepted your invitation.

ARRELSFORD: I'm greatly obliged Miss Varney! As a matter of justice to 300
me it was — (*Lt. Foray puts revolver back on shelf under table.*)

EDITH (*interrupting*):   I didn't come to oblige you! I'm here to see that no
more — murders are committed in order to satisfy your singular curiosity.

ARRELSFORD (*low voice*):   Where has he been? (*brief pause*) Is the man dead?

EDITH (*looking at him steadily*):   The man is dead. (*pause*) 305

ARRELSFORD (*Turns to her; with cutting emphasis but low voice*):   It's a curious thing, Miss Varney, that a Yankee prisoner more or less should
make so much difference to you. They're dying down in Libby by the
hundreds!

EDITH: At least they're not killed in our houses — before our very eyes! 310

(*Enter an Orderly who is a Special Agent of the War Department at door up right. He
comes quickly in and crosses to Arrelsford, then glances around toward Lt. Foray. Arrelsford moves down stage to speak to the Orderly, in a low voice.*)

ARRELSFORD: Well, have you kept track of him?

ORDERLY (*in low voice throughout scene*):   He's coming up Fourth Street, sir!

ARRELSFORD: Where has he been?

ORDERLY: To his quarters on Cary Street. We got in the next room and
watched him through a transom. 315

ARRELSFORD: What was he doing?

ORDERLY: Working at some papers or documents.

ARRELSFORD: Could you see them? Could you see what it was?

ORDERLY: Headings looked like orders from the War Department.

ARRELSFORD: He's coming in here with forged orders! 320

ORDERLY: Yes sir.

ARRELSFORD: His game is to get control of these wires and then send out
dispatches to the front that'll take away a battery from some vital point!

ORDERLY: Looks like it sir.

ARRELSFORD: And that vital point is what the Yankees mean by Plan Three! 325
That's where they'll hit us. (*Glances round quickly considering — goes up left above
line of middle window — turns to Orderly.*) Is there a guard in this building?

ORDERLY (*going near Arrelsford*):   Not inside — there's a guard in front and
sentries around the barracks over in the square.

ARRELSFORD: They could hear me from this window, couldn't they? 330

ORDERLY: The guard could hear you. (*glance toward door right*) He must be
nearly here sir, you'd better look out!

EDITH (*up center, low voice*):   Where shall I go?

ARRELSFORD: Outside here — on the balcony — I'll be with you!

EDITH: But — if he comes to the window!   335

ARRELSFORD: We'll step in at the next one. (*to Orderly*) See if the window of the Commissary-General's office is open.

ORDERLY (*Steps quickly out of window up left through middle window, and goes off along balcony left. He returns at once re-entering through middle window.*):   The next window's open sir.

ARRELSFORD: That's all I want of you — report back to Corporal Matson.   340 Tell him to get the body of that prisoner out of the Varney house — he knows where it's to go!

ORDERLY: Very well sir! (*Salutes, crosses and exits door up right.*)

ARRELSFORD (*to Edith*):   This way please! (*Conducts her out through middle window to balcony. He is closing the window to follow when he sees a Messenger enter up right and thereupon he stops just in the window keeping out of sight behind window frame.*)

(*Enter Messenger 1; takes position up stage waiting for message as before. Arrelsford eyes him sharply an instant — then comes forward a step.*)

ARRELSFORD: Where did you come from?   345

MESSENGER I: War Department sir.

ARRELSFORD: Carrying dispatches?

MESSENGER I: Yes sir.

ARRELSFORD: You know me don't you?

MESSENGER I: I've seen you at the office sir.   350

ARRELSFORD: I'm here on Department business. All you've got to do is to keep quiet about it! (*Exit Arrelsford at middle window which he closes after him and then disappears from view along balcony to left.*)

(*Enter Messenger 2; takes his place with Messenger 1 at up left. Lt. Foray busy at table. Moment's wait. Enter Captain Thorne at door up right center. As he comes down he gives one quick glance about the room but almost instantly to front again, so that it would hardly be noticed. He wears cap and carries an order in his belt. Thorne goes down at once to table and face[s] Lt. Foray.*)

THORNE (*saluting*):   Lieutenant! (*Hands Lt. Foray the order which he carried in his belt.*)

LT. FORAY (*Turns, sees Thorne, rises, saluting briefly, takes order, opens and looks at it.*): Order from the Department. (*Moves a little to give Thorne chance to get to back of table.*)

THORNE (*motionless, facing to right*):   I believe so. (*Quickly glances at door up right   355 as Lt. Foray is looking at the order.*)

LT. FORAY: They want me to take a cipher dispatch ovah to the President's house.

THORNE (*moving to take Lt. Foray's place at table — pulls chair back a little and then tosses cap over on table right.*):   Yes — I'm ordered on here till you get back. (*Goes to place back of table right center and stands arranging things on the table.*)

LT. FORAY (*at table right, looking front*):   That's an odd thing. They told me the President was down here with the Cabinet! He must have just now gone home I reckon. 360

THORNE (*standing at table and arranging papers, etc. on it*):   Looks like it. — If he isn't there you'd better wait. (*looking through a bunch of dispatches*)

LT. FORAY (*Gets cap from table right, puts it on.*):   Yes — I'll wait! (*pause*) You'll have to look out for Allison's wires, Cap'n. He was called ovah to the De- 365 partment.

(*Thorne stops and looks front an instant on mention of Lt. Allison.*)

THORNE (*easy manner again*):   Ah ha — Allison!

LT. FORAY: Yes.

THORNE: Be gone long? (*Throws used sheets in waste-basket and fixes a couple of large envelopes ready for quick use.*)

LT. FORAY: Well, you know how it is — they generally whip around quite 370 a while before they make up their minds what they want to do. I don't ex- pect they'll trouble you much! It's as quiet as a church down the river. (*starting toward door up right*)

THORNE (*seeing a cigar on the table near instrument*):   See here — wait a minute — you'd better not walk out and leave a — no matter! (*Lt. Foray stops and turns back to Thorne — comes center a little.*) It's none of my business 375 (*tapping with the end of a long envelope on table where the cigar is*). Still, if you want some good advice, that's a dangerous thing to do!

LT. FORAY (*coming down*):   What is it Cap'n?

THORNE: Leave a cigar lying around this office like that! (*Picks it up with left hand and lights a match with right.*) Somebody might walk in here any 380 minute and take it away! (*about to light cigar*) I can't watch your cigars all day (*lighting it*).

LT. FORAY (*laughing*):   Oh! Help yourself Cap'n!

THORNE (*suddenly snatching cigar out of mouth with left hand and looking at it*): What's the matter with it? Oh well — I'll take a chance. (*Puts it in his mouth and resumes lighting.*)

LT. FORAY (*Hesitates a moment, goes down near Thorne, confidentially.*):   Cap'n, if 385 there's any trouble around here you'll find a revolver under there. (*indicat- ing shelf under table. Thorne stops lighting cigar an instant; eyes motionless front; match blazes up.*)

THORNE (*at once resuming nonchalance — finishing lighting cigar*):   What about that? What makes you think — (*pulling in to light cigar*) there's going to be trouble?

LT. FORAY: Oh well, there might be! 390

THORNE (*tossing match away*):   Been having a dream?

LT. FORAY: Oh no — but you never can tell! (*Starts toward door.*)

THORNE (*cigar in mouth; going at papers again*):   That's right! You never can tell. But see here — hold on a minute! (*reaching down and getting revolver from shelf and tossing it on table near left end*) If you never can tell you'd better 395 take that along with you. I've got one of my own. (*rather sotto voce*) I can tell!

(*Click of instrument A. Thorne answers on instrument A. at right end of table right center and slides into chair.*)

LT. FORAY: Well, if you've got one here, I might as well. (*Takes revolver.*) Look out for yourself, Cap'n! (*Goes up. Instrument A. begins clicking off a message. Thorne sits at table listening and ready to take down what comes.*)

THORNE: Same to you old man — and many happy returns of the day! 400 (*Exit Lt. Foray door up right center. Thorne writes message, briefly addresses long envelope. Instrument A. stops receiving as Thorne addresses envelope. He okays dispatch.*) Ready here! (*Messenger 1 down to Thorne and salutes.*) Quartermaster-General (*handing dispatch to Messenger*).

MESSENGER 1:   Not at his office, sir!

THORNE: Find him! He's got to have it!

MESSENGER 1:   Very well sir! (*Salutes and exits quickly up right.*)

(*Thorne turns slowly left looking to see if there is a Messenger there; sees there is one without looking entirely around. A second's wait. Instrument C. upper end of table right begins to click. Thorne quickly rises and going to instrument C. answers call — on instrument — drops into chair up right and writes message — puts it in envelope and okays call.*)

THORNE: Ready here! (*Messenger 2 goes quickly across to Thorne and salutes.*) Sec- 405 retary of the Treasury — marked private. Take it to his house. (*Begins to read a dispatch he twitched off from a file.*)

MESSENGER 2:   He's down yere at the Cabinet, sir.

THORNE: Take it to his house and wait till he comes!

(*Messenger 2 salutes and exits door up right center, closing the door after him. On the slam of door Thorne crushes dispatch in right hand and throws it to floor — and wheels front — his eyes on the instrument down right center. All one quick movement. Then he rises and with cat-like swiftness springs to the door up right and listens — opens the door a little and looks off. Closes it quickly, turning swiftly to center and opens the door*) *up center glancing in. Then he goes to the window up left center — the nearest. Pushes it open a little and looks off through window and begins at same time to unbuckle belt and unbutton coat. Turns and moves down toward the telegraph table right center at same time throwing belt over to right above right table, and taking off coat. Glances back up left — looks to see that a document is in breast pocket of coat — letting audience see that it is there — and lays coat over back of chair above table right center with document in sight so that he can get it without delay. Takes revolver from hip pocket and quickly but quietly lays it on the table right center, just to right of the instrument, and then seizes key of instrument A. and gives a certain call: (— ....). Waits. A glance rapidly to left. He is standing at table — cigar in mouth. Makes the call again. Waits again. Gives the call third time. Goes to lower end of table right and half sits on it, folding arms, eyes on instrument, chewing cigar, with a glance or two up stage, but his eyes come quickly back to the instrument. Slides off table — takes cigar out of his mouth with left hand and gives the call again with right: (— ....) putting cigar in mouth again and turning and walking upstage, looking about. Soon he carelessly throws papers which he took from right pocket — off up stage. Just as he throws papers — facing to left — the call is answered: (— ....). Thorne is back at the table right center in an instant and telegraphing rapidly — cigar in mouth. When he has sent for about five seconds steps are heard in corridor outside up right. He quickly strikes a match — which is close at hand to right of instrument — and sinks into the chair, appearing to be lazily lighting his cigar as a Messenger comes in at door up right center. Messenger 4 enters as soon as he hears match strike and goes down at once to Thorne with dispatch. Salutes and extends it toward Thorne — on Thorne's left.)*

MESSENGER 4: Secretary of War, Cap'n! Wants to go out right now! (*Thorne tosses away match, takes dispatch and opens it. Messenger 4 salutes, turns and starts up toward door.*)

THORNE: Here! Here! What's all this! (*looking at the dispatch. Messenger 4 returns to him, salutes.*) Is that the Secretary's signature?   410

MESSENGER 4: Yes sir — I saw him sign it.

(*Thorne looks closely at the signature. Turns it so as to get gas light. Turns and looks sharply at the Messenger and then back to dispatch again; puts it on table and writes an O.K. on it.*)

THORNE: Um hm — saw him sign it did you?

MESSENGER 4: Yes sir.

THORNE (*writing*): Got to be a little careful tonight! (*holding dispatch up from   415 table in left hand so that audience can see it is the same one — with the Secretary's signature*)

MESSENGER 4: I can swear to that one sir. (*Salutes, turns and goes up and exits.*)

(*Thorne listens — faced front for exit of Messenger. Dispatch in left hand. Instantly on slam of door he puts cigar down at end of table, rises, folds and very dexterously and rapidly cuts off the lower part of the paper which has the signature of the Secretary of*

War upon it, holds it between his teeth and tears the rest of the order in pieces, which he is on the point of throwing into waste-basket at left of table when he stops and changes his mind, stuffing the torn-up dispatch into his right hand trousers pocket. Picks up coat from back of chair and takes the document out of inside breast pocket. Opens it out on table and quickly pastes to it the piece of the real order bearing the signature, wipes quickly with handkerchief, puts handkerchief back into pocket, picks up cigar which he laid down on table and puts it in mouth, at same time sitting and at once beginning to telegraph rapidly on instrument A.; rapid click of the instrument. Thorne intent, yet vigilant. During business of Thorne pasting dispatch, Arrelsford appears outside windows up left at side of columns. He motions off toward left. Edith comes into view there also. Arrelsford points toward Thorne, calling her attention to what he is doing. They stand at the window watching Thorne — the strong moonlight brings them out sharply. After a few seconds Arrelsford accidentally makes a slight noise with latch of window. Instantly on this faint click of latch Thorne stops telegraphing and sits absolutely motionless — his eyes front. Arrelsford and Edith exit quickly and noiselessly on balcony to left. Dead silence. After a motionless pause, Thorne begins to fumble among papers on the table with his left hand, soon after raising the dispatch or some other paper with that hand in such a way that it will screen his right hand and the telegraph instrument on the key of which it rests, from an observer on the left. While he appears to be scanning this paper or dispatch with the greatest attention, his right hand slowly slips off the telegraph key and toward his revolver which lies just to the right of the instrument. Reading it, he very slowly moves it over the right edge of the table, and down against his right leg. He then begins to push things about on the table with left hand as if looking for something and soon rises as if not able to find it, and looking still more carefully. Thorne keeps revolver close against right side — looks about on table, glances over to table on right as if looking for what he wanted there, puts cigar down on table before him — after about to do so once and taking a final puff — and steps over to table at right still looking for something and keeping revolver out of sight of anyone at window up left. As he looks he raises left hand carelessly to the cock of the gas bracket and instantly shuts off light. Stage dark. Instantly on lights off, Thorne drops on one knee at right of table right center — facing toward left. Revolver covering windows up left. Light from windows gauged to strike across to Thorne at table with revolver. After holding it a short time, he begins slowly to edge up stage, first seizing chair with his coat on it, and crouching behind it — then edges cautiously up on right until within reach of the door, when he suddenly slides the heavy bolt, thus locking the doors on the inside. From doors up right Thorne glides with a dash — throwing aside the chair in the way — at the door of closet up center which opens down stage and hinges on its left side. With motion of reaching it he has it open — if not already open — and pushing it along before him as he moves left toward window. When moving slowly behind this door with his eyes and revolver on window the telegraph instrument down right suddenly gives two or three sharp clicks. Thorne makes an instantaneous turn front covering the instrument with revolver. Sees what it was. Turns left again. Just as he gets door nearly wide open against wall at back he dashes at windows up left center and bangs them open with left hand covering all outside with revolver in his right. In an instant sees that no one is there. Straightens up — looking. Quick spring past first window stopping close behind the upright between first and second windows, and at same time banging these windows open and covering with revolver. Sees no one. Looks this way and that. Makes quick dash outside and covers over balustrade — as if someone might be below. In again quick. Looks about with one or two quick glances. Concludes he must have been mistaken, and starts down toward table right center — stops after going two or three steps and looks back. Turns and goes rapidly down to table. Picks up cigar with left hand. Puts revolver at right end of table with right hand, and gets a match with that hand. Stands an instant looking left. Strikes match and is about to relight cigar. Pause — eyes front. Match burning. Listening. Looks left — lights cigar — as he is lighting cigar thinks of gas being out, and steps to right, turns it on and lights it. Lights full on. Thorne turns quickly, looking left as lights on. Then steps at once — after glancing quickly about room — to telegraph table, puts down cigar near upper right corner of table with left hand and begins to telegraph with left hand, facing front. Suddenly sharp report of revolver outside through lower window, up left with crash of glass and on it Arrelsford springs on at middle window left with revolver in his hand. Thorne does not move on shot except quick recoil from instrument, leaning back a little, expression of pain an instant. His left hand — with which he was telegraphing — is covered with blood. He stands motionless an instant. Eyes then down toward his own revolver. Slight pause. He makes a sudden plunge for it getting it in his right hand. At same instant quick turn on Arrelsford but before he can raise the weapon Arrelsford covers him with revolver and Thorne stops where he is, holding position.)

ARRELSFORD: Drop it! (*pause*) Drop that gun or you're a dead man! Drop it I say! (*a moment's pause. Thorne gradually recovers to erect position again, looking easily front, and puts revolver on the table, picking up cigar with same hand and putting it casually into his mouth as if he thought he'd have a smoke after all, instead of killing a man. He then gets handkerchief out of pocket with right hand and gets hold of a corner of it not using his left. Arrelsford advances a step or two, lowering revolver, but holding it ready.*) Do you know why I didn't kill you like a dog just now?

THORNE (*back of table right center as he twists handkerchief around his wounded hand*): Because you're such a damn bad shot. 420

ARRELSFORD: Maybe you'll change your mind about that!

THORNE (*Arranging handkerchief to cover his wounded hand — leaving fingers free. Speaks easily and pleasantly.*):   Well I hope so I'm sure. It isn't pleasant to be riddled up this way you know!

ARRELSFORD: Next time you'll be riddled somewhere else besides the hand! There's only one reason why you're not lying there now with a bul- 425 let through your head!

THORNE: Only one, eh?

ARRELSFORD: Only one!

THORNE (*still fixing hand and sleeve*):   Do I hear it?

ARRELSFORD: Simply because I gave my word of honor to someone out- 430
side there that I wouldn't kill you now!

(*Thorne on hearing "someone outside there" turns and looks at Arrelsford with interest.*)

THORNE (*taking cigar out of mouth and holding it in right hand as he moves toward Arrelsford*):   Ah! Then it isn't a little tête-à-tête between ourselves! You have someone with you! (*stopping near center, coolly facing him*)

ARRELSFORD (*sarcastically*):   I *have* someone with me Captain Thorne! Someone who takes quite an interest in what you're doing tonight! 435

THORNE (*Puts cigar in mouth.*):   Quite an interest, eh! That's kind I'm sure. (*Takes cigar out of mouth facing front.*) Is the gentleman going to stay out there all alone on the cold balcony, or shall I have the pleasure — (*Enter Edith from balcony through the upper window, where she stands supporting herself by the sides. She is looking toward right as if intending to go, but not able for a moment, to move; avoids looking at Thorne.*) — of inviting him in here and having a charming little three-handed — (*glancing up toward window he sees Edith and* 440 *stops motionless. Looks at her quietly a moment — then turns slowly and looks at Arrelsford — who has a slight smile on his lips; then turns front and holds position motionless.*)

EDITH (*Does not speak until after Thorne looks front; low voice*):   I'll go, Mr. Arrelsford!

ARRELSFORD: Not yet, Miss Varney!

EDITH (*coming blindly into room a few steps as if to get across to the door up right*):   I don't wish to stay — any longer! 445

ARRELSFORD: One moment please! We need you!

EDITH (*Stops.*):   For what?

ARRELSFORD: A witness.

EDITH: You can send for me. I'll be at home. (*about to start toward door*)

ARRELSFORD (*sharply*):   I'll have to detain you till I turn him over to the 450 guard — it won't take a moment! (*Steps to the middle window, still keeping an eye on Thorne and calls off in loud voice.*) Corporal o' the guard! Corporal o' the guard! Send up the guard will you!

(*Edith shrinks back up center not knowing what to do.*)

VOICE (*outside in distance, as if down below in the street*):   What's the matter up there! Who's calling the guard! 455

ARRELSFORD (*at window*):   Up here! Department Telegraph! Send 'em up quick!

VOICES (*outside*):   Corporal of the Guard Post Four! (*repeated more distant*) Corporal of the Guard Post Four! (*repeated again almost inaudible*) Corporal

of the Guard Post Four! Fall in the guard! Fall in! (*These orders gruff — in-* 460
distinct — distant. Give effect of quick gruff shouts of orders, barely audible.)

EDITH (*turning suddenly on Arrelsford*):   I'm not going to stay! I don't wish to
be a witness!

ARRELSFORD (*after an instant's look at Edith — suspecting the reason for her refusal*):
Whatever your feelings may be Miss Varney, we can't permit you to
refuse!

EDITH (*with determination*):   I do refuse! If you won't take me down to the 465
street I'll find the way out myself! (*Stops as she is turning to go, on hearing the
Guard outside running through lower corridors and coming up stairway and along hall-
ways outside up right. Thorne holds position looking steadily front, cigar in right hand.*)

ARRELSFORD (*loud voice to stop Edith*):   Too late! The guard is here! (*Steps down
left center with revolver, his eye on Thorne.*)

(*Edith stands an instant and then as the Guard is heard nearer in the corridor she moves
up to window and remains there until sound of Guard breaking in the door. Then she
makes her exit off to left on balcony, disappearing so as to attract no attention.*)

ARRELSFORD (*shouting across to Thorne*):   I've got you about where I want you
at last! (*Thorne motionless; sound of hurried tread of men outside as if coming on double quick toward the door, on bare floor of corridor*) You thought you was 470
almighty smart — but you'll find we can match your tricks every time!

(*Sound of the Guard coming suddenly ceases close outside the door up right.*)

SERGEANT OF THE GUARD (*close outside door*):   What's the matter here! Let
us in!

THORNE (*loud, incisive voice, still facing front*):   Break down the door Sergeant!
Break it down! (*As he calls begins to back up stage toward right center.*) 475

(*Officers and men outside at once begin to smash in the door with the butts of their
muskets.*)

ARRELSFORD (*surprised*):   What are you saying about it!

THORNE: You want 'im in here, don't you!

ARRELSFORD (*Moves up a little as Thorne does, and covers him with revolver; speaks
through noise of breaking door.*):   Stand where you are!

(*Thorne has backed up until nearly between Arrelsford and the door, so that the latter
cannot fire on him without hitting others. But he must stand a trifle to right of line the
men will take in rushing across to Arrelsford.*)

THORNE (*facing Arrelsford*):   Smash in the door! What are you waiting for!
Smash it in Sergeant! (*Keeps up this call till door breaks down and men rush in —* 480

which must be at once. Door is quickly battered in and Sergeant and Men rush on. Thorne, continuing without break from last speech, above all the noise, pointing to Arrelsford with left hand) Arrest that man! (*Sergeant and six Men spring forward past Thorne and seize Arrelsford before he can recover from his astonishment, throwing him nearly down in the first struggle, but pulling him to his feet and holding him fast. As soon as quiet, Thorne moves down center.*) He's got in here with a revolver and he's playing Hell with it!

ARRELSFORD: Sergeant — my orders are —

THORNE (*facing him*): Damn your orders! You haven't got orders to shoot 485
everybody you see in this office! (*Arrelsford makes a sudden effort to break loose.*)
Get his gun away — he'll hurt himself! (*Turns at once and goes to table right
center putting his coat in better position on back of chair, and then getting things in
shape on the table. At same time putting cigar back in mouth and smoking. Sergeant
and Men twist revolver out of Arrelsford's hands.*)

ARRELSFORD (*continuing to struggle and protest*): Listen to me! Arrest him!
He's sending out a false —

SERGEANT OF THE GUARD: Now that'll do! (*silencing Arrelsford roughly by hand* 490
across his mouth — to Thorne) What's it all about, Cap'n?

THORNE (*at table arranging things*): All about! I haven't got the slightest (*sudden snatch of cigar out of mouth with right hand and then to Sergeant as if remembering something*) He says he came out of some office! Sending out dispatches
here he began letting off his gun at me. (*Turns back arranging things on table.*)
Crazy lunatic! 495

ARRELSFORD (*struggling to speak*): It's a lie! Let me speak — I'm from the —

SERGEANT (*quietly to avoid laugh*): Here! That'll do now! (*silencing him, then to
Thorne*) What shall we do with him?

THORNE (*tossing things into place on table with one hand*): I don't care a damn —
get him out o' here — that's all I want! 500

SERGEANT: Much hurt, Cap'n?

THORNE (*carelessly*): Oh no. Did up one hand a little — I can get along
with the other all right. (*Sits at table and begins telegraphing.*)

ARRELSFORD (*struggling desperately*): Stop him! He's sending a — wait! Ask
Miss Varney! (*Speaks until stopped; wildly, losing all control of himself*) She saw 505
him! Ask her! Ask Miss Varney!

SERGEANT (*breaking in*): Here! Fall in there. We'll get him out. (*The guard
quickly falls in behind Arrelsford, who is still struggling.*) Forward —

(*Enter quickly an Officer striding in at door up right.*)

OFFICER (*loud voice, above the noise*): Halt! (*Men on motion from Sergeant stand
back, forming a double rank behind Arrelsford. Two Men hold him in front rank. All
face to center, Sergeant up left center.*)

(*Enter Major General Harrison Randolph striding in at door up right center. Caroline comes to door after the General, and stands just within, up right center. Arrelsford has been so astonished and indignant at his treatment that he can't find his voice at first. Officers salute as General Randolph comes in. Thorne goes on working instrument at table, cigar between his teeth. He has the dispatch with signature pasted on it spread on table before him.*)

GENERAL RANDOLPH (*Comes down center and stops.*): What's all this about 510
refusing to send Miss Mitford's telegram! Is it some of your work
Arrelsford?

ARRELSFORD (*breathless, violent, excited*): General! They've arrested me. A
conspiracy! A — (*Sees Thorne working at telegraph instrument.*) Stop that
man — for God's sake stop him before its too late! 515

(*Caroline edging gradually up right center quietly slips out at door up right center, unnoticed.*)

GENERAL RANDOLPH: Stop him! What do you mean?

THORNE (*back of table, quickly rising so as to speak on cue, with salute*): He means
me sir! He's got an idea some dispatch I'm sending out is a trick of the
Yankees!

ARRELSFORD (*excitedly*): It's a conspiracy! He's an imposter — a — a — 520

THORNE: Why the man must have gone crazy General! (*Stands facing left
motionless.*)

ARRELSFORD: I came here on a case for —

GENERAL RANDOLPH (*sharply*): Wait! I'll get at this! (*to Sergeant without turning to him*) What was he doing?

SERGEANT (*with salute*): He was firing on the Cap'n sir. 525

ARRELSFORD: He was sending out a false order to weaken our lines at
Cemetery Hill and I — ah — (*suddenly recollecting*) Miss Varney! (*looking
excitedly about*) She was here — she saw it all!

GENERAL RANDOLPH (*gruffly*): Miss Varney!

ARRELSFORD: Yes sir! 530

GENERAL RANDOLPH: The General's daughter?

ARRELSFORD (*nodding affirmatively with excited eagerness*): Yes sir!

GENERAL RANDOLPH: What was she doing here?

ARRELSFORD: She came to see for herself whether he was guilty or not!

GENERAL RANDOLPH: Is this some personal matter of yours? 535

ARRELSFORD: He was a visitor at their house — I wanted her to know!

GENERAL RANDOLPH: Where is she now? Where is Miss Varney?

ARRELSFORD (*looking about excitedly*): She must be out there on the balcony!
Send for her!

GENERAL RANDOLPH: Sergeant! (*Sergeant steps down to him and salutes.*) Step 540 out there on the balcony. Present my compliments to Miss Varney and ask her to come in!

(*Sergeant salutes and steps quickly out through middle window on the balcony. Walks off at left, reappears walking back as far as balcony goes. Turns and re-enters room, coming down and saluting.*)

SERGEANT: No one there sir!

(*Thorne turns and begins to send dispatch, picking up the forged order with left hand as if sending from that copy and quickly opening instrument A. and telegraphing with right, all on nearly same motion.*)

ARRELSFORD: She must be there! She's in the next office! The other window. Tell him to — (*Sees Thorne working at instrument.*) Ah! (*almost screaming*) Stop him! He's sending it now!   545

GENERAL RANDOLPH (*to Thorne*):   One moment Cap'n! (*Thorne stops. Salutes. Drops dispatch in left hand to table. Pause for an instant — all holding their positions. General Randolph after above pause, to Arrelsford*) What have *you* got to do with this?

ARRELSFORD: It's a Department Case! They assigned it to me!   550

GENERAL RANDOLPH: What's a Department Case?

ARRELSFORD: The whole plot — to send the order — it's the Yankee Secret Service! His brother brought in the signal tonight!

(*General Randolph looks sharply at Arrelsford.*)

THORNE (*very quietly, matter-of-fact*):   This ought to go out sir — it's very important.   555

GENERAL RANDOLPH: Go ahead with it!

(*Thorne salutes and quickly turns to instrument A. dropping dispatch on table and begins sending rapidly as he stands before the table, glancing at the dispatch as he does so as if sending from it.*)

ARRELSFORD (*seeing what is going on*):   No no! It's a —

GENERAL RANDOLPH: Silence!

ARRELSFORD (*excitedly*):   Do you know what he's telling them!

GENERAL RANDOLPH: No! Do you?   560

ARRELSFORD: Yes! If you'll —

GENERAL RANDOLPH (*to Thorne*):   Wait! (*Thorne stops, coming at once to salute, military position a step back from table facing front.*) Where's that dispatch? (*Thorne goes to General Randolph and hands him the dispatch; then [moves] back a step. General Randolph takes the dispatch. To Arrelsford*) What was it? What has he been telling them? (*Looks at dispatch in his hand.*)   565

ARRELSFORD (*excitedly*):   He began to give an order to withdraw Marston's Division from its present position!

GENERAL RANDOLPH: That is perfectly correct.

ARRELSFORD: Yes — by that dispatch — but that dispatch is a forgery! (*Thorne with a look of surprise turns sharply toward Arrelsford.*) It's an order to   570 withdraw a whole division from a vital point! A false order! He wrote it himself! (*Thorne stands as if astounded.*)

GENERAL RANDOLPH: Why should he write it? If he wanted to send out a false order he could do it without setting it down on paper, couldn't he?

ARRELSFORD: Yes — but if any of the operators came back they'd catch   575 him doing it! With that order and the Secretary's signature he could go right on! He could even order one of them to send it!

GENERAL RANDOLPH: How did he get the Secretary's signature?

ARRELSFORD: He tore it off from a genuine dispatch! Why General — look at that dispatch in your hand! The Secretary's signature is pasted on!   580 I saw him do it!

THORNE: Why — they often come that way! (*Turns away nonchalantly toward front.*)

ARRELSFORD: He's a liar! They never do!

THORNE (*Turns indignantly on "liar" and the two men glare at each other a moment; recovering himself*):   General, if you have any doubts about that dispatch send it back to the War Office and have it verified!   585

(*Arrelsford is so thunderstruck that he starts back a little unable to speak. He stands with his eyes riveted to Thorne until cue of telegraph click below.*)

GENERAL RANDOLPH (*slowly, his eyes on Thorne*):   Quite a good idea! (*pause*) Sergeant! (*holding out dispatch; Sergeant salutes and waits for orders.*) Take this dispatch over to the Secretary's office and — (*sudden loud, click of telegraph instrument A. General Randolph stops, listening. To Thorne*) What's that?

(*Arrelsford looking at the instrument. Thorne stands motionless, excepting that he took his eyes off Arrelsford and looked front listening on click of instrument.*)

THORNE (*slight wait*):   Adjutant General Chesney.   590

GENERAL RANDOLPH: From the front?

THORNE: Yes, sir.

GENERAL RANDOLPH: What does he say?

THORNE (*Turns and steps to table, stands eyes front, listening to instrument.*):   His compliments sir — (*pause — continued click of instrument*) He asks —   595 (*pause — continued click of instrument*) for the rest — (*pause — click of instrument*) of that dispatch — (*pause — click; then stops*) It's of vital importance. (*Thorne stands motionless.*)

GENERAL RANDOLPH (*After very slight pause abruptly turns and hands the dispatch back to Thorne.*):   Let him have it! (*Thorne [delivers] hurried salute, takes dispatch — sits at table and begins sending.*)

ARRELSFORD: General — if you —

GENERAL RANDOLPH (*sharply to him*):   That's enough! We'll have you examined at headquarters! (*Hurried steps in corridor outside up right and enter quickly at door Lt. Foray, breathless and excited.*) 600

ARRELSFORD (*catching sight of Lt. Foray as he comes in*):   Ah! Thank God! There's a witness! He was sent away on a forged order! Ask him! Ask him! (*pause; Lt. Foray standing up stage looking at others surprised, Thorne continuing business at instrument*)

GENERAL RANDOLPH (*after instant's pause during which click of instrument is heard*):   Wait a moment, Cap'n! 605

(*Thorne stops telegraphing, sits motionless, hand on the key. An instant of dead silence. General Randolph moves up center to speak to Lt. Foray.*)

GENERAL RANDOLPH (*gruffly*):   Where did you come from?

LT. FORAY (*not understanding exactly what is going on; salutes*):   There was some mistake sir!

(*Arrelsford gives gasp of triumph quick on cue; brief pause of dead silence.*)

GENERAL RANDOLPH: Mistake eh? Who made it?

LT. FORAY: I got an order to go to the President's house, and when I got there the President — ! 610

THORNE (*rising at telegraph table*):   This delay will be disastrous sir! Permit me to go on — if there's any mistake we can rectify it afterwards! (*Turns to instrument and begins sending as he stands before it.*)

ARRELSFORD (*half suppressed cry of remonstrance*):   No!

GENERAL RANDOLPH (*who has not given heed to Thorne's speech — to Lt. Foray*):   Where did you get the order? 615

ARRELSFORD: He's at it again sir!

GENERAL RANDOLPH (*Suddenly sees what Thorne is doing.*):   Halt there! (*Thorne stops telegraphing.*) What are you doing! I ordered you to wait!

THORNE (*Turns to General Randolph.*):   I was sent here to attend to the business of this office and that business is going on! (*turning again as if to telegraph*) 620

GENERAL RANDOLPH (*temper rising*):   It's not going on sir, until I'm ready for it!

THORNE (*turning back to the General; loud voice, angrily*):   My orders came from the War Department — not from you! This dispatch came in half an hour ago — they're calling for it — and it's my business to send it out! (*Turning at end of speech and seizing the key endeavors to rush off the dispatch.*)

GENERAL RANDOLPH: Halt! (*Thorne goes on telegraphing. To Sergeant*) Sergeant!   625
(*Sergeant salutes.*) Hold that machine there! (*pointing at telegraph instrument.
Sergeant and two men spring quickly across to right; Sergeant rushes against Thorne
with arm across his breast forcing him over to right against chair and table on right —
chair a little away from table to emphasize with crash as Thorne is flung against it —
and holds him there. The two men cross bayonets over instrument and stand motionless. All done quickly, business-like and with as little disturbance as possible. General
Randolph strides down center and speaks across to Thorne.*) I'll have you court-
martialed for this!

THORNE (*breaking loose and coming down right*):   You'll answer yourself sir, for
delaying a dispatch of vital importance!   630

GENERAL RANDOLPH (*sharply*):   Do you mean that!

THORNE: I mean that! And I demand that you let me proceed with the
business of this office!

GENERAL RANDOLPH: By what authority do you send that dispatch?

THORNE: I refer you to the Department!   635

GENERAL RANDOLPH: Show me your order for taking charge of this office!

THORNE: I refer you to the Department! (*Stands motionless facing across to left.*)

(*Edith appears at upper window up left, coming on from balcony left, and moves a
little into room. Sergeant remains at right above table when Thorne broke away
from him.*)

GENERAL RANDOLPH: By God then I'll *go* to the Department! (*Swings
round and striding up center a little way*) Sergeant! (*Sergeant salutes.*) Leave your
men on guard there and go over to the War Office — my compliments   640
to the Secretary and will he be so good as to —

ARRELSFORD (*suddenly breaking out on seeing Edith*):   Ah! General! (*pointing to
her*) Another witness! Miss Varney! She was here! She saw it all!

(*Thorne on Arrelsford's mention of another witness glances quickly up left toward
Edith, and at once turns front and stands motionless, waiting. General Randolph
turns left and sees Edith.*)

GENERAL RANDOLPH (*bluffly touching hat*):   Miss Varney! (*Edith comes forward
a little.*) Do you know anything about this?   645

EDITH (*Speaks in low voice.*):   About what, sir?

GENERAL RANDOLPH: Mr. Arrelsford here claims that Captain Thorne is acting without authority in this office and that you can testify to that effect.

EDITH (*very quietly*):   Mr. Arrelsford is mistaken! He has the highest authority!   650

(*Arrelsford aghast, General Randolph surprised. Thorne faces left listening, motionless.*)

GENERAL RANDOLPH (*after pause of surprise*):   What authority has he?

EDITH (*drawing the commission from her dress*):   The authority of the President of the Confederate States of America! (*handing the commission to General Randolph, who takes it and at once opens and examines it. Edith stands a moment where she was, looking neither at Arrelsford nor Thorne, then slowly retires up and stands back of others out of the way.*)

GENERAL RANDOLPH (*looking at commission*):   What's this! Major's Commission! Assigned to duty on the Signal Corps! In command of the Tele- ⟨655⟩ graph Department!

ARRELSFORD (*breaking out*):   That commission — let me explain how she —

GENERAL RANDOLPH: That'll do! — I suppose this is a forgery too?

ARRELSFORD: Let me tell you sir —

GENERAL RANDOLPH: You've told me enough! Sergeant — take him to ⟨660⟩ headquarters!

SERGEANT (*quick salute*):   Fall in there! (*motioning men at instrument, who hurry across and fall into rank*) Forward march!

(*Sergeant and Guard quickly rush Arrelsford across to door up right and off.*)

ARRELSFORD (*resisting and protesting as he is forced off*):   No! For God's sake, General, listen to me! It's the Yankee Secret Service! Never mind me, but ⟨665⟩ don't let that dispatch go out! He's a damned Yankee Secret Agent! His brother brought in the signal tonight!

(*Sound of footsteps of the Guard outside dying away down the corridor and of Arrelsford's voice protesting and calling for Justice. Short pause, Thorne motionless through above looking front; General Randolph, who crossed to up left center on men forcing Arrelsford off, goes down center and looks across at Thorne.*)

GENERAL RANDOLPH (*gruffly*):   Cap'n Thorne! (*Thorne comes to straight military position, goes to the General and salutes. General gruffly*) It's your own fault Cap'n! If you'd had the sense to mention this before we'd have been saved ⟨670⟩ a damned lot o' trouble! There's your commission! (*Hands [it] to Thorne, who takes it saluting — General turns to go.*) I can't understand why they have to be so cursed shy about their Secret Service Orders! (*Goes up toward exit, stops and speaks to Lt. Foray who is standing at right of door.*) Lieutenant! (*Lt. Foray salutes. Very gruffly*) Take your orders from Cap'n Thorne! (*Turns and ⟨675⟩ goes heavily off, very much out of temper.*)

(*Lt. Foray goes down right and sits at telegraph table on extreme right. Busy with papers. No noise. Thorne stands facing left, commission in right hand, until the General is off. Turns right glancing round to see that he is gone, and at once glides to telegraph instrument A. and begins sending with right hand — still holding commission in it. Edith comes quickly down to Thorne.*)

EDITH (*at upper corner of table, very near Thorne*):   Cap'n Thorne! (*Thorne stops and turns quickly to her, hand still on key. She goes on in low voice, hurried, breathless.*) That gives you authority — long enough to escape from Richmond!

THORNE: Escape? Impossible! (*Seizes key and begins to send.*)

EDITH: Oh! You wouldn't do it now! (*Thorne instantly stops sending and looks at her.*) I brought it — to save your life! I didn't think you'd use it — for any- 680 thing else! Oh — you wouldn't.

(*Thorne stands looking at her. Sudden sharp call from instrument A. turns him back to it. Edith looks at him — covers her face and moans, at same time turning away left. She moves up to the door up right and goes out. Thorne stands in a desperate struggle with himself as instrument A. is clicking off the same signal that he made when calling up the front. He almost seizes the key — then resists — and finally, with a bang of right fist on the table, turns and strides up left center, the commission crushed in his right hand.*)

LT. FORAY (*who has been listening to calls of instrument, rising as Thorne comes to a stand up left center*):   They're calling for that dispatch sir! What shall I do?

THORNE (*turning quickly*):   Send it!

(*Lt. Foray drops into seat at table right center and begins sending at the same time arranging dispatch at left of table for Thorne to seize. Thorne stands motionless on the order an instant. As Lt. Foray begins to send he turns round a little up to right slowly and painfully, right arm up across eyes in a struggle with himself. Suddenly he breaks away and dashes toward table right center.*)

THORNE: No no — stop! (*Seizes the dispatch from the table in his right hand which still has the commission crumpled in it.*) I won't do it! I won't do it! (*Lt. Foray rises 685 in surprise on Thorne seizing the dispatch, and stands facing him. Thorne points at instrument unsteadily.*) Revoke the order! It was a mistake! I refuse to act under this commission! (*throwing the papers in his right hand down on the floor and standing center slightly turned away to left*)

ACT IV

Drawing-room at General Varney's. Same as Acts I and II. Eleven o'clock. The furniture is somewhat disordered as if left as it was after the disturbances at the close of the second act. Nothing is broken or upset. Half light on in room. Lamps lighted but not strong on. Portieres on window down right are closed. Thunder of distant cannonading and sounds of volleys of musketry and exploding shells on very strong at times during this act. Quivering and rather subdued flashes of light — as the artillery is some miles distant — shown at windows right from time to time. Violent and hurried ringing of church bells in distant parts of the city — deep, low tones booming out like a fire bell. Sounds of hurried passing in the street outside of bodies of soldiers — artillery —

*cavalry, etc. on cues, with many horse-hoof and rattling gun-carriage and chain ef-
fects — shouting to horses — orders, bugle calls, etc. The thunder of cannonading,
shelling fortifications, musketry, flashes, etc., must be kept up during the act, coming in
now and then where it will not interfere with dialogue, and so arranged that the idea
of a desperate attack will not be lost. Possible places for this effect are marked thus in the
script: (XXX). At rise of curtain, thunder of artillery and flashes of light now and then.
Ringing of church and fire bells in distance. Caroline is discovered in window up right
shrinking back against curtains and looking out through window with fright. Enter
Mrs. Varney coming hurriedly down the stairs from up left and in at door.*

MRS. VARNEY: Caroline! (*Caroline goes to her.*) Tell me what happened? She
won't speak! Where has she been? Where was it?

CAROLINE (*frightened*):   It was at the telegraph office!

MRS. VARNEY: What did she do? What happened? Try to tell!

(*Flashes — cannonading — bells, etc., kept up strong. Effect of passing artillery begins
in the distance very softly.*)

CAROLINE: Ah don't know! Ah was afraid and ran out! (*alarm bell very   5
strong*) It's the alarm bell, Mrs. Varney — to call out the reserve!

MRS. VARNEY: Yes — yes! (*glance of anxiety toward windows right*) They're
making a terrible attack tonight. Lieutenant Maxwell was right! That
quiet spell was the signal! (*artillery effect louder*)

CAROLINE (*Goes to window, turns to Mrs. Varney and speaks above noise, which is not
yet on full.*):   It's another regiment of artillery goin' by! They're sendin'   10
'em all over to Cemetery Hill! That's where the fighting is! Cemetery
Hill! (*effect on loud*)

(*Caroline watches from window. Mrs. Varney crosses over left and rings bell. As effect
dies away Martha enters up left from door right of stairs.*)

MRS. VARNEY: Go up and stay with Miss Edith till I come. Don't leave her
a moment! (*Martha turns and hurries up the stairway. Alarm bell and cannon on
strong*) Shut the curtains Caroline!   15

CAROLINE: (*Closes the window curtains at right.*):   Ah'm afraid they're goin' to
have a right bad time tonight! (*going to Mrs. Varney*)

MRS. VARNEY: Indeed I'm afraid so! Now try to think dear, who was at the
telegraph office? Can't you tell me something?

CAROLINE (*shaking her head*):   No — only they arrested Mr. Arrelsford!   20

MRS. VARNEY: Mr. Arrelsford! Why, you don't mean that!

CAROLINE: Yes, Ah do! An' General Randolph — he came — Ah went an'
brought him there — an' oh — he was in a frightful temper!

MRS. VARNEY: And Edith — now you can tell me — what — what did
she do?   25

CAROLINE: Ah can't Mrs. Varney. Ah don't know! Ah just waited for her outside an' when she came out she couldn't speak — an' then we hurried home! That's all Ah know, Mrs. Varney — truly!

(*Loud ringing of door bell in another part of the house. Caroline and Mrs. Varney turn toward door up left. Noise of heavy steps outside left and Arrelsford almost immediately strides into the room, followed by two privates, who stand at the door. Caroline steps back up stage a little as Arrelsford enters, and Mrs. Varney faces him.*)

(*XXX*)

ARRELSFORD (*roughly, as he advances on Mrs. Varney*):   Is your daughter in the house?   30

MRS. VARNEY (*after a second's pause*):   Yes!

(*XXX*)

ARRELSFORD: I'll see her if you please!

MRS. VARNEY: I don't know that she'll care to receive you at present.

ARRELSFORD: What she cares to do at present is of small consequence! Shall I go up to her room with these men or will you have her come   35 down?

MRS. VARNEY: Neither one nor the other until I know your business.

(*Effect of passing cavalry and artillery — strong*)

ARRELSFORD (*excitedly*):   My business! I've got a few questions to ask! Listen to that! (*XXX on strong*) Now you know what "Attack Tonight Plan Three" means!   40

MRS. VARNEY (*change of manner; surprise*):   Is that — the attack!

ARRELSFORD: That's the attack Madam! They're breaking through our lines at Cemetery Hill! That was PLAN THREE! We're rushing over the reserves but they may not get there in time!

(*XXX*)

(*Caroline has crossed at back to left door as if going out, but waits to see what happens.*)

MRS. VARNEY: What has my daughter to do with this?   45

ARRELSFORD: Do with it! She did it!

MRS. VARNEY (*astonished*):   What!

(*Noise of passing Cavalry Officer going by singly*)

ARRELSFORD: We had him in his own trap — under arrest — the telegraph under guard — when she brought in that commission!

MRS. VARNEY (*horrified*):   You don't mean she —   50

ARRELSFORD: Yes — that's it! She put the game in his hands. He got the wires! His cursed dispatch went through. As soon as I got to headquarters they saw the trick! They rushed the guard back — the scoundrel had got away! But we're after him hot, an' if she knows where he is — (*about to turn and to toward door up left*) I'll get it out of her!   55

(*XXX*)

MRS. VARNEY: You don't suppose my daughter would —
ARRELSFORD: I suppose anything!
MRS. VARNEY: I'll not believe it!
ARRELSFORD: We can't stop for what you believe! (*as if to go to stairs*)

(*Stop alarm bells.*)

MRS. VARNEY: Let me speak to her!   60

(*Passing cavalry effect has died away by this time.*)

ARRELSFORD: I'll see her myself! (*going up left*)
CAROLINE (*Has stepped quietly down so that as Arrelsford turns to go toward stairway she confronts him.*):   Where is your order for this?
ARRELSFORD (*after instant's surprise*):   I've got a word or two to say to you — after I've been upstairs!
CAROLINE: Show me your order for going upstairs!   65
ARRELSFORD: Department business — I don't require an order!
CAROLINE (*shaking head*):   Oh, you've made a mistake about that! This is a private house! It isn't the telegraph office! If you want to go up any stairs or see anybody about anything you'll have to bring an order! Ah don't know much — but Ah know enough for that!   (*Exit upstairs.*)   70

(*XXX light*)

ARRELSFORD (*Turns sharply to Mrs. Varney.*):   Am I to understand Madam, that you —

(*Loud ringing of door bell in distant part of house, followed almost immediately after by the sound of door outside left and tramp of many feet in the hallway*)

(*XXX cavalry effect begins again.*)

(*Arrelsford and Mrs. Varney turn. Enter quickly a Sergeant and four Men. Men are halted near left. Officer advances to Mrs. Varney. Arrelsford steps back a little.*)

SERGEANT (*touching cap roughly*):   Are you the lady that lives here, ma'am?
MRS. VARNEY: I am Mrs. Varney.

SERGEANT (*interrupting*):   I've got an order to search the house! (*showing her* 75 *the order*)

ARRELSFORD: Just in time! (*coming down*) I'll go through the house if you please!

SERGEANT (*shortly*):   You can't go through on this order — it was issued to me!

MRS. VARNEY: You were sent here to — 80

SERGEANT: Yes, ma'am! Sorry to trouble you but we'll have to be quick about it! If we don't get him here we've got to follow down Franklin Street — he's over this way somewhere! (*Turns left about to give orders to men.*)

MRS. VARNEY: Who? Who is it you —

SERGEANT (*hurriedly*):   Man named Thorne — Cap'n of Artillery — that's 85 what he went by! (*Turns to his Men.*) Here — this way! That room in there! (*Indicates room up center.*) Two of you outside! (*pointing to windows*) Cut off those windows.

(*Two Men run into room up center and two off at windows right, throwing open curtains and windows as they do so. Mrs. Varney stands aside. Sergeant glances quickly round the room — pushing desk out and looking behind it, etc. Keep up cavalry effects and flashes during business; artillery strong during this. These effects distant — as if going down another street several blocks away. During business, Arrelsford goes to door left, gives an order to his men, then exits, followed by men who came with him.*)

(*XXX*)

(*The two Men who went off at door up center to search, re-enter shoving the old negro Jonas roughly into the room. He is torn and dirty and shows signs of rough handling. They force him down center a little way and he stands crouching.*)

SERGEANT (*to Men*):   Where did you get that?

PRIVATE: Hiding in a closet sir. 90

SERGEANT (*going to Jonas*):   What are you doing in there? If you don't answer me we'll kick the life out of you! (*short pause; to Mrs. Varney*) Belongs to you, Ah reckon?

MRS. VARNEY: Yes — but they want him for carrying a message —

SERGEANT: Well if they want him they can get him — we're looking for 95 someone else! (*Motions to Men.*) Throw him back in there! (*Men shove Jonas off at door up center. Other Men re-enter from windows at right.*) Here — this room! Be quick now! Cover that door! (*Two Men have quick business of searching room down right and left. The other two Men stand on guard [at] door up left.*) Sorry to disturb you ma'am! (*Bell rings off left.*)

MRS. VARNEY: Do what you please — I have nothing to conceal! (*sound of* 100
door outside up left)

(*XXX*)

ORDERLY (*outside door up left*):   Here! Lend a hand will you!

(*Two Men at door up left exit to help someone outside. Enter the Orderly who took
Wilfred away in Act II, coming on hurriedly at door up left. He stands just below
door — a few steps into room — splashed with foam and mud from hard riding. He
sees Sergeant and salutes. Sergeant salutes back and goes over, looking out of window up
right. Mrs. Varney upon seeing the Orderly gives a cry of alarm.*)

ORDERLY: Ah've brought back the boy, ma'am!

MRS. VARNEY (*starting forward*):   Oh! What do you — (*breathless*) What —

ORDERLY: We never got out there at all! The Yankees made a raid down at
Mechanicsville not three miles out! The Home Guard was goin' by on 105
the dead run to head 'em off an' before I knew it he was in with 'em riding like mad! There was a bit of a skirmish an' he got a clip across the
neck — nothing at all ma'am — he rode back all the way an' — (*Cavalry
effects die away gradually.*)

MRS. VARNEY: Oh — he's hurt — he's hurt!

ORDERLY: Nothing bad ma'am — don't upset yourself. 110

MRS. VARNEY (*Starts toward door.*):   Where did you — (*Stops on seeing Wilfred,
who enters supported by two Men. He is pale and has a bandage about his neck. Mrs.
Varney after the slight pause on his entrance goes to him at once.*)

MRS. VARNEY: Oh Wilfred!

WILFRED (*motioning Mrs. Varney off*):   It's all right — you don't understand!
(*Tries to free himself from the man who is supporting him.*) What do you want to
hold me like that for? (*Frees himself and walks toward center a few steps a little
unsteadily but not too much so.*) — You see — I can walk all right! (*Mrs. Var-* 115
*ney comes down anxiously and holds him. Wilfred turns and sees his mother and takes
her hand with an effort to do it in as casual a manner as possible.*) How-dy-do
Mother! — Didn't expect me back so soon, did you? — Tell you how it
was — (*Turns and sees Orderly.*) Don't you go away now — Ah'm going
back with you — just wait till I rest about a minute. See here! They're
ringing the bells to call out the reserves! (*starting weakly toward door left*) 120
Ah'll go right now!

(*XXX*)

MRS. VARNEY (*gently holding him back*):   No no Wilfred — not now!

(*XXX louder*)

WILFRED (*weakly*): Not now! — You hear that — you hear those bells — and tell me — not now! — I — (*Sways a little.*) I — (*Mrs. Varney gives a cry of alarm seeing Wilfred is going to faint.*)

SERGEANT (*quick undertone to Men*): Stand by there! (*Wilfred faints. Mrs. Varney supports him, but almost immediately the two Men come to her assistance. Sergeant and two Men push couch forward down right center and they quickly lay him on it, head to the right. Mrs. Varney goes to head of couch, and holds Wilfred's head as they lay him down.*) 125

(*Cannonading gradually ceases.*)

SERGEANT (*to one of the Men*): Find some water will you? (*to Mrs. Varney*) Put his head down ma'am — he'll be all right in a minute!

(*A Private hurries off at door up left on order to get water. Sergeant gets chair from up center and puts it back of couch. Mrs. Varney goes back of couch, attending to Wilfred. Private re-enters with basin of water and gives it to Mrs. Varney.*)

SERGEANT (*to Men*): This way now!

(*Men move quickly to door up left. Sergeant gives quick directions to Men at door up left. All exit. One or two go right. Sergeant with most of men are seen going up the stairway. Orderly is left standing a little below door, exactly as he was. Mrs. Varney kneeling back of Wilfred and bathing his head tenderly — using her handkerchief.*)

ORDERLY (*after brief pause*): If there ain't anything else ma'am, Ah'd better report back. 130

MRS. VARNEY: Yes — don't wait! — The wound is dressed, isn't it?

ORDERLY: Yes'm. I took him to the Winder Hospital — they said he'd be on his feet in a day or two — but he wants to keep quiet a bit.

MRS. VARNEY: Tell the General just how it happened!

ORDERLY (*touching cap*): Very well ma'am. (*Exit at door up left.*) 135

(*Short pause. Mrs. Varney gently bathing Wilfred's head and wrists. Alarm bells die away excepting one which continues to ring in muffled tones. Caroline appears coming down the stairway absent-mindedly, stopping when part way down; sees somebody in the room. She looks more intently, then runs suddenly down the rest of the way and into the room, stopping dead when a little way in and looking at what is going on. Mrs. Varney does not see her at first — Caroline stands motionless — face very white. Mrs. Varney after a moment's pause for above, sees Caroline.*)

(*XXX*)

MRS. VARNEY (*rising quickly*): Caroline dear! (*Goes to her.*) It's *nothing!* (*Holds Caroline, though the girl seems not to know it, her face expressionless and her eyes fixed on Wilfred.*) He's hardly hurt at all! There — there — don't you faint too, dear!

CAROLINE (*very low voice*): Ah'm not going to faint! (*Sees the handkerchief in Mrs. Varney's hand.*) Let me — (*Takes handkerchief and goes across toward Wilfred,* 140 *toward front of couch; turns to Mrs. Varney.*) — Ah can take care of him. Ah don't need anybody here at all! (*Goes toward Wilfred.*)

MRS. VARNEY: But, Caroline —

CAROLINE (*still with a strange quiet; looks calmly at Mrs. Varney.*):   Mrs. Varney — there's a heap o' soldiers goin' round upstairs — lookin' in all the rooms. 145 Ah reckon you'd better go an' attend to 'em.

MRS. VARNEY: Yes yes — I must go a moment! (*Going up toward door, stops and turns to Caroline.*) You know what to do?

CAROLINE: Oh yes! (*dropping down on the floor beside Wilfred*)

MRS. VARNEY: Bathe his forehead — he isn't badly hurt! — I won't be 150 long! (*Exit hurriedly up left closing the portieres or curtains together after her.*)

(*Caroline on her knees close to Wilfred, tenderly bathing his forehead and smoothing his hair. Wilfred soon begins to show signs of revival.*)

CAROLINE (*speaking to him in low tone as he revives — not a continued speech, but with pauses, business, etc.*):   Wilfred dear! — Wilfred! You're not hurt much are you? — Oh, no — you're not! There there! — You'll feel better in just a minute! — Yes — just a minute!

WILFRED (*weakly, before he realizes what has happened*):   Is there — are you — 155 (*Looks round with wide open eyes.*)

CAROLINE: Oh Wilfred — don't you know me?

WILFRED (*Looks at her.*):   What are you talking about — of course Ah know you! — Say — what am I doing anyhow — taking a bath?

CAROLINE: No no! — You see Wilfred — you just fainted a little an' —

WILFRED: Fainted! (*Caroline nods.*) I fainted! (*weak attempt to rise; begins to re-* 160 *member.*) Oh — (*Sinks back weakly.*) — Yes of course! — Ah was in a fight with the Yanks — an' got knocked — (*Begins to remember that he was wounded; thinks about it a moment, then looks strangely at Caroline.*)

CAROLINE (*after looking at him in silence*):   Oh, what is it?

WILFRED: Ah'll tell you one thing right yere! Ah'm not going to load you up with a cripple! Not much! 165

CAROLINE: Cripple!

WILFRED: Ah reckon Ah've got an arm knocked off haven't I?

CAROLINE (*quickly*):   No no! You haven't Wilfred! (*shaking head emphatically*) They're both on all right!

WILFRED (*after thinking a moment*):   Maybe I had a hand shot away? 170

CAROLINE: Oh — not a single one!

WILFRED: Are my — are my ears on all right?

CAROLINE (*Looks on both sides of his head.*): Oh yes! You needn't trouble about them a minute! (*Wilfred thinks a moment, then turns his eyes slowly on her.*)

WILFRED: How many legs have Ah got left? 175

CAROLINE (*Looks to see.*): All of 'em — every one!

(*Last alarm bell ceases.*)

WILFRED (*after pause*): Then — if there's enough of me left to — to amount to anything — (*Looks in Caroline's face a moment.*) you'll take charge of it just the same? — How about that?

CAROLINE (*after pause*): That's all right too! (*Caroline suddenly buries face on his* 180 *shoulder. Wilfred gets hold of her hand and kisses it. She suddenly raises head and looks at him.*) Ah tried to send you a telegram — an' they wouldn't let me!

WILFRED: Did you? (*Caroline nods.*) What did you say in it? (*pause*) Tell me what you said!

CAROLINE: It was something nice! (*Looks away.*)

WILFRED: It was, eh? (*Caroline nods with her head turned away from him; Wilfred* 185 *reaches up and turns her head toward him again.*) You're sure it was something nice!

CAROLINE: Well Ah wouldn't have gone to work an' telegraphed if it was something *bad* would Ah?

WILFRED: Well if it was good, why didn't you send it? 190

CAROLINE: Goodness gracious! How could Ah when they wouldn't let me!

WILFRED: Wouldn't let you!

CAROLINE: Ah should think not! (*Moves back for Wilfred's getting up.*) Oh they had a dreadful time at the telegraph office! 195

WILFRED: Telegraph office. (*Tries to recollect.*) Telegr — were you there when — (*raising himself*)

(*Alarm bell begins to ring again.*)

(*XXX*)

(*Caroline moves back a little frightened — without getting up — watching him. Wilfred suddenly tries to get up.*)

That was it! — They told me at the hospital! (*Attempts to rise.*)

(*XXX*)

CAROLINE (*rising, trying to prevent him*): Oh, you mustn't!

WILFRED (*Gets partly on his feet and pushes Caroline away with one hand, holding to the chair near the desk right for support with the other.*): He gets hold of our 200

Department Telegraph — sends out a false order — weakens our defense at Cemetery Hill — an' they're down on us in a minute! An' she gave it to him! The commission! — My sister Edith!

(*XXX*)

CAROLINE: Oh you don't know —

WILFRED (*imperiously*):   Ah know this — if the General was here he'd see her! The General isn't here — Ah'll attend it!   205

(*XXX*)

(*Wilfred begins to feel a dizziness and holds on to desk for support. Caroline starts toward him in alarm. He braces himself erect again with an effort and motions her off. She stops.*)

WILFRED (*weakly but with clear voice and commandingly*):   Send her to me! (*Caroline stands almost frightened with her eyes upon him.*)

(*Enter Mrs. Varney at door up left. Caroline hurries toward Mrs. Varney in a frightened way — glancing back at Wilfred.*)

CAROLINE: He wants to see Edith!

MRS. VARNEY (*going toward Wilfred*):   Not now Wilfred — you're too weak and ill!   210

WILFRED: Tell her to come here!

MRS. VARNEY: It won't do any good — she won't speak!

WILFRED: Ah don't want her to speak — Ah'm going to speak to her!

MRS. VARNEY: Some other time!

WILFRED (*Leaves the chair that he held to and moves toward door up left as if to pass his mother and Caroline.*):   If you won't send her to me — Ah'll —   215

MRS. VARNEY (*stopping him*):   There there! If you insist I'll call her!

WILFRED: Ah insist!

(*XXX*)

MRS. VARNEY (*Turns toward door and goes a few steps; stops, turns back to Caroline.*): Stay with him, dear!

WILFRED (*weak voice but commandingly*):   Ah'll see her alone!

(*Mrs. Varney looks at him an instant, sees that he means what he says, and motions Caroline to come. Caroline looks at Wilfred a moment, then turns and slowly goes to door up left where Mrs. Varney is waiting for her, looks sadly back at Wilfred again, and then they both go off at door.*)

(*XXX*)

(*Wilfred stands motionless an instant down right center as he was when the ladies left. Noise of approaching men — low shouts — steps on gravel, etc., outside up right, begins in distance. On this Wilfred turns and moves up center looking off to right, then goes up into the doorway opening up center but does not open the door.*)

(*XXX*)

(*Alarm bell ceases. Low sound of distant voices and the tramp of hurrying feet quickly growing louder and louder outside right. When it is on strong, Thorne appears springing over balustrade of veranda above window up right and instantly runs forward into the room — knocking over pedestal and vase at right, but quickly back against wall or curtains at right so that he will not be seen. He stands there panting — face pale — eyes hunted and desperate. His left hand is bandaged roughly. He has no hat, or coat, hair is disheveled, shoes dusty, trousers and shirt torn and soiled. As the noise of his pursuers dies away he turns into the room and makes a rapid start across toward left, looking quickly about as if searching for someone. Wilfred, who has been watching him from up center, darts down center as Thorne goes across and comes down right of him catching hold of him by right arm and shoulder.*)

WILFRED: Halt! You're under arrest!   220

THORNE (*with a quick glance back at Wilfred*):   Wait a minute! (*shaking loose from Wilfred*) Wait a minute an' I'll go with you! (*going up left, looking this way and that*)

WILFRED (*a step toward Thorne as if to follow*):   Halt I say! You're my prisoner!

THORNE (*turning and going quickly down to him*):   All right — prisoner — anything you like! (*drawing revolver from right hip pocket and pushing it into his*   225 *hands*) Take this — shoot the life out of me — but let me see my brother first!

WILFRED (*taking the revolver*):   Your brother!

THORNE (*Nods, breathless.*):   One look in his face — that's all!

WILFRED: Where is he?   230

THORNE (*quick glance about; points toward the door up center*):   Maybe they took him in there! (*striding toward door as he speaks*)

WILFRED (*springing up between door and Thorne and covering him with revolver*): What is he doing?

THORNE (*facing Wilfred*):   Ha!

WILFRED (*still covering him*):   What's he doing in there?   235

THORNE: Nothing! . . . He's dead!

WILFRED (*Looks at Thorne a moment, then begins to back slowly up to door, keeping eyes on Thorne and revolver ready but not aimed; opens door, takes quick look into the room, and faces Thorne again.*):   It's a lie!

THORNE (*turning up toward him*):   What!

WILFRED: There's no one there! — it's another trick of yours! (*Starts toward window up right.*) Call in the Guard! Call the Guard! Captain Thorne is 240 here in the house!

(*Wilfred exits at window, calling the Guard. His voice is heard outside right, becoming more and more distant. Thorne stands a moment until Wilfred is off, then springs to the door up center, opens it and looks into the room, going part way off at the door. He glances this way and that within room, then attitude of failure — left hand dropping from frame of door to his side as he comes to erect position; right hand retaining hold of knob of door, which he pushed open. On Thorne standing erect, Edith enters through the portieres of the door up left, expecting to find Wilfred. She stands just within the doorway. Thorne turns and comes out of room, closing the door as he does so. Turning away from the door, right hand still on the knob, he sees Edith and stops motionless facing her.*)

THORNE (*going to Edith*):   You wouldn't tell me would you! He was shot in this room — an hour ago — my brother Harry! — I'd like one look in his dead face before they send me the same way! Can't you tell me that much Miss Varney? Is he in the house? (*Edith looks in his face an instant motionless —* 245 *then turns and moves slowly down left center and stands near the table there.*)

THORNE (*Turns and moves toward window up right. A sudden burst of shouts and calls outside up right in distance on Thorne's turning away to right as if Wilfred had reached a posse of the Guard. Turning near center, a flash of distant artillery on him from outside*):   Ha ha — they're on the scent, you see! — They'll get me in a minute — an' when they do it won't take long to finish me off! (*Looks at her.*) And as that'll be the last of me Miss Varney — maybe you'll listen to one thing! We can't all die a soldier's death — in the roar and glory of battle — our friends around us — under the flag we love! — no — not 250 all! Some of us have orders for another kind of work — desperate — dare-devil work — the hazardous schemes of the Secret Service! We fight our battles alone — no comrades to cheer us on — ten thousand to one against us — death at every turn! If we win we escape with our lives — if we lose — dragged out and butchered like dogs — no soldier's 255 grave — not even a trench with the rest of the boys — alone — despised — forgotten! These were my orders Miss Varney — this is the death I die tonight — and I don't want you to think for one minute that I'm ashamed of it — not for one minute!

(*Suddenly shouts and noise of many men rushing up outside up right and also outside up left. Thorne swings round and walks up center in usual nonchalant manner, and stands up center waiting and faced a little to right of front, leaning on side of door with outstretched right arm. Edith moves to left and stands near mantel. As shouts become nearer, Thorne turns and stands waiting, faced to front. No assumption of bravado. Enter from both windows on right — bursting open the one down right — and from*) *door up left a Squad of Confederate Soldiers in gray uniforms — not too old and dirty — those on right headed by the Sergeant who searched the house early in this act, and those on left by a Corporal. Wilfred Varney with revolver still in his hand, enters at windows in lead of others, coming to right center. They rush on — with a shout of exultation, and stand on charge at each side.)*

WILFRED (*to Sergeant*):   There's your man Sergeant — I hand him over to you! 260

SERGEANT (*advancing to Thorne and putting hand roughly on his shoulder*):   Prisoner!

(*XXX*)

(*Enter Arrelsford hurriedly at door up left.*)

ARRELSFORD (*breaking through between men at left and standing left center*): Where is he? (*Sees him.*) Ah! We've got him have we!

SERGEANT: Young Varney here captured him, sir! (*Enter Mrs. Varney up left.* 265 *She goes down left side near fireplace and stands looking on.*)

ARRELSFORD: So! — Run down at last! (*Thorne pays no attention to him; he merely waits for the end of the disturbance.*) Now you'll find out what it costs to play your little game with our Government Telegraph Lines! (*to Sergeant*) Don't waste any time! Take him down the street and shoot him full of lead! — Out with him! (*going down left center on last of speech. Low shouts of ap-* 270 *proval from Men, and general movement as if to start, the Sergeant at same time shov-ing Thorne a little toward left*)

SERGEANT (*gruffly, as he starts*):   Come along!

WILFRED (*a step toward center, revolver still in hand*):   No! — Whatever he is — whatever he's done — he has the right to a trial! (*Thorne turns suddenly round and looks at Wilfred.*)

ARRELSFORD: General Tarleton said to me, "If you find him shoot him on sight!" 275

WILFRED: I don't care what General Tarleton said — I captured the man — he's in this house — and he's not going out without he's treated fair! (*Looks up toward Thorne; their eyes meet, then Thorne turns away up stage, rest-ing left hand against left side of door frame.*)

ARRELSFORD (*suddenly, angrily*):   Well — let him have it! — We'll give him a drum-head, boys — but it'll be the quickest drum-head ever held on 280 earth! (*to Sergeant*) Stack muskets here an' run 'em in for the Court!

SERGEANT (*stepping a little down center and facing about, back to audience*):   Fall in here! (*Men break positions each side and run up stage, falling quickly into a double rank just above Sergeant.*) Fall in the Prisoner! (*Men separate right and left, leav-ing space at center; Thorne steps down into position and stands.*) Stack — arms! 285

(Front rank Men stack — rear rank Men pass pieces forward. Front rank Men lay them on stacks. Turning right to Mrs. Varney and touching cap) Where shall we find a vacant room, ma'am?

MRS. VARNEY: At the head of the stairs — there's none on this floor.

SERGEANT *(turning up to Men)*: Escort — left face! *(Men left face — Thorne obeying the order with them.)* Forward — march! — File left!   290

(Soldiers with Thorne march rapidly out of the room at door up left and disappear up the stairway. The Sergeant exits after men.)

(XXX)

(The door up center slowly opens a little way and soon the old negro Jonas enters cautiously — almost crawling on. He looks this way and that and off at door up left and up the stairway. Suddenly his eyes light on the stacks of muskets. He goes to the one up left center — looks about fearfully, apprehensively, hesitates an instant. During his business, artillery and cavalry effects on strong. Cannon and musketry fire in distance — alarm bells on strong — begin as Men go upstairs. Jonas makes up his mind. He drops down on knees by stack of muskets — snaps the breech lock of one — without moving it from the stack — gets out the cartridge, looks at it, bites it with his teeth and looks at it again. Bites again and makes motions of getting the ball off and putting it in his pocket. Puts cartridge back in the musket, snaps the lock shut, and moves on to the next. Repeats the movement of taking the cartridge out, but is much quicker, biting off the ball at once. Repeats more rapidly and quickly with another musket, crawling quickly round the stack. Moves over to second stack; same business. As Jonas gets well to work on muskets Edith turns at window up right and sees him. She stands a moment motionless — then comes down on right, and stands looking at him without moving. Jonas, who began after leaving stack left center at upper side of stack right center has worked around down stage on the stack, and has come to the lower side. Edith stands near the desk at right and drops a book upon it on cue to make Jonas look up after the last musket but one. Jonas looks up and sees Edith watching. He stops. Stop loud effects as Jonas speaks, but keep up bells and far distant cannon.)

JONAS *(after pause, very low voice)*: Dhey's a-goin' ter shoot 'im — shoot 'im down like a dog, Missy — an' Ah couldn't b'ar to see 'em do dat! Ah wouldn't like it noways! You won't say nuffin' 'bout dis — fer de sake of ole Jonas what was always so fond o' you — ebber sense ye was a little chile! *(Sees that Edith does not appear angry and goes on with his work of drawing*   295 *the bullets out of the last musket.)* Ye see — I jiss take away dis yer — an' den dar won't be no harm to 'im what-some-ebber — less'n day loads 'em up again! *(Slowly hobbles to his feet as he speaks.)* When dey shoots — an' he jiss draps down, dey'll roll 'im over inter de gutter an' be off like dey was mad! Den Ah can be near by — an' — *(Suddenly thinks of something; a look of consternation comes over his face. He speaks in almost whisper.)* How's he goin' ter*   300 know! Ef he don't drap down dey'll shoot him agin — an dey'll hab bullets in 'em nex' time! (*Anxiously glances around an instant.*) Dey'll hab bullets in 'em next time! (*Looks about. Suddenly to Edith.*) *You* tell 'im! *You* tell him Missy — it's de ony-est way! Tell 'im to drap down! (*supplicatingly*) Do dis 305 fur ole Jonas, honey — do it fur me — an' Ah'll be a slabe to ye ez long ez Ah lib! (*slight pause; sudden subdued yell outside up left sounding as if from men shut inside a room on the floor above. Jonas starts and turns on the yell; half whisper*) Dey's a-goin' ter kill 'im!

(*XXX*)

(*Noise of heavy tramp of feet outside left above, doors opening, etc.; an indistinct order or two before regular order heard. Jonas goes hurriedly up to door up center.*)

SERGEANT (*outside, above*): Fall in! — Right face! — Forward — March!
JONAS (*at door*): Oh tell 'im Missy! Tell 'im to drap down for God's sake! 310 (*Exit at door, carefully closing it after him.*)

(*XXX*)

(*Edith crosses to left center and stands waiting, her face expressionless, in front of table.*)

(*XXX*)

(*Enter Wilfred up left coming down the stairs. He enters the room coming down center. Enter Caroline at door up left as Wilfred goes down center. She hurries to him with an anxious glance up stairway as she passes.*)

CAROLINE (*almost whisper*): What are they — going to do?
WILFRED: Shoot him!
CAROLINE: When?
WILFRED: Now.
CAROLINE (*low exclamation of pity*): Oh! 315

(*Wilfred goes below couch; Caroline stands near him looking on as Soldiers and others enter. Sergeant enters first followed by escort of Soldiers. They enter room and turn right marching to position they were formerly in above the stacks of muskets. Enter Arrelsford after the men. He goes across to up right center. Mrs. Varney enters and goes down left.*)

SERGEANT (*at center facing up*): Halt! (*Men halt.*) Left face! (*Men face front.*) (*Enter Thorne up left coming down the stairway, followed by Corporal with his carbine. Thorne comes into position at left of front line of men. Corporal stands left of Thorne.*)
SERGEANT: Take arms! (*Men at once take muskets, all very quick.*) Carry arms! (*Men stand in line waiting.*) Fall in the Prisoner! (*Thorne walks in front of Men to center and falls into position.*) Left face! (*Thorne and Men face to left on order, ready to march out.*) Forward — 320
EDITH: Wait! — (*motion of hand to stop them without looking round*) Who is the officer in command?

SERGEANT: I'm in command, Miss! (*touching cap*)

EDITH: I'd like to — speak to the prisoner!

SERGEANT: Sorry Miss, but we haven't got time! (*turning as though to give* 325 *orders*)

EDITH (*sudden turn on him*):   Only a word!

SERGEANT (*Hesitates an instant, turns to Men, stepping up left center.*):   Right face! (*Men face to front again on order, Thorne obeying order with others.*) Fall out the prisoner! (*Thorne moves forward one step out of rank and stands motionless.*) Now Miss!   330

WILFRED (*starting indignantly toward center*):   No!

(*Sergeant turns in surprise.*)

CAROLINE (*holding to Wilfred and speaking in a low voice full of feeling*):   Oh Wilfred — let her speak to him — let her say good-bye!

(*Wilfred looks at Caroline a moment; then with gesture to Sergeant indicates that he may go on, and turns away with Caroline.*)

SERGEANT (*turning to Thorne*):   The lady!

(*A brief motionless pause — Thorne looking front as before. Then he turns slowly and looks at Sergeant. Sergeant turns and looks meaning[ful]ly toward Edith. Thorne walks down to her, stopping close on her right, standing in military position, faced, as he walked, a little left of front. Arrelsford looks at Edith and Thorne. Caroline with Wilfred gives an occasional awed and frightened glance at Thorne and Edith. All this arranged so that there is no movement after Sergeant's order to "fall out the prisoner." Edith, after slight pause, speaks slowly in almost a whisper and as if with an effort, but without apparent feeling, and without turning to Thorne.*)

EDITH (*slowly, distinctly, without inflection; an occasional tremor*):   One of the ser-   335 vants — has taken the musket balls — out of the guns. If you care to fall on the ground when they fire — you may escape with your life!

THORNE (*after pause, to Edith in low voice*):   Do you wish me to do this?

EDITH (*low voice, without turning*):   It's nothing to me.

THORNE (*With slight sudden movement at the cue, turns slowly away to front; brief pause, then he turns toward her again and speaks in low voice.*):   Were you re-   340 sponsible in any way for — (*Edith shakes her head slightly without looking at him. He turns and walks right a step or two, makes turn there and walks up center and turns to left facing the Sergeant, saluting.*) Sergeant — (*as if making an ordinary military report*) You'd better take a look at your muskets — they've been tampered with.

SERGEANT (*snatching musket from man nearest him*):   What the — (*Quickly snaps*   345 *it open. Cartridge drops to floor. Sergeant picks it up and looks at it.*) Here! — (*handing musket back to man. Turns to squad and gives orders quickly.*) Squad — ready!

(*Men come in one movement from "carry" to position for loading.*) Draw — cartridge! (*Men draw cartridges. The click and snap of locks and levers ringing out simultaneously along the line*) With ball cartridge — reload! (*Men quickly reload.*) Carry — arms! (*Men come to carry on the instant; motionless, eyes front. To Thorne — with off-hand smile*) Much obliged sir!

THORNE (*low voice, off-hand as if of no consequence*): That's all right. (*Stands facing left waiting for order to fall in. Wilfred, after Thorne's warning to officer about muskets, watches him with undisguised admiration.*)

WILFRED (*suddenly walking to Thorne*): Ah'd like to shake hands with you!

THORNE (*Turns and looks at Wilfred; a smile breaks gradually over his face.*): Is this for yourself — or your father?

WILFRED (*earnestly*): For both of us sir! (*putting out his hand a little way — not raising it much. Thorne grasps his hand, they look into each other's faces a moment, let go hands; Wilfred turns away to down right center to Caroline. Thorne looks after Wilfred to front an instant, then turns left.*) That's all, Sergeant!

SERGEANT (*lower voice than before*): Fall in the Prisoner! (*Thorne steps to place in the line and turns front.*) Escort — left face! (*Men with Thorne left face*) Forward ma — (*sharp cry of "Halt! Halt" outside up left, followed by bang of heavy door outside*) Halt! (*Men stand motionless at left face. On seeing the Orderly approaching — just before he is on*) Right face!

(*Men with Thorne face to front. Enter quickly at door an Aid, wearing Lieutenant's uniform. Sergeant, faced front up left center just forward of his men, salutes. Aid salutes.*)

SERGEANT (*low voice to Men*): Present arms! (*Men present.*) Carry arms! (*Men come to carry again.*)

(*XXX*)

AID (*standing up left center, facing right*): General Randolph's compliments sir, and he's on the way with orders!

ARRELSFORD (*up right center*): What orders, Lieutenant? — Anything to do with this case?

AID (*no salute to Arrelsford*): I don't know what the orders are, sir. He's been with the President.

ARRELSFORD: I sent word to the Department we'd got the man and were going to drum-head him on the spot.

AID: Then this must be the case sir. I believe the General wishes to be present.

ARRELSFORD: Impossible! We've held the Court and I've sent the finding to the Secretary! The messenger is to get his approval and meet us at the corner of Copley Street.

AID: I have no further orders sir! (*Retires up with quick military movement and turns facing front, stands motionless.*)

(*XXX*)

(*Sound of door outside up left and the heavy tread of the General as he strides across the hall.*)

SERGEANT (*low voice to Men*):   Present — arms! (*Men present.*)

(*Sergeant, Orderly, etc., on salute. Enter General Randolph at door up left, striding on hurriedly, returning salutes as he goes down center glancing about. Enter, after General Randolph, as if he had come with him, Lt. Foray. He stands waiting near door, faced front, military position.*)

SERGEANT (*low order to Men*):   Carry — arms! (*Men come to carry again.*)   38c

GENERAL RANDOLPH: Ah, Sergeant! — (*going to him*) Got the prisoner in here have you?

SERGEANT (*saluting*):   Just taking him out sir!

GENERAL RANDOLPH: Prison?

SERGEANT: No sir! To execute the sentence of the Court!   38

GENERAL RANDOLPH: Had his trial then!

ARRELSFORD (*stepping toward him with a salute*):   All done according to regulations, sir! The finding has gone to the Secretary!

GENERAL RANDOLPH (*to Arrelsford*):   Found guilty I judge?

ARRELSFORD: Found guilty sir! — No time for hanging now — the Court   39c ordered him shot!

GENERAL RANDOLPH: What were the grounds for this?

ARRELSFORD: Conspiracy against our government and the success of our arms by sending a false and misleading dispatch containing forged orders!   39

GENERAL RANDOLPH: Court's been misinformed. The dispatch wasn't sent!

(*Edith looks up with sudden breathless exclamation. Wilfred turns with surprise. General astonishment.*)

ARRELSFORD (*recovering*):   Why General — the dispatch — I saw him —

GENERAL RANDOLPH: I say the dispatch wasn't sent! I expected to arrive in time for the trial and brought Foray here to testify. (*Calls to Lt. Foray without looking round.*) Lieutenant!   40c

(*Lt. Foray comes quickly down facing General Randolph — salutes.*)

Did Captain Thorne send out any dispatches after we left you with him in the office an hour ago?

LT. FORAY: No sir. I was just going to send one under his order, but he countermanded it.

GENERAL RANDOLPH: What were his words at the time?   405

LT. FORAY: He said he refused to act under that commission.

(*Edith turns toward Thorne and looks at him steadfastly.*)

GENERAL RANDOLPH: That'll do, Lieutenant! (*Lt. Foray salutes and retires up left.*) In addition we learn from General Chesney that no orders were received over the wire — that Marston's Division was not withdrawn — and that our position was not weakened in any way. The attack at that   410 point has been repulsed. It's plain that the Court has been acting under error. The President is therefore compelled to disapprove the finding and it is set aside.

ARRELSFORD (*with great indignation*):   General Randolph, this case was put in my hands and I —   415

GENERAL RANDOLPH (*interrupting bluffly, but without temper*):   Well I take it out of your hands! Report back to the War Office with my compliments!

ARRELSFORD (*Turns and starts toward up left, turns back again after going a few steps.*):   Hadn't I better wait and see —

GENERAL RANDOLPH: No — don't wait to see anything! (*Arrelsford looks at him an instant, then turns and exits at door up left; sound of door outside closed with force. General Randolph in front of couch.*) Sergeant! (*Sergeant quickly down to him*   420 *on salute*) Hold your men back there. I'll see the prisoner. (*Sergeant salutes, turns, marches straight up from where he is to the right division of the escort so that he is a little to right of Thorne and turns front.*)

SERGEANT: Order — arms! (*Squad obeys with precision.*) Parade — rest! (*Squad obeys.*) Fall out the Prisoner! (*Thorne steps forward one step out of the rank and stands.*) The General! (*Thorne starts down center to go to General Randolph. As he steps forward, Edith starts quickly toward center and intercepts him about two-thirds of the way down, on his left. Thorne stopped by Edith shows slight surprise for an instant, but quickly recovers and looks straight front.*)

EDITH (*to Thorne as she meets him, impulsively in low voice*):   Oh — why didn't   425 you tell me! — I thought you sent it! I thought you —

GENERAL RANDOLPH (*surprised*):   Miss Varney!

EDITH (*crossing Thorne and to the General*):   There's nothing against him, General Randolph! — He didn't send it! — There's nothing to try him for now!   430

GENERAL RANDOLPH: You're very much mistaken, Miss Varney. The fact of his being caught in our lines without his uniform is enough to swing him off in ten minutes.

(Edith moans a little, at same time moving back from General Randolph a trifle.)

GENERAL RANDOLPH: Cap'n Thorne — *(Thorne steps down and faces General.)* or whatever your name may be — the President is fully informed regard- 435 ing the circumstances of your case, and I needn't say that we look on you as a cursed dangerous character! There isn't any doubt whatever that you'd ought to be exterminated right now! — But considering the damned peculiarity of your behavior — and that you refused for some reason — to send that dispatch when you might have done so, we've de- 440 cided to keep you out of mischief some other way. The Sergeant will turn you over to Major Whitfield sir! *(Sergeant salutes.)* You'll be held as a pris- oner of war! *(Turns and goes right a few steps.)*

(Edith turns suddenly to Thorne, coming down before him as he faces right.)

EDITH *(looking in his face)*: Oh — that isn't nearly so bad!
THORNE *(Holds her hand in his right.)*: No? 445
EDITH: No! — Because — sometime — *(Hesitates.)*
THORNE *(his face nearer hers)*: Ah — if it's sometime, that's enough!

(Slight pause. Edith sees Mrs. Varney at left and crosses to her, Thorne retaining her hand as she crosses — a step back to let her pass — following her with his eyes — re- leasing her hand only when he has to.)

EDITH: Mama, won't you speak to him?

(Mrs. Varney and Edith talk quietly.)

WILFRED *(suddenly leaving Caroline and striding to Thorne, extending hand)*: I'd like to shake hands with you! 450
THORNE *(turning to Wilfred)*: What, again? *(taking Wilfred's hand)* All right — go ahead.

(Wilfred, shaking hands with Thorne and crossing him to left as he does so — back to audience, laughing and very happy about it.)

CAROLINE *(coming quickly down to Thorne)*: So would I! *(holding out her hand)*

(Thorne lets go of Wilfred's hand — now on his left — and takes Caroline's.)

WILFRED: Don't you be afraid now — it'll be all right! They'll give you a parole and — 455
CAROLINE *(breaking in enthusiastically)*: A parole! Goodness gracious! Why they'll give you hundreds of 'em! *(turning away with funny little comprehen- sive gesture of both hands on end of her speech)*

GENERAL RANDOLPH (*gruffly*):   One moment if you please! (*Thorne turns at once, facing General near center. Caroline and Wilfred go up above couch. Edith stands left center. Mrs. Varney near table left*) There's only one reason on earth why the President has set aside a certain verdict of death. You held up that 460 false order and made a turn in our favor. We expect you to make the turn complete and enter our service.

(*All motionless — watching the scene*)

THORNE (*after instant's pause, quietly*):   Why General — that's impossible!
GENERAL RANDOLPH: You can give us your answer later!
THORNE: You have it now! 465
GENERAL RANDOLPH: You'll be kept in close confinement until you come to our terms!
THORNE: You're making me a prisoner for life!
GENERAL RANDOLPH: You'll see it in another light before many days. And it wouldn't surprise me if Miss Varney had something to do with your 470 change of views!
EDITH (*coming toward center*):   You're mistaken General Randolph — I think he's perfectly right!

(*Thorne turns to Edith.*)

GENERAL RANDOLPH: Very well — we'll see what a little prison life will do. (*a sharp order*) Sergeant! (*Sergeant comes down stage and salutes.*) Report 475 with the prisoner to Major Whitfield! (*Turns away to front.*)

(*Sergeant turns at once to Thorne. — Thorne and Edith look in each other's eyes.*)

THORNE (*low voice to Edith*):   What is it — love and good-bye?
EDITH (*almost a whisper*):   Oh no — only the first! — And that one every day — every hour — every minute — until we meet again!
THORNE: Until we meet again! 480
SERGEANT: Fall in the Prisoner!

(*Thorne turns and walks up, quickly taking his place in the squad. Edith follows him up a step or two as he goes, stopping a little left of center.*)

SERGEANT (*quick orders*):   Attention! (*Squad obeys order.*) Carry arms! (*Squad obeys order.*) Escort — left — face! (*Squad with Thorne turn left face on order.*) Forward — march!

(*Escort with Thorne marches out at door up left and off to left.*)

CURTAIN

FIGURE 9 *Walter Hampden as George Rand (l.) and Tully Marshall as Hannock (r.) in the climactic scene of Act II of* The City, *in its original production.*

CLYDE WILLIAM FITCH

The City

>‹—

Clyde William Fitch (1865–1909), author of approximately twenty-two
adaptations and thirty-three original plays written between 1890 and 1909,
established social comedy in America and was arguably the most successful
playwright of the early twentieth century. Fitch attended Amherst College,
where, though a loner, he was a leader in the dramatic club, excelling in
women's roles. After graduating from college in 1886, he went to New York
to pursue a career, at his parent's behest, as an architect and interior decora-
tor. Instead, he wrote short plays and stories until, in 1890, he wrote *Beau
Brumell* for actor Richard Mansfield — the beginning of his short-lived but
meteoric rise to fame. Though prolific, Fitch carefully and cleverly crafted
his many plays, usually directing the initial production of each. Of the almost sixty credited to him, the best known include: *Nathan Hale* (1898); *The
Moth and the Flame* (1898); *The Cowboy and the Lady* (1899); *Lover's Lane,
Captain Jinks of the Horse Marines* (with the young Ethel Barrymore), *The
Climbers,* a study of the viciousness of social climbers in New York society,
and *Barbara Frietchie* (all 1901, running simultaneously in New York); *The
Girl with the Green Eyes* (1902); *Her Great Match* (1905); *The Truth* (1907),
about the consequences of being a congenital liar and one of his best plays;
and *The City* (1909). Fitch died suddenly at Châlons-sur-Marne, France,
having never reached his full potential.

→ The City

1909

A Modern Play of American Life in Three Acts

Dramatis Personae

GEORGE D. RAND	ELEANOR VORHEES
GEORGE D. RAND, JR.	GEORGE FREDERICK HANNOCK
MRS. RAND	DONALD VAN VRANKEN
TERESA RAND	SUSAN, *maidservant in Middleburg*
CICELY RAND	JOHN, *the coachman in Middleburg*
ALBERT F. VORHEES	FOOT, *butler in New York*

Act i

SCENE: *At the Rands'. The library of a substantial house in Middleburg. Front doors open out into the "front hall." It is furnished in a "set" of rosewood furniture, upholstered in brown and red figured velvet. The walls are covered with dark maroon wall-paper, with framed photographs of Thorwaldsen's "Four Seasons," and over the mantel there is an engraving of "Washington Crossing the Delaware." A rocking chair and an armchair are in front of the grate fire. Lace curtains and heavy curtains are draped back from two French windows that look out on a covered piazza. There are a desk, a bookcase with glass doors, a "centre table" on which stands a double, green-shaded "Student's lamp," a few novels, and some magazines. Near the bookcase is a stand holding a "Rogers' Group."[1] There are jars and bowls filled with flowers everywhere.*

Rand enters with the New York evening papers, the Post, *the* Sun; *he half yawns, half sighs with fatigue. He starts to make his armchair ready before the fire; stops and goes over to his desk, where he finds a letter which he dislikes, recognizing the handwriting.*

RAND (*Angry*):   Yes, still keeping it up, the young blackguard! (*He tears the letter in two, and throws it into the fire without reading it. He watches it burn a second, lighting a cigar; then takes his papers, makes himself comfortable in his chair before the fire, and starts to read. After a second, Mrs. Rand and Cicely, a very pretty girl of about seventeen, enter. Mrs. Rand carries a pitcher of water, scissors, and a newspaper. Cicely has her arms full of yellow tulips and a big bowl*)

MRS. RAND: Why, father! Aren't you home early? Teresa's train won't be in for an hour or so yet. (*Mrs. Rand, filling the bowl with water, spreads the newspaper on the table; then cuts off the stems, and hands the flowers one by one to Cicely, who arranges them*)

RAND: I felt tired to-day, Molly. My head bothers me!

---

[1] U.S. Sculptor John Rogers (1829–1904) was famous for a series of small groups illustrating literary, historical, and humorous subjects. They were replicated for popular consumption.

MRS. RAND (*Going to him with affection and solicitude*):　Why don't you lie down?　5
(*She lays her hand on his head*) You haven't any fever. (*She kisses his forehead*)
You're just overtired! (*He pats her hand affectionately, and holds it*) When are
you going to give up business entirely, darling, and leave it all to George?

RAND:　Never, I'm afraid, dear. (*Letting go her hand*) I've tried to face the idea,
but the idleness appalls me.　10

CICELY:　Mother, have you the scissors?

MRS. RAND:　Yes, dear. (*Joins her, and continues with the flowers*)

RAND:　Besides, George is too restless, too discontented yet, for me to trust
him with my two banks! He's got the New York bee in his bonnet.

CICELY (*Glances at her mother before she speaks*):　Oh! We all have that, father, —　15
except you.

RAND:　And mother!

CICELY:　Humph! Mother's just as bad as the rest of us. Only she's afraid to
say so. (*Smiling*) Go on, mother, own up you've got villiageitis and city-
phobia!　20

MRS. RAND (*Smiling*):　I *dare*, only I don't want to bother your father!

RAND:　That's the effect of George — and Teresa. I've noticed all the innu-
endos in her letters home. Europe's spoiled the girl! The New York school
started the idea, but I hoped travel would cure her, and instead — !

MRS. RAND:　Wait till you see her. Remember, in spite of letters, what a year　25
may have done for her. Oh, I'm so eager to see her! What a long hour this
is! (*The telephone bell rings out in the hall. Mrs. Rand goes out and is heard saying,*
"Hello! Yes, who is it? Oh, is it you, Katherine?")

RAND (*Reading his paper*):　Who's that talking to your mother?

CICELY:　One of Middleburg's Social Queens, Mrs. Mulholland — known　30
in our society as the lady who can wear a décolleté gown, cut in accordance with the Middleburg limit, and not look as if she'd dressed in a
hurry and forgotten her collar!

Rand laughs.

MRS. RAND (*Off stage*):　Really! I should think she was much too old to be so
advanced in the styles as that!　35

CICELY:　The flowers are lovely all over the house. Father, you ought to see
them! They came from a New York florist. (*Mrs. Rand off stage* "Good-by.
See you at five.") Our man here hadn't anything but ferns and aniline-
dyed pinks.

MRS. RAND (*Reenters*):　Kate Mulholland called up to tell me Mary Carter-　40
son's mother-in-law is visiting her from South Norwalk, and went down
[the] street this morning wearing one of those new washtub hats, — and
she's sixty, if she isn't over! She was born in 1846, — at least she *used* to be!

RAND (*Still reading*): When do you expect your crowd to come this afternoon?

CICELY: Crowd? (*She laughs derisively*) The only thing that can get a crowd in Middleburg is a fire or a funeral!

MRS. RAND: As we expect Teresa at four, I asked everybody to come in at five. But you know, father, "*everybody*" in Middleburg isn't *many!*

CICELY: Not many — nor *much!*

RAND: You have the best the town affords, and it's good old stock!

CICELY: I'm afraid Tess'll think it's rather tame for a girl who has been presented at *two European courts!*

MRS. RAND: Yes, I'm afraid she'll find it awfully dull. Don't you think, father, we could go to New York, if only for the winter months?

RAND: Don't tell me *you're* ambitious, too?

MRS. RAND: Well, I've done all, in a social way, a woman can in Middleburg, and I want to do more.

CICELY: You can't tell the difference in Middleburg between a smart afternoon tea and a Mother's Meeting, or a Sunday-school teacher's conclave, or a Lenten Sewing Circle, or a Fair for the Orphan Asylum, or any other like "Event"! It's always the same old people and the same old thing! Oh, Lord, we live in a cemetery!

RAND: Molly, wouldn't you rather be *it* in Middleburg — than *nit* in the City?

MRS. RAND: But with your influence and our friends, — we'd take letters, — I would soon have the position your wife was entitled to in the City, too.

CICELY: I don't care a darn about the position, if I can only have something to do, and something to see! Who wants to smell new-mown hay if he can breathe in gasoline on Fifth Avenue instead! Think of the theatres! the crowds! *Think* of being able to go out on the street and *see some one you didn't know even by sight!*

RAND (*Laughs, amused*): Molly! How can *you* deceive yourself? A banker from a small country town would give you about as much position as he could afford to pay for on the West Side, above Fifty-ninth Street.

MRS. RAND: But, *George* said you'd been asked to join a big corporation in New York, which would make the family's everlasting fortune, and social position beside.

RAND (*Looks up, angry*): George had no right telling you that. I told him only in confidence. What is this anyway, — a family conspiracy?

CICELY: No, it is the American legation shut up in Peking, longing for a chance to escape from social starvation.

RAND (*Thoroughly irritated*):   Now listen! This has got to stop, once and for all! So long as I'm the head of this family, it's going to *keep its head* and not lose it! And our home is *here,* and *will be here,* if to hold it I have to die in harness. 85

MRS. RAND (*Going to him affectionately*):   Father, don't be angry! You know *your will is law* with all of us. And so long as you want it, we'll stay right here.

CICELY: Giving teas to the wallflower brigade, and dinners to the Bible class! And our cotillion favors will be articles appropriate for the missionaries boxes! Oh, Lord! 90

RAND: Mother, Cicely has convinced me of *one thing.*

CICELY (*Delighted*):   Not really! Good! What?

RAND: *You* go to no *finishing school* in *New York!* You get *finished* all you're going to, right here in Middleburg. New York would completely turn your head! 95

CICELY: Well, don't worry; Middleburg will *"finish"* me all right! Good and strong! Maybe New York would turn your head, but Middleburg turns my — (*She is going to say "Stomach," but her mother interrupts*) 100

MRS. RAND: Cicely!

Enter George. He is a handsome, clean-cut young American, of about twenty-seven.

GEORGE: Hello, everybody!

RAND (*Surprised*):   Hello, George! What's the matter? It's only half past four! Nothing happened in the office?

GEORGE: Nothing! *All day!* That's why I am here. I thought I'd be in good time for Tess; and, so far as missing anything *really doing in the office* is concerned, I could have left at ten this morning — (*Adds half aside*) or almost any morning, *in this* — our city! 105

CICELY: Look out! The word *"city"* is a red rag to a bull with father, to-day! And it's for good in the graveyard! I'm going to dress. Thank the Lord, I've actually got somebody new to look smart for, if it's only my sister! (*Yawns and starts to go*) 110

RAND: Who's coming to your tea party?

CICELY (*As she goes out*):   All the names are on the tombstones in the two churchyards, plus Miss Carterson's mother-in-law from South Norwalk!

MRS. RAND: I must dress, too. (*Going over to Rand*) Dear, aren't you going to change your coat, and help me? 115

RAND: Oh, Molly, don't ask me to bore myself with your old frumps!

MRS. RAND: *I have to!* And I don't know that *I* take any more interest than *you* do in what sort of a hat Mary Carterson's mother is wearing! But if it were in New York — 120

RAND (*Sneers*):   Stop! I meant what I said — let's drop that!

MRS. RAND: All right, — I didn't say anything!

GEORGE: Look here, father, — mother's right.

RAND (*Interrupting*):   No, *you* do the *"looking,"* George, and straight *in my eyes!* (*He does so.*) Your mother's wrong, but it isn't *her* fault, — it's *you* children. 125

MRS. RAND (*Remonstrating*):   Now, father —

GEORGE: But we're *not children,* and that's the mistake you make! *I'm* twenty-seven.

MRS. RAND: Yes, father, you forget, — George is twenty-seven! 130

GEORGE: I'm no longer a *boy!*

RAND: Then why did you tell your mother about this offer I had from New York, when I told you it was absolutely *confidential!* And a man in business knows what the word *"confidential"* means.

MRS. RAND: It was *my* fault; *I* wormed it out of George! 135

GEORGE: Nonsense, mother! (*To his father*) I told, because I thought you needed a good, big hump, and I believed, if all of us put our shoulders to it, we could move you.

RAND: Out of Middleburg?

GEORGE: Yes! 140

RAND: *Into New York?*

GEORGE: Yes!

RAND: Listen, George —

GEORGE (*Going on*):   What position is there for a fellow like me in a hole like this? 145

Rand tries to interrupt.

MRS. RAND (*Stops him*):   No, father, let George have his say out!

RAND: All right! Come on, George, we'll have it out now, — but this must *settle it!*

GEORGE: You grew up with this town. You and Middleburg reached your prime together, — so she's good enough for you. Besides, you are *part of it,* so you haven't any point of view, — you're too close! 150

RAND: What's good enough for your father ought to be good enough for you.

MRS. RAND: That's true, George.

GEORGE: *Grandfather Rand* was a real estate dealer in East Middleburg, with an income of about two thousand a year. I notice *your father's limit* wasn't good enough for you! 155

RAND: No, but *my* father turned me loose, without a cent, to make my own way! *Your* father will leave you the *richest man in your town,* — with the best established name, with two banks as safe as Gibraltar behind you!

GEORGE: But, I tell you, Middleburg and her banks are just as picayune to 160
me, in comparison with the City and a *big career there,* as *East Middleburg*
and *real estate* were to *you* in 1860!

RAND: Good God, how little you know of the struggle and fight *I* went
through!

GEORGE: No, sir! Good God — 165

RAND (*Interrupting*): Don't swear before your father. I don't like it!

GEORGE: Well — what *you* don't realize is that *I* am just starving after a big
fight and a big struggle — for even bigger stakes than *you* fought for! I'm
my father's own son — (*Going up to him with a sudden impulse of pride and affection, and putting his arm about his shoulder*) Accept this great city chance, fa- 170
ther! There's millions in it, *and no fight!* They're offering the position to
you on a gold plate. All I'll ask of you afterward is to launch me. Give me
a start; the rest will be up to me! All I'll ask you to do then is *watch.*

RAND: No, I'm too old now.

MRS. RAND: Now *I* must join in! It's ridiculous you calling yourself too old. 175
Besides, it reflects on me! (*Smiling*) Men and women of our age in the
City dress and act just as young as their children, more or less. *Old age* has
gone out of fashion! There's no such thing, except in dull little *country
towns!*

GEORGE: Exactly! That's just what stagnation in the small place does for 180
you. Come to the City, father! It'll give you a new lease of life!

RAND: No, I *don't want* to!

GEORGE: I wouldn't have the selfish courage to go on persuading you, if I
didn't feel you'd be *glad of it in the end.* And besides, you're *one* against *all
the rest* of us, — Mother, Teresa; Cicely — we're all choking here, dying 185
of exasperation, *dry-rotting* for *not enough to do!*

RAND: Not at all! It's only amusement and excitement you children are after, and you've inoculated your mother with the germ.

MRS. RAND: No! If I'm restless and dissatisfied here, it's my own fault. I
sympathize with Teresa having to come back to this, after New York and 190
all Europe. I'm tired, myself, of our humdrum, empty existence. I'm tired
of being the leading woman in a society where there's nobody to lead! I'm
tired of the narrow point of view here! I'm tired of living to-day on yesterday's news, and wearing styles adapted to what Middleburg will stand
for! I sympathize with Cicely. I want her to have a chance with the *real* 195
world — not our expurgated edition! I know what she means when she
says the quiet of the country gets on her nerves! that the birds keep her
awake! that she longs for the rest of a cable-car and the lullaby of a
motor-bus! Yes, I want the City for myself, but even more for my children, and most of all for George to make a name and career for himself! 200

RAND: You've got an exaggerated idea of the importance of the City. This country isn't *made* or run by New York or its half dozen sisters! It's in the smaller towns, — and spread all over the country, — that you find the bone and sinew of the United States!

GEORGE: But for a young man to make a career for himself — I don't mean in business only, — in politics, in —   205

RAND (*Interrupting*):   You don't need the *City!* What's the matter with here?

GEORGE: Look at what Bert Vorhees has done, going to New York! He's going to be District Attorney, they say. And how long has he been there? Five or six years! I had a long talk with Eleanor Vorhees when she was   210
here last month; it's wonderful what Bert's accomplished! And look at Eleanor herself! By George, she's the finest girl I've ever seen!

RAND: Still, did Lincoln need New York? Did Grant? Did a metropolis turn out McKinley, or have anything to do with forming the character and career of Grover Cleveland? You're cheating yourself, if you're hon-   215
est in your talk with me! All you want of the City is what you can get out of it, — not what you can do for it!

GEORGE: No, you judge from your own point of view! Middleburg makes you look through the wrong end of the opera-glass. You *can't* judge from *my* point of view.   220

RAND: When you're *my* age, if you've kept as abreast of the times as I have, you'll be lucky. But if you're in New York, you won't have had time. There, you'll know one thing to perfection — but only one — where your interests are centered! All city men specialize — they have to *get* success, and *keep* it! Every walk in life, there, is a marathon! But the worst of it is, the   225
goal isn't stationary. It's like the horizon, — no man can reach it!

GEORGE: But why blame the City?

RAND: Because the City turns ambition into selfish greed! There, no matter what you get, you want more! And when you've got more, at God knows what price sometimes, it's not enough! There's no such thing as   230
being satisfied! First, you want to catch up with your neighbor; then you want to pass him; and then you die disappointed if you haven't left him out of sight!

MRS. RAND: I'm afraid your father's determined. And forty years with him has taught me two things, — first, when he *is* determined, you might just   235
as well realize it in the beginning; and second, in the end you're sure to *be glad he was!*

RAND: Thank you, Molly. And I was never more determined than I am this time.

MRS. RAND (*With a sigh of half-amused resignation*):   Then I'll go and put on the   240 dress I got in New York, which the dressmaker said I'd made her spoil in order that my neighbors at home shouldn't say I'd gone out of my senses. (*She exits*)

GEORGE: Well father, if *you* won't leave, let me go away! Let me go to the City on my own account. Bert Vorhees has been urging me to come for over a year. He says politics in the City are crying for just such new, clean men as me. He wants me to help *him*; that, in itself, is a big opening. I won't ask for any help from you. Just let me go, as *your father* let *you* go, to work out, myself, my own salvation!

RAND: Your own damnation it would be! No, sir, you stay here as long as I live and have any power over or influence with you.

GEORGE: Suppose *I'm* stubborn as *you* are, and go, even if it has to be against your will.

RAND: Look here, boy! You're trained in my methods, for my job. Those methods are all right for Middleburg, where I'm known and respected. No one has been to this town more, in a civic way, than I have. The Park Street Congregational Church couldn't have been built, nor halfway supported as it has been, without my help; and I could go on for some length, if I liked, in much the same sort of strain. What *I* do in this town is *right*. But the public libraries of Middleburg wouldn't help me in the City, nor the Park Street Church be a sufficient guarantee for my banking methods, to let me risk myself in the hornet's nest New York is at present.

GEORGE (*Almost laughing at the idea*): You don't mean you would be afraid of any investigation — ?

RAND: *Here,* no! I've always kept to the right side of the line, but I've kept very close, and the line may be *drawn* differently here. My conscience is clear, George, but my common sense is a good watch-dog.

The Maidservant enters.

MAIDSERVANT: Here's a man says he has an appointment with you, sir.

RAND (*Startled and a little angry*): *No one* has an appointment with me!

MAIDSERVANT: Well, I didn't know!

Enter Hannock, during the speech. The Maidservant looks a little alarmed at what she has done, as she goes out.

HANNOCK (*Very hard*): I told you, in the letter I sent here to-day, I was going to call this afternoon.

RAND: I destroyed that letter without reading it, — as I have the last half dozen you've sent me.

HANNOCK: That's what made it necessary for me to call in person!

George looks from one to the other, dumbfounded.

GEORGE: Father?

RAND (*To Hannock, referring to George*):   This is my son. I'm glad he is here, to be a witness. Go ahead! I take it, as you seem to be *in the business,* you've made yourself acquainted with the *law of blackmail!*   280

HANNOCK: I know what you've already told me — but I don't give a damn! I've got nothing to lose, and nothing to get, except money, from you. *You won't jail me,* anyway, for you know a trial here would ruin *you,* no matter what happened to me!

GEORGE: Here, you — !   285

RAND (*Taking a step forward*):   No, George! Keep your temper. This man says I ruined his mother — (*In great shame and emotion*)

GEORGE (*To Hannock*):   You *liar!*

HANNOCK: Then why did he give her a regular allowance till she died? and why did he keep on giving to me? — for a while!   290

RAND: George, I feel badly. Get me some whiskey and water. (*George hurries out. Rand, in rising anger*) I kept on giving to you, till I found out you were a sot and a degenerate blackguard — a drug fiend and a moral criminal. I kept on helping you after three houses of correction had handled you, and one prison! *Then I stopped!* What was the use, — money   295 was only helping you on!

HANNOCK: Still, for my mother's sake, you can't let me *starve!* You oughtn't to have torn up those letters; then you'd have had the blackmail in writing. I told you, if you didn't give me what I want, I'd print your letters to my mother right here in this town. The anti-saloon paper, that hates you   300 for not joining its movement, would be glad to get them and show you up for a God damn whited sepulchre!

RAND (*Quiet, controlling himself by a terrific effort*):   And suppose that didn't frighten me!

HANNOCK: I've just got on to something bigger yet, I can use by way of a   305 lever! The two years you had me working in the bank, I kept my eyes open. If it hadn't been for the yellow streak in me, I guess I'd have made a banker, all right. I liked it, and I seem to catch on to things sorter by instinct. You were the *big thing,* and I watched and studied your methods to make 'em mine!   310

RAND: Well?

HANNOCK: Yes! "Well," by God! I guess you realize just as plain as I do that those very methods in New York, that have been raising hell with the insurance companies and all sorts of corporations, aren't a patch on

some of *your deals* I know of! And I tell you, if there should be a State in-   315
vestigation in Middleburg, you'd go under as sure as I stand here; and if
I had to go to prison, I'd stand a sure chance of passing you in the yard
some day — wearing the same old stripes yourself.

RAND (*In a paroxysm of rage*):   It's a lie! It's a lie! Just to get money out of me!
I told you, before you began, you'd come to blackmail! (*He chokes*)   320

HANNOCK: Well, you know how to prove it! Have me arrested; charge me
with it; and *let the whole thing be thrashed out!* (*A second's pause*) Aw — you
don't dare. You know you don't!

Enter Cicely, looking girlishly lovely in a fresh white dress and corn-colored sash.

CICELY: Father, aren't you going to dress — and help us?

Hannock looks at Cicely, admiring her.

RAND: Excuse me, Cicely, I'm engaged just now.   325

CICELY: I beg your pardon.   (*She goes out*)

HANNOCK (*Following her with his eyes*):   She's growing into a lovely girl, your
daughter! It would be a pity — (*He speaks in broken sentences.*)

RAND (*Giving in*):   How much do you want?

HANNOCK: I want two thousand dollars.   330

RAND: For how long?

HANNOCK: *For as long as it lasts!*

RAND (*With a reaction*):   No, I won't do it! You'll gamble, or squander this in
some low way, and be back before the week's out! What's the use! I can't
keep this up for ever!   335

HANNOCK (*Bringing a pistol out of his pocket, quickly*):   Do you see that? (*He puts
it on the desk.*)

RAND (*Greatly frightened*):   Good God!

HANNOCK: Don't be frightened! It's not for *you.* I'm no murderer! It's for
myself.

RAND (*Suffering from shock*):   How do you mean?   340

HANNOCK (*Taking up the pistol, and handling it almost affectionately*):   I'm never
without it. And when I can't get anything more out of you, when I'm
clean empty, — not a crust, or drink, or drug to be had, — then I'll take
this friend to my heart, so — (*Placing pistol over his heart*)

RAND (*Frightened, calls feebly*):   George!   345

HANNOCK: Oh, not yet! (*Taking pistol from his chest*) I'm not ready yet. But remember, when you've signed your last check for me, *you will be respon-
sible for this.* (*He touches the pistol; then hides it quickly in his pocket, as George enters
with whiskey and water*)

GEORGE: I'm sorry to take so long, but I had to persuade mother not to

come with me, when she heard you were faint. And I thought you 350
wouldn't want —

RAND: Yes, quite right — (*He drinks, excitedly, tremblingly, feebly*)

GEORGE (*To Hannock*):   You can see my father is ill; surely, ordinary human
feeling will make you realize today is no time for you to —

RAND (*Interrupting*):   It's all right, George. Hannock and I have had it out 355
while you were gone. (*Writing a check*) We understand each other now!

HANNOCK: I've made my position quite clear to your father.

RAND (*Giving Hannock the check*):   Here — and for God's sake try to behave
yourself! (*Looking at him intently, with a strange, almost yearning look, as if he
really cared whether Hannock behaved himself or not*) *Try* to do right! 360

HANNOCK: Thanks for your advice *and money!* (*To George*) Good-by!

RAND: Good-by!

*George only nods his head, looking at Hannock with unconcealed dislike. Hannock goes
out. Rand sinks on his arms, his head falling on the table. George goes to him in alarm.*

GEORGE: Father!

RAND: I'm not well. I've felt dizzy all day. It was more than I could stand!

GEORGE: I don't approve of your giving him money! Till you once take a 365
firm stand, there'll never be any let up.

RAND: But I owe it to him, George! I owe it to him.

GEORGE: Nonsense! What sort of a woman was his mother?

RAND: She was a dressmaker in East Middleburg; hadn't a very good reputation. I doubt very much if what he says is *true.* 370

GEORGE: *Well then?*

RAND: Yes, but more than he knows *is true!* — and worse!

GEORGE: How do you mean?

RAND: Yes, the whole thing is more than I can carry any longer! I'm too
old! Your younger shoulders must help me bear it, George. It breaks my 375
heart to tell you, and shames me, George, but I must unburden myself.
Besides, I need help — I need advice! And besides, you'll see how you
can't go away and leave me alone here! (*He rises in fear and excitement*) I'm
your father, and you've got to stand by me and help me! I can't stand
alone any longer! 380

GEORGE: Father! (*He goes to him*)

RAND: Promise me, George, promise me you won't leave me here! You'll
stand by me!

GEORGE: Yes, father, *I promise you!*

RAND (*Sinks back exhausted into his chair. A second's pause*):   That man who just 385
left here don't know it, but — (*He stops from dread and shame of finishing*)

GEORGE: But what?

RAND: I'm his father!

GEORGE (*Astounded*): That *fellow's?*

RAND: *That* fellow's!

GEORGE: *Then of course he knows it!*

RAND: No, it would be a stronger lever for money than any he has used, and he doesn't hesitate to use the strongest he can find — or *invent!* In return for the financial arrangement I made with her, his mother swore he should never know. As a matter of fact, she was anxious, for her own sake, to keep it quiet. She moved to Massachusetts, passed herself off as a widow, and married a man named Hannock, there; but he died, and so back she came, passing off this boy, *here,* as Hannock's son! (*He groans*) What a story for a father to own up to, before a son like you. (*After a second's pause*)

GEORGE: Don't think of that! *Don't mind me!* After all, I'm a twentieth century *son,* you know, and *New York at heart!*

RAND: Of course your mother's never dreamed. *That* I couldn't bear —

GEORGE: That's right. Mother's not me, — she's *nineteenth century* and Middleburg!

RAND: Now, you see I do owe this young man something. I can't shut my eyes to it!

GEORGE: Yes. I'm even wondering, father, if you don't owe him — the *truth!*

RAND: No, no, I couldn't trust him with it!

GEORGE: *Still,* father, don't *you owe it to him?* Even more than money! And don't you suppose he suspects it, anyway?

RAND: No, and he *mustn't know.* He'd tell *everybody!* It would be my ruin; and your mother? — break her heart, — and for what good?

GEORGE (*With a sudden idea*): Father, why not come to the City and escape him?

RAND: Escape him! He'd follow! That's his hunting ground! When you came back home from college, I'd had him in the bank a couple of years. But I didn't want you two to meet, so I got him a good place in Boston. But in six months he'd lost it, and was mixed up in some scrape in New York! No! Remember, George, you gave me your promise you wouldn't leave me! You'll stay with me here. We must take care of this man, of course, for our own sakes, as well as his. I am his father!

GEORGE: And I'm his brother, and Cicely and Tess are his sisters! It's hard lines on him! I can't help feeling, father, we owe him a good deal.

RAND: You'll stand by me — so long as I live. (*Excitedly*) Promise me solemnly!

GEORGE: I have promised you, father.

RAND: And, if anything should ever happen to *me,* you'd look after — Hannock, wouldn't you, George?

GEORGE: Yes, father. I consider you — we — owe Hannock a future!   430

RAND: But you'll keep my secret — promise me that, too!

GEORGE: I give you my word of honor, father.

RAND (*Half collapses and sways*):   I feel so badly again! I — I'm going to my room to lie down. Don't let them disturb me till suppertime. (*George goes to help him out. Rand smiles, though with an effort.*) No, no! I'm not so far gone   435 as all that, — not yet a while, boy, not quite yet — ! (*Goes out alone*)

GEORGE (*Coming back*):   Who'd *have thought it! Who'd have thought it! Father!* (*A heavy fall is heard in the hall outside. George looks up, and then starts on, but stops and lifts his head suddenly to listen. A look of fright and dread is on his face. Then he turns to the door and walks into the hall. A moment after, off stage, he cries, "*Father!*")*

The following scene takes place off stage.

MRS. RAND (*In a voice of excitement*):   What was it? Father? Did he faint? (*Calling*) James! *James,* bring me water, *quick!*   440

GEORGE: I'll telephone for the doctor. I'll get Dr. Hull from across the street. He'll be the quickest. (*Passes by the door from Left to Right. The telephone bell is heard. The Maidservant hurries past the door with water*) Hello. Give me sixteen —

MRS. RAND (*To Maidservant*):   Is John in the kitchen having his supper?   445

MAIDSERVANT: Yes, ma'am.

GEORGE: Hello?

MRS. RAND: Tell him to come here to help us carry Mr. Rand into the parlor, and you come right back.

MAIDSERVANT: Yes, ma'am. (*She again goes hurriedly past the door from Left to*   450 *Right, as George is talking*)

GEORGE (*At 'phone, off stage*):   Is that you, Dr. Hull? Can you come right over? Father — looks to me like a stroke! Good-by. (*Rings telephone bell, and passes before the door on his way from Right to Left*)

MRS. RAND: I've sent for John. I thought between us we could carry him. (*Maidservant passes through hall from Right to Left*) Susan, get a pillow from upstairs, and put it on the sofa in the parlor, and send Miss Cicely.   455

MAIDSERVANT: Yes, ma'am.

Before doorway, John passes from Right to Left.

GEORGE: Here, John! Father's very ill. John, we want to get him on to the sofa in the parlor.

CICELY: What's the matter? What is it, mother?

MRS. RAND: We don't know ourselves, dear, but we're waiting for Dr. Hull.   460

GEORGE: You hold his head up, mother. And John — that's right!

MRS. RAND: Give me the pillow, Susan, — help me.

GEORGE: Cicely, go into the library, close the door, and wait for me. As soon as the doctor comes — (*Front doorbell rings outside*)

MRS. RAND: There he is! Susan, go to the door.   465

Enter Cicely. She closes the door behind her, frightened, and leans against it, listening.

CICELY (*Whispers*):   He's dead, — I know it, — he's *dead!* (*She carefully opens the door on a crack to listen. She sees Maidservant*) Susan! (*Maidservant approaches in the hall beyond the half-open door.*) Was it the doctor?

MAIDSERVANT (*In doorway*):   Yes, Miss.

CICELY: What did he say?   470

MAIDSERVANT: I don't know, Miss. I didn't go in the room.

JOHN (*Appearing in the hall*):   Susan! (*Whispers*)

CICELY: What is it, John? What does the doctor say?

JOHN (*Embarrassed*):   I — I — don't know, Miss. Mr. George'll tell you. He wants you, Susan, to telephone to his aunt, Mrs. Loring, and ask her to   475 have word 'phoned round to the guests for this afternoon not to come. You're to say Mr. Rand has been taken suddenly ill, and will she come over at once.

MAIDSERVANT: All right. (*She goes*)

CICELY: Poor papa! He isn't dead, then?   480

Susan is heard ringing the 'phone.

JOHN: Mr. George'll tell you. (*He goes off*)

MAIDSERVANT: Hello! Give me thirty-one, please.

George comes into the room to Cicely.

CICELY: How is he?

GEORGE: Cicely!

CICELY (*Frightened*):   What?   485

MAIDSERVANT (*Heard outside*):   Is that Mrs. Loring, please — this is Susan —

George shuts the hall door; he puts his arm around Cicely.

GEORGE: Cicely, father's dead.

CICELY: Oh, George! (*Bursts into tears*)

GEORGE (*Putting his arms around her again*):   Cicely, dear, don't cry, little girl! Go upstairs to mother; she wants you. And stay with her till Aunt Nellie   490 comes —

CICELY (*Crying*):   Oh, poor mother, poor mother! (*Cicely goes out, leaving door open*)

MAIDSERVANT (*Off stage at the telephone*): Yes ma'am. Good-by.

GEORGE: Susan?

MAIDSERVANT (*In the doorway*): Yes, sir?   495

GEORGE: If any strangers come to the door to ask questions, tell them nothing. Do you know Mr. Straker?

MAIDSERVANT: No, sir.

GEORGE: Well, he's on the evening newspaper here. He's sure to hear we've put off our little party, and come around to find out. If any one asks, 500 never mind who, — you know nothing except that Mr. Rand was taken suddenly sick. That's all. You don't know how, or what it is. You understand?

MAIDSERVANT: Yes, sir.

GEORGE: All right. (*Nods to her to go. She goes out. He walks over to the desk and* 505 *looks where his father sat and stood*) Why, it was only a minute ago he was there, talking with me! It doesn't seem possible — that now — he's dead — dead — (*He wipes the tears out of his eyes, and gives a long sigh; sinks in the seat*) gone for good out of this life! I don't understand it! What does it all mean? (*He is staring straight ahead of him. Suddenly a thought comes to him and* 510 *takes possession of him*) I know one thing it *means for me!* — (*He rises and stands straight.*) It means *New York.* (*There is a tapping on the glass of the window. He doesn't hear it at first. It is Teresa, outside, tapping. She taps again. He looks up and sees her*) Tess!! (*He hurries to the window and opens it*) Tess! (*Embraces her enthusiastically*)

TERESA: I thought I'd stroll in and surprise you! It's the same old room! — (*Smiling around, as she recognizes things*) not a thing changed! — nor in the 515 town, either, from the smelly old barn of a depot — past the same gray houses with the empty old iron urns, right up to *ours,* — bigger and uglier than all the rest! Nothing's changed! And oh, George, how can I live here? I'll never be able to stand it! I can't do it! I know I can't do it! (*Kisses him again.*)

GEORGE: Tess! You won't have to! We're going to live in New York!   520

TERESA: George!! What do you mean?

GEORGE: We're going to live in the City!

TERESA: Oh, George! You don't know how much that means to me! I can be married in New York, then!

GEORGE (*Amazed*): Married!   525

TERESA: Sh! That's my surprise! Heavens, how hard it's been to keep it out of my letters! I met him first in Egypt, and then he joined us at Nice, at Paris, and in London, and *there* he proposed.

GEORGE: But who?

TERESA: I just told you!   530

GEORGE (*Smiling*): No, you didn't!

TERESA: Oh! Donald Van Vranken.

GEORGE: Don Van Vranken?

TERESA: Yes! Think what my position will be in New York!

GEORGE: But Tess! He's the fastest fellow going! He's notorious! Look at   535
the scandals that have been more or less public property about him. It's
the last one that drove him abroad, afraid of the witness bench!

TERESA: Oh, you can't believe everything you hear! He's a handsome darling, and I love him, and he loves me, — so don't worry!

GEORGE: But I can't help worrying! Your happiness isn't safe with a man   540
like Don Van Vranken.

TERESA: Oh, come, you haven't been away from Middleburg enough!
Here, *maybe,* the husbands do go to the altar like Easter lilies! But in the
City, you don't marry a man for what he has or hasn't been; you marry
him for what he is and what you hope he's going to be! But I did dread a   545
wedding here — with his people and friends! How in the world did you
persuade father?

A second's pause, as George suddenly comes back with a terrific shock.

GEORGE: Good God! I forgot! I've some awful news!

TERESA: Mother — !

GEORGE: No, — father.   550

TERESA: What? — not — ?

GEORGE: Yes. To-day, — just a little while ago! Suddenly — in a second!
His heart gave out — I was talking with him two minutes before.

TERESA: Oh, poor mother! Where is she? Let me go to her!

GEORGE: She's up in her room.   555

TERESA: Mother! — (*As she goes out in great distress, she is heard again in the distance*) Mother!!

GEORGE (*Stands where she left him — alone — his head bowed. He straightens up and
lifts his head; and his face flashes with the uncontrolled impulses of youth and ambition.
With a voice of suppressed excitement, full of emotion, and with a trembling ring of triumph, he says*): The CITY. . . !

ACT II

SCENE: *Several years later. The library in the Rands' house in New York. The walls are
panelled in light walnut. Two French windows, with the sun shining in, are on the
left. There are small doors, Right and Left Centre, opening into other rooms. Between
the bookcases, which occupy most of the wall space, are marble busts, standing in deep
niches. There are flowers about. The sofa, chairs, hangings, and cushions are of golden*

yellow brocade, except one big armchair, upholstered in red, standing in front of the open wood fire. A Sargent portrait is built in over the mantel. A small typewriting table is at one side. Almost in the centre of the room, with chairs grouped near it, is a long carved table, with all the desk fittings of a luxurious but busy man; there is also a bunch of violets on it, in a silver goblet — and at present it is strewn with papers, etc.

Foot is arranging the fire. There is a knock at the door. Hannock enters. He comes in, in evident and only partly suppressed nervous excitement. He wears a white flower in his buttonhole.

HANNOCK: Hello, Foot. Is Mr. Rand out?

FOOT: Yes, sir. (*Rises, having finished the fire*)

HANNOCK: He left no message for me?

FOOT: Yes, sir. He left some papers on the desk, which he said he'd like you to go over carefully, at once, and two letters he wanted you to answer.   5

HANNOCK: All right. Get me a package of longish papers, with an elastic band around them, in my overcoat in the hall.

FOOT: Yes, sir.

HANNOCK: Has the stenographer been here?

FOOT: Yes, but he's gone; said he couldn't wait any longer, as he has an appointment.   10

HANNOCK (*Angry; making nervous, irritable movements*):   He'll be sorry! I'll see to it he loses Mr. Rand's job, that's all, if he don't knuckle down to me!

FOOT: Yes, sir. It's none of my business, but Mr. Rand didn't like your being late. He said you knew it was an important day for him, and he couldn't understand it.   15

HANNOCK: He'll understand all right when I explain! It's an *important day* for *me* too!

FOOT (*Eagerly*):   Is he going to get the nomination for governor, sir?

HANNOCK: Nothing surer! — except his election. That'll be a knockout,   20 and then you'll see us both forging ahead.

FOOT: I'm sure I wish you luck, sir.

HANNOCK: Thanks! Oh, yes, I shall tie my fortune up to Mr. Rand's!

FOOT: Yes, sir — (*He goes out*)

HANNOCK: Yes, sir, (*Imitating Foot*) — *damned "important"* day for me, too!   25 Phew! (*A great sigh, showing he is carrying something big on his mind*) I wonder just how he'll take it? I wish it was over. (*He goes to the typewriting table, rummages in a drawer, takes out a little box, containing a hypodermic needle, and tries it; then, putting it to his arm just above the wrist, he presses it, half grinning and mumbling to himself, — looking furtively over his shoulder, fearing an interruption. Just as he finishes, the door opens. Cicely half comes in. She is in hat, gloves, etc.*)

CICELY (*Half-whispering*):   You're back first. (*He nods, hiding the hypodermic needle*) I've just this minute come in, and I didn't meet a soul. I've sent for Eleanor Vorhees — she's the best.   30

Enter Teresa hurriedly, in great and angry emotional excitement, pushing past Cicely.

TERESA: Good morning, Cicely. Where's George?

CICELY: Give it up! (*Following her in*)

HANNOCK: He'll be in soon, Mrs. Van Vranken. He's an appointment with Mr. Vorhees.

Enter Foot.

FOOT: I can't find any papers with an elastic band, sir.   35

HANNOCK (*Irritated*):   Oh, well, perhaps there wasn't a band! Use your *common sense!* I'll look myself. (*To the ladies*) Excuse me. (*Goes out, followed by Foot*)

CICELY: What's the matter with you, Tess? Don on the loose again?

TERESA: I don't know and I don't care! I've *left* him.

CICELY: *Left your husband!* — for good? Honest? Or has *he* left you?   40

TERESA: What do you mean by that? That's a nice thing for my sister to say?

CICELY: My dear! — even donkeys — I mean sisters — have ears, — and you must know how every one has been talking about you and Jimmy Cairns!   45

TERESA: Well, if I can't depend upon my own family, I don't suppose I can expect my husband to protect me.

CICELY: After all, what can Don say? He can't find any fault with *you!*

TERESA: Exactly! — and I went to him, perfectly calm and reasonable, and said very sweetly: "Don, I'm going to divorce you. We needn't have any   50
disagreeable feeling about it, or any scandal. I will simply bring the divorce, mentioning this woman" —

CICELY: Mrs. Judly?

TERESA: Of course — but doing it as quietly as possible, behind closed doors, or with sealed papers, or whatever they call it. Only, of course he   55
must give me the children!

CICELY: Oh! — and he refused?

TERESA: *Absolutely refuses,* — and to let me get the divorce as I propose! He will only agree to a legal separation, the children's time to be divided between us. That's all he'll stand for.   60

CICELY: Let him agree to what he likes! You've got your case, all right. You could prove everything you want to, couldn't you?

TERESA (*Getting angry*):   Yes, but he — Oh, the beast! — he dares to *threaten!* If I attempt to do this, he'll bring a counter suit, mentioning Mr. Cairns!   65

CICELY: Tess!

TERESA: You see! He ties my hands!

CICELY: But not if he couldn't —

TERESA: Sh-h! Let's talk about something else. I don't want that horrid Hannock to know anything. I despise him!   70

CICELY (*On the defensive*):   I don't know why!

TERESA: Well, I'm not alone in my feelings. I don't know any one who *likes* him.

CICELY: Yes, you do, because *I'm* one.

TERESA: He always affects me like a person who would listen at keyholes!   75

CICELY: Some day you'll be very sorry you said that.

Hannock reenters.

HANNOCK: Mr. Vorhees is here with Miss Vorhees.

CICELY: I asked Eleanor to come. (*She goes out to greet them*)

TERESA (*To Hannock*):   Let me know the minute Mr. Rand comes in. (*She goes out. Hannock takes up letters on desk which are for him to answer, goes to the type-writing table, and sits down to write, reading over to himself one of the letters — mumbling the words. He laughs to himself*)

HANNOCK: Ha! And I suppose he thinks this is legitimate business! —   80 that *this sort of a deal* goes hand in hand with his "clean record," with his "white politics," with the Vorhees "good government." Humph! "Teddy, Jr." is a good nickname for him, — I guess not! The *public* would put George Rand in the Roosevelt class with a vengeance, wouldn't they! — if they were on to this one piece of manipulation! Following in father's   85 footsteps, all right, and going popper one better! That's what! And he *pretends* to think his methods are on the level! All the same, I guess he is just as square as the rest of 'em. You can't tell me Vorhees isn't feathering *his nest* good! You bet *I'm* on to Vorhees! (*He looks up, half startled*) Damn it, when am I going to stop talking in my sleep when I'm wide awake?   90 (*Looking at the place on his arm, and smoothing it over*) Too much of the needle, I guess!

Enter Servant with Vorhees. Servant goes out.

VORHEES: Good morning, Hannock.

HANNOCK: Good morning, Mr. Vorhees. You're ten minutes early for your appointment, sir.   95

VORHEES: Mr. Rand is generally ready ahead of time. I thought I'd probably find him.

HANNOCK: He isn't here yet. I *hope* he gets the nomination for governor!

VORHEES: Well, I'm inclined to think it's all *up to him* now, Hannock, and that to-day will decide. 100

HANNOCK: Isn't it wonderful how far he's got in barely five years!

VORHEES: Well, it was Rand's good luck — to come along at the right psychological moment — the party tired of the political gambler, the manipulator. We wanted a candidate with just the freshness, the force and stability of a *small town's bringing up.* The whole of Middleburg, no matter what the party, will come forward unanimously, and speak for their young fellow townsman. His family is the boast of the place! His father's name stands for everything that's best and finest in public and private life, and, when George took hold in New York, with all the political vitality and straightforward vigor of his blood and bringing up, [he] not only helped along *our reforms,* but *created new ones of his own,* giving his time and his strength and his money to the public good! Well, you know what the man in the street's been calling him for a year now? 105 110

HANNOCK (*With a covert sneer*): "*Teddy, Jr.!*"

VORHEES: Yes, "Teddy Jr." That idea ought to land him in Albany, all right! 115

HANNOCK (*With the bare suggestion of a bully's manner*): I hope, Mr. Vorhees, I haven't been altogether overlooked in all the enthusiasm.

VORHEES (*With a big drop*): How do you mean?

HANNOCK: Well, I've been George Rand's right hand, you know! I've done my share of the work. Where do *I* come in on the *reward* end? 120

VORHEES (*Strongly*): I *really* don't understand you.

HANNOCK (*Smiling, but serious and determined, and speaking deliberately*): *What do I get out of it?*

VORHEES (*After a pause*): You get a damned lot of pride in the man you've had the honor of serving, that's what you get! 125

HANNOCK (*Angry at the snub, and suspicious that he is to be thrown down*): And a hell of a lot of good that'd do me! Look here, Mr. Vorhees, I might as well have my say out now! If George Rand wants to be elected Governor of New York, he and his electors have got to square me!

VORHEES: Why, you talk like a fool — or a scoundrel! 130

HANNOCK: Well, never mind what I talk *like*; I know what I'm talking *about,* and I say there's something good in the way of a job coming to his confidential secretary out of *"Gov." Rand's* election!

Vorhees half laughs, half sneers, but still is slightly disturbed. George enters.

GEORGE: Hello! Am I late? Sorry!

VORHEES: No, I'm early. Well!! Can we have our talk?   135

GEORGE (*Smiling at himself*):   I believe I'm nervous! Go ahead! Fire your first gun! (*Takes a chair. Hannock also sits*)

VORHEES (*With a glance toward Hannock*):   I'll wait, if you have any business to discuss with Mr. Hannock.

GEORGE: No, nothing in a hurry; that's all right, go on —   140

VORHEES: Well, if you don't mind, I'd like to talk with *you privately.*

GEORGE: Certainly. Would you mind, Hannock, waiting in —

VORHEES (*Interrupting; to Hannock*):   Eleanor's in the drawing-room. Cicely sent for her; wants her advice, I believe, about something or other, *very important!* (*Guying the latter with a smile*)   145

GEORGE: Well, suppose you go to my room, Hannock, and use the desk there.

HANNOCK (*In a hard voice, reluctant to leave them*):   Very good. (*Rises, takes papers, and starts to go*)

VORHEES (*With the tone of a final good-by*):   Good morning, Hannock.

HANNOCK: Good morning, sir. (*Stops at the door.*) If I wanted to speak with   150
you later on to-day, after I've had a talk with Mr. Rand, could I call you up on the 'phone, and make an appointment?

VORHEES: Certainly.

HANNOCK (*In a satisfied voice*):   Thank you. (*Goes out*)

GEORGE: Well?   155

VORHEES: How do you *feel?* Eager, eh?

GEORGE: That depends on what I'm going to get! I'm eager, all right, if you've come to tell me what I want to hear!!

VORHEES: You're *warm,* as the children say!

GEORGE: What wouldn't I give — that was honest to give — for this   160
chance, not just to *talk,* not to *boast,* not to *promise,* only —

VORHEES (*Interrupting him*):   Exactly! That's exactly what we want — the man behind the gun in *front of the gun!* We don't want a Fourth of July orator *only,* in the Capitol! We want a man who'll be *doing something,* George!   165

GEORGE (*Enthusiastically*):   Every minute!!

VORHEES: We can hire a human phonograph to do the talking. The party's full of them!

GEORGE: I want to make *my name mean,* in this *whole country,* what *father's* meant in *that small, up-State town we came from!!*   170

VORHEES: Your name can take care of itself. Don't think of any glory *you're* going to get! You'll get most by keeping busy for the good of the State, for the welfare of the people —

GEORGE (*Eagerly, not waiting for Vorhees to finish*):   I know! But I'm going to show the gods and the demi-gods, the rabble and the riff-raff, that one   175 good lesson we've learned from the success of the last administration is that the real leader of a party must be its independent choice, and not its tool.

VORHEES (*Approving*):   Right!

GEORGE: Machine politics are a *back number.* The public has got on to the   180 engine, and smashed the works!

VORHEES: Man is greater than a machine, because God's soul is in him.

GEORGE: Yes, and what I'm going to show is that the soul of a political party is the uncompromising honesty of its leader.

VORHEES: Don't always be emphasizing the leader; — let it go at the   185 *party's* honesty! You're inclined, George, to overemphasize the personal side of it! It's E Pluribus *Unum,* not E Pluribus *me*-um!

GEORGE: All right, all right! Only, don't forget that I've got an inordinate ambition, and you're dangling in front of my eyes the talisman that may land me, God knows how high!   190

VORHEES: Well, come back to earth! Now, I've come here with the nomination in one hand —

George draws a long, excited breath.

GEORGE: And a *string* in the other?

VORHEES: Yes.

GEORGE: Well, give it to us!   195

VORHEES: The Committee decided it was up to me! I've known you as a boy. You're going to marry my sister. We're brothers practically. I can speak frankly, without giving any offence — that's sure, isn't it?

GEORGE: Nothing surer!

VORHEES: It's just this! Of course the minute you're nominated, our political opponents will get busy! The muckrakes are all ready!   200

GEORGE: You bet they are, and the searchlights haven't any Foolish Virgins in charge of them. They're trimmed, all right, and filled with *gasoline!*

VORHEES (*Very seriously*):   You can stand it, George?

GEORGE: I can.   205

VORHEES: You've got a wonderful popularity, and the Committee believes in you, but it wants your word confirming its confidences, — that's all.

GEORGE: That's the least it can ask.

VORHEES: Is there anything in your life that isn't absolutely above board, George? No skeleton in your heart, or your *cupboard?* It's safe for us to   210 put you up? You're sure not a particle of the mud they'll rake can stick?

GEORGE: Not a particle.

VORHEES: Look back a little. Sometimes I think you're a little *too* cocksure of yourself. No man can be, absolutely, till he's been tried in the furnace, and you haven't been, yet. But we're getting the fires ready! (*Smiles*) You're all right at heart, I'm sure of it. Nobody in this world believes more in you than *I* do, — (*Again smiling*) except, perhaps, you yourself. But there's nothing, nothing that could be ferreted out? You know they'll dig, and dig, and dig!! 215

GEORGE: But I give you my word of honor, so help me God, I've never done a dishonest or dishonorable act, or an act — 220

VORHEES (*Interrupting*): In business?

GEORGE (*Hesitates just one moment*): You know what my father stood for, — and my business methods *he* taught me. I've gone ahead of him, of course, — gone on with the times, — but on the road father blazed for me! I've not deviated from a single principle. 225

VORHEES: Good! I know what George Rand, Sr., stood for in Middleburg! That's good enough for me. And in your private life? Oh, this is just going through the form; personally, I'd stake my life on your answer, and Eleanor's instinct would have kept her from loving you. 230

GEORGE: I was brought up in a small town, in the old-fashioned family life that's almost ancient history in the bigger cities. I loved my father and my mother, and their affection meant everything to me. From their influence, I went under Eleanor's. You needn't have one worry about my private life. 235

VORHEES: Of course I knew you were clean and above board, but different men have different ideas about some things.

GEORGE: Listen, — I'm no little tin god! I'm as full of faults as the next man, but I'm not afraid to own up my mistakes; I'm not afraid to tell the truth to my own disadvantage; I'm not afraid to stand or fall by my sincere conviction! In a word, I'm game to be put to any test you or the party want to put me, and I'll stand straight as I know how, so long as there's a drop or a breath of life left in me! 240

VORHEES: Then that's all! And unofficially — *unofficially* — I can tell you, barring the unexpected accident, the nomination is yours! (*Holding out his hand, he grips George's in his*) 245

GEORGE: *Isn't it great? It's wonderful!* Oh, God, if *I can only do it big!*

VORHEES: You mean *do it well!*

GEORGE (*Taken aback only for a second*): Er — yes, of course — same thing! — Do half I dream of and want to!

VORHEES (*Smiling*): Well — I'm taking any bets!! 250

GEORGE: I owe the whole business to you, you know, and *I* know it!

VORHEES: Nonsense! With that overwhelming ambition of yours! Perhaps I taught you your *primer* of politics, your *grammar* of public life; that's all — except that I'm a *damned proud* teacher!!!

Enter Foot.

FOOT: Mr. Van Vranken must see you at once, sir, — says it's very urgent. 255

GEORGE: All right.

VORHEES: Say in two or three minutes.

FOOT: Yes, sir. (*Goes out*)

VORHEES: There is just one more thing before I can go.

GEORGE: What? 260

VORHEES: Nothing that really concerns you, though it may cause you some inconvenience. The Committee thinks you'd better get rid of your secretary.

GEORGE (*Astounded*): *Hannock?*

VORHEES: Yes, — he's no good! 265

GEORGE: No good?

VORHEES: A damn rotten specimen. We've found out enough about him to make sure we don't want him mixed up with us in *any way* in the election.

GEORGE: You — you take me off my feet! 270

VORHEES: If you want more detailed information, ask any detective with tenderloin experience.

GEORGE: I've never liked him. I can't say I've really trusted him. And yet I laid my prejudice to a personal source.

VORHEES: He's dishonest besides. You can't have him in a confidential position. You couldn't help getting tarred with some of his pitch! 275

GEORGE: But are you sure of what you say?

VORHEES: Sure! Why, just now, here, he showed me the hoof of a blackmailer.

GEORGE (*Looks up quickly*): *At that again!* 280

VORHEES: How do you mean "*again*"?

GEORGE: Explain to *me* what *you* mean.

VORHEES: Oh, he didn't get far — we were interrupted! He put out a feeler, which was very like a *demand,* as to what he was going to get out of this election. 285

GEORGE (*Carelessly, and not very loudly*): He needn't think I'm *father!*

VORHEES (*Not understanding*): What's that?

GEORGE: You leave Hannock to me. I'll take care of *him!*

VORHEES: You'll *discharge* him? (*A pause*)

GEORGE: No, — I can't.   290

VORHEES (*Astonished*):   How do you mean, — "can't?"

GEORGE: I couldn't turn him out, if he insists on staying.

VORHEES: *Why not?*

GEORGE (*A short second's pause*):   That I cannot tell you —

VORHEES: Look here, George! What hold has this man got on you?   295

GEORGE: On me personally, none. But I owe him a certain duty, and in a way he could do harm to —

VORHEES: I thought you said you had no skeleton?

GEORGE: It isn't in *my* closet, but it concerns those that are nearest and dearest to me.   300

VORHEES: Then you must risk sacrificing them, if you want the position.

GEORGE: I'd have to sacrifice a memory, too, — and I haven't the right!

VORHEES: If I went to the Committee, and said to them, — Rand refuses to dismiss Hannock; doesn't deny he may be a scoundrel; owns up, in fact, that his family is in some way in the man's power; says he himself is   305
not; but still he doesn't dismiss him, — do you believe for a minute the Committee will go on with your nomination?

GEORGE: No! For God's sake don't tell the Committee anything of the sort! Perhaps I can handle Hannock — beg him off!

VORHEES: I don't like the sound of that. There's one thing about you I'm   310
afraid of, George. You're one of those men who think wrong means are justified by right ends; — unsafe and dishonest policy!

GEORGE: I tell you he can't hurt *me*, George Rand — (*after a second*) "Jr."

VORHEES: That don't do for the Committee. You can't handle mud and not —   315

GEORGE (*Interrupting*):   Very well, then if I can't buy him off, I *will* dismiss him! And the others must face the music! There's too much at stake for the future, to over-consider the past.

VORHEES: All right!

Enter Van Vranken, excited and angry; perhaps he's had a little too much to drink.

VAN VRANKEN: Look here!   320

GEORGE: Good morning, Don.

VORHEES: Good morning.

GEORGE: I'm very busy now.

VAN VRANKEN (*With a jeer*):   I won't interrupt you long!

VORHEES: Would you like *me* to hunt up Eleanor and Cicely, and come   325
back later?

VAN VRANKEN: Oh, you might as well stop. You're as good as in the family, now. You'll be sure to be asked to put *your* oar in!

GEORGE: Sit down, Don, and cool off!

VAN VRANKEN: I haven't time. I'm on the way to my lawyer! I understand 330
my wife's here. Has she talked with you?

GEORGE: No. I've been very busy with Vorhees.

VAN VRANKEN: I know — the governorship! Well, your sister'll put a spoke
in that wheel, if you don't side with *me!*

GEORGE: What do you mean? 335

VAN VRANKEN: She threatens to take my children from me by bringing a
suit for divorce, — mentioning Nellie Jud — Mrs. Judly.

GEORGE: Well, can you blame her?

VAN VRANKEN: It's a pity you haven't gone out, once in a while, into the society that bores you so, and kept your ears open. 340

GEORGE: What for?

VAN VRANKEN: You'd have heard a whisper, or caught a look that would
have kept you from being surprised at what I'm going to tell you.

GEORGE: What?

VAN VRANKEN: If your sister starts a suit against me, bringing in Nellie's — 345
Mrs. Judly's — name, I'll bring a *counter suit* against her, naming Jim
Cairns!

GEORGE: You drunken liar! (*Going for him. Vorhees holds George back*)

VAN VRANKEN: You didn't *know* I could win. I wouldn't put such a stum-
bling block in the way of my little daughter's happiness! 350

GEORGE: Liar!! (*Struggles to free himself*)

VORHEES: No, George! Even *I've* heard enough to wonder something of it
hasn't come your way.

VAN VRANKEN (*Thickly, whiningly*): All I ask for is a noiseless, dignified separation, — that's all I want, and God, I want that bad! Legal or not, as *she* 355
wishes, — only she's got to agree to cut out Cairns. I give her this chance
for my little daughter's sake, — not for hers! But in another day, maybe,
it'll be too late. I get my children six months of the year, and she the
other six. I ask no more than I give, — that's fair! I'd like my complete
freedom as well as she. So far as love goes, it's a pretty even thing between 360
us! And when the children are grown up and settled in life, she can do
what she damn pleases, and good luck to her!

VORHEES: I've heard the gossip, Van Vranken, but you know enough of our
world to realize half that gets about, gets about wrong.

GEORGE: Granted Tess has been *foolish.* That's bad *enough,* God knows! 365
Still — I can't *believe* worse than that! *I grew up with her,* — *I know her!*

VAN VRANKEN: You knew her before she came to New York. She hadn't
developed yet, in that *mud*hole you all lived in! There's no smoke without —

GEORGE: Yes, there is! There's a smoldering that never breaks into a flame! 370
And you know, Don, you've given every reason for Tess's heart to smol-
der, yes, and burn, too — though I don't believe it. While we're about it,
let's finish the whole ugly business here, now. You're a drunkard, and your
best friends are the most depraved crew in town, — a crowd that is used
individually as markers to tally off each smart scandal that crops up. It 375
never occurred to you, before you married Tess, that you would be faithful to her afterwards; and you didn't disappoint yourself.

VAN VRANKEN: What right had she to be disappointed? I never made any
bluff or pose, and you all fought the match! She married me with her eyes
open. 380

GEORGE: You had the glamour of the City about you. Tess was a *real*
woman, full of good and bad; she was ready to be what the man she loved
would make of her. And, poor girl, she married *you!*

VORHEES: Well, all that's done. What about the present? Van Vranken is
right in saying any divorce scandal would endanger your election. We 385
might lose the entire Catholic vote, and the support of the anti-divorce
party, — both of which we're banking on. And besides, one of the strongest
planks of our platform is the Sanctity of the Home! We're putting you up
as the representative of the great section of the country which stands for
the Purity of Family Life. We'd have to drop that platform, or be ridiculed 390
off the face of the earth. And it doesn't seem right in any way to me! And
it's not up *to you* to suffer for your sister. (*To Van Vranken*) If we persuade
Mrs. Van Vranken to a dignified separation such as you want —

VAN VRANKEN: And she gives her promise to call off Cairns — !

GEORGE (*Quickly*): Tess will be as anxious to stop gossip, when she hears its 395
extent, as you. I'll take that on *my* shoulders.

Van Vranken looks at him, and half smiles cynically at his confidence.

VORHEES: Very well! Will you, Van Vranken, be willing to hush the whole
business up?

VAN VRANKEN: Glad to!

VORHEES: Live on with Mrs. Van Vranken in your house as if nothing had 400
happened?

VAN VRANKEN: No! Not by a damned sight!

VORHEES: Come, don't be a yellow dog! Do all or nothing.

VAN VRANKEN: She left my house of her own accord, and I've sworn she
shall never put her foot in it again. 405

VORHEES: Oh, well, what's an oath more or less to you! It will be only till
after the election! Rand's nomination is practically settled on —

VAN VRANKEN: Oh, I see! Why didn't you say that at first? I've nothing personal against Rand.

VORHEES: I'm sure Mrs. Van Vranken, on her side, will do all she can to protect his interests.   410

VAN VRANKEN: I suppose I'll have to give in —

VORHEES: *Good!*

GEORGE: I'll see her now, if she's in the house.

VORHEES (*To Van Vranken*):   I will communicate something to you, after Rand has seen your wife.   415

VAN VRANKEN: Very good. She took both the children when she left this morning. One child must go back with me now.

VORHEES: *Both must go back,* to-day, and Mrs. Van Vranken, herself, — to live under your roof till after the election.   420

VAN VRANKEN: That's true! Of course! All right! God, it'll be a *hell* of a life! However, there'll be an end of it to look forward to! Good-by.

VORHEES and GEORGE: Good-by.

Enter Teresa and Mrs. Rand. Mrs. Rand is very altered. Her hair is dressed fashionably, etc., and, instead of the sweet, motherly woman she was, in Act I, she is now a rather overdressed, nervous-looking woman, ultra-smart, but no longer comfortable-looking and happy.

TERESA (*As she enters*):   George!

MRS. RAND: George!   425

They both stop short, as they see Van Vranken. He bows to Teresa; she only glares at him.

VAN VRANKEN (*To Mrs. Rand*):   Good morning.

MRS. RAND (*Looking at him — outraged and angry*):   You *wicked* man!

Van Vranken is somewhat taken aback; from her, he turns and looks at the two men; he raises his eyebrows, smiles, shrugs his shoulders, and slouches out indifferently.

VORHEES: I must go, too.

TERESA: Good morning, Bert.

VORHEES: Good morning, Tess. How do you do, Mrs. Rand.   430

MRS. RAND: I don't know where I am, Bert. I never felt the need of Mr. Rand more than to-day!

GEORGE: Bert, will you have to tell the Committee about this? Won't it queer my nomination?

VORHEES: Not if Tess will do what we expect. I'll leave you to explain to her. (*Moving to go*)   435

GEORGE: No, — stay, Bert!

MRS. RAND: George! Tess couldn't possibly tell you everything she wants to, before Bert.

TERESA: Oh, don't worry, mother. I guess *Don* hasn't left much for me to   440
tell! Besides, Bert's a lawyer. I'd like his advice. (*To George*) Don gave you
his version, didn't he?

GEORGE: Listen! My whole future is at stake, and it's in *your* hands!

TERESA: Nonsense! My hands are full of my own troubles.

MRS. RAND (*To nobody in particular, and nobody pays any attention to her*):   What a   445
tragedy!

VORHEES: George is right. His nomination for governor was decided on,
this morning, provided he had an open chance. If you make a scandal
now, he'll lose the nomination, sure, — and if not, what's worse, the election!   450

TERESA: You are trying to influence me against what I want to do, through
George. I will never live with Don again!

GEORGE: Won't you? Only till after the election?

TERESA: No! I intend to begin proceedings for a divorce to-day.

GEORGE: But Don *offers* you a legal separation, and to share the children.   455

TERESA: That's done purposely to keep me *tied,* so I couldn't marry again!
I want the children all the time, and I want my freedom!

GEORGE: But you know what he threatens to do?

TERESA: *He won't dare!*

VORHEES: That's not his reputation in New York.   460

MRS. RAND (*At random*):   If she only wouldn't decide at once — all of a sudden. That's where women always slip up!

TERESA: Did he pretend he wanted me to come back?

GEORGE (*Smiling in spite of himself*):   No, but we persuaded him to be willing.

VORHEES: For George's sake, till after the election, on one condition —   465

TERESA (*Quickly*):   *What* condition?

VORHEES: That you agree to the sort of separation he planned.

GEORGE: And promise to put an end, once [and] for all, to the Cairns gossip.

TERESA: Just what I told you! The whole thing with him is only a mean
spirit of revenge! He would sacrifice the children and me and everything   470
else, to keep me from being happy with Jim.

GEORGE (*Surprised at the apparent confession*):   Do you mean you *do* love
Cairns?

TERESA: Yes.

MRS. RAND (*Breaking in*):   No, she doesn't mean that! She doesn't love him   475
now, but she *will,* if she gets her divorce.

GEORGE (*To Teresa*):   What you really want to divorce Don for, then, is not
because of Mrs. Judly but so you can marry Cairns?

TERESA: Exactly.

VORHEES (*Looking at his watch*):   I must go. (*To George*) The Committee will 480
be waiting now for me.

MRS. RAND (*Mortified*):   You've shocked Bert, Tess.

VORHEES (*Smiling*):   Oh, no, I've a report to make before George's nomination can be official, and I don't see, now, just how I'm going to make that
report exactly as I wish. 485

GEORGE: You mean on account of *Tess!*

TERESA: I'll make any sacrifice I can for George, except my own personal
happiness. That, I haven't the right to sacrifice, because that belongs half
to some one else.

GEORGE: You go on and call me up by telephone when you get there. I'll 490
have had a longer talk with Tess, and I may have something different to
say to you.

VORHEES: All right. (*Going to Teresa*)

TERESA: I shall want you for my lawyer, Bert.

VORHEES: Thanks. That isn't exactly in my line, but I hope you won't *need* 495
a lawyer. Do what you can for George, won't you?

TERESA: Of course.

Mrs. Rand goes out with Vorhees.

MRS. RAND (*As they go out*):   Bert, you mustn't get the wrong impression
from what Tess said, will you? She's her father's own daughter, and you
know a Rand *couldn't* do a really wrong thing; it's not in the blood. 500

GEORGE: Now, look here, Tess! On one side is a great career and me, and a
dignified life for you, with independence and the happiness and the love
and the respect of your children; on the other is probable failure for me,
and worse than failure for you. Don'll do what he says, and if he wins his
suit, you'll lose *both* children and everything else you ought to care 505
about —

TERESA: Except Jim!

GEORGE: Would he make up for any thing?

TERESA: Everything!

GEORGE: Even the children? 510

TERESA (*Almost breaking down*):   How can you say that? You know I wouldn't
have to give up my children!

GEORGE: Ten chances to one you'd have to.

TERESA: I don't believe any judge would give *Don* the children in prefer-
ence to *me*. 515

GEORGE: Believe me, it'll be taking awful chances.

TERESA: All life is that. (*She turns aside, crying quietly*)

GEORGE (*Going over to her*):   Tess! But you don't realize what this nomination means to me — more than anything in the world! I want it with every nerve and sinew in my body, with every thought in my brain, with every ambition I've got! Just let me get this one big thing in my hands, and nothing *shall stop me!* I'll climb on up the ladder of achievement and fame, and I'll take you all up with me! Remember our boy and girl days, Tess, in Middleburg. We were never selfish, you and I, with each other. It used to be a fight between us as to which should give up! Don't go back on me this time. You've got it in your power to give me a *great boost,* or push the whole scaffolding of my career from under my feet. For the love of God, stand by me to-day!

TERESA: It's your future against my future! Why should you expect me to sacrifice mine for yours? We aren't children now, and this isn't Middleburg! I love you very much, but not in that old-fashioned way.

GEORGE: But has any one in this world the right to absolutely ignore everybody else, and think only of one's self?

TERESA: It sounds to me *exactly* like *what you're doing!*

GEORGE: I suppose I do sound like a selfish brute; but I can't help feeling that what I ask of you, if six for me, is half a dozen for you, too, in the end.

TERESA: If Don'll give me a full divorce, I'll do anything for you — live with the beast *two years,* if necessary, and not see Jim all that time. But don't ask me to give up *Jim* — (*With emotion again*) because I love him, and I won't, I couldn't; if I said I would, I'd lie!

GEORGE: But Don won't give you what you want, and if you insist, he'll do what *he* says — divorce you, with a filthy scandal!

TERESA: The *hour after* the divorce was granted, Jim Cairns and I would be married.

GEORGE: Listen! Would you do *this?* Deceive *me* now?

TERESA: How?

GEORGE: Well — agree to what Don asks —

TERESA: Never!

GEORGE: Wait! After the election, you might change your mind. Whatever course you took then, wouldn't interfere with me.

TERESA: Does that seem to you quite square? Isn't it a good deal like breaking your word?

GEORGE: Has Don done much else beside *break* his since he answered "I will" with you to the Bishop in the chancel?

TERESA: His word was cracked before I knew him! But I wasn't thinking of Don and me. Aren't you playing a trick on the party that is putting its trust in you?

GEORGE: I don't see it! If your divorce comes out after my election, it needn't affect the party. My acts will be speaking for themselves, then. I 560 intend to be square in office, and to succeed or fail by that standard. I don't mind a failure, *doing* the *right thing*; what I can't stand is failure *doing nothing* with having had my chance!

TERESA: I see; a sort of the-end-justifying-the-means principle.

GEORGE: Not exactly, because I don't see anything wrong. It's just election 565 tactics! the others'd do it; we must fight them with their weapons.

TERESA (*Rather cunningly*): Will you tell Bert Vorhees?

GEORGE (*After a second's pause*): No.

TERESA: *That's just what I mean!* It's something father wouldn't do.

GEORGE: He *wouldn't!* Why, father's whole business success was due to his 570 not letting his left hand know what his right hand was after, but to square things in the end by a good division! — *one third* to the left hand on the basis that the *right hand* had done *all the work!* And you know what father's name stood for — the very criterion of business honor!

TERESA: Well, George, suppose I do it. I'm in no position to criticise, any- 575 way. I'll go back till you're elected, and pretend I'm going to carry out Don's plan.

GEORGE: Thank you, Tess. (*But the enthusiasm is gone*)

TERESA: Only, somehow it doesn't coincide with my idea of what I *thought* you were being and striving for. Maybe you're on your way up the ladder, 580 but you, at the same time, are coming down from the pedestal I'd put you on, to join me at the bottom of *mine*.

There is a moment's pause, both looking straight ahead, not liking to look into each other's eyes. Enter Hannock.

HANNOCK: Excuse me, Mr. Rand. Mr. Vorhees is on the 'phone.

TERESA (*Quickly, to George*): I'll tell him. Then you won't have to *lie,* if he asks any difficult questions. 585

GEORGE: I wouldn't lie; I'd just beg anything I don't want to answer — and tell Eleanor to be sure and let me see her before she goes.

TERESA (*Very serious*): I wonder if *she'd* approve of this little plot of ours? I wish it didn't seem contemptible to me!

GEORGE (*Hurt and showing a hint of shame for the first time*): For God's sake, 590 Tess, don't suggest such a thing! Eleanor is the one thing in the world I wouldn't give up to get this election.

Teresa looks at him meaningly as she goes out.

What did you mean by looking for personal graft out of this election just now, with Mr. Vorhees?

HANNOCK: I was showing my hand, that's all. I was calling the pot! It's   595
time!

GEORGE: You don't know the men you're dealing with!

HANNOCK (*Looking George squarely and meaningly in the face*):   I know one of
them better than he knows himself!

GEORGE: Listen, Hannock! That day my father died, I promised myself   600
and his memory I'd look after you, and look after you well — not like a
dependent on father's charity —

HANNOCK (*Interrupts*):   Damned unwilling charity — he was *afraid* —

GEORGE: We won't go into the story of your mother — (*Hannock winces*)
I've tried to treat you as I would a — brother who was unlucky — some-   605
body I was *glad* to give a hand to —

HANNOCK (*Interrupting*):   Well, haven't I made good? What complaints
have you —

GEORGE (*Going on*):   You've been of the greatest service to me in every way.
There's no question about that! But it's time for us now to open a new   610
pack, and each go his own way —

HANNOCK (*Thunderstruck*):   What's that you say?

GEORGE: I'm going to offer you a fixed yearly income, — a sum we'll agree
on, — and you're to get a job elsewhere, that's all —

HANNOCK (*Dry and ugly*):   Is it!   615

GEORGE: What do you say?

HANNOCK: Oh, I've got a hell of lot to say!

GEORGE: Cut it down to yes or no, and we'll discuss the amount of the income!

HANNOCK: *No!!!* You haven't got to give half of what I expect to get out of   620
the present situation!

GEORGE (*Angry, but controlled*):   If you don't look out, you'll get *nothing*.

HANNOCK (*Sneers*):   Pah! Just wait till I begin to open your eyes for you! For
instance, how about the New Brunswick deal?

GEORGE: *What about* it? (*On the defensive*)   625

HANNOCK: As crooked as anything that's ever been in "high finance"!
(*With a sneer*)

GEORGE: What do you mean? You knew that deal from the very beginning — you knew every step I took in it?

HANNOCK: Yes, *I* did! I notice you kept the transaction pretty quiet from
everybody else.   630

GEORGE: It was nobody else's business. My father taught me that —

HANNOCK (*Not listening out*):   *Yes!* — and he taught you a lot of *other* things,
too! But you go farther than he would have dared.

GEORGE: That's enough!

HANNOCK: What's the difference between your deal, and the Troy busi-   635
ness that sent Pealy to State's Prison?

GEORGE: Every difference!

HANNOCK (*Triumphantly*):   *Is* there? *Think* a minute! (*A second's pause*) You
gambled with your partner's money: Pealy gambled with his bank's.

GEORGE: It wasn't my *partner's* money; it was the *firm's*.   640

HANNOCK: But you were the only one who knew what was being done
with it.

GEORGE: My partner got his fair share, didn't he?

HANNOCK: Yes, but you got the *unfair!* You got paid pretty high for your
"*influence.*" Nobody else had any chance to sell theirs! If that isn't taking   645
money under false pretences, if it isn't using funds you haven't the right
to use, — there was a miscarriage of justice in the Pealy case, that's all.

GEORGE: But — !

HANNOCK: Go over the two deals with *Vorhees*, if you don't believe *me!*
Show him the differences between the Brunswick Transaction and the   650
Pealy case, — if he can *see* any!

Enter Eleanor, breezily, enthusiastically.

ELEANOR: Good morning! (*She sees Hannock, her manner changes to a cold one*)
Good morning, Mr. Hannock.

HANNOCK: Good morning, Miss Vorhees. Excuse me!

*He passes Miss Vorhees, and goes out; as he goes, with his back to them, he is seen taking
out from his pocket his hypodermic needle, and a small bottle, — and, by then, he is out.
Eleanor and George silently follow him with their eyes.*

ELEANOR (*Turning*):   What *is* it about him?   655

GEORGE (*Kisses her*):   *You* don't like him either?

ELEANOR: I *detest* him! What Cicely can see in him I —

GEORGE (*Quietly*):   Cicely?

ELEANOR: Yes, I've come to-day as a go-between — between you and
Cicely —   660

GEORGE: Ha! Cicely's clever enough to know how to get what she wants
from me. She has only to use you —

ELEANOR: She's in love with your secretary.

GEORGE (*Not taking it in*):   What?

ELEANOR: Cicely and Mr. Hannock are in love with each other —   665

GEORGE (*Aghast*):   Impossible —

ELEANOR: I know; I felt the same as you do. I detest him; he's no match for
Cicely — I feel instinctively [he's] the last man in the world for her.

GEORGE: Even *not* that —

ELEANOR: But Cicely insists. They wish to marry. 670

GEORGE: Never!

ELEANOR: She guessed you would be against it. She says we none of us like Hannock, and nobody's fair to him; and so she begged me to persuade you. She asked me to remember how much *I* loved *you*, and what *our* marriage meant to *us*. You see, I couldn't refuse! But I'm afraid I'm not a 675 very good go between; my heart isn't in it!

GEORGE (*Hardly hearing Eleanor*): It's beyond believing! (*He touches the bell with decision*) I must talk to Cicely now, before she sees Hannock again.

ELEANOR: Wouldn't it be better without me? She might resent your refusing and giving your reasons before me. 680

Enter Foot.

GEORGE: Ask Miss Cicely to come here at once, please.

FOOT: Yes, sir. (*He goes out*)

GEORGE: Perhaps it *would* be better.

ELEANOR: George, it doesn't make any difference to *you* that Hannock has no family or position? Cicely thinks you're prejudiced against him be- 685 cause his mother was a milliner or dressmaker — or something —

GEORGE: Of course that makes no difference to me —

ELEANOR: And you wouldn't be influenced against a man by your personal feeling, where your sister's happiness was concerned, would you? (*He shakes his head*) If you don't *know* anything against Hannock, you'll let him 690 have a *chance* to prove himself worthy of Cicely, won't you?

GEORGE: Eleanor, it can't be! Don't ask me any questions, but believe me, nothing could make such a thing possible, — personal prejudice and any other kind aside! I want you to help me pull Cicely through it. I may even ask you to take Cicely into your house for a while. Would you do this for 695 me? Teresa and Don, you know, would be no comfort, and, on the other hand, would set her a bad example, and fan every little rebellious flame in her!

ELEANOR: Of course, I'll do whatever I possibly can, dear. This is the very sort of thing I want to *share* with you, if I can't take it *entirely* off your 700 shoulders.

Enter Cicely.

CICELY (*Half defiant, half timid and hopeful*): Well?

ELEANOR (*Going. To Cicely, speaking tenderly*): I won't go home yet. I'll wait for you upstairs.

CICELY: Humph! *Thank* you; I know what *that* means! 705

Eleanor goes out.

GEORGE: My dear girl, it isn't possible that you care for Hannock?

CICELY (*Determined*): Yes, *very much!*

GEORGE: Well, even that may be, but still not in the way you think.

CICELY: *I love him!* Oh, I knew you'd be against it! Nobody cares for him in this house! 710

GEORGE (*Quickly*): And that's *why you* do! You're *sorry* for him, my dear girl! It's *pity,* not *love!*

CICELY (*Increasing her resentment and determination*): Nothing of the sort! He doesn't need my pity in any way.

GEORGE: It's just as I would feel toward a girl who seemed to me to be ig- 715 nored.

CICELY: Abused! As good as *insulted here,* by everybody!

GEORGE: You *think* so, and your sympathy is aroused, — but that's not love.

CICELY: You don't know what you're talking about!

GEORGE: Yes, I do, — better than you. You've never been in love in your 720 life, and so you mistake something, that is probably like a sisterly affection for this man, for the other thing.

CICELY: *Ridiculous!*

GEORGE: You don't know the difference now —

CICELY: Nonsense! 725

GEORGE: But you'll realize it some day when the right man comes along —

CICELY (*Satirically*): I hope not! It would be awkward, as *I shall be married* to Fred Hannock.

GEORGE: No, you'll never be married to Hannock!

CICELY: *You're* not my father! 730

GEORGE: But I represent him, and I tell you you must give up this idea —

CICELY (*Interrupting angrily*): And I tell you I won't! Good-by! (*Starting to go*)

GEORGE: Wait a minute. (*Rings bell*) You can't marry this man. He isn't good enough for you!

CICELY: Humph! 735

GEORGE: Or for any self-respecting woman to marry, as far as that goes.

CICELY: Your opinion as to whom I shall marry, or not, means absolutely nothing to me.

GEORGE: Very well, I'll go even farther. I'll tell you that, even if both my reasons for disapproving of Hannock were done away with, — still, I say 740 for you to marry him is *impossible,* and I, as your elder brother, *representing your father,* forbid it.

Enter Foot.

FOOT: Yes, sir?

GEORGE: Ask Mr. Hannock to come here.

FOOT: Yes, sir. (*Goes out*) 745

GEORGE: I shall tell him, *before you,* anything between him and you is absolutely impossible, — that I forbid it, and that he is dismissed from my service.

CICELY: Then I will go with him, if he wants me to. Do you think I'm going to have *him* lose his position and everything *through me,* and not stick 750 to him?

GEORGE (*With tension*): *Sorry for him!* That's all it is! *Sorry for him!*

CICELY: *It's not* — and you can forbid now till doomsday. I'm my own mistress, and I shall do as I *darn please!* I shall marry the man I want to, in spite of you — and the whole family, if necessary, — but I wanted to give 755 you the chance to stand by me — (*Her voice falters, and she turns away; she cries*) I felt you *wouldn't,* but I wanted you to, and that's why — I've come here now — and let you — humiliate me — in this — way. I wanted my own brother to sympathize with me, to help me. Everybody will follow your lead! 760

GEORGE (*Goes to her, and puts his arms about her*): Cis! I can't tell you how sorry I am! Not since father died have I felt as I do now. I've nothing to gain or lose except your affection, dear girl, and your happiness, so you can believe me when I say this marriage *can't* be — (*She pushes his arm away and faces him*)

CICELY (*Literal and absolutely unconvinced or frightened*): *Why* not? 765

GEORGE: I *can't tell* you.

CICELY: Well, you know me well enough to realize such reasoning with me is a waste of breath.

GEORGE (*Suffering*): I want to *spare* you —

CICELY: *What?* It doesn't seem to me you're *sparing* me much! 770

GEORGE: But listen — Vorhees just now told me — Hannock isn't on the level, — he isn't *honest!*

CICELY: I won't take Bert Vorhees' word for that! Fred's been your right-hand man here for four years and over. Have you ever found him doing a single dishonest thing? I'm sure you haven't, or you wouldn't have kept 775 him. I don't know why you did *anyway!* It was perfectly evident you didn't like him!

Hannock enters.

GEORGE (*Quickly, before he is fully in the room, and going to the door*): Hannock, please excuse me. Will you wait one minute in the hall?

HANNOCK (*In the doorway. He looks questioningly at Cicely. She nods her head*): Certainly. (*He goes out*) 780

GEORGE (*Intensely, with his hand on the knob, holding the door closed behind him*): *Listen* to me, for God's sake! You're my *sister*, I'm your *brother*. Have I ever showed that I did anything but love you?

CICELY: No, that's why I hoped —

GEORGE (*Interrupting, almost beside himself*): *But it can't be!!* Won't you *trust* me, — *won't* you? Let me tell Hannock, without going any deeper into 785 it, that — you realize the marriage can't be; that you and he mustn't meet again! You can say what kind things you —

CICELY (*Flashing*): Never!! You ought to know me better than to propose any such thing! (*She moves toward the door*)

GEORGE (*With a movement to stop her*): For your *own* sake, *his* sake, for *mother's*, 790 for *everybody's* — trust me and —

CICELY (*Looking him directly in the face after a second's silence, speaks with the note of finality*): Listen! I *married Fred Hannock* this morning!

George looks at her, his eyes dilating. There is a pause.

GEORGE (*In horror*): What!!

CICELY: I *married* Fred Hannock half an hour ago. We walked home from the church, separately. He went to his work, and I sent for Eleanor. 795

GEORGE (*In a voice of terrible but suppressed rage, goes to the door, throws it open with violence, and calls loudly*): Come in!

Hannock enters quietly, expecting a fight or a scene; he is on the defensive and not in any way frightened.

GEORGE (*Controlling himself by a big effort*): Is this *true*, what my sister says, that behind my back you've been making love to her —

CICELY (*Interrupting him*): I *never* said that!

GEORGE: That you've repaid all that I've done for you, and all my father 800 did, by taking advantage of our kindness and your position here to run off with —

CICELY (*Interrupting*): I was as anxious to run off as he —

GEORGE: But why wasn't I told? Why do it secretly? (*To Hannock*) Why didn't you go about it in the square, open way, unless you *knew* you were 805 doing wrong?

HANNOCK: I knew you'd fight it for all you were worth, and I wasn't going to run any risk of losing her!

CICELY: But you wouldn't have! My brother would have wasted his words then, as much as he is now — 810

HANNOCK: I was afraid — any fool in my place could see how I've really stood in this family. The only friend I had in the house, or who ever came to it, was *she!* (*With a wave of his hand toward Cicely*)

GEORGE: And that's *why!* Can't you see it? Don't you know the difference between *pity* and *love?*   815

CICELY: *I* love *him* and *he knows it*; — *don't* you, Fred?

HANNOCK: Yes, *I do know it!* As well as I know your brother only kept me here because — (*Turning to George*) you were afraid of me!

GEORGE: *Afraid of you?*

HANNOCK: Yes! Do you suppose I didn't guess your father must have told   820
you I was on to him in the bank!

GEORGE: Leave the dead alone! You've got your hands full with the *living!*

HANNOCK: Well, I know my business well enough to realize that once Cicely and I were married, you'd have to make the best of it!

GEORGE: Never! I tell you this marriage is *no* marriage!   825

Cicely and Hannock exclaim in derision.

CICELY: What's the use of talking any more about it? We aren't getting anywhere! It's *done* — and George has *got* to make the best of it!

GEORGE: I tell you it can't be! Will you take my word, Hannock?

HANNOCK: No! (*Laughs loudly*)

GEORGE: Then, I must go ahead without you! You're dismissed. Do you   830
hear? You're *discharged* from my employ!

HANNOCK (*Getting very angry, but controlled*):   *You take care!*

GEORGE (*Continues determinedly*):   You'll leave this house to-day. I'll give you an hour to pack up and get out, and you'll never lay your eyes on this girl again.   835

CICELY: If he goes now, I'll go with him. I'm his wife!

GEORGE: You *won't go* with him!

HANNOCK: Who'll prevent her?

GEORGE: *I will!*

HANNOCK (*In a blaze*):   Try it!!   840

CICELY: I've just promised to love, honor and obey him — and if he says to come, I'll go!

GEORGE (*Slowly but strongly*):   *He won't say it.*

HANNOCK: I *do* say it! Come on, Cicely! But if you want to come back, you can, because, before I'm through with your brother, I'll get him down on   845
to his knees, begging me to come back, and I won't come *without you!*

GEORGE (*Going to the door and holding it open*):   Cicely, will you wait in here with Eleanor for a few minutes?

HANNOCK: Oh, we can speak out before her! I want my wife to know the truth about everything! I don't intend to be the goat in this family any 850 longer!

GEORGE: Well, you can tell Cicely, afterward, what I'm going to tell you, if you like. God keep me from ever having to tell her! (*After a look straight at Hannock, he looks at Cicely very seriously. She responds to his look, impressed by it, and turns her eyes to Hannock. Neither quite understands, but each feels the depth of seriousness in George's attitude*)

HANNOCK (*Doggedly to Cicely*): Go on.

CICELY (*To Hannock*): I'll wait there for you. Don't do anything without 855 me. I'm so sorry my brother takes this attitude! Don't think it can influence *me*, any more than the disgraceful way you've always been treated here has; *nothing* they say can change *me* toward you, Fred! (*She leaves them*)

GEORGE: I didn't *want to* have to tell you this. I'd rather almost die than have to tell Cicely! I must break faith with father, but of course he'd be 860 the first to ask me to. I must dig out a skeleton that is rotting in its closet — that's the trouble! I must do this, and a lot more, if you make me, and give *you* a couple of blows which will come pretty near to knocking you out, if you've anything at all of a man in you. And every bit of it can be spared *everybody*, if you'll go away and let Cicely — divorce you. 865

HANNOCK: Well, I *won't!*

GEORGE: Because you won't give up Cicely?

HANNOCK: Exactly. I love her better than anything, — money, comfort, happiness, everything you can think of, — so go on, fire your last gun, and let's get through with it! My wife — 870

GEORGE (*With excitement*): She *isn't* your wife! — (*Hannock looks at him and sneers. George's rage at Hannock is only governed by the tragedy of the whole thing*) Your *marriage wasn't any marriage!*

HANNOCK (*A little frightened, and very angry now*): What do you mean? —

GEORGE (*Looks towards the door where Cicely has gone, and, with difficulty, manages to control his voice, as he lowers it*): Cicely is your *sister!*

HANNOCK (*With a cry*): Cicely is *what?* 875

GEORGE: *Your sister!*

HANNOCK (*Sees "red," and goes nearly mad*): You're a God damn liar!

GEORGE: It's the truth —

HANNOCK (*Out of his mind, with an insane laugh*): You're a liar! (*Cicely, alarmed, opens the door to come in. Hannock shouts at her angrily, in an ugly voice*) You go 880 back! — and shut the door! Do *you hear!* Get *out of this room!*

GEORGE (*Strong, but more kind*): Wait in the room till I call you.

HANNOCK (*Brokenly — ugly*):   I don't want her hanging round here now! This is none of her business, none o' hers!

GEORGE (*Speaks toward the doorway*):   Eleanor, I don't want Cicely to hear what we're saying. 885

ELEANOR (*Answering*):   Very good. (*She is seen shutting the door*)

HANNOCK (*Making guttural sounds, and unable to pronounce the words clearly*): Hugh — hugh — hah! — You'd play any game to get rid of me, wouldn't you? But you can't fool me like that!! (*He sits in a chair, mumbling to himself incoherently every other minute, working his hands, his mouth and his chin wet with saliva*)

GEORGE: That day I saw you first, just before he died, my father told me. 890

HANNOCK: I don't believe it!

GEORGE: He made me promise two things: — that I wouldn't tell you — never! — and that I would look out for you.

HANNOCK: I don't *believe it!*

GEORGE: That's why your mother got her allowance, — and to buy her si- 895 lence —

HANNOCK: I don't *believe it!* (*Laughing and weeping*)

GEORGE: Now, you see why you must leave here to-day — leave New York! Why there was no marriage this morning and never can be! Why —

HANNOCK (*His mind deranged, rises unevenly; he is loud, partly incoherent, and his face is twitching and distorted, his hands clutching and clenching, his whole body wracked and trembling, but still strong, with a nervous madman's strength*):   It's all a *lie* — 900 to separate Cicely from me!

GEORGE (*Goes to him and sees the change*):   Hannock!

HANNOCK: I'll never believe it!

GEORGE (*Taking him by the shoulder*):   Have you gone out of your mind!

HANNOCK: I'll never give her up! 905

GEORGE: *What!! I tell you, she's your sister!*

HANNOCK: And I say *I don't believe it!* I *love* her, she *loves* me. I won't give her up!!

GEORGE: *Yes, you will!!*

HANNOCK: I *won't!* Do you think I'd give her up to some other fellow to 910 hold in his arms! For some other man to *love* and *take care of!!* You're crazy!! She said if I said come, she'd go with me, and I'll say it!! (*He starts toward the door. George takes hold of him to stop him from calling her*)

GEORGE: Wait! If you don't give her up now, after what I've told you, and *leave here* before she comes out of that room, I'll have to do the only thing left, — *tell her!* 915

HANNOCK (*Furious*):   No, you won't! You shan't tell her! It isn't *true!* And if it was, by God, she shan't know it! It *would separate* us!

GEORGE (*Horrified at what this means, calls sternly and with determination*): Cicely!

HANNOCK (*Wildly*): *Don't you dare to tell her that lie!*

ELEANOR (*Opening the door*): You want Cicely to come in? 920

GEORGE: Yes.

Eleanor turns away from the door, leaving it open behind her. Cicely appears, and enters, — leaving the door open.

HANNOCK: There isn't any lie too big for him to make up to separate us! I'm going! Will you come with me?

CICELY: Of course!

GEORGE: Cicely! Are you strong? Are you brave? You must hear something 925 *unbelievably terrible!*

HANNOCK (*Holding out his hand beggingly*): Come along, don't listen to him! (*She makes a movement toward Hannock*)

GEORGE: You *can't!* (*Taking hold of her*)

CICELY: I *will!* Leave go of me! (*Struggling desperately*)

GEORGE (*Puts his arms about her, and holds her in his arms — her back to him*): My 930 poor child, he's your —

Hannock, without warning, pulls out a pistol from his hip pocket, and shoots her dead in George's arms.

ELEANOR (*Calls, in fright*): George!!

GEORGE: Cicely! (*He holds her in his arms, and carries her over to sofa. Calls brokenly*) Cicely!

Eleanor enters quickly and goes to them.

ELEANOR (*In horror as she sees*): *Oh!* 935

GEORGE: Take her.

Eleanor takes Cicely tenderly from him.

HANNOCK: Now, you nor nobody else can separate us! (*Lifts the pistol to his heart to shoot, feeling for the place he showed in Act I. George springs forward and gets hold of him and the pistol before he can shoot*)

GEORGE: No! *That's too good for you!* That's too easy! By God, you've got to *pay.*

Enter Foot in excitement.

FOOT: Excuse me, sir, I heard — 940

GEORGE: All right. Telephone for the police. Is she breathing, Eleanor? (*Eleanor shakes her head*) Oh, God! (*Bowing his head, emotion surges up in him.*

Hannock, in this moment of weakness, almost frees himself and almost gets hold of the pistol)

ELEANOR (*Who is watching, cries out in alarm*):   George! George, be careful! (*George pulls himself together too quickly for him, and prevents Hannock. Foot starts to go. To Foot*) Help me; it won't take you a moment!

GEORGE: No! Foot, I know I can trust you. (*Giving him the pistol*) Keep this, 945 yourself, and don't let him get out of the room.

FOOT: Yes, sir. (*Takes the pistol, and stands before Hannock. George goes to Cicely, and takes her in his arms*)

GEORGE: Poor little woman! little sister! Why did this have to be! I wonder if *this* is what they call the sins of the fathers? (*He carries her out of the room, Left, followed by Eleanor. Hannock, the moment they are gone, makes a movement. Foot at once covers him with the pistol*)

HANNOCK: Give *me* that pistol!   950

FOOT: No, sir.

HANNOCK: Name your own *price!*

FOOT: Miss Cicely's life back, sir!

HANNOCK: *You're* against me too, *are* you! Every one's against *me!*

George comes back.

GEORGE (*Taking the pistol from Foot*):   Thank you. Now, telephone, and ask 955 them to be quick, please.

FOOT: Shall I come back, sir?

GEORGE: No, I think this job had better be mine. (*Looking hard at Hannock*)

HANNOCK (*Quickly*):   I won't try to get away, — I give you my word of honor.   960

GEORGE: Your word of honor! (*To Foot*) When you've telephoned, go to Miss Vorhees.

FOOT: Yes, sir.

GEORGE: Ask her to keep my mother and Mrs. Van Vranken from coming here.   965

FOOT: Yes, sir. (*Goes out*)

HANNOCK (*Makes a move for George*):   Give me that gun! (*There is a short struggle. George breaks from Hannock, and, crossing to the table, lays the pistol on it. Hannock makes a tricky attempt to get to it quickly, but is caught by George, who holds him. The following scene takes place with George keeping hold of Hannock, who sometimes struggles and sometimes tries to break, suddenly or craftily, away from George's grip, and at other times remains quiescent*) You're a damn fool! Don't you see it's the easiest way all around for us? I've got to die anyway.

GEORGE: But not that way. That's too easy for you!   970

HANNOCK: Well, it's easier for you, too, with me out of the way! There's no arrest, no trial, no scandal! Nobody'll know I was her brother; nobody'll know about your father! Think what it'll save your mother! Think what it'll save you! Think what it'll save everybody!

GEORGE: Including *you*, — and you don't deserve to be saved *anything!*   975

HANNOCK: Still, even *I* am your own blood! For God's sake, go on, let me! All you have to do is to turn your back a minute — it won't take *two!* Please! Think of *her* — what'll it save her memory!

GEORGE: No!

HANNOCK: Then for your mother's sake! How can *she* go through a trial   980 and all *that* means!

GEORGE: Your work in the next room is worse than any trial for her to bear.

HANNOCK: Think of yourself, of the election! What will my trial do to your election?

GEORGE: I'm not thinking of my election now, — I'm thinking of that   985 little, still figure lying in the next room!

HANNOCK (*Emotionally, almost crying*):   There'd have been two, if you hadn't stopped me! For the love of God, give me the gun —

GEORGE: No! *You've got to sit in the chair!*

HANNOCK (*With an ugly change*):   Well, you'll get *your* punishments, too, —   990 don't you forget that!! I know how eaten up with ambition you are! And every single wish nearest to your heart will die just as dead as I do, if you let me go to trial!

GEORGE: What do you think you're doing?

HANNOCK: If I have to pay *my price,* I'll make you pay *yours.* And you'll be   995 dead, publicly and politically, before I go into the condemned cell.

GEORGE: You're crazy, and that's the only thing that may save you, if *Matteawan* is salvation!

HANNOCK: I knew your father was dishonest, and I told him that day; I guess it killed him. And I've watched you, and tempted you, and helped   1000 you go on with his methods! Every bit of this will come out in my trial. I'll get a clever enough lawyer to manage *that!* And you'll lose, not only your ambition, but your position in the world, and one more thing besides, — *the woman you're in love with!* For that kind of a high-browed moral crank wouldn't stand for one half *you* stand for   1005 in business, and when she finds out how deceived she's been in you, if I know human nature, she won't have that much love left for you — (*Snapping his fingers*) And *she'll find out,* and they'll *all know!* — *your party* and the *other* party! That election'll be a hell of a walkover for the other side!   1010

Eleanor enters.

GEORGE: What is it, Eleanor? I don't want you here.

HANNOCK (*Half aside, with a half jeer, and a half smile*):   Hah!

ELEANOR: Excuse me. Bert wants you on the telephone. Shall I answer?

GEORGE: Yes, please. (*Hannock begins to steal behind, toward the pistol*) Does mother know? 1015

ELEANOR: Yes, and she's very plucky. But I'm surprised how full she is of the desire for revenge! (*George turns and sees Hannock, and quickly but quietly intercepts him, and stands with his hand on the pistol*) She wants Hannock punished! She's watching for the police!

GEORGE: They ought to be here soon, now. 1020

ELEANOR: Teresa is with me. She feels it terribly. (*Goes out*)

HANNOCK: Do you realize how completely you'll be done for, if you don't let me do it? The New Brunswick business isn't a patch on some of your other deals I know about!

GEORGE: I've never done a thing in business that couldn't stand the 1025 strictest overhauling.

HANNOCK: If you believe that, you're a bigger fool than I thought! *I'd* rather be a *crook* than a *fool*, any day! Quick, before she comes from the telephone! Turn your back; walk to the door there! It's easily explained; — you're not to blame! 1030

GEORGE: *No!*

HANNOCK (*Hysterically*):   If you *don't*, I'll explain now, *before her*, where and how your standard in business is rotten, and your dealings crooked, — and you *can begin to take* your medicine!

GEORGE: I dare you! 1035

Eleanor comes back.

ELEANOR: Bert wants me to tell you it's settled, — your nomination — and he adds, *"good luck!"*

GEORGE: Did you tell him about — ?

ELEANOR: No — I — I told him to come here as soon as he could.

GEORGE: All right. 1040

Eleanor starts to go.

HANNOCK (*Excitedly*):   Wait a minute, Miss Vorhees!

GEORGE: No, Eleanor, go back, please!

HANNOCK (*Quickly*):   This man, who thinks he has it on me, is afraid to have you hear the truth about himself. That's why he don't want you to stay. 1045

GEORGE (*To Eleanor*): Stay!

HANNOCK: You think George Rand stands for honesty, and the square deal in the business world! Well, he does, but *it's a lie!* And if he wasn't paying up to the hilt — East, West, North and South — to protect himself, everybody in this country would know what we, on the inside, do! 1050

ELEANOR: George, unless you'd really rather I stayed, I don't want to hear what he has to say about you.

HANNOCK (*Quickly*): I don't blame you for not wanting to hear about the suicide of Henry Bodes! (*To George*) Do you know who killed Bodes? *You did!* 1055

GEORGE: The man's out of his mind still, Eleanor.

HANNOCK: Am I? Bodes was on to your Copper Pit scheme, and *saw it succeed* — so he tried one like it, and it failed!

GEORGE: Was that *my* fault?

HANNOCK: Yes! It was your example set him on, and do you think your 1060 scheme was legitimate?

GEORGE: So help me God, I *do!*

HANNOCK: Then why, when it failed, did Bodes kill himself? He wasn't *broke!* It wasn't *money* that drove him to it! It was *shame,* because his scheme was *crooked,* just as yours was. Success covered it, but failure 1065 showed it up.

ELEANOR: Don't ask me to listen to this any longer! (*She goes out. George watches her go, but Hannock only gives a quick glance after her*)

HANNOCK: Bodes was one of your sweet, weak family men, who can't stand on disgrace!

GEORGE: Disgrace!! 1070

HANNOCK: Ask Vorhees, — and about the New Brunswick case! And get him to *tell you the truth!*

GEORGE (*Half to himself*): Good God! If there is something in all this?

HANNOCK: What are you paying Elmer Caston ten thousand a year for?

GEORGE: For his legal services! 1075

HANNOCK: Rot! The firm's never used him —

GEORGE: But keeping him on our pay list keeps him from working against us.

HANNOCK: Hush money!

GEORGE: No! 1080

HANNOCK: *Why* were all these Amsterdam tunnel bonds made over to Parker Jennings?

GEORGE: He helped us get the bill passed!

HANNOCK: *Ask Vorhees* if he wouldn't put that down in the expense-book under the name of Blackmail. 1085

GEORGE: No!

HANNOCK: Ask Vorhees!

GEORGE: You can't alter the diplomacy of the business world — calling it by ugly names.

HANNOCK: No, I can't but *Roosevelt did!*   1090

GEORGE: If you think I'm afraid of what you —

HANNOCK: Oh, come! Stop bluffing! If you don't realize I know what I'm talking about, I'll go on. I know at least *five* separate deals of yours so damned crooked, if any *one* of them were made public you'd be out of business over night, and out of the country, if you know your job. (*He*   1095 *waits. No answer. George is weighing the truth or the lie of what he is saying. He evidently sees some truth in it*) And I've got proof of what I say! Every proof! I've got copies of letters and telegrams, when I couldn't get the originals. I've got shorthand reports of private telephone conversations. I've got data enough for fifty trials, if it should come to that. I've been preparing for a   1100 deal of my own *with you* ever since I came to you! Only — God! (*He is moved as he thinks of Cicely*) I didn't think it would be trying to get rid of my life! I'd planned to make you finance a big game for me!

GEORGE: If what you say is true — and I don't know but what some of it may be, — then it's good-by to everything for me, and it'll be about all   1105 I'm worth having come to me.

HANNOCK: That's it! Even Middleburg'll be too small for you, if I show you up! But you know what'll shut my lips tight! Gimme the gun —

GEORGE (*Quickly*):   No.

HANNOCK (*Pleadingly*):   You've *everything* to get, and *nothing* to lose by it!   1110

GEORGE: Yes, I have something to lose! — what rag of honor I've got left!

HANNOCK: No! Think a minute — if *I'm* out of the way? There's no real scandal — your father's old story — *our* father's old story — isn't even known by *your mother.* I shot Cicely, and killed myself, — it's an ordinary story. I was drunk or crazy — she wouldn't have me. Any story you want   1115 to make up, and there'll not be a murmur against Cicely, then! But can you see the papers if the *real story comes out!!* All over this country, and all the countries, it'll be telegraphed and pictured and revelled in. It'll even get into the cinematograph shows in Europe — with some low down girl masquerading as Cicely.   1120

GEORGE: Stop! *Stop!*

HANNOCK: And the story will come out, if I go to trial. I'll stop at nothing to take it out of you. Whether you believe or not what I say about your business methods, you take my word for it, my arrest will put a quietus on your election, and *finish you,* not only in a political career, but any old ca-   1125 reer at all!

GEORGE: What a finish! What a finish of all I hoped to do and be!

HANNOCK: And — you'll lose the woman who's just left this room. Whether all *her brother's* high-browed talk is bunkum or not, even *I* know *hers* is serious; and if she finds you've deceived her all the time, that your high ideals are *fake* — !   1130

GEORGE (*Interrupts, crying, in an agony, half to himself*):   They're not! They're not! God knows, nobody's been more deceived in me than I've been myself!

HANNOCK: Well, you know she won't stand for it. A girl like her — her heart couldn't stomach it! Go on, bring me to trial and lose everything   1135 you've banked on for a career! Lose your business standing, lose your best friends, lose the woman you want, and raise the rottenest scandal for your family, for your mother, to bear, and your little sister's memory to go foul under! Do it all, and be damned to you!! (*He falls on his knees with exhaustion*)

GEORGE: My God, how can I?   1140

HANNOCK (*Whining, pleading*):   All you have to do, to save every mother's son of us, is to let me do what the law'll do anyway! Leave that pistol where I can get it, and walk half a dozen steps away. That's all you need do! (*He sees George hesitate*) It's *all* or nothing for you!! It's the finish or the beginning! Are you ready and willing to be down and out, and go through the hell my   1145 living'll mean for you? (*He sees George weaken more*) You'll be Governor! Sure, you'll marry Miss Vorhees! You'll find all the proofs I told you about in my safety deposit box at the Manhattan. And there'll be only *white* flowers and pity on the new little grave! It'll be your *chance* to prove by the future that you were made of the right stuff at heart, after all!   1150

George puts down the pistol not far from Hannock's reach, and starts to walk away with a set face — suffering. Hannock makes a slow, silent step towards the pistol, but, before he can get it, George turns and recovers it, with a terrific revulsion of feeling. He seizes the pistol and throws it through the big glass window.

GEORGE: No! I haven't the right! You must take your punishment as it comes, and I *must take mine!* (*He suddenly breaks down; tears fill his throat and pour from his eyes. Hannock is crouching and drivelling on the floor*) This is my *only chance to show I can be on the level!* That I *can be straight*, when it's plain what *is* the right thing to do! God help me *do it!*   1155

The door opens and a Policeman enters with Foot.

ACT III

SCENE: *Same room as Act II, only seen from another point of view. The mantel is now Right and the windows Back. Left is the wall not seen before. Later the same day. Vorhees and George are seated at the desk before a mass of business papers. There is a tall whiskey-and-soda glass, nearly empty, and a plate with the remnants of some sandwiches, beside George. The shades of the windows are drawn, but it is still daylight. George looks crushed, mentally and physically, but is calm and immovable. Vorhees looks stern and disappointed. There is a pause; neither man moves.*

GEORGE: That's all? (*Vorhees nods his head. George drinks, and gathers up the papers*) What's to be done with these papers? Are they Hannock's or mine?

VORHEES: They have only to do with *your* affairs. Hannock hadn't any right to them! In any case, you don't pretend to deny anything these papers prove. Destroy them!   5

GEORGE: But — (*Getting up all the papers, except some of his own, which he separates and leaves on the desk*)

VORHEES: I doubt if, when it comes to the point, Hannock will go into all this business! He will have had months to cool down, and his hands will be full enough. (*He gives George a couple of papers he has had in his hand, and motions to the fireplace*) Here! don't wash your dirty linen, *burn* it!   10

George goes to the fireplace with a mass of papers, and burns them.

GEORGE (*As the papers burn*):   Has Eleanor gone home?

VORHEES: Yes, but she promised your mother to come back later and stop over-night with her.

GEORGE: I wonder if she'd be willing to see me?

VORHEES: Yes, because I'm sure she didn't believe Hannock.   15

GEORGE: Tess can stay with mother. There'll be no need of her pretending to go back to Don, now.

VORHEES: *Pretending!*

GEORGE: Yes, that's something else I did, — persuaded Tess to make Don believe she'd come back in accordance with his conditions. But it was   20
agreed between us she was to break her word to him, *after the election!* (*He burns his last batch of papers*)

VORHEES: It's a pity you can't burn that, too! I'd have staked my reputation on your being absolutely on the level! How I have been taken in by you!

GEORGE: I know, it sounds ridiculous, and I don't expect you to understand it; but I've been taken in by myself, too! Shall I write my withdrawal from   25
the nomination, or will you take a verbal message?

VORHEES: Write it. It will make less for me to say by way of explanation. (*George goes to the desk and writes*) I'm sorry, I'm sorry, George. I *know* what it means to you!

GEORGE: Somehow now, it doesn't seem so much, after all; I suppose that's   30
Cicely — poor little girl — poor little girl, — and — Eleanor. (*He adds the last, almost in a whisper*)

VORHEES: You're a *young* man, George! You've got a good chance yet to make good, and it's all up to you!

GEORGE: I know that —

VORHEES: I suppose you won't want to go back to Middleburg? 35

GEORGE: No! No!! For everybody's sake! But, *would it have* been wrong — leave *me out of it,* — to have saved *father's memory,* to have saved mother — could I have let him do it?

VORHEES: You know you couldn't!

GEORGE: Yes, and anyway, I didn't. Why can't I forget it! 40

VORHEES: Oh, it'll be many a day before you *deserve* to forget it!

GEORGE: But, will *you* ever have any confidence in me? Can any one ever believe in me again? (*Buries his face in his hands, and groans*)

VORHEES: *I can.* Whether I *do* or not, is entirely up to you.

GEORGE: You're sure of that? 45

VORHEES (*Takes his hand and shakes it*): Sure.

GEORGE: And Eleanor?

VORHEES: Well — there's no use in my lying about it. If I know her, you must give up all idea of marrying her. Eleanor's husband must be a man she can *look up* to. That's a necessity of her nature — she can't help it. But *I do* believe she'll *help you* with *her friendship.* If you don't go back to Middleburg, where will you go? 50

GEORGE: Here! I stay *right here!*

VORHEES (*Surprised*): Here! It'll be *hard.*

GEORGE: I suppose it will! 55

VORHEES: How will you start?

GEORGE: First, make a clean breast to my partners! Give back all the money I've made in ways which you've proved to me are illegal. Publish every form of graft I've benefited by, for the sake of future protection! Resign from all — 60

VORHEES: It's gigantic! It's colossal! *Can* you *do* it?

GEORGE (*Simply*): I can try. I'm going to have a go at it, anyway!

VORHEES: The Press! Among your professional associates — here and all over the State — it'll be hell for you to go through!

GEORGE: I know it! I know it! But to get back where I want to be — if I 65 ever can! I've got to fight it out right here, and make good *here,* or not at all. I don't care what it costs me!

TERESA (*Opening the door*): May I come in?

GEORGE: Yes, come in, Tess. Where's mother?

TERESA: She's locked herself in her room! She's *turned against me* in the 70 most extraordinary manner! Says my influence over Cicely is at the bottom of everything! (*She begins to cry*) She goes so far as to say, if I'd be-haved like a decent woman, she doesn't believe this would have hap-pened! I didn't care what other people believe of me, but this I didn't bargain for! I have been unfaithful to Don in my heart — and in my mind, perhaps, — but that's all — 75

GEORGE: I always felt it, Tess!

TERESA: Can't you persuade mother?

GEORGE: *Bert could,* because he represents the outside world.

TERESA: But you know Bert. He wouldn't persuade her, unless he believed in me himself. 80

VORHEES: That's true, and I'll go talk with her now, if Mrs. Rand will see me. (*He goes toward door*)

TERESA (*Deeply moved, and grateful*):   Thank you!

VORHEES: That's all right.   (*He goes out*) 85

TERESA: George, I don't know — but everything, even Jimmy Cairns, seems so little now, in comparison with *Cicely — dead,* the bottom fallen out of everything!

GEORGE: Even worse than that, for me. I've given up the nomination.

TERESA: I'm sorry! Did Bert feel you had to? 90

GEORGE: No more than I did. You won't have to act a lie for me after all, Tess.

TERESA: I'm glad! I know, if Eleanor Vorhees knew I was doing it —

GEORGE: She's going to know it, — and that I'm a liar! She's going to know much worse things than that! Everybody's going to know them, I 95 guess! Father was a crook in business, — that's the ugly, unvarnished fact, — and I've been a worse one! But I'd rather she'd learn these things from me, — what Hannock hasn't already told her — rather than she learned them outside.

TERESA: But George! George!! Don't you realize you'll lose her? 100

GEORGE: Well, I've lost everything else, except —

TERESA: Except what?

GEORGE: Except that! After all, I don't believe, way down at the bottom, I'm not fundamentally straight! I mean to give myself, all by myself, a chance to prove it! I know there are lots of "good men" who are born 105 crooks. I want to see if I'm not a crook who was born good!

Vorhees reenters.

VORHEES: It's all right. They've told Mrs. Rand she can go in and see Cicely now, and she wants you to go with her.

TERESA (*Holds his hand in her two, for a moment*):   Thank you!   (*She goes out*)

VORHEES: And give me that paper you wrote. The sooner we get that off 110 our hands, the better. (*George takes up the paper and, reading it over to himself, goes slowly to Vorhees, and gives it to him*)

VORHEES: Too bad, old man, too bad! But it *can't* be helped.

GEORGE: I know! (*Vorhees starts to go*) Bert, — Eleanor hasn't come yet?

VORHEES: No. Are you sure you want to see her, or shall I first —

GEORGE: No, leave it to me! I'd rather. I don't want a loophole, anywhere, for her thinking me a coward. I want to make a clean breast of it all! That's what I'm after, — a clean breast, no matter what the doing it costs me!

VORHEES: You're right. (*About to go*)

Enter Foot.

FOOT: A gentleman from a newspaper, sir.

GEORGE: Will you see him, Bert?

VORHEES: Yes. (*To Foot*) You refer all the reporters to me. You know my address?

FOOT: Yes, sir.

VORHEES (*To Foot*):   Say no one here can be seen. (*To George*) I'll see you early to-morrow.

GEORGE: Thank you. I'd like your help in laying out a plan of action. Of course I shan't do anything till after — (*He hesitates, and raises his head and eyes to upstairs*)

VORHEES: I wouldn't.   (*Goes out*)

Foot exits. George stands alone in the room, a picture of utter dejection, of ruin and sorrow, but with a bulldog look all the while, — the look of a man who is licked, beaten, but not dead yet. He stands immovable almost — in complete silence. Slowly and softly, the door opens. Van Vranken looks in. He speaks in a sullen, hushed, and somewhat awed voice. He is pale; all evidence of drinking and excitement are gone.

VAN VRANKEN: George?

GEORGE (*In a monotonous voice*):   Hello, Don — you know?

VAN VRANKEN: I just heard. It's *true?* (*George, with a set face and stern lips, nods his head firmly, still standing. Van Vranken collapses in a chair.*) God! Poor Cicely!

GEORGE: Tough, isn't it? (*With a great sigh*)

VAN VRANKEN: I was having an awful time, George, with Mrs. Judly. She was giving it to me good for being willing to patch it up, temporarily, with Tess! She *didn't care about you!* I've come to the conclusion she don't care about anybody, anyway, but herself. Her brother telephoned it from his Club, and *she* (*His anger rises*) had the rottenness to say she believed there was something between Hannock and Cicely. That was more than I could stand for! God knows I'm as bad as they make them, but, with that little girl dead like that — to think such a thing, let alone say it — I don't know! — It took it out of me, somehow! It didn't seem to me it was the time to have a low quarrel between two people like us! It made us seem so beastly small! Death's such an awful — such a big — I suppose I'll feel differently to-morrow — but to-day — now — George, I *couldn't* 145 stand for it! She kicked me out, and I give you my word of honor I'm glad she did!

GEORGE (*Not deeply impressed, but civil*):   As you say, you'll feel differently to-morrow.

VAN VRANKEN: Very likely! Still, I've got these few decent hours, anyway, 150 to put on your sister's grave. (*A pause. George sits*)

GEORGE: I've given up running for governor.

VAN VRANKEN (*Surprised*):   Because — ?

GEORGE: No. You'll hear all the reasons soon enough. The point for the moment is, you and Tess needn't fake any further — living together. 155

VAN VRANKEN (*Thoughtfully*):   I see. (*After a pause*) George — ?

GEORGE: What?

VAN VRANKEN: Could I see Cicely?

GEORGE (*Hesitating*):   Tess is there.

VAN VRANKEN (*After a moment*):   Then, perhaps I'd better not go — ? 160

GEORGE: I think I *would*, if I were you.

Van Vranken looks at George questioningly. Teresa enters.

TERESA (*Quietly*):   Don — (*Her voice fills; she turns aside, and hastily wipes her eyes*)

VAN VRANKEN (*Moved*):   I was going upstairs.

TERESA: Not now! Mother and I have just left. They've come to — (*She stops, and again turns aside*)

VAN VRANKEN: Where are the children? 165

TERESA: Home!

VAN VRANKEN: "Home"? (*Very meaningly*)

TERESA: At the house.

VAN VRANKEN: Oh, Tess! — I'm — I'm not fit to take care of them! You'd better take them both, Tess, but let me see them off and on — 170

TERESA: I'm going back now with you, Don.

VAN VRANKEN: You needn't. I take it all back, Tess. You can have it your own way entirely. Leave Mrs. Judly out of it, — that's all I'll ask. Outside that, I'll fix it easy for you.

TERESA: Thank you, Don, (*After a second's pause*) but, if you don't mind, I'd 175 rather go back with you for the present, anyway. It seems to me, between us, we've pretty well spoiled everything except — well, — perhaps, in

ACT III | 533
thinking of the children's happiness we might find something for ourselves! What do you say?

VAN VRANKEN: It's worth a try — so long as you're willing!   180

Enter Mrs. Rand in a flurry.

MRS. RAND: Has any one thought to send for a dressmaker? (*Nobody answers*) Did *you* think of it, Teresa?

TERESA: No, I'm afraid I didn't.

MRS. RAND (*Her eyes filling*):   I haven't the remotest idea what's the thing to
wear! In Middleburg, I'd have known, — but here, I'm always wrong! If   185
I'd had my way, I'd never have taken off my crepe veil for your father, and
now *I wish I hadn't!* (*She sees Don*) Oh! I didn't see you, Don. Have you
come to beg Tess's pardon? Has this terrible thing reformed you?

VAN VRANKEN: I don't know, mother, how much reform is possible, but I
came to tell Tess I'm ashamed — (*He and Teresa exchange a look of almost sym-*   190
pathy, — at least, all antagonism has gone from them)

MRS. RAND: I confess, if I were Tess I could never forgive you! *Her father*
spoiled me for that sort of thing!

GEORGE: Tess isn't thinking now only of herself.

MRS. RAND: Oh, why did we ever come here! That was the first and *great
mistake!* I haven't had a happy moment since I left their father's and my   195
old home!

TERESA: Mother! Mother!!

MRS. RAND: It's the truth, — I haven't! I've never been anything, in New
York, but a fizzle! I've been snubbed right and left by the people I wanted
to know! I'm lonesome for my church, and if I died I wouldn't have a   200
handful of people at my funeral!

GEORGE: But you're going to *live*, mother, and you'll see we'll make you
happy yet!

MRS. RAND: Not here! You can't do it yourself! Bert says you have given up
running for governor, and Tess says everything's off between you and   205
Eleanor. I don't have to be told how disappointed and unhappy you are,
and Tess's made a miserable mess of it! And now, Cicely, the baby of you
all! — killed, like this! (*She breaks down into hysterical sobbing*) It's more than
I can bear! I tell you, children, I can't bear it! And it's all thanks to coming *here!!* This is what we get for not doing what your father wished.   210
Why didn't we stay home? I amounted to something there. I had as
much sense as my neighbors. I could hold my own! Here, I've been made
to understand I was such a nonentity — that I've grown actually to be
the fool they believe me! Oh, what the City has done for the whole of us!

TERESA: Yes, you're right, mother. I was happy too, till I came here. It was   215
the City that taught me to make the worst of things, instead of the best
of them.

GEORGE (*Gently*):   No, Tess — let's be honest with ourselves to-day. After
all, it's our own fault —

VAN VRANKEN: I agree with Tess! She and I, in a small town, would have   220
been happy always! I'd not have been tempted like I am here — I couldn't
have had the chances —

GEORGE (*Rising and speaking with the fulness of conviction*):   No! You're all wrong!
Don't blame the City. It's not her fault! It's our own! What the City does
is to bring out what's strongest in us. If at heart we're good, the good in   225
us will win! If the bad is strongest, God help us! Don't blame the City!
She gives the man his opportunity; it is up to *him* what he makes of it! A
man can live in a small town all his life, and deceive the whole place and
himself into thinking he's got all the virtues, when at heart he's a hypocrite! But the village gives him no chance to find it out, to prove it to his   230
fellows — the small town is too easy! *But the City!!!* A man goes to the
gates of the City and knocks! — New York or Chicago, Boston or San
Francisco, no matter *what* city so long as it's big, and busy, and selfish,
and self-centered. And she comes to her gates and takes him in, and she
stands him in the middle of her market place — where Wall Street and   235
Herald Square and Fifth Avenue and the Bowery, and Harlem, and
Forty-second Street all meet, and there she strips him naked of all his
disguises — and all his hypocrisies, — and she paints his ambition on
her fences, and lights up her skyscrapers with it! — what *he wants* to be
and *what he thinks he is!* — and then she says to him, Make good if you   240
can, or to Hell with you! And what is in him comes out to clothe his
nakedness, and to the City he can't lie! I *know*, because I *tried!* (*A short
pause*)

Foot enters.

FOOT: Miss Vorhees.

GEORGE: Ask her to come in here.

Teresa rises quickly.

TERESA: Don, I think —   245

VAN VRANKEN: I've a taxi outside.

MRS. RAND: All this time, and that clock going on every minute!

TERESA (*To Mrs. Rand*):   Mother, if you want to see us after dinner, telephone. (*Kisses her*)

MRS. RAND: What about our clothes?   250

TERESA: I'll attend to everything in the morning. (*Teresa and Don go out together*)

MRS. RAND: I think I'd rather be alone with you, George, to-night, if the things are off between you and Eleanor. At a time like this, there is no excuse for her going back on you —

GEORGE: Hush, mother! You don't understand. She has every excuse. I'll 255 tell you about it afterward.

MRS. RAND: No, tell her for me not to stop. I wanted her, because I thought she loved you — and was to be one of us — that's all! (*Enter Eleanor*) Thank you for coming back, Eleanor, but good night. George will explain. (*She goes out*) 260

ELEANOR: What's the matter with your mother? and Teresa? And Bert seemed strange, too, when I met him outside. What have I done?

GEORGE: Nothing, Eleanor.

ELEANOR (*Realizing what it may mean*): They think I believed what Hannock said? That anything he would say against *you* could for *one* moment 265 mean anything to *me!*

GEORGE: You didn't believe Hannock?

ELEANOR: Not for one second! That's why I left the room.

GEORGE: You'd better have stayed.

ELEANOR: Why? 270

GEORGE: Because he told the truth!

ELEANOR: How do you mean?

GEORGE: Everything he told me here, this afternoon, was true.

ELEANOR: Not when *I* was here! When I was here, he was calling you a thief, and a cheat, and a liar! 275

GEORGE: He was right!

ELEANOR: No! I don't understand you!

GEORGE: Your brother understands — and I've withdrawn my name from the nomination! I'm giving up all the things it seemed to me I wanted most, — and *you,* most of all, Eleanor! I thought I minded losing the 280 others, but in comparison with what I feel now!!! *You loved* me because I was honest!

ELEANOR: Not *because,* — but, of course, if you were not *honest* —

GEORGE: Well, I'm not — I'm *not!*

ELEANOR: *You are! I know you are!* 285

GEORGE: No! I've lied and tricked and cheated in business, and I've got to pay for it!

ELEANOR: And all this you did *deliberately?*

GEORGE: The only excuse I have, if you can call it an excuse, is that I didn't realize what I was doing! I did what others I had been taught to respect, 290 to pattern on, did before me, — what others were doing around me! I accepted cheating for business diplomacy. I explained lying as the commercial code! I looked on stealing as legitimate borrowing! But I was a grown man, and in possession of my senses, and I had no real excuse! Eleanor, I've been a *business* "*crook*," in a big way, perhaps, but still a "*crook*," and I'm not good enough for *you!* (*A pause*) 295

ELEANOR: What are you going to do?

GEORGE: Give up all the positions I haven't any right to fill. Pay back interest I hadn't any right to get, and money I hadn't any right to use! Give up principal I gained on somebody else's risk than my own! Begin all over again at 300 the bottom, but on the *level*, and climb, only if I can do it on the square!

ELEANOR: I understand! I understand it all, now! You've done wrong?

GEORGE: Yes.

ELEANOR: Oh, so wrong, but you're owning all up, and *giving* all up!

GEORGE: Yes. 305

ELEANOR: You aren't being pressed to?

GEORGE: Of course I could fight it, but what's the use? *It's true!* Now *I realize that*, I can't own up fast enough! I can't begin over again soon enough! I can't eat or sleep or take a long breath even, till I'm on the level again with myself. Even at the price of *you!* But I'll make you believe in 310 me again, Eleanor, — you'll see, if we live long enough!

ELEANOR: We don't have to live *any longer* for that.

GEORGE: In what way?

ELEANOR: The man who has done wrong, and can own it up, — face life all over again empty-handed, emptying his own hands of his own accord, 315 turn his back on everything he counted on and lived for, because it is the right thing to do, and because — leaving the world out of it — he *had to be honest with himself!* — that — George — is the man I look up to ten times more than the one who was *born* good and lived good because he never was tempted to enjoy the spoils of going wrong! It's the man whom 320 it costs something to be good, — that's what makes real character! And to me — (*She goes up to him, and puts her hand on his arm*) you, here, *to-day*, are twice the man you were yesterday! You needed a test, though we didn't know it! And at the same time we found that out, you had to go through it; and thank God, your real self has triumphed! *To-day* you *are* the man 325 I loved yesterday!

GEORGE (*Looking away*): Now, I know what those people mean who say a man gets all the *Hell* that's coming to him *in this world*, — (*Looking at her*) — and *all the Heaven, too!*

FINIS

Selected Prologues and Epilogues

→ Prologue to *The Contrast*

The Contrast was first staged at the John Street Theatre, New York, on April 16, 1787 with the actor Thomas Wignell, the company's principal low comedian, as the Yankee Jonathan. He also spoke the prologue credited to a "young gentleman of New York," possibly Tyler himself. On the title page of the first published text of the play in 1790, Tyler modestly referred to himself only as "A Citizen of the United States." The prologue appeared in the published version, though in later revivals it is rarely spoken. It is noteworthy that one of the rare reviews of the original production echoes many of the same sentiments and nationalist feelings found in the prologue. "Candour" in *The Daily Advertiser* (April 18, 1787) wrote:

> "The characters are drawn with spirit, particularly Charlotte's; the dialogue is easy, sprightly, and often witty, but wants the pruning knife very much. The author has made frequent use of soliloquies, but I must own, I think, injudiciously; Maria's song and her reflections after it are pretty, but certainly misplaced. Soliloquies are seldom so conducted as not to wound probability. If we ever talk to ourselves, it is when the mind is much engaged in some very interesting subject, and never to make calm reflections on indifferent things. . . . Colonel Manly's advice to America, tho' excellent is yet liable to the same blame, and perhaps greater. A man can never be supposed to be in conversation with himself, to point out examples of imitation to his countrymen. . . ."

Prologue

Exult each patriot heart! — this night is shewn
A piece, which we may fairly call our own;
Where the proud titles of "My Lord! Your Grace!"
To humble Mr. and plain Sir give place.
Our Author pictures not from foreign climes   5
The fashions, or the follies of the times;
But has confin'd the subject of his work
To the gay scenes — the circles of New-York.
On native themes his Muse displays her pow'rs;
If ours the faults, the virtues too are ours.   10
Why should our thoughts to distant countries roam,
When each refinement may be found at home?
Who travels now to ape the rich or great,
To deck an equipage and roll in state;
To court the graces, or to dance with ease,   15
Or by hypocrisy to strive to please?
Our free-born ancestors such arts despis'd;
Genuine sincerity alone they priz'd;
Their minds, with honest emulation fir'd,
To solid good — not ornament — aspir'd;   20
Or, if ambition rous'd a bolder flame,
Stern virtue throve, where indolence was shame.

    But modern youths, with imitative sense,
Deem taste in dress the proof of excellence;
And spurn the meanness of your homespun arts,   25
Since homespun habits would obscure their parts;
Whilst all, which aims at splendour and parade,
Must come from Europe, and be ready made.
Strange! we should thus our native worth disclaim,
And check the progress of our rising fame.   30
Yet once, whilst imitation bears the sway,
Aspires to nobler heights, and points the way,
Be rous'd, my friends! his bold example view;
Let your own Bards be proud to copy you!
Should rigid critics reprobate our play,   35
At least the patriotic heart will say,
"Glorious our fall, since in a noble cause.

"The bold attempt alone demands applause."
Still may the wisdom of the Comic Muse
Exalt your merits, or your faults accuse.   40

↹ Prologue and Epilogue to Stone's *Metamora*

When *Metamora* premièred on December 15, 1829, at the Park Theatre in New
York, actor Edwin Forrest, "proprietor of the tragedy," included a prologue and
an epilogue to counteract strong anti-American feelings, attitudes especially
negative toward native-authored plays. Forrest chose two writers who had been
judges in the playwriting contest that had produced *Metamora* for Forrest. Prosper M. Wetmore, a poet, wrote the prologue, and poet, playwright, and editor
James Lawson wrote the epilogue.

Prologue

Not from the records of Imperial Rome,
Or classic Greece — the muses' chosen home —
From no rich legends of the olden day
Our bard hath drawn the story of his play;
Led by the guiding hand of genius on,   5
He here hath painted Nature on her throne;
His eye hath pierced the forest's shadowy gloom,
And read strange lessons from a nation's tomb:
Brief are the annals of that blighted race —
These halls usurp a monarch's resting-place —   10
Tradition's mist-enshrouded page alone
Tells that an empire was — we know 'tis gone!
From foreign climes full oft the muse has brought
Her glorious treasures of gigantic thought;
And here, beneath the witchery of her power,   15
The eye hath poured its tributary shower:
When modern pens have sought th' historic page,
To picture forth the deeds of former age —
O'er soft Virginia's sorrows ye have sighed,
And dropt a tear when spotless beauty died;   20
When Brutus "cast his cloud aside"; to stand
The guardian of the tyrant-trampled land —

When patriot Tell his clime from thraldom freed,
And bade th' avenging arrow do its deed,
Your bosoms answered with responsive swell,   25
For freedom triumphed when th' oppressors fell!
These were the melodies of humbler lyres,
The lights of Genius, yet without his fires;
But when the master-spirit struck the chords,
And inspiration breathed her burning words —   30
When passion's self stalked living o'er the stage,
To plead with love, or rouse the soul to rage —
When Shakespeare led his bright creations forth,
And conjured up the mighty dead from earth —
Breathless — entranced — ye've listened to the line,   35
And felt the minstrel's power, all but divine!
While thus your plaudits cheer the stranger lay,
Shall native pens in vain the field essay?
To-night we test the strength of native powers,
Subject, and bard, and actor, all are ours —   40
'Tis yours to judge, if worthy of a name,
And bid them live within the halls of fame!

Epilogue

Before this bar of beauty, taste, and wit,
This host of critics, too, who throng the pit,
A trembling bard has been this night arraigned;
And I am counsel in the cause retained.
Here come I, then, to plead with nature's art,   5
And speak, less to the law, than to the heart.
   A native bard — a native actor too,
Have drawn a native picture to your view;
In fancy, this bade Indian wrongs arise,
While that embodied all before your eyes;   10
Inspired by genius, and by judgment led,
Again the Wampanoag fought and bled;
Rich plants are both of our own fruitful land,
Your smiles the sun that made their leaves expand;
Yet, not that they are native do I plead,   15
'Tis for their worth alone I ask your meed.

How shall I ask ye? Singly? Then I will —
But should I fail? Fail! I must try my skill.
    Sir, I know you — I've often seen your face;   20
And always seated in that selfsame place;
Now, in my ear — what think you of our play?
That it has merit truly, he did say;
And that the hero, prop'd on genius' wing,
The Indian forest scoured, like Indian king!   25
    See that fair maid, the tear still in her eye,
And hark! hear not you now that gentle sigh?
Ah! these speak more than language could relate,
The woe-fraught heart o'er Nahmeokee's fate;
She scans us not by rigid rules of art,   30
Her test is feeling, and her judge the heart.
    What dost thou say, thou bushy-whiskered beau?
He nods approval — whiskers are the go.
    Who is he sits the fourth bench from the stage?
There; in the pit! — why he looks wondrous sage!   35
He seems displeased, his lip denotes a sneer —
O! he's a critic that looks so severe!
    Why, in his face I see the attic salt —
    A critic's merit is to find a fault.
What fault find you, sir? eh! or you, sir?   40
    None!
Then, if the critic's mute, my cause is won.
Yea, by that burst of loud heartfelt applause,
I feel that I have gained my client's cause.
    Thanks, that our strong demerits you forgive,   45
And bid our bard and Metamora live.

→ **Prologue to *Fashion***

Epes Sargent (1813–1880), critic and author of four plays, was a family friend of
the Mowatts who had suggested that Anna Cora write *Fashion*. He also assisted
her with technical details in the composition. When the play premièred on
March 24, 1845, it was preceded by this prologue written by Sargent. The play's
epilogue (see pp. 177–79), written in dialogue form, is by Mowatt herself.

Prologue

(Enter a Gentleman, reading a Newspaper.)

" '*Fashion, a Comedy.*' I'll go; but stay —
Now I read farther, 'tis a native play!
Bah! homemade calicoes are well enough,
But homemade dramas *must* be stupid stuff.
Had it the *London* stamp, 'twould do — but then,   5
For plays, we lack the manners and the men!"
    Thus speaks one critic. Hear another's creed: —
" '*Fashion!*' What's here? (*Reads.*) It never can succeed!
What! from a woman's pen? It takes a man
To write a comedy — no woman can."   10
    Well, sir, and what say you, and why that frown?
His eyes uprolled, he lays the paper down: —
"Here! take," he says, "the unclean thing away!
'Tis tainted with the notice of a play!"
    But, sir! — but, gentlemen! — you, sir, who think   15
No comedy can flow from native ink, —
Are we such *perfect* monsters, or such *dull,*
That Wit no traits for ridicule can cull?
Have we no follies here to be redressed?
No vices gibbeted? no crimes confessed?   20
"But then a female hand can't lay the lash on!"
How know you that, sir, when the theme is FASHION?
    And now, come forth, thou man of sanctity!
How shall I venture a reply to thee?
The Stage — what is it, though beneath thy ban,   25
But a daguerreotype of life and man?
Arraign poor human nature, if you will,
But let the DRAMA have her mission still;
Let her, with honest purpose, still reflect
The faults which keeneyed Satire may detect.   30
For there *be* men who fear not an hereafter,
Yet tremble at the hell of public laughter!
    Friends, from these scoffers we appeal to you!
Condemn the false, but O, applaud the true.
Grant that *some* wit may grow on native soil,   35
And Art's fair fabric rise from woman's toil.
While we exhibit but to *reprehend*
The social voices, 'tis for *you* to mend!

Play Summaries

><

→ **ROYALL TYLER**

The Contrast

I. In a New York apartment friends Charlotte and Letitia quibble over appropriate clothing fashions. Letitia accuses Charlotte of being a libertine; Charlotte calls Letitia a prude. The imminent marriage of their acquaintance, Maria, is discussed, and it is revealed that she is giving her hand "without her heart," that her fiancé Billy Dimple's absence in Europe has given her time and freedom to discover true sentiment in novels of manners, especially when compared with the inadequacy of Dimple's own love letters. This difference — this contrast — sets the drama in motion.

The scene shifts to Van Rough's house, where a morose Maria sits at a table, lamenting her marital predicament and ruminating on the allure of noble acts and masculinity. Her father, Van Rough, counsels his daughter, assures her of the wisdom of her "choice" in hopes of steering her from a too-serious consideration of marriage. Maria is left unconsoled, even more troubled. She finds her heart "militating with her filial duty" over whether to be true to herself or dutiful to her father.

II. What begins as a loud and discursive dialectic between Charlotte and

543

Letitia on sense, style, and sentimentalism turns to Charlotte's character analysis of her brother, Colonel Manly, who is due to visit. She counts him as the antithesis of her own gaiety and buoyancy, attributes that intrigue her counterpart. Manly arrives, exploiting his heroic manner and gravity so as to cast a pall over the women's previously boisterous conversation and flamboyant speech.

On the mall, Dimple's man, Jessamy the intriguer, and Jonathan, Manly's waiter and the consummate Yankee, discuss servitude and mastery in an archly comic, ironic manner. The bullish and naïve Jonathan prides himself on his true-blooded American character. His surprise at learning of Jessamy's vocation as a fellow waiter demonstrates his perpetual delusion with appearances. A girl he meets in the city turns out, with Jessamy's good observation, to be a prostitute. Jessamy takes advantage of his lesser's blindness by instructing him to kiss Jenny the maid, the woman he wishes to court, as requisite procedure, an action that, Jessamy plans, will fill her with disgust and make Jessamy's conquest of her easier. Jonathan's acceptance of Jessamy's proposition crystallizes the contrast of their sensibilities — a point of which Jessamy is acutely aware.

III. Dimple's own reservation about the marriage seems surprising, and his schemes, outlandish. He considers it necessary to sever ties with Maria, marry Letitia for her fortune, and keep Charlotte close by for her beauty. He sends two letters with Jessamy to each of his love interests so as to profess his devotion to each. Soon after, his mission complete, Jessamy plays matchmaker to a reluctant Jenny and oblivious Jonathan. Art and life for the hapless servant are exploded beyond repair when he mistakes the goings-on at a playhouse ("the devil's drawing-room") as real-life high jinks. He commits another social blunder when he lands the misguided kiss on Jenny and proposes marriage. She flies off in a rage.

On the mall, Dimple introduces himself to Manly and wins his confidence by praising soldiery and playing sycophant. To Dimple's surprise, he learns that Manly is Charlotte's brother.

IV. In Charlotte's apartment Maria still bemoans her fate. The inclination not to marry Dimple sits well with Charlotte, who has designs of her own on him. Following Charlotte's curt lecture on caprice, Maria announces her affections for a gentleman who turns out to be Charlotte's brother, Manly. Dimple and Manly come on the scene, and Maria and Manly are immediately, visibly smitten with each other. After Manly enumerates America's virtues, he escorts Maria out. Dimple confirms his appointments *d'amour* with Charlotte and Letitia.

At Van Rough's house Van Rough is disgruntled over Dimple's money troubles. He hides in a closet as Maria and Manly enter, then discuss their feelings about marriage and filial obligations. Manly learns of Maria's engagement and entreats her to "follow the path of rectitude" and obey her father's wishes.

v. At Dimple's lodgings Jessamy, assuring Jonathan that he has lost out with Jenny because he lacks the social graces, schools the Yankee in laughing etiquette; but Jonathan is a disappointment to his mentor.

In Charlotte's apartment the incorrigible Dimple leads on both Letitia and Charlotte alternately. Dimple makes advances on Charlotte, and Manly bursts forth with a sword to defend her honor. All the characters begin to converge at this locus of animation: Van Rough reprimands Manly on his false heroics; Jonathan throws himself into the fray; and Letitia sheds light on Dimple's amatory intentions toward both herself and Charlotte. Dimple has lost his real and potential marriage partners, his money, and his respect. He departs from the company, reminding all present of the superiority of the European polished man over "an unpolished, untravelled American." Van Rough grants Manly his daughter's hand. Maria accepts Letitia and Charlotte's apologies; the women have learned the pitfalls of their conduct and their emphasis on style, and Manly has acquired an understanding of the real American honor, virtue, and probity that wins women.

→ JOHN AUGUSTUS STONE

Metamora; or, the Last of the Wampanoags

I. Mordaunt, a leading New England settler, anticipates the arrival of his daughter Oceana's suitor from England, the brutish Lord Fitzarnold. After his exit, Oceana arrives with the orphan Walter, describing her rescue from a panther by an Indian. Just as Walter identifies him as Metamora — "the white man's dread, the Wampanoags' hope" — the Indian chief appears. Oceana and the Indian exchange tokens of mutual affection, a scarf and an eagle plume, and Metamora departs. Walter demurs Oceana's wishes to convert him to Christianity (despite his valor and dignity, "he is a heathen," as she notes), explaining Heaven's perfect adjudication of human vocation and worship. Soon after, Walter and his guardian, Sir Arthur Vaughan, debate Fitzarnold's worthiness to be Oceana's husband, with Walter airing his own strong feelings about her. Fitzarnold arrives, makes Mordaunt and

Walter's acquaintance, and waits for Oceana's arrival. A tramp informs Walter of an imminent Indian attack, urging him to send word to Mordaunt. The younger agrees, recalling Metamora's promise of benignity to Oceana.

II. In Metamora's wigwam his wife, Nahmeokee, inquires into her husband's affairs and well-being. He admits to nightmarish dreams that auger bloody struggle with the white man. Otah, his son, notifies his father of an English offensive against the Indians, and Nahmeokee suspects Annawandah's betrayal of the Wampanoags. A brigade of soldiers arrives meanwhile, besieging Metamora with demands that he attend an upcoming council to unify the Indians and the English settlers. He agrees and departs immediately.

Mordaunt, troubled by his daughter's rejection of her betrothed, bids her to decide "between my honor and instant death." She expresses her disapproval to both her father and the smitten Walter. Mordaunt assuages Fitzarnold, who discerns her hesitancy to marry him, and convinces him that she will change her position.

In the council chamber Metamora is a bastion of easy confidence and candor, denying any malicious intents toward the English and refusing to make known his complicity in the murder of a traitor. When the duplicitous Annawandah appears to testify against the chief, Metamora stabs him to death and flees, threatening the Englishmen with the mighty wrath of the wronged Indian. Mordaunt is critically wounded in the hail of bullets and ricochets that follows the escaping Metamora.

III. Fitzarnold has decided to sail hastily to England with a kidnapped Oceana. Metamora has safely returned to his family, pledging revenge upon the English. Fitzarnold tries unsuccessfully to woo Oceana into matrimony. Walter intercedes and a duel nearly ensues. Metamora, vindictive and resolute, desires to kill Mordaunt in exchange for the wrongdoing inflicted on the Indians. Oceana, however, reminds him of his earlier declaration of protection and friendship to her. Metamora leaves both father and daughter unscathed. Walter and Oceana embrace.

IV. The English vow to annihilate the Wampanoag tribe. Oceana pleads with Fitzarnold for the release of Nahmeokee, who has been interrogated about her husband and his whereabouts. Walter, trying to make symbolic peace with Metamora, is summarily detained pending Nahmeokee's return. The increasingly bloody showdown between Metamora and the English moves forward; the chief renews his promise to vanquish the enemies who threaten his people's land, food, and homes, as well as their burial grounds.

V. Metamora's pledge is realized when he kills Fitzarnold, having interrupted the latter's insidious advances on Oceana. Sir Arthur informs his cohorts of Metamora's escape through the secret passages of Mordaunt's house; Mordaunt turns out to be one of the regicides of King Charles. It was because of Fitzarnold's knowledge of this secret that Mordaunt felt obligated to marry her off to him to avoid exposure. Wolfe, Walter's companion, reveals to Sir Arthur that Walter, whom he abducted as a boy, is his son. Metamora prepares his people for one last confrontation. In the ensuing chaos, he almost kills the oracle Kaneshine, who has envisaged the great chief's defeat and death. Walter informs Errington, the Puritan chief of council, of Oceana's safekeeping. In Metamora's secret stronghold, with its waterfall, craggy rocks, and bridges, it is discovered that his infant son is dead, shot by a burning shaft. After extolling death as freedom and denouncing life with the white man as servitude, Metamora kills his wife to save her from an uncertain fate. The Indian chief is executed by the English, though not before unleashing imprecations against them and their families, with his last words directed to his dead wife, Nahmeokee.

→ JOHN BROUGHAM

Metamora; or, The Last of the Pollywogs

I. Oceana discusses with Walter her rescue from a hungry bear by "one of the natyves." The free verse integrated into the dialogue attaches more insipidness to Oceana's description of the Indian:

His hair was glossy as the raven's wing;
He looked and moved a certain savage king;
His speech was pointed, at the same time blunt —
Something between a whisper and a grunt.

Oceana's father (now Vaughan; in Stone's original, Mordaunt) appears, replete with a clumsy brogue and a stubborn, urgent desire for his daughter not to marry Walter. The Indian hero enters with a thunderous "Ugh!," diffusing the situation by his ridiculous presence rather than intensifying the company's passions. He gives a mongrel rooster tail to Oceana to ward off "red-man's wrath" and leaves in a huff. In the kitchen of Metamora's home, Metamora's wife, Tapiokee (Nahmeokee in the original) tends her child as her husband returns. Metamora's dreams of an internecine struggle in the Stone play have been transformed into a fantasia of triumphant Indian massacre. Old Tar alerts him of the nearness of English soldiers. Badenough (the Puritan Goodenough in the original) and Worser (Captain Church, military leader in the original) and their soldiers arrive to demand Metamora's presence at a peace council. In the white man's chamber, Metamora is interrogated about the Pollywogs' claim to the land, the murder of the traitor Sassinger (Sasamond), and his involvement in a brick-throwing incident. Then the traitor Anaconda (Annawandah in the original) appears to testify, is stabbed by Metamora, and the scene ends, with Metamora professing his bloodthirst and stupidly throwing his hatchet into the stage.

II. In the woods the poseur Fitzfaddle (Fitzarnold) fails miserably in his bid to court Oceana and to speak convincingly romantic French. When she refuses to capitulate to him, he threatens bodily harm. Walter cowers, while Metamora emerges predictably from the shadows, first to murder everybody, then to save her. In another part of the woods, Badenough and Worser browbeat Tapiokee for information about her husband, but she refuses to divulge anything. Metamora comes to her rescue, but Kantshie (Kaweshine) prophesies a pig turning its tail, allegorizing the Pollywogs' cowardice, retreat, and defeat. Kantshie is banished by Metamora, who rallies his people to combat. In a setting parallel to Metamora's secret hiding place in Stone's play, Tapiokee's child winds up dead; Metamora's response is to kill the interloper Fitzfaddle and stab his wife. Metamora succumbs to a volley issued by toy popguns, though is resurrected of his own accord (as is Tapiokee and also Vaughan, who never really died). After his rebirth, Metamora appeals to audience generosity in applauding the play and the Pollywogs. The chorus sings "We're all dying . . ." to the tune of "We're all nodding." The ending degenerates further into a routine of comic dances and the chanting of "Pollywog, Polly, Polly, Pollywog" as the parody ends.

→ ANNA CORA OGDEN MOWATT

Fashion; or, Life in New York

I. In the embellished drawing room of socialite Mrs. Elizabeth Tiffany, Zeke, the black servant (who speaks in a broad stage-Negro dialect), is admiring his gaudy livery with the French maid, Millinette, who has been brought from Paris by Mrs. Tiffany to teach her the French mode. Millinette digresses on the habits of her employers, Mr. and Mrs. Tiffany. He is shown to be a man of business; she, a lady of fashion. Their daughter, Seraphina, and Prudence, a "Maiden Lady," are similarly scrutinized. Millinette also describes the drudgery of Zeke's occupation for him. With Mrs. Tiffany's arrival, Zeke exits. As she arrives, Mrs. Tiffany exudes affectation with simpering phrases, mostly a butchered hybrid of French and English. Finding in French a grace and precision lacking in the coarse strains of English, she begins to rename her possessions and Zeke, who becomes "Adolphe." Prudence enters and commits a faux pas by divulging the meager beginnings of her girlhood friends. Mr. T. Tennyson Twinkle, first of the day's guests, is a bad poet who woos Seraphina with his saccharine verses. Mrs. Tiffany, however, is pleased to host him, as poets are "the aristocrats of literature" (though unsuitable as husbands). The eccentric Mr. Augustus Fogg, a "drawing room appendage," is the next visitor and suitor for Seraphina. He is a tired, misanthropic, toad of a man who negates everyone's appraisals, being indifferent to everything but food. The entrance of Count Jolimaitre, a fashionable European import, foils all appeals for Seraphina's heart from Fogg and Twinkle. Jolimaitre lies about his background and lets forth frivolous observations on American fashion. The aptly named farmer, Adam Trueman, an old friend of Mr. Tiffany's, arrives on the scene, indignant that Mrs. Tiffany has instructed Zeke to tell him she was away. His directness is unfashionable to the throng, and Mrs. Tiffany, upset and exasperated by his criticisms of her, sends Millinette for a glass of water and her husband. Mrs. Tiffany is aware neither of the Count's startled response when he recognizes Millinette nor of Millinette's similar reaction on seeing the Count.

II. Mr. Tiffany is in his countinghouse quarreling with his assistant Snobson about the younger man's salary. Snobson has designs on Seraphina Tiffany, which disappoints her father greatly. Trueman is reunited with his old chum Tiffany and elaborates on the "fashion-worship" and deception found in the Tiffany household. He also remarks on the dourness of Tiffany and the "hang-dog face" of Snobson. They depart, leaving a fuming Snobson to contemplate their levity and his own source of joy — Seraphina.

In the Tiffany's conservatory Gertrude, gossipmonger, governess, and orphan, and the chivalrous Colonel Howard converse. He is about to say something crucial when the Count interrupts them, titillating and then crushing Gertrude with wooing passions and his resolve to marry another, Seraphina. Trueman intervenes amid this verbal abuse, striking the Count with a hickory switch. Mrs. Tiffany then intercedes and takes the Count's side. Trueman, in a pedantic overture, cautions Gertrude about deception and its manifestations in image and fashion. The old maid Prudence, who is attempting to attract Trueman, is left alone with him and reveals all the other guests' amatory pursuits.

III. In Mrs. Tiffany's parlor the Tiffanys haggle over costs and material possessions. Mrs. Tiffany discharges numerous insults at her husband, primarily accusing him of being "plebeian" and "American." To his chagrin, she announces her plans for a ball the next Friday to save her husband's reputation. Furthermore, she riles him about the marriage of their daughter to the Count. Tiffany agrees to the arrangement as long as Snobson is invited, and ensuing fireworks turn the affair into an unfashionable scene. When Snobson arrives, Mrs. Tiffany attempts to educate him about foreign fashion influences and the American "ee-light." He is introduced to the Count and ushered upstairs. Meanwhile, the Count proposes to make Seraphina his Countess as long as she keeps it secret. Snobson feels shortchanged and threatens to cause a scene if his love isn't requited. In the housekeeper's room the Count pretends to disclose his intentions to stay true to Millinette, which the eavesdropping Gertrude learns, and to notify Seraphina so her heart isn't broken. Gertrude, who plans to entrap the Count (who believes that Gertrude has fallen for his charms), confronts him and agrees not to betray his true intentions if he will do her bidding.

IV. At the ball, Trueman arrives unfashionably late. The crowd has already started its night of merriment and blackmail, the Count whispering to Seraphina his plan to marry her the next day. Gertrude devises a scheme to get Millinette away from the Count, and Fogg is at last found not to be indifferent to food! In the darkened housekeeper's room Gertrude enters the circle of intrigue by imitating Millinette's voice and asking the Count to divulge all. Trueman bursts into the room abruptly; Gertrude and the Count rush to conceal themselves but are discovered by Mrs. Tiffany and her retinue. Gertrude is accused of being a malingerer, while the Count buys time to explain himself.

V. In Mrs. Tiffany's drawing room Gertrude commits her wisdom to paper. Trueman demands to peruse the letter and is finally convinced of her sincerity. Howard announces his departure because of the presumed disgrace of Gertrude's liaison with the Count in the closet. He, too, reads the missive and apologizes to Gertrude. Mr. and Mrs. Tiffany again squabble about finances. Prudence informs everyone that Seraphina has eloped with the Count. At this point, Trueman relates how the "orphan" Gertrude is his granddaughter and, therefore, heiress to his fortunes. He gives Howard permission to marry her. Millinette enters in tears, telling Mrs. Tiffany of the Count's transgressions and his falsehood. Intoxicated and going mad, Snobson declares entitlement to Seraphina and insults Trueman and Tiffany. He reveals his business associate's forgeries, implicating himself and leaving promptly for California to avoid prosecution as an accessory. Seraphina returns, unmarried. Trueman agrees to absolve Tiffany as long as he sells his house and brings his family to the country so they can learn "economy, true independence, and home virtues, instead of foreign follies." The Count confesses to deception, agreeing that he is actually Gustave Treadmill, a Parisian head cook, and unites with Millinette. Trueman, who has arbitrated the confessions and play's conclusion, takes a part in the epilogue along with Prudence, the Count, Howard, Tiffany, Gertrude, Mrs. Tiffany, and Seraphina. Fashion is shown to be grounded in falsehood; the characters are vindicated in their reform and, in the case of Howard, Trueman, and Gertrude, in their steadfastness.

GEORGE L. AIKEN

Uncle Tom's Cabin

I. Married houseslaves George and Eliza discuss their bondage, and George's immediate plan to flee to freedom in Canada. Their exchange ponders servitude in relation to Christianity and American principles of democracy and liberty. Although Eliza counsels George to embrace faith and patience, he resolves to run, to "be free or die," promising to buy his wife and child when he gains freedom. In a dining-room setting, slave-traders Shelby and Haley debate a transaction that concludes in Shelby's decision to sell off his prized manservant Tom and Eliza's young child, Harry. Eliza, who overhears this pact, immediately readies herself and her child for a daring escape. At Uncle Tom's cabin, laden with snow, she informs Tom and Aunt Chloe of her intentions to flee. As mother and child leave to begin their flight, Chloe urges Tom also to run away, but he refuses, assuring his wife of God's good and His will to free his shackled Christian subjects.

When Eliza arrives at a riverside tavern to inquire about a ferry, she and Harry encounter Phineas, a flamboyant gentleman whose love for a Quaker girl has forced him to give up his slaves and become a Quaker. Phineas entertains another visitor, the lawyer Marks, and leaves. Soon, a society of men congregates — hucksters, swindlers, speculators, and worse, slave-traders — who are pursuing Eliza and Harry. As she hears this, she flees across the landscape with the ravening bounty hunters hot on her trail, finally attempting to cross the Ohio River on ice floes. As the act ends, Eliza and Harry are seen drifting downstream on a "cake of ice," with her hunters on the bank mutely observing and Phineas in wait on the opposite side.

II. St. Clare returns to his Lake Pontchartrain, Louisiana, estate after a two-week absence, in which time he has purchased Tom, at his daughter Eva's insistence, and brought his cousin Ophelia for a visit. A series of exchanges between characters reveals Ophelia's puritanism, St. Clare's wife Marie's garrulousness, and St. Clare's daughter Eva's sweetness. St. Clare tells his wife how Eva fell into the water by the ferry and was rescued by the courageous Tom.

On a riverbank, Eva sits on Tom's lap, garnishing his head with flowers and a wreath. St. Clare meanwhile imparts Christian morality to Ophelia, who clings to racial prejudices. He also introduces her to a slave he has bought for Ophelia to educate, Topsy — a wild girl who rails against the convention and civility expected of her. A distrustful Ophelia interrogates Topsy about her background, concluding she is both "heathenish and shiftless." Topsy steals Ophelia's ribbon and, when charged with the theft, confesses her "wickedness."

Back at the Tavern, Phineas greets a Mr. Wilson, previously George Harris's owner. George enters disguised but is recognized by Phineas. He is informed of his wife's whereabouts and vehemently defends his actions to Wilson. They argue over legality and liberty, and George leaves. Shortly after, the slave-hunters Marks, Loker, and Haley bumble onto the scene, seeking information about Eliza and Harry. An irate Phineas threatens them with injury.

Back on the St. Clare estate, Topsy tells Eva her life story and her history of being unloved. She subsequently bursts into tears when Eva expresses love and sympathy for her. Meanwhile George reunites with Eliza and Harry. As they start out on a freedom journey to Canada through a rocky pass in the hills, they are beset by Loker and his gang, who are forced to retreat — unable to match the marksmanship of George or the brute strength of Phineas. George shoots Loker and his body is thrown off a large rock by Phineas.

III. Tom preaches a temperance sermon to his master, St. Clare, stating that by denying Christianity, St. Clare is denying himself. Ophelia enters, complaining of Topsy's disobedience and imperviousness to her educational attempts.

At the edge of a lake Tom sings spirituals to Eva. St. Clare arrives and detects a sadness in his daughter's disposition. He learns that she cries for humanity and its servitude. St. Clare promises to free Tom when Eva dies a prophesied, unexplained death soon after. Tom explains to Ophelia the imminence of this event, and finally, in the following scene, with St. Clare kneeling by her side in prayer, Eva dies.

IV. A street in New Orleans serves as a meeting place for the greasy speculator Gumption Cute and Lawyer Marks. Marks tries to persuade his acquaintance to assist him in the business of slave-catching, but Cute rejects the offer. At the St. Clare estate, Tom expresses fealty and compassion to his owner, who, in exchange, grants Tom freedom at an unspecified future time and then leaves for town. A charity of sorts is extended to Topsy by Ophelia, who grants her young slave freedom and an opportunity for employment and education in Ophelia's home in Vermont. While in town, St. Clare has been mysteriously fatally wounded and dies in Tom's arms without having signed his freedom papers.

V. Wicked slave-owner Simon Legree buys at auction St. Clare's former slaves Emmeline for one thousand dollars and Tom for twelve hundred.

At Ophelia's home in Vermont, distant relation Gumption Cute comes to request part of the family fortune but is stopped at the door by Topsy, whom he verbally abuses. Back in Louisiana, Tom is brutally whipped by Legree for not following orders to beat another slave. In Vermont, Cute's intrusion upsets the household, but he leaves with his money scheme unhatched and unsuccessful. Ophelia plans to wed Deacon Perry, who, though shocked by Topsy and southern accents assimilated by his soon-to-be-wife, is madly devoted to her.

VI. In a darkened landscape back in Louisiana, Tom is again preaching Christian doctrine to a despairing fellow slave, Cassy. Back in New Orleans, Shelby, original owner of Tom, Eliza, and Harry, learns from Marks that Tom has been sold to Legree; Marks agrees for a fee to show him the location of Legree's property. In a rough chamber, where Legree is badly mistreating Cassy, Legree admits to his evil inclinations and recalls the origins of his malevolence. Marks runs into Cute, who tells of his misfortunes. The slave-owner Legree is discussed, and it is revealed that he killed St. Clare, mistaking him for Cute. They decide to blackmail Legree for two thousand dollars.

Legree informs Tom of his intention to kill him. In the ensuing episode, he beats Tom virtually to death. Shelby, Marks, and Cute arrive to apprehend Legree, but he tries to resist their efforts and is shot dead in the confrontation. The dying Tom peacefully awaits enshrinement in heaven and the end to his mortal poverty. In a final scene, a white-robed Eva, revealed on the back of a milk-white dove, extends a benediction to St. Clare and Tom, who are kneeling and gazing up at her.

→ DION BOUCICAULT

The Poor of New York

I. In the midst of the Commercial Panic of 1837, unscrupulous banker Gideon Bloodgood is making plans to leave New York. He is both ruined and ruinous, indebted but remorseless. His assistant Edwards is oblivious to his intentions and only slightly aware of his moral bankruptcy. In contrast, Badger, the last remaining clerk, knows all. Discharged by Bloodgood, he threatens to divulge his employer's fraudulence unless he is paid remittance. Meanwhile, Fairweather, a sea captain in the India Trade, deposits $100,000 to be invested later for his two children. The captain is eager to embark for Calcutta the next day. He and Bloodgood become sentimental about their children, professing aloud their love for them. The captain leaves, and Bloodgood embezzles the money and pays off a share to Badger.

Fairweather, having caught wind of Bloodgood's deviousness at a shipowner's dinner, soon returns and asks to cancel his account. Bloodgood hesitates and Fairweather threatens death. Fairweather drops dead of apoplexy, leaving Bloodgood his fortune and Badger the original receipt of Fairweather's doomed transaction for blackmailing purposes.

II. Twenty years have intervened, and the country is in the grip of the Panic of 1857. In a park near Tammany Hall impoverished yacht-owner Mark Livingstone talks with Puffy, a street vendor, about Fairweather's widow and her now-grown children who live in Puffy's tenement. Livingstone learns that Fairweather's son Paul has been discharged from a clerkship in the Navy Yard and that his sister, Lucy, works at a milliner's on Broadway.

Paul and Mrs. Fairweather arrive, commemorating the twentieth anniversary of the captain's death. Paul reiterates an account of Fairweather's demise: how he left home with $100,000 and was found dead and robbed on the sidewalk of Liberty Street. Paul needles Livingstone, formerly a suitor of Lucy's, about why he forsook her. In an aside, Mark reveals how he lost everything in speculation and was too ashamed of his failure to pursue the marriage.

Bloodgood arrives on the scene, advises all to settle their accounts, refuses employment to Paul and Livingstone, and departs. Livingstone then expounds on poverty in a soliloquy that waxes full of unrestrained vigor. A crowd convenes, but a policeman promptly stops the speech and dismisses the gathering.

In front of Bloodgood's Bank on Nassau Street, Bloodgood reminisces on the fortune accruing from Fairweather's funds, while his daughter, Alida, demands $2,000. A foreign duke, one of Alida's lovers, has requested such a sum to cover gambling debts that must be paid off immediately. A spoiled despot, Alida is her father's motivating force for all his wrongdoing. She is a repository for all his greed and therefore a lecherous creature.

At the modest flat of the Puffys, the Fairweathers are being temporarily housed. The class strictures are shown to be implacable, as the indigent Puffys treat the destitute Fairweathers as if they were still aristocracy. During dinner, two sheriff's officers arrive in response to a suit that Bloodgood has directed against Susan Fairweather and Jonas Puffy for a debt of $150. Livingstone is here revealed a ruined man.

III. In Bloodgood's pretentiously decorated apartment Alida reads a scathing newspaper article about her father to Bloodgood, asking if his cruelty is the cause for her expulsion from the finest homes in New York. Livingstone enters and once again confesses his ruined state, this time to Bloodgood. Thinking she can win his hand in marriage by rescuing him from his poverty, Alida requests that her father write Livingstone a check to save him. Badger comes in, demanding an additional $5,000 as he flashes the Fairweather receipt of twenty years ago. Paul Fairweather then wanders in, asking pardon from his creditor, Bloodgood. To rid himself of the Fairweathers, Bloodgood offers Paul a bookkeeping position in Rio de Janeiro, but he must leave on a ship sailing early the next morning.

After Livingstone and Lucy again express their love for each other, Alida confronts Lucy. She happily apprises her rival in love that Livingstone will marry her for her money. When Livingstone reenters, Lucy informs him of her inability to marry him. Later, Badger is framed by Bloodgood for purloining the receipt from his desk. Badger is escorted to jail by the police.

IV. In Union Square at night, with snow falling, the Puffys peddle their wares, as does Badger (opera libretto and matchbooks), now impoverished and just out of jail. He encounters Bloodgood and relates his plans to confess to Fairweather's death and to implicate Bloodgood as well. They agree to meet at Badger's residence to negotiate a settlement. In a montagelike shifting of scene, Mrs. Fairweather tries to pawn a ring, Paul is shown begging, and Lucy, due to pride, stumbles in her attempt to beg. They reunite cheerfully, despite their misery. In the vestibule of the Academy of Music, Paul happens on Livingstone and Alida, the latter shooing him away. Livingstone, observing his friend's hardship, agrees to meet him with money.

In the area of New York known as "Five Points," in two adjoining attic rooms belonging to Badger and the Fairweather family, the familiar disharmonic partnership of Bloodgood and Badger is reestablished as persecutor and blackmailer. Bloodgood pulls a revolver on Badger, demanding the receipt, but his would-be victim pulls two revolvers from his pillow. Bloodgood exits, promising remuneration for Badger.

In a suicide attempt Lucy lights a brazier of charcoal, ostensibly to suffocate herself and her mother with smoke inhalation. She and her mother lie down in darkness but are rescued by Livingstone and Paul. Badger conceals the receipt and later, in the final act and in Paul's presence, denounces Bloodgood as an incendiary murderously intent on destroying the receipt.

v. Upscale Brooklyn Heights is the environs for the financially revived Puffys and Fairweathers. Livingstone has agreed to marry Alida, but her extortion is soon revealed. With the truth known, Livingstone no longer feels obligated to marry Alida; instead, the reunited lovers, Lucy and Livingstone, embrace. Badger confesses the crime against Captain Fairweather to the family, only to learn that the proof (the receipt) is in an old tenement that is burning down. The group quickly runs out to recover the evidence.

In a brief but tense scene Bloodgood is seen amid the flames, basking in the glow of presumed triumph. He flees. The Puffys' son races into the house and emerges soon after, black and burned. Badger, who has made his way to the upper floor, falls as the building is gutted by flames, and is rescued by Dan.

In the drawing room of Bloodgood's mansion, preparation is made for the marriage of Alida and Livingstone; Bloodgood expresses worry over the groom's absence. Livingstone arrives to decline Alida's hand. Badger bursts in with two policemen and a warrant for Bloodgood's arrest. Bloodgood fails in a last-ditch effort to free himself by wielding a knife, and he is handcuffed. As the truth unfolds, Alida abandons her father. Bloodgood, having lost his child, asks to be taken away. This, to Paul, is an example of Bloodgood's one virtue — selflessness toward his daughter. Paul orders him to be freed and his fortunes restored to him. The marriage of Livingstone and Lucy commences as the whole cast assembles. Mrs. Fairweather ends the play with a monologue expressing compassion for the poor and urging the audience to do likewise.

Shore Acres

I. Set in rustic Bar Harbor, Maine, the play opens with young Millie Berry playing with sand and pieces of old crockery when the mailman arrives with letters and candies. Her older sister, Helen, is haggling with Uncle Nat over the merits of her love interest, Sam Warren. Her father, we learn, does not approve of Warren because of his newfangled, unconventional approach to life. Helen talks about running away and proclaims a greater love for her uncle than for her father, farm-owner Martin Berry. Impoverished farmworker Joel Gates comes on the scene with his shy young daughter, Mandy, to borrow a gun to rid himself of an animal spoiling his crops. He departs soon after, and Helen remonstrates with her uncle about not pursuing the matter of a government pension long due to him.

Martin Berry intends Helen to marry postmaster-storekeeper-entrepreneur Josiah Blake. Martin and Blake enter with Blake trying to persuade Martin to sell acres of the farm for a lucrative real-estate development venture. Despite his reservations (he had promised his dead mother that he would never sell the farm), Martin finally agrees to Blake's conditions. They turn to a discussion of Helen's intractability and her rejection of Blake as a prospective husband, which they blame on modernity and the radicalism of the new woman. Young Nat also tries to convince his sister to marry Blake, though to no avail.

Sam and Helen rendezvous; Sam gives her a book by William Dean Howells, of whom her father disapproves. Sam jolts Helen by announcing his plans to move west to escape the intolerance and parochialism of Shore Acres. Martin walks in on them, disrupts their talk, and verbally attacks Sam for his iconoclasm and his belief in evolution. Soon the lovers are forced to exchange farewells, Sam revealing the need of $100 for his journey. Martin confronts Uncle Nat about the real-estate scheme, only to find that his brother cares little for the idea or for moving their mother's remains to nearby Bangor.

II. The scene opens on "The Silver Weddin' " — a huge dinner party at the Berry farmhouse. Helen and her mother are preparing foods and utensils, while other family members and guests fulfill their own obligations. The loosely framed proceedings include the children playing, Uncle Nat titillating his family with wild hijinks, and Joel Gates revealing that a skunk was the cause of his garden woes. Blake informs Helen that he refused to lend $100 to Sam, and Helen renews her refusal of marriage to Blake. Blake discovers, much to his distress, that Squire Andrews is his chief competitor for the speculative development of Shore Acres. Ann Berry, Martin's wife, informs him of her lack of enthusiasm for his business deals and voices strong opposition to moving the family.

Young Nat reports that a hundred-dollar package of money had been stolen from the safe in Blake's store. Sam is immediately suspected, and general opinion turns against him. Uncle Nat secretly tells Helen that Sam cannot be the thief — he himself took money from his savings and inheritance and gave it to Sam. He arranges for Helen and Sam to leave Shore Acres by a boat owned by his friend Captain Ben. He bids them a good, safe trip, and they depart hurriedly.

III. A scene in the interior of the Berry Lighthouse, subtitled "Havin' an Understandin'," provides the setting for Uncle Nat's revelation to Martin of Helen's and Sam's flight. Martin proceeds contemptuously to disown her and obstructs Uncle Nat's path to the lighthouse landing to beam light to the storm-wracked schooner in which Sam and Helen are traveling. Uncle Nat finally convinces Martin of the need for understanding and goes on to confess his early love for Martin's wife, a love suppressed when Martin expressed interest in her. Martin makes one last-ditch effort to prevent Nat from reaching the lighthouse lantern, but Nat pushes him away and ignites the lamp.

A scene called "The 'Liddy Ann' in a Sou'easter" shows the exterior of the Berry Lighthouse. The beam from the lighthouse cascades onto the figures aboard the ship, who celebrate their rescue.

IV. In a scene dubbed "Me an' the Children" at the Berry farmhouse, fifteen months later, on Christmas Eve, Uncle Nat amuses the children and tries to put them to bed. He and Martin have not spoken in the intervening time but Martin now bursts forth with imprecations and ends the silence. Blake arrives to announce the land boom has ended; he and Martin are now ruined. Sam and Helen announce their return to Uncle Nat through the window. Nat presents their baby to Martin as a baby found on the doorstep. Martin steadfastly refuses to care for the baby until he realizes that it is his grandson and namesake. He is reconciled with both Helen and Sam, while Blake and Young Nat reveal that the purportedly stolen money was only misplaced.

Martin, in a return to his former fatalistic character, announces his financial ruin to the party. The levity is hardly broken, as Sam (who has been financially successful in the West) and Helen agree to mortgage their house and lend money to Martin. A well-timed letter arrives from Washington, D.C., to announce an adjusted pension of $1,768.92 to go to Uncle Nat, who offers this sum to Martin. Uncle Nat fires his old army-issue musket, which belches smoke and little bang, to the amusement of the gathering. Martin chats with Sam briefly, and they go out with everyone else. Uncle Nat, left by himself, tends to house chores and goes off to bed.

→ **WILLIAM HOOKER GILLETTE**

Secret Service

I. In the drawing room of General Varney's house in Civil War–torn Richmond, it is learned that the General is dispatched in battle, while his wife tends to a stricken son. Their other son, Wilfred, seventeen, longs to join his father in combat. Mrs. Varney promises to write her husband a notification of their son's conscription but delays indefinitely. As mother and son debate the merits of his joining the southern battalion, their maid Martha ushers in a messenger for Wilfred. Mrs. Varney and hospital intern Mrs. Kitteridge meanwhile argue over whether the elder Varney son deserves more medical attention. The ebullience of young Edith Varney as she arrives quickly disengages the two from their conversation.

Edith has spoken to Confederate President Jefferson about an appointment in the War Department Telegraph Service for Captain Thorne. Subtly, her affections for this seemingly beleaguered veteran emerge; her desire to obtain a job for him is a ploy to keep him out of combat. The President's messenger, Lieutenant Maxwell, delivers to Edith a note verifying Thorne's appointment.

Captain Thorne arrives, quietly informing Edith of his intention to join his battalion at the front and pass up the War Department position. Wilfred's former sweetheart, the ravishing Caroline Mitford, enters, disrupts the heated talk in progress, and invites the Captain to a starvation party — a gathering short on refreshment but long on camaraderie.

Wilfred soon arrives, carrying in a paper bag the Confederate uniform taken from a dead soldier. He enlists Caroline to hem the trousers. She obliges, and her still-strong affections for Wilfred are readily revealed. When Mrs. Varney enters the room later on, she sees Caroline's scissors and an unidentified uniform but does not realize it is Wilfred's. Southern gentleman Benton Arrelsford, working under the auspices of the Southern militia, arrives accusing Mrs. Varney's slave Jonas of transporting messages from a Yankee prisoner in Libby Prison to a secret agent in Richmond. The agent provocateurs have been identified as brothers Lewis and Henry

Dumont, the former still at large while the latter remains in Confederate custody. The military secret in question — a note that reads "ATTACK TONIGHT — PLAN 3 — USE TELEGRAPH" — is thought to be a false order sent through the War Department telegraph lines to weaken the position of the Southern army. Arrelsford reveals that Captain Thorne is actually Lewis Dumont, a crack Yankee secret agent. Edith refuses to believe this accusation but nevertheless goes along with the plan to entrap Thorne/Dumont (or prove his innocence) by entertaining him on the veranda so that Arrelsford can bring Henry Dumont around to identify him as either a complicit sibling or innocent, wrongly accused citizen.

II. At the Varney's home, Wilfred reads Caroline a letter he has addressed to his father about his imminent military service. An orderly arrives with orders to take Wilfred to the front with him. Edith reluctantly meets Thorne on the veranda as soldiers take watch outside. Thorne pledges his love to Edith, and she interrogates him on the meaning of the secret letter. Thorne denies knowledge of the note and feigns curiosity. Edith partly divulges her scheme; Thorne pulls a revolver when he hears a voice outside. It is a Corporal announcing the supposed escape of Thorne's brother, and Thorne holsters his weapon. Henry is quickly pushed into the room by Confederate soldiers without Thorne seeing this action. During a scuffle with the prisoner, Thorne is able to isolate Dumont from his eavesdropping military captors; Dumont then shoots himself to cover his brother Thorne's tracks and belie his espionage mission.

III. At the War Department Telegraph Office, Caroline has come to send a telegram to Wilfred. The operators refuse the dispatch per orders from Arrelsford, who appears on the scene but quickly leaves. Thorne surreptitiously enters and a pantomimic episode ensues: Thorne crushes the incoming dispatch and transmits a series of messages. A messenger enters with a dispatch for Thorne from the Secretary of War. Thorne rips off the signature, affixes it to the fake dispatch in his coat, and telegraphs the message. Thorne acts suspiciously, puffing a cigar and fingering his revolver repeatedly. Arrelsford, who along with Edith has watched Thorne for some time now, shoots him in the hand and apprehends him. As reinforcements arrive, Thorne in a strange, bold move, directs the men to arrest Arrelsford. He comically depicts Arrelsford as a maniacal vigilante with a revolver.

Amidst the chaos, Thorne dispatches another message, ostensibly from the forged copy. It turns out that Thorne has not sent out a vital order to withdraw Marston's division from its present position; for Edith's sake he has not gone through with his sabotage of the Confederate army. He tries to send another dispatch, but Arrelsford's pleading has finally convinced the authorities of Thorne's mischievous plans. Edith testifies to Thorne's truthfulness and his sanction by the Confederate president. A dispatch is called for, but Thorne revokes the order that would betray the Southern forces.

IV. Back in General Varney's drawing room, amid gunblasts and explosions, Caroline explains the disturbances at the War Department to Mrs. Varney. Arrelsford comes on the scene, demanding to see Edith, having implicated her in the espionage conspiracy, and revealing that Thorne has escaped. A battered Wilfred comes home with the orderly. Caroline tends to Wilfred's wounds, and soon their romance is rekindled. Wilfred spies Thorne vaulting over the veranda. He orders Thorne over and summarily arrests him. Thorne begs Wilfred, then Edith, to let him see his dead brother. Neither relents, and he soliloquizes on the degrading life of the Secret Service man. Arrelsford intends to shoot him, but Wilfred protests and insists on a trial.

While the drumhead trial proceeds, Jonas busies himself with disengaging the ammunition and powder from the soldiers' stacked weapons and muskets. Edith begs to see Thorne and posits yet another method of escape. He refuses and notifies the sergeant of Jonas's actions; the muskets are reloaded. The order to shoot Thorne has been delayed, as General Randolph has requested to be present before the prisoner is touched. He arrives, announcing that the false order was never sent. Thorne is nevertheless remanded as a prisoner of war. General Randolph tries to persuade him to join the Confederate forces, but Thorne is still a man of loyalty — as a Yankee, the thought of being traitorous is reprehensible. Edith makes a final pledge of fidelity to Thorne, and he is escorted out by the arresting squad.

→ CLYDE WILLIAM FITCH

The City

I. Cantankerous Middleburg businessman George Rand reads a newspaper while waiting for his daughter Theresa to arrive home from a trip to Europe. Mrs. Rand, fresh from her daily chores, looks disapprovingly on her weary husband. She suggests he give over the business to their son, George, but quickly agrees with her husband's assessment: their son is too taken with

New York City to settle in their small town and turn entrepreneur. Much to Mr. Rand's dismay, their youngest daughter, Cicely, extols the praises of the big city, hoping to go there one day herself.

Mrs. Rand tries to persuade her husband of the wisdom of moving to the city. He has been asked to join a large corporation there and all the family, except Mr. Rand, is behind the idea. George Jr. quickly enters, only to have his good cheer nipped by his father's reprimand for divulging news of the offer he has received in the city to the rest of the family. An argument between father and son then ensues, George Jr. defending his right to follow his own ambitions, make a break with family business obligations, and go to the city to pursue a political career. None of the other family members heed Mr. Rand's warnings about the city and its proclivity to turn "ambition into selfish greed" as they badger him into taking the job.

Meanwhile George Hannock, an extortionist with a secret past, arrives to collect money from Mr. Rand. Long ago Mr. Rand had made arrangements to provide for Hannock and his mother for unstated reasons. When Rand refuses to pay him, Hannock threatens to take his own life out of despair. He finagles the money from Rand and leaves. Rand confesses to his son a transgression he has kept to himself for years: Hannock is his son, rightfully receiving money through a bargain Rand made with Hannock's mother. After volunteering this information, Rand drops dead. A moment later, before hearing of her father's death, Teresa informs George of her plans to marry one Donald Van Vranken and move to the city. Only after her burst of joy does her brother tell her of their father's death. Nevertheless, as the act ends, after the entire family has resolved to move to the city, George exults in the prospect of the move.

II. In the library of the new Rand house in New York City, Hannock, now George Rand's aide, reveals that George is a candidate for the nomination of governor. Hannock, a drug addict, injects himself with a hypodermic needle and is almost caught in the act by Teresa and Cicely, who are looking for George. Hannock exits; Teresa confides her extramarital affair and her plans to leave Van Vranken; Cicely hints of her affection for Hannock. Neither woman approves of the other's romantic interest.

Before George arrives, Hannock tries to blackmail his political mentor, Bert Vorhees, into giving him a significant bonus for his troubles. Vorhees refuses; George comes in. George and Vorhees both boast of George's good character, his political prowess, and his chances in the upcoming election. George prides himself on his good family name and the reputable business conducted by his father, and he looks to his native Middleburg as cultivating virtue in his person. He swears he has no skeletons in the closet, though this will prove to be not wholly true. When Vorhees demands that George dismiss Hannock as his secretary, he says he cannot — suspicions soon crystallize. Van Vranken informs George of Teresa's plan to divorce him, a move that would be disastrous to George's bid for the governorship. George pleads for reconciliation, then for a delay of the divorce proceedings, but to no avail. The two men then accuse each other of selfishness.

George tries to get rid of Hannock by offering him a fixed yearly income if he will leave his employ. Hannock rejects the offer, opting to blackmail George for a series of scandals his political administration has been involved with, scandals that he rattles off with painstaking deviltry. Eleanor Vorhees, George's fiancée, enters. On behalf of Cicely, she comes to George to plead Hannock's goodness and moral rectitude. Cicely herself then comes to argue her case; George tries in vain to convince her that she doesn't truly love Hannock. Cicely explodes in indignation. George, undeterred, tells Cicely she may under no circumstances marry Hannock but will not say why. To George's horror, Cicely reveals that she and Hannock were married earlier that morning.

When Hannock enters, George urges Cicely to leave. He then tells Hannock his father's secret history: Hannock cannot be married to Cicely because they are brother and sister. Hannock goes mad as he moves from disbelief to wretched realization. He shoots Cicely dead as she enters the room, an action motivated more out of possessive love than homicidal hatred. He turns the gun on himself, but George apprehends him before he can perform the deed.

Hannock begs George to let him kill himself (rationalizing that the scandals that would hurt George in his political life would remain undisclosed), but George chooses to bring both Cicely's assailant and himself to justice. Hannock taunts George and Eleanor with stories of George's indiscretions. George strategically places the revolver so Hannock can kill himself, reconsiders, and takes hold of the gun. "You must take your punishment as it comes," cries George, "and I must take mine!"

III. Vorhees attempts to persuade George to destroy incriminating papers and be "on the level." He has also urged him to decline the nomination. George agrees to make amends and discusses his woes with Van Vranken. He and Teresa have agreed to forgive each other and go back to living together. Mrs. Rand confesses her disgust with the city, only to be cut off by George who declares that human evil initiates all wrongdoing — this city is not autonomous. When Eleanor arrives, George apologizes for his dishonesty and is surprised to find Eleanor sympathetic and willing to help him reform himself. They walk out together.

Chronology

><

<table>
<tr><td>HISTORICAL</td><td>THEATRICAL / CULTURAL</td></tr>
<tr><td>

1757: Royall Tyler born.

1775: First Continental Congress meets in Philadelphia.

1777: Articles of Confederation approved by the Continental Congress. • First U.S. Independence Day celebrated on July 4.

1781: British Gen. Cornwallis surrenders to George Washington at Yorktown, Virginia.

1784: New York chosen as temporary U.S. capital.

1789: U.S. Constitution ratified by eleven of thirteen states. • French Revolution begins. • George Washington inaugurated as first president.

</td><td>

1752: Lewis Hallam and his company from London first appear in U.S. (Virginia).

1766: Southwark Theatre established in Philadelphia.

1767: Thomas Godfrey, *Prince of Parthia*, first native-authored play to be produced professionally • John Street Theatre established in New York.

1777: John Street renamed Theatre Royal under British control.

1784: Hallam company returns from Jamaica after Revolutionary War.

1787: Tyler, *The Contrast*.

</td></tr>
</table>

HISTORICAL	THEATRICAL / CULTURAL
1791: U.S. Bill of Rights ratified.	**1790:** Mercy Otis Warren, *Poems, Dramatic and Miscellaneous* published.
1794: Boston repeals 1750 law prohibiting plays.	**1793:** First circus in the U.S. • Elihu Hubbard, *American Poems* (first native verse anthology).
1797: John Adams inaugurated as second president.	
1800: Washington, D.C., becomes permanent capital of the United States. • John Augustus Stone born.	**1796:** Playwright William Dunlap becomes theater manager in New York. • British actor Thomas Abthorpe Cooper debuts in U.S.
1801: Thomas Jefferson inaugurated as third president.	**1798:** Park or New Theatre opens in New York. • Novelist Charles Brockden Brown, *Wieland.*
1804: Lewis and Clark begin first expedition across the continent to the Pacific coast.	**1802–15:** Washington Irving writes theater criticism (as Jonathan Oldstyle).
1807: Congress passes Embargo Act. • Henry Wadsworth Longfellow and John Greenleaf Whittier born.	**1808:** James Nelson Barker, *The Indian Princess,* first produced "Indian" play, about Pocahontas.
1809: James Madison inaugurated president.	**1809:** Acting debut of native playwright/actor John Howard Payne.
1810: John Brougham born.	**1810–12:** Tour of British actor George Frederick Cooke.
1812: U.S. goes to war with England (War of 1812).	**1815:** Tour under Samuel Drake begins westward movement of theater.
1814: British capture and burn Washington, D.C.	**1820:** Washington Irving, *Sketch Book.* • First tour of actor Edmund Kean (second in 1825). • First appearances of native actor Edwin Forrest.
1815: Andrew Jackson defeats British at New Orleans; War of 1812 ends.	
1817: James Monroe inaugurated president.	
1819: Anna Cora Mowatt, Herman Melville, and Walt Whitman born.	**1824:** Camp St. or American Theatre opens in New Orleans, Louisiana.
1820: Dion Boucicault born.	**1825:** Hudson River School of painting founded by artist Thomas Cole.
1823: The Monroe Doctrine proclaimed.	

HISTORICAL	THEATRICAL / CULTURAL
1825: John Quincy Adams named president by House of Representatives due to lack of electoral vote.	**1826:** James Fenimore Cooper, *The Last of the Mohicans*. • New York's Bowery Theatre opens.
1829: Andrew Jackson inaugurated president.	**1827:** James Kirke Paulding pleads for "American" drama in *American Quarterly Review*.
1830: Passage of Removal Bill, establishing Indian Territory in what becomes the state of Oklahoma. • George L. Aiken and Emily Dickinson born.	**1829:** Stone, *Metamora; or, The Last of the Wampanoags*.
	1830: Thomas S. Hamblin begins thirty-year control of Bowery Theatre. • James Kirke Paulding, *The Lion of the West*.
1832: Black Hawk Indian War in Illinois and Wisconsin.	
1834: Department of Indian Affairs established.	**1832:** Dunlap, *History of the American Theatre*.
1837: Martin Van Buren inaugurated president. • Major financial crash followed by depression after period of prosperity.	**1835:** Phineas T. Barnum enters show business.
	1839: Longfellow, *The Village Blacksmith*.
1841: Benjamin Harrison becomes president, succeeded by John Tyler.	**1843:** Debut of The Virginia Minstrels in New York.
1843: Yellow fever sweeps Mississippi Valley (13,000 die).	**1845:** Mowatt, *Fashion; or, Life in New York*. • Edgar Allan Poe, *The Raven and Other Poems*. • Margaret Fuller, *Woman in the Nineteenth Century*.
1845: James Polk becomes president. • Mass emigrations from Ireland due to famine.	
1846–48: Mexican War.	**1847:** Brougham, *Metamora; or, The Last of the Pollywogs*.
1847: Frederick Douglass founds abolitionist newspaper.	
1848: Gold discovered in California.	**1849:** Edwin Forrest-William Charles Macready feud climaxes with Astor Place Opera House riot. • Stage debut of Edwin Booth.
1849: Zachary Taylor becomes president, followed in 1850 by Millard Fillmore.	
1850: Fugitive Slave Act passed.	**1850:** Hawthorne, *The Scarlet Letter*.
	1851: Harriet Beecher Stowe's novel, *Uncle Tom's Cabin* (in serial form). • Melville, *Moby Dick*.

HISTORICAL	THEATRICAL / CULTURAL
1853: Franklin Pierce inaugurated president. • William Gillette born.	**1852:** Aiken's play, *Uncle Tom's Cabin.*
1856: James Buchanan elected president.	**1854:** Thoreau, *Walden.*
1857: Short-lived economic panic.	**1855:** George Henry Boker, *Francesca da Rimini* (romantic drama). • Whitman, *Leaves of Grass.*
1859: John Brown's raid on Harper's Ferry.	**1856:** First American copyright law.
1860: Abraham Lincoln elected president.	**1857:** Boucicault, *The Poor of New York.*
1861: U.S. Civil War begins.	**1858:** Tom Taylor's *Our American Cousin* produced first in U.S. by actress Laura Keene.
1863: Emancipation Proclamation issued.	**1861:** Variety entrepreneur Tony Pastor establishes his first variety theater in New York.
1865: Civil War ends. • Abraham Lincoln, assassinated by actor John Wilkes Booth, is succeeded by Andrew Johnson. • Clyde Fitch born.	**1865:** Actor Joseph Jefferson III first appears in Boucicault's version of *Rip Van Winkle.*
1869: Transcontinental railroad completed. • U.S. Grant becomes president.	**1866:** *The Black Crook,* forerunner of American musical.
1875: Congress passes early Civil Rights Act.	**1867:** Augustin Daly, *Under the Gaslight.*
1877: Rutherford B. Hayes elected president. • Post–Civil War Reconstruction officially ends.	**1869:** Ned Buntline, *Buffalo Bill, The King of Border Men* (dime novel). • Mark Twain, *The Innocents Abroad.*
	1873: Italian actor Tommaso Salvini tours.
	1876: Twain, *Tom Sawyer.*
	1879: Edward Harrigan's *Mulligan Guard* series begins. • Bartley Campbell, *My Partner.* • Henry James, *Daisy Miller.*
	1880: Steele Mackaye's Madison Square Theatre in New York.

HISTORICAL	THEATRICAL / CULTURAL
1881: James A. Garfield inaugurated president; assassinated, and succeeded by Chester A. Arthur.	**1883:** B. F. Keith, future vaudeville king, opens dime museum in Boston. • First Ibsen play (*A Doll's House* in adaptation called *Thora*) seen in America. • British stars Henry Irving and Ellen Terry tour (first of many).
1882: Immigration restrictions imposed for the first time.	
1885: Grover Cleveland becomes 22nd president; reelected in 1893.	
1889: Benjamin Harrison inaugurated president.	**1884:** Twain, *Huckleberry Finn.*
1890: Sherman Antitrust Act passed.	**1880:** Theatrical club, The Players, founded by Edwin Booth and others.
1893: Henry Ford road tests his first automobile.	**1889:** Charles Frohman emerges as producer with Bronson Howard, *Shenandoah.*
1897: William McKinley becomes president.	**1890:** Herne, *Margaret Fleming,* first American problem play in Ibsen tradition. • Charles Hoyt, *A Trip to Chinatown.*
	1891: Augustus Thomas, *Alabama.*
	1893: World's Columbian Exposition in Chicago. • Eleonora Duse appears as Camille in New York.
	1894: Bernard Shaw introduced to America by Richard Mansfield in *Arms and the Man.* • Actress Minnie Maddern Fiske appears successfully as Nora in *A Doll's House.* • *Billboard,* first true theatrical trade paper, begins.
	1895: Gillette, *Secret Service.* • David Belasco, *The Heart of Maryland.* • Stephen Crane, *The Red Badge of Courage.*
	1896: Theatrical Syndicate organized. • Weber and Fields open their Music Hall.

HISTORICAL	THEATRICAL / CULTURAL
1898: Spanish-American War. **1901:** Theodore Roosevelt becomes president after assassination of McKinley. **1906:** San Francisco earthquake. **1909:** William Taft becomes president.	**1898:** Bob Cole and Billy Johnson musical, *A Trip to Coontown.* • Henry James, *Turn of the Screw.* **1899:** Herne's *Sag Harbor.* • Spectacular production of *Ben-Hur.* • George M. Cohan begins musical theater career. • Kate Chopin, *The Awakening.* **1900:** Theodore Dreiser, *Sister Carrie.* **1902:** Winslow Homer, "Early Morning after a Storm at Sea" (painting). **1903:** Iroquois Theatre fire in Chicago (nearly 600 die). • First American narrative films by Edwin Porter (*The Life of an American Fireman* and *The Great Train Robbery*). • W. E. B. Du Bois, *The Souls of Black Folk.* **1905:** George Pierce Baker begins playwriting course at Harvard. • Shubert brothers begin to challenge Syndicate. **1906:** Langdon Mitchell, *The New York Idea.* • William Vaughn Moody, *The Great Divide.* **1907:** Belasco Theatre opens in New York. • Augustus Thomas, *The Witching Hour.* • First of Florenz Ziegfeld's *Follies.* **1908:** Edward Sheldon, *Salvation Nell.* **1909:** Fitch, *The City.* • The New Theatre under direction of Winthrop Ames opens as art theater in New York; fails within two years.

Suggestions for Further Reading

General overviews of American theater and its drama covering the period to 1910 include: Travis Bogard, Richard Moody, and Walter J. Meserve, *The Revels History of Drama in English: Volume VIII, American Drama* (London: Methuen & Co., 1977); Barnard Hewitt, *Theatre U.S.A., 1665 to 1957* (New York: McGraw-Hill, 1959), narrative with key documents and critical commentaries; Garff Wilson, *Three Hundred Years of American Drama and Theatre* (Englewood Cliffs, N.J: Prentice-Hall, 1973), designed as a general-student text; Gary A. Richardson, *American Drama From the Colonial Period Through World War I: A Critical History* (New York: Twayne, 1993), though focused on the text, includes cultural context; Don B. Wilmeth and Tice L. Miller, *Cambridge Guide to American Theatre* (Cambridge and New York: Cambridge University Press, 1993), with overview essays and entries on many specifics; and Mary C. Henderson, *Theater in America: 200 Years of Plays, Players, and Productions* (New York: Harry N. Abrams, 1996). A unique and very relevant volume is *Theatre in the United States: A Documentary History. Volume I: 1750–1915, Theatre in the Colonies and United States*, edited by Barry B. Witham with contributions by Martha Mahard, David Rinear, and Don Wilmeth. Volume one of the forthcoming *Cambridge History of American Theatre*, coedited by Wilmeth and C. W. E. Bigsby, covers aspects of the subject to 1870; volume two to 1945.

More specific studies (coverage is clear by titles) include: Hugh F. Rankin, *The Theater in Colonial America* (Chapel Hill: University of North Carolina, 1965); Jared Brown, *The Theatre in America During the Revolution* (New York and Cambridge: Cambridge University Press, 1995); Walter J. Meserve, *An Emerging Entertainment: The Drama of the American People to 1828* (Bloomington: Indiana University Press, 1977) and *Heralds of Promise: The Drama of the American People in the Age of Jackson, 1829–1849* (Westport, Conn., and London: Greenwood Press, 1986); Rosemarie K. Bank, *Theatre Culture in America, 1825–1860* (New York and Cambridge: Cambridge University Press, 1997); and Lawrence W. Levine, *Highbrow/Lowbrow: The Emergence of Cultural Hierarchy in America* (Cambridge, Mass.: Harvard University Press, 1988), with a focus on the nineteenth century.

Of studies of genres (placed in context) represented in this collection, the most useful are: Daniel G. Gerould, *American Melodrama* (New York: Performing Arts Journal Publications, 1983), with plays and commentary; David Grimsted, *Melodrama Unveiled: American Theater and Culture, 1800–1850* (Chicago: University of Chicago Press, 1968); Bruce A. McConachie, *Melodramatic Formations: American Theatre and Society 1820–1870* (Iowa City: University of Iowa Press, 1992); Jeffrey D. Mason, *Melodrama and the Myth of America* (Bloomington: Indiana University Press, 1993), with a chapter on Stone's *Metamora;* and Brenda Murphy, *American Realism and American Drama, 1880–1940* (Cambridge and New York: Cambridge University Press, 1987).

In addition to sources mentioned in the introduction, the following are recommended for additional insights and information on the playwrights in this collection. Royall Tyler: Ada Lou Carson and Herbert L. Carson, *Royall Tyler* (Boston: Twayne, 1979); and G. Thomas Tanselle, *Royall Tyler* (Cambridge, Mass.: Harvard University Press, 1967). John Brougham: Pat M. Ryan, *John Brougham, The Gentle Satirist. A Critique, with a Handlist and Census* (New York: New York Public Library, 1959). Anna Cora Mowatt: Eric Wollencott Barnes, *The Lady of Fashion: The Life and Theatre of Anna Cora Mowatt* (New York: Charles Scribner's Sons, 1954); and Mowatt's *Autobiography of an Actress* (Boston: Ticknor, Reed, and Fields, 1854). Dion Boucicault: a fairly comprehensive biography is Richard Fawkes's *Dion Boucicault* (London: Quartet Books, 1979); Peter Thomson's edition of *Plays by Dion Boucicault* (Cambridge: Cambridge University Press, 1984) provides selected plays, bibliography, and a complete handlist of plays. James A. Herne: John Perry, *James A. Herne: The American Ibsen* (Chicago: Nelson-Hall, 1978); Murphy, above, includes extensive coverage of Herne. Clyde Fitch: Montrose Moses and Virginia Gerson, eds., *Clyde Fitch and His Let-*

ters (Boston: Little, Brown, 1924); also recommended is an unpublished doctoral dissertation, Thomas L. Hellie's "Clyde Fitch, Playwright of New York's Leisure Class" (Columbia: University of Missouri, 1985).

Finally, of the few anthologies of American drama that include a sampling of pre-twentieth century plays, especially recommended because of notes and commentary are John Gassner, *Best Plays of the Early American Theatre* (New York: Crown, 1967); Richard Moody's *Dramas from the American Theatre* (see the Introduction); Arthur Hobson Quinn, *Representative American Plays,* 7th ed. (New York: Appleton-Century-Crofts, 1953); and, the most recent and only ones currently in print: Stephen Watt and Gary A. Richardson, *American Drama: Colonial to Contemporary* (Fort Worth, Tex.: Harcourt Brace, 1995) and Walter Meserve, *On Stage, America!* (Brooklin, Maine: Feedback Theatrebook, 1996).

Acknowledgments (continued from page iv)

Figure 6. Act V, scene II of *The Poor of New York*. An advertising woodcut from *Specimans of Theatrical Cuts*. Ledger Job Printing Office, Philadelphia, c. 1875. By permission of the Wilmeth Collection.

Figure 7. Cover of an advertising herald for *Shore Acres*. By permission of the Laurence Senelick Collection.

Figure 8. William Gillette in *Secret Service*. Photograph by Pach Brothers, NY. By permission of the Laurence Senelick Collection.

Figure 9. Walter Hampden as George Rand and Tully Marshall as Hannock in Act II of *The City*. From *The Theatre* (Feb., 1910). By permission of the Laurence Senelick Collection.